ANGLO-AMERICAN TORT LAW CASE BOOK

English/Chinese

英美侵权法
经典案例教程

英汉对照

王竹 吴震宇 吴至诚 编译

图书在版编目(CIP)数据

英美侵权法经典案例教程：英汉对照 / 王竹，吴震宇，吴至诚编译. —北京：北京大学出版社，2021.6
 ISBN 978-7-301-32078-5

Ⅰ. ①英… Ⅱ. ①王… ②吴… ③吴… Ⅲ. ①侵权法—英国—教材—英、汉 ②侵权法—美国—教材—英、汉 Ⅳ. ①D956.13 ②D971.23

中国版本图书馆 CIP 数据核字(2021)第 055097 号

书　　　　名	英美侵权法经典案例教程（英汉对照） YING-MEI QINQUANFA JINGDIAN ANLI JIAOCHENG （YING-HAN DUIZHAO）
著作责任者	王竹　吴震宇　吴至诚　编译
策 划 编 辑	陆建华
责 任 编 辑	陆建华　张文桢
标 准 书 号	ISBN 978-7-301-32078-5
出 版 发 行	北京大学出版社
地　　　　址	北京市海淀区成府路 205 号　100871
网　　　　址	http://www.pup.cn　http://www.yandayuanzhao.com
电 子 信 箱	yandayuanzhao@163.com
新 浪 微 博	@北京大学出版社　@北大出版社燕大元照法律图书
电　　　　话	邮购部 010-62752015　发行部 010-62750672 编辑部 010-62117788
印 刷 者	北京中科印刷有限公司
经 销 者	新华书店 965 毫米×1300 毫米　16 开本　43.5 印张　730 千字 2021 年 6 月第 1 版　2021 年 6 月第 1 次印刷
定　　　　价	168.00 元

未经许可，不得以任何方式复制或抄袭本书之部分或全部内容。
版权所有，侵权必究
举报电话：010-62752024　电子信箱：fd@pup.pku.edu.cn
图书如有印装质量问题，请与出版部联系，电话：010-62756370

编译者简介

王竹

（1981— ），男，四川大学法学院教授、博士生导师，四川大学市场经济法治研究所所长，"天府万人计划"天府社科菁英，兼任中国人民大学民商事法律科学研究中心法治大数据研究所所长。1999—2009年相继在中国人民大学获得管理学学士、民商法学硕士和博士学位，先后赴我国台湾地区东吴大学、美国康奈尔大学和耶鲁大学求学，2015—2016年赴英国牛津大学法学部访学。

主持国家重点研发计划项目1项、国家社科基金2项、教育部基地重大项目1项、司法部项目2项。在《法学研究》、TEL、CKLR等杂志发表论文160余篇，其中多篇被《新华文摘》、中国人民大学《复印报刊资料》转载。独著 *On the Constitutionality of Compiling a Civil Code of China*、《侵权责任分担论》《编纂民法典的合宪性思考》《侵权责任法疑难问题专题研究》，主编《民法典·侵权责任编）（编纂建议稿）附立法理由书》《慕课的制作与运行指南》，总主编《民法典关联法规与权威案例提要丛书》《法律大数据·案由法条关联丛书》，合写专著11部、教材4部，编著若干。

主持"首批国家精品在线开放课程"和"国家级虚拟仿真实验教学项目"各1门。荣获教育部人文社科二等奖、三等奖，四川省社科优秀成果奖三等奖2次和教学成果奖三等奖，宝钢优秀教师奖等学术、教学成果奖励。

吴震宇

（1986— ），男，四川大学法学院助理研究员。2005—2013年相继在中国政法大学获得法学学士学位和民商法学硕士学位；2011年在美国圣路易斯华盛顿大学获得法律硕士学位（LL.M.），并获得纽约州律师资格；2013—2018年在法国蒙彼利埃大学获得私法和刑事科学博士学位。出版英文专著1部，主持四川省社科基金项目1项。

吴至诚

（1990— ），男，中国人民大学法学院助理教授，中国人民大学民商事法律科学研究中心副研究员，未来法治研究院研究员、普通法中心主任助理、营商环境法治研究中心副秘书长、国际商事争端预防与解决研究院副秘书长。相继在苏州大学取得法学学士学位，在牛津大学取得法律硕士、法学硕士、法学博士学位。主持国家社科基金青年项目1项，在中英文刊物上发表论文若干。

以课育人、以书传趣(代前言)

一、判例盛宴,以课育人

《美国侵权法:实体与程序(第七版)》出版的时候,北京大学出版社蒋浩老师希望用醒目的一句话来向学界介绍这本书,我酝酿了一下,建议表述为"超越成文法经验,品味判例法盛宴",后来这段话便成为了该书的"腰封",并且刊登在了《政法论坛》2014年第3期的封底。①

2008年我去美国之前,就已经和四川大学法学院初步商定就业意向。为任教后开展教学,2007年在我国台湾地区东吴大学和2008—2009年在美国康奈尔大学、耶鲁大学访学期间,我就认真观察了潘维大教授、Henderson教授和Kysar教授对该教材的具体使用方式。潘维大教授和美国学者在教学中对该书的使用方式的最大的差别就是,由于母语差异,美国法学院授课对象是J.D.,在一学期就完成该书近1000页的阅读和教学;而东吴大学法律学院授课对象为大二本科生,一个学期仅能完成该书第一章"侵权程序介绍:致害性和攻击性殴击行为的责任",将其作为介绍性内容,然后每学年再选取后续的1—2章来作为授课内容,通过多年循环来完成一轮的授课。在教学方法上,美国法学院是采用苏格拉底式教学法,而东吴大学法学院采用教师讲授加同学们分组报告的方式来授课。

2009年我回国后到四川大学法学院任教。从2010年开始,结合当时正在进行的《美国侵权法:实体与程序(第七版)》翻译工作,开始在四川大学开设"英美侵权法"全英文课程。尤其要感谢东吴大学法学院黄心怡教授无私分享了她的介绍性内容PPT和几份东吴大学同学们的报告PPT,让我能够借鉴摸索适合中国大陆法学院的"英美侵权法"教学模式。

综合借鉴美国法学院和我国台湾地区东吴大学法学院的教学模式,经过10年坚持不懈的逐步探索,现在四川大学法学院已经形成较为成熟的"英美侵权法"教学体系,按照每学期16周(2学分,32课时)安排,分为3个教

---

① 〔美〕小詹姆斯·A.亨德森、理查德·N.皮尔森等著,王竹等译,《美国侵权法:实体与程序(第七版)》北京大学出版社2014年版。

学阶段，分别是：

第一阶段（1—4周）：引导和介绍。这部分主要是由教师介绍美国侵权法的法源、基本诉讼程序和侵权法的基本原理。这一阶段教师的英语口语语速尽量地慢，让同学们熟悉全英文的学习环境，并且不允许学生在课堂上使用中文，坚持全英文教学和课堂交流。

第二阶段（5—8周）：案例教学和思考题。这部分是由教师通过案例教学逐步引导学生进入到美国侵权法的论证方式，并根据教材的思考题引导学生建立用已经学过的案例来论证的判例法思考方式。在这一阶段使用的案例均提供中英文对照版本，但全英文授课，让同学们逐步进入全英文学习的状态。

第三阶段（9—16周）：学生案例报告和教师评论。这部分由学生分组用PPT轮值报告一个案例，报告内容包括：（1）案件事实；（2）审理程序；（3）原告诉求；（4）被告辩护意见；（5）案件争议焦点；（6）案件的法律适用；（7）案件说理；（8）判决结果；（9）其他报告人认为值得说明的内容。为了方便同学们深入交流，我们建设了"Comparative Tort Law"课程中心（可以直接访问：www.comparativetortlaw.com）。轮值报告案例的组提前一周将报告PPT传到课程中心，不轮值报告的组根据PPT提问，然后轮值报告组在完成报告后，再回答其他各组的提问，接着再由其他各组交叉提问。最后由教师对案例和报告进行评论。

二、同源有别，以书传趣

2015—2016年，我的第一个休息年（Sabbatical）是在牛津大学度过的。为了不中断"英美侵权法"课程，我将原本上半年开课的课程移到了下半年我回国后开设。在备课期间，我和当时在牛津大学法学院攻读博士学位的吴至诚博士聊起我前5年授课的一个缺憾，就是课程叫做"英美侵权法"，但使用的教材却只是我主持翻译的《美国侵权法：实体与程序》。虽然其中也有不少早期英国侵权法的经典判例，但是却缺乏对现代英国侵权法的介绍。正好他刚完成了 Donoghue v Stevenson [1932] AC 562 的全文翻译并在国内期刊发表[1]，就主动提议何不由他来选择英国侵权法判例，然后与我之前翻译的美国法案例一起，出版一本英汉对照的真正意义上的"英美侵权法"教材？于是，

---

[1] 本案全文翻译可参见吴至诚译：《英国法中基于过失的一般侵权责任——多诺霍诉史蒂文森案》，载《苏州大学学报（法学版）》2015年第1期。

就有了本书的策划。

经过比较，我们选择了牛津大学出版社出版的 Lunney, Nolan & Oliphant, *Tort Law: Text and Materials*（6th edn）[1] 作为英国侵权法主要的参考书，并参考其他英国侵权法的通行教材。主要考虑到这三位教授都是世界侵权法学会的理事，在英联邦国家具有普遍的影响力，可以使后续该书新版更新的情况能够更方便地纳入我们的教学活动和本书更新（如果能够得到读者认可出版后续版本的话）。2018年吴至诚博士学成归国，入职中国人民大学法学院，和我一起最终选定了54个美国法案例和46个英国法案例，然后对应编入一个相对兼容的侵权法框架中。正好2018年年底吴震宇博士入职四川大学法学院，他是美国华盛顿大学的 L.L.M. 和法国蒙彼利埃大学的法学博士，精通英文和法文，也和我一起进行"英美侵权法"的授课，我们就邀请他一起参与翻译工作。最后由吴至诚博士对全书进行了校对，确保翻译的准确性。

需要说明的是，尽管美国侵权法和英联邦侵权法具有同源性，但随着各自的发展，也有较大区别。比如，在引注体例上，美国法使用 Bluebook（The Bluebook: A Uniform System of Citation），英国法使用 OSCOLA（The Oxford University Standard for Citation of Legal Authorities）；在案例引注格式上，最直观的差别就是美国案例使用"v."，英国案例使用"v"而没有小圆点。

我一直觉得英美侵权法的判例本身读起来就很有意思，但不少读者可能囿于英文水平和阅读习惯，无法欣赏到这些判例中的趣味。所以我和编辑商量，该书采用特殊排版方式，书打开之后，左侧和右侧是对应的英文和中文。这样这本书既可以当英文书读，或当中文书读，又可以英文、中文对照阅读。这是我特别设计的体例，希望得到读者的认可。如果读者在阅读过程中，发现部分术语在一般的英汉词典上无法找到合适的解释，可以尝试登录我主持编写的线上《简明中英文侵权法词典》（http://www.qinquanfa.com/ct.asp），专供侵权法领域术语的查漏补缺。

三、致谢

英汉对照的出版体例，给本书的编辑添了不少麻烦；我指导的吴玉章学院学生王安娜和焦祎晨在后期编辑过程中提供了大量协助，在此一并致谢！徐铁英教授长期和我一起开设"英美侵权法"课程，这次是因为他喜得千金

---

[1] Lunney, Nolan & Oliphant, *Tort Law: Text and Materials (6th edn)*, OUP, 2017.

没有参加编译工作，但能够与他一起授课并交流，也是我能够长期坚持的重要动力！

  特别感谢教育部人文社会科学重点研究基地重大项目"中国侵权责任法改革研究"（16JJD820015）对本书的资助，感谢北京大学出版社对我的"英美侵权法"学术道路的长期支持！

王竹
庚子年 端午 于 成都·白鹿镇

CONTENTS

Chapter 1. Intentional Torts — 002

Section 1. Intent — 002
1. Vosburg v. Putney, 80 Wis. 523, 50 N.W. 403 (1891) — 002
2. Garratt v. Dailey, 46 Wash. 2d 197, 279 P.2d 1091 (1955) — 004
3. Fowler v Lanning [1959] 1 QB 426 — 012

Section 2. Contact — 018
4. Fisher v. Carrousel Motor Hotel, 424 S.W.2d 627 (Tex. 1967) — 018
5. Leichtman v. WLW Jacor Communications, Inc., 634 N.E.2d 697 (1994) — 022
6. Wilson v Pringle [1987] QB 237 — 026

Chapter 2. Negligence — 048

Section 1. Duty of Care: Basic Formula — 048
7. Brown v. Kendall, 60 Mass. 292 (1850) — 048
8. Tubbs v. Argus, 140 Ind. App. 695, 225 N.E.2d 841 (1967) — 054
9. Rowland v. Christian, 69 Cal. 2d 108, 443 P.2d 561, 70 Cal. Rptr. 97 (1968) — 056
10. Donoghue v Stevenson [1932] AC 562 — 066
11. Caparo Industries plc v Dickman [1990] 2 AC 605 — 084

Section 2. Breach of Duty: Standard of Care — 096
12. Washington v. Louisiana Power and Light Co., 555 So. 2d 1350 (La. 1990) — 096
13. Weirum v. RKO General, Inc., 15 Cal. 3d 40, 539 P.2d 36, 123 Cal. Rptr. 468 (1975) — 102
14. Palsgraf v. Long Island R.R. Co., 248 N.Y. 339, 162 N.E. 99 (1928) — 108
15. United States v. Carroll Towing Co., 159 F.2d 169 (2d Cir. 1947) — 122

16. Bolton v Stone [1951] AC 850   124

17. Bolam v Friern Hospital Management Committee [1957] 1 WLR 582   134

Chapter 3. Defenses   140

Section 1. Defences in Intentional Torts   140

18. O'Brien v. Cunard Steamship Co., 154 Mass. 272, 28 N.E. 266 (1891)   140

19. Barton v. Bee Line, Inc., 238 App. Div. 501, 265 N.Y.S. 284 (1933)   142

20. Bang v. Charles T. Miller Hospital, 251 Minn. 427, 88 N.W.2d 186 (1958)   144

21. Kennedy v. Parrott, 243 N.C. 355, 90 S.E.2d 754 (1956)   150

22. Hackbart v. Cincinnati Bengals, Inc., 601 F.2d 516 (10th Cir. 1979)   156

23. Chatterton v Gerson [1981] QB 432   162

24. Balmain New Ferry Co Ltd v Robertson (1906) 4 CLR 379   166

25. Courvoisier v. Raymond, 23 Colo. 113, 47 P. 284 (1896)   170

26. Katko v. Briney, 183 N.W.2d 657 (Iowa 1971)   176

27. Ashley and Another v Chief Constable of Sussex [2008] UKHL 25, [2008] 1 AC 962   188

28. Ploof v. Putnam, 81 Vt. 471, 71 A. 188 (1908)   196

29. In Re F (Mental Patient: Sterilisation) [1990] 2 AC 1   198

Section 2. Defences in Negligence   206

30. Butterfield v Forrester (1809) 11 East 60, 103 ER 926   206

31. Davies v Mann (1842) 10 M & W 546, 152 ER 588   206

32. Knight v. Jewett, 3 Cal. 4th 296, 834 P.2d 696, 11 Cal. Rptr. 2d 2 (1992)   210

33. Jones v Livox Quarries [1952] 2 QB 608   214

34. Froom v Butcher [1976] QB 286   218

35. Meistrich v. Casino Arena Attractions, Inc., 31 N.J. 44, 155 A.2d 90 (1959)   224

36. Morris v Murray [1991] 2 QB 6   228

Chapter 4. Causations   240

Section 1. Causation: Factual or Legal   240

37. Hoyt v. Jeffers, 30 Mich. 181 (1874)   240

38. Smith v. Rapid Transit Inc., 317 Mass. 469, 58 N.E.2d 754 (1945)   244

39. Summers v. Tice, 33 Cal. 2d 80, 199 P.2d 1 (1948)   246

40. Ybarra v. Spangard, 25 Cal. 2d 486, 154 P.2d 687 (1944)   250

41. Barnett v Chelsea and Kensington Hospital Management Committee [1969] 1 QB 428   254
42. Gregg v Scott [2005] UKHL 2, [2005] 2 AC 176   258
43. Bonnington Castings Ltd v Wardlaw [1956] AC 613   278
44. Fairchild v Glenhaven Funeral Services Ltd [2002] UKHL 22, [2003] 1 AC 32   282

Section 2. Concurrent and Sccessive Causation   288

45. Dillon v. Twin State Gas & Electric Co., 85 N.H. 449, 163 A. 111 (1932)   288
46. Kingston v. Chicago & N.W. Ry.Co., 191 Wis. 610, 211 N.W. 913 (1927)   290
47. Baker v Willoughby [1970] AC 467   294

Chapter 5. Trespass to Land and Nuisance   304

Section 1. Trespass to Land and Nuisance in US Cases   304

48. Peters v. Archambault, 361 Mass. 91, 278 N.E.2d 729 (1972)   304
49. Davis v. Georgia-Pacific Corp., 251 Or. 239, 445 P.2d 481 (1968)   310
50. Jost v. Dairyland Power Cooperative, 45 Wis. 2d 164, 172 N.W.2d 647 (1969)   314
51. Spur Industries, Inc. v. Del E. Webb Development Co., 108 Ariz. 178, 494 P.2d 700 (1972)   316

Section 2. Trespass to Land and Nuisance in English Cases   322

52. Graham v Peat (1801) 1 East 244, 102 ER 95   322
53. Smith v Stone (1647) Sty 65, 82 ER 533   322
54. Cambridge Water Co Ltd v Eastern Counties Leather plc [1994] 2 AC 264   322
55. Sedleigh-Denfield v O'Callaghan [1940] AC 880   326
56. Hunter v Canary Wharf Ltd [1997] AC 655   334

Chapter 6. Strict Liability   352

Section 1. Common Starting Point: Rylands v Fletcher   352

57. Fletcher v Rylands (1865–66) LR 1 Ex 265   352
58. Rylands v Fletcher (1868) L.R. 3 H.L. 330   358

Section 2. Development in US Law: Abnormally Dangerous Activities   **360**

59. Turner v. Big Lake Oil Co., 128 Tex. 155, 96 S.W.2d 221 (1936)   360
60. Siegler v. Kuhlman, 81 Wash. 2d 448, 502 P.2d 1181 (1972)   364
61. PSI Energy, Inc. v. Roberts, 829 N.E.2d 943 (Ind. 2005)   370

Section 3. Development in English Law: Escape of Dangerous Things in the Course of Non-natural Use of Land — 376
62. Cambridge Water Co Ltd v Eastern Counties Leather Plc [1994] 2 AC 264 — 376
63. Transco Plc v Stockport Metropolitan Borough Council [2003] UKHL 61, [2004] 2 AC 1 — 382

Chapter 7. Products Liability — 394

Section 1. US Law: A Three-fold Taxonomy of Defect — 394
64. MacPherson v. Buick Motor Co., 217 N.Y. 382, 111 N.E. 1050 (1916) — 394
65. Vandermark v. Ford Motor Co., 391 P.2d 168 (Cal. 1964) — 398
66. Sheckells v. AGV Corp., 987 F.2d 1532 (11th Cir. 1993) — 404

Section 2. English Law: From Negligence to Strict Liability — 412
67. A v National Blood Authority [2001] 3 All ER 289 — 412

Chapter 8. Damages — 426

Section 1. Medical Expenses — 426
68. Williams v. Bright, 230 A.D.2d 548, 658 N.Y.S.2d 910, appeal dismissed, 90 N.Y.2d 935, 686 N.E.2d 1368 (1997) — 426
69. Coyne v. Campbell, 11 N.Y.2d 372, 183 N.E.2d 891 (1962) — 434
70. Hunt v Severs [1994] 2 AC 350 — 440

Section 2. Loss of Earnings — 448
71. Ruzzi v. Butler Petroleum Company, 527 Pa. 1, 588 A.2d 1 (1991) — 448
72. Grayson v. Irvmar Realty Corp., 7 A.D.2d 436, 184 N.Y.S.2d 33 (1959) — 452
73. Pickett v British Rail Engineering Ltd [1980] AC 136 — 458

Section 3. Non-Pecuniary Losses — 466
74. Walters v. Hitchcock, 237 Kan. 31, 697 P.2d 847 (1985) — 466
75. McDougald v. Garber, 73 N.Y.2d 246, 536 N.E.2d 372 (1989) — 474
76. H West & Son Ltd v Shephard [1964] AC 326 — 486

Section 4. Punitive or Exemplary Damages — 494
77. State Farm Mutual Automobile Insurance Company v. Campbell, 123 S. Ct. 1513 (2003) — 494
78. Rookes v Barnard [1964] AC 1129 — 512

79. Cassell v Broome [1972] AC 1027	516
80. Kuddus v Chief Constable of Leicestershire Constabulary [2001] UKHL 29, [2002] 2 AC 122	518

Chapter 9. Dignitary Wrongs and Intentional Infliction — 524

Section 1. Assault — 524
81. Read v Coker [1853] 13 C.B. 850, 138 ER 1437 — 524
82. Beach v. Hancock, 27 N.H. 223 (1853) — 526
83. Stephens v Myers (1830) 4 C & P 349, 172 ER 735 — 528

Section 2. False Imprisonment — 530
84. Whittaker v. Sanford, 110 Me. 77, 85 A. 399 (1912) — 530
85. Sindle v. New York City Transit Authority, 33 N.Y.2d 293, 307 N.E.2d 245 (1973) — 532
86. Bird v Jones (1845) 7 QB 742, 115 ER 668 — 536
87. Davidson v Chief Constable of North Wales and another [1994] 2 All ER 597 — 540

Section 3. Intentional Infliction of Mental Upset — 544
88. State Rubbish Collectors Association v. Siliznoff, 38 Cal. 2d 330, 240 P.2d 282 (1952) — 544
89. Ford v. Revlon, Inc., 153 Ariz. 38, 734 P.2d 580 (1987) — 550
90. Wainwright v Home Office [2003] UKHL 53, [2004] 2 AC 406 — 562

Chapter 10. Defamation — 572

Section 1. US Law: Constitutional Issues — 572
91. Gertz v. Robert Welch, Inc., 418 U.S. 323, 94 S. Ct. 2997, 41 L. Ed. 2d 789 (1974) — 572
92. Milkovich v. Lorain Journal Co., 497 U.S. 1, 110 S. Ct. 2695, 111 L. Ed. 2d 1 (1990) — 582

Section 2. English Law: Definition, Remedies, and Free Speech — 590
93. Cassidy v Daily Mirror [1929] 2 KB 331 — 590
94. John v MGN Ltd [1997] QB 586 p 752 — 596
95. Derbyshire County Council v Times Newspapers [1993] AC 534 — 606

Chapter 11. Invasion of Privacy — 614

Section 1. Invasion of Privacy in US Law — 614

96. Hamberger v. Eastman, 106 N.H. 107, 206 A.2d 239 (1964) — 614

97. Shulman v. Group W Productions, Inc., 18 Cal. 4th 200, 955 P.2d 469, 74 Cal. Rptr. 2d 843 (1998) — 618

98. Godbehere v. Phoenix Newspapers, Inc., 162 Ariz. 335, 783 P.2d 781 (1989) — 630

Section 2. Invasion of Privacy in English Law — 638

99. Wainwright v Home Office [2003] UKHL 53, [2004] 2 AC 406 — 638

100. Campbell v Mirror Group Newspapers Ltd [2004] UKHL 22, [2004] 2 AC 457 — 646

目 录

第一章　故意侵权责任　　003

第一节　意图　　003
1. Vosburg v. Putney, 80 Wis. 523, 50 N.W. 403 (1891)　　003
2. Garratt v. Dailey, 46 Wash. 2d 197, 279 P.2d 1091 (1955)　　005
3. Fowler v Lanning [1959] 1 QB 426　　013

第二节　接触　　019
4. Fisher v. Carrousel Motor Hotel, 424 S.W.2d 627 (Tex. 1967)　　019
5. Leichtman v. WLW Jacor Communications, Inc., 634 N.E.2d 697 (1994)　　023
6. Wilson v Pringle [1987] QB 237　　027

第二章　过失侵权责任　　049

第一节　注意义务：基本规则　　049
7. Brown v. Kendall, 60 Mass. 292 (1850)　　049
8. Tubbs v. Argus, 140 Ind. App. 695, 225 N.E.2d 841 (1967)　　055
9. Rowland v. Christian, 69 Cal. 2d 108, 443 P.2d 561, 70 Cal. Rptr. 97 (1968)　　057
10. Donoghue v Stevenson [1932] AC 562　　067
11. Caparo Industries plc v Dickman [1990] 2 AC 605　　085

第二节　义务的违反：注意的标准　　097
12. Washington v. Louisiana Power and Light Co., 555 So. 2d 1350 (La. 1990)　　097
13. Weirum v. RKO General, Inc., 15 Cal. 3d 40, 539 P.2d 36, 123 Cal. Rptr. 468 (1975)　　103
14. Palsgraf v. Long Island R.R.Co., 248 N.Y. 339, 162 N.E. 99 (1928)　　109
15. United States v. Carroll Towing Co., 159 F.2d 169 (2d Cir. 1947)　　123

16. Bolton v Stone [1951] AC 850   125

17. Bolam v Friern Hospital Management Committee [1957] 1 WLR 582   135

第三章 抗辩事由   141

第一节 故意侵权责任中的抗辩事由   141

18. O'Brien v. Cunard Steamship Co., 154 Mass. 272, 28 N.E. 266 (1891)   141

19. Barton v. Bee Line, Inc., 238 App. Div. 501, 265 N.Y.S. 284 (1933)   143

20. Bang v. Charles T. Miller Hospital, 251 Minn. 427, 88 N.W.2d 186 (1958)   145

21. Kennedy v. Parrott, 243 N.C. 355, 90 S.E.2d 754 (1956)   151

22. Hackbart v. Cincinnati Bengals, Inc., 601 F.2d 516 (10th Cir. 1979)   157

23. Chatterton v Gerson [1981] QB 432   163

24. Balmain New Ferry Co Ltd v Robertson (1906) 4 CLR 379   167

25. Courvoisier v. Raymond, 23 Colo. 113, 47 P. 284 (1896)   171

26. Katko v. Briney, 183 N.W.2d 657 (Iowa 1971)   177

27. Ashley and Another v Chief Constable of Sussex [2008] UKHL 25, [2008] 1 AC 962   189

28. Ploof v. Putnam, 81 Vt. 471, 71 A. 188 (1908)   197

29. In Re F (Mental Patient: Sterilisation) [1990] 2 AC 1   199

第二节 过失侵权责任中的抗辩事由   207

30. Butterfield v Forrester (1809) 11 East 60, 103 ER 926   207

31. Davies v Mann (1842) 10 M & W 546, 152 ER 588   207

32. Knight v. Jewett, 3 Cal. 4th 296, 834 P.2d 696, 11 Cal. Rptr. 2d 2 (1992)   211

33. Jones v Livox Quarries [1952] 2 QB 608   215

34. Froom v Butcher [1976] QB 286   219

35. Meistrich v. Casino Arena Attractions, Inc., 31 N.J. 44, 155 A.2d 90 (1959)   225

36. Morris v Murray [1991] 2 QB 6   229

第四章 因果关系   241

第一节 事实因果关系或法律因果关系   241

37. Hoyt v. Jeffers, 30 Mich. 181 (1874)   241

38. Smith v. Rapid Transit Inc., 317 Mass. 469, 58 N.E.2d 754 (1945)   245

39. Summers v. Tice, 33 Cal. 2d 80, 199 P.2d 1 (1948)   247

40. Ybarra v. Spangard, 25 Cal. 2d 486, 154 P.2d 687 (1944)   251

41. Barnett v Chelsea and Kensington Hospital Management Committee [1969] 1 QB 428　　255
42. Gregg v Scott [2005] UKHL 2, [2005] 2 AC 176　　259
43. Bonnington Castings Ltd v Wardlaw [1956] AC 613　　279
44. Fairchild v Glenhaven Funeral Services Ltd [2002] UKHL 22, [2003] 1 AC 32　　283

第二节　并发因果关系和继发因果关系　　289
45. Dillon v. Twin State Gas & Electric Co., 85 N.H. 449, 163 A. 111 (1932)　　289
46. Kingston v. Chicago & N.W. Ry.Co., 191 Wis. 610, 211 N.W. 913 (1927)　　291
47. Baker v Willoughby [1970] AC 467　　295

第五章　侵入土地与妨害　　305

第一节　美国法上的侵入土地与妨害　　305
48. Peters v. Archambault, 361 Mass. 91, 278 N.E.2d 729 (1972)　　305
49. Davis v. Georgia-Pacific Corp., 251 Or. 239, 445 P.2d 481 (1968)　　311
50. Jost v. Dairyland Power Cooperative, 45 Wis. 2d 164, 172 N.W.2d 647 (1969)　　315
51. Spur Industries, Inc. v. Del E. Webb Development Co., 108 Ariz. 178, 494 P.2d 700 (1972)　　317

第二节　英国法上的侵入土地与妨害　　323
52. Graham v Peat (1801) 1 East 244, 102 ER 95　　323
53. Smith v Stone (1647) Sty 65, 82 ER 533　　323
54. Cambridge Water Co Ltd v Eastern Counties Leather plc [1994] 2 AC 264　　323
55. Sedleigh-Denfield v O'Callaghan [1940] AC 880　　327
56. Hunter v Canary Wharf Ltd [1997] AC 655　　335

第六章　严格责任　　353

第一节　共同的起点：Rylands v Fletcher 案　　353
57. Fletcher v Rylands (1865–66) LR 1 Ex 265　　353
58. Rylands v Fletcher (1868) L.R. 3 H.L. 330　　359
第二节　美国法上的发展：异常危险活动　　361
59. Turner v. Big Lake Oil Co., 128 Tex. 155, 96 S.W.2d 221 (1936)　　361
60. Siegler v. Kuhlman, 81 Wash. 2d 448, 502 P.2d 1181 (1972)　　365
61. PSI Energy, Inc. v. Roberts, 829 N.E.2d 943 (Ind. 2005)　　371

第三节　英国法上的发展：在土地非自然利用中溢出的
　　　　危险物　　　　　　　　　　　　　　　　　　　　　377
62. Cambridge Water Co Ltd v Eastern Counties Leather Plc [1994] 2 AC 264　　377
63. Transco Plc v Stockport Metropolitan Borough Council [2003] UKHL 61,
　　[2004] 2 AC 1　　　　　　　　　　　　　　　　　　　　　383

第七章　产品责任　　　　　　　　　　　　　　　　　　　　395

第一节　美国法：缺陷三分法　　　　　　　　　　　　　　　　395
64. MacPherson v. Buick Motor Co., 217 N.Y. 382, 111 N.E. 1050 (1916)　　395
65. Vandermark v. Ford Motor Co., 391 P.2d 168 (Cal. 1964)　　399
66. Sheckells v. AGV Corp., 987 F.2d 1532 (11th Cir. 1993)　　405
第二节　英国法：从过失责任到严格责任　　　　　　　　　　　413
67. A v National Blood Authority [2001] 3 All ER 289　　413

第八章　损害赔偿金　　　　　　　　　　　　　　　　　　　　427

第一节　医疗费用　　　　　　　　　　　　　　　　　　　　　427
68. Williams v. Bright, 230 A.D.2d 548, 658 N.Y.S.2d 910, appeal dismissed,
　　90 N.Y.2d 935, 686 N.E.2d 1368 (1997)　　　　　　　　　　427
69. Coyne v. Campbell, 11 N.Y.2d 372, 183 N.E.2d 891 (1962)　　435
70. Hunt v Severs [1994] 2 AC 350　　441
第二节　收入损失　　　　　　　　　　　　　　　　　　　　　449
71. Ruzzi v. Butler Petroleum Company, 527 Pa. 1, 588 A.2d 1 (1991)　　449
72. Grayson v. Irvmar Realty Corp., 7 A.D.2d 436, 184 N.Y.S.2d 33 (1959)　　453
73. Pickett v British Rail Engineering Ltd [1980] AC 136　　459
第三节　非金钱损失　　　　　　　　　　　　　　　　　　　　467
74. Walters v. Hitchcock, 237 Kan. 31, 697 P.2d 847 (1985)　　467
75. McDougald v. Garber, 73 N.Y.2d 246, 536 N.E.2d 372 (1989)　　475
76. H West & Son Ltd v Shephard [1964] AC 326　　487
第四节　惩罚性或惩戒性损害赔偿金　　　　　　　　　　　　495
77. State Farm Mutual Automobile Insurance Company v. Campbell, 123 S. Ct.
　　1513 (2003)　　　　　　　　　　　　　　　　　　　　　　495
78. Rookes v Barnard [1964] AC 1129　　513

79. Cassell v Broome [1972] AC 1027   517

80. Kuddus v Chief Constable of Leicestershire Constabulary [2001] UKHL 29, [2002] 2 AC 122   519

第九章　不法侵害尊严与故意致人精神损害　　525

第一节　威吓　　525

81. Read v Coker [1853] 13 C.B. 850, 138 ER 1437   525
82. Beach v. Hancock, 27 N.H. 223 (1853)   527
83. Stephens v Myers (1830) 4 C & P 349, 172 ER 735   529

第二节　非法拘禁　　531

84. Whittaker v. Sanford, 110 Me. 77, 85 A. 399 (1912)   531
85. Sindle v. New York City Transit Authority, 33 N.Y.2d 293, 307 N.E.2d 245 (1973)   533
86. Bird v Jones (1845) 7 QB 742, 115 ER 668   537
87. Davidson v Chief Constable of North Wales and another [1994] 2 All ER 597   541

第三节 故意致人精神损害　　545

88. State Rubbish Collectors Association v. Siliznoff, 38 Cal. 2d 330, 240 P.2d 282 (1952)   545
89. Ford v. Revlon, Inc., 153 Ariz. 38, 734 P.2d 580 (1987)   551
90. Wainwright v Home Office [2003] UKHL 53, [2004] 2 AC 406   563

第十章　诽　谤　　573

第一节　美国法：宪法性问题　　573

91. Gertz v. Robert Welch, Inc., 418 U.S. 323, 94 S. Ct. 2997, 41 L. Ed. 2d 789 (1974)   573
92. Milkovich v. Lorain Journal Co., 497 U.S. 1, 110 S. Ct. 2695, 111 L. Ed. 2d 1 (1990)   583

第二节 英国法：定义、救济与言论自由　　591

93. Cassidy v Daily Mirror [1929] 2 KB 331   591
94. John v MGN Ltd [1997] QB 586 p 752   597
95. Derbyshire County Council v Times Newspapers [1993] AC 534   607

第十一章　侵犯隐私　　　　　　　　　　　　　　　　　　615

第一节　美国法上的侵犯隐私之诉　　　　　　　　　　　　615

96. Hamberger v. Eastman, 106 N.H. 107, 206 A.2d 239 (1964)　　615

97. Shulman v. Group W Productions, Inc., 18 Cal. 4th 200, 955 P.2d 469, 74 Cal. Rptr. 2d 843 (1998)　　619

98. Godbehere v. Phoenix Newspapers, Inc., 162 Ariz. 335, 783 P.2d 781 (1989)　　631

第二节　英国法上的侵犯隐私之诉　　　　　　　　　　　　639

99. Wainwright v Home Office [2003] UKHL 53, [2004] 2 AC 406　　639

100. Campbell v Mirror Group Newspapers Ltd [2004] UKHL 22, [2004] 2 AC 457　　647

巨人已逝、巨著长存（代后记）　　　　　　　　　　　　　673

Chapter 1. Intentional Torts

Section 1. Intent

1. Vosburg v. Putney, 80 Wis. 523, 50 N.W. 403 (1891)

Supreme Court of Wisconsin, United States

The action was brought to recover damages for battery, alleged to have been committed by the defendant upon the plaintiff on February 20, 1889. The answer is a general denial. At the date of the alleged the plaintiff was a little more than fourteen years of age, and the defendant a little less than twelve years of age.

The injury complained of was caused by a kick inflicted by defendant upon the leg of the plaintiff, a little below the knee. The transaction occurred in a schoolroom in Waukesha, during school hours, both parties being pupils in the school. A former trial of the cause resulted in a verdict and judgment for the plaintiff for $2,800. The defendant appealed from such judgment to this court, and the same was reversed for error, and a new trial awarded. 78 Wis. 84.

The case has been again tried in the circuit court, and resulted in a verdict for plaintiff for $2,500. The facts of the case, as they appeared on both trials, are sufficiently stated in the opinion by Mr. Justice Orton on the former appeal....

On the jury found a special verdict, as follows: "(1) Had the plaintiff during the month of January, 1889, received an injury just above the knee, which became inflamed, and produced pus? *Answer.* Yes. (2) Had such injury on the 20th day of February, 1889, nearly healed at the point of the injury? A. Yes. (3) Was the plaintiff, before said 20th of February, lame, as the result of such injury? A. No. (4) Had the *tibia* in the plaintiff's right leg become inflamed or diseased to some extent before he received the blow or kick from the defendant? A. No. (5) What was the exciting cause of the injury to the plaintiff's leg? A. Kick. (6) Did the defendant, in touching the plaintiff with his foot, intend to do him any harm? A. No. (7) At what sum do you assess the damages of the plaintiff? A. $2,500."

The defendant moved for judgment in his favor on the verdict, and also for a new trial. The plaintiff moved for judgment on the verdict in his favor. The motions of defendant were overruled, and that of the plaintiff granted. Thereupon judgment for plaintiff for $2,500 damages and costs of

第一章　故意侵权责任

第一节　意图

1. Vosburg v. Putney, 80 Wis. 523, 50 N.W. 403 (1891)

美国威斯康星州最高法院

本案原告提起的诉求是对被告于 1889 年 2 月 20 日向原告实施的殴击造成的损害进行赔偿。被告在答辩状中对指控进行了全部否定。指控的殴击行为发生当天，原告刚满 14 岁，而被告则快满 12 岁。

原告控诉的伤害是由被告脚踢原告膝盖略下部位引起的。事件发生在 Waukesha 的一间教室里，当时是在校期间，当事人双方都是该校的学生。在初审中陪审团裁断和法官判决被告向原告赔偿 2 800 美元。被告不服该判决提起上诉，该判决因存在错误而被推翻，并发回重审。（78 Wis. 84.）

本案在巡回法庭再次审理，判决结果要求被告向原告赔偿 2 500 美元。对于在两次初审中都审理过的案件事实，Orton 法官在首次上诉的判决意见书中进行了充分的说明……

陪审团作出的特殊裁断内容如下："（1）原告是否在 1889 年 1 月膝盖以上受伤，而伤口发炎灌脓？回答：是的。（2）该伤口在 1889 年 2 月 20 日是否已经接近愈合？回答：是的。（3）原告是否在 2 月 20 日之前由于第一次受伤而瘸腿？回答：没有。（4）在被告接触或踢打原告之前，原告右腿的胫骨是否已经有一定程度的发炎或感染？回答：没有。（5）原告腿伤的刺激因素是什么？回答：脚踢。（6）被告在用脚接触原告时是否意图伤害他？回答：没有。（7）你们确定原告应得到多少赔偿款？回答：2 500 美元。"

被告要求法官根据陪审团裁断作出有利于自己的判决，并要求重审。原告要求法官根据陪审团裁断作出有利于自己的判决。被告的要求被驳回了，原告的要求得到了支持。由此，支持原告 2 500 美元的赔偿和诉讼费用请求的判决书被依法记录在案。被告对判决结果提起了上诉。

suit was duly entered. The defendant appeals from the judgment.

Lyon, J. Several errors are assigned, only three of which will be considered.

1. The jury having found that the defendant, in touching the plaintiff with his foot, did not intend to do him any harm, counsel for defendant maintain that the plaintiff has no cause of action, and that defendant's motion for judgment on the special verdict should have been granted. In support of this proposition counsel quote from 2 Greenl. Ev. §83, the rule that "the intention to do harm is of the essence of an assault." Such is the rule, no doubt, in actions or prosecutions for mere assaults. But this is an action to recover damages for an alleged assault and battery. In such case the rule is correctly stated, in many of the authorities cited by counsel, that plaintiff must show either that the intention was unlawful, or that the defendant is in fault. If the intended act is unlawful, the intention to commit it must necessarily be unlawful. Hence, as applied to this case, if the kicking of the plaintiff by the defendant was an unlawful act, the intention of defendant to kick him was also unlawful.

Had the parties been upon the play-grounds of the school, engaged in the usual boyish sports, the defendant being free from malice, wantonness, or negligence, and intending no harm to plaintiff in what he did, we should hesitate to hold the act of the defendant unlawful, or that he could be held liable in this action. Some consideration is due to the implied license of the play-grounds. But it appears that the injury was inflicted in the school, after it had been called to order by the teacher, and after the regular exercises of the school had commenced. Under these circumstances, no implied license to do the act complained of existed, and such act was a violation of the order and decorum of the school, and necessarily unlawful. Hence we are of the opinion that, under the evidence and verdict, the action may be sustained.

…

3. Certain questions were proposed on behalf of defendant to be submitted to the jury, founded upon the theory that only such damages could be recovered as the defendant might reasonably be supposed to have contemplated as likely to result from his kicking the plaintiff. The court refused to submit such questions to the jury. The ruling was correct. The rule of damages in actions for torts was held in Brown v. C., M. & St. P.R. Co., to be that the wrong-doer is liable for all injuries resulting directly from the wrongful act, whether they could or could not have been foreseen by him.…

2. Garratt v. Dailey, 46 Wash. 2d 197, 279 P.2d 1091 (1955)

Supreme Court of Washington, United States

Hill, J.

The liability of an infant for an alleged battery is presented to this court for the first time.

Lyon 法官主笔①:

几个错误被陈述,但只有三个错误将得到考虑。

(1)陪审团已经发现被告在用脚接触原告时并不打算伤害他,被告的律师因此坚持认为原告没有诉因,因此被告对特定裁断作出有利于自己的判决的要求应该被准予。为了支持这种主张,被告律师援引了 2 Green 1. Ev. §83 中的规则:"威吓的关键在于是否有伤害的意图。"毫无疑问,任何威吓行为案件的诉讼和检举都要依据这个规则。但是这是一个为获得因被指控的威吓行为和殴击行为所导致损害的赔偿的诉讼。在本案中,该规则得到了正确的援引,律师引用的许多法源都要求原告必须证明被告的意图是违法的,或者被告有过错。如果被告意图实施的行为是违法的,那么实施该行为的意图也应该是违法的。因此,适用到这个案件中,如果被告踢原告是违法的行为,那么被告踢原告的意图也是违法的。

如果原告和被告双方在学校的操场上参加男孩常见的体育活动,被告不存在任何的恶意、肆意或过失,而且在没有伤害原告意图的情况下伤害到了原告,那么我们便不宜轻易认定被告的行为是非法的,或者被告应该为自己的行为承担责任。这样考虑是出于特殊行为发生的地点,即操场。但是原告受伤的地点是在学校,被告的行为出现在老师整顿了纪律以及学校的各项常规正常开始之后。在这样的情况下,原告指控的行为不存在任何的特殊情况,而且被告的行为违反了学校的秩序和规范,因此是非法的。所以我们认为,基于证据和陪审团的裁断,该申请可以得到支持。

……

(3)一些代表被告立场的被提出并提交给陪审团的问题基于这样一个理论,即被告在踢到原告之后,有理由相信这样的伤是可以恢复的。法院拒绝将这些问题提交给陪审团。法庭的裁决是正确的。在 Brown v. C., M. & St. P.R.Co.,一案中提到的侵权行为伤害规则这样写道:不法行为人应该对违法行为直接导致的所有伤害承担责任,无论过错人是否预见到该伤害……

2. Garratt v. Dailey, 46 Wash. 2d 197, 279 P.2d 1091 (1955)

美国华盛顿州最高法院

Hill 法官主笔:

本法院第一次审理由幼儿实施的殴击行为而引起的侵权责任案件。1951

---

① 美国法院判决书中的多数意见和相同的反对意见都是由一名法官主笔,其他法官在其同意的意见之后被列出,以表示对多数意见或者反对意见的同意。因此,译者添加"主笔"一词,来表明意见的撰写者,以区别于该意见的同意者。以下作相同处理。——译者注

Brian Dailey (age five years, nine months) was visiting with Naomi Garratt, an adult and a sister of the plaintiff, Ruth Garratt, likewise an adult, in the backyard of the plaintiff's home, on July 16, 1951. It is plaintiff's contention that she came out into the backyard to talk with Naomi and that, as she started to sit down in a wood and canvas lawn chair, Brian deliberately pulled it out from under her. The only one of the three persons present so testifying was Naomi Garratt. (Ruth Garratt, the plaintiff, did not testify as to how or why she fell.) The trial court, unwilling to accept this testimony, adopted instead Brian Dailey's version of what happened, and made the following findings:

"III....that while Naomi Garratt and Brian Dailey were in the back yard the plaintiff, Ruth Garratt, came out of her house into the back yard. Some time subsequent thereto defendant, Brian Dailey, picked up a lightly built wood and canvas lawn chair which was then and there located in the back yard of the above described premises, moved it sideways a few feet and seated himself therein, at which time he discovered the plaintiff, Ruth Garratt, about to sit down at the place where the lawn chair had formerly been, at which time he hurriedly got up from the chair and attempted to move it toward Ruth Garratt to aid her in sitting down in the chair; that due to the defendant's small size and lack of dexterity he was unable to get the lawn chair under the plaintiff in time to prevent her from falling to the ground. That plaintiff fell to the ground and sustained a fracture of her hip, and other injuries and damages as hereinafter set forth.

"IV. That the preponderance of the evidence in this case establishes that when the defendant, Brian Dailey, moved the chair in question *he did not have any wilful or unlawful purpose in doing so;* that *he did not have any intent to injure the plaintiff, or any intent to bring about any unauthorized or offensive contact with her person* or any objects appurtenant thereto; that the circumstances which immediately preceded the fall of the plaintiff established that the defendant, *Brian Dailey, did not have purpose, intent or design to perform a prank or to effect an assault and battery upon the person of the plaintiff.* " (Italics ours, for a purpose hereinafter indicated.)

It is conceded that Ruth Garratt's fall resulted in a fractured hip and other painful and serious injuries. To obviate the necessity of a retrial in the event this court determines that she was entitled to a judgment against Brian Dailey, the amount of her damage was found to be eleven thousand dollars. Plaintiff appeals from a judgment dismissing the action and asks for the entry of a judgment in that amount or a new trial.

The authorities generally, but with certain notable exceptions (see Bohlen, "Liability in Tort of Infants and Insane Persons," 23 Mich. L. Rev. 9), state that, when a minor has committed a tort with force, he is liable to be proceeded against as any other person would be.

In our analysis of the applicable law, we start with the basic premise that Brian, whether five or fifty-five, must have committed some wrongful act before he could be liable for appellant's injuries.

年 7 月 16 日，被告 Brian Dailey（5 岁零 9 个月）与原告 Ruth Garratt 的一位成年姐姐 Naomi Garratt 和另一位成年人 Ruth Garratt 一同来到原告家的后院拜访原告。原告的主张是，她来到后院与 Naomi 交谈，当她开始坐在一个木质帆布草坪躺椅上时，Brian 蓄意地将椅子从她身下抽走。现场三个人中唯一能提供证词的是 Naomi Garratt（原告 Ruth Garratt 并没有就她如何摔倒或为什么摔倒进行说明）。初审法院并没有采信该证词，而接受了 Brian Dailey 对事件经过的陈述，并且作出了以下裁决：

"III……当 Naomi Garratt 和 Brian Dailey 在后院时，原告 Ruth Garratt 从自己的房间走出来，来到后院。过了一会儿，被告 Brian Dailey 将上述地方放置的一张轻巧的木质帆布草坪躺椅抬起来，将之向旁边挪了几英尺，然后在椅子上坐了下来，而这时被告发现原告 Ruth Garratt 正打算在椅子原先放置的位置坐下，因此 Brian 赶紧起身想将椅子放回原处，以便帮助 Ruth 坐下；由于被告体形过小，而且动作也不太灵活，他没能及时把椅子拖到原告身下，也没能避免原告摔在地上。原告摔倒在地，造成臀部骨折，由此还引发了其他的伤情和损失。"

"IV. 本案的优势证据显示，[当被告 Brian Dailey 挪动本案涉及的椅子时，他并不存有意的或违法的目的；他没有伤害原告的意图，也不存在任何未经许可的或攻击性的接触原告本人或所属物品的意图]；原告摔倒前的情形显示出，[被告 Brian Dailey 并没有实施恶作剧或对原告人身进行威吓或殴击的目的、意图或企图]。"

得到承认的是，Ruth Garratt 的摔倒导致她臀部骨折和其他痛苦和严重的伤害。为了避免该案重审的必要，初审法院决定作出对她有利的判决，判定 Brian Dailey 向原告支付 11 000 美元的赔偿。原告提出上诉，要求判决驳回该诉讼，并对该赔偿金额进行判决登记，或重新审理。

除了一些值得注意的例外（参见 Bohlen 的《幼儿和精神病患者的侵权责任》，23 Mich. L. Rev. 9），权威人士普遍认为，如果未成年人以武力实施了侵权行为，那么他仍然应和其他人一样承担侵权责任。

在分析适用法律时，我们有一个基本前提，即 Brian 无论是 5 岁还是 55 岁，在造成上诉人受伤之前，一定实施了某种不法行为。

初审法院查明的 Brian 是 Garratt 后院的造访者的事实得到了证据的支持，而且否认了上诉人关于 Brian 是侵入者，因而无权接触、挪动院子中的椅子，或坐在椅子上的主张，法院将不再考虑该争议。

The trial court's finding that Brian was a visitor in the Garratt backyard is supported by the evidence and negatives appellant's assertion that Brian was a trespasser and had no right to touch, move, or sit in any chair in that yard, and that contention will not receive further consideration.

It is urged that Brian's action in moving the chair constituted a battery. A definition (not all-inclusive but sufficient for our purpose) of a battery is the intentional infliction of a harmful bodily contact upon another. The rule that determines liability for battery is given in 1 Restatement, Torts, 29, §13, as:

> An act which, directly or indirectly, is the legal cause of a harmful contact with another's person makes the actor liable to the other, if
> (a) the act is done with the intention of bringing about a harmful or offensive contact or an apprehension thereof to the other or a third person, and
> (b) the contact is not consented to by the other or the other's consent thereto is procured by fraud or duress, and
> (c) the contact is not otherwise privileged.

We have in this case no question of consent or privilege. We therefore proceed to an immediate consideration of intent and its place in the law of battery. In the comment on clause (a), the Restatement says:

> Character of actor's intention. In order that an act may be done with the intention of bringing about a harmful or offensive contact or an apprehension thereof to a particular person, either the other or a third person, the act must be done for the purpose of causing the contact or apprehension or with knowledge on the part of the actor that such contact or apprehension is substantially certain to be produced.

See also, Prosser on Torts 41, §8.

We have here the conceded volitional act of Brian, i.e., the moving of a chair. Had the plaintiff proved to the satisfaction of the trial court that Brian moved the chair while she was in the act of sitting down, Brian's action would patently have been for the purpose or with the intent of causing the plaintiff's bodily contact with the ground, and she would be entitled to a judgment against him for the resulting damages. Vosburg v. Putney (1891), 80 Wis. 523, 50 N.W. 403.

The plaintiff based her case on that theory, and the trial court held that she failed in her proof and accepted Brian's version of the facts rather than that given by the eyewitness who testified for the plaintiff. After the trial court determined that the plaintiff had not established her theory of a battery (i.e., that Brian had pulled the chair out from under the plaintiff while she was in the act of

Brian 移动椅子的行为被极力地主张为构成殴击。殴击的定义（尽管不全面但足以适用于本案）是，殴击是对他人故意施加的致害性身体接触。决定殴击责任的规则在《侵权法第一次重述》第 13 条（1 Restatement, Torts, 29, §13）规定如下：

> 满足下列条件时，如果其行为直接或间接地成为他人身体致害性接触的法律原因，那么该行为人应向该他人承担责任：
> (a) 该行为以引起对他人或第三人的致害性或攻击性接触，或者使其产生此类恐惧为意图的；并且
> (b) 该接触没有征得该他人的同意，或该他人的同意是通过欺诈或者强迫得到的；并且
> (c) 该接触并非可以被特免。

在本案中，不存在同意或特免的问题。因此，我们可以直接考虑意图，以及意图在殴击法中的地位。《重述》中该条（a）款的评论如下：

> 行为人意图的特征。如果某一行为可能以引起致害性或攻击性接触，或者以使其产生此类恐惧为意图的，针对某一特定人，无论是他人或第三人，那么该行为必须是以引起该接触或恐惧为目的，或者对行为人而言明知实质上确定会造成这样的接触或恐惧。

另参见 Prosser on Torts 41, §8。

我们这里姑且认为 Brian 移动椅子的行为是有意的。如果原告向初审法院充分证实了 Brian 在她即将坐下时移动了椅子，那么 Brian 的行为显然存在导致原告身体与地面接触的目的或意图，因此原告有权要求法院作出被告承担损害的判决。[Vosburg v. Putney（1891），80 Wis. 523, 50 N.W. 403]

原告的理由基于上述理论，而初审法院认为原告没有能够充分举证，于是采纳了 Brian 的说法，而没有采信为原告作证的目击证人的证词。在初审法院认定原告没有能够证实殴击理论成立之后（即被告在原告即将坐下时将椅子从她身下拖走的说法），在已有事实的基础上，殴击行为是否成立成为了考虑的对象。

在这个连结点上，我们引用了与《重述》该条第 a 款有关的另一部分关

sitting down), it then became concerned with whether a battery was established under the facts as it found them to be.

In this connection, we quote another portion of the comment on the "Character of actor's intention," relating to clause (a) of the rule from the Restatement heretofore set forth:

> It is not enough that the act itself is intentionally done and this, even though the actor realizes or should realize that it contains a very grave risk of bringing about the contact or apprehension. Such realization may make the actor's conduct negligent or even reckless but unless he realizes that to a substantial certainty, the contact or apprehension will result, the actor has not that intention which is necessary to make him liable under the rule stated in this Section.

A battery would be established if, in addition to plaintiff's fall, it was proved that, when Brian moved the chair, he knew with substantial certainty that the plaintiff would attempt to sit down where the chair had been. If Brian had any of the intents which the trial court found, in the italicized portions of the findings of fact quoted above, that he did not have, he would of course have had the knowledge to which we have referred. The mere absence of any intent to injure the plaintiff or to play a prank on her or to embarrass her, or to commit an assault and battery on her would not absolve him from liability if in fact he had such knowledge. Without such knowledge, there would be nothing wrongful about Brian's act in moving the chair, and, there being no wrongful act, there would be no liability.

While a finding that Brian had no such knowledge can be inferred from the findings made, we believe that before the plaintiff's action in such a case should be dismissed there should be no question but that the trial court had passed upon that issue; hence, the case should be remanded for clarification of the findings to specifically cover the question of Brian's knowledge, because intent could be inferred therefrom. If the court finds that he had such knowledge, the necessary intent will be established and the plaintiff will be entitled to recover, even though there was no purpose to injure or embarrass the plaintiff. Vosburg v. Putney, supra. If Brian did not have such knowledge, there was no wrongful act by him, and the basic premise of liability on the theory of a battery was not established.

It will be noted that the law of battery as we have discussed it is the law applicable to adults, and no significance has been attached to the fact that Brian was a child less than six years of age when the alleged battery occurred. The only circumstance where Brian's age is of any consequence is in determining what he knew, and there his experience, capacity, and understanding are of course material.

From what has been said, it is clear that we find no merit in plaintiff's contention that we can

于"行为人意图的特征"的评论：

> 即使行为人认识到或者应当认识到该行为有造成接触或恐惧的非常重大潜在风险，仍然不能说明行为本身是故意被实施的这一点。行为人的这种认识会导致其行为被认为是有过失的或者鲁莽的，但除非他认识到该接触或恐惧确定会发生，都不能认为行为人并不具备依照本条所述的规则必须承担责任的意图。

除原告摔倒之外，如果可以证明 Brian 在移动椅子时非常确信原告将在椅子原来放置的位置坐下，那么殴击行为成立。如果初审法院查明 Brian 具有初审法院所查明的意图，而事实上他并没有，那么他当然对我们提及的内容有相当的认识。如果 Brian 真的具有这样的认识，那么即使没有伤害原告或捉弄原告或令原告尴尬或对原告实施威吓或殴击的意图，也不能免除被告的侵权责任。如果没有这样的认识，那么 Brian 移动椅子的行为便没有过错，也就没有不法行为，就更不会有责任。

从法院查明的事实中，无法推断出 Brian 存在这种认识，我们认为在该案中原告的诉讼被驳回之前，并不存在问题，但初审法院对该问题并未予以考虑；因此，应将该案发回，澄清事实，以便回答 Brian 是否具备这样的认识这一问题，因为意图可以从中得到推断。如果法院查明他存在这样的认识，那么必备的意图就成立，原告便会获得救济，哪怕被告并没有伤害原告或使原告难堪的目的。（前引 Vosburg v. Putney 案。）如果 Brian 没有这样的认识，那么他的不法行为便不存在，基于殴击理论的侵权责任的前提也便不存在。

应该注意到的是，我们讨论的殴击法是一种适用于成年人的法律，在被诉殴击行为发生时，并不强调 Brian 是一个不满 6 岁的儿童。唯一受到 Brian 的年龄影响的问题是他到底认识到什么，他的经历、能力和理解力当然都是重要的。

如上文所述，很明显，我们没有找到案卷中原告主张法院作出对她有利的 11 000 美元判决的依据。

同时我们也没有在案卷中找到任何使得重审获得授权的错误……

案件被发回重审以澄清事实，指示陪审团明确 Brian Dailey 是否知道原告即将在椅子原来放置的位置坐下。如果事实裁决使改变判决显得必要，则应

direct the entry of a judgment for eleven thousand dollars in her favor on the record now before us.

Nor do we find any error in the record that warrants a new trial....

The case is remanded for clarification, with instructions to make definite findings on the issue of whether Brian Dailey knew with substantial certainty that the plaintiff would attempt to sit down where the chair which he moved had been, and to change the judgment if the findings warrant it....

Remanded for clarification.

Schwellenbach, Donworth, and Weaver, JJ., concur.

3. Fowler v Lanning [1959] 1 QB 426

Queen's Bench Division, United Kindgom

DIPLOCK J.read the following judgment.

"The distinction between actions of trespass on the case and trespass vi et armisshould be most carefully and precisely observed. Otherwise we shall introduce much confusion and uncertainty." So said de Grey C.J. in 1773 in *Scott v. Shepherd*. It must gratify the ghosts of generations of special pleaders that today, nearly a century after the passing of the Judicature Act 1875, I should be invited to decide whether such a distinction still exists where an unintentional injury to the person of the plaintiff arises directly from an act of the defendant, and should be invited to decide this point upon what is the modern equivalent of demurrer.

The writ in this case claims damages for trespass to the person committed by the defendant at Corfe Castle, in the county of Dorset, on November 19, 1957. The statement of claim alleges laconically that at that place and on that date "the defendant shot the plaintiff," and that by reason thereof the plaintiff sustained personal injuries and has suffered loss and damage. By his defence the defendant, in addition to traversing the allegations of fact, raises the objection "that the statement of claim is bad in law and discloses no cause of action against him on the ground that the plaintiff does not allege that the said shooting was either intentional or negligent."

An order has been made that this point of law be disposed of before the trial of the issues of fact in the action. That order is binding upon me, and, in disposing of it, I can look no further than the pleadings. I must confess that at first glance at the pleadings I felt some anxiety lest I was being invited to decide a point which has long puzzled the professors (see the article by Professors Goodhart and Winfield, 1933 Law Quarterly Review, vol. 49, p. 359; Pollock on Torts, 15th ed., p. 128; Salmond on Torts, 12th ed., p. 311; Winfield on Torts, 5th ed., p. 213), only to learn ultimately that, just as in *Donoghue v. Stevenson,* there was in fact no snail in the ginger-beer bottle, so in this case there was in fact no pellet in the defendant's gun.

The point of law is not, however, a mere academic one even at the present stage of the action. The alleged injuries were, I am told, sustained at a shooting party; it is not suggested that the

改变判决……

发回重审以澄清事实。

Schwellenbach 法官、Donworth 法官和 Weaver 法官赞同判决。

3. Fowler v Lanning [1959] 1 QB 426

联合王国高级法院王座分庭

Diplock 法官宣读了以下判决:

De Grey 首席法官在 1733 年的 *Scott v Shepherd* 一案中曾说:"若不仔细地区分'间接侵害之诉'和'人身侵害之诉',必然会造成混乱和不确定。"而经过几代特别辩护人的努力,我得以有幸在百年后的今天,通过英国 1875 年《司法组织法》,在原告受到的损伤并非由被告过失造成的情境下,判断这样的区分仍然存在;也在与抗辩(demurrer)对等的现代概念中,判断这样的区分是否依然存在。

原告 McCreery 诉称被告于 1957 年 11 月 19 日在 Dorset 郡的 Corfe 城堡侵害其人身,遂提起"人身侵害之诉",请求判决被告赔偿原告相应损失。原告的起诉状中只是粗略地声称在某地某时"被告枪击了原告",使原告受到了人身侵害和其他的损失。被告除了否认原告主张的事实,还另外辩称"起诉状在法律上并不合适,没有表明任何针对被告的诉由,因为原告既未主张枪击是被告故意所为,也未主张是被告过失所为"。

本席被指令要求在审查本案事实前先处理涉及的法律上的争议焦点。因为该指令对本席有约束力,本席只能对起诉书中提到的部分进行审查。本席必须承认,在刚看到本案的起诉书时本席有一丝忧虑,因为本席担心需要对一个长期困扰学者们的问题给出最终答案。[参见 Goodhart 和 Winfield 的文章,载 Law Quarterly Review, vol. 49, p. 359;《Polloc 论侵权》(第十五版),第 128 页;《Salmond 论侵权》(第十二版),第 311 页;《Winfield 论侵权》(第五版),第 213 页]。然而,后来本席发现,如同 *Donoghue v Stevenson* 一案中的姜汁啤酒的瓶子里并没有蜗牛,本案中被告的枪里也没有子弹。

然而,法律上的争议焦点,即便在现在这个诉讼阶段,也并非仅仅是个学理问题。原告主张在一个射击聚会上他受伤了;然而他却并没有主张射击行为是被告故意所为。因此,这里的关键问题就是,假设原告确实是被被告开枪所伤,此时是由原告承担证明被告过失的责任——现代法律要求这种情

shooting was intentional. The practical issue is whether, if the plaintiff was in fact injured by a shot from a gun fired by the defendant, the onus lies upon the plaintiff to prove that the defendant was negligent, in which case, under the modern system of pleading, he must so plead and give particulars of negligence (see R.S.C., Ord. 19, r. 4), or whether it lies upon the defendant to prove that the plaintiff's injuries were not caused by the defendant's negligence, in which case the plaintiff's statement of claim is sufficient and discloses a cause of action (see R.S.C., Ord. 19, r. 25). The issue is thus a neat one of onus of proof.

…

In trespass on the case the onus of proof of the defendant's negligence undoubtedly lay upon the plaintiff. Where it lay in trespass is much more difficult to determine. The defence that the accident "was inevitable and that the defendant had committed no negligence to give occasion to the hurt" was available to the defendant upon a plea to the general issue by the end of the seventeenth century: see *Gibbons v. Pepper*; and this appears to have been accepted by the Court of Common Pleas as late as 1823: see *Wakeman v. Robinson* - a case still cited as authority in the third edition of Bullen&Leake in 1868. Since the plea to the general issue merely denied the existence of the necessary ingredients of the tort, this would suggest that in the case of trespass to the person the onus lay upon the plaintiff to show that the defendant's act was either intentional or negligent. Lord Ellenborough, on the other hand, sitting at nisi prius in 1810, had already decided in *Knapp v. Salsbury* that such a defence must be specially pleaded, and the Court of King's Bench in 1842 in *Hall v. Fearnley* appears to have come down on the pleading point on the side of Lord Ellenborough, although the differences between the two reports of this case make it difficult to elicit the ratio decidendi. But although the two last-cited cases destroy the force of any inference as to onus of proof which might be drawn from *Gibbons v. Pepper*, they do not themselves give rise to the contrary inference. With the growth of special pleading, and in particular after the "general rules" of Hil. Term, 1834, there were many matters the onus of proof of which, if disputed, lay upon the plaintiff, which were not regarded as traversed by a plea to the general issue: see Bullen&Leake, 3rd ed., pp. 699-704.

…

I think that what appears to have been the practice of the profession during the present century is sound in law. I can summarise the law as I understand it from my examination of the cases as follows:

(1) Trespass to the person does not lie if the injury to the plaintiff, although the direct consequence of the act of the defendant, was caused unintentionally and without negligence on the defendant's part.

(2) Trespass to the person on the highway does not differ in this respect from trespass to the person committed in any other place.

况下原告提出这个主张并给出能证明过失的事实（参见《最高法院规则》第19号命令第4号规则）；抑或是由被告来证明原告所受伤害并非由其过失所致——这种情况下原告的诉讼请求是充分的，是有明确诉由的（参见《最高法院规则》第19号命令第25号规则）。因此，本案关键的争议焦点是一个纯粹的举证责任分配问题。

……

毫无疑问，在"间接侵害之诉"中，被告过失的举证责任应由原告来承担。而在"人身侵害之诉"中，谁来承担举证责任就不是那么好判断了。在17世纪末的一个案件中，在被告提出的"概括否认答辩"中，他被允许提起如下抗辩：涉案事故"是不可避免的，而被告对伤害的产生不具有任何过失"。（参见 Gibbons v Pepper。）至迟在1823年，这种观点也被"民事诉讼法院"所接受［参见 Wakeman v Robinson，该案在 Bullen&Leake（第三版）中依然被视为有效的法律渊源。］由于"概括否认答辩"仅仅旨在否认侵权责任构成要件的存在，这说明在"人身侵害之诉"中，原告承担证明被告故意或者过失的责任。相反，在1810年的一个独任初审案件 Knapp v Salsbury 中，Ellenborough 大法官判决这种抗辩必须以"特别答辩"的形式来进行。而在1842年的 Hall v Fearnley 一案中，王座法院似乎在这一点上和 Ellenborough 大法官意见一致，虽然本案在两个判例汇编中的记录有所不同，使得我们很难理解它的判决理由。然而，虽然上文引用的两个判决否定了 Gibbons v Pepper 在举证责任分配上的约束力，这两个判决本身却没有给出相反的观点。随着"特别答辩"的发展，特别是随着1834年春季开庭期的"一般规则"的产生，很多案件事实的举证责任，如果有争议，都由原告来承担，且不会仅因被告的"概括否认答辩"就被推翻［参见 Bullen&Leake（第三版），第699至704页］。

……

本席认为本世纪我们的职业中的这种做法，在法律上是有效的。本席通过对相关判例的审视，现将本案所涉及的法律规范总结如下：

（1）即便被告的行为确实是损害造成的直接原因，只要被告对此行为不是故意或者过失的，"人身侵害之诉"即不成立。

（2）涉及道路交通事故的"人身伤害"，在这一点上与其他任何地方发生的人身伤害没有任何区别。

（3）1866年 Blackburn 法官认为只有当客观情况显示原告是自愿承担

(3) If it were right to say with Blackburn J. in 1866 that negligence is a necessary ingredient of unintentional trespass only where the circumstances are such as to show that the plaintiff had taken upon himself the risk of inevitable injury (i.e., injury which is the result of neither intention nor carelessness on the part of the defendant), the plaintiff must today in this crowded world be considered as taking upon himself the risk of inevitable injury from any acts of his neighbour which, in the absence of damage to the plaintiff, would not in themselves be unlawful - of which discharging a gun at a shooting party in 1957 or a trained band exercise in 1617 are obvious examples. For Blackburn J., in the passage I have quoted from *Fletcher v. Rylands*, was in truth doing no more than stating the converse of the principle referred to by Lord Macmillan in *Read v. J. Lyons & Co. Ltd.,* that a man's freedom of action is subject only to the obligation not to infringe any duty of care which he owes to others.

(4) The onus of proving negligence, where the trespass is not intentional, lies upon the plaintiff, whether the action be framed in trespass or in negligence. This has been unquestioned law in highway cases ever since *Holmes v. Mather*, and there is no reason in principle, nor any suggestion in the decided authorities, why it should be any different in other cases. It is, indeed, but an illustration of the rule that he who affirms must prove, which lies at the root of our law of evidence.

I am glad to be able to reach this conclusion, and to know that the Supreme Court of British Columbia has recently done the same (*Walmsley v. Humenick*, for "while admiring the subtlety of the old special pleaders our courts are primarily concerned to see that rules of law and procedure should serve to secure justice between the parties": per Lord Simon in *United Australia Ltd. v. Barclays Bank Ltd.*

If, as I have held, the onus of proof of intention or negligence on the part of the defendant lies upon the plaintiff, then, under the modern rules of pleading, he must allege either intention on the part of the defendant, or, if he relies upon negligence, he must state the facts which he alleges constitute negligence. Without either of such allegations the bald statement that the defendant shot the plaintiff in unspecified circumstances with an unspecified weapon in my view discloses no cause of action.

This is no academic pleading point. It serves to secure justice between the parties. If it is open to the plaintiff - as Mr. McCreery must, I think, contend - on the pleadings as they at present stand to prove that the defendant shot him deliberately, failure to allege such intention deprives the defendant of his right to apply to stay the action pending prosecution for the felony: *Smith v. Selwyn*. I should repeat that there is, of course, in fact no suggestion that the shooting here was intentional, and thus felonious. But if Mr. McCreery be right, proof of intention would be open upon the pleading in its present form.

Turning next to the alternative of negligent trespass to the person, there is here the bare allegation that on a particular day at a particular place "the defendant shot the plaintiff." In what

风险的（即损害并非由被告的故意或者过失造成），被告的过失才是"非过失的人身侵害之诉"的构成要件。我们认为这是正确的，然而在今天这样一个拥挤的世界里，我们必须认为原告是自愿承担了其邻居的行为带来的不可避免的风险，只要这些风险本身——不包括给原告造成伤害的意义上——不是非法的，而在 1957 年在一个射击聚会上开枪和在 1617 年参加民兵训练的案件便正是这样的典型情况。Blackburn 法官在我所引用的 *Fletcher v Rylands* 的段落中，不过是在阐述一个原则的逆命题，该原则是 Macmillan 大法官在 *Read v J. Lyons & Co. Ltd.* 提出的：一个人的行为自由仅仅受到一处限制，即不违反他对其他人的注意义务。

（4）无论在"人身侵害之诉"还是"过失之诉"中，只要侵害不是故意的，对过失的证明就属于原告的责任。这点自 *Holmes v Mather* 一案起，在涉及道路交通事故的"人身侵害之诉"中就是无可否认的。同样，没有任何法律原则或者其他选定的法律渊源支持我们在其他案件中不这么处理。这其实不过是在重申一个证据法的基础规则：谁主张，谁举证。

本席很高兴能得出这个结论，也欣然得知英属哥伦比亚最高法院最近也得出了相同的结论。（*Walmsley v Humenick*，"我们固然敬佩过往的特别辩护人的精明，然而我们法院最看重的还是法律规则和程序应当用来实现当事人之间的正义"——Simon 大法官在 *United Australia Ltd. v Barclays Bank Ltd.* 一案中所言。）

在现代的诉讼主张提出规则下，如果原告承担被告存在故意或者过失的证明责任，那么他必须要么主张被告存在故意，要么主张被告存在过失并证明能够构成过失的事实。如果两者都不主张，而仅仅是主张被告在一个未指明的场合下用未指明的武器枪击了他，在本席看来，诉由就不存在。

关于这点，我觉得在学理上也不会有什么争议。这是用来确保实现双方当事人之间的正义的。如果原告有权——我想 McCreery 先生也会同意——在起诉书中主张被告故意枪击他，不这么主张则反而使得原告丧失了请求中止民事诉讼直至刑事诉讼被提起的权利（*Smith v Selwyn*）。我想再次重申，我们当然没有证据证明枪击是故意的，因此是穷凶极恶的。但是如果 McCreery 先生是对的，证明故意的证据应该早已在现在的起诉书中开示。

让我们来看看另一个可能的诉由"过失侵害人身"。原告仅仅主张在某日某地被告枪击了他，而完全没有提及在什么情况下，用什么武器，是弓箭还是核弹头。这样苍白的指控的内容与被告尽到了注意义务的可能性是并行

circumstances, indeed with what weapon, from bow and arrow to atomic warhead, is not stated. So bare an allegation is consistent with the defendant's having exercised reasonable care. It may be - I know not - that, had the circumstances been set out with greater particularity, there would have been disclosed facts which themselves shouted negligence, so that the doctrine of res ipsa loquitur would have applied. In such a form the statement of claim might have disclosed a cause of action even although the word "negligence" itself had not been used, and the plaintiff in that event would have been limited to relying for proof of negligence upon the facts which he had alleged. But I have today to deal with the pleading as it stands. As it stands, it neither alleges negligence in terms nor alleges facts which, if true, would of themselves constitute negligence. If Mr. McCreery is right, he would be entitled to prove that the defendant's gun was to his knowledge defective or even that he was short-sighted and had left his spectacles at home, nor would the plaintiff be bound at any time before the trial to disclose to the defendant what facts he relies upon as constituting negligence.

I do not see how the plaintiff will be harmed by alleging now the facts upon which he ultimately intends to rely. On the contrary, for him to do so will serve to secure justice between the parties. It offends the underlying purpose of the modern system of pleading that a plaintiff, by calling his grievance "trespass to the person" instead of "negligence," should force a defendant to come to trial blindfold; and I am glad to find nothing in the authorities which compels justice in this case to refrain from stripping the bandage at least from the defendant's eyes.

I hold that the statement of claim in its present form discloses no cause of action.

Section 2. Contact

4. Fisher v. Carrousel Motor Hotel, 424 S.W.2d 627 (Tex. 1967)

Supreme Court of Texas, United States

Greenhill, J. This is a suit for actual and exemplary damages growing out of an alleged assault and battery. The plaintiff Fisher was a mathematician with the Data Processing Division of the Manned Spacecraft Center, an agency of the National Aeronautics and Space Agency, commonly called NASA, near Houston. The defendants were the Carrousel Motor Hotel, Inc., located in Houston, the Brass Ring Club, which is located in the Carrousel, and Robert W. Flynn, who as an employee of the Carrousel was the manager of the Brass Ring Club. Flynn died before the trial, and the suit proceeded as to the Carrousel and the Brass Ring. Trial was to a jury which found for the plaintiff Fisher. The trial court rendered judgment for the defendants notwithstanding the verdict. The Court of Civil Appeals affirmed. 414 S.W.2d 774. The questions before this Court are whether there was evidence that an actionable battery was committed, and, if so, whether the

不悖的。有一种可能，当然我不确定，就是如果情况被描述得更具体一些，也许就会有一些提到的事实能够直接证明过失，因此"事实自证"理论可能被适用。在这种情况下，即便没有明确提到"过失"二字，起诉书是可以标明一个诉由的；而原告也可以在他提到的这些事实范围内，通过举证来证明被告的过失。然而，本席今天需要面对的是现实中已经呈上来的起诉书，它既没有明确提到"过失"二字，也没有提到任何足以本身构成"过失"的事实。如果 McCreery 先生是对的，那他就有权证明被告的枪在他看来是有问题的，或者被告是近视却把眼镜放在了家里；原告也就不会在开庭之前被要求证明他据以主张被告存在过失的事实了。

本席看不出原告现在宣称的他主张的事实最终将会如何对他产生损害。相反，他这么做将有助于确保双方当事人的公正。如果原告可以仅仅依靠将他的诉由从"过失"变成"人身侵害"就让被告蒙上眼睛受审，那么这一定违背了现代诉讼制度所蕴含的目的。本席也欣然发现，现存的法律渊源至少并不禁止法官除去被告眼睛上蒙着的布条。

本席因此判决目前的起诉书并未表示诉由。

第二节　接触

4. Fisher v. Carrousel Motor Hotel, 424 S.W.2d 627 (Tex. 1967)

美国得克萨斯州最高法院

Greenhili 法官主笔：这是一起以威吓和殴击为由提起的要求实际损害赔偿和惩戒性赔偿的案件。原告 Fisher 是载人飞船中心（Manned Spacecraft Center）数据处理部的一名数学家，该中心是休斯顿附近的美国航天航空局（National Aeronautics and Space Agency，简称 NASA）下属的一个机构。被告是位于休斯顿的 Carrousel 汽车旅馆和位于 Carrousel 汽车旅馆内的 Brass Ring 俱乐部，以及 Brass Ring 俱乐部的经理 Robert W. Flynn，他同时也是 Carrousel 汽车旅馆的雇员。Flynn 在案件审理之前便去世了，因此诉讼的被告变为了 Carrousel 汽车旅馆和 Brass Ring 俱乐部。案件由陪审团裁断，作出了支持原告 Fisher 的裁断。但初审法院作出了与陪审团裁断相反的支持被告的判决。民事上诉法院维持原判。（414 S.W.2d 774.）本院面临的问题是，是否有证据证明被告实施了可以提起诉讼的殴击行为，如果有，那么作为被告的两家企业是否必须在为 Flynn 的恶意行为支付实际损害赔偿的同时支付惩戒性赔偿。

two corporate defendants must respond in exemplary as well as actual damages for the malicious conduct of Flynn.

The plaintiff Fisher had been invited by Ampex Corporation and Defense Electronics to a one day's meeting regarding telemetry equipment at the Carrousel. The invitation included a luncheon. The guests were asked to reply by telephone whether they could attend the luncheon, and Fisher called in his acceptance. After the morning session, the group of 25 or 30 guests adjourned to the Brass Ring Club for lunch. The luncheon was buffet style, and Fisher stood in line with others and just ahead of a graduate student of Rice University who testified at the trial. As Fisher was about to be served, he was approached by Flynn, who snatched the plate from Fisher's hand and shouted that he, a Negro, could not be served in the club. Fisher testified that he was not actually touched, and did not testify that he suffered fear or apprehension of physical injury; but he did testify that he was highly embarrassed and hurt by Flynn's conduct in the presence of his associates.

The jury found that Flynn "forceably dispossessed plaintiff of his dinner plate" and "shouted in a loud and offensive manner" that Fisher could not be served there, thus subjecting Fisher to humiliation and indignity. It was stipulated that Flynn was an employee of the Carrousel Hotel and, as such, managed the Brass Ring Club. The jury also found that Flynn acted maliciously and awarded Fisher $400 actual damages for his humiliation and indignity and $500 exemplary damages for Flynn's malicious conduct.

The Court of Civil Appeals held that there was no assault because there was no physical contact and no evidence of fear or apprehension of physical contact. However, it has long been settled that there can be a battery without an assault, and that actual physical contact is not necessary to constitute a battery, so long as there is contact with clothing or an object closely identified with the body....

Under the facts of this case, we have no difficulty in holding that the intentional grabbing of plaintiff's plate constituted a battery. The intentional snatching of an object from one's hand is as clearly an offensive invasion of his person as would be an actual contact with the body....

...Damages for mental suffering are recoverable without the necessity for showing actual physical injury in a case of willful battery because the basis of that action is the unpermitted and intentional invasion of the plaintiff's person and not the actual harm done to the plaintiff's body. Personal indignity is the essence of an action for battery; and consequently the defendant is liable not only for contacts which do actual physical harm, but also for those which are offensive and insulting. We hold, therefore, that plaintiff was entitled to actual damages for mental suffering due to the willful battery, even in the absence of any physical injury....

We now turn to the question of the liability of the corporations for exemplary damages. In this regard, the jury found that Flynn was acting within the course and scope of his employment on the occasion in question; that Flynn acted maliciously and with a wanton disregard of the rights

原告 Fisher 受 Ampex 公司和防卫电子公司（Defense Electronics）的邀请，来到 Carrousel 汽车旅馆参加一个为期一天的关于遥感勘测设备的会议。该邀请包括午餐。客人们被要求通过电话回复是否参加午餐，Fisher 打电话接受了邀请。在参加完早上的会议之后，与会的 25~30 位客人来到 Brass Ring 俱乐部用午餐。午餐是自助餐，Fisher 与其他客人一道排队，当时他身后站着的是赖斯大学（Rice University）的研究生，该学生后来也出庭作了证。就在 Fisher 快排到时，Flynn 走到他面前，从他手中抢下盘子，冲他大喊："本俱乐部不为黑鬼提供服务！"Fisher 作证说，当时并没有发生身体接触，但并没有作证说他感到害怕或者恐惧受到身体伤害；但他的确作证说在同事都在场的情况下，当时他感到非常尴尬，被 Flynn 的行为伤害到了。

陪审团调查发现，Flynn"将盘子从原告手中强行抢下"，"对原告攻击性地高声喊道"不为 Fisher 提供服务，因此使 Fisher 感觉受到了羞辱和侮辱。根据诉讼协议，Flynn 是 Carrousel 汽车旅馆的一名雇员，而且管理 Brass Ring 俱乐部。同时陪审团还裁定，Flynn 的行为是恶意行为，Fisher 因受到羞辱和侮辱获得 400 美元的实际损害赔偿，因 Flynn 的恶意行为获得 500 美元的惩戒性赔偿。

民事上诉法院则认为，并没有发生威吓行为，因为双方并没有发生身体接触，而且也没有证据证明原告害怕或者恐惧受到身体接触。然而，只要与原告的衣服或者与身体紧密相关的物品发生接触……那么即使没有威吓的情况下殴击也可以成立，实际的身体接触并非构成殴击行为的必备要素，这个问题早已成为定论。

以本案的事实为依据，我们不难看出，故意抢夺原告的盘子这一行为构成殴击。从某人手中故意抢下一个物品，和与此人的身体发生实际接触一样，都是对此人的一种攻击性的侵犯……

……在一起故意的殴击案中，获得精神损害赔偿不一定必须有实际的身体伤害，因为这类诉讼的基础是未经原告同意的、对原告本人的故意侵犯，而非对原告身体造成的实际损害。人格侮辱是殴击诉讼的精髓；因此，被告不仅需要对造成实际身体损害的接触行为承担责任，同时还必须对攻击性和侮辱性的行为承担责任。所以，我们认为，在故意的殴击案中，原告有权获得精神损害的实际损害赔偿，即便被告没有对原告造成身体伤害……

我们现在着手研究公司的惩戒性赔偿责任问题。在这方面，陪审团认为 Flynn 的行为在本案涉及的场合属于在工作过程和范围中；Flynn 的行为具有恶意，肆意地极度漠视原告在本案涉及场合的权利和感受。对于陪审团查明

and feelings of plaintiff on the occasion in question. There is no attack upon these jury findings. The jury further found that the defendant Carrousel did not authorize or approve the conduct of Flynn. It is argued that there is no evidence to support this finding. The jury verdict concluded with a finding that $500 would "reasonably compensate plaintiff for the malicious act and wanton disregard of plaintiff's feelings and rights.…"

The rule in Texas is that a principal or master is liable for exemplary or punitive damages because of the acts of his agent, but only if: (a) the principal authorized the doing and the manner of the act, or (b) the agent was unfit and the principal was reckless in employing him, or (c) the agent was employed in a managerial capacity and was acting in the scope of employment, or (d) the employer or a manager of the employer ratified or approved the act.

…At the trial of this case, the following stipulation was made in open court: "It is further stipulated and agreed to by all parties that as an employee of the Carrousel Motor Hotel the said Robert W. Flynn was manager of the Brass Ring Club." We think this stipulation brings the case squarely within part (c) of the rule.…

The judgment of the courts below are reversed, and judgment is here rendered for the plaintiff for $900 with interest.…

5. Leichtman v. WLW Jacor Communications, Inc., 634 N.E.2d 697 (1994)

Court of Appeals of Ohio, United States

Per Curiam.

The plaintiff-appellant, Ahron Leichtman, appeals from the trial court's order dismissing his complaint against the defendants-appellees, WLW Jacor Communications ("WLW"), William Cunningham and Andy Furman, for battery.…In his single assignment of error, Leichtman contends that his complaint was sufficient to state a claim upon which relief could be granted and, therefore, the trial court was in error when it granted the defendants' motion to dismiss the complaint. We agree in part.

In his complaint, Leichtman claims to be "a nationally known" antismoking advocate. Leichtman alleges that, on the date of the Great American Smokeout, he was invited to appear on the WLW Bill Cunningham radio talk show to discuss the harmful effects of smoking and breathing secondary smoke. He also alleges that, while he was in the studio, Furman, another WLW talk-show host, lit a cigar and repeatedly blew smoke in Leichtman's face "for the purpose of causing physical discomfort, humiliation and distress."…

Leichtman contends that Furman's intentional act constituted a battery. The Restatement of the Law 2d, Torts (1965), states:

的事实，双方没有任何的异议。陪审团随后发现，被告 Carrousel 汽车旅馆并未授权也未允许 Flynn 的这种行为。对于这一点，因为缺乏证据予以支持而存在争议。陪审团认为 500 美元是"因为恶意的行为和肆意地极度漠视原告的感受和权利而对原告进行合理的赔偿……"

得克萨斯州的规则是，负责人或者雇主应该为其代理人的行为承担惩戒性或者惩罚性赔偿责任，但仅适用于以下情形：（a）雇主对行为和行为方式进行了授权；或（b）代理人不符合条件，但雇主在雇佣他时存在放任；或（c）代理人受雇从事管理工作，而该行为发生在其工作范围以内；或（d）雇主或雇主的管理人员认可或批准了该行为。

……在判决该案的过程中，在公开法庭上作出了如下诉讼协议："各方进一步协定并同意，作为 Carrousel 汽车旅馆的一名雇员，本案中的 Robert W. Flynn 是 Brass Ring 俱乐部的经理。"我们认为这一诉讼协定使得本案正好符合上述规定的（c）部分……

下级法院的判决被推翻，这里作出原告获得 900 美元的赔偿外加利息的判决……

5. Leichtman v. WLW Jacor Communications, Inc., 634 N.E.2d 697 (1994)

美国俄亥俄州上诉法院

法庭全体同意：

上诉人即原告 Ahron Leichtman 因主审法院驳回他对被上诉人即被告 WLW Jacor Communications（以下简称"WLW"）、William Cunningham 和 Andy Furman 提起的殴击民事起诉状，提起上诉……Leichtman 在他唯一的错误陈述中主张，他的民事起诉状足以提出他的请求并基于该请求使他获得救济，因此，主审法院同意被告提出的驳回原告起诉的申请存在错误。我们部分认可。

Leichtman 在民事起诉状中声称自己是一个"全国知名"的反吸烟倡导者。Leichtman 声称，在"全美无烟日"（Great American Smokeout）那天，他在受邀参加 WLW Bill Cunningham 的广播脱口秀节目中，讨论吸烟以及吸二手烟的致害性影响。他还声称，就在他在广播室时，WLW 脱口秀的另一名主持人 Furman 点燃了一支香烟，并且不断地向 Leichtman 吐着烟雾，"其目的在于造成生理上的不适、羞辱和痛苦"……

Leichtman 主张 Furman 的故意行为已经构成了殴击。《侵权法重述·第二次》（1965）规定如下：

An actor is subject to liability to another for battery if

(a) he acts intending to cause a harmful or offensive contact with the person of the other..., and

(b) a harmful contact with the person of the other directly or indirectly results;

(c) an offensive contact with the person of the other directly or indirectly results.

In determining if a person is liable for a battery, the Supreme Court has adopted the rule that "contact which is offensive to a reasonable sense of personal dignity is offensive contact." Love v. Port Clinton (1988), 37 Ohio St. 3d 98, 99, 524 N.E.2d 166, 167. It has defined "offensive" to mean "disagreeable or nauseating or painful because of outrage to taste and sensibilities or affronting insultingness." State v. Phipps (1979), 58 Ohio St. 2d 271, 274, 12 O.O.3d 273, 275, 389 N.E.2d 1128, 1131. Furthermore, tobacco smoke, as "particulate matter," has the physical properties capable of making contact. R.C. 3704.01(B) and 5709.20(A); Ohio Adm. Code 3745-17.

As alleged in Leichtman's complaint, when Furman intentionally blew cigar smoke in Leichtman's face, under Ohio common law, he committed a battery. No matter how trivial the incident, a battery is actionable, even if damages are only one dollar....

Other jurisdictions also have concluded that a person can commit a battery by intentionally directing tobacco smoke at another. Richardson v. Hennly (1993), 209 Ga. App. 868, 871, 434 S.E.2d 772, 774-775. We do not, however, adopt or lend credence to the theory of a "smoker's battery," which imposes liability if there is substantial certainty that exhaled smoke will predictably contact a nonsmoker. Ezra, Smoker Battery: An Antidote to Second-Hand Smoke (1990), 63 S. Cal. L. Rev. 1061, 1090. Also, whether the "substantial certainty" prong of intent from the Restatement of Torts translates to liability for secondary smoke via the intentional tort doctrine in employment cases...need not be decided here because Leichtman's claim for battery is based exclusively on Furman's commission of a deliberate act. Finally, because Leichtman alleges that Furman deliberately blew smoke into his face, we find it unnecessary to address offensive contact from passive or secondary smoke under the "glass cage" defense of McCracken v. Sloan (1979), 40 N.C. App. 214, 217, 252 S.E.2d 250, 252, relied on by the defendants....

Arguably, trivial cases are responsible for an avalanche of lawsuits in the courts. They delay cases that are important to individuals and corporations and that involve important social issues. The result is justice denied to litigants and their counsel who must wait for their day in court. However, absent circumstances that warrant sanctions for frivolous appeals...we refuse to limit one's right to sue. Section 16, Article I, Ohio Constitution states, "All courts shall be open, and every person, for an injury done him in his land, goods, person, or reputation, shall have remedy by due course of law, and shall have justice administered without denial or delay."

满足下列条件时,行为人应对他人承担殴击的责任:
（a）行为人意图使他人或第三人的身体遭受伤害性或攻击性的接触,或使其对此类接触濒临恐惧……；并且
（b）对该他人身体的伤害性接触,直接或间接地发生；
（c）对该他人身体的攻击性接触,直接或间接地发生。

在判断某人是否应为殴击承担责任时,最高法院采取的规则是"使人合理地感觉尊严受到了攻击性的接触就是攻击性接触"。[Love v. Port Clinton（1988）, 37 Ohio St. 3d 98, 99, 524 N.E.2d 166, 167 案。] 对"攻击性"的定义为"因味觉和感观上的暴行或当众侮辱而使人感到不快,或恶心,或疼痛"。[参见 State v. Phipps（1979）, 58 Ohio St. 2d 271, 274, 12 O.O. 3d 273, 275, 389 N.E.2d 1128, 1131 案。] 此外,香烟烟雾作为一个"特殊问题",具有造成接触的物理属性。[R.C. 3704.01（B）and 5709.20（A）; Ohio Adm. Code 3745-17。]

正如 Leichtman 在民事起诉状中提出的,当 Furman 故意将烟雾吹在 Leichtman 脸上时,依据俄亥俄州的法律,他实施了殴击。无论事件多么的微不足道,殴击行为都是可诉的,哪怕损害赔偿只有 1 美元……

其他法域同样也赞成某人故意将烟雾吐到另一人脸上的行为构成殴击。[Richardson v. Hennly（1993）, 209 Ga. App. 868, 871, 434 S.E.2d 772, 774-775 案。] 但是,我们并不采纳或者采信"吸烟者的殴击"理论,即如果实质确信呼出的烟雾可预见地会接触非吸烟者就对吸烟者施加责任。[Ezra 的《吸烟者殴击：对抗二手烟的良方》Smoker Battery: An Antidote to Second-Hand Smoke（1990）, 63 S. Cal. L. Rev. 1061, 1090] 同时,是否可以将《侵权法重述》中意图的"实质确信"分支理论通过雇佣关系案件中的故意请求法律学说解释适用于二手烟责任……并不需要在这里决定,因为 Leichtman 提出的殴击诉讼请求排他性地以 Furman 实施的蓄意行为为基础。最后,由于 Leichtman 声称 Furman 蓄意将烟雾吹到他的脸上,我们认为没有必要基于[McCracken v. Sloan（1979）, 40 N.C. App. 214, 217, 252 S.E.2d 250, 252] 案中被告抗辩依据的"玻璃笼子",强调被动吸烟或二手烟的攻击性接触……

存在争议的是,微不足道的案件应该为法院案件的雪崩负责。这些案件耽误了那些对个人、公司来说重要的案件,以及涉及重要社会问题的案件。导致的结果是诉讼当事人得不到公正,而他们的律师则需等待开庭时间。然而,如果没有一个允许琐碎案件诉讼的环境……我们不能限制人们诉讼的权利。《俄亥俄州宪法》第 16 节第 1 条规定："所有法院都应开放,每个人在其土地、财产、人身或名誉受到伤害时都可以通过正当法律程序获得救济,都应获得

This case emphasizes the need for some form of alternative dispute resolution operating totally outside the court system as a means to provide an attentive ear to the parties and a resolution of disputes in a nominal case. Some need a forum in which they can express corrosive contempt for another without dragging their antagonist through the expense inherent in a lawsuit. Until such an alternative forum is created, Leichtman's battery claim, previously knocked out by the trial judge in the first round, now survives round two to advance again through the courts into round three.

We…reverse that portion of the trial court's order that dismissed the battery claim in the second count of the complaint. This cause is remanded for further proceedings consistent with law on that claim only.

Judgment accordingly.

DOAN, P.J., and HILDEBRANDT and GORMAN, JJ., concur.

6. Wilson v Pringle [1987] QB 237

Court of Appeal, United Kingdom

The plaintiff and the defendant, both aged 13, were schoolboys in the same class. The plaintiff suffered serious injury as a result, so the plaintiff alleged, of the defendant having intentionally jumped on him, and he claimed damages from the defendant for, inter alia, trespass to the person (battery). The defendant denied liability, claiming that he had merely pulled the plaintiff's schoolbag off his shoulder in the course of ordinary horseplay and that as a result the plaintiff had fallen to the ground and sustained his injuries.

…

CROOM-JOHNSON L.J.

This is an appeal from Judge Wilson Mellor Q.C. sitting as a judge of the Queen's Bench Division, giving judgment under R.S.C., Ord. 14, r. 3, in favour of the plaintiff for damages to be assessed. It is necessary to set out the facts.

On 4 December 1980 the plaintiff and defendant were both schoolboys aged 13. On that day at school the plaintiff had a fall which caused an injury to his left hip, from which he still suffers. In the statement of claim it is alleged:

> "the defendant jumped on the plaintiff, causing him to suffer personal injury, loss and damage.... The matters aforesaid constitute a trespass to the person of the plaintiff and/or were caused by the defendant's negligence."

> In further and better particulars it is said that the defendant jumped on the plaintiff intentionally.

正义不可剥夺或延误的眷顾。"

本案突显了对某种完全在司法系统之外运行的替代性纠纷解决方式的需要，这种方式能够听取各方意见，并解决微不足道的纠纷。有些人需要一个讲坛，这样他们可以表达对其他人恶意的蔑视，而不通过诉讼必然存在的成本将其对手卷进来。在这个替代性的讲坛被建立之前，Leichtman 的殴击诉讼请求，虽然在第一回合对阵的法庭初审中败下阵来，现在在第二回合获得了重生，并再次通过法院向第三回合进发。

我们……推翻初审法院关于驳回民事起诉状第二项诉因中的殴击诉讼请求的部分。为了将来的诉讼过程与法律仅在诉讼请求上保持一致性，该诉因被发回了。

因此作出判决。

Doan 首席法官，Hildebrandt 法官和 Gorman 法官赞同判决。

6. Wilson v Pringle [1987] QB 237

联合王国上诉法院

原被告双方均为13岁的同班在校男生。据原告陈述，被告故意将他扑倒，导致他受到严重伤害。他因此提起人身侵害之诉（殴击之诉），请求被告赔偿损失。被告则否认对此负有责任，宣称他仅仅是在平常的打闹中把原告的书包从其肩上拉了下来，而原告因此摔倒受伤。

……

Croom-johnson 上诉法院法官主笔：

被邀请来高等法院王座分庭审案的巡回法官 Wilson Mellor 御用大律师[①]，依据《最高法院规则》第 14 号命令第 3 号规则，作出了有利于原告的判决；被告因此上诉。在这里，我们有必要总结一下案件的事实。

1980年12月4日，原被告双方均为13岁的男生，那天在学校，原告摔倒，其左臀部受伤，此伤迄今犹未痊愈。在起诉状中，原告诉称：

被告猛扑向原告，致其遭受人身伤害以及其他损失。上述事实说明，

---

① 英国的御用大律师（Queen's Counsel, QC 或 King's Council, KC，取决于在任国君的性别）有机会被选任为低级法院的法官。称谓体例如下：假设有 John Smith QC，如果他被选任为基层的郡法院法官或巡回法官（Circuit Judge），则他被称为 Judge John Smith QC 或 Judge Smith QC；如果他被选任为高等法院的暂委法官（Deputy Judge），则他被称为 Deputy Judge John Smith QC 或 Deputy Judge Smith QC；如果他被选任为高等法院的正式法官（Judge），则他被称为 John Smith J 或 Smith J（读为'Mr Justice Smith'）。感谢香港大律师及莫斯科国立法学院访问教授苏颖（Wing W So）的帮助。——编者注

The defendant put in a defence. It is there denied that the defendant jumped on the plaintiff. Trespass to the person and negligence are both denied. The defendant's version of what happened is set out in paragraph 5, as follows:

> "The defendant will aver that... after the Maths class which both plaintiff and defendant had attended, the plaintiff was in front of the defendant in a corridor and was carrying his school bag over his right shoulder. The bag was of the hand grip type, and the plaintiff was holding the handle in his right hand and holding the bag over his shoulder so that the bag hung down over his back. The defendant on this occasion pulled the bag off the plaintiff's shoulder. The defendant will aver that this act was one of ordinary horseplay as between pupils in the same school and the same class, and that it was induced by the plaintiff because it was a school regulation that bags should not be carried over the shoulder."

The plaintiff took out a summons under Order 14 . It can be rare indeed that actions for damages for personal injuries are suitable for proceedings under Order 14. This summons was argued on the ground that the defendant had committed a trespass to the person of the plaintiff. If it had been argued on the basis that the defendant had been guilty of negligence there could have been no question of the plaintiff obtaining summary judgment. The question of foreseeability alone would have required a trial on the facts. And whether the argument were based on trespass to the person or on negligence, the first triable issue would be how the plaintiff came to fall. The plaintiff filed an affidavit in which he stated that "the defendant jumped on to me in a way that was consistent with an attempt to grab my sports bag causing me to fall to the ground." On behalf of the defendant an affidavit was filed denying that he had jumped on the plaintiff.

The hearing came before the district registrar. He refused leave to sign judgment. The plaintiff appealed to the judge. The judge was not able to reconcile the two accounts of the incident. He adjourned the hearing with a view to further evidence being filed. It is recorded that on the resumed hearing

> "On behalf of the defendant it is admitted that when the defendant pulled the sports bag off the plaintiff's shoulder the plaintiff fell to the ground and apparently suffered injury."

The note of the judgment continues:

> "Therefore I only address myself to whether paragraph 5 of the defence leads

被告的行为或者满足人身侵害之诉的要件或者满足过失之诉的要件。

需要补充并强调的是，原告诉称被告是故意扑向他的。

被告对此作了辩护。被告辩称他并没有扑向原告；他也拒绝承认其行为满足人身侵害之诉或者过失之诉的要件。在其答辩书的第5段中，被告版本的事实如下：

> 被告极力声明，原被告上完同一堂数学课后，同在走廊里，原告在被告前面，把书包搭在自己的右肩上。书包本是手提包，原告却用右手握住把手把书包搭在肩上，这样书包就挂在了他背上。在这种情况下，被告拉了一下原告的书包，使其从原告的肩上掉了下来。被告认为这种行为不过是同班同学间的日常打闹。而且被告的行为还是被原告所招惹的，因为根据校规，学生不允许把书包搭在肩上。

原告依据第14号命令就一些细节问题向法官提起申请。我们必须承认对人身侵害的损害赔偿适用于第14号命令的诉讼程序的情况确实可能很少。在申请中，原告主张被告实施了人身侵害之诉意义上的侵权行为。我们认为，如果原告是以过失为诉由，那么他毫无疑问可以获得即席判决。当然，对于被告是否能够预见到期行为的后果这一事实，也许需要通过开庭才能查明。然而，无论原告的诉由是人身侵害还是过失，被告到底是怎么摔倒的这一事实，都是首先必须开庭查明的。对此，原告曾提交证词说"被告扑向我身上这一行为与抓住我的书包使我摔倒的意图是一致的"。被告方提交证词否认其扑向原告。

听证会在地区司法常务官面前进行。他拒绝直接签署判决书。因此原告上诉到原审法官处。然而该法官也无法判断这两种版本的说法中哪个是真的，所以他中止了听证，要求双方提交更多的证据。在前述听证会上，以下事实被记录下来：

> 被告方承认，被告拉扯原告的书包并将它从其肩上拉下来后，原告摔倒在地并显然地因此而受伤。

原审法官由此认为：

to an arguable basis for suggesting the defendant's act did not involve battery or was done with consent express or implied, or justification. I say without hesitation that the pleading as to the school regulations is not one I regard as sufficient to justify the exercise of discipline over the plaintiff, and is inconsistent with horseplay. The assertion in paragraph 5 of horseplay... might be well-founded but does not raise any averment that the plaintiff was playing or horse-playing with the defendant so as to suggest reciprocation. The assertions in paragraph 5 of the defence amount to express admissions that the defendant was doing something in relation to the plaintiff and his bag which brought the plaintiff to the ground. In the absence of any allegation of express or implied consent it is a clear admission on the part of the defendant of an unjustified trespass amounting to a battery.... There is no basis for saying that the defendant has an arguable case that he was not responsible in law for the results of his acts in seizing the plaintiff's bag and bringing him to the ground."

He accordingly gave leave to the plaintiff to sign judgment. Since we have decided that the judge was wrong, we must state our reasons for the guidance of whoever tries the action.

The action of trespass to the person, in its sense where there is an assault to or a battery of the plaintiff, is of great antiquity. The court has been referred to a number of authorities in which the ingredients constituting that tort have been discussed and ruled upon. In the early days the result of the case sometimes depended on whether a particular issue had been raised in the pleadings. Even if it had been raised, it might not amount to a defence to the action. The technicalities were great. One can detect in the reports the development not only of the action of trespass on the case (leading to the modern action of negligence) but also of the action of trespass to the person itself.

A convenient starting point is *Weaver v. Ward* (1617) Hob. 134. The plaintiff and defendant were exercising in the trained band with live ammunition. The defendant shot the plaintiff. The plaintiff sued the defendant in trespass. The defendant confessed and avoided. He pleaded that he had not shot the plaintiff intentionally. That plea was held to be demurrable. The defendant could not be excused of trespass "except it be judged utterly without his fault." In other words the defendant would be liable in trespass if he acted negligently, even though he had no intention to shoot the plaintiff. Nowadays an action such as that could only be brought in trespass on the case, in negligence.

Tuberville v. Savage (1669) 1 Mod. 3 was an action for assault. The defendant clapped his hand upon his sword and said to the plaintiff, "If it were not assize-time, I would not take such language." The court ruled that there was no threat, and accordingly no assault. This case is authority that there must be not only a deliberate threat (in an assault) or a deliberate touching (in battery) but also hostile behaviour. If the intention is obviously hostile, that will suffice, but it was

因此，本席认为问题的焦点是判断被告在其答辩状第5段中的行为，是否足以作为以下事项的判断依据：其行为到底是（可非难的）"人身侵害"，抑或是在原告明示或者暗示的同意下作出的，抑或被告的行为有其他的正当化事由。本席可以毫不犹豫地说，即便有校规的存在，被告也无正当化的理由用自己的前述行为来对原告实施这样的行为，而且这种贯彻校规的说法也与他主张的他只是在跟原告打闹的说法冲突。另外，无论第5段中所主张的被告只是在和原告打闹的说法是否站得住脚，这都不能证明原告这方也在和被告玩耍或者打闹，因此不能说明原被告双方的打闹行为是相互的。相反，被告在答辩书第5段中的陈述，其实恰恰是在明示地自认其行为与原告的摔倒存在因果关系。在其并未同时明示或暗示地主张其行为得到了原告的同意的情况下，这明显是在承认其行为构成对原告的"人身侵害之诉"意义下的人身侵害。被告找不出任何的依据来主张其抓扯原告书包以致原告摔倒在地的行为不会使其承担法律上的责任。

原审法官因此作出了不许被告再答辩而支持原告请求的判决。本席认为这种做法是错误的，故在此，本席有必要给任何再次审理本案的法官一点本席的指导意见。

本意含有对原告的威吓或殴击的人身侵害之诉有着悠久的历史。本庭参考了一系列判例，这些判例讨论并确定了一系列"侵权行为"的构成要件。早先，案件的结果有时取决于被告在辩护词中是否提出了特定的抗辩事由。即使它已经被提出，也可能对诉讼辩护没有意义。但这些案件的程序性细节很精彩。从这些判例报告中，我们不仅可以发现间接侵权之诉（现代过失之诉的前身）的发展，还可以发现人身侵害之诉本身的发展。

最早的有意义的判例是 *Weaver v Ward* 一案。该案中，原被告双方均参与实弹演习，在演习中，被告对原告开枪了。原告控告被告侵权。被告承认事实的发生，但是却不承认原告的诉讼请求成立。他辩称其行为并非出于故意。该案的法官没有接受这个答辩，因为他们认为"只有在能够判断被告完全没有任何过错"的情况下，侵权之诉才不成立。换言之，即使被告并非故意向原告开枪，但只要被告的行为有过失，那么他就要承担侵权责任。如今这样的诉讼只能以过失之诉的方式提起。

Tuberville v Savage 一案涉及威吓。本案中被告按剑而对原告说："若非巡回法官在，我必不受尔折辱！"法院判决该案因为被告并未有威胁行为，因此也就不构成威吓。该案所确定的规则是人身侵害之诉除了需要有威胁的存在（在

recognised that there are many circumstances in life where contact with one's fellow men is not only unavoidable but even if deliberate may also be innocent. It was said,

> "if one strike another upon the hand, or arm, or breast in discourse, it is no assault, there being no intention to assault; but if one, intending to assault, strike at another and miss him, this is an assault:..."

Cole v. Turner (1704) 6 Mod. 149 was an action in trespass for assault and battery. Holt C.J. ruled that the least touching is a battery if it is done in anger, but that touching without violence or design of harm is no battery, and that violence in a rude and inordinate manner is a battery. Again, the case is authority for the proposition that for a battery there must be either an intention to harm or overt hostility.

Perhaps the most technical of the old cases is *Williams v. Jones* (1736) Cas.t.Hard. 298. The report bristles with pleading points, especially on the subject of what makes an arrest lawful. What it does support is that the use of only a slight degree of force is not a battery every time. The intention of the defendant and the degree of force used are both relevant. A slight degree of force is no battery if done by way of a joke, or in friendship. As Lord Hardwicke C.J. expressed it, a molliter manus in joke is no battery. It also indicates that the onus of proof in an action for trespass is on the plaintiff, a matter which was eventually clearly decided by Diplock J. in *Fowler v. Lanning* [1959] 1 Q.B. 426 .

Cases in the 19th century such as *Stanley v. Powell* [1891] 1 Q.B. 86 (a shooting accident) and *Holmes v. Mather* (1875) L.R. 10 Ex. 261 (a non-negligent highway accident) are of interest for present purposes in that they illustrate the distinction which has to be drawn between an unintended accident (when the action must be brought in negligence) and a deliberate accident (when it may be brought in trespass to the person). In the later cases some of the dicta are not easy to follow because of the synonymous use of words like "wilful," "direct," and "wrongful."

It is not possible, even if it were desirable, to ignore the distinction between torts of negligence and torts of trespass strictly so called. This distinction has to be borne in mind in view of a submission made on behalf of the defendant, which would have had the effect of blurring the lines of demarcation between the two causes of action. In a situation (such as the present) in which both causes of action are sought to be raised it is necessary to be as precise as possible in seeing which of the facts giving rise to that situation are appropriate to which cause of action.

The first distinction between the two causes of action where there is personal injury is the element of contact between the plaintiff and defendant: that is, a touching of some sort. In the action for negligence the physical contact (where it takes place at all) is normally though by no means always unintended. In the action for trespass, to constitute a battery, it is deliberate. Even so

威吓之诉中）或者直接的身体接触（在殴击之诉中），这种威胁或者身体接触还必须是怀有敌意的。如果某人的行为明显可以看出其主观上存在敌意，那么就满足了人身侵害之诉的构成要件。然而，该案同时还确认，生活中有许许多多的场合，身体接触他人不但是不可避免的，而且即便是在故意的情况下，也是没有可非难性的。以下是该判决的原文：

> 在交谈中碰到他人的手、臂或者胸不能被认定为威吓，因为这里没有侵害的故意；但是如果某人意图侵害，并确实有付诸实施，但却未遂，这就是侵害……

Cole v. Turner（1704）6 Mod. 149 一案涉及威吓和殴击的人身侵害之诉。Holt 首席法官判决认为在愤怒中，即便是细微的身体接触也是侵害，然而如果没有任何意图使用暴力或者伤害他人的表征，那么就不是侵害：须知，侵害需要粗鲁而无节制的暴力。该判例再次证明其确定的规则是构成侵害需要具有伤害的故意或者明显的敌意。

或许最富技术性的判例当属 Williams v. Jones（1736）Cas.t.Hard. 298 一案。该案充斥着恳切的答辩状观点，特别是在合法逮捕一事上。然而该案在一点上对本案有所帮助，即它确定轻微地使用强制力并不一定构成侵害，是否构成侵害取决于两点：被告的意图和强制力的大小。如果是出于玩笑或者友谊而实施的轻微的强制力并不构成侵害。正如 Hardwicke 首席大法官所表达的那样，把手轻轻放在一个人身上并不构成殴击。该判例另外还提到侵害之诉的举证责任由原告承担，这点由 Diplock 法官在 Fowler v. Lanning [1959] 1 Q.B. 426 一案中予以明确。

十九世纪的判例，比如 Stanley v Powell [1891] 1 Q.B. 86（枪击事件）和 Holmes v Mather（1875）L.R. 10 Ex. 261（非故意的道路交通事件）在以下意义上与本案有关：这些案件阐释了非故意事件（应该提起过失之诉）和故意事件（应该提起人身侵害之诉）之间的区别。后期的一些案件中的某些附带意见，由于混用诸如"故意""直接"或者"不正当的"等同义词而显得难以理解。

忽略严格意义上的过失之诉和人身侵害之诉的区别，即使有可取之处，也是不可能的。我们需要充分认识到这两者的区别，而被告方的意见恰恰就模糊了这两种不同的诉由的界限。在类似于本案的情况下，如果原告同时恰恰提起了这两种不同的诉由，那么我们就需要尽量精确地判断，哪些导致了这种情况的事实符合哪种诉由。

在存在人身伤害的情形下，这两种诉由的首要区别在于"作用于原被告之间的肢体接触"这一要件。在确实发生了肢体接触的过失之诉中，这种接

it is not every intended contact which is tortious. Apart from special justifications (such as acting in self-defence) there are many examples in everyday life where an intended contact or touch is not actionable as a trespass. These are not necessarily those (such as shaking hands) where consent is actual or to be implied. They may amount to one of the instances had in mind in Tuberville v. Savage,1 Mod. 3 which take place in innocence. A modern instance is the batsman walking up the pavilion steps at Lord's after making a century. He receives hearty slaps of congratulation on his back. He may not want them. Some of them may be too heavy for comfort. No one seeks his permission, or can assume he would give it if it were asked. But would an action for trespass to the person lie?

Another ingredient in the tort of trespass to the person is that of hostility. The references to anger sufficing to turn a touch into a battery (*Cole v. Turner*, 6 Mod. 149) and the lack of an intention to assault which prevents a gesture from being an assault are instances of this. If there is hostile intent, that will by itself be cogent evidence of hostility. But the hostility may be demonstrated in other ways.

The defendant in the present case has sought to add to the list of necessary ingredients. He has submitted that before trespass to the person will lie it is not only the touching that must be deliberate but the infliction of injury. The plaintiff's counsel, on the other hand, contends that it is not the injury to the person which must be intentional, but the act of touching or battery which precedes it: as he put it, what must be intentional is the application of force and not the injury. In support of his contention, counsel for the defendant has relied on passages in the judgments in *Fowler v. Lanning* [1959] 1 Q.B. 426 and *Letang v. Cooper* [1965] 1 Q.B. 232.

Fowler v. Lanning [1959] 1 Q.B. 426 was tried at first instance by Diplock J. on a preliminary point. The allegation in the statement of claim stated simply "the defendant shot the plaintiff." No particulars were given. The defendant objected that the pleading disclosed no cause of action. If the case was brought in negligence, it did not tell the defendant what case he had to meet. If the case was brought for trespass to the person (battery), it was necessary to state whether the shooting was intentional. Diplock J. analysed the issues which might arise, and decided that the defendant was right, and that if the shooting was said to be intentional the plaintiff must say so. Equally, if it was said to be negligent, the facts must be pleaded. In both cases, the onus of proof was on the plaintiff.

In the course of his judgment, Diplock J., at p. 439, summarised the present law on the onus of proof in four propositions. The first is relied upon by the present defendant:

> "(1) Trespass to the person does not lie if the injury to the plaintiff, although the direct consequence of the act of the defendant, was caused unintentionally and without negligence on the defendant's part."

触往往是无意的,当然有些情况下也可能是有意的。而在人身侵害之诉中,这种接触必然是故意的。当然,并非所有的故意的肢体接触都构成侵权行为。除有正当性事由的场合(比如正当防卫)外,在日常生活中我们还会发现许许多多的故意的肢体接触并不被认为是可以被起诉的侵权行为。这些肢体接触不构成侵权行为,并不一定需要被接触人的明示或者默示的同意。这些接触完全可能符合 *Tuberville v Savage* 一案中发生情况,该案中被告对原告的肢体接触是善意的。上述的这种虽然是故意,但是并非侵权的情况,有个现代社会中的例子:若板球的击球手,打满了一百分,便能够走上伦敦大板球场中场馆的台阶。人们纷纷拍打他的背部来衷心地祝贺他。他可能并不喜欢这样,因为有的人拍得太重了,并不舒服。这时,拍他背的人没人征求他的意见,这些人也不能预见如果他们征求了意见,这个击球手就会同意。然而这时候有任何的人身侵害的诉由存在吗?

另外一个构成人身侵害之诉的要件是敌意。如果在肢体接触的时候伴有"愤怒",那么这个肢体接触就足够被判定为殴击(*Cole v Turner*, 6 Mod 149);在不存在威胁、恐吓的主观意图时,我们就很难讲一个行为是威吓;以上这些情况都是例证。如果存在敌对的意图,那么这个意图本身就是敌意的证明。当然,敌意也可以通过其他方式来证明。

本案被告意图增加原告的诉讼请求需要满足的要件。他主张,如果要支持人身侵害之诉,那么被告不但须对侵权行为是故意的,而且对损害结果也必须是故意的。与之相反,原告的律师则主张,他并不需要证明被告有故意伤害原告的意图,他仅须要证明造成这种伤害的肢体接触是被告故意为之的:正如原告律师所说,需要证明是故意的要件是被告使用了暴力这一事实而非原告受到伤害这一结果。被告律师以 *Fowler v Lanning* [1959] 1 Q.B. 426 一案和 *Letang v Cooper* [1965] 1 Q.B. 232 一案两个判例来支持其主张。

Fowler v Lanning [1959] 1 Q.B. 426 的一审法官是 Diplock 法官,他主要是对一个前置问题作出了判决。该案起诉书中仅仅陈述了"被告枪击了原告",而没有提到任何的其他细节。被告抗辩称,原告诉讼请求的内容不符合任何诉由。如果原告主张的是过失之诉,那么他并没有清晰地向被告说明诉由。如果原告提起的是人身侵害之诉,那么他需要陈述被告的行为是故意的。Diplock 法官分析了可能的争议焦点,并判决支持被告:该法官认为如果像原告所说被告的行为是故意的,原告必须说明这点。同理,如果原告主张的是过失之诉,那么需要提出支持这一诉由的事实。这两种情况下,举证责任都是原告来承担的。

在判决书中,Diplock 法官通过四段话总结了当时的法律对举证责任的规定。本案被告依据的是第一段话:

That case was considered in *Letang v. Cooper* [1965] 1 Q.B. 232, where the plaintiff was sunbathing in the car park of a country hotel, with the result that her legs were run over by the defendant's motor car. She sued him for both negligence and trespass to the person more than three years afterwards. She proved negligence but could not recover because her action was barred by the Limitation Act 1939 . But she contended that she could recover in trespass to the person which, she said. was not caught by the three year period. The Court of Appeal held that it was so caught. The court also held that her action lay only in negligence and not in trespass to the person.

The nature of the modern action of trespass was much discussed. Lord Denning M.R. (with whose judgment Danckwerts L.J. agreed) said, at p. 239:

"The truth is that the distinction between trespass and case is obsolete. We have a different sub-division altogether. Instead of dividing actions for personal injuries into trespass (direct damage) or case (consequential damage), we divide the causes of action now according as the defendant did the injury intentionally or unintentionally. If one man intentionally applies force directly to another, the plaintiff has a cause of action in assault and battery, or, if you so please to describe it, in trespass to the person. 'The least touching of another in anger is a battery,' *per* Holt C.J. in *Cole v. Turner*, 6 Mod. 149 . If he does not inflict injury intentionally, but only unintentionally, the plaintiff has no cause of action today in trespass. His only cause of action is in negligence, and then only on proof of want of reasonable care. If the plaintiff cannot prove want of reasonable care, he may have no cause of action at all."

Lord Denning M.R. then referred to the facts of *Fowler v. Lanning* [1959] 1 Q.B. 426, and continued, at p. 240:

"The modern law on this subject was well expounded by Diplock J. in *Fowler v. Lanning,* with which I fully agree. But I would go this one step further: when the injury is not inflicted intentionally, but negligently, I would say that the only cause of action is negligence and not trespass. If it were trespass, it would be actionable without proof of damage; and that is not the law today. In my judgment, therefore, the only cause of action in the present case, where the injury was unintentional, is negligence..."

Diplock L.J. dealt with the issues more narrowly, basing his decision on the fact that the injury to Miss Letang had been caused unintentionally and therefore was to be sued for in case. On

(1)如果原告所受到的伤害既非故意也非过失，即便这样的伤害是被告行为的直接后果，人身侵害之诉也不能被支持。

刚说到的这个判例被引用在了 Letang v Cooper [1965] 1 Q.B. 232 一案中。该案中，原告正在一个乡村旅馆的停车场晒日光浴时，其双腿被被告的汽车碾压。此后三年，原告既提起了过失之诉，又提起了人身侵害之诉。上诉法院判决，人身侵害之诉是受到3年诉讼时效的限制的。该法院同时还指出，她的诉讼请求只能以过失之诉来提出，而不能主张人身侵害之诉。

现代意义上的侵害之诉是一个常常被讨论的问题。丹宁勋爵曾说（上诉法院 Danckwerts 法官在第 239 页支持了他的判断）：

> 事实上，直接侵害之诉和间接侵害之诉之间的区分已经过时了。我们有另一种完全不同的分法。我们现在并不把涉及人身伤害的诉由分为产生直接损害的诉由和产生间接损害的诉由。相反，我们把这些诉由，按照被告人是故意侵权还是过失侵权来划分。如果某人故意直接对他人使用暴力，那么原告的诉讼请求就是威吓之诉或者殴击之诉，也可以描述为人身侵害之诉。按照 Cole v Turner 一案中 Holt 首席法官的说法，任何细微的身体接触，只要是出于愤怒作出的，就是殴击。如果被告的行为并非出于故意，在现代法上原告就不能以人身侵害之诉来起诉。他的唯一诉由是过失，这里他必须证明被告没有尽到注意义务。如果他无法证明被告没有尽到注意义务，他就没有任何可用的诉由。

丹宁勋爵接着提到了 Fowler v Lanning [1959] 1 Q.B. 426 一案：

> 关于现代法上的这个问题，Diplock 法官已经说得很明确了，对此我非常同意。然而，我想再多说一句：当原告受到的伤害并非被告故意实施的，而是过失造成时，我认为这里原告唯一能用的诉由是过失而非人身侵害。如果我们认为原告可以在此时提起侵害之诉，那么我们就在承认他可以不用证明损害，而这是和现代法相抵牾的。因此在我看来，当损害是非故意造成时，可用的诉由只有过失。

Diplock 上诉法院法官对于上述的争议焦点的处理更加谨慎，他的判决是基于以下事实作出的：Letang 小姐所受到的伤害并非被告故意为之，因此她应当提起的只能是间接侵害之诉。根据 Letang 小姐所主张的事实，在

the facts as pleaded, her action had to be brought in negligence. He also agreed that in any event an action for trespass to the person where the damages claimed included damages for personal injuries was subject to a limitation period of three years.

The judgment of Lord Denning M.R. was widely phrased, but it was delivered in an action where the only contact between the plaintiff and the defendant was unintentional. It has long been the law that claims arising out of an unintentional trespass must be made in negligence. A careful reading of his judgment shows that he was not adverting to the point now being made by this defendant. Similarly, the first proposition of Diplock J. in *Fowler v. Lanning* [1959] 1 Q.B. 426, 439 was not meant to bear the interpretation now given to it by counsel for the defendant. In our view, the submission made by counsel for the plaintiff is correct. It is the act and not the injury which must be intentional. An intention to injure is not essential to an action for trespass to the person. It is the mere trespass by itself which is the offence.

That does not answer the question, what does entitle an injured plaintiff to sue for the tort of trespass to the person? Reference must be made to one further case: Williams v. Humphrey (unreported), 12 February 1975, a decision of Talbot J. There the defendant, a boy just under 16, pushed the plaintiff into a swimming pool and caused him physical injury. The judge found the defendant acted negligently and awarded damages. But there was another claim in trespass. Talbot J. rejected the submission that the action would not lie unless there was an intent to injure. He held that it was sufficient, if the act was intentional, that there was no justification for it. In the present Order 14 proceedings the judge relied upon that decision. The reasoning in Williams v. Humphrey is all right as far as it goes, but it does not go far enough. It did not give effect to the reasoning of the older authorities, such as *Tuberville v. Savage*, 1 Mod. 3, *Cole v. Turner*, 6 Mod. 149 , and *Williams v. Jones*, Cas.t.Hard. 298 that for there to be either an assault or a battery there must be something in the nature of hostility. It may be evinced by anger, by words or gesture. Sometimes the very act of battery will speak for itself, as where somebody uses a weapon on another.

What, then, turns a friendly touching (which is not actionable) into an unfriendly one (which is)? We have been referred to two criminal cases. *Reg. v. Sutton (Terence)* [1977] 1 W.L.R. 182 was decided in the Court of Appeal (Criminal Division). It was a case concerning alleged indecent assaults on boys who consented in fact although in law they were too young to do so. They were asked to pose for photographs. The only touching of the boys by the appellant was to get them to stand in poses. It was touching on the hands, arms, legs or torso but only for the purpose of indicating how he wanted them to pose; it was not hostile or threatening. The court which was presided over by Lord Widgery C.J. held these were therefore not assaults.

A more recent authority is *Collins v. Wilcock* [1984] 1 W.L.R. 1172. This case was not cited to the judge. It had not been reported at the time of the hearing of the Order 14 appeal. The facts were that a woman police officer, suspecting that a woman was soliciting contrary to the Street Offences

我们今天看来她应该提起过失之诉。Diplock 上诉法院法官还认为在任何情况下，为了获得人身伤害赔偿而提起的诉讼，都受到三年的诉讼时效的限制。

丹宁勋爵的判决书讨论的范围是宽泛的，然而该案直接涉及的事实却是被告对原告无意的肢体接触。法律早已规定，对于非故意的人身伤害提起的诉讼，其诉由只能是过失。如果我们认真读一读丹宁勋爵的这一判决，我们就会发现他其实并未提及现在被告主张的问题。同样，Diplock 法官在 *Fowler v Lanning* [1959] 1 Q.B. 426, 439 一案中所作出的第一项结论，也不能被像被告律师主张的那样解释。在本席看来，原告律师的主张更正确：人身侵害之诉中需要被证明的，是被告对其做出的侵权行为必须是故意的，而不是伤害结果。被告意图造成原告的伤害并非这种诉由中需要证明的关键事实。仅仅被告对原告的行为本身就是这种诉由所关注的事实。

我们上述的分析并没有回答这个问题：到底是什么使得受到伤害的原告可以人身侵害之诉来起诉？为此，我们需要看一看另一个判例：*Williams v Humphrey*（未被收入判例集），该案于 1975 年 2 月 12 日由 Talbot 法官判决。该案中，一名未满 16 岁的男孩将原告推入游泳池并对其造成了身体上的伤害。该法官判决被告的行为有过失，因此须支付赔偿金。但是，该案原告同时也提起了人身侵害之诉。关于人身侵害之诉，Talbot 法官否认了伤害的故意为其要件的说法。他主张要满足这种诉由，只要行为本身是故意的，且行为人对其行为无正当理由即可。*Williams v Humphrey* 这一判例的分析是正确的，然而却不够深入。这个判例并没有提到更早的那些判例（比如 *Tuberville v Savage*, 1 Mod. 3, *Cole v Turner*, 6 Mod. 149, 和 *Williams v Jones*, Cas.t.Hard）所确认的规则：敌意是人身侵害之诉的必要条件。这里的敌意可以表现为愤怒，或者表现为一定的语言或者行为。有时，击打他人的行为本身就说明了敌意，特别是行为人对他人使用了武器的场合。

那么，在何种情况下，友好的、不可诉的肢体接触会变得不友好且可诉？本庭参考两个判例。*R. v Sutton*（*Terence*）[1977] 1 W.L.R. 182 一案是由上诉法院刑庭所判决的。该案中，原告诉称，被告和一些男孩有不合适的肢体接触。而虽然这些肢体接触在事实上是这些男孩同意的，然而因为其年龄太小，不具有法律上的同意的能力。被告要求这些男孩为拍照片摆造型。而他和这些男孩的身体接触的唯一目的是指导他们摆出正确的造型，为此他接触了这些男孩的手、臂、腿和躯干：这种行为绝非有敌意或者是为了威胁他们。该案的法庭（由 Widgery 首席大法官主持）最终判决，被告的行为并非人身侵害之诉意义上的侵害。

另一个比较近的判例是 *Collins v Wilcock* [1984] 1 W.L.R. 1172. 当事人并未引用这一案例，因为在第十四号命令听证会发生时，该案尚未被编入判例集。该案的事实是，一女警官怀疑一女子在招嫖，而这一行为是违反《英国 1959

Act 1959, tried to question her. The woman walked away, and was followed by the police officer. The officer took hold of her arm in order to restrain her. The woman scratched the officer's arm. She was arrested, charged with assaulting a police officer in the execution of her duty, and convicted. On appeal by case stated, the appeal was allowed, on the ground that the officer had gone beyond the scope of her duty in detaining the woman in circumstances short of arresting her. The officer had accordingly committed a battery.

The judgment of the Divisional Court was given by Robert Goff L.J. It is necessary to give a long quotation to do full justice to it. He said, at pp. 1177-1178:

"The law draws a distinction, in terms more easily understood by philologists than by ordinary citizens, between an assault and a battery. An assault is an act which causes another person to apprehend the infliction of immediate, unlawful, force on his person; a battery is the actual infliction of unlawful force on another person. Both assault and battery are forms of trespass to the person. Another form of trespass to the person is false imprisonment, which is the unlawful imposition of constraint upon another's freedom of movement from a particular place. The requisite mental element is of no relevance in the present case.

"We are here concerned primarily with battery. The fundamental principle, plain and incontestable, is that every person's body is inviolate. It has long been established that any touching of another person, however slight, may amount to a battery. So Holt C.J. held in *Cole v. Turner* (1704) 6 Mod. 149 that 'the least touching of another in anger is a battery.' The breadth of the principle reflects the fundamental nature of the interest so protected. As Blackstone wrote in his *Commentaries,* 17th ed. (1830), vol. 3, p. 120: 'the law cannot draw the line between different degrees of violence, and therefore totally prohibits the first and lowest stage of it; every man's person being sacred, and no other having a right to meddle with it, in any the slightest manner.' The effect is that everybody is protected not only against physical injury but against any form of physical molestation.

"But so widely drawn a principle must inevitably be subject to exceptions. For example, children may be subjected to reasonable punishment; people may be subjected to the lawful exercise of the power of arrest; and reasonable force may be used in self-defence or for the prevention of crime. But, apart from these special instances where the control or constraint is lawful, a broader exception has been created to allow for the exigencies of everyday life. Generally speaking, consent is a defence to battery; and most of the physical contacts of ordinary life are not actionable because they are impliedly consented to by all who move in society and

年街头犯罪法》的。女警官因此盘问了该女子。在此过程中,女警官为了留置该女子抓握了其手臂,该女子因此抓伤了警官的手臂。该女子最终被逮捕,并以在警官执行任务期间袭警的罪名被起诉并定罪。该女子的上诉被二审法院支持,因为二审法院认为该案中的女警官的行为已经超出了其职责范围:该案中女警官的职责是留置该女子而非逮捕她。由此,该女警官的行为构成人身侵害之诉意义上的侵害。

该案的判决书由上诉法院法官 Robert Goff 撰写。为了能准确理解该判决的意思,我们有必要多引用一点判决书的原文。在第 1177 到 1178 段中,该法官写道:

> 这部法律以语言学家比普通公民更容易理解的方式,将 assualt(威吓)和 battery(殴击)区分开来。assualt 是指让他人感到行为人将要对他当场实施非法的暴力;而 battery 是指行为人已经对他人实施了非法的暴力。assault 和 battery 是人身侵害之诉的两种形式。另一种形式的人身侵害之诉是非法拘禁,即非法地限制他人从某个地方离开的行动自由。而主观要件与本案并无太多关联性。
>
> 本案中涉及的主要是 battery。每个人的身体都不容侵犯是一个不言而喻且不可否认的基本原则。很早以前我们就确定了这么一个规则:对他人的肢体接触,无论多么轻微,都很可能构成一个 battery。所以 Holt 首席法官在 *Cole v Turner* (1704) 6 Mod. 149 一案中判决到:"任何细微的身体接触,只要是出于愤怒做出的,就是 battery。"该原则的广泛实用性其实反映了其所保护的利益的基本性。正如布莱克斯通在其《英国法释义》中说的那样(1830 年第 17 版第三卷第 120 页):"法律不可能区分不同程度的暴力,因此法律是完全禁止最低层次的暴力的;所有人的身体都是神圣的,因此他人没有任何权利来干涉它,无论多么轻微。"这句话的意思是,人并非仅仅免于身体的伤害,还应该免于任何形式的对其身体的骚扰。
>
> 然而作为适用范围如此之广的基本原则,它不可避免地会受到一些例外的限制。比如,孩童可能受到合理的惩罚;人们可能受到合法的逮捕;在正当防卫或者预防犯罪时,人们可能适用合理的暴力。上述情况下,人身神圣的原则受到了一定的合法的限制,而除了这些特殊的情况,为了满足日常生活的需要,还存在一种一般的对人身神圣原则的例外。一般说来,受害人同意是对人身侵害的抗辩;大部分日常生活中的肢体接触都是不可诉的,因为我们默认被接触者是同意这种接触的,因为他

so expose themselves to the risk of bodily contact.So nobody can complain of the jostling which is inevitable from his presence in, for example, a supermarket, an underground station or a busy street; nor can a person who attends a party complain if his hand is seized in friendship, or even if his back is, within reason, slapped: see *Tuberville v. Savage(1669) 1 Mod. 3* . Although such cases are regarded as examples of implied consent, it is more common nowadays to treat them as falling within a general exception embracing all physical contact which is generally acceptable in the ordinary conduct of daily life.We observe that, although in the past it has sometimes been stated that a battery is only committed where the action is 'angry, revengeful, rude, or insolent' (see Hawkins, Pleas of the Crown, 8th ed. (1824), vol. 1, c. 15, section 2), we think that nowadays it is more realistic, and indeed more accurate, to state the broad underlying principle, subject to the broad exception.

"Among such forms of conduct, long held to be acceptable, is touching a person for the purpose of engaging his attention, though of course using no greater degree of physical contact than is reasonably necessary in the circumstances for that purpose. So, for example, it was held by the Court of Common Pleas in 1807 that a touch by a constable's staff on the shoulder of a man who had climbed on a gentleman's railing to gain a better view of a mad ox, the touch being only to engage the man's attention, did not amount to a battery: see *Wiffin v. Kincard* (1807) 2 Bos. & Pul. 471; for another example, see *Coward v. Baddeley* (1859) 4 H. & N. 478. But a distinction is drawn between a touch to draw a man's attention, which is generally acceptable, and a physical restraint, which is not. So we find Parke B. observing in *Rawlings v. Till* (1837) 3 M. & W. 28, 29, with reference to *Wiffin v. Kincard*, that 'There the touch was merely to engage [a man's] attention, not to put a restraint upon his person.' Furthermore, persistent touching to gain attention in the face of obvious disregard may transcend the norms of acceptable behaviour, and so be outside the exception. We do not say that more than one touch is never permitted; for example, the lost or distressed may surely be permitted a second touch, or possibly even more, on a reluctant or impervious sleeve or shoulder, as may a person who is acting reasonably in the exercise of a duty. In each case, the test must be whether the physical contact so persisted in has in the circumstances gone beyond generally acceptable standards of conduct; and the answer to that question will depend upon the facts of the particular case."

This rationalisation by Robert Goff L.J. draws the so-called "defences" to an action for trespass to the person (of which consent, self-defence, ejecting a trespasser, exercising parental

们穿梭于社会之中，自然将自己暴露于受到肢体接触的风险之下。故而，不可避免进入推挤之地，如发生在超市、地铁站或繁忙的街道上，则其人不可抱怨推挤；进入聚会之地，则其人不可抱怨来自他人的友好的握手或者适度的拍背［参见 *Tuberville v Savage*（1669）1 Mod 3］。虽然上述的情况可以看作行为人对被接触人的身体接触因为被接触人默认的同意而正当化，然而这并非唯一的正当化思路。我们现在更通常的做法是将上述情况总结为一种更一般的对人身神圣原则的例外——在这种例外下，在日常生活中通常被接受的身体接触，不再能够被视为人身侵害之诉意义上的人身侵害。在以前，人们对人身侵害之诉的构成要件要求非常严格，要求构成侵害的行为必须伴随着"愤怒、仇恨、粗鲁或者无礼"［参见 *Hawkins, Pleas of the Crown, 8th ed.*（1824），vol. 1, c. 15, section 2］，而现在我们认为更现实且更精确的做法是坚持一个更宽泛的人身神圣的原则并且让其受到更多的限制。

为了引起某人注意而实施的身体接触，就是一个在生活中可被接受的例子，当然此时的身体接触不能超过引起他人注意这一目的所必要的限度。比如1807年民诉法院就判决，当某人为了获得更好的视野来围观疯牛，而爬上某个绅士的栏杆时，警察为了引起他的注意而拍打他的肩膀，并不属于人身侵害之诉意义上的人身侵害。［参见 *Wiffin v Kincard*（1807）2 Bos. & Pul. 471；*Coward v Baddeley*（1859）4 H & N 478］当然，我们应该区分两种情况：一种是为社会所普遍接受的，为引起他人注意而为的身体接触；另一种是不为社会所普遍接受的身体强制。在对 *Rawlings v Till* 一案的评注中，Parke 就说（他援引了 *Wiffin v Kincard* 这一判例）："这里，身体接触仅仅是为了获得［某人］的注意，而并非对其身体进行强制。"当然，即便是为了获得他人的注意，当他人已经明显拒绝理睬的情况下，持续的身体接触就不再是社会所接受的行为，因而不再属于这一例外的范围。我们并不是说对他人只能拍打一次；当我们希望引起其注意的人对于我们的行为无动于衷时，失望的我们当然可以通过再次拍打他的肩膀或者拉扯他的衣袖来引起他的注意，我们甚至可以再这么做不止一次，就像一个在履行职责时行为合理的人。在每个个案中，我们重复的身体接触到底是不是属于上述的例外，取决于在具体情况下我们的行为是否超出了社会公认地可接受的行为标准；而我们是否超出了这个标准取决于个案中的具体的案件事实。

Robert Goff 上诉法院法官将各种各样的人身损害之诉的抗辩事由（典型的例子包括：受害人同意、正当防卫、驱逐侵入者、行使亲权或者法定权力）

authority, and statutory authority are some examples) under one umbrella of "a general exception embracing all physical contact which is generally acceptable in the ordinary conduct of daily life." It provides a solution to the old problem of what legal rule allows a casualty surgeon to perform an urgent operation on an unconscious patient who is brought into hospital. The patient cannot consent, and there may be no next-of-kin available to do it for him. Hitherto it has been customary to say in such cases that consent is to be implied for what would otherwise be a battery on the unconscious body. It is better simply to say that the surgeon's action is acceptable in the ordinary conduct of everyday life, and not a battery. It will doubtless be convenient to continue to tie the labels of the "defences" to the facts of any case where they are appropriate. But the rationalisation explains and utilises the expressions of judicial opinion which appear in the authorities. It also prevents the approach to the facts, which, with respect to the judge in the present case, causes his judgment to read like a ruling on a demurrer in the days of special pleading.

Nevertheless, it still remains to indicate what is to be proved by a plaintiff who brings an action for battery. Robert Goff L.J.'s judgment is illustrative of the considerations which underlie such an action, but it is not practicable to define a battery as "physical contact which is not generally acceptable in the ordinary conduct of daily life."

In our view, the authorities lead one to the conclusion that in a battery there must be an intentional touching or contact in one form or another of the plaintiff by the defendant. That touching must be proved to be a hostile touching. That still leaves unanswered the question "when is a touching to be called hostile?" Hostility cannot be equated with ill-will or malevolence. It cannot be governed by the obvious intention shown in acts like punching, stabbing or shooting. It cannot be solely governed by an expressed intention, although that may be strong evidence. But the element of hostility, in the sense in which it is now to be considered, must be a question of fact for the tribunal of fact. It may be imported from the circumstances. Take the example of the police officer in *Collins v. Wilcock* [1984] 1 W.L.R. 1172. She touched the woman deliberately, but without an intention to do more than restrain her temporarily. Nevertheless, she was acting unlawfully and in that way was acting with hostility. She was acting contrary to the woman's legal right not to be physically restrained. We see no more difficulty in establishing what she intended by means of question and answer, or by inference from the surrounding circumstances, than there is in establishing whether an apparently playful blow was struck in anger. The rules of law governing the legality of arrest may require strict application to the facts of appropriate cases, but in the ordinary give and take of everyday life the tribunal of fact should find no difficulty in answering the question "was this, or was it not, a battery?" Where the immediate act of touching does not itself demonstrate hostility, the plaintiff should plead the facts which are said to do so.

Although we are all entitled to protection from physical molestation we live in a crowded world in which people must be considered as taking on themselves some risk of injury (where

一般化为一种概括的"一切在日常生活中按照一般观念可接受的身体接触"。这种做法解决了一个古老的问题：到底是什么法律规则允许在紧急状态下外科医生为昏迷的病人做手术？此时，病人是无法同意的，而且很可能也没有近亲属来代他同意这个手术。之前对这个问题的解决办法是，试图论证在这种情况下病人对这种本来可算作对其身体的侵害的行为给出了默示的同意。然而其实更简单的解决办法是直接把这种行为看作并非人身侵害的日常生活中可接受的行为。当然，继续就每个个案的具体情况来判断是否应该接受某个具体的抗辩事由，依然是正确的做法。但是之前的合理化解释及其利用还是会出现在现存法律渊源当中。这也阻碍了接近真相的路径，就本案的法官而言，这使得他的判决读起来就像"特别答辩"时代对异议者的裁决。

然而，其提出方案对解决本案的问题来说依然是不够的：我们依然不知道在人身侵害之诉中，原告胜诉需要证明什么样的事实。上诉法院法官 Robert Goff 的判决揭示了这种诉由存在背后的考量因素，但仅仅将人身伤害定义为"在日常生活中所通常不被接受的身体接触"，似乎对解决本案的问题来说并无太大实效。

在我们看来，上述判例可以确定这样一个结论：只有在原告以某种方式故意地接触被告，他才能提起人身侵害之诉；并且这种接触必须是有敌意的。那么到底什么叫做有敌意的接触呢？需要指出的是，敌意并不等同于恶意。我们可以通过具体的行为（如拳打、刀捅或者枪击）所体现出来的明显的主观意思来判断恶意的存在；而敌意的存在就不能如此判断。恶意的存在也可以通过明确表达出来的意思来判断，而这种办法在是否存在敌意的判断中就很难适用，虽然明确表达出来的意思可以作为判断敌意的存在的有力的证据。就本案涉及问题来说，被告是否存在敌意完全是一个事实问题，应该由负责事实审的法院来回答这个问题。一般回答这个问题需要考虑当时的情况。比如 *Collins v Wilcock* [1984] 1 W.L.R. 1172 一案中的女警官侵害了该案中的女士的权利，妨碍了她的身体自由。通过询问的方式，或者直接通过当时的情况推测，我们就能明确该案中女警官的主观状态。这么做并不比判断看起来像是玩闹的一拳是否暗含着愤怒容易。根据法治原则，我们在判断逮捕的合法形式，可能需要严格地审查案件事实，然而在日常生活中，事实审法庭判断是否构成人身侵害并非难事。当行为人的行为自身并不能直接证明其敌意的存在时，原告有义务援引相关事实来证明这种敌意的存在。

虽然我们每个人都有权免受身体上的骚扰，但是我们须知自己生活在一

it occurs) from the acts of others which are not in themselves unlawful. If negligence cannot be proved, it may be that an injured plaintiff who is also unable to prove a battery, will be without redress.

Defences like self-defence, and exercising the right of arrest, are relevant here. Similarly, it may be that allowances must be made, where appropriate, for the idiosyncrasies of individuals or (as was demonstrated in *Walmsley v. Humenick* [1954] 2 D.L.R. 232) the irresponsibility of childhood and the degree of care and awareness which is to be expected of children.

In our judgment the judge who tried the Order 14 proceedings took too narrow a view of what has to be proved in order to make out a case of trespass to the person. It will be apparent that there is a number of questions which must be investigated in evidence.

Accordingly we would allow this appeal, and give unconditional leave to defend. The court will invite submissions as to what directionsare required for the further conduct of the action.

个拥挤的世界上。在这里，我们应该假定每个人都承担了一定的因他人所作出的本身并非违法的行为而受害的风险。因此，如果受害人无法证明原告的过失（此时往往他也无法证明人身侵害的存在），他也就无法获得任何的救济。

正当防卫或者行使逮捕权这样的抗辩事由可以用来在人身侵害之诉中抗辩。同样的，行为人自身的特征 [参见 *Walmsley v Humenick*（1954）2 D.L.R. 232 一案]、儿童所固有的无责任特性，以及我们所能预见到的儿童的注意和认识能力的低下，也应该被允许作为被告的抗辩事由。

对于在人身侵害之诉中，原告需要证明的事实的范围，依照第 14 号命令来审理本案的原审法官的理解过于狭窄了些。很明显，要审理该案，我们需要先调查很多的事实问题。

因此，我们支持被告的上诉，并无条件地允许他提出抗辩意见。本庭希望双方提交后续诉讼程序所必需的相关文书。

Chapter 2. Negligence

Section 1. Duty of Care: Basic Formula

7. Brown v. Kendall, 60 Mass. 292 (1850)

Supreme Judicial Court of Massachusetts, United States

This was an action of trespass for assault and battery....

It appeared in evidence, on the trial,...that two dogs, belonging to the plaintiff and the defendant, respectively, were fighting in the presence of their masters; that the defendant took a stick about four feet long, and commenced beating the dogs in order to separate them; that the plaintiff was looking on, at the distance of about a rod, and that he advanced a step or two towards the dogs. In their struggle, the dogs approached the place where the plaintiff was standing. The defendant retreated backwards from before the dogs, striking them as he retreated; and as he approached the plaintiff, with his back towards him, in raising his stick over his shoulder, in order to strike the dogs, he accidentally hit the plaintiff in the eye, inflicting upon him a severe injury.

Whether it was necessary or proper for the defendant to interfere in the fight between the dogs; whether the interference, if called for, was in a proper manner, and what degree of care was exercised by each party on the occasion; were the subject of controversy between the parties, upon all the evidence in the case, of which the foregoing is an outline.

The defendant requested the judge to instruct the jury, that "if both the plaintiff and defendant at the time of the blow were using ordinary care, or if at that time the defendant was using ordinary care and the plaintiff was not, or if at that time both plaintiff and defendant were not using ordinary care, then the plaintiff could not recover."

The defendant further requested the judge to instruct the jury, that, "under the circumstances, if the plaintiff was using ordinary care and the defendant was not, the plaintiff could recover, and that the burden of proof on all these propositions was on the plaintiff."

The judge declined to give the instructions, as above requested, but left the case to the jury under the following instructions: "If the defendant, in beating the dogs, was doing a necessary act, or one which it was his duty under the circumstances of the case to do, and was doing it in a proper way; then he was not responsible in this action, provided he was using ordinary care at the

第二章　过失侵权责任

第一节　注意义务：基本规则

7. Brown v. Kendall, 60 Mass. 292 (1850)

美国马萨诸塞州最高法院

本案是关于威吓和殴击的侵权诉讼……

在初审中，有证据证明……有两只分别属于原告与被告的狗，在它们的主人面前打架；被告拿了一根大约4英尺长的棍子开始打狗，试图将它们分开；原告当时则站在约5米①距离远的地方旁观，之后朝前走了一两步。在打架的过程中，这两只狗逐渐接近了原告所站的位置。被告在狗前面一边向后退，一边继续敲打；当他背对着后退到原告附近，为了打狗，他把棍子举过头顶时，意外地打到了原告的眼睛，造成了严重伤害。

被告干涉狗打架的行为是否必要与合理；如果干涉实属必要，是否是一种合理方式，并且在此种场合原告、被告双方各自需要履行何种程度的注意义务。根据所有的证据，双方当事人主要争议点就是前述几点。

被告要求法官指示陪审团决定："如果原告与被告在当时都尽到了普通注意义务，或者如果被告尽到了而原告未尽到普通注意义务，或者原告与被告都未尽到普通注意义务，那么原告不能获得救济。"

被告进一步要求法官指示陪审团决定："在此情形之下，如果原告尽到普通注意义务而被告没有，原告可以获得救济，而所有的这些主张的证明都应由原告来承担。"

法官拒绝按照上述请求给出指示，而是把案件留给陪审团并给出了如下指示："如果被告打狗是一个必要的行为，或者在本案情形之下他有义务去那样做并且是以一种合理的方式去做；如果他在当时尽到了普通注意义务，那么他在这个诉讼中就不用负责。如果不是一个必要的行为；如果他没有义务

---

① 原文为"a rod"，直译为"一杆"。"杆"是一种英制长度单位，等于16.5英尺（5.03米）。——译者注

time of the blow. If it was not a necessary act; if he was not in duty bound to attempt to part the dogs, but might with propriety interfere or not as he chose; the defendant was responsible for the consequences of the blow, unless it appeared that he was in the exercise of extraordinary care, so that the accident was inevitable, using the word inevitable not in a strict but a popular sense.

"If, however, the plaintiff, when he met with the injury, was not in the exercise of ordinary care, he cannot recover, and this rule applies, whether the interference of the defendant in the fight of the dogs was necessary or not. If the jury believe, that it was the duty of the defendant to interfere, then the burden of proving negligence on the part of the defendant, and ordinary care on the part of the plaintiff, is on the plaintiff. If the jury believe, that the act of interference in the fight was unnecessary, then the burden of proving extraordinary care on the part of the defendant, or want of ordinary care on the part of the plaintiff, is on defendant."

The jury under these instructions returned a verdict for the plaintiff; whereupon the defendant alleged exceptions....

Shaw, C.J. The facts set forth in the bill of exceptions preclude the supposition, that the blow, inflicted by the hand of the defendant upon the person of the plaintiff, was intentional. The whole case proceeds on the assumption, that the damage sustained by the plaintiff, from the stick held by the defendant, was inadvertent and unintentional; and the case involves the question how far, and under what qualifications, the party by whose unconscious act the damage was done is responsible for it. We use the term "unintentional" rather than involuntary, because in some of the cases, it is stated, that the act of holding and using a weapon or instrument, the movement of which is the immediate cause of hurt to another, is a voluntary act, although its particular effect in hitting and hurting another is not within the purpose or intention of the party doing the act.

It appears to us, that some of the confusion in the cases on this subject has grown out of the long-vexed question, under the rule of the common law, whether a party's remedy, where he has one, should be sought in an action of the case, or of trespass. This is very distinguishable from the question, whether in a given case, any action will lie. The result of these cases is, that if the damage complained of is the immediate effect of the act of the defendant, trespass vi et armis lies; if consequential only, and not immediate, case is the proper remedy.

In these discussions, it is frequently stated by judges, that when one receives injury from the direct act of another, trespass will lie. But we think this is said in reference to the question, whether trespass and not case will lie, assuming that the facts are such, that some action will lie. These dicta are no authority, we think, for holding, that damage received by a direct act of force from another will be sufficient to maintain an action of trespass, whether the act was lawful or unlawful, and neither wilful, intentional, or careless....

We think, as the result of all the authorities, the rule is correctly stated by Mr. Greenleaf, that the plaintiff must come prepared with evidence to show either that the *intention* was unlawful, or

必须把狗分开，并且本该有合适的干涉方式而他没有选择；被告应当对下述后果负责。除非有证据表明他尽到了高度的注意义务，而该事故仍不可避免，此'不可避免'不是严格意义上而是通常意义上的。"

"然而，如果适用原告在受伤之时没有尽到普通注意义务就不该被赔偿的规则，那么被告干涉狗打架的必要性是否还有必要。如果陪审团判定被告有义务干涉，那么证明被告一方有过失和原告一方有普通注意义务的负担就在原告一方。如果陪审团判定，被告的干涉是不必要的，那么证明被告一方的高度注意义务和原告缺乏普通注意义务的负担就在被告一方。"

陪审团根据这些指示作出了有利于原告的裁断；由此，被告主张异议……

Shaw 大法官主笔……：

详尽展示的异议清单排除了推想，事实是被告的手打到原告的身体是故意的。整个案件的进行基于猜想，原告因被告所持的棍子而遭受的损害是疏忽大意的和非故意造成的；案件隐含着疑问，那就是到什么程度和在何种条件下，当事人应对其无意识的行为所致之损害负责。我们用术语"非故意"而不是非自愿，因为在某些情形下，其指称握有和使用武器或工具行为、直接导致他人损害的动作是自愿行为，尽管其打击或者射击他人的具体结果并不在当事人做这个行为的目的或意图之中。

这向我们揭示了，该案件中的种种疑惑均来自于长期困扰我们的普通法规则上的问题，即一方的救济，如果存在的话，必须通过间接侵害之诉（action of the case），或者直接侵害之诉（action of trespass）来寻求。由此引发的一个明显的问题是，在给定的一个案件中，哪种诉由可被受理？这些案件的结果是，如果该诉请的损失是由被告的行为直接造成的，那么暴力侵害之诉（trespass vi et armis）就可被受理；如果是间接引起的，而不是直接的，间接侵害之诉将是合适的救济。

在这些讨论中，法官经常作如下表述，当某人因他人的直接行为而受到损害时，直接侵权可被受理。但我们认为，这是根据下面的问题而言的，该问题是直接侵权而非间接侵权可被受理，均假设了一个事实，存在一个诉由可被受理。我们认为，这些法官附带意见（dictum/ 复数 dicta）并无法源，因为其认为，因他人的直接暴力侵害而受到损害是支持直接侵害之诉的充分条件，而不论该行为合法还是不合法，也不论其是蓄意的、故意的，或者过失的……

我们认为，作为所有这些言论的结论，Greenleaf 先生正确地表述了以下规则，即原告必须用证据证明该故意是非法的，或者证明被告有过错；因

that the defendant was *in fault;* for if the injury was unavoidable, and the conduct of the defendant was free from blame, he will not be liable. If, in the prosecution of a lawful act, a casualty purely accidental arises, no action can be supported for an injury arising therefrom. In applying these rules to the present case, we can perceive no reason why the instructions asked for by the defendant ought not to have been given; to this effect, that if both plaintiff and defendant at the time of the blow were using ordinary care, or if at that time the defendant was using ordinary care, and the plaintiff was not, or if at that time, both the plaintiff and defendant were not using ordinary care, then the plaintiff could not recover.

In using this term, ordinary care, it may be proper to state, that what constitutes ordinary care will vary with the circumstances of cases. In general, it means that kind and degree of care, which prudent and cautious men would use, such as is required by the exigency of the case, and such as is necessary to guard against probable danger. A man, who should have occasion to discharge a gun, on an open and extensive marsh, or in a forest, would be required to use less circumspection and care, than if he were to do the same thing in an inhabited town, village, or city. To make an accident, or casualty, or as the law sometimes states it, inevitable accident, it must be such an accident as the defendant could not have avoided by the use of the kind and degree of care necessary to the exigency, and in the circumstances in which he was placed....

The court instructed the jury, that if it was not a necessary act, and the defendant was not in duty bound to part the dogs, but might with propriety interfere or not as he chose, the defendant was responsible for the consequences of the blow, unless it appeared that he was in the exercise of extraordinary care, so that the accident was inevitable, using the word not in a strict but a popular sense. This is to be taken in connection with the charge afterwards given, that if the jury believed, that the act of interference in the fight was unnecessary (that is, as before explained, not a duty incumbent on the defendant), then the burden of proving extraordinary care on the part of the defendant, or want of ordinary care on the part of plaintiff, was on the defendant.

The court are of opinion that these directions were not conformable to law. If the act of hitting the plaintiff was unintentional, on the part of the defendant, and done in the doing of a lawful act, then the defendant was not liable, unless it was done in the want of exercise of due care adapted to the exigency of the case, and therefore such want of due care became part of the plaintiff's case, and the burden of proof was on the plaintiff to establish it.

Perhaps the learned judge, by the use of the term extraordinary care, in the above charge, explained as it is by the context, may have intended nothing more than that increased degree of care and diligence, which the exigency of particular circumstances might require, and which men of ordinary care and prudence would use under like circumstances, to guard against danger. If such was the meaning of this part of the charge, then it does not differ from our views, as above explained. But we are of opinion, that the other part of the charge, that the burden of proof was on

为，如果该损害是不可避免的，并且被告的行为无需责罚，他就将不负责任。如果起诉的是一个合法行为，即使有纯粹事故性的伤亡，一项由此引起的损害提起的诉讼也不能得到支持。将这些规则应用在该案件当中，我们认为，法院没有理由支持被告所请求的指示；这样如果原告与被告在当时都尽到了普通注意义务，或者如果被告尽到了而原告未尽到普通注意义务，或者原告与被告都未尽到普通注意义务，那么原告不能获得救济。

通过使用"普通注意"这个术语，可以恰当地表述如下，构成普通注意的那些要素将因案件的情况有所变化。一般情况下，其意味着一个小心谨慎的人所拥有的那种程度的注意，即为该案件中的紧急事件所要求，亦为避免可能发生的危险所必需的注意。一个人，如果有机会在空旷而广阔的沼泽地带或森林中开枪，其所要求具备的谨慎和注意就比其在城镇、乡村或是城市里做同样的事情所要求的要低。要想使之构成一次事故，或者伤亡，或者像法律有时候所表述的那样——不可避免的事故，其就必须满足以下条件：被告在其所处的环境中，即使尽到了应对该紧急事件所要求的种类和程度的注意义务，仍然不能避免⋯⋯

法庭指示陪审团说，如果那不是一个必要的行为，并且被告也没有义务去把狗分开，以及如果用其他适当的方式而不是像他所选择的那样，被告就应对接下来的后果负责。除非有证据显示被告实施了超乎寻常的注意，而该事故仍无法避免，不是在严格意义上而是在普通意义上使用该词。这一点被认为与后来提出的起诉有关，即如果陪审团认定干涉狗打架这个行为不是必要的（如前述所解释的，这并不是被告所负有的义务），那么证明被告有超乎寻常的注意或者原告欠缺普通注意的责任义务就在被告一方。

法庭认为这些指令不符合法律。如果被告一方当事人打击原告的行为不是故意的，并是在从事一个合法行为，那么被告就是没有责任的，除非该行为欠缺应对该案件中的紧急事件的合理注意，而举证责任就在原告一方。

上述案件的初审中，在相应的场景下所使用的"超乎寻常的注意"，所表达的不过是在特殊的环境下，若尽到了普通注意义务之人会提到注意程度，则当事人也应当提高注意程度。如果这就是该初审中这一部分的含义，那么其就如前面我们所解释的那样，与我们的观点并无不同。但是，我们认为，该案初审中的另一部分，即证明责任在被告一方，是不正确的。这些事实对于原告获得赔偿是非常关键的，他应当予以证明。证据可以由

the defendant, was incorrect. Those facts which are essential to enable the plaintiff to recover, he takes the burden of proving. The evidence may be offered by the plaintiff or by the defendant; the question of due care, or want of care, may be essentially connected with the main facts, and arise from the same proof; but the effect of the rule, as to the burden of proof, is this, that when the proof is all in, and before the jury, from whatever side it comes, and whether directly proved, or inferred from circumstances, if it appears that the defendant was doing a lawful act, and unintentionally hit and hurt the plaintiff, then unless it also appears to the satisfaction of the jury, that the defendant is chargeable with some fault, negligence, carelessness, or want of prudence, the plaintiff fails to sustain the burden of proof, and is not entitled to recover.

New trial ordered.

8. Tubbs v. Argus, 140 Ind. App. 695, 225 N.E.2d 841 (1967)

Appellate Court of Indiana, United States

Pfaff, J. This appeal arises as a result of demurrer to appellant's Second Amended Complaint which was sustained and judgment entered thereon upon the failure and refusal of the appellant to plead over.

The facts material to a determination of the issues raised on this appeal may be summarized as follows:…

…The appellant was riding as a guest passenger in the right front seat of an automobile owned and operated by the appellee when it was driven over the south curb of West Hampton Drive and into a tree, resulting in injury to the appellant. After the said collision, the appellee abandoned the automobile and did not render reasonable aid and assistance to the injured appellant. Appellant alleges that she suffered additional injuries as a result of appellee's failure to render reasonable aid and assistance and seeks to recover only for these additional injuries.

In her assignment of errors, the appellant avers that the trial court erred in sustaining the demurrer to appellant's Second Amended Complaint. More specifically, the appellant alleges that appellee's failure to render reasonable aid and assistance constituted a breach of a common law duty.…

The appellant herein is seeking recovery for additional injuries arising from the appellee's failure to render reasonable aid and assistance, and not for the initial injuries which resulted from the operation of the automobile.

At common law, there is no general duty to aid a person who is in peril. L. S. Ayres & Company v. Hicks (1941), 220 Ind. 86, 40 N.E.2d 334. However, in L. S. Ayres & Company, supra, page 94, 40 N.E.2d page 337, the Supreme Court of Indiana held that "under some circumstances, moral and humanitarian considerations may require one to render assistance to another who has

原告或者是被告提供；合理注意或者欠缺注意的问题也许与主要事实有着核心关联，也可以由同样的证据得出。但是，证明责任规则的效果就是这样，一旦证据全部提交给陪审团，无论其来自何方当事人，无论其是直接证明，还是由条件间接得出，如果其显示被告在从事合法行为，且并非故意打击而伤害到原告，那么除非其展示了能说服陪审团的下述情况——被告有可归责的过错、过失、疏忽，或者缺乏谨慎。但原告未能承担证明责任，因此不能获得救济。

发回重审。

8. Tubbs v. Argus, 140 Ind. App. 695, 225 N.E.2d 841 (1967)

美国印第安纳州上诉法院

Pfaff 法官主笔：该上诉是对上诉人二次修正起诉状的诉求不充分抗辩被准许且在上诉人再答辩失败和被拒的情况下，作出判决产生的结果。

对确定上诉引起的争议具有实质性的事实可以概括如下：……

……上诉人是一名被告所有并驾驶的车上的乘客，当时坐在车右前座上。那时车开出了 West Hampton 快速路的南侧并撞上了一棵树，导致上诉人受了伤。在发生上述碰撞事故后，被上诉人抛弃了车，且没有为受伤的上诉人提供合理的救助和帮助。上诉人声称，由于被上诉人未能为其提供合理的救助和帮助，其受到了额外的伤害，并仅针对这些额外的伤害寻求救济。

在其错误陈述中，上诉人主张初审法院错误地准许了上诉人二次修正起诉状的诉求进行的不充分抗辩，更具体地说，上诉人声称被告未能为其提供合理的救助和帮助的行为构成了对普通法义务的违反……

在这里，上诉人是针对其因被上诉人未能提供合理的救助和帮助造成的额外伤害寻求救济，而不是针对最初被告的驾驶行为导致她受到的伤害。

在普通法中，人们并没有普遍的义务去救助处于危险情形中的人。［参见 L. S. Ayres & Company v.Hicks（1941），220 Ind. 86,40 N.E.2d 334 案。］然而在上引案例 L. S. Ayres & Company, supra, page 94, 40 N.E.2d page 337 中，印第安纳州最高法院认为："在某些情况下，出于道德和人道主义考量，可能会要求一个人去对伤者提供帮助，即使该伤害不是因他的过失造成的并且可能是因受伤者自己的过失引起的。如果由于缺少适当的注意而加重了损害的话，那么在这种情况下，不去提供帮助就可能构成可诉的过失。"［Tippecanoe

been injured, even though the injury was not due to negligence on his part and may have been caused by the negligence of the injured person. Failure to render assistance in such a situation may constitute actionable negligence if the injury is aggravated through lack of due care." Tippecanoe Loan, etc., Co. v. Cleveland, etc., R. Co., 57 Ind. App. 644, 104 N.E. 866, 106 N.E. 739 (1915).

In Tippecanoe Loan, etc., Co. v. Cleveland, etc. R. Co., supra, this court held that a railroad company was liable for failing to provide medical assistance to an employee who was injured through no fault of the railroad company, but who was rendered helpless and by reason of which the employee's injuries were aggravated.

The Supreme Court of Indiana in *L. S. Ayres,* supra, found the appellant liable for aggravation of injuries when it failed to extricate the appellee, a six-year-old boy, whose fingers were caught in the moving parts of an escalator, even though the jury conclusively established that the appellant was not negligent with respect to the choice, construction, or manner of operating the elevator. In so holding, the Supreme Court stated that it may be deduced from Tippecanoe Loan, etc. Co. v. Cleveland, etc. R. Co., supra, "that there may be a legal obligation to take positive or affirmative steps to effect the rescue of a person who is helpless and in a situation of peril, when the one proceeded against is a master or an invitor or when the injury resulted from use of an instrumentality under the control of the defendant."

The doctrine of law as set forth in Restatement (Second) of Torts, §322, p. 133, adds credence to these two Indiana cases. "…If the actor knows or has reason to know that by his conduct, whether tortious or innocent, he has caused such bodily harm to another as to make him helpless and in danger of future harm, the actor is under a duty to exercise reasonable care to prevent such further harm."…

In the case at bar, the appellant received her injuries from an instrumentality under the control of the appellee. Under the rule stated above and on the authority of the cases cited, this was a sufficient relationship to impose a duty to render reasonable aid and assistance, a duty for the breach of which the appellee is liable for the additional injuries suffered.

We are of the opinion that the court below erred in sustaining the demurrer to appellant's Second Amended Complaint.

This cause is reversed and remanded for proceedings not inconsistent with this opinion.

Judgment reversed.

Bierly and Smith, JJ., concur.

9. Rowland v. Christian, 69 Cal. 2d 108, 443 P.2d 561, 70 Cal. Rptr. 97 (1968)

Supreme Court of California, United States

Peters, J.…Section 1714 of the Civil Code provides: "Every one is responsible, not only for

Loan, etc., Co. v. Cleveland, etc., R. Co., 57 Ind. App. 644, 104 N.E. 866, 106 N.E. 739（1915）。]

在案例 Tippecanoe Loan, etc., Co. v. Cleveland, etc. R. Co. 中，法庭认为铁路公司应为其没有对受伤的雇员提供医疗帮助而负责，因为铁路公司虽不存在过错，但是却由于没有提供任何帮助而加重了雇员的损伤程度。

印第安纳州最高法院在上引案例 L.S. Ayres & Compang v. Hicks 中认为，被上诉人是一个6岁的小男孩，最终他的手指被卡在了自动扶梯活动部分之间，上诉人未能将其解救出来。尽管陪审团最终确定上诉人在电梯运营的选择、构造以及方式等方面不存在过失，上诉人仍然需要对加重的伤害部分负责。据此，最高法院表示可以从上引案例 Tippecanoe Loan,etc.Co.v. Cleveland,etc.R.Co. 中推论出："当被起诉的人是雇主、邀请者或者伤害是因使用被告所控制的设施而造成的情况下，也许其有法定的义务去采取积极或者肯定的措施来救助无助或处于危险之中的人。"

《侵权法重述·第二次》第322条在第133页所确立的法律学说进一步确认了这两起印第安纳州的判决。"……无论是侵权行为还是无害行为，如果行为人知道或有理由知道其行为造成了他人的身体伤害导致其无助且有发生未来损害的危险，行为人就有义务给予合理的注意以防止发生未来损害。"……

在本案的情形中，上诉人的伤害是由被上诉人控制的设施所造成的。依以上列举的规则以及引用的判例法源，被上诉人与伤害存在充分的关系，有施加合理的救助与帮助的义务，并且因违反了上述义务的行为，被上诉人有义务对遭受的额外损伤负责。

我们的意见是，下级法院错误地准许了对上诉人二次修正起诉状的诉求进行的不充分抗辩。

本案被撤销，发回重审，诉讼不得与本法律意见相悖。

撤销判决。

Bierly 法官和 Smith 法官赞同。

9. Rowland v. Christian, 69 Cal. 2d 108, 443 P.2d 561, 70 Cal. Rptr. 97 (1968)

美国加利福尼亚州最高法院

Peters 法官主笔：……《加利福尼亚州民法典》第1714条规定："每个人不仅应为其故意的行为造成的结果负责，而且还应该为其因在管理其财物和

the result of his willful acts, but also for an injury occasioned to another by his want of ordinary care or skill in the management of his property or person, except so far as the latter has, willfully or by want of ordinary care, brought the injury upon himself...." This code section, which has been unchanged in our law since 1872, states a civil law and not a common law principle.

Nevertheless, some common law judges and commentators have urged that the principle embodied in this code section serves as the foundation of our negligence law. Thus in a concurring opinion, Brett, M. R. in Heaven v. Pender (1883) 11 Q.B.D. 503, 509, states: "whenever one person is by circumstances placed in such a position with regard to another that every one of ordinary sense who did think would at once recognize that if he did not use ordinary care and skill in his own conduct with regard to those circumstances he would cause danger of injury to the person or property of the other, a duty arises to use ordinary care and skill to avoid such danger."

California cases have occasionally stated a similar view: "All persons are required to use ordinary care to prevent others being injured as the result of their conduct." Although it is true that some exceptions have been made to the general principle that a person is liable for injuries caused by his failure to exercise reasonable care in the circumstances, it is clear that in the absence of statutory provision declaring an exception to the fundamental principle enunciated by section 1714 of the Civil Code, no such exception should be made unless clearly supported by public policy.

A departure from this fundamental principle involves the balancing of a number of considerations; the major ones are the foreseeability of harm to the plaintiff, the degree of certainty that the plaintiff suffered injury, the closeness of the connection between the defendant's conduct and the injury suffered, the moral blame attached to the defendant's conduct, the policy of preventing future harm, the extent of the burden to the defendant and consequences to the community of imposing a duty to exercise care with resulting liability for breach, and the availability, cost, and prevalence of insurance for the risk involved.

One of the areas where this court and other courts have departed from the fundamental concept that a man is liable for injuries caused by his carelessness is with regard to the liability of a possessor of land for injuries to persons who have entered upon that land. It has been suggested that the special rules regarding liability of the possessor of land are due to historical considerations stemming from the high place which land has traditionally held in English and American thought, the dominance and prestige of the landowning class in England during the formative period of the rules governing the possessor's liability, and the heritage of feudalism.

The departure from the fundamental rule of liability for negligence has been accomplished by classifying the plaintiff either as a trespasser, licensee, or invitee and then adopting special rules as to the duty owed by the possessor to each of the classifications. Generally speaking a trespasser is a person who enters or remains upon land of another without a privilege to do so; a licensee is a person like a social guest who is not an invitee and who is privileged to enter or remain upon land

员工时缺少一般的注意和技能而造成他人伤害的结果负责。除非后者无论是因故意还是缺少一般的注意而自己造成了伤害……"该法条从1872年开始就没有在法律中改变过,它表述了一条成文法而非普通法的原则。

然而,有一些普通法的法官和评论者认为,包含该法条的原则是被当作我们的过失责任规则中的基本原理去应用的。因此,Heaven v. Pender (1883) 11 Q.B.D. 503, 509案中,掌卷法官Brett的一条协同意见认为:"无论何时,如果一个人由环境置于一种位置,处在这种涉及他人利益的位置时,每一个有普通常识并且在思考的人都会立刻认识到,如果在那种环境下,他在行事过程中没有尽到一般的注意以及应用相应的技巧的话,他将引起导致他人人身及财产损失的危险,那么就产生了通过一般的注意和技能避免这类危险发生的义务。"

加利福尼亚州的案例也偶然地表达了类似的观点:"所有人都须尽到一般的注意义务以防止因其行为对他人造成伤害。"虽然该一般原则确实存在一些例外,即一个人对于其在相应环境下没有尽到合理注意义务所造成的伤害是负有责任的。但该原则很明显不满足《加利福尼亚州民法典》第1714条所明确规定的基本原则例外的法定条件(除非得到了公共政策的明显支持,否则不构成这种例外)。

背离基本的原则需要权衡很多因素,其中主要的一些为:原告对损害的可预见性、原告伤害的确定性、被告的行为与损害结果之间联系的密切性、被告行为在道德上的应受谴责性、防止发生未来损害的方式、被告负担的范围以及若这种注意义务存在时对社会的影响,以及应对这样的风险的保险险种是否存在,如果有是否又过于昂贵。

本法院及其他法院背离了一个人应为其疏忽大意所造成的损害负责的基本原则的领域之一就是土地所有人对进入其土地的人受到伤害的责任问题。已经有人提出,关于土地所有人责任的特殊规定是出于英美思维中历史性地持有的对土地赋予较高地位和在规定土地所有人责任的规则形成时期英国地主阶级的统治和声望,以及封建制度遗产这三个方面的考虑。

对过失责任基本规则的背离是通过将原告划分为侵入者、准入者以及应邀者来实现的,并且对土地占有人在各种类型原告的义务上都采纳了专

by virtue of the possessor's consent, and an invitee is a business visitor who is invited or permitted to enter or remain on the land for a purpose directly or indirectly connected with business dealings between them.

Although the invitor owes the invitee a duty to exercise ordinary care to avoid injuring him, the general rule is that a trespasser and licensee or social guest are obliged to take the premises as they find them insofar as any alleged defective condition thereon may exist, and that the possessor of the land owes them only the duty of refraining from wanton or willful injury. The ordinary justification for the general rule severely restricting the occupier's liability to social guests is based on the theory that the guest should not expect special precautions to be made on his account and that if the host does not inspect and maintain his property the guest should not expect this to be done on his account.

An increasing regard for human safety has led to a retreat from this position, and an exception to the general rule limiting liability has been made as to active operations where an obligation to exercise reasonable care for the protection of the licensee has been imposed on the occupier of land. In an apparent attempt to avoid the general rule limiting liability, courts have broadly defined active operations, sometimes giving the term a strained construction in cases involving dangers known to the occupier....

Another exception to the general rule limiting liability has been recognized for cases where the occupier is aware of the dangerous condition, the condition amounts to a concealed trap, and the guest is unaware of the trap....

The cases dealing with the active negligence and the trap exceptions are indicative of the subtleties and confusion which have resulted from application of the common law principles governing the liability of the possessor of land. Similar confusion and complexity exist as to the definitions of trespasser, licensee, and invitee.

In refusing to adopt the rules relating to the liability of a possessor of land for the law of admiralty, the United States Supreme Court stated: "The distinctions which the common law draws between licensee and invitee were inherited from a culture deeply rooted to the land, a culture which traced many of its standards to a heritage of feudalism. In an effort to do justice in an industrialized urban society, with its complex economic and individual relationships, modern common-law courts have found it necessary to formulate increasingly subtle verbal refinements, to create subclassifications among traditional common-law categories, and to delineate fine gradations in the standards of care which the landowner owes to each. Yet even within a single jurisdiction, the classifications and subclassifications bred by the common law have produced confusion and conflict. As new distinctions have been spawned, older ones have become obscured. Through this semantic morass the common law has moved, unevenly and with hesitation, towards imposing on owners and occupiers a single duty of reasonable care in all the circumstances." ...

门的规定。一般来说，所谓侵入者是指没有权限而进入或停留在他人土地之上的人；所谓的准入者并非是受邀者，而是一种作为社交访客那样得到土地所有人的同意而有权进入或留在其土地上的人；所谓的受邀者是指出于二者之间直接或间接的事务目的而被邀请或允许进入或留在其土地上的事务拜访者。

邀请者有义务对受邀者尽到一般的注意义务以避免其受到损害，而对于侵入者和准入者以及作为社交的客人而言，普遍的规则是，其有义务承受场地内发生的任何可能存在的风险。土地所有者仅仅对他们承担防止其受到肆意或蓄意伤害的义务。对于普遍规则严重限制了占有人对作为社交客人的责任问题通常是基于以下理论，即客人无权期待为其提供特殊的保护并且如果主人怠于检查和维护其财产，客人无权期待为其完成这些行为。

普遍规则中有限责任的另一个例外情形是：占有人注意到了存在危险的情形，该情形含有一个隐蔽的陷阱而客人没有察觉到该陷阱……

本案对这种积极的过失以及存在陷阱的例外的分析处理体现了在应用普通法原则确定土地所有者责任时的微妙之处以及相应的困惑所在。在对侵入者、准入者和受邀者进行定义时也存在类似复杂的、困惑的问题。

美国最高法院在拒绝采纳海事法中有关土地所有者责任的规则时表明："普通法中对准入者和受邀者的区分来自于一种深深植根于土地的文化，该文化保留了很多封建制度遗留的准则，致力于在一个工业化的城市化社会中维护公平正义。在复杂的经济及人际关系中，现代普通法法院认为很有必要越来越多地进行一些微妙的用词上的改进，来对传统普通法上的分类进行进一步细化，以形成一种土地所有者对每类人的注意义务标准的令人满意的层次划分。然而，即使在一个单独的法域中，由普通法所带来的（对相关标准的）分类和进一步细分都会产生相应的困惑及冲突。由于产生了大量的新的区分标准，旧有标准就变得晦涩了。通过这种语义上的混乱，普通法在犹豫不决的情况下发生了变化，其已经开始对所有者和占有者施加一种单独的、在任何情形下都应履行合理注意的义务。"……

所有者责任的确定依赖于普通法对受伤一方作为侵入者，准入者以及受邀者的法律地位所进行的划分。对于该责任问题，还有另一种根本性的

There is another fundamental objection to the approach to the question of the possessor's liability on the basis of the common law distinctions based upon the status of the injured party as a trespasser, licensee, or invitee. Complexity can be borne and confusion remedied where the underlying principles governing liability are based upon proper considerations. Whatever may have been the historical justifications for the common law distinctions, it is clear that those distinctions are not justified in the light of our modern society and that the complexity and confusion which has arisen is not due to difficulty in applying the original common law rules—they are all too easy to apply in their original formulation—but is due to the attempts to apply just rules in our modern society within the ancient terminology.

Without attempting to labor all of the rules relating to the possessor's liability, it is apparent that the classifications of trespasser, licensee, and invitee, the immunities from liability predicated upon those classifications, and the exceptions to those immunities, often do not reflect the major factors which should determine whether immunity should be conferred upon the possessor of land. Some of those factors, including the closeness of the connection between the injury and the defendant's conduct, the moral blame attached to the defendant's conduct, the policy of preventing future harm, and the prevalence and availability of insurance, bear little, if any, relationship to the classifications of trespasser, licensee and invitee and the existing rules conferring immunity.

Although in general there may be a relationship between the remaining factors and the classifications of trespasser, licensee, and invitee, there are many cases in which no such relationship may exist. Thus, although the foreseeability of harm to an invitee would ordinarily seem greater than the foreseeability of harm to a trespasser, in a particular case the opposite may be true. The same may be said of the issue of certainty of injury. The burden to the defendant and consequences to the community of imposing a duty to exercise care with resulting liability for breach may often be greater with respect to trespassers than with respect to invitees, but it by no means follows that this is true in every case. In many situations, the burden will be the same, i.e., the conduct necessary upon the defendant's part to meet the burden of exercising due care as to invitees will also meet his burden with respect to licensees and trespassers. The last of the major factors, the cost of insurance, will, of course, vary depending upon the rules of liability adopted, but there is no persuasive evidence that applying ordinary principles of negligence law to the land occupier's liability will materially reduce the prevalence of insurance due to increased cost or even substantially increase the cost....

A man's life or limb does not become less worthy of protection by the law nor a loss less worthy of compensation under the law because he has come upon the land of another without permission or with permission but without a business purpose. Reasonable people do not ordinarily vary their conduct depending upon such matters, and to focus upon the status of the injured party as a trespasser, licensee, or invitee in order to determine the question whether the landowner has

反对意见。如果规范相关责任的根本原则是基于适当的考量的话，是可以忍受复杂性并补救的。不论普通法进行分类的历史因素为何，很明显，从现代社会来看，这些分类并不合理而且出现的复杂性及困惑问题并不在于原始的普通法规则难以应用——事实上应用那些原始的表述太容易了——而是在于试图在我们现代社会中，在古代的专业用语范围之内应用这些规则。

不用去试图详细分析关于所有者责任的所有规定，就可以很明显地看出：对于侵入者、准入者和受邀者的分类以及这些分类所表明的免责规定，还有这些免责规定的例外，通常都没有反映出决定是否应对这些土地所有者予以免责的主要因素。其中一些因素，包括被告的行为以及损害结果之间联系的密切性、被告行为在道德上的可谴责性、预防发生未来损害的法律目的、保险的普遍性和可行性，都几乎很少出现，即使有，也与侵入者、准入者和受邀者的分类以及现存的免责规定有关。

尽管一般说来，剩下的因素与侵入者、准入者和受邀者的分类可能有关系，但是很多情况下它们仍然没有关系。因此，尽管一般看来，可以预见到对受邀者的损害的可能性可能大于对侵入者，但是在特定情况下，情况可能截然相反。对于伤害的确认问题也是如此，通常来说，被告的责任以及施加这种如违反将导致承担责任的注意义务对社会的结果，对侵入者来说可能重于受邀者，但这并不意味着每起案件中都应如此。在许多情况下，责任是相同的。例如，为达到对受邀者尽到适当注意义务的要求，被告方所做的必要的行为同样适用于准入者及侵入者。这些主要因素的最后一点是保险的成本，它必然将会改变对所采纳的责任规则的依赖，但是没有有说服力的证据表明对于土地占有者的责任采纳过失责任规则中的一般原则，将会因成本的增长或成本的大幅增长而能够实质性地降低保险的普遍性……

法律不能因其未经允许或虽经允许但不是出于事务目的而进入他人的土地，而使一个人的生命或身体变得不那么值得保护或损失不那么值得赔偿。理性人通常情况下不会依这些原因而改变其行为。把注意力集中在受伤害一方的身份究竟是侵入者、准入者还是受邀者上，并以此来决定是否土地所有者应负有注意义务的问题，有悖于我们现代的社会公德以及人道主义价值。

a duty of care, is contrary to our modern social mores and humanitarian values. The common law rules obscure rather than illuminate the proper considerations which should govern determination of the question of duty.

It bears repetition that the basic policy of this state set forth by the Legislature in section 1714 of the Civil Code is that everyone is responsible for an injury caused to another by his want of ordinary care or skill in the management of his property. The factors which may in particular cases warrant departure from this fundamental principle do not warrant the wholesale immunities resulting from the common law classifications, and we are satisfied that continued adherence to the common law distinctions can only lead to injustice or, if we are to avoid injustice, further fictions with the resulting complexity and confusion. We decline to follow and perpetuate such rigid classifications. The proper test to be applied to the liability of the possessor of land in accordance with section 1714 of the Civil Code is whether in the management of his property he has acted as a reasonable man in view of the probability of injury to others, and, although the plaintiff's status as a trespasser, licensee, or invitee may in the light of the facts giving rise to such status have some bearing on the question of liability, the status is not determinative.

Once the ancient concepts as to the liability of the occupier of land are stripped away, the status of the plaintiff relegated to its proper place in determining such liability, and ordinary principles of negligence applied, the result in the instant case presents no substantial difficulties. As we have seen, when we view the matters presented on the motion for summary judgment as we must, we must assume defendant Miss Christian was aware that the faucet handle was defective and dangerous, that the defect was not obvious, and that plaintiff was about to come in contact with the defective condition, and under the undisputed facts she neither remedied the condition nor warned plaintiff of it. Where the occupier of land is aware of a concealed condition involving in the absence of precautions an unreasonable risk of harm to those coming in contact with it, the trier of fact can reasonably conclude that a failure to warn or to repair the condition constitutes negligence. Whether or not a guest has a right to expect that his host will remedy dangerous conditions on his account, he should reasonably be entitled to rely upon a warning of the dangerous condition so that he, like the host, will be in a position to take special precautions when he comes in contact with it....

The judgment is reversed.

Traynor, C.J., Tobriner, J., Mosk, J., and Sullivan, J., concurred.

Burke, J. I dissent. In determining the liability of the occupier or owner of land for injuries, the distinctions between trespassers, licensees and invitees have been developed and applied by the courts over a period of many years. They supply a reasonable and workable approach to the problems involved, and one which provides the degree of stability and predictability so highly prized in the law. The unfortunate alternative, it appears to me, is the route taken by the majority

普通法规则没有予以阐明，而是使应当确定有关义务问题的适当的考量变得模糊起来。

请允许我重复本州立法机构在《加利福尼亚州民法典》第1714条所阐明的在此情形下所采纳的基本法律目的，即每个人应该为其因在管理其财物时缺少一般的注意和技能而造成他人伤害的结果负责。在特定案例中准许背离基本原则的因素并不准许普通法分类所导致的大量免责情形的出现，并且我们确信如果继续坚持进行普通法上的分类只能导致不公正，或者如果我们试图避免不公正和未来将导致的复杂而困惑的主观臆断的话。我们拒绝服从及保持这种僵化的分类。依据《加利福尼亚州民法典》第1714条，正确检验土地所有者责任的方式应该是看其在管理其财产时，是否在考虑其他人受伤的可能性方面做到了理性行事。并且，尽管原告作为侵入者、准入者以及受邀者的身份可能鉴于产生这种身份的事实而与责任问题有一些关系，但是这种身份并非是决定性的。

一旦关于土地占有者责任的古代概念被去除，原告的身份问题就转为，在确定责任时其所应处的正确位置为何，并且可以应用一般的过失责任原则，在本案的结果中就没有设置实质性的困难。像我们看到的那样，对于被告主张作出简易裁判的申请，我们必须假设被告 Christian 小姐注意到了龙头把手存在缺陷且具有危险，而这种缺陷并不明显且原告确定将处于这种情形之中，因此毫无疑问的是，被告既没有采取补救措施，也没有提醒原告注意它。当土地占有者注意到了这种隐蔽的情形但没有采取预防措施避免使处于该情形下的人承担不合理的损害风险时，通过分析事实可以得出一个合理的结论，即：如果责任者没有提出警告或对这种情况进行补救，其就构成了过失。无论客人是否有权期待主人会为客人的利益而对危险情形作出补救措施，他都理应有权得到对危险情形的警告，以便使其能够在这种情况下得到像主人那样的专门保护……

撤销判决。

Traynor 大法官和 Tobriner 法官、Mosk 法官、Sullivan 法官同意。

Burke 法官撰写反对意见：我反对。在确定土地占有者或所有者的损害责任问题时，对于侵入者、准入者、受邀者的区分在许多年间一直被法院所采纳并发展着，它们提供了一种合理可行的解决相关问题的途径并赋予了其稳定性以及可预见性，在法律上得到了很高的评价。依我来看，这不幸的替代是本案多数意见所采纳的惯常做法。这些问题未来将适用有关过失的基本法

in their opinion in this case; that such issues are to be decided on a case by case basis under the application of the basic law of negligence, bereft of the guiding principles and precedent which the law has heretofore attached by virtue of the relationship of the parties to one another.

Liability for negligence turns upon whether a duty of care is owed, and if so, the extent thereof. Who can doubt that the corner grocery, the large department store, or the financial institution owes a greater duty of care to one whom it has invited to enter its premises as a prospective customer of its wares or services than it owes to a trespasser seeking to enter after the close of business hours and for a nonbusiness or even an antagonistic purpose? I do not think it unreasonable or unfair that a social guest (classified by the law as a licensee, as was plaintiff here) should be obliged to take the premises in the same condition as his host finds them or permits them to be. Surely a homeowner should not be obliged to hover over his guests with warnings of possible dangers to be found in the condition of the home (e.g., waxed floors, slipping rugs, toys in unexpected places, etc., etc.). Yet today's decision appears to open the door to potentially unlimited liability despite the purpose and circumstances motivating the plaintiff in entering the premises of another, and despite the caveat of the majority that the status of the parties may "have some bearing on the question of liability…" whatever the future may show that language to mean.

In my view, it is not a proper function of this court to overturn the learning, wisdom and experience of the past in this field. Sweeping modifications of tort liability law fall more suitably within the domain of the Legislature, before which all affected interests can be heard and which can enact statutes providing uniform standards and guidelines for the future.

I would affirm the judgment for defendant.

10. Donoghue v Stevenson [1932] AC 562

House of Lords, United Kingdom

LORD BUCKMASTER

(read by LORD TOMLIN). My Lords, the facts of this case are simple. On August 26, 1928, the appellant drank a bottle of ginger-beer, manufactured by the respondent, which a friend had bought from a retailer and given to her. The bottle contained the decomposed remains of a snail which were not, and could not be, detected until the greater part of the contents of the bottle had been consumed. As a result she alleged, and at this stage her allegations must be accepted as true, that she suffered from shock and severe gastro-enteritis. She accordingly instituted the proceedings against the manufacturer which have given rise to this appeal.

The foundation of her case is that the respondent, as the manufacturer of an article intended for consumption and contained in a receptacle which prevented inspection, owed a duty to her as consumer of the article to take care that there was no noxious element in the goods, that he

律逐案裁判，失去了指导性的原则和法律迄今为止所遵循的依照双方关系效力的先例。

有无过失的责任取决于是否负有注意义务，如果有的话，其程度为何。谁能质疑食品店、大型百货商场或金融机构对作为其商品或服务的潜在消费者而被邀请进入其营业场所的人负有的注意义务，比试图出于非商业的甚至是有敌意的目的，在营业时间结束后进入其营业场所的侵入者更大呢？我不认为一个作为社交访客（法律上归为准入者，就像本案的原告）在主人发现他们或允许他们在那里时，在营业场所中应得到同样的对待是不合理的或不公平的。当然，也不应强迫房主绕着圈地提醒他客人房中目前可能存在的任何危险之处（例如打过蜡的地板、打滑的地毯以及无法预料之处的玩具等）。然而现在的判决似乎不顾鼓励原告进入他人营业场所的动机和情况，就打开了通往潜在的无限责任之门，并且不顾大多数人的告诫——即原告方的身份可能"与责任承担问题是有一些关系的……"将来的证据。

依我来看，在这个领域中，法庭不应推翻过去该领域的经验、智慧以及认知。在所有相关利益都能被考虑到并且颁布能为未来提供统一标准和指导原则的法规之前，大规模地修正侵权责任法更应该属于立法机构的权限范围。

我宁可维持对被告有利的原判。

10. Donoghue v Stevenson [1932] AC 562

联合王国上议院

Buckmaster 大法官

（由 Tomlin 大法官宣读）尊敬的大法官阁下们，本案的事实很简单。1928 年 8 月 26 日，本案上诉人饮用了由被上诉人生产的，上诉人的朋友从一零售商处买给她喝的姜汁啤酒。啤酒瓶中含有解体的蜗牛，且此问题未能（且不可能）在上诉人已然饮完大半瓶酒前被其发现。基于此，她宣称自己遭受了巨大的震惊以及因此而患急性胃炎（考虑到我们已经进入终审阶段，此宣称的真实性已经不容置疑），进而提交了诉讼申请。此诉讼经过层层上诉，最终来到了这里。

上诉人的主张的基础是：作为生产商的被上诉人因为生产了供人消费的商品、而且外包装使人难以事前察觉，就应对作为消费者的上诉人负担保证货物中不存在有害物质的义务。被上诉人因疏忽导致其未能履行上述义务，

neglected such duty and is consequently liable for any damage caused by such neglect. After certain amendments, which are now immaterial, the case came before the Lord Ordinary, who rejected the plea in law of the respondent and allowed a proof. His interlocutor was recalled by the Second Division of the Court of Session, from whose judgment this appeal has been brought.

Before examining the merits two comments are desirable: (1.) That the appellant's case rests solely on the ground of a tort based not on fraud but on negligence; and (2.) that throughout the appeal the case has been argued on the basis, undisputed by the Second Division and never questioned by counsel for the appellant or by any of your Lordships, that the English and the Scots law on the subject are identical. It is therefore upon the English law alone that I have considered the matter, and in my opinion it is on the English law alone that in the circumstances we ought to proceed.

The law applicable is the common law, and, though its principles are capable of application to meet new conditions not contemplated when the law was laid down, these principles cannot be changed nor can additions be made to them because any particular meritorious case seems outside their ambit.

…

In my view, therefore, the authorities are against the appellant's contention, and, apart from authority, it is difficult to see how any common law proposition can be formulated to support her claim.

The principle contended for must be this: that the manufacturer, or indeed the repairer, of any article, apart entirely from contract, owes a duty to any person by whom the article is lawfully used to see that it has been carefully constructed. All rights in contract must be excluded from consideration of this principle; such contractual rights as may exist in successive steps from the original manufacturer down to the ultimate purchaser are ex hypothesi immaterial. Nor can the doctrine be confined to cases where inspection is difficult or impossible to introduce. This conception is simply to misapply to tort doctrine applicable to sale and purchase.

The principle of tort lies completely outside the region where such considerations apply, and the duty, if it exists, must extend to every person who, in lawful circumstances, uses the article made. There can be no special duty attaching to the manufacture of food apart from that implied by contract or imposed by statute. If such a duty exists, it seems to me it must cover the construction of every article, and I cannot see any reason why it should not apply to the construction of a house. If one step, why not fifty? Yet if a house be, as it sometimes is, negligently built, and in consequence of that negligence the ceiling falls and injures the occupier or any one else, no action against the builder exists according to the English law, although I believe such a right did exist according to the laws of Babylon. Were such a principle known and recognized, it seems to me impossible, having regard to the numerous cases that must have arisen to persons injured by its

就应对其基于此项疏忽所造成的损失承担侵权损害赔偿责任。经过一些对此处无关紧要的修改后，本案被提交至苏格兰最高民事法院独任法官处。作为一审法官的独任法官拒绝了被诉人的答辩意见，而允许上诉人呈递证据以查明事实。但是，最高民事法院第二分庭判决驳回了独任法官的这一裁定。本判决所有处理的即是对二审法院判决的上诉。

在展开实质性的讨论之前，有两点需要在此声明：第一，上诉人此次诉讼请求的法律基础是基于过失的侵权（negligence）而非基于欺诈的侵权（fraud）。第二，在整个上诉的前后过程中，有一点是毫无争议的（无论是苏格兰第二分庭，还是上诉人，抑或是尊敬的大法官阁下们），那就是：苏格兰法与英国法（英格兰法）就本问题的立场是一样的。因此，虽然本案来自苏格兰，我却只需考虑英国法，且我认为此次诉讼也只需立足于英国法即可。

具体而言，此次适用的法律是普通法。需要注意的是，虽然每一个普通法的原则最初产生时都是为了处理当时的法律所未能调整的新情况，但是我们却不能仅仅因为在这个原则之后不能实现某个个案的正义，就主张改变或增补它。

……

所以在我看来，上诉人的主张与先例不符。且就算不考虑先例，我们也很难通过对普通法的再解读得出对上诉人有利的规则。

可想而知，被上诉人主张的大原则是：任何产品的生产商（也包括修理商），无论合同存在与否，都对合法使用该产品的第三人负有保证产品被仔细组装的义务。此项义务与合同无关，哪怕在整个链条中涉及一份又一份的合同，这些合同对于义务的存在也无关紧要。这项大原则也不限定于受害人很难发现或根本没有机会发现潜在缺陷的情形。在我看来，这项大原则根本就是错误地把侵权法的原则类推适用到了买卖关系中。

如果这项大原则存在，那么它的适用范围就没有理由只局限在上诉人考虑的情形中。换言之，任何人使用任何形式的产品都可以触发这种义务。毕竟食物这类产品没有什么特殊性，即除了合同和制定法以外，食物的提供者和消费者之间不会有什么特殊的义务存在。如果按照被上诉人所主张的这项大原则，真的有一项特殊义务的话，那么我们没有理由不将这项义务也类推适用于房屋建筑关系中。既开先例，何以限之？但我们知道，如果一个房子在建造时存在疏忽，且此房屋天花板掉落时正好砸伤了房屋的占用人或随便一个走进房屋的陌生人，那么根据英国法，此受害人是无法根据过失侵权起诉房屋建造人的。当然，我相信在巴比伦这个案件结果会不一样。如果这项大原则真的存在于英国法，那么为什么先前那么多受害者因为此类产品生产中的过失而受伤的案件，除了 *George v Skivington* 案，其他全输了呢？为什么

disregard, that, with the exception of George v. Skivington, no case directly involving the principle has ever succeeded in the Courts, and, were it well known and accepted, much of the discussion of the earlier cases would have been waste of time, and the distinction as to articles dangerous in themselves or known to be dangerous to the vendor would be meaningless.

In *Mullen v. Barr & Co.*, a case indistinguishable from the present excepting upon the ground that a mouse is not a snail, and necessarily adopted by the Second Division in their judgment, Lord Anderson says this: "In a case like the present, where the goods of the defenders are widely distributed throughout Scotland, it would seem little short of outrageous to make them responsible to members of the public for the condition of the contents of every bottle which issues from their works. It is obvious that, if such responsibility attached to the defenders, they might be called on to meet claims of damages which they could not possibly investigate or answer."

In agreeing, as I do, with the judgment of Lord Anderson, I desire to add that I find it hard to dissent from the emphatic nature of the language with which his judgment is clothed. I am of opinion that this appeal should be dismissed, and I beg to move your Lordships accordingly.

LORD ATKIN.

My Lords, the sole question for determination in this case is legal: Do the averments made by the pursuer in her pleading, if true, disclose a cause of action? I need not restate the particular facts. The question is whether the manufacturer of an article of drink sold by him to a distributor, in circumstances which prevent the distributor or the ultimate purchaser or consumer from discovering by inspection any defect, is under any legal duty to the ultimate purchaser or consumer to take reasonable care that the article is free from defect likely to cause injury to health. I do not think a more important problem has occupied your Lordships in your judicial capacity: important both because of its bearing on public health and because of the practical test which it applies to the system under which it arises. The case has to be determined in accordance with Scots law; but it has been a matter of agreement between the experienced counsel who argued this case, and it appears to be the basis of the judgments of the learned judges of the Court of Session, that for the purposes of determining this problem the laws of Scotland and of England are the same. I speak with little authority on this point, but my own research, such as it is, satisfies me that the principles of the law of Scotland on such a question as the present are identical with those of English law; and I discuss the issue on that footing. The law of both countries appears to be that in order to support an action for damages for negligence the complainant has to show that he has been injured by the breach of a duty owed to him in the circumstances by the defendant to take reasonable care to avoid such injury. In the present case we are not concerned with the breach of the duty; if a duty exists, that would be a question of fact which is sufficiently averred and for present purposes must be assumed. We are solely concerned with the question whether, as a matter of law in the circumstances alleged, the defender owed any duty to the pursuer to take care.

先前我们的先例会确立一项明确的标准，即需要区分产品依其本身属性危险与否，或出卖人明知其产品危险与否呢？难道我们应该认为这种区分只是无意义的徒劳吗？

再看 Mullen v A.G.Barr & Co., Ltd. 案，一个几乎与本案相同的案子，只是标的物所含的瑕疵从蜗牛换成了老鼠。苏格兰民事最高法院第二分庭大法官 Anderson 在该案判决中说道："就本案以及类似的案件而言，考虑到作为标的物的商品在苏格兰境内广泛销售，如果我们认为生产商对全社会成员都负有保证产品质量的义务，那似乎就对他们太苛刻了。如果真有这种义务，那么生产商就得时刻面对各种他们根本无法预料到，也不该回应的损害赔偿请求。"

总而言之，我赞同 Anderson 大法官的判决，而且说实话我已经被判决书中他那无可辩驳的语言说服了。所以我认为本次上诉的请求应予驳回，请尊敬的大法官阁下们考虑。

Atkin 大法官：

尊敬的大法官阁下们，本案要裁决的唯一问题是法律上的问题，即：如果上诉人对事实的宣称是真实的，那么她的上诉是否具有一个有效的诉由呢？本案的具体事实我就不再赘述了。简而言之，本案的争议点就是：饮料的生产商将产品卖给了销售商，且当时的情形决定了无论是销售商、最终购买者抑或实际消费者都无法通过检验来发现饮料中的缺陷，那么该生产商对最终购买者或实际消费者是否有义务通过施加合理的注意，以保证产品不会造成人身伤害呢？我想各位在行使司法权时还没有遇到过比这个案件更重要的案件：不仅因为本案关乎大众健康，更因为本案牵涉到我们法律体系中判断一项义务是否存在的实用标准。本案之前都是根据苏格兰法裁判的，但我们经验丰富的双方律师以及苏格兰民事最高法院博学的法官同事们都认为，就本案的法律问题而言，英格兰法与苏格兰法是一样的。我不敢说我在法律适用问题上是权威，但就我个人的研究而言，我也认为原则上苏格兰法与英格兰法在本案核心问题上是相同的，所以我接下来的讨论都会建立在这样一个基础之上。两个地区的法律看来都是：原告如果想以过失侵权为诉由追究被告的侵权责任，则必须证明被告在特定的情境下对原告负有注意义务以免原告遭受人身伤害，且被告因为违反了此项注意义务导致原告遭受了人身伤害。本案的关键点不在于此项义务是否被违反，因为假如此项义务真的存在，那么根据我们对事实的审理，则可以确认被告违反了此项义务。本案的关键点

It is remarkable how difficult it is to find in the English authorities statements of general application defining the relations between parties that give rise to the duty. The Courts are concerned with the particular relations which come before them in actual litigation, and it is sufficient to say whether the duty exists in those circumstances. The result is that the Courts have been engaged upon an elaborate classification of duties as they exist in respect of property, whether real or personal, with further divisions as to ownership, occupation or control, and distinctions based on the particular relations of the one side or the other, whether manufacturer, salesman or landlord, customer, tenant, stranger, and so on. In this way it can be ascertained at any time whether the law recognizes a duty, but only where the case can be referred to some particular species which has been examined and classified. And yet the duty which is common to all the cases where liability is established must logically be based upon some element common to the cases where it is found to exist. To seek a complete logical definition of the general principle is probably to go beyond the function of the judge, for the more general the definition the more likely it is to omit essentials or to introduce non-essentials. The attempt was made by Brett M.R. in Heaven v. Pender, in a definition to which I will later refer. As framed, it was demonstrably too wide, though it appears to me, if properly limited, to be capable of affording a valuable practical guide.

At present I content myself with pointing out that in English law there must be, and is, some general conception of relations giving rise to a duty of care, of which the particular cases found in the books are but instances. The liability for negligence, whether you style it such or treat it as in other systems as a species of "culpa," is no doubt based upon a general public sentiment of moral wrongdoing for which the offender must pay. But acts or omissions which any moral code would censure cannot in a practical world be treated so as to give a right to every person injured by them to demand relief. In this way rules of law arise which limit the range of complainants and the extent of their remedy. The rule that you are to love your neighbour becomes in law, you must not injure your neighbour; and the lawyer's question, Who is my neighbour? receives a restricted reply. You must take reasonable care to avoid acts or omissions which you can reasonably foresee would be likely to injure your neighbour. Who, then, in law is my neighbour? The answer seems to be - persons who are so closely and directly affected by my act that I ought reasonably to have them in contemplation as being so affected when I am directing my mind to the acts or omissions which are called in question. This appears to me to be the doctrine of Heaven v. Pender, as laid down by Lord Esher (then Brett M.R.) when it is limited by the notion of proximity introduced by Lord Esher himself and A. L. Smith L.J. in *Le Lievre v. Gould*. Lord Esher says: "That case established that, under certain circumstances, one man may owe a duty to another, even though there is no contract between them. If one man is near to another, or is near to the property of another, a duty lies upon him not to do that which may cause a personal injury to that other, or may injure his property." So A. L. Smith L.J.: "The decision of Heaven v. Pender was founded upon the principle, that a duty

在于，在本案特定的情境下，被告是否对原告负有法律上的某项注意义务。

值得注意的是，在英国法的先例中，我们很难找到一般性的标准以判定某项义务是否存在于当事人双方。法院只关注那些已经提交到庭上的具体诉讼案件，然后判定某项义务在那种特定情境中是否存在。所以法院一直在忙于对财产领域的注意义务进行繁杂的列举，从最初的动产和不动产的区分，到后来根据所有、占有或控制对问题进一步区分，再看当事人双方是否有特定的关系，比如一方是否是生产商、销售商或是房东、消费者、承租人，抑或只是陌生人，等等。这种方法的好处是我们可以迅速判定在某类情形下法律是否承认某项义务的存在，坏处则是我们只能判定那些先前已经被确立和区分完毕的情形。但是从逻辑上说，那些先前被确立的情形总该是基于共同的标准才被确立的。我知道，寻找一般性原则的任务已经超出了法官的职责范围，毕竟这种定义越宽泛，那些关键的东西就越容易被忽略，而那些不那么关键的东西就越容易被提及。就本案的核心问题而言，掌卷法官 Brett 在 *Heaven v Pender* 案中第一次作出了尝试，这个尝试我稍后还会提到。尽管从架构上看，他给出的原则显然太宽泛，但在我看来，如果对这个原则作一些限定，它完全可以成为一个很有价值的实践指南。

现在我认为，英国法一定也的确有某种一般性的关于义务在特定关系下是否存在的认识，且目前我们在书籍中看到的那些就是，但也仅仅是其例证。过失侵权责任，无论你是这样称呼还是像其他国家那样把它归为过失（culpa）的一种，你都是基于道德情感上的一般性立场，即侵害人应当向受害人赔偿损失。但道德上会被谴责的某种作为或不作为本身不能作为受害人申请救济的权利依据。在这种情况下，法律就起到了限定适格受害人的范围以及限定他们可以获取救济的程度的作用。如果说"你应当关爱你附近的人以免使他因为你受到伤害"成为了法律规则，那么我们法律人就会问：什么是"附近的人"？这显然需要限定。你必须对你的某项作为或不作为施以合理的注意义务，并在你可预见的范围内使附近的人免受伤害。那么在法律上，到底谁才是我"附近的人"？这个问题的答案也许是：那些会被我的行为近距离以及直接影响的人，以至于我在为一定行为或不为一定行为时必须把他们考虑在内的那些人。在我看来，这就是当年掌卷法官 Brett 在 *Heaven v Pender* 案中提出的原理（也是后来被 Esher 大法官确立的原理）。不过 Esher 大法官以及 A.L. Smith 上诉法院法官在 *Le Lievre v Gould* 案中对此原理作出了限制，那就是加入了"接近"（proximity）的观念。在该案中，Esher 大法官写道："*Heaven v Pender* 案确立了这样的原则，即在特定情形下，一人可能对与其无合同关系的另一人负有义务。如果某甲离某乙很近，或离某乙的财产很近，这项义务就会落在他头上，使他不得做那些可能对某乙的人身造成伤害或财产造成

to take due care did arise when the person or property of one was in such proximity to the person or property of another that, if due care was not taken, damage might be done by the one to the other." I think that this sufficiently states the truth if proximity be not confined to mere physical proximity, but be used, as I think it was intended, to extend to such close and direct relations that the act complained of directly affects a person whom the person alleged to be bound to take care would know would be directly affected by his careless act. That this is the sense in which nearness of "proximity" was intended by Lord Esher is obvious from his own illustration in Heaven v. Pender of the application of his doctrine to the sale of goods.

> "This" (i.e., the rule he has just formulated) "includes the case of goods, etc., supplied to be used immediately by a particular person or persons, or one of a class of persons, where it would be obvious to the person supplying, if he thought, that the goods would in all probability be used at once by such persons before a reasonable opportunity for discovering any defect which might exist, and where the thing supplied would be of such a nature that a neglect of ordinary care or skill as to its condition or the manner of supplying it would probably cause danger to the person or property of the person for whose use it was supplied, and who was about to use it. It would exclude a case in which the goods are supplied under circumstances in which it would be a chance by whom they would be used or whether they would be used or not, or whether they would be used before there would probably be means of observing any defect, or where the goods would be of such a nature that a want of care or skill as to their condition or the manner of supplying them would not probably produce danger of injury to person or property."

I draw particular attention to the fact that Lord Esher emphasizes the necessity of goods having to be "used immediately" and "used at once before a reasonable opportunity of inspection." This is obviously to exclude the possibility of goods having their condition altered by lapse of time, and to call attention to the proximate relationship, which may be too remote where inspection even of the person using, certainly of an intermediate person, may reasonably be interposed. With this necessary qualification of proximate relationship as explained in *Le Lievre v. Gould*, I think the judgment of Lord Esher expresses the law of England; without the qualification, I think the majority of the Court in Heaven v. Pender were justified in thinking the principle was expressed in too general terms. There will no doubt arise cases where it will be difficult to determine whether the contemplated relationship is so close that the duty arises. But in the class of case now before the Court I cannot conceive any difficulty to arise. A manufacturer puts up an article of food in a container which he knows will be opened by the actual consumer. There can be no inspection by

损害的事情。"所以 A.L. Smith 上诉法院法官写道："*Heaven v Pender* 案的判决基于如下原则，即若一个人或他的财产与另一个人或他的财产足够接近，那么一项注意义务就会被触发，如果此义务人没有施以应有的注意，那么他就应当对该受害人承担损害赔偿责任。"我认为这番话充分阐释了如下真理，即接近不应当只限于物理上的接近，而应当适用于人与人之间那些已经足够接近和直接的关系，即这种接近已经到了义务人明确知晓如果他不履行注意义务，那么他的过失行为就足以直接影响到对方的程度。这也是 Esher 大法官在解释 *Heaven v Pender* 案并把此原理适用于货物买卖情境时加上"接近"这一限制的真意：

> 这（即他刚刚建构的规则）包括买卖货物的情形，即这些货物是提供给特定的一个人或一群人，或一个群体中的某些人，且在这种情况下如果货物的提供者明知此货物将会被消费者一次性使用，且该消费者没有合理的机会发现货物中潜在的缺陷，且此货物的属性决定了只要提供者没有就货物的品质或提供方式施以合理的注意义务和技术义务就有可能对消费者造成人身伤害或财产损害的情形。这不包括另外两种情形，即实际消费者有机会在使用前就发现货物中潜在的缺陷，或此货物的属性决定了即使提供者没有就货物的品质或提供方式施以合理的注意义务和技术义务，它也不太可能对消费者造成人身伤害或财产损害的情形。

我尤其注意到 Esher 大法官强调了货物必须是"立刻被使用"以及"在合理的发现机会到来之前就被一次性使用"。这显然就排除了那些根据货物本身的属性决定了货物的品质会因为时间的推移而改变的情形。这也提醒我们注意此标准与"接近"的关系：因为有些"接近"可能会很遥远，以至于实际使用者在检验时可能已经有别的因素介入货物了。有了"接近关系"的限制，正如 *Le Lievre v Gould* 案解释的那样，我认为 Esher 大法官正确表达了英国法在本问题上的立场。反之，如果没有这项限制，那么就如 *Heaven v Pender* 案中大多数法官反应的那样，这个原则就失之过宽了。当然，以后肯定会发生一些案件，让我们难以判断个案中当事人双方的关系是否足够"接近"从而触发这项义务，但就目前我们能看到的案件而言，我不认为这里面

any purchaser and no reasonable preliminary inspection by the consumer. Negligently, in the course of preparation, he allows the contents to be mixed with poison. It is said that the law of England and Scotland is that the poisoned consumer has no remedy against the negligent manufacturer. If this were the result of the authorities, I should consider the result a grave defect in the law, and so contrary to principle that I should hesitate long before following any decision to that effect which had not the authority of this House. I would point out that, in the assumed state of the authorities, not only would the consumer have no remedy against the manufacturer, he would have none against any one else, for in the circumstances alleged there would be no evidence of negligence against any one other than the manufacturer; and, except in the case of a consumer who was also a purchaser, no contract and no warranty of fitness, and in the case of the purchase of a specific article under its patent or trade name, which might well be the case in the purchase of some articles of food or drink, no warranty protecting even the purchaser-consumer. There are other instances than of articles of food and drink where goods are sold intended to be used immediately by the consumer, such as many forms of goods sold for cleaning purposes, where the same liability must exist. The doctrine supported by the decision below would not only deny a remedy to the consumer who was injured by consuming bottled beer or chocolates poisoned by the negligence of the manufacturer, but also to the user of what should be a harmless proprietary medicine, an ointment, a soap, a cleaning fluid or cleaning powder. I confine myself to articles of common household use, where every one, including the manufacturer, knows that the articles will be used by other persons than the actual ultimate purchaser - namely, by members of his family and his servants, and in some cases his guests. I do not think so in of our jurisprudence as to suppose that its principles are so remote from the ordinary needs of civilized society and the ordinary claims it makes upon its members as to deny a legal remedy where there is so obviously a social wrong.

It will be found, I think, on examination that there is no case in which the circumstances have been such as I have just suggested where the liability has been negatived. There are numerous cases, where the relations were much more remote, where the duty has been held not to exist. There are also dicta in such cases which go further than was necessary for the determination of the particular issues, which have caused the difficulty experienced by the Courts below. I venture to say that in the branch of the law which deals with civil wrongs, dependent in England at any rate entirely upon the application by judges of general principles also formulated by judges, it is of particular importance to guard against the danger of stating propositions of law in wider terms than is necessary, lest essential factors be omitted in the wider survey and the inherent adaptability of English law be unduly restricted. For this reason it is very necessary in considering reported cases in the law of torts that the actual decision alone should carry authority, proper weight, of course, being given to the dicta of the judges.

......

有什么难处。生产商把一份食物放入容器中，且他知道容器会被最终消费者打开，且在整个过程中销售者不可能有机会检验，最终消费者也不太可能事前检查，且在装瓶的过程中，生产商因为自己的疏忽导致毒物混入了此产品。如果英格兰和苏格兰的法律都认为在这种情况下中毒的消费者不能对疏忽的生产商追究侵权责任的话，我就必须要说，法律在这个问题上是有严重问题的，也是违背基本原则的。虽然我在上议院的职责是遵循先例，但我还是会在本问题上踌躇不定。而且我必须提醒各位，在我们现行法律的框架内，中毒的消费者不仅不能从生产商处获得任何救济，他也很可能无法从整个链条上的其他人处获得救济，至少他根本不知道链条上的任何一人存在疏忽。另外，除非该消费者同时也是买受人，否则合同中的质量瑕疵担保责任也不能触发。其实除了食品和饮料，还有其他货物以其属性是供消费者立刻使用的，比如清洁用品，那么此类侵权责任也应该存在。下面诸案支持的原理不仅没有否定那些因为饮用了有毒啤酒或食用了巧克力的消费者对有过失的生产商寻求救济的权利，而且也支持了那些因使用无害专卖药、软膏、肥皂、洗衣液、洗衣粉而受害的消费者。我此处的论述被限定在了家用产品，这意味着几乎任何人，包括生产商在内，都明知此类产品最终肯定会被某个家庭的成员、仆人或是在某些情况下被客人使用。我不认为从我国的法理能得出这样的结论，即此原则离文明社会的需求以及对社会成员的要求还很遥远，以至于即使社会上发生了明显的不法行为，我们的法律也不能赋予此项救济。

　　只要仔细考察一下我们就可以发现，关于本问题的先例，没有一个明确否认了此项侵权责任的存在。还有很多案子是因为与本问题的关系实在太远才认为此项义务不存在。在下面我们会提及的案件中，还有不少已经超越案件主争点的附带意见，给法院的审判制造了困难。在此我敢断言，在侵权法领域，我们法官看上去是在适用那些已存在的一般性原则，但别忘了这些原则也是由我们法官一手建构的。这意味着，我们需要时刻警惕，避免使用那些不必要的大概念，以免一些重要因素在笼统描述中被抛弃，甚至英国法的内在适应性也被削减。基于这个原因，我们不仅要考虑那些可作为法源的判决本身，还要适当考虑那些法官的附带意见。

I do not find it necessary to discuss at length the cases dealing with duties where the thing is dangerous, or, in the narrower category, belongs to a class of things which are dangerous in themselves. I regard the distinction as an unnatural one so far as it is used to serve as a logical differentiation by which to distinguish the existence or non-existence of a legal right. In this respect I agree with what was said by Scrutton L.J. in *Hodge & Sons v. Anglo-American Oil Co.*, a case which was ultimately decided on a question of fact.

> "Personally, I do not understand the difference between a thing dangerous in itself, as poison, and a thing not dangerous as a class, but by negligent construction dangerous as a particular thing. The latter, if anything, seems the more dangerous of the two; it is a wolf in sheep's clothing instead of an obvious wolf."

The nature of the thing may very well call for different degrees of care, and the person dealing with it may well contemplate persons as being within the sphere of his duty to take care who would not be sufficiently proximate with less dangerous goods; so that not only the degree of care but the range of persons to whom a duty is owed may be extended. But they all illustrate the general principle.

My Lords, if your Lordships accept the view that this pleading discloses a relevant cause of action you will be affirming the proposition that by Scots and English law alike a manufacturer of products, which he sells in such a form as to show that he intends them to reach the ultimate consumer in the form in which they left him with no reasonable possibility of intermediate examination, and with the knowledge that the absence of reasonable care in the preparation or putting up of the products will result in an injury to the consumer's life or property, owes a duty to the consumer to take that reasonable care.

It is a proposition which I venture to say no one in Scotland or England who was not a lawyer would for one moment doubt. It will be an advantage to make it clear that the law in this matter, as in most others, is in accordance with sound common sense. I think that this appeal should be allowed.

LORD MACMILLAN.

… In addition to George v. Skivington there is the American case of Thomas v. Winchester, which has met with considerable acceptance in this country and which is distinctly on the side of the appellant. There a chemist carelessly issued, in response to an order for extract of dandelion, a bottle containing belladonna which he labelled extract of dandelion, with the consequence that a third party who took a dose from the bottle suffered severely. The chemist was held responsible. This case is quoted by Lord Dunedin, in giving the judgment of the Privy Council in *Dominion Natural Gas Co. v. Collins & Perkins*, as an instance of liability to third parties, and I think it was a

……

我认为花费大篇幅去讨论那些涉及有危险的产品（或狭义上那些依其属性本身就属于危险物的物）的案例中的注意义务是否存在是没有必要的。这种区分如果被用以划定逻辑上某种权利是否存在的话，就是一种不自然的区分。在这点上我同意上诉法院法官 Scrutton 在 *Hodge & Sons v Anglo-American Oil Co.* 案中说的话。该案裁判最终的焦点是事实问题。他说：

> 就我个人而言，我不理解那些依其本身属性就危险的物和那些作为一类物并不危险但因为疏忽组装导致危险存在于其中的特定物之间到底有什么区别。后者，如果真有的话，其实比前者更危险。这就好比披着羊皮的狼和真狼之间的关系。

的确，物的属性决定了应施以注意的程度。处理某物的人其实大可将那些因标的物不危险而使关系似乎不那么近的人放在他的注意义务范围内加以考虑。如此，注意义务的程度上升了，注意义务施加的对象也增加了。但无论如何，这些都阐释了一般性的原则。

尊敬的大法官阁下们，如果你们接受我的观点，那么本案的上诉就构成了有效的诉因。进而可以得出这样的结论：即在苏格兰法和英格兰法以及类似的法律体系中，产品的制造商如果根据出售商品的形式表明此产品会流至最终消费者，且最终消费者没有合理的可能性中途检测出产品的缺陷，且制造商知道消费者会因为自己在准备和组装产品的过程中未尽合理的注意义务而遭受人身伤害或财产损害的话，那么制造商就对消费者负有施以此合理注意的义务。

关于这个主张，我敢断言苏格兰和英格兰的每一个非法律人在看到时都不会产生片刻的质疑。和我们作出的其他尝试一样，这里我们又一次在冒险地用一般性原则的方法来让我们的法律变得更清晰，以便使法律与合理的常识接轨。所以，我认为对此次上诉应该予以支持。

Macmillan 大法官：

……另一个可以作为 *George v Skivington* 案补充的案子是来自美国的 *Thomas v. Winchester* 案。该案在我国受到了普遍的积极评价，也和本案上诉人的主张很接近。该案中，一位化学家本来被要求制作蒲公英提取液，结

sound decision.

In the American Courts the law has advanced considerably in the development of the principle exemplified in Thomas v. Winchester. In one of the latest cases in the United States, MacPherson v. Buick Motor Co., the plaintiff, who had purchased from a retailer a motor-car manufactured by the defendant company, was injured in consequence of a defect in the construction of the car, and was held entitled to recover damages from the manufacturer. Cardozo J., the very eminent Chief Judge of the New York Court of Appeals and now an Associate Justice of the United States Supreme Court, thus stated the law:

> "There is no claim that the defendant knew of the defect and wilfully concealed it. .... The charge is one, not of fraud, but of negligence. The question to be determined is whether the defendant owed a duty of care and vigilance to anyone but the immediate purchaser. .... The principle of Thomas v. Winchester is not limited to poisons, explosives, and things of like nature, to things which in their normal operation are implements of destruction. If the nature of a thing is such that it is reasonably certain to place life and limb in peril when negligently made, it is then a thing of danger. Its nature gives warning of the consequences to be expected. If to the element of danger there is added knowledge that the thing will be used by persons other than the purchaser and used without new tests, then, irrespective of contract, the manufacturer of this thing of danger is under a duty to make it carefully. That is as far as we are required to go for the decision of this case. There must be knowledge of a danger, not merely possible, but probable. .... There must also be knowledge that in the usual course of events the danger will be shared by others than the buyer. Such knowledge may often be inferred from the nature of the transaction. .... The dealer was indeed the one person of whom it might be said with some approach to certainty that by him the car would not be used. Yet the defendant would have us say that he was the one person whom it the defendant company was under a legal duty to protect. The law does not lead us to so inconsequent a conclusion."

The prolonged discussion of English and American cases into which I have been led might well dispose your Lordships to think that I had forgotten that the present is a Scottish appeal which must be decided according to Scots law. But this discussion has been rendered inevitable by the course of the argument at your Lordships' Bar, which, as I have said, proceeded on the footing that the law applicable to the case was the same in England and Scotland. Having regard to the inconclusive state of the authorities in the Courts below and to the fact that the important question involved is now before your Lordships for the first time, I think it desirable to consider the matter

果不慎配制成了颠茄提取液，但标记上还是蒲公英的字样。这导致合同外的第三人因为服用了一定剂量的液体导致身体严重受损。该案的结果是这位化学家被判应承担侵权责任。此案在 Dunedin 大法官在枢密院司法委员会判决 *Dominion Natural Gas Co v Collins & Perkins* 一案时被引用，作为向第三人承担侵权责任的例子。我认为这是个合理的判决。

在 Thomas v. Winchester 案以后，美国法在本问题上的发展很快。在 MacPherson v. Buick Motor Co. 案中，某汽车制造商因其生产的有缺陷汽车给在场的第三方造成人身伤害而被判对其承担侵权责任。卡多佐法官，这位纽约上诉法院非常著名的首席法官，是这样表述法律的：

> 原告本来就没有指控被告知道此缺陷然后故意隐瞒此缺陷……原告的指控是基于疏忽而非欺诈。本案需要裁决的问题是：被告是否只对直接买受人负有注意义务……Thomas v. Winchester 案确立的原则不仅限于毒药，爆炸物，以及其他依其属性正常使用都具有破坏能力的物。如果某物的性质决定了只要不谨慎制造，它就会危及人的生命或四肢，那么它就是危险物。它的属性决定了我们希望能得到来自提供人的警示。如果生产商明知此物会被买受人以外的人使用，且该人不知道具体方法，那么生产商对那个实际使用人也负有说明清楚的义务。这就是我们处理本案应当遵循的规则。需要强调的是，对危险的明知必须是很可能的（probable），而非仅仅是可能的（possible）……对该物会被他人使用的明知必须限定在惯常事件范围内。对这种明知的要求也许可以从交易的性质上推测出……比如，从卖家那儿我们可以确定汽车不可能被他自己使用。但被告却非要说他（作为公司）是法律需要保护的对象。我想法律不会让我们推导出这种莫名其妙的结论。

经过上述关于英国和美国判例的大段讨论，我想你们可能会觉得我已经忘了本案是来自苏格兰的上诉案子，必须依照苏格兰法判决。但正如此次上诉双方律师共同承认的，就像我刚才说的那样，英格兰和苏格兰法律就本案的核心问题在原则上是一样的。鉴于先例没有给我们一个确定的答案，也鉴于我们是第一次一起处理此问题，我认为我们可以从

from the point of view of the principles applicable to this branch of law which are admittedly common to both English and Scottish jurisprudence.

The law takes no cognizance of carelessness in the abstract. It concerns itself with carelessness only where there is a duty to take care and where failure in that duty has caused damage. In such circumstances carelessness assumes the legal quality of negligence and entails the consequences in law of negligence. What, then, are the circumstances which give rise to this duty to take care? In the daily contacts of social and business life human beings are thrown into, or place themselves in, an infinite variety of relations with their fellows; and the law can refer only to the standards of the reasonable man in order to determine whether any particular relation gives rise to a duty to take care as between those who stand in that relation to each other. The grounds of action may be as various and manifold as human errancy; and the conception of legal responsibility may develop in adaptation to altering social conditions and standards. The criterion of judgment must adjust and adapt itself to the changing circumstances of life. The categories of negligence are never closed. The cardinal principle of liability is that the party complained of should owe to the party complaining a duty to take care, and that the party complaining should be able to prove that he has suffered damage in consequence of a breach of that duty. Where there is room for diversity of view, it is in determining what circumstances will establish such a relationship between the parties as to give rise, on the one side, to a duty to take care, and on the other side to a right to have care taken.

To descend from these generalities to the circumstances of the present case, I do not think that any reasonable man or any twelve reasonable men would hesitate to hold that, if the appellant establishes her allegations, the respondent has exhibited carelessness in the conduct of his business. For a manufacturer of aerated water to store his empty bottles in a place where snails can get access to them, and to fill his bottles without taking any adequate precautions by inspection or otherwise to ensure that they contain no deleterious foreign matter, may reasonably be characterized as carelessness without applying too exacting a standard. But, as I have pointed out, it is not enough to prove the respondent to be careless in his process of manufacture. The question is: Does he owe a duty to take care, and to whom does he owe that duty? Now I have no hesitation in affirming that a person who for gain engages in the business of manufacturing articles of food and drink intended for consumption by members of the public in the form in which he issues them is under a duty to take care in the manufacture of these articles. That duty, in my opinion, he owes to those whom he intends to consume his products. He manufactures his commodities for human consumption; he intends and contemplates that they shall be consumed. By reason of that very fact he places himself in a relationship with all the potential consumers of his commodities, and that relationship which he assumes and desires for his own ends imposes upon him a duty to take care to avoid injuring them. He owes them a duty not to convert by his own carelessness an article which he

原则的角度试着解决本案，只要这种原则被英格兰和苏格兰的法学界双双承认即可。

关于疏忽，我们的法律没有一个抽象的认识。我们只会在特定的注意义务存在且违约导致的损害已经发生的时候才会去考虑疏忽的定义。在那种情况下，疏忽是过失侵权的法律基础，也是过失侵权法律体系的一部分。那么到底在哪些情况下，这种注意义务会被触发呢？如果我们把问题投放在日常的社会或商业生活中，或者把它投放在随机的社会成员间的关系中，法律只能使用一般理性人的标准去判定，某情境是否会在当事人双方间触发这种注意义务。那么此问题的诉讼基础就会像人犯的错误一样多种多样。法律责任的概念也就会随之改变，以适应新的社会条件和新的行为规范。司法裁判的标准也必须随着社会环境的变迁而适当调整，以适应社会需要。过失侵权的分类永远不是有限的。关于此种责任，最核心的原则就是被告对原告负有一项注意义务，原告必须证明被告违约，且原告的损失与被告的违约有因果关系。我们有空间容纳多样性，但这空间指的也只是那些帮助我们判别注意义务是否存在的情形。

把上面这些普适性的话落实到本案，我不认为任何人或任何12个人会质疑这样的观点，即如果上诉人证明了事实上的真实性，被上诉人就确实在他的生产过程中存在疏忽。作为一家汽水生产商，他把自己的瓶子存放在了蜗牛可以爬进去的地方，而且在封装时也没有注意查看瓶子来保证没有异物混入产品，那么我们可以很合理地认为它已经构成了疏忽。但是，正如我之前说的那样，证明被上诉人在生产过程中的疏忽还是不够的。现在的问题是：他是否负有注意义务，以及他对谁负有注意义务？现在我可以确定，一个以盈利为目的的生产商，如果他的经营方法是向公众提供消费的货物，那么该生产商就在生产环节负有注意义务。至于这个注意义务的对象，包括所有他能想象到的消费者。他如果卖的是人类可饮用的产品，那么他就能想象得到，所有人类都有可能喝到他的产品。基于这种原因，他将自己和所有潜在消费者绑定了关系，这种关系足以触发一种注意义务，要求他防止消费者的健康由于他的产品受损。他有义务防止他的产品转化为对人体有害的物质。有时候我们可以说，如果一个理性的人能够预见这

issues to them as wholesome and innocent into an article which is dangerous to life and health. It is sometimes said that liability can only arise where a reasonable man would have foreseen and could have avoided the consequences of his act or omission. In the present case the respondent, when he manufactured his ginger-beer, had directly in contemplation that it would be consumed by members of the public. Can it be said that he could not be expected as a reasonable man to foresee that if he conducted his process of manufacture carelessly he might injure those whom he expected and desired to consume his ginger-beer? The possibility of injury so arising seems to me in no sense so remote as to excuse him from foreseeing it. Suppose that a baker, through carelessness, allows a large quantity of arsenic to be mixed with a batch of his bread, with the result that those who subsequently eat it are poisoned, could he be heard to say that he owed no duty to the consumers of his bread to take care that it was free from poison, and that, as he did not know that any poison had got into it, his only liability was for breach of warranty under his contract of sale to those who actually bought the poisoned bread from him? Observe that I have said "through carelessness," and thus excluded the case of a pure accident such as may happen where every care is taken. I cannot believe, and I do not believe, that neither in the law of England nor in the law of Scotland is there redress for such a case. The state of facts I have figured might well give rise to a criminal charge, and the civil consequence of such carelessness can scarcely be less wide than its criminal consequences. Yet the principle of the decision appealed from is that the manufacturer of food products intended by him for human consumption does not owe to the consumers whom he has in view any duty of care, not even the duty to take care that he does not poison them.

11. Caparo Industries plc v Dickman [1990] 2 AC 605

House of Lords, United Kingdom

BINGHAM LJ (judgment at the Court of Appeal, [1989] QB 653, 677–80)

"It is not easy, or perhaps possible, to find a single proposition encapsulating a comprehensive rule to determine when persons are brought into a relationship which creates a duty of care upon those who make statements towards those who may act upon them and when persons are not brought into such a relationship."

Thus the Lord Ordinary, Lord Stewart, in *Twomax Ltd. v. Dickson, McFarlane & Robinson, 1983 S.L.T 98*, 103. Others have spoken to similar effect. In Hedley Byrne & Co. Ltd. v. Heller & Partners Ltd. [1964] A.C. 465 Lord Hodson said, at p. 514: "I do not think it is possible to catalogue the special features which must be found to exist before the duty of care will arise in a given case," and Lord Devlin said, at pp. 529-530:

种情况，此种情况就本该被避免，那么如果生产商没有避免，他就应负法律责任。本案中，被上诉人在生产姜汁啤酒的时候，明确知道这些啤酒会被公众饮用。他是不是一个理性的人，他是不是本该预见这种情况呢？答案显然是肯定的。另外，上诉人健康受损的情况告诉我，从因果关系上看，此损害与被上诉人的疏忽关系很近，这也就说明了被上诉人不能推脱这种预见义务。假设有一家面包店，因为疏忽让一定量的砷混入了一批面包，并导致部分消费者中毒，那么我们可以认为这家面包店对消费者不负防止面包有毒的注意义务吗？另外，我们可以因为面包店事实上不知道砷的混入，他的合同瑕疵担保责任就可以免除了吗？注意我刚才使用了"疏忽"二字，这意味着我排除了纯意外事件的情形。我不敢相信，也不会相信英格兰和苏格兰的法律对此案的被害人没有提供任何救济。要知道，一般都是民法的责任比刑法的责任宽，何以在此案中，面包店店主虽应承担刑事责任，却不需要承担民事责任了呢？但我们的先例确立的原则偏偏就是，生产供大众食用的食物的生产者不对消费者负有任何注意义务，甚至不负防止消费者被毒害的注意义务。

11. Caparo Industries plc v Dickman [1990] 2 AC 605

联合王国上议院

上诉法院法官 Bingham［上诉法院判决，（1989）*QB 653, 677-80*］：

要找到这样的一个单一的规则即使不是不可能的，也是极其困难的。这个规则要用来判断何时某人会被带入一段关系中，这段关系会给制作财务报表的人施加一个对使用这些报表之人的注意义务。

Ordinary 大法官和 Stewart 大法官，在 *Twomax Ltd. v Dickson, McFarlane & Robinson*, 1983 S.L.T 98, 103 一案中也持有这样的观点。其他人也说过类似的话。在 *Hedley Byrne & Co. Ltd. v. Heller & Partners Ltd.* [1964] A.C. 465 一案中，Hodson 大法官（在第 514 页）写道："我认为我们不可能列举出所有的判断注意义务的条件。注意义务的条件只能在每个具体的案子中来判定。"

"I do not think it possible to formulate with exactitude all the conditions under which the law will in a specific case imply a voluntary undertaking any more than it is possible to formulate those in which the law will imply a contract."

In *Mutual Life and Citizens' Assurance Co. Ltd. v. Evatt [1971] A.C. 793* Lord Reid and Lord Morris of Borth-y-Gest said, at p. 810: "In our judgment it is not possible to lay down hard-and-fast rules as to when a duty of care arises in this or in any other class of case where negligence is alleged." In *Rowling v. Takaro Properties Ltd. [1988] A.C. 473*, 501, Lord Keith of Kinkel emphasised the need for careful analysis case by case:

"It is at this stage that it is necessary, before concluding that a duty of care should be imposed, to consider all the relevant circumstances. One of the considerations underlying certain recent decisions of the House of Lords*(Governors of the Peabody Donation Fund v. Sir Lindsay Parkinson & Co. Ltd. [1985] A.C. 210*) and of the Privy Council (*Yuen Kun Yeu v. Attorney-General of Hong Kong [1988] A.C. 175*) is the fear that a too literal application of the well-known observation of Lord Wilberforce in *Anns v. Merton London Borough Council* [1978] A.C. 728 , 751-752, may be productive of a failure to have regard to, and to analyse and weigh, all the relevant considerations in considering whether it is appropriate that a duty of care should be imposed. Their Lordships consider that question to be of an intensely pragmatic character, well suited for gradual development but requiring most careful analysis. It is one upon which all common law jurisdictions can learn much from each other; because, apart from exceptional cases, no sensible distinction can be drawn in this respect between the various countries and the social conditions existing in them. It is incumbent upon the courts in different jurisdictions to be sensitive to each other's reactions; but what they are all searching for in others, and each of them striving to achieve, is a careful analysis and weighing of the relevant competing considerations."

The many decided cases on this subject, if providing no simple ready-made solution to the question whether or not a duty of care exists, do indicate the requirements to be satisfied before a duty is found.

The first is foreseeability. It is not, and could not be, in issue between these parties that reasonable foreseeability of harm is a necessary ingredient of a relationship in which a duty of care will arise: *Yuen Kun Yeu v. Attorney-General of Hong Kong [1988] A.C. 175*, 192A. It is also common ground that reasonable foreseeability, although a necessary, is not a sufficient condition of the existence of a duty. This, as Lord Keith of Kinkel observed in *Hill v. Chief Constable of West*

而 Devlin 大法官则写道（在第 529—530 页）：

> 我认为我们不可能找到这样的一种条件，这种条件能够确定地判断在任何一个特殊案件中，某个人是否自愿地承担了注意义务；正如我认为我们不可能找到那种能够一般化地判断一个默示合同是否存在的条件一样。

在 *Mutual Life and Citizens' Assurance Co. Ltd. v Evatt* [1971] A.C. 793 一案中，Reid 大法官和 Morris 大法官说道（在第 810 页）："在我们看来，我们是不可能找到那种严格的规则来判断'过失之诉'所必须的注意义务是否存在的，无论是对本案还是对任何类型的其他案件。"在 *Rowling v Takaro Properties Ltd.* [1988] A.C. 473, 501 一案中，Keith 大法官强调了个案审查是否存在注意义务的必要性：

> 在此阶段，在确定应该施加注意义务之前，有必要考虑所有相关情况。上议院 [*Governors of the Peabody Donation Fund v Sir Lindsay Parkinson & Co. Ltd.*（1985）A.C. 210] 和枢密院 [*Yuen Kun Yeu v Attorney-General of Hong Kong*（1988）A.C. 175] 在最近判决的一系列案件中表达出了一点担心：他们担心太过于字面意义地适用在 *Anns v. Merton London Borough Council* [1978] A.C. 728, 751-752 一案中 Wilberforce 大法官所发表的著名的意见，这将会使得法官在判断是否应该存在注意义务时，不能考虑、分析和权衡所有的相关因素。大法官们认为这是一个非常实务性的问题，解决这个问题的方法在未来当然可能有所发展，但是必须经过严密的分析才行。对于这个问题，所有普通法法域都可以互相学习；因为除了特殊情况外，在这方面，各国的社会条件不具有明显的区别。不同法域的法院对其他法域的法院在这个问题上的反应应该敏感，但是他们在别的法院的判决中所寻求的以及他们各自所想努力实现的，都是如何仔细地分析并权衡相关的互相冲突的各种因素。

上述就这个问题作出的各个判决，虽说并不能直接提供一个现成的判断注意义务是否存在的标准，但是却可以给我们一些提示。

注意义务存在的第一个要件是可预见性。只有损害是足够可预见时，才能使得双方处在一个能产生注意义务的关系中，这点不会也不应该成为当时双方的争议焦点。[参见 *Yuen Kun Yeu v Attorney-General of Hong Kong*（1988）A.C. 175, 192A] 同样没有争议的是损害的可预见性，仅仅是注意义务的必要

Yorkshire [1989] A.C. 53, 60B, has been said almost too frequently to require repetition.

The second requirement is more elusive. It is usually described as proximity, which means not simple physical proximity but extends to

"such close and direct relations that the act complained of directly affects a person whom the person alleged to be bound to take care would know would be directly affected by his careless act:" *Donoghue v. Stevenson [1932] A.C. 562,* 581, *per* Lord Atkin.

Sometimes the alternative expression "neighbourhood" is used, as by Lord Reid in the Hedley Byrne case [1964] A.C. 465 , 483 and Lord Wilberforce in Anns v. Merton London Borough Council [1978] A.C. 728 , 751H, with more conscious reference to Lord Atkin's speech in the earlier case. Sometimes, as in the Hedley Byrne case, attention is concentrated on the existence of a special relationship. Sometimes it is regarded as significant that the parties' relationship is "equivalent to contract" (see the Hedley Byrne case, at p. 529, *per* Lord Devlin), or falls "only just short of a direct contractual relationship" *(Junior Books Ltd. v. Veitchi Co. Ltd. [1983] 1 A.C. 520 ,* 533B, *per* Lord Fraser of Tullybelton), or is "as close as it could be short of actual privity of contract:" see p. 546C, *per* Lord Roskill. In some cases, and increasingly, reference is made to the voluntary assumption of responsibility: *Muirhead v. Industrial Tank Specialities Ltd. [1986] Q.B. 507,* 528A, *per* Robert Goff L.J.; *Yuen Kun Yeu v. Attorney-General of Hong Kong [1988] A.C. 175 ,* 192F, 196G; *Simaan General Contracting v. Pilkington Glass Ltd. (No. 2) [1988] Q.B. 758 ,* 781F, 784G;*Greater Nottingham Co-operative Society Ltd. v. Cementation Piling and Foundations Ltd. [1989] Q.B. 71 ,* 99, 106, 108. Both the analogy with contract and the assumption of responsibility have been relied upon as a test of proximity in foreign courts as well as our own: see, for example, Glanzer v. Shepard (1922) 135 N.E. 275 , 276; Ultramares Corporation v. Touche (1931) 174 N.E. 441 , 446; State Street Trust Co. v. Ernst (1938) 15 N.E. 2d 416, 418; *Scott Croup Ltd. v. McFarlane [1978] 1 N.Z.L.R. 553,* 567. It may very well be that in tortious claims based on negligent misstatement these notions are particularly apposite. The content of the requirement of proximity, whatever language is used, is not, I think, capable of precise definition. The approach will vary according to the particular facts of the case, as is reflected in the varied language used. But the focus of the inquiry is on the closeness and directness of the relationship between the parties. In determining this, foreseeability must, I think, play an important part: the more obvious it is that A's act or omission will cause harm to B, the less likely a court will be to hold that the relationship of A and B is insufficiently proximate to give rise to a duty of care.

The third requirement to be met before a duty of care will be held to be owed by A to B is that the court should find it just and reasonable to impose such a duty: *Governors of the Peabody*

条件，而不是充分条件。这点，正如 Keith 大法官在 Hill v Chief Constable of West Yorkshire [1989] A.C. 53, 60B 一案中所强调的那样，已经被大家无数次提及，就不用我们赘述了。

注意义务存在的第二个要件是一个不那么好把握的概念。通常我们称它为"紧密性"。这里的紧密性不仅仅指的是物理上的紧密性，也包括

"那些紧密且直接的关系：在这种关系中，行为人的行为直接地影响了受害人（受害人一般主张行为人对他有注意义务），且行为人应当知道他那粗心的行为是会直接影响到受害人的。"［Donoghue v Stevenson（1932）A.C. 562, 581 Atkin 大法官意见。］

这里所说的"紧密性"，有人把它称作"邻近性"：就像 Reid 大法官在 Hedley Byrne 一案中［（1964）A.C. 465, 483］所做的那样。Wilberforce 大法官在 Anns v. Merton London Borough Council [1978] A.C. 728, 751H 一案中也用到了"邻近性"这个词，并且他还特意提到了 Atkin 大法官在之前我们提到的那个案子中的话。所谓的"邻近性"，有时关注的是加害人和受害人之间是否存在某种特殊的关系，就像 Hedley Byrne 一案中那样。这种"邻近性"，关注的重点时而是双方之间存在一种"等同于合同"的关系（参见 Hedley Byrne 一案，第529页，Devlin 大法官的意见），时而是指一种"仅次于直接合同关系的紧密关系"［Junior Books Ltd. v Veitchi Co. Ltd.（1983）1 A.C. 520, 533B, Fraser 大法官的意见］，时而是一种"除了没有合同的相对性外非常接近"的关系（参见同案第546C 页，Roskill 大法官的意见）。有时候，这个"邻近性"关注的是加害人是否自愿地承担了某种责任［参见 Muirhead v Industrial Tank Specialities Ltd.（1986）Q.B. 507, 528A, per Robert Goff L.J.；Yuen Kun Yeu v Attorney-General of Hong Kong（1988）A.C. 175, 192F, 196G; Simaan General Contracting v Pilkington Glass Ltd.（No. 2）（1988）Q.B. 758, 781F, 784G; Greater Nottingham Co-operative Society Ltd. v Cementation Piling and Foundations Ltd.（1989）Q.B. 71, 99, 106, 108］。看是否存在类似合同的关系，或者看加害人有没有自愿承担某种责任，这两种对紧密性的判断标准，我们都可以在外国法庭和我国法庭的判决中找到。［参见 Glanzer v Shepard（1922）135 N.E. 275, 276; Ultramares Corporation v. Touche（1931）174 N.E. 441, 446; State Street Trust Co. v Ernst（1938）15 N.E. 2d 416, 418; Scott Croup Ltd. v McFarlane（1978）1 N.Z.L.R. 553, 567.］在涉及过时陈述的诉讼中，这些判断标准可能尤为合适。然而，"紧密性"这一要件的内容归根结底是无法用任何语词来定义清楚的。根据不同的案件事实，我们需要有不同的描述"紧密性"的方法，就如同前文列举的这些案件中所作的不同的描述。然而，我们需要关注的核心是不变的：即双方当事人之间是否存在密切而直接的关系。要

Donation Fund v. Sir Lindsay Parkinson & Co. Ltd. [1985] A.C. 210 , 241, per Lord Keith of Kinkel. This requirement, I think, covers very much the same ground as Lord Wilberforce's second stage test in Anns v. Merton London Borough Council [1978] A.C. 728 , 752A, and what in cases such as *Spartan Steel & Alloys Ltd. v. Martin & Co. (Contractors) Ltd. [1973] Q.B. 27* and *McLoughlin v. O'Brian [1983] 1 A.C. 410* was called policy. It was considerations of this kind which Lord Fraser of Tullybelton had in mind when he said that "some limit or control mechanism has to be imposed upon the liability of a wrongdoer towards those who have suffered economic damage in consequence of his negligence:" *Candlewood Navigation Corporation Ltd. v. Mitsui O.S.K. Lines Ltd. [1986] A.C. 1*, 25A. The requirement cannot, perhaps, be better put than it was by Weintraub C.J. in Goldberg v. Housing Authority of the City of Newark (1962) 186 A. 2d 291 , 293:

> "Whether a *duty* exists is ultimately a question of fairness. The inquiry involves a weighing of the relationship of the parties, the nature of the risk, and the public interest in the proposed solution."

If the imposition of a duty on a defendant would be for any reason oppressive, or would expose him, in Cardozo C.J.'s famous phrase in Ultramares Corporation v. Touche, 174 N.E. 441, 444, "to a liability in an indeterminate amount for an indeterminate time to an indeterminate class," that will weigh heavily, probably conclusively, against the imposition of a duty (if it has not already shown a fatal lack of proximity). On the other hand, a duty will be the more readily found if the defendant is voluntarily exercising a professional skill for reward, if the victim of his carelessness has (in the absence of a duty) no means of redress, if the duty contended for, as in *McLoughlin v. O'Brian [1983] 1 A.C. 410*, arises naturally from a duty which already exists or if the imposition of a duty is thought to promote some socially desirable objective.

...

LORD BRIDGE (judgment at the House of Lords, [1990] 2 AC 605, 616–18)

In determining the existence and scope of the duty of care which one person may owe to another in the infinitely varied circumstances of human relationships there has for long been a tension between two different approaches. Traditionally the law finds the existence of the duty in different specific situations each exhibiting its own particular characteristics. In this way the law has identified a wide variety of duty situations, all falling within the ambit of the tort of negligence, but sufficiently distinct to require separate definition of the essential ingredients by which the existence of the duty is to be recognised. Commenting upon the outcome of this traditional approach, Lord Atkin, in his seminal speech in *Donoghue v. Stevenson [1932] A.C. 562*, 579-580, observed:

判断这一点，我认为"可预见性"这一要件，又起了关键作用：A 的作为或者不作为会导致 B 的损害这一事实越明显，法院越不可能认为 A 和 B 之间的关系过于疏远因此不足以支持认定 A 存在对 B 的注意义务。

注意义务存在的第三个要件是法院认为对加害人施加这样的义务是合理的：*Governors of the Peabody Donation Fund v Sir Lindsay Parkinson & Co. Ltd.* [1985] A.C. 210，241，Keith 大法官意见。在我看来，这个条件和 Wilberforce 大法官在 *Anns v. Merton London Borough Council* [1978] A.C. 728，752A 一案中提出的"第二阶段的考量"，和 *Spartan Steel & Alloys Ltd. v. Martin & Co.（Contractors）Ltd.* [1973] Q.B. 27 和 *McLoughlin v. O'Brian* [1983] 1 A.C. 410 等判例中条的"政策"，涉及的是同样的东西。Fraser 大法官曾说，"因为过失而致人遭受经济损失的人，应承担责任。但是这种责任应该受到某种限制或者控制"。[参见 *Candlewood Navigation Corporation Ltd. v. Mitsui O.S.K. Lines Ltd.*（1986）A.C. 1, 25A] 他也是出于同样的考量。对这个要件最好的总结，也许要属 Weintraub 首席法官，他在 *Goldberg v. Housing Authority of the City of Newark*（1962）186 A. 2d 291，293 一案中说：

> 某个义务是否存在，归根结底是一个公平的问题。要回答这个问题，我们需要衡量的因素有：双方当事人的关系，涉及的风险的性质，以及可能的解决方案对公共利益的影响。

如果对某人施加某个义务是显然不公的，或者如著名的卡多佐首席法官在 *Ultramares Corporation v Touche,* 174 N.E. 441, 444 一案中说的那样，施加该义务是会使他面临一种"无限数额、无限时间、无限类型"的责任，那么很可能，甚至说一定，我们不会给他施加这个义务（就算没有证据证明此人和受害人之间缺乏紧密的关系）。相反，我们很可能向一个人施加某种义务，如果他是自愿地、有偿地发挥他的职业技能，如果受害人在他不存在义务的情况下就没有救济途径，如果我们讨论的要不要施加的这个义务是由另一个已经存在的义务自然而然地产生的 [如 *McLoughlin v O'Brian*（1983）1 A.C. 410 一案中的那样]，如果我们认为施加这种义务能实现某种欲达的社会目标。

……

Bridge 大法官 [上议院判决，（1990）2 AC 605, 616-18]

在无穷无尽的不同类型的人类关系中，要判断一个人是否对另一个人负有注意义务以及在多大程度上负担注意义务，通常要遵循两种方法。传统上，法律是将各种要负担这种义务的情形分类，并且具体规定每种类型的特征。这样，在法律上我们就可以得到许多不同情形，这些情形下法官都会认定行为人应该承担注意义务且都属于过失之诉的范围，然而这些情形彼此不同，以至于在每种情形下，要认定存在注意义务的构成要件也是不同的。对于这种传统的方法会造成的后果，Atkin 大法官在 *Donoghue v Stevenson* [1932] A.C.

'The result is that the courts have been engaged upon an elaborate classification of duties as they exist in respect of property, whether real or personal, with further divisions as to ownership, occupation or control, and distinctions based on the particular relations of the one side or the other, whether manufacturer, salesman or landlord, customer, tenant, stranger, and so on. In this way it can be ascertained at any time whether the law recognises a duty, but only where the case can be referred to some particular species which has been examined and classified. and yet the duty which is common to all the cases where liability is established must logically be based upon some element common to the cases where it is found to exist.'

It is this last sentence which signifies the introduction of the more modern approach of seeking a single general principle which may be applied in all circumstances to determine the existence of a duty of care. Yet Lord Atkin himself sounds the appropriate note of caution by adding, at p. 580:

'To seek a complete logical definition of the general principle is probably to go beyond the function of the judge, for the more general the definition the more likely it is to omit essentials or to introduce non-essentials.'

Lord Reid gave a large impetus to the modern approach in *Dorset Yacht Co. Ltd. v. Home Office [1970] A.C. 1004*, 1026-1027, where he said:

'In later years there has been a steady trend towards regarding the law of negligence as depending on principle so that, when a new point emerges, one should ask not whether it is covered by authority but whether recognised principles apply to it. *Donoghue v. Stevenson* [1932] A.C. 562 may be regarded as a milestone, and the well known passage in Lord Atkin's speech should I think be regarded as a statement of principle. It is not to be treated as if it were a statutory definition. It will require qualification in new circumstances. But I think that the time has come when we can and should say that it ought to apply unless there is some justification or valid explanation for its exclusion.'

The most comprehensive attempt to articulate a single general principle is reached in the well known passage from the speech of Lord Wilberforce in Anns v. Merton London Borough Council [1978] A.C. 728 , 751-752:

562, 579-580 一案的判决中，发表了他那影响巨大的观点：

> 这种方法的后果是法院需要对各种条件下的注意义务进行精细地分类。或按照财产的性质分类——是动产还是不动产，接着进一步划分是所有、占据还是控制关系；或按照双方当事人的关系来分类，进一步划分是制造者、销售者、土地所有者、顾客、承租人还是陌生人等。这么做的话，对任何一个特定情况，我们好像在任何时候都能判断法律是否承认这时的注意义务，然而能够判断的前提是这种情况符合我们预先分类并检验过的一种类型。然而，对于所有应该确认注意义务的情形下所共有的注意义务，在逻辑上必定基于一些共同的应该确认注意义务的要素。

上面这段话的最后一句话向我们介绍了另一种更现代的方法：这种方法旨在寻找一种能够适用于所有情况下的一般原则，以判断是否存在注意义务。然而，对这种方法 Atkin 大法官自己提出了他的一点担忧（参见第 580 页）：

> 要找到一种完备而富有逻辑的一般原则，也许超出了法官所承担的角色，因为这个原则越是一般化，那么就越可能漏掉某些必要的要件或者增添某些不必要的要件。

Reid 大法官则大大推动了这种现代方法。在 *Dorset Yacht Co. Ltd. v Home Office* [1970] A.C. 1004, 1026-1027 一案的判决中，他说：

> 近几年发展出来一种把过失之诉视为建立于一般原则上的稳定趋势。因此，当发生了新的争议问题时，我们不仅要去看这个问题已有的判例是否对它有处理的方法，同时也要看公认的原则是否能对其适用。*Donoghue v Stevenson* [1932] A.C. 562 一案就是这种趋势的一个里程碑，Atkin's 那段著名的话则是对这个判断过失之诉的一般原则的陈述。然而，这段话不应该被理解成一种成文法般的定义。在遇到新问题时，我们是一定需要具体分析的。然而我认为，现在这个时代我们已经可以，并且应该认同这用一般原则来判断是否存在注意义务的做法应该在一般意义上适用，除非有具体的排除适用的理由或者解释。

Wilberforce 大法官在 *Anns v. Merton London Borough Council* [1978] A.C. 728, 751-752 一案判决中发表的著名观点，可以说是对这种用一个单一的统一的原

'Through the trilogy of cases in this House - *Donoghue v. Stevenson [1932] A.C. 562, Hedley Byrne & Co. Ltd. v. Heller & Partners Ltd. [1964] A.C. 465*, and *Dorset Yacht Co. Ltd. v. Home Office [1970] A.C. 1004*, the position has now been reached that in order to establish that a duty of care arises in a particular situation, it is not necessary to bring the facts of that situation within those of previous situations in which a duty of care has been held to exist. Rather the question has to be approached in two stages. First one has to ask whether, as between the alleged wrongdoer and the person who has suffered damage there is a sufficient relationship of proximity or neighbourhood such that, in the reasonable contemiplation of the former, carelessness on his part may be likely to cause damage to the latter - in which case a prima facie duty of care arises. Secondly, if the first question is answered affirmatively, it is necessary to consider whether there are any considerations which ought to negative, or to reduce or limit the scope of the duty or the class of person to whom it is owed or the damages to which a breach of it may give rise: see *Dorset Yacht case* [1970] A.C. 1004 per Lord Reid at p. 1027.'

But since the Anns case a series of decisions of the Privy Council and of your Lordships' House, notably in judgments and speeches delivered by Lord Keith of Kinkel, have emphasised the inability of any single general principle to provide a practical test which can be applied to every situation to determine whether a duty of care is owed and, if so, what is its scope: see *Governors of Peabody Donation Fund v. Sir Lindsay Parkinson & Co. Ltd.* [1985] A.C. 210, 239f-241c;*Yuen Kun Yeu v. Attorney-General of Hong Kong* [1988] A.C. 175, 190e-194f; *Rowling v. Takaro Properties Ltd.* [1988] A.C. 473, 501d-g; *Hill v. Chief Constable of West Yorkshire* [1989] A.C. 53, 60b-d. What emerges is that, in addition to the foreseeability of damage, necessary ingredients in any situation giving rise to a duty of care are that there should exist between the party owing the duty and the party to whom it is owed a relationship characterised by the law as one of 'proximity' or 'neighbourhood' and that the situation should be one in which the court considers it fair, just and reasonable that the law should impose a duty of a given scope upon the one party for the benefit of the other. But it is implicit in the passages referred to that the concepts of proximity and fairness embodied in these additional ingredients are not susceptible of any such precise definition as would be necessary to give them utility as practical tests, but amount in effect to little more than convenient labels to attach to the features of different specific situations which, on a detailed examination of all the circumstances, the law recognises pragmatically as giving rise to a duty of care of a given scope. Whilst recognising, of course, the importance of the underlying general principles common to the whole field of negligence, I think the law has now moved in the direction of attaching greater significance to the more traditional categorisation of distinct and recognisable

则来判断是否存在注意义务的做法，最完整的尝试：

> 本院（上议院）通过三个判例［*Donoghue v Stevenson*（1932）A C 562, *Hedley Byrne & Co. Ltd. v Heller & Partners Ltd.*（1964）A.C. 465, 和 *Dorset Yacht Co. Ltd. v Home Office*（1970）A.C. 1004］总结出了以下观点：要证明在某个特定情况下某人要承担注意义务，我们并不需要去找到一个已经被认定了的承担注意义务的情况，然后再证明我们要证明的情况和这个已经被认定了的情况是一样的。相反，我们需要运用两个步骤来解决这个问题。首先，我们需要讨论的是在所谓的加害人和受害人之间，是否存在一个足够紧密或者邻近的关系，足以使得前者能够合理地意识到，他的不小心足以使得后者遭受损失。如果在这个阶段我们的答案是肯定的，那么我们可以初步判定加害者应该承担对受害者的注意义务。其次，在第一个阶段的答案是肯定的情况下，我们需要考虑是否存在能够否定这个义务，或者限制这个义务的范围、权利人或者赔偿金的情节［参见 *Dorset Yacht Co Ltd v Home Office*（1970）A C 1004, Reid 大法官的意见，第 1027 页］。

然而，自从 Anns 案一来，一系列枢密院和上议院的判决——尤其是 Keith 大法官所作出的那些——都强调一点，即用单一的、一般化的原则来判断某个情况下是否存在注意义务，以及在存在的情况下这种注意义务的范围，是不可行的。［参见 *Governors of Peabody Donation Fund v Sir Lindsay Parkinson & Co. Ltd.*（1985）A.C. 210, 239f-241c; *Yuen Kun Yeu v Attorney-General of Hong Kong*（1988）A C 175 190e-194f; *Rowling v Takaro Properties Ltd.*（1988）A.C. 473, 501d-g; *Hill v Chief Constable of West Yorkshire*（1989）A.C. 53, 60b-d］在这些判决中我们可以看到，在一般的情况下，要判定存在注意义务，其构成要件除了加害人对其行为所造成的损害要有可预见性，还需要在注意义务的义务人和权利人之间存在法律所认为"紧密"或者"邻近"的关系，以及法院认为该注意义务的存在及其范围是公平且合理的。然而，这些判决的文字其实暗示了一点：即紧密性或者公正性这样的作为注意义务构成要件的概念，其实并不能精确定义，因此并不能被用作判断注意义务的标准。这些概念最多可以被看作对每个具体的法律所实用主义地确认了的存在注意义务及其范围的情形所做的正当化论证。我当然认同过失之诉背

situations as guides to the existence, the scope and the limits of the varied duties of care which the law imposes. We must now, I think, recognise the wisdom of the words of Brennan J. in the High Court of Australia in *Sutherland Shire Council v. Heyman* (1985) 60 A.L.R. 1, 43-44, where he said:

> 'It is preferable, in my view, that the law should develop novel categories of negligence incrementally and by analogy with established categories, rather than by a massive extension of a prima facie duty of care restrained only by indefinable 'considerations which ought to negative, or to reduce or limit the scope of the duty or the class of person to whom it is owed."

Section 2. Breach of Duty: Standard of Care

12. Washington v. Louisiana Power and Light Co., 555 So. 2d 1350 (La. 1990)

Supreme Court of Louisiana, United States

Dennis, Justice.

We granted certiorari in this power line accident case to review the Court of Appeal's judgment setting aside a jury award to the adult children of a man who was electrocuted when he accidentally allowed a citizens band radio antenna to come into contact with an uninsulated 8,000 volt electrical wire that spanned the backyard of his residence. We affirm. The jury verdict for the plaintiffs was manifestly erroneous....

After a trial on the merits, a jury found LP & L at fault in the accident and awarded plaintiffs $500,000 for pain and suffering and the loss of life of the decedent and $75,000 for each plaintiff's loss of love, affection, and support. LP & L appealed suspensively. The Court of Appeal, noting that the decedent had five years earlier received an electrical shock when he touched the antenna to the same line, and had since that time been extremely careful to never move the antenna alone or toward the line until the day of the fatal accident, reversed, concluding that LP & L did not breach any duty owed to the decedent....

When the evidence is clear, as in the present case, that the power company either knew or should have known of the possibility of an accident that materialized in the decedent's electrocution, the remaining negligence issue is whether the possibility of such injury or loss constituted an unreasonable risk of harm. Such a case invites "a sharp focus upon the essential balancing process that lies at the heart of negligence." Malone, Work of Appellate Courts, 29 La. L. Rev. 212, 212 (1969). In this regard, we recently held that the power company's duty to provide

后的一般原则对其是极其重要的,然而实在法现在更倾向于更传统的类型化方法,即把各个互相区别又能被识别的情形列举出来,以判断每个情形下是否存在注意义务,及其范围和例外。我认为我们有必要重温澳大利亚高等法院的 Brennan 法官在 *Sutherland Shire Council v Heyman*(1985)60 A.L.R. 1, 43-44 一案中说的话:

> 我认为,与其去创造一个范围极大的一般性的注意义务(对这个注意义务,只存在泛泛的一些"否定条件或者限制范围、义务人的条件"),不如一点点地、通过类比已有类型的方法去创造新的过失类型。

第二节 义务的违反:注意的标准

12. Washington v. Louisiana Power and Light Co., 555 So. 2d 1350 (La. 1990)

美国路易斯安那州最高法院

Dennis 法官主笔。

我们签发调卷令(certiorari)对这一电线事故案件进行重审。本案中,上诉法院撤销了陪审团对一位男士的几名成年子女的赔偿裁断,该男子由于意外地使其民用波段天线同越过自家后院的一条高达 8 000 伏特的无绝缘的电线相接触而触电身亡。我们确定,陪审团对原告作出的裁断显然是错误的……

经过对本案的审理,陪审团认为路易斯安那电力和照明公司对事故的发生有过错,判决被告因痛苦和受难以及死者生命的丧失赔偿所有原告共计 50 万美元,每位原告还各自因失去所爱、慈爱和抚养而获得 7.5 万美元的赔偿。路易斯安那电力和照明公司提起终止判决执行的上诉。上诉法院认为,死者 5 年前就因为天线和高压线相接触而遭受过电击,自此以后应当极端谨慎,不要单独移动天线或者向高压线方向移动天线。上诉法院推翻了原审判决,认为路易斯安那电力和照明公司没有违背任何对死者负有的义务……

本案的证据十分清晰,电力公司已经或者应当知道该实际导致受害人触电身亡事故的可能性,存疑的过失问题在于这种伤害或损失的可能性能否构成不合理的损害风险。本案引发对"处于过失核心地位的基本衡量过程的强烈关注"。[Malone 的《上诉法院的工作》, Work of Appellate Courts, 29 La. L.

against resulting injuries, as in similar situations, is a function of three variables: (1) the possibility that the electricity will escape; (2) the gravity of the resulting injury, if it does; (3) the burden of taking adequate precautions that would avert the accident. When the product of the possibility of escape multiplied times the gravity of the harm, if it happens, exceeds the burden of precautions, the risk is unreasonable and the failure to take those precautions is negligence.

Applying the negligence balancing process, we conclude that although there was a cognizable risk that the antenna stationed in the corner of Mr. Washington's backyard could be lowered and moved to within a dangerous proximity of the power line, that possibility could not be characterized as an unreasonable risk and the power company's failure to take additional precautions against it was not negligence.

Under the circumstances, there was not a significant possibility before the accident that Mr. Washington or anyone acting for him would detach the antenna and attempt to carry it under or dangerously near the power line. Standing alone, Mr. Washington's 1980 accident might have caused an objective observer to increase his estimate of the chances that this particular antenna might be handled carelessly. The other surrounding circumstances, however, overwhelmingly erase any pre-accident enlargement of the risk at that site. Except for the single occasion of the 1980 accident, the antenna was stationed safely in the corner of the backyard for many years, one to three years before the 1980 mishap and five years afterwards. Most of that time it was maintained safely in the pipe receptacle which, by Mr. Washington's design, allowed it to be lowered only in a safe direction. Between his close call in 1980 and his fatal accident in 1985, Mr. Washington had never been known to handle the antenna carelessly. Indeed, after he and his son narrowly escaped death or serious injury in 1980, his remarks to friends and relatives indicated that the experience had convinced him to keep the antenna far away from the power line. That he continued to be aware of the danger and take exemplary precautions to avoid it until his fatal accident was further illustrated by the care that he and his friend took when they lowered and laid it next to the fence several days before the accident.

The likelihood that the antenna in this case would be brought into contact with the power line was not as great as the chances of an electrical accident in situations creating significant potential for injuries to victims who may contact or come into dangerous proximity with the powerline due to their unawareness of or inadvertence to the charged wire.

Prior to the accident, the anticipated gravity of the loss if the risk were to take effect was, of course, of a very high degree. The deaths and serious injuries in this and other electrical accidents verify that the weight of the loss threatened by a power line accident is not trivial. While some accidents, such as Mr. Washington's 1980 mishap, do not lead to dire consequences, a consideration of all losses resulting from this type of risk indicates that the gravity of the loss if it occurs is usually extreme.

Rev. 212, 212（1969）〕。在这一点上，我们新近认为，电力公司在类似情况下应该负有针对导致损害的义务，是由以下三个变量所决定的：（1）漏电的可能性大小；（2）如果发生损害，其导致损害的程度；（3）对此采取充分预防措施以避免损害发生的负担。当漏电可能性数倍大于损害的严重程度时，如果损害发生的话，超过了预防措施的负担，则风险就是不合理的并且未采取预防措施就构成过失。

适用上述过失衡量过程，我们认为尽管存在可被察觉的风险，即Washington先生家后院角落安置的天线可能会降低高度，并发生移动进而接近高压线，该种可能性并不能被定性为不合理的风险，并且电力公司未采取额外的预防措施以避免损害发生并不构成过失。

在这种情况下，事故发生前并不存在该种重大可能性，即Washington本人或者为其工作的人将天线拆下来，试图将其拿到高压线之下或者接近的地方。独立地看，Washington先生1980年经历的意外理应使其客观地注意到提高对该天线不慎处理的可能性估量。但是，其他相关情况压倒性地排除了任何事故发生前该地点风险的扩大。除了1980年发生的这起单一事故外，其他时间，包括1980年前的一到三年间和其后的五年时间里，这根天线一直安全地放置在后院角落。根据Washington先生的设计，这根天线在绝大部分时间里，都安全地放置在管状容器管内，只能向一个安全方向降低高度。在1980年幸免于难之后和1985年这场致命事故发生之前，Washington先生从未不慎地处理过这根天线。实际上，在他和他儿子险些丧命于1980年事故之后，他曾向朋友和亲戚说过，这次的经历使他确信一定要使天线远离高压输电线。直到事故发生前，Washington也一直注意采取必要的措施以避免危险发生，这可以从直到事故发生前几天，他还和朋友小心翼翼地降低天线的高度，并将其安置在栅栏旁中得到进一步的印证。

本案中天线同高压线发生接触的可能性，要小于对受害人产生显著潜在损害情形的电力事故发生几率。在这些情形中，受害人因为没有意识到或者疏忽了通电的电线而可能接触电线或者进入到电线的危险区域。

在事故发生前，如果考虑到风险的话，预计的损害程度会非常高。这类事故及其他类型的电力事故中发生的伤亡损害证明，由电线事故所造成的损失并非无关紧要。尽管在某些事故中，比如Washington 1980年遭遇的事故，并未导致可怕的后果，但是考虑到此类风险所导致的所有损失，表明损害发

Yet when this high degree of gravity of loss is multiplied by the very small possibility of the accident occurring in this case, we think it is clear that the product does not outweigh the burdens or costs of the precautions of relocating or insulating the power line. This does not mean, of course, that it would not have been worth what it would have cost to place the line underground or to insulate it in order to save the decedent's life if it had been known that the accident would happen or even if the chance of it occurring had been greater. Nor does it mean, on the other hand, that we stop with a consideration of only the burden of an effective precaution in this single case. Common knowledge indicates that within any power company's territory there probably are a great number of situations involving antennas that have been safely installed, but which conceivably could be detached and carelessly moved about dangerously near a power line. In fairness, in this case, in which the coexistence of the power line and the safely installed antenna was no riskier than countless other similar coexistences not considered to involve negligence, the burden to the company of taking precautions against all such slight possibilities of harm should be balanced against the total magnitude of all these risks, including the relatively few losses resulting from the total of all those insignificant risks. Just as single case applications of the Hand formula can understate the benefits of accident prevention by overlooking all other accidents that could be avoided by the same safety expenditures, the burdens of taking precautions in all similar cases may be depreciated by single case consideration here.

The foregoing, of course, is merely a shorthand expression of the mental processes involved in such considerations. We cannot mathematically or mechanically quantify, multiply, or weigh risks, losses, and burdens of precautions. As many scholars have noted, the formula is primarily helpful in keeping in mind the relationship of the factors involved and in centering attention upon which of them may be determinative in any given situation. Nevertheless, the formula would seem to be of greater assistance in cases of the present type, in which the power company's ability to perceive risks is superior and its duty is utmost, than other notions, such as "reasonable man," "duty," or "foreseeability," for example, which must be little more than labels to be applied after some sort of balancing or weighing that the formula attempts to describe. In the present case, the balancing process focuses our attention on the fact that the possibility of an accident appeared to be slight beforehand and on the reality that precautions against such slight risks would be costly and burdensome because they exist in great number and have not usually been considered unreasonable or intolerable.

For the reasons assigned, the judgment of the court of appeals is affirmed.

生的程度是非常严重的。

但是，如果这种高程度的损失和此种情形下事故发生的小几率值相乘，可以明显看出，二者的乘积不会超过采取重新安置电线或者添置绝缘设备等预防措施所支出的负担或者成本。当然，这并不意味着，如果电力公司知道事故可能发生或者事故发生概率变大时，花费一些成本将电线放置在地下或使其绝缘以挽救死者性命是没有价值的。当然，从另一方面讲，这也绝非意味着我们只考虑个案中采取有效措施预防风险所支出的成本大小问题。从基本常识来看，每一家电力公司在其所覆盖范围之内，可能会存在大量的本应当被安全安装的天线，可以想象将其被拆下并不慎地移动到电线附近。本案中，从公平角度考量，电线同安全安装的天线的共存状态并不比其他不计其数的类似的不被认为有过失的共存状态更危险。电力公司采取措施以避免极小可能会发生的损害成本与所有风险可能造成的总损失大小相权衡，其中包括由所有微不足道的风险总和所导致的相对而言较小的损失。正如汉德公式在个案中的运用可能由于忽略了所有其他可以通过同样安全措施即可避免的事故，从而低估了事故预防的好处一样，在所有类似案件中采取预防措施的成本也可能会由于此处对个案的考量而被轻视。

当然，上述内容仅仅是对案件思维过程的简单描述。我们不能数学地或者机械地定量，做乘法，或者衡量各种风险、损失和预防负担。正如一些学者所言，该公式主要的作用在于帮助我们记住涉案因素之间的关系以及关注既定条件下何种因素占据决定性地位。虽然，在当前这一类型案件中，该公式似乎能发挥更大的作用，这类案件中的电力公司对风险的觉察能力比其他概念诸如"理性人""义务""预测能力"等要大，并且其义务是最大的，比如，在公式试图描述的某种平衡或衡量后，肯定会比所适用的标签稍微多一点。在本案中，运用平衡机制，我们认为事故发生的可能性很小。并且，我们认为针对轻微风险而采取预防措施成本高昂且负担沉重，因为这些风险是广泛存在的，并且被认为是合理且可承受的。

基于上述理由，我们维持上诉法院的判决。

13. Weirum v. RKO General, Inc., 15 Cal. 3d 40, 539 P.2d 36, 123 Cal. Rptr. 468 (1975)

Supreme Court of California, United States

Mosk, J. A rock radio station with an extensive teenage audience conducted a contest which rewarded the first contestant to locate a peripatetic disc jockey. Two minors driving in separate automobiles attempted to follow the disc jockey's automobile to its next stop. In the course of their pursuit, one of the minors negligently forced a car off the highway, killing its sole occupant. In a suit filed by the surviving wife and children of the decedent, the jury rendered a verdict against the radio station. We now must determine whether the station owed decedent a duty of due care.

The facts are not disputed. Radio station KHJ is a successful Los Angeles broadcaster with a large teenage following. At the time of the accident, KHJ commanded a 48 percent plurality of the teenage audience in the Los Angeles area. In contrast, its nearest rival during the same period was able to capture only 13 percent of the teenage listeners. In order to attract an even larger portion of the available audience and thus increase advertising revenue, KHJ inaugurated in July of 1970 a promotion entitled "The Super Summer Spectacular." The "spectacular," with a budget of approximately $40,000 for the month, was specifically designed to make the radio station "more exciting." Among the programs included in the "spectacular" was a contest broadcast on July 16, 1970, the date of the accident.

On that day, Donald Steele Revert, known professionally as "The Real Don Steele," a KHJ disc jockey and television personality, traveled in a conspicuous red automobile to a number of locations in the Los Angeles metropolitan area. Periodically, he apprised KHJ of his whereabouts and his intended destination, and the station broadcast the information to its listeners. The first person to physically locate Steele and fulfill a specified condition received a cash prize. In addition, the winning contestant participated in a brief interview on the air with "The Real Don Steele." The following excerpts from the July 16 broadcast illustrate the tenor of the contest announcements:

"9:30 and The Real Don Steele is back on his feet again with some money and he is headed for the Valley. Thought I would give you a warning so that you can get your kids out of the street."…

"The Real Don Steele is moving into Canoga Park—so be on the lookout for him. I'll tell you what will happen if you get to The Real Don Steele. He's got twenty-five dollars to give away if you can get it…and baby, all signed and sealed and delivered and wrapped up."…

In Van Nuys, 17-year-old Robert Sentner was listening to KHJ in his car while searching for "The Real Don Steele." Upon hearing that "The Real Don Steele" was proceeding to Canoga Park, he immediately drove to that vicinity. Meanwhile, in Northridge, 19-year-old Marsha Baime heard and responded to the same information. Both of them arrived at the Holiday Theater in Canoga Park to find that someone had already claimed the prize. Without knowledge of the other, each

13. Weirum v. RKO General, Inc., 15 Cal. 3d 40, 539 P.2d 36, 123 Cal. Rptr. 468 (1975)

美国加利福尼亚州最高法院

  Mosk 法官主笔：一家拥有众多青少年听众的摇滚乐无线广播电台举办了一期竞赛节目，第一个发现巡回中的电台主持人的参赛者将会得到奖励。有两个未成年人驾驶各自的汽车跟着主持人的汽车去下一站。在跟随的过程中，其中一人因过失将一辆汽车撞出了公路，导致车主死亡。在死者幸存的妻子和孩子提起的诉讼中，陪审团提交了一份对电台不利的裁断。我们现在必须确定的问题是电台对死者是否负有合理的注意义务。

  事实并无争议。KHJ 无线电台是一家成功的洛杉矶广播公司，拥有很多青少年听众。事件发生时，KHJ 拥有洛杉矶地区 48% 的青少年听众。而相比之下，其最强竞争对手在同一时期仅获得 13% 的青少年听众。为了吸引更多的听众，以及随之而增加的广告收入，KHJ 于 1970 年 7 月举行了一个名为"超级夏季盛典"的宣传活动。该月活动预算约 4 万美元，策划的目标是让电台节目"更令人兴奋"。1970 年 7 月 16 日，也就是事故的发生日，"盛典"的广播节目中有一个竞赛节目。

  在那天，一位 KHJ 的电台节目主持人和电视明星，被业内称为"真正的 Don Steele"的 Donald Steele Revert，乘坐一辆显眼的红色汽车去洛杉矶市区的数个地点。他每隔一段时间通知 KHJ 一次他的位置以及预定目的地，电台再把这些信息广播给听众。第一个找到 Steele 并且满足一定条件的人将会获得一笔奖金。另外，获胜者将参加由"真正的 Don Steele"在广播中进行的简短采访。下面的内容来自于 7 月 16 日的广播，竞赛通告大意如下：

  "9 点 30 分，真正的 Don Steele 将再次徒步带着一些钱回来，并正向着山谷进发。届时我们将会给出警告，以便您能让您的孩子离开街道……"

  "真正的 Don Steele 正在进入 Canoga 公园——请时刻注意。如果您找到真正的 Don Steele，我告诉您将会发生什么。如果您能发现他，他将赠送您 25 美元……而且各位，所有都是他签名、盖章、送到并且包好的……"

  在 Van Nuys，17 岁的 Robert Sentner 正一边在车里听着 KHJ 的广播，一边搜寻着"真正的 Don Steele"。一听到"真正的 Don Steele"在去往 Canoga 公园的路上，他立即驱车赶往附近。同一时间，在 Northridge，19 岁的 Marsha Baime 也听到了广播，并向 Canoga 公园赶去。两人都到达了 Canoga 公园的假日剧场，却发现已经有人获得了奖金。尽管两个人互不相识，但都决定跟随

decided to follow the Steele vehicle to its next stop and thus be the first to arrive when the next contest question or condition was announced.

For the next few miles the Sentner and Baime cars jockeyed for position closest to the Steele vehicle, reaching speeds up to 80 miles an hour. [However, the plaintiff did not contend that Steele exceeded the speed limit at any time.] About a mile and a half from the Westlake offramp the two teenagers heard the following broadcast: "11:13—The Real Don Steele with bread is heading for Thousand Oaks to give it away. Keep listening to KHJ....The Real Don Steele out on the highway—with bread to give away—be on the lookout, he may stop in Thousand Oaks and may stop along the way...Looks like it may be a good stop Steele—drop some bread to those folks."

The Steele vehicle left the freeway at the Westlake offramp. Either Baime or Sentner, in attempting to follow, forced decedent's car onto the center divider, where it overturned. Baime stopped to report the accident. Sentner, after pausing momentarily to relate the tragedy to a passing peace officer, continued to pursue Steele, successfully located him and collected a cash prize.

Decedent's wife and children brought an action for wrongful death against Sentner, Baime, RKO General, Inc. as owner of KHJ, and the maker of decedent's car. Sentner settled prior to the commencement of trial for the limits of his insurance policy. The jury returned a verdict against Baime and KHJ in the amount of $300,000 and found in favor of the manufacturer of decedent's car. KHJ appeals from the ensuing judgment and from an order denying its motion for judgment notwithstanding the verdict. Baime did not appeal.

The primary question for our determination is whether defendant owed a duty to decedent arising out of its broadcast of the giveaway contest. The determination of duty is primarily a question of law. It is the court's "expression of the sum total of those considerations of policy which lead the law to say that the particular plaintiff is entitled to protection." (Prosser, Law of Torts (4th ed. 1971) pp. 325-326.) Any number of considerations may justify the imposition of duty in particular circumstances, including the guidance of history, our continually refined concepts of morals and justice, the convenience of the rule, and social judgment as to where the loss should fall. While the question whether one owes a duty to another must be decided on a case-by-case basis, every case is governed by the rule of general application that all persons are required to use ordinary care to prevent others from being injured as the result of their conduct. However, foreseeability of the risk is a primary consideration in establishing the element of duty. Defendant asserts that the record here does not support a conclusion that a risk of harm to decedent was foreseeable.

While duty is a question of law, foreseeability is a question of fact for the jury. The verdict in plaintiffs' favor here necessarily embraced a finding that decedent was exposed to a foreseeable risk of harm. It is elementary that our review of this finding is limited to the determination whether there is any substantial evidence, contradicted or uncontradicted, which will support the conclusion

Steele 的车去下一个地点,以便能够在下一个竞赛问题或条件给出时成为第一个到达的人。

在接下来的几公里中,Sentner 和 Baime 的车一直跟随在离 Steele 的车最接近的位置,车速都达到了每小时 80 英里以上(然而,原告并没有提出 Steele 的车在任何时候有超速行为)。在离 Westlake 匝道大约一公里半的地方,两个未成年人听到了如下的广播:"11 点 13 分——带着面包的真正的 Don Steele 正朝着 Thousand Oaks 进发准备将其分发。请继续收听 KHJ……真正的 Don Steele 已经出了高速公路……带着将要分发的面包……看来 Steele 要好好停一下了——给那些听众发一些面包。"

Steele 的车子在 Westlake 匝道离开了高速公路。Sentner 或者 Baime 在追逐的过程中,迫使死者的车子驶向了分道线中央,造成了翻车。Baime 停车报了警。Sentner 则在短暂停车,向一个过路的治安人员讲述了这起悲剧之后,继续追赶 Steele 的车,并且成功地追到了,还获得了现金奖励。

死者的妻子和孩子以不法致死状告了 Sentner、Baime 和作为 KHJ 所有者的 RKO General 公司,以及死者车辆的制造者。Sentner 在案件审理之前就在保险限额之内达成和解。陪审团作出了 Baime 和 KHJ 支付 30 万美元以及对死者车辆的制造商有利的裁断。KHJ 对随后的判决提起上诉,并对拒绝其提出的与陪审团裁断相反的申请的法庭命令提起上诉。Baime 没有上诉。

我们作出决定的第一个前提是,在其提供分发竞赛的广播中,被告对于死者是否负有义务。义务的判断首先是一个法律问题。是法院的"表达的那些法律目的考虑因素的全部总和使得某一具体的原告有权被保护"。[Prosser 的《侵权法》(Law of Torts ,4th. ed. 1971,pp. 325-326)]。任何考量因素都需要被证明在具体情形之下施加义务是正当的,包括历史性的指引,对道德和正义概念的持续淳化,规则的便利性,以及对于损失应该由谁承担的社会判断。然而,某人是否对另外一个人负有义务的问题,必须根据具体案件来判断,每一个案件的判断需要根据一项一般应用规则,即所有的人都被要求尽到一般注意去防止他人受到其行为的伤害。但是,风险的可预见性在判断义务要素时是一个基础要素。被告声称,依据本案所有的案卷,不能支持得出结论认为死者的损害风险是可以预见的。

尽管义务问题是一个法律问题,但是可预见性问题却是一个由陪审团决定的事实问题。本案中有利于原告的裁断,包含了认定使原告面临可以预见损害风险之中的判定。初步来看,我们对判定的观点受制于这个决定,即是

reached by the jury.

We conclude that the record amply supports the finding of foreseeability. These tragic events unfolded in the middle of a Los Angeles summer, a time when young people were free from the constraints of school and responsive to relief from vacation tedium. Seeking to attract new listeners, KHJ devised an "exciting" promotion. Money and a small measure of momentary notoriety awaited the swiftest response. It was foreseeable that defendant's youthful listeners, finding the prize had eluded them at one location, would race to arrive first at the next site and in their haste would disregard the demands of highway safety.

Indeed, "The Real Don Steele" testified that he had in the past noticed vehicles following him from location to location. He was further aware that the same contestants sometimes appeared at consecutive stops. This knowledge is not rendered irrelevant, as defendant suggests, by the absence of any prior injury. Such an argument confuses foreseeability with hindsight, and amounts to a contention that the injuries of the first victim are not compensable. "The mere fact that a particular kind of an accident has not happened before does not…show that such accident is one which might not reasonably have been anticipated." (*Ridley v. Grifall Trucking Co.*, 136 Cal. App. 2d 682, 686 [289 P.2d 31] (1955).) Thus, the fortuitous absence of prior injury does not justify relieving defendant from responsibility for the foreseeable consequences of its acts.

It is of no consequence that the harm to decedent was inflicted by third parties acting negligently. Defendant invokes the maxim that an actor is entitled to assume that others will not act negligently. This concept is valid, however, only to the extent the intervening conduct was not to be anticipated. If the likelihood that a third person may react in a particular manner is a hazard which makes the actor negligent, such reaction whether innocent or negligent does not prevent the actor from being liable for the harm caused thereby. Here, reckless conduct by youthful contestants, stimulated by defendant's broadcast, constituted the hazard to which decedent was exposed.

It is true, of course, that virtually every act involves some conceivable danger. Liability is imposed only if the risk of harm resulting from the act is deemed unreasonable—i.e., if the gravity and likelihood of the danger outweigh the utility of the conduct involved.

We need not belabor the grave danger inherent in the contest broadcast by defendant. The risk of a high speed automobile chase is the risk of death or serious injury. Obviously, neither the entertainment afforded by the contest nor its commercial rewards can justify the creation of such a grave risk. Defendant could have accomplished its objectives of entertaining its listeners and increasing advertising revenues by adopting a contest format which would have avoided danger to the motoring public.

Defendant's contention that the giveaway contest must be afforded the deference due society's interest in the First Amendment is clearly without merit. The issue here is civil accountability for

否存在实质证据,与之矛盾或者不矛盾,支持陪审团得出这样一个结论。

我们得出结论认为案卷完全支持可预见性认定。这些悲剧性事件发生在7月,在这个时间里,年轻人正好处在脱离学校控制的自由阶段,需要在无聊的假期中寻求放松。为了吸引新的听众,KHJ设计了一个"令人兴奋的"促销。现金和一些小的可以短时出名的措施等待着那些最迅速的回应。可以预见的是,作为被告的年轻听众,在发现奖金在某地被他人获得之后,将会争着第一个到达下一个地点,他们匆忙之中一定会忽视对高速公路的安全要求。

事实上,"真正的 Don Steele"作证说他曾经注意到跟着他从一个地方到另外一个地方的车辆。他还发现,同一个参赛者有时会出现在连续的停车点。这些认识并非是无关的推理,就像被告所说的那样,此前从未出现损害。此种说法混淆了可预见性和后见之明,进而会得出结论认为第一个受害人是无需赔偿的。"仅仅是某一具体类型的事故此前从未发生的事实并不……表明该事故就是一个不能合理被预测的事故。"〔Ridley v. Grifall Trucking Co., 136 Cal. App. 2d 682,686(289 P. 2d 31)(1955).〕因此,之前并没有出现的偶然的损害并不能使得被告免于承担其行为的可预见性后果。

如果证明死者的损害是由第三人的过错行为所致,则可以不承担责任。被告援引行为人有权假设他人将不会出现过失行为的格言。但是,这种观念只是在介入行为是不可预期的情形下有效。如果第三人可能会以一种危险的行为方式反应,并导致行为人有过失,此种反应无论是无辜的还是有过失的,都不能阻止行为人对其行为所发生的后果承担责任。在本案中,被告广播所激发的年轻参赛者的鲁莽行为,构成了死者面临的危险。

事实上,每一个行为都包含了某种可能的危险。责任仅被施加在那些被认为是不合理的行为所导致的损害风险之上——例如,如果风险的重要性和可能性都超出了行为的有益性的时候。

我们无需过多地讨论被告广播竞赛固有的重大危险。高速车辆追逐的风险就是死亡或者严重伤害。很明显,无论是该竞赛的娱乐性还是其商业奖金都不能将这样一种重大风险正当化。被告本来应该通过一种能够避免在公共场合驾车的竞赛形式去达到娱乐听众并增加其广告收入的目标。

由于社会对《美国宪法第一修正案》的关注,被告关于必须对赠品竞赛给予尊重的主张,显然没有根据。本案的问题是一个因可预见结果的广播所导致的一种对死者的损害风险具有民事可责难性的问题。《美国宪法第一修正案》并不制裁仅仅是由言语而非行为所导致的人身损害。

the foreseeable results of a broadcast which created an undue risk of harm to decedent. The First Amendment does not sanction the infliction of physical injury merely because achieved by word, rather than act.

We are not persuaded that the imposition of a duty here will lead to unwarranted extensions of liability. Defendant is fearful that entrepreneurs will henceforth be burdened with an avalanche of obligations: an athletic department will owe a duty to an ardent sports fan injured while hastening to purchase one of a limited number of tickets; a department store will be liable for injuries incurred in response to a "while-they-last" sale. This argument, however, suffers from a myopic view of the facts presented here. The giveaway contest was no commonplace invitation to an attraction available on a limited basis. It was a competitive scramble in which the thrill of the chase to be the one and only victor was intensified by the live broadcast which accompanied the pursuit. In the assertedly analogous situations described by defendant, any haste involved in the purchase of the commodity is an incidental and unavoidable result of the scarcity of the commodity itself. In such situations there is no attempt, as here, to generate a competitive pursuit on public streets, accelerated by repeated importuning by radio to be the very first to arrive at a particular destination. Manifestly the "spectacular" bears little resemblance to daily commercial activities....

The judgment and the orders appealed from are affirmed. Plaintiffs shall recover their costs on appeal. The parties shall bear their own costs on the cross-appeal.

Wright, C.J., McComb, J., Tobriner, J., Sullivan, J., Clark, J., and Richardson, J., concurred.

14. Palsgraf v. Long Island R.R. Co., N.Y. 339, 162 N.E. 99 (1928)

Court of Appeals of New York, United States

Appeal from a judgment of the Appellate Division of the Supreme Court in the second judicial department...affirming a judgment in favor of plaintiff entered upon a verdict.

Cardozo, C.J. Plaintiff was standing on a platform of defendant's railroad after buying a ticket to go to Rockaway Beach. A train stopped at the station, bound for another place. Two men ran forward to catch it. One of the men reached the platform of the car without mishap, though the train was already moving. The other man, carrying a package, jumped aboard the car, but seemed unsteady as if about to fall. A guard on the car, who had held the door open, reached forward to help him in, and another guard on the platform pushed him from behind. In this act, the package was dislodged, and fell upon the rails. It was a package of small size, about fifteen inches long, and was covered by a newspaper. In fact it contained fireworks, but there was nothing in its appearance to give notice of its contents. The fireworks when they fell exploded. The shock of the explosion threw down some scales at the other end of the platform, many feet away. The scales struck the plaintiff, causing injuries for which she sues.

我们坚持认为，在本案中施加义务将会导致一种没有根据的责任扩张。被告担心企业将会因此承担一种雪崩式的责任：体育部门将会对热心的体育迷因疯狂地去购买限量门票而引起的损害承担责任；销售商店将会因对"最后狂甩"促销导致的伤害承担责任。然而，此种观点，其实是一种对与所呈现事实近似的观点。免费礼物竞赛不是在有限的基础上邀请。这种因要争抢那个唯一一个胜利者的冲动而导致的竞赛性混乱，通过伴随无线电的重复输入加快了它成为最早到达特定目的地的速度。在被告所描述的类似情形之下，任何为了购买商品的匆忙，都是商品本身不可避免的结果。就此而言，在这种情形之下并不试图，没有像在这里那样试图在公共街道上产生竞争性追求。通过无线电的重复运作它成为第一个到达特定目的地的人。很明显，"盛典"与日常商业行为具有较少的相似性……

判决维持原判和法庭命令。原告应获得上诉费用的赔偿。当事人各自承担交叉上诉的费用。

Wright 大法官、Mccomb 法官、Tobriner 法官、Sullivan 法官、Clark 法官和 Richardson 法官赞同。

14. Palsgraf v. Long Island R.R. Co., 248 N.Y. 339, 162 N.E. 99 (1928)

美国纽约州上诉法院

这是由最高法院上诉分庭第二法庭的判决引发的上诉……该判决维持了根据陪审团裁断作出的有利于原告的判决。

Cardozo 大法官主笔：原告购买了一张前往 Rockaway Beach 的火车票后，站在被告的铁路站台上。一辆火车在站前停了下来，准备前往另一个地方。两个人跑过来想赶上这辆火车。尽管当时火车已经开动，但是其中一个人还是跳上了火车末尾的站台，没有发生意外。另一个人拿着一个包裹，跳上火车，但是似乎没有站稳，马上就要摔倒。车上的保安列车员当时没有关门，上前将他拉进车厢，并且站台上的另一名保安从后面推他。结果，包裹掉了下来，掉在了铁轨上。这个包裹很小，长约 15 英寸，表面上包着报纸。实际上，包裹里装着鞭炮，但是从表面看不出里面装的是什么。包裹落下时鞭炮发生了爆炸。爆炸产生的冲击力推倒了数英尺之外站台末尾的磅秤。磅秤打到了原告，导致其受到伤害，原告由此提起了诉讼。

被告保安的行为，就与包裹持有人的关系来看是存在过错的，但是就与站在很远之外的原告之间的关系来看，却没有过错。与原告有联系，但是却

The conduct of the defendant's guard, if a wrong in its relation to the holder of the package, was not a wrong in its relation to the plaintiff, standing far away. Relative to her it was not negligence at all. Nothing in the situation gave notice that the falling package had in it the potency of peril to persons thus removed. Negligence is not actionable unless it involves the invasion of a legally protected interest, the violation of a right. "Proof of negligence in the air, so to speak, will not do" (Pollock, Torts [11th ed.], p. 455....). The plaintiff as she stood upon the platform of the station might claim to be protected against intentional invasion of her bodily security. Such invasion is not charged. She might claim to be protected against unintentional invasion by conduct involving in the thought of reasonable men an unreasonable hazard that such invasion would ensue. These, from the point of view of law, were the bounds of her immunity, with perhaps some rare exceptions, survivals for the most part of ancient forms of liability, where conduct is held to be at the peril of the actor.

If no hazard was apparent to the eye of ordinary vigilance, an act innocent and harmless, at least to outward seeming, with reference to her, did not take to itself the quality of a tort because it happened to be a wrong, though apparently not one involving the risk of bodily insecurity, with reference to some one else....The plaintiff sues in her own right for a wrong personal to her, and not as the vicarious beneficiary of a breach of duty to another.

A different conclusion will involve us, and swiftly too, in a maze of contradictions. A guard stumbles over a package which has been left upon a platform. It seems to be a bundle of newspapers. It turns out to be a can of dynamite. To the eye of ordinary vigilance, the bundle is abandoned waste, which may be kicked or trod on with impunity. Is a passenger at the other end of the platform protected by the law against the unsuspected hazard concealed beneath the waste? If not, is the result to be any different, so far as the distant passenger is concerned, when the guard stumbles over a valise which a truckman or a porter has left upon the walk? The passenger far away, if the victim of a wrong at all, has a cause of action, not derivative, but original and primary. His claim to be protected against invasion of his bodily security is neither greater nor less because the act resulting in the invasion is a wrong to another far removed. In this case, the rights that are said to have been violated, the interests said to have been invaded, are not even of the same order. The man was not injured in his person nor even put in danger. The purpose of the act, as well as its effect, was to make his person safe. If there was a wrong to him at all, which may very well be doubted, it was a wrong to a property interest only, the safety of his package. Out of this wrong to property, which threatened injury to nothing else, there has passed, we are told, to the plaintiff by derivation or succession a right of action for the invasion of an interest of another order, the right to bodily security. The diversity of interests emphasizes the futility of the effort to build the plaintiff's right upon the basis of a wrong to some one else. The gain is one of emphasis, for a like result would follow if the interests were the same. Even then, the orbit of the danger as disclosed to

绝对不是过失。当时的情况并没有显示出落下的包裹内部存在致人伤亡的潜在可能。除非过失侵犯到受法律保护的利益，侵犯到权利，否则过失都不具有可诉性。"凭空的过失证据，可以说，不起作用。"[Pollock 的《侵权法》，Torts（11th ed.），p.455…]当原告站在车站的站台上时，可以声称自己受到保护，其人身安全不应受到故意的侵犯。这种侵犯没有被指控。在理性人看来，会产生不合理危险的行为会对原告造成非故意的侵犯，原告可以声称自己受到保护，不应该受到这种侵犯。从法律的角度来看，这些都是原告豁免权的界限，可能在极少情况下还会有一些例外，这些例外大多来源于古老形式的责任，行为人要为自己的行为承担责任。

如果保持普通的警惕性无法轻易地看清危险，那么对于原告而言，该行为便是无罪无害的，至少从外表上看不具有侵权性质，因为行为只是凑巧存在过错，尽管在表面上看并没有威胁到他人的人身安全……原告有权起诉对她本人造成损害的过错行为，而不是因违背对他人的义务而作为间接受益人来提起起诉。

一个不同的结论很快会将我们卷入一个矛盾的谜团中。一名保安被放在站台上的一个包裹绊了一下。包裹似乎是一捆报纸，结果却是一筒炸药。保持普通的警惕性，人们会认为这捆东西就是一堆废品，可以随意地踢它或踩踏它。那么，对于这种废品下面隐藏的未被人们发现的危险，站在站台另一端的乘客是否受到法律保护？如果不受法律保护，那么保安被卡车司机或搬运工留在走道上的小提箱绊倒，对于站在很远位置的乘客而言，结果是否会有所不同？如果乘客成为过错行为的受害人，那么远处的乘客便有了诉因，该诉因不是衍生结果，而是原生的和主要的。他要求得到保护，确保人身不受侵犯，这一主张不多也不少，因为造成侵犯结果的行为对于远处的某个人来说是一种过错行为。在这个案件中，所谓被冒犯了的权利和所谓被侵犯了的利益甚至都不在同一个层次上。这个人并没有受伤，甚至没有身处危险之中。本诉讼的目的在于，其实际效果也在于保持其人身安全。如果确实对他实施了不法行为，尽管这是值得怀疑的，那么也只是损害了财产利益的不法行为，即威胁其包裹的安全。除了针对财产的不法行为之外，对其他任何事物都没有构成威胁，我们认为，通过推导或演替，本属于另一个层次的因侵犯一种利益而获得的起诉权被传递给了原告，成为了原告保护人身安全的权利。由于利益具有多样性，因此以对他人实施的不法行为为基础，努力建立原告的权利是没有意义的。收益是值得强调的，因为如果利益是相同的，就会得到相同的结果。即使这样，保持合理警惕性的人眼中的危险范围就是其履行义务的范围。当一个人在人群中推撞自己身旁的人，无意中将一枚炸弹撞到了地上，他的行为并没有侵犯到站在外圈的其他人的权利。对于他们来说，不

the eye of reasonable vigilance would be the orbit of the duty. One who jostles one's neighbor in a crowd does not invade the rights of others standing at the outer fringe when the unintended contact casts a bomb upon the ground. The wrongdoer as to them is the man who carries the bomb, not the one who explodes it without suspicion of the danger. Life will have to be made over, and human nature transformed, before prevision so extravagant can be accepted as the norm of conduct, the customary standard to which behavior must conform.

The argument for the plaintiff is built upon the shifting meanings of such words as "wrong" and "wrongful," and shares their instability. What the plaintiff must show is "a wrong" to herself, i.e., a violation of her own right, and not merely a wrong to some one else, nor conduct "wrongful" because unsocial, but not "a wrong" to any one. We are told that one who drives at reckless speed through a crowded city street is guilty of a negligent act and, therefore, of a wrongful one irrespective of the consequences. Negligent the act is, and wrongful in the sense that it is unsocial, but wrongful and unsocial in relation to other travelers, only because the eye of vigilance perceives the risk of damage. If the same act were to be committed on a speedway or a race course, it would lose its wrongful quality. The risk reasonably to be perceived defines the duty to be obeyed, and risk imports relation; it is risk to another or to others within the range of apprehension.... The range of reasonable apprehension is at times a question for the court, and at times, if varying inferences are possible, a question for the jury. Here, by concession, there was nothing in the situation to suggest to the most cautious mind that the parcel wrapped in newspaper would spread wreckage through the station. If the guard had thrown it down knowingly and willfully, he would not have threatened the plaintiff's safety, so far as appearances could warn him. His conduct would not have involved, even then, an unreasonable probability of invasion of her bodily security. Liability can be no greater where the act is inadvertent.

Negligence, like risk, is thus a term of relation. Negligence in the abstract, apart from things related, is surely not a tort, if indeed it is understandable at all....

The law of causation, remote or proximate, is thus foreign to the case before us. The question of liability is always anterior to the question of the measure of the consequences that go with liability. If there is no tort to be redressed, there is no occasion to consider what damage might be recovered if there were a finding of a tort. We may assume, without deciding, that negligence, not at large or in the abstract, but in relation to the plaintiff, would entail liability for any and all consequences, however novel or extraordinary. There is room for argument that a distinction is to be drawn according to the diversity of interests invaded by the act, as where conduct negligent in that it threatens an insignificant invasion of an interest in property results in an unforeseeable invasion of an interest of another order, as, e.g., one of bodily security. Perhaps other distinctions may be necessary. We do not go into the question now. The consequences to be followed must first be rooted in a wrong.

法行为人是携带炸弹的人,而不是那个没有意识到危险却引爆炸弹的人。在如此过度的规定作为行为规范和必须遵守的行为习惯标准被人们所接受之前,必须改变生活,改变人类的本性。

  对原告有利的观点都建立在偷换一些词的概念基础上,如"不法"和"不法的",利用了它们内涵的不确定性。原告必须证明对她本人实施的是"不法",即冒犯了她本人的权利,而不只是对其他人的过错,也不是某个不符合社会规范的"不法的"但却不对任何人构成"不法"的行为。我们被告知,如果一个人不计后果地高速驾车穿过拥挤的城市街道,那么因为他的过失,他是有罪的,因此无论后果如何,他的行为都是有不法的。虽然行为存在过失,由于不符合社会规范而在某种意义上是不法行为,但是这只对其他驾驶员来说是不法的和不符合社会规范的,只是因为有警惕性的人看到了发生损害的风险。如果同样的行为发生在高速公路或赛车道上,那么该行为就完全没有了过错的特质。以合理的方式可以预见到的风险决定了需要遵守什么样的义务,风险使得关系的确认变得非常重要;是对他人的风险,或者在可理解范围内对其他多人的风险……合理的理解范围有时是法院需要回答的问题,有时,如果可以作出不同的推断,这个问题需要陪审团来回答。经过让步,当时的情况丝毫没有让最谨慎的人们认为,包在报纸里的那个包裹会毁掉整个车站。如果保安在知情的情况下故意将包裹扔下来,那么他不会威胁到原告的安全,因为他已经从包裹的外表得到了警示。他的行为没有任何侵犯到原告人身安全的不合理的可能性。当行为是无意造成的,责任也不会更大。

  和风险一样,过失是一个和"关系"有关的用语。从抽象层面来讲,如果人们确实可以理解什么是过失,那么离开了相关事物的过失责任便不是一种侵权行为……

  因果关系法,无论是近因还是远因,与我们面前的这个案件都是不相关的。责任问题往往总是先于如何衡量伴随责任而来的后果问题。如果没有需要矫正的侵权行为,那么即使认定了存在侵权行为,也不用考虑损害赔偿问题。我们可以设想而不用去决定,不用一般性地或抽象地去设想,而是以与原告的关系出发去设想,那么只要有过失行为,就需要对行为产生的所有后果承担责任,无论这些后果是多么的离奇和不寻常。有人可以提出,应当根据行为侵犯的不同利益对行为进行区分,因为这个过失行为对财产利益造成的侵犯虽然并不重大,但是却以不可预见的方式对另一层次的另一种利益造成了侵犯,即人身安全利益。也许还有必要作出其他方面的区分。我们现在不谈论这个问题。需要追踪的后果首先必须立足于过错。

  上诉分庭和陪审团初审的判决被撤销,驳回起诉,并承担在各级法院中

The judgment of the Appellate Division and that of the Trial Term should be reversed, and the complaint dismissed, with costs in all courts.

Andrews, J. (dissenting)....

...The result we shall reach depends upon our theory as to the nature of negligence. Is it a relative concept—the breach of some duty owing to a particular person or to particular persons? Or where there is an act which unreasonably threatens the safety of others, is the doer liable for all its proximate consequences, even where they result in injury to one who would generally be thought to be outside the radius of danger? This is not a mere dispute as to words. We might not believe that to the average mind the dropping of the bundle would seem to involve the probability of harm to the plaintiff standing many feet away whatever might be the case as to the owner or to one so near as to be likely to be struck by its fall. If, however, we adopt the second hypothesis we have to inquire only as to the relation between cause and effect. We deal in terms of proximate cause, not of negligence....

But we are told that "there is no negligence unless there is in the particular case a legal duty to take care, and this duty must be one which is owed to the plaintiff himself and not merely to others." (Salmond, Torts [6th ed.], 24.) This, I think too narrow a conception. Where there is the unreasonable act, and some right that may be affected there is negligence whether damage does or does not result. That is immaterial. Should we drive down Broadway at a reckless speed, we are negligent whether we strike an approaching car or miss it by an inch. The act itself is wrongful. It is a wrong not only to those who happen to be within the radius of danger but to all who might have been there—a wrong to the public at large. Such is the language of the street....Due care is a duty imposed on each one of us to protect society from unnecessary danger, not to protect A, B or C alone.

It may well be that there is no such thing as negligence in the abstract. "Proof of negligence in the air, so to speak, will not do." In an empty world negligence would not exist. It does involve a relationship between man and his fellows. But not merely a relationship between man and those whom he might reasonably expect his act would injure. Rather, a relationship between him and those whom he does in fact injure. If his act has a tendency to harm some one, it harms him a mile away as surely as it does those on the scene....

In the well-known Polemis Case (1921, 3 K. B. 560), Scrutton, L. J., said that the dropping of a plank was negligent for it might injure "workman or cargo or ship." Because of either possibility the owner of the vessel was to be made good for his loss. The act being wrongful the doer was liable for its proximate results. Criticized and explained as this statement may have been, I think it states the law as it should be and as it is.

The proposition is this. Every one owes to the world at large the duty of refraining from those acts that may unreasonably threaten the safety of others. Such an act occurs. Not only is he

的全部费用。

Andrews 法官撰写反对意见……

……我们将要得出的结论取决于关于过失本质的理论。这是一个相对概念吗——违反了对某个人或某些人所负的义务？或者，当某个行为不合理地威胁到他人的安全时，即使一般情况下认为这个人并没有处在危险范围之内，那么行为人是否应该为其行为导致的近因结果负责？这并非文字之争。我们可能不会认为，对于一般人来说，丢下一捆物品似乎有可能危害到站在数英尺之外的原告，无论该物品的所有人当时情况如何，或者离现场近的可能受伤的人当时情况如何。然而，如果我们选择第二种假设，那么我们只需要研究原因和结果之间的关系问题。我们解决的问题是近因，而不是过失……

但是，我们被告知"除非在特殊的情况下需要尽到法律义务，否则便不存在过失，且该法律义务必须是对原告本人的义务，而不只是对他人的义务。"[Salmond 的《侵权法》，Torts（6th ed.），24。]我认为这个概念太过狭窄。如果存在不合理的行为，而且有一些人可能被行为影响到，那么就存在过失，无论行为是否造成了损害。这是非实质性的。如果我们在百老汇上肆意地高速行驶，那么无论我们是否撞上了迎面过来的汽车还是与之擦肩而过，我们都是有过失的。行为本身就是不法的。不光对于恰好身处危险范围之内的人而言是不法的，而且对于所有在场的人都是不法的——对普遍的公众是不法的。这就是街道法则……我们每个人都有保护社会免受不必要危险的注意义务，而不是保护作为个体的 A、B 或 C 的安全。

有可能根本就没有抽象的过失概念。"凭空的过失证据，可以说，不起作用。"在一个空虚的世界中，过失是不存在的。过失确实涉及一个人和他的同伴之间的关系。一个人可能合理地预料到自己的行为可能对他人造成损害，但是过失却不仅仅是这个人和这些人之间的关系。相反，过失是这个人与他实际伤害到的人之间的关系。如果他的行为有伤害到他人的意图，那么该行为伤害到现场的人和伤害到一英里之外的人是一样的……

在著名的 Polemis（1921, 3 K. B. 560）案中，Scrutton 上议院议员法官 Lord Justice 说，掉下一块厚木板的行为是有过失的，因为厚木板可能伤到"工人或货物或船只"。由于存在其中一种可能性，因此船只的所有人应该就其损失获得赔偿。行为本身是不法的，因此行为人应该为行为造成的直接后果承担责任。虽然这一陈述被人们批评和解释，但是我认为它陈述了法律应该是怎样的，而且确实是怎样的。

观点如下。每个人对这个世界都有义务，即避免自己的行为不合理地威胁到他人的安全。但却发生了这样的行为。对于可能受到伤害的那些人，他的行为是不法的，而且事实上在一般情况下被认为处在危险区外的一些人也

wronged to whom harm might reasonably be expected to result, but he also who is in fact injured, even if he be outside what would generally be thought the danger zone. There needs be duty due the one complaining but this is not a duty to a particular individual because as to him harm might be expected. Harm to some one being the natural result of the act, not only that one alone, but all those in fact injured may complain. We have never, I think, held otherwise....Unreasonable risk being taken, its consequences are not confined to those who might probably be hurt.

If this be so, we do not have a plaintiff suing by "derivation or succession." Her action is original and primary. Her claim is for a breach of duty to herself—not that she is subrogated to any right of action of the owner of the parcel or of a passenger standing at the scene of the explosion.

The right to recover damages rests on additional considerations. The plaintiff's rights must be injured, and this injury must be caused by the negligence. We build a dam, but are negligent as to its foundations. Breaking, it injures property down stream. We are not liable if all this happened because of some reason other than the insecure foundation. But when injuries do result from our unlawful act we are liable for the consequences. It does not matter that they are unusual, unexpected, unforeseen and unforeseeable. But there is one limitation. The damages must be so connected with the negligence that the latter may be said to be the proximate cause of the former.

These two words have never been given an inclusive definition. What is a cause in a legal sense, still more what is a proximate cause, depend in each case upon many considerations, as does the existence of negligence itself. Any philosophical doctrine of causation does not help us. A boy throws a stone into a pond. The ripples spread. The water level rises. The history of that pond is altered to all eternity. It will be altered by other causes also. Yet it will be forever the resultant of all causes combined. Each one will have an influence. How great only omniscience can say. You may speak of a chain, or if you please, a net. An analogy is of little aid. Each cause brings about future events. Without each the future would not be the same. Each is proximate in the sense it is essential. But that is not what we mean by the word. Nor on the other hand do we mean sole cause. There is no such thing....

...What we do mean by the word "proximate" is, that because of convenience, of public policy, of a rough sense of justice, the law arbitrarily declines to trace a series of events beyond a certain point. This is not logic. It is practical politics. Take our rule as to fires. Sparks from my burning haystack set on fire my house and my neighbor's. I may recover from a negligent railroad. He may not. Yet the wrongful act as directly harmed the one as the other. We may regret that the line was drawn just where it was, but drawn somewhere it had to be. We said the act of the railroad was not the proximate cause of our neighbor's fire. Cause it surely was. The words we used were simply indicative of our notions of public policy. Other courts think differently. But somewhere they reach the point where they cannot say the stream comes from any one source.

Take the illustration given in an unpublished manuscript by a distinguished and helpful writer

受到了伤害，对于这些人，他也是不法的。由于有人起诉，所以需要履行义务，但是这并非对某个人的义务，因为对于他而言，损害可能是预期的。作为行为自然而然损害到的个人，而且不止这个人，还包括所有实际上受到了伤害的人都可能起诉。我认为，产生了不合理的风险，否则（风险也不会产生）该风险的结果并不仅仅限于那些可能被伤害到的人。

如果确实如此，那么我们的原告就不是因为"衍生或承接"而起诉。她提起的诉讼是原生的和主要的。她提出的主张是行为人违反了对她本人应尽到的义务——她并没有替代包裹所有人或处在爆炸现场的乘客的诉讼权利。

获得损害赔偿的权利是基于其他的考量。原告的权利一定是受到了损害，而造成损害的原因一定是过失。我们修建了一座大坝，但是在修建大坝基础时我们存在过失。大坝崩溃，对下游的财产造成了损失。如果发生事故的原因不是大坝基础的安全问题，那么我们就不需要承担责任。但是，当我们的不法行为造成了损害时，我们就应该对后果承担责任。即使后果是不寻常的、出乎意料的、未预见到的和无法预料的，也必须承担责任。损失必须与过失紧密相关，以至于可以认为过失是造成损失的近因。

这两个词从来就没有被赋予包含性的定义。什么是原因，在法律意义上，更进一步讲，什么是近因，在每个案件中取决于许多考量，就像是否存在过失本身一样。哲学上有关因果关系的任何定义对我们都没有帮助。一个男孩向池塘里扔了一块石头，水波散布开去，水平面上升。那个池塘的历史成为了永恒的过去。池塘还可能会因为其他原因而发生变化。但是这些变化永远都是所有原因综合在一起的结果。每个原因都会产生影响。影响有多大，只有全能的上帝才知道。你可以说是连锁反应，或者你还可以说是网状反应。无论如何比喻都无济于事。每一个原因都会引发未来的事件。缺少任何一个原因，未来都会有所不同。每一个原因都具有接近性，因为每一个原因都很重要。但是这并非我们想通过文字进行说明的。另一方面，我们也不仅仅指原因。并没有单纯的原因的存在……

……为了方便起见，因为公共政策和大致的正义感，我们的确用"接近性"表示，法律武断地拒绝追究超过某一个点的一连串事件。这并不符合逻辑。这是一个实用主义的策略。将我们的规则用在火灾案件中。从燃烧的草堆上溅出的火花点燃了我和我邻居的房子。我可以从存在过失的铁路公司获得赔偿。而邻居却不行。但是过错行为却直接地损害了一个人，也损害了另一个人。对于划分界线的位置我们可能感到遗憾，但是却必须划清界线。我们说铁路公司的行为并非造成邻居房屋失火的近因。这肯定是原因。我们采用的措辞仅仅表明了我们的公共政策意见。其他法院则有不同的看法。但是他们也会在某一点上说不清溪流的根源到底在哪里。

on the law of torts. A chauffeur negligently collides with another car which is filled with dynamite, although he could not know it. An explosion follows. A, walking on the sidewalk nearby, is killed. B, sitting in a window of a building opposite, is cut by flying glass. C, likewise sitting in a window a block away, is similarly injured. And a further illustration. A nursemaid, ten blocks away, startled by the noise, involuntarily drops a baby from her arms to the walk. We are told that C may not recover while A may. As to B it is a question for court or jury. We will all agree that the baby might not. Because, we are again told, the chauffeur had no reason to believe his conduct involved any risk of injuring either C or the baby. As to them he was not negligent.

But the chauffeur, being negligent in risking the collision, his belief that the scope of the harm he might do would be limited is immaterial. His act unreasonably jeopardized the safety of any one who might be affected by it. C's injury and that of the baby were directly traceable to the collision. Without that, the injury would not have happened. C had the right to sit in his office, secure from such dangers. The baby was entitled to use the sidewalk with reasonable safety.

The true theory is, it seems to me, that the injury to C, if in truth he is to be denied recovery, and the injury to the baby is that their several injuries were not the proximate result of the negligence. And here not what the chauffeur had reason to believe would be the result of his conduct, but what the prudent would foresee, may have a bearing. May have some bearing, for the problem of proximate cause is not to be solved by any one consideration.

It is all a question of expediency. There are no fixed rules to govern our judgment. There are simply matters of which we may take account....There is in truth little to guide us other than common sense.

There are some hints that may help us. The proximate cause, involved as it may be with many other causes, must be, at the least, something without which the event would not happen. The court must ask itself whether there was a natural and continuous sequence between cause and effect. Was the one a substantial factor in producing the other? Was there a direct connection between them, without too many intervening causes? Is the effect of cause on result not too attenuated? Is the cause likely, in the usual judgment of mankind, to produce the result? Or by the exercise of prudent foresight could the result be foreseen? Is the result too remote from the cause, and here we consider remoteness in time and space....Clearly we must so consider, for the greater the distance either in time or space, the more surely do other causes intervene to affect the result....

Here another question must be answered. In the case supposed it is said, and said correctly, that the chauffeur is liable for the direct effect of the explosion although he had no reason to suppose it would follow a collision. "The fact that the injury occurred in a different manner than that which might have been expected does not prevent the chauffeur's negligence from being in law the cause of the injury." But the natural results of a negligent act—the results which a prudent man would or should foresee—do have a bearing upon the decision as to proximate cause. We have

举一个例子，这个例子出现在侵权法上的一名杰出的且乐于助人的作者未发表的手稿中。一名司机因过失撞上了另一辆装载着炸药的汽车，引发了爆炸。行走在旁边人行道上的 A 死于爆炸。而坐在对面楼房窗户旁边的 B 则被因爆炸飞起来的玻璃划伤。坐在一个街区之外楼房的窗户旁边的 C 也受到了类似的伤害。再举一个例子。10 个街区之外的一名育婴女佣被爆炸声吓到，不小心将怀里的孩子掉在了人行道上。我们被告知，C 没有获得赔偿，而 A 获得了。对于 B 的问题，由法院或陪审团来裁断。我们都同意，婴儿无法获得赔偿。我们再次被告知，因为司机没有理由相信自己的行为会为 C 或婴儿带来任何的风险。对于他们而言，司机没有过失。

但是司机在撞车中存在过失，他认为自己可能造成的损害范围是有限的，但是他的这种认识却不具有实质性的意义。他的行为不合理地威胁到了任何可能受到影响的人的安全。C 受到的伤害和婴儿受到的伤害都可以直接追溯到撞车事故。如果没有撞车事故，就不会发生伤害。C 有权利坐在办公室，不受到任何危险的威胁。婴儿也有权安全地使用人行道。

真正的理论在我看来是这样的：C 受到的伤害如果不能获得赔偿，那么他所受到的和婴儿受到的这些个别伤害并非是过失行为产生的近因结果。这里，可能有影响的并不是司机有理由认为自己的行为可能产生什么样的结果，而是一个谨慎的人可以预见到什么样的结果。可能有影响的，是因为解决近因问题并不能只靠一个考量因素。

这一切都是权宜之计。并没有固定的规则来规范我们的判决。只是有一些需要我们考虑的问题……除了常识之外，实际上很少有什么可以给予我们指导。

有一些线索可以帮助我们。近因与许多其他原因混淆在一起，但是至少，如果没有近因，事件便不会发生。法院必须问自己，在原因和效果之间是否存在自然的和连续性的顺序。一个因素是否是产生另一个因素的实质性因素？它们之间是否存在直接联系，没有过多干预性的原因？原因对结果产生的效果是否被过分削弱？就人类正常的判断力来看，该原因是否可能产生该结果？或者，经过慎重的预见，是否可以预见到结果？结果和原因是否过于疏远，这里我们考虑的是时间和地点上的疏远……显然，我们必须考虑这些问题，因为时间越长或地点越远，其他原因影响到结果的可能性就越大……

这里还必须回答另一个问题。在假设的案件中，据说，而且说得很对，司机应该对爆炸产生的直接效果承担责任，尽管他没有理由预计到撞车之后会发生爆炸。"尽管损害发生的方式与预计的方式有所不同，但是这并不妨碍司机的过失行为在法律上成为造成损害的原因。"但是过失行为产生的自然结果——谨慎的人可以或应该预见到的结果——确实影响到有关近因的决

said so repeatedly. What should be foreseen? No human foresight would suggest that a collision itself might injure one a block away. On the contrary, given an explosion, such a possibility might be reasonably expected. I think the direct connection, the foresight of which the courts speak, assumes prevision of the explosion, for the immediate results of which, at least, the chauffeur is responsible.

It may be said this is unjust. Why? In fairness he should make good every injury flowing from his negligence. Not because of tenderness toward him we say he need not answer for all that follows his wrong. We look back to the catastrophe, the fire kindled by the spark, or the explosion. We trace the consequences—not indefinitely, but to a certain point. And to aid us in fixing that point we ask what might ordinarily be expected to follow the fire or the explosion.

This last suggestion is the factor which must determine the case before us. The act upon which defendant's liability rests is knocking an apparently harmless package onto the platform. The act was negligent. For its proximate consequences the defendant is liable. If its contents were broken, to the owner; if it fell upon and crushed a passenger's foot, then to him. If it exploded and injured one in the immediate vicinity, to him also as to A in the illustration. Mrs. Palsgraf was standing some distance away. How far cannot be told from the record—apparently twenty-five or thirty feet. Perhaps less. Except for the explosion, she would not have been injured. We are told by the appellant in his brief "it cannot be denied that the explosion was the direct cause of the plaintiff's injuries." So it was a substantial factor in producing the result—there was here a natural and continuous sequence—direct connection. The only intervening cause was that instead of blowing her to the ground the concussion smashed the weighing machine which in turn fell upon her. There was no remoteness in time, little in space. And surely, given such an explosion as here it needed no great foresight to predict that the natural result would be to injure one on the platform at no greater distance from its scene than was the plaintiff. Just how no one might be able to predict. Whether by flying fragments, by broken glass, by wreckage of machines or structures no one could say. But injury in some form was most probable.

Under these circumstances I cannot say as a matter of law that the plaintiff's injuries were not the proximate result of the negligence. That is all we have before us. The court refused to so charge. No request was made to submit the matter to the jury as a question of fact, even would that have been proper upon the record before us.

The judgment appealed from should be affirmed, with costs.

Pound, Lehman and Kellogg, JJ., concur with Cardozo, C.J.; Andrews, J., dissents in opinion in which Crane and O'Brien, JJ., concur.

Judgment reversed, etc.

定。我们已经说了很多遍。应该预见到什么？人类不会预见到一场撞车事故可能会伤害到一个街区外的人。相反，若存在爆炸，便有理由预见到这种可能性。我认为，法院讲到的关于直接联系的预见问题，假设爆炸是可以预见的，司机至少应该对爆炸产生的直接结果承担责任。

有人可能会说这不正当。为什么？要做到公平，他需要对自己的过失所产生的所有损害都进行赔偿。我们说他不需要对由自己过错造成的所有后果承担责任，这并不是为了善待他。我们回顾那场灾难，由火星引燃了大火，或者引起了爆炸。我们在追究后果时并没有无限制地追究下去，而是到某一个点为止。要使我们确定这个临界点，我们要问这样一个问题：在火灾或爆炸发生后一般还会发生什么？

最后一个问题正是帮助我们判决这个案件的要素。被告需要承担责任的行为就是打翻了一个看似无害的包裹，将其掉在了站台上。这个行为是过失行为。被告需要对行为产生的直接后果承担责任。如果包裹内的东西被打碎，那么被告需要对包裹的主人承担责任；如果包裹掉在一名乘客的脚上，并使其骨折，那么被告需要对该乘客承担责任。如果包裹爆炸并炸伤了附近的人，那么被告需要对他承担责任，就像在例子中司机需要对 A 承担责任一样。Palsgraf 太太站在一定距离之外。从案卷中无法得知她到底有多远——可能 25 至 30 英尺开外。也可能没有那么远。如果不是因为爆炸，她不会受到伤害。我们从上诉人的诉讼摘要获知"不能否认，爆炸是造成原告受伤的直接原因"。因此，爆炸是造成结果的实质性因素——这里有一个自然的连续性的顺序——直接联系。唯一的介入原因是，爆炸没有将她冲倒在地，反而是冲击波打碎了一台称重器，称重器砸在了原告的身上。这里没有时间的间隔，距离也不是太远。可以肯定的是，假设出现了这里的这种爆炸，不需要太多的远见便可以预见到，爆炸自然而然地会伤害到站在站台上的人，这个人站的距离不会超过原告的距离。只是没有人可以预测发生伤害的方式是什么。究竟是被飞起来的碎片伤到，还是被破碎的玻璃伤到，还是被机器或建筑物的残片伤到，没有人说得清。但是发生某种形式的伤害是极其可能的。

在这样的情况下，我不能说，作为法律问题，原告受到的伤害不是过失行为的直接结果。这就是我们所面对的问题。法院拒绝作出这样的裁判。没有人要求将这一问题作为事实问题提交给陪审团裁断，即使从我们面前的案卷来看，提交给陪审团是更合适的做法。

应当维持被上诉的判决，由败诉方承担费用。

Pound 法官、Lehman 法官和 Kellogg 法官同意 Cardozo 大法官的意见。Crane 法官和 O'Brien 法官同意 Andrews 法官的反对意见。

撤销被判决，等等。

15. United States v. Carroll Towing Co., 159 F.2d 169 (2d Cir. 1947)

Second Circuit, Court of Appeals, United States

L. Hand, J....

It appears...that there is no general rule to determine when the absence of a bargee or other attendant will make the owner of the barge liable for injuries to other vessels if she breaks away from her moorings. However, in any cases where he would be so liable for injuries to others, obviously he must reduce his damages proportionately, if the injury is to his own barge. It becomes apparent why there can be no such general rule, when we consider the grounds for such a liability. Since there are occasions when every vessel will break from her moorings, and since, if she does, she becomes a menace to those about her; the owner's duty, as in other similar situations, to provide against resulting injuries is a function of three variables: (1) The probability that she will break away; (2) the gravity of the resulting injury, if she does; (3) the burden of adequate precautions. Possibly it serves to bring this notion into relief to state it in algebraic terms: if the probability be called P; the injury L; and the burden, B; liability depends upon whether B is less than L multiplied by P: i.e., whether $B < PL$. Applied to the situation at bar, the likelihood that a barge will break from her fasts and the damage she will do, vary with the place and time; for example, if a storm threatens, the danger is greater; so it is, if she is in a crowded harbor where moored barges are constantly being shifted about. On the other hand, the barge must not be the bargee's prison, even though he lives aboard; he must go ashore at times. We need not say whether, even in such crowded waters as New York Harbor a bargee must be aboard at night at all; it may be that the custom is otherwise...and that, if so, the situation is one where custom should control. We leave that question open; but we hold that it is not in all cases a sufficient answer to a bargee's absence without excuse, during working hours, that he has properly made fast his barge to a pier, when he leaves her. In the case at bar the bargee left at five o'clock in the afternoon of January 3rd, and the flotilla broke away at about two o'clock in the afternoon of the following day, twenty-one hours afterwards. The bargee had been away all the time, and we hold that his fabricated story was affirmative evidence that he had no excuse for his absence. At the locus in quo—especially during the short January days and in the full tide of war activity—barges were being constantly "drilled" in and out. Certainly it was not beyond reasonable expectation that, with the inevitable haste and bustle, the work might not be done with adequate care. In such circumstances we hold—and it is all that we do hold—that it was a fair requirement that the owner of the barge, should have a bargee aboard (unless he had some excuse for his absence), during the working hours of daylight.

15. United States v. Carroll Towing Co., 159 F.2d 169 (2d Cir. 1947)

美国联邦上诉法院第二巡回法庭

L. Hand 法官主笔……

看起来……并不存在一个一般规则来决定船员或者其他服务人员何时离开将会使得驳船的所有者对其他突然从其停泊处离开的船只造成的损失负责。但是，在任何情况下，只要其对他人的伤害负有责任，如果该伤害是对他自己的驳船，他就必须相应比例地减少他的损害赔偿金。在我们考虑这样的一个责任基础的时候，没有这样一个一般规则的原因很清楚。因为在有些场合，每一艘船都可能会从其停泊处脱离，因此，如果其脱离了，就变成了那些在它周围的船的威胁；所有人的义务，就像在其他类似情况下一样，就是提供所导致的损害函数的三种变量：（1）其脱离的可能性；（2）所致损害的程度（如果其脱离了）；（3）充分预防的成本负担。或许它的作用在于把该观念缩减为用数学公式来表达：如果可能性被看做是 P，损害是 L，成本（burden）是 B，那么责任就取决于 B 是否会小于 L 乘以 P，即判断是否 B<PL。应用到当前的情形中，驳船脱离其固定处的可能性和其将产生的损害，将会因为地点和时间的不同而不同。例如，如果有风暴威胁，危险可能很大；确实如此，如果其处在一个拥挤的港口，停泊的船只进进出出。另外一方面，驳船不是船员的监狱，即使他生活其上，他必然有时会上岸。我们不能说，即使是在这样一个像纽约港一样拥挤的水域，船员是否必须整夜待在船上；习惯也许是另外一种情况……如果是这样，这种情形下就应该按照习惯处理。我们对这个问题持开放态度；但是我们认为，船员离开时将驳船栓牢，这并不构成在任何情况下船员在工作时间没有理由离开的充分答辩。在审案件中，船员在 1 月 3 日下午 5 点离开，该小型船队大概在第二天下午 2 点脱离，即在 21 个小时之后。船员在此期间一直处于离开状态，我们认为他所造成的事实是一个肯定的关于其没有离开借口的证据。在这一点上——特别是在 1 月白天较短和波涛汹涌的涨潮之时——驳船被"反复操练"进出频繁。在不可避免的匆忙中，工作没有尽到完全的注意，其当然没有超出合理预期。在此情形下，我们认定——这就是我们认定的所有事实——驳船的所有者应当要求其船员在白天工作时间待在船上，除非有离开的某些借口。

16. Bolton v Stone [1951] AC 850

House of Lords, United Kingdom

The facts, as stated by Lord Porter, were as follows:- On August 9, 1947, Miss Stone, the plaintiff, was injured by a cricket ball while standing on the highway outside her house, No. 10 Beckenham Road, Cheetham Hill, Manchester. The ball was hit by a batsman playing in a match on the Cheetham Cricket Ground which was adjacent to the highway. She brought an action for damages against the committee and members of the club. The striker of the ball, a member of a visiting team, was not a defendant.

The club had been in existence, and matches regularly played on this ground, since about 1864. Beckenham Road was constructed and built up in 1910. For the purpose of its lay-out, the builder made an arrangement with the club that a small strip of ground at the Beckenham Road end should be exchanged for a strip at the other end. The match pitches had always been, and still were, kept along a line opposite the pavilion, which was the mid-line of the original ground. The effect was that for a straight drive - the hit in the case in question - Beckenham Road had for some years been a few yards nearer the batsman than the opposite end. The cricket field, at the point at which the ball left it, was protected by a fence seven feet high but the upward slope of the ground was such that the top of the fence was some seventeen feet above the cricket pitch. The distance from the striker to the fence was about seventy-eight yards, not ninety yards as Oliver, J., stated, and to the place where the plaintiff was hit just under 100 yards.

Beckenham Road was an ordinary side-road giving access to private houses. It followed the western half of the northern edge of the ground, with houses on the far side only, and then, approximately opposite the line of the wickets, turned northeastwards with houses thereafter on both sides of the highway. The plaintiff's house was the second after the house in the angle of the turn. Opposite there was a row of six houses, No. 11, occupied by one Brownson, standing nearest the ground, with its side towards the northern boundary, and being substantially closer to it than the spot where the plaintiff was injured.

Brownson, giving evidence, said that five or six times during the last few years he had known balls hit his house or come into the yard. His evidence was vague as to the number of occasions. Members of the club of twenty years' standing or more agreed, in evidence, that the hit was altogether exceptional in comparison with anything previously seen on that ground. They also said (and Oliver, J., accepted their evidence) that it was only very rarely indeed that a ball was hit over the fence during a match. A club member of thirty-three years' standing said that he knew of no complaints of balls being hit into the road. Another member estimated that balls had been hit into that road about six times in twenty-eight years, but said that there had been no previous accident,

16. Bolton v Stone [1951] AC 850

联合王国上议院

  Porter 大法官确认了如下事实：原告 Stone 小姐住在曼彻斯特 Cheetham 山上的 Beckenham 路 10 号。1947 年 8 月 9 日，她在其住宅外的公路上，被一个板球击中而受伤。击伤原告的球是被一位击球手在一场举办于 Cheetham 板球场的比赛上击打出去的，Cheetham 板球场与涉事公路相邻。原告因此提起诉讼，要求涉事俱乐部的管委会和其成员赔偿其损失。至于实际击打板球的击球手（该选手来自客队），则并没有被作为被告。

  涉事俱乐部自 1864 年就一直存在，并经常在其板球场上举办比赛。而 Beckenham 路则是 1910 年才建设的。出于布局的考虑，这条路的建设者和涉事俱乐部达成协议：俱乐部将 Beckenham 路一侧的板球场场地的一部分交给道路的建设方以拓宽该路，而球场缩小的部分则在另一侧得到补偿。球场的投球区（pitch）一直是设在一条正对着板球亭的球场线上的，这条线本来是球场的中线，在修路之后则不再是球场中线。如此，修路就产生了这样的后果：在击球手打出了直线抽击（straight drive）的情况下（本案就是这样的情况），好几年来，Beckenham 路要比另一侧到击球手的距离更近。板球场的边界是由 7 英尺高的栅栏围起来的；然而由于场地向上倾斜，栅栏的顶部大概比投球区高 17 英尺。击球手到栅栏的距离并非 Oliver 法官所认为的 90 码，而是只有 78 码；击球手到原告被球击中的地方，则相距不到 100 码。

  Beckenham 路是通向私人住宅的小路。它紧靠球场的北部边缘延伸开来，在三柱门线的位置折向东北。在紧靠球场北部的部分，只有远离球场的一侧有房屋，在折向东北的部分，则道路两侧都有房屋。原告家住在拐角处的第二座房屋。此处有并排的六栋房屋。其中第 11 号为一位叫做 Brownson 的人所居住。该房屋是离板球场最近的，房屋的一侧刚好正对着球场的北部边界，远近于原告受伤的案发地点。

  Brownson 作证：据他所知，过去数年间，他的房子有数次被板球击中，有时板球也会被打进他的院子。他的证词并未明确这种事件发生的次数。板球俱乐部中的一些有 20 年或以上会籍的成员认为，相比于球场上发生的其他事，球打到房子是非常异常的。他们同时指出（Oliver 法官采信了这些证言），球被打出球场周围的栅栏，是极其罕见的。一位有 33 年会籍的老成员指出，他从未听说过有人投诉球被打到了街上。另一位成员则估计在 28 年中，球可

so far as he knew.

The plaintiff claimed damages in respect of injuries said to be caused by the defendants' negligence or as the result of a nuisance for which they were responsible. The particulars of negligence were that they "(A) pitched the cricket pitch too near to the said road; (B) failed to erect a ... fence ... of sufficient height to prevent balls being struck into the said road; (C) failed to ensure that cricket balls would not be hit into the said road".

On the facts found by him Oliver, J., acquitted the defendants of negligence and held that nuisance was not established. The Court of Appeal, reversing this decision, held that a public nuisance was not established but that the defendants were guilty of negligence and were liable in damages. The defendants appealed to the House of Lords.

LORD OAKSEY.

My Lords, I have come to the conclusion in this difficult case that Oliver, J.'s decision ought to be restored.

Cricket has been played for about ninety years on the ground in question and no ball has been proved to have struck anyone on the highways near the ground until the respondent was struck, nor has there been any complaint to the appellants. In such circumstances was it the duty of the appellants, who are the committee of the club, to take some special precautions other than those they did take to prevent such an accident as happened? The standard of care in the law of negligence is the standard of an ordinarily careful man, but in my opinion an ordinarily careful man does not take precautions against every foreseeable risk. He can, of course, foresee the possibility of many risks, but life would be almost impossible if he were to attempt to take precautions against every risk which he can foresee. He takes precautions against risks which are reasonably likely to happen. Many foreseeable risks are extremely unlikely to happen and cannot be guarded against except by almost complete isolation. The ordinarily prudent owner of a dog does not keep his dog always on a lead on a country highway for fear it may cause injury to a passing motor cyclist, nor does the ordinarily prudent pedestrian avoid the use of the highway for fear of skidding motor cars. It may very well be that after this accident the ordinarily prudent committee man of a similar cricket ground would take some further precaution, but that is not to say that he would have taken a similar precaution before the accident. The case of Castle v. St. Augustine's Links Ld. is obviously distinguishable on the facts and there is nothing in the judgment to suggest that a nuisance was created by the first ball that fell on the road there in question.

There are many footpaths and highways adjacent to cricket grounds and golf courses on to which cricket and golf balls are occasionally driven, but such risks are habitually treated both by the owners and committees of such cricket and golf courses and by the pedestrians who use the adjacent footpaths and highways as negligible and it is not, in my opinion, actionable negligence not to take precautions to avoid such risks.

能只有 6 次被打到了街上，并且据他所知没有一次酿成了事故。

原告则根据两个诉由请求被告承担损害赔偿责任：一个诉由是"过失"，另一个诉由则是"妨害"。对于"过失"之诉，原告具体主张以下事实构成了被告的过失：首先，被告把板球场建得离道路太近了；其次，被告没有竖立足够高的、能够避免板球被打到道路上的栅栏；最后，被告没有采取措施来确保球不会被打到路上。

依据 Oliver 法官所确认的事实，他否认被告存在过失，同时也否认了被告的行为构成妨害。上诉法院维持了公有妨害并不成立的判决，但就被告的过失问题进行了改判，认定被告存在过失并因此需要承担损害赔偿责任。被告因此上诉到上议院。

Oaksey 大法官主笔：

各位大法官，我对这个疑难案件的结论是应当推翻上诉法院的判决，维持 Oliver 法官的判决。

在这座球场上，人们打板球已经打了约 90 年的时间。直到被上诉人被击伤之前，并没有证据证明有人曾在球场附近的公路上被球击中，因此上诉人也没有收到过任何这类的投诉。在这样的前提下，上诉人（也就是俱乐部的管委会）是否有义务采取其他的预防措施，来防止像本案中这样的事故？过失之诉中的过失标准是一般理性人的标准；而这种标准在我看来，是并不要求对所有可预见的风险采取预防措施的。一个人当然是可以预见到许多事故是有发生的可能性的，然而如果他试图采取预防措施应对他可以预见的每一种风险，生活就几乎过不下去了。许多风险虽然是可预见的，但是却是极其不可能发生的，因此一个人除非与世隔绝，否则是不可能防范相应的事故发生的。乡村公路上的一般谨慎的狗主人不会仅仅因为害怕他的狗会对经过的摩托车骑手造成伤害，就一直给他的狗系上狗绳；一般谨慎的行人也不会仅仅因为汽车可能打滑就不上公路。发生了本案这样的事故之后，类似的板球场的管委会成员如果是一般谨慎的，很可能会采取一定的预防措施，但这并不是说他在事故发生之前就会采取类似的预防措施。*Castle v. St. Augustine's Links Ltd* 这一判例在其事实上显然跟本案是有区别的，并且即便根据这个判决也并不能推出第一个落在涉案道路上的球就构成妨害。

板球场和高尔夫球场附近有许多人行道和公路，板球和高尔夫球偶尔会被打到这些路上。然而这类风险，不论对板球场和高尔夫球场的所有者或管委会，还是对使用相邻道路的行人，一般都被认为是可以忽略不计的。因此，

LORD REID

My Lords, it was readily foreseeable that an accident such as befell the respondent might possibly occur during one of the appellants' cricket matches. Balls had been driven into the public road from time to time and it was obvious that, if a person happened to be where a ball fell, that person would receive injuries which might or might not be serious. On the other hand it was plain that the chance of that happening was small. The exact number of times a ball has been driven into the road is not known, but it is not proved that this has happened more than about six times in about thirty years. If I assume that it has happened on the average once in three seasons I shall be doing no injustice to the respondent's case. Then there has to be considered the chance of a person being hit by a ball falling in the road. The road appears to be an ordinary side road giving access to a number of private houses, and there is no evidence to suggest that the traffic on this road is other than what one might expect on such a road. On the whole of that part of the road where a ball could fall there would often be nobody and seldom any great number of people. It follows that the chance of a person ever being struck even in a long period of years was very small.

This case, therefore raises sharply the question what is the nature and extent of the duty of a person who promotes on his land operations which may cause damage to persons on an adjoining highway. Is it that he must not carry out or permit an operation which he knows or ought to know clearly can cause such damage, however improbable that result may be, or is it that he is only bound to take into account the possibility of such damage if such damage is a likely or probable consequence of what he does or permits, or if the risk of damage is such that a reasonable man, careful of the safety of his neighbour, would regard that risk as material?

I do not know of any case where this question has had to be decided or even where it has been fully discussed. Of course there are many cases in which somewhat similar questions have arisen. but generally speaking if injury to another person from the defendants' acts is reasonably foreseeable the chance that injury will result is substantial and it does not matter in which way the duty is stated. In such cases I do not think that much assistance is to be got from analysing the language which a judge has used. More assistance is to be got from cases where judges have clearly chosen their language with care in setting out a principle, but even so, statements of the law must be read in light of the facts of the particular case. Nevertheless, making all allowances for this, I do find at least a tendency to base duty rather on the likelihood of damage to others than on its foreseeability alone.

The definition of negligence which has perhaps been most often quoted is that of Alderson, B., in *Blyth v. Birmingham Waterworks Co.*: "Negligence is the omission to do something which a reasonable man, guided upon those considerations which ordinarily regulate the conduct of human affairs, would do, or doing something which a prudent and reasonable man would not do". I think that reasonable men do in fact take into account the degree of risk and do not act on a bare

在我看来，未对这类风险采取预防措施，并不是可诉的过失。

Reid 大法官主笔：

各位大法官。上诉人所举办的板球比赛是非常可能造成这次发生在被上诉人身上的这类事故的，而且这种事故也是可预见的：板球不时地会落入公共道路，而很明显，如果一个人碰巧处在球的落点，这个人会受到伤害，不管这种伤害是严重还是不严重。但是从另一个角度来看，这种情况发生的机会，明显是很小的：板球落入公共道路的确切次数虽然不清楚，但没有证据证明在过去的大约三十年中，这种情况发生了六次以上。如果我假设这种情况平均仅仅每三个季度发生一次，那么满足被上诉人的请求就并非是不公正的。然后，我们还必须考虑下一个人被落在路上的板球击中的机会。看起来，这条道路是一条通向私人住宅的普通小路，而且没有证据表明这条道路上的人流量与一般的这种小路上的人流量有什么不同。在可能落下板球的那部分道路上，通常是一个人也没有的，有很多人经过的情况更是极少的。因此我们可以说，板球击中行人的可能性，即使放在很长一段时间内，也是很小的。

本案的焦点其实是，如果一个人在自己的土地上从事可能损害到邻近道路上的他人的活动，那么他应该负担何种性质的责任及这种责任的范围。一种可能是只要他知道或者应该知道某个活动会对他人造成损害，即便该损害是的概率是非常非常低的，他也不应该开展或者批准开展这个活动；另一种可能是只有活动非常可能造成损害，他才必须将这种可能的损害列入考量因素；最后一种可能性只有在一个会考虑到其邻居福祉的一般理性人看来，这种活动的风险是重大时，这个活动的批准者或者实施者才应该承担责任。

据我所知，本案的这个焦点问题并未被之前的判例所判决过，甚至没有深入地讨论过。毋庸置疑，之前的判例中肯定有很多类似的情况。然而，总体来说在之前的案件中，只要被告的行为对他人的损害是合理可预期的，那么这种损害发生的可能性就是极大的，因此无论我们采取上述的哪一种责任的标准，结果都没有太大的区别。所以，对于之前的这些判例，我并不认为去细究其中法官所使用的词句有什么帮助。那种法官的用语明确表明其希望设置一种原则的判决能提供多一点的帮助，但即便是这种案件，其对法律的表达也需要和案件的具体事实结合起来一起分析。然而，考虑到这一点，我确实发现了一种趋势：责任的构成现在不仅需要对损害后果可预见性，还需要考虑这种损害的可能性。

对于"过失"一词的定义，我们所最常引用的也许是财税法院 Alderson 法官在 *Blyth v Birmingham Waterworks Co.* 一案中的判词："所谓过失，是指不去做理性人在通常规范指导着人类事务的那种考虑的指引之下会做的事情，或者做了谨慎理性人不会做的事情。"而我认为，一个理性人在考虑做或不做某件事时，

possibility as they would if the risk were more substantial.

A more recent attempt to find a basis for a man's legal duty to his neighbour is that of Lord Atkin in *Donoghue v. Stevenson*. I need not quote the whole passage: for this purpose the important part is: "You must take reasonable care to avoid acts or omissions which you can reasonably foresee would be likely to injure your neighbour". Parts of Lord Atkin's statement have been criticized as being too wide, but I am not aware that it has been stated that any part of it is too narrow. Lord Atkin does not say "which you can reasonably foresee could injure your neighbour": he introduces the limitation "would be likely to injure your neighbour".

Counsel for the respondent in this case had to put his case so high as to say that, at least as soon as one ball had been driven into the road in the ordinary course of a match, the appellants could and should have realized that that might happen again and that, if it did, someone might be injured; and that that was enough to put on the appellants a duty to take steps to prevent such an occurrence. If the true test is foreseeability alone I think that must be so. Once a ball has been driven on to a road without there being anything extraordinary to account for the fact, there is clearly a risk that another will follow, and if it does there is clearly a chance, small though it may be, that someone may be injured. On the theory that it is foreseeability alone that matters it would be irrelevant to consider how often a ball might be expected to land in the road and it would not matter whether the road was the busiest street, or the quietest country lane; the only difference between these cases is in the degree of risk.

It would take a good deal to make me believe that the law has departed so far from the standards which guide ordinary careful people in ordinary life. In the crowded conditions of modern life even the most careful person cannot avoid creating some risks and accepting others. What a man must not do, and what I think a careful man tries not to do, is to create a risk which is substantial. Of course there are numerous cases where special circumstances require that a higher standard shall be observed and where that is recognized by the law. But I do not think that this case comes within any such special category. It was argued that this case comes within the principle in *Rylands v. Fletcher*, but I agree with your Lordships that there is no substance in this argument. In my judgment the test to be applied here is whether the risk of damage to a person on the road was so small that a reasonable man in the position of the appellants, considering the matter from the point of view of safety, would have thought it right to refrain from taking steps to prevent the danger.

In considering that matter I think that it would be right to take into account not only how remote is the chance that a person might be struck but also how serious the consequences are likely to be if a person is struck; but I do not think that it would be right to take into account the difficulty of remedial measures. If cricket cannot be played on a ground without creating a substantial risk, then it should not be played there at all. I think that this is in substance the test which Oliver, J.,

一定会考虑到这么做的风险的大小，而不会只考虑这么做是不是有造成损害的可能性；风险大和风险小时，理性人是否会行动的可能性是不一样的。

最近 Atkin 大法官在 *Donoghue v Stevenson* 一案中，再一次尝试了给一个人对他邻居的义务找一个法律基础。为了表达这个目的，我只需引用以下内容："你需要尽到一定的注意义务，以避免那些你可以预见到的，很可能会损害你的邻居的作为或者不作为行为。"Atkin 大法官的话被有些人批评太宽泛，但据我所知好像没有人说他的话太狭窄。Atkin 大法官并没有说"那些你可以预见到的可能会损害你的邻居的"；他加了一个限定成分"那些很可能会损害你的邻居的"。

如果被上诉人的律师要赢的话，他需要提出一个非常高的标准。根据这个标准，只要在正常的比赛中，至少有一个球落在了那条道路上，上诉人就可能并且应该预见到这种事会再次发生，并且只要它再次发生，有人就有可能会因此受伤；并且，这种预见义务足够给上诉人施加采取相应措施避免事故发生的义务。如果责任的构成仅仅需要可预见性这一个要件，那么我觉得上诉人的律师需要提出的这个标准是正确的。一旦有一个球落到了道路上，那么只要在没有其他的特殊情况下，显然会有下一个球同样落在道路上，如果真是这样，那么即便可能性很小，显然也会有人因此受伤。根据只需要可预见性这一个要件的理论，讨论板球落在道路上的频率有多高是没有意义的；并且涉案道路是繁忙的大道还是僻静的小路也是无关紧要的，因为这些情节的不同，仅仅影响产生损害的风险的程度。

如果法律是这样规定的话，它便会极大地偏离指导负有一般注意义务的人在日常生活中如何行动的准则，这将使我难以置信。在现代社会这样拥挤的生活条件下，即便是最谨慎的人也很难避免会制造一些风险，同时也会承受另外一些风险。人们所不被允许做的，同时也是谨慎的人会尝试避免的，只是不要制造重大的风险。毋庸置疑，某些特殊的情形要求人们遵守更高的注意标准，这些情形往往也会被法律所规定。然而，我并不认为本案属于这些法定的特别类型。有人主张本案应该被 *Rylands v Fletcher* 一案所确立的原则所调整，但我认为这种说法毫无道理。在我看来，我们在本案中需要考虑的是，本案涉及的行为对路上行人的损害风险足够得小，以至于跟上诉人面对同样情形的理性人考虑到安全性时，会认为不采取措施去避免危险是正确的。

对于这个问题，我认为考虑有人被砸中的可能有多小是正确的，考虑一旦被砸中后果有多严重也是正确的。然而我不认为我们需要考虑采取避免的措施有多困难。如果在一块场地上打板球时很难避免给别人造成危险，那么就根本不该在这里打。我认为，我的这种说法和 Oliver 法官所采取的标准是一致的。他考虑了上诉人是否为使用目的提供了足够大的场地因而足够安全，

applied in his case. He considered whether the appellants' ground was large enough to be safe for all practical purposes and held that it was. This is a question not of law but of fact and degree. It is not an easy question and it is one on which opinions may well differ. I can only say that having given the whole matter repeated and anxious consideration I find myself unable to decide this question in favour of the respondent. But I think that this case is not far from the borderline. If this appeal is allowed, that does not in my judgment mean that in every case where cricket has been played on a ground for a number of years without accident or complaint those who organize matches there are safe to go on in reliance on past immunity. I would have reached a different conclusion if I had thought that the risk here had been other than extremely small, because I do not think that a reasonable man considering the matter from the point of view of safety would or should disregard any risk unless it is extremely small.

…In my judgment the appeal should be allowed.

LORD RADCLIFFE.

My Lords, I agree that this appeal must be allowed. I agree with regret, because I have much sympathy with the decision that commended itself to the majority of the members of the Court of Appeal. I can see nothing unfair in the appellants being required to compensate the respondent for the serious injury that she has received as a result of the sport that they have organized on their cricket ground at Cheetham Hill. But the law of negligence is concerned less with what is fair than with what is culpable, and I cannot persuade myself that the appellants have been guilty of any culpable act or omission in this case.

Those being the facts, a breach of duty has taken place if they show the appellants guilty of a failure to take reasonable care to prevent the accident. One may phrase it as "reasonable care" or "ordinary care" or "proper care" - all these phrases are to be found in decisions of authority - but the fact remains that, unless there has been something which a reasonable man would blame as falling beneath the standard of conduct that he would set for himself and require of his neighbour, there has been no breaks of legal duty. And here, I think, the respondent's case breaks down. It seems to me that a reasonable man, taking account of the chances against an accident happening, would not have felt himself called upon either to abandon the use of the ground for cricket or to increase the height of his surrounding fences. He would have done what the appellants did: in other words, he would have done nothing. Whether, if the unlikely event of an accident did occur and his play turn to another's hurt, he would have thought it equally proper to offer no more consolation to his victim than the reflection that a social being is not immune from social risks, I do not say, for I do not think that that is a consideration which is relevant to legal liability.

I agree with the others of your Lordships that if the respondent cannot succeed in negligence she cannot succeed on any other head of claim.

他的结论是肯定的。这并不是一个法律问题,而是一个事实和程度的问题。这并不是一个容易回答的问题,对此,人们也是各执己见。我只能说,当我多次认真考虑了整个事件的经过之后,我很难作出有利于被上诉人的决定。但我认为,本案与那些边界案例的距离并不遥远。如果本案的上诉得到了支持,在我看来并不意味着,只要板球比赛在一块场地上举办了很多年而未造成事故或者投诉,板球比赛的组织者就可以根据过往的平安无事而毫无顾忌地继续举办比赛。如果我认为风险并非特别小,我可能就会得出不同的结论:因为在我看来,从安全的角度,理性人只有在风险非常小的时候才会忽略这些风险。

……在我看来,上诉应该得到支持。

Radcliffe 大法官主笔:

各位大法官,我赞同本案的上诉应该得到支持。我对此表示遗憾,因为我对上诉法院大多数法官作出的这一判决深表同情。被上诉人因为上诉人在 Cheetham Hill 的场地所组织的体育比赛而遭受了严重的伤害,因而要求上诉人对被上诉人进行赔偿,在我看来是完全公平的。然而,"过失之诉"所关注的更多的是加害人的可非难性,而非整个事件的公平,而我很难说服自己上诉人在本案中有什么过错,或者其作为或者不作为有什么可非难性。

如果已经查明的事实能够证明,被告因为未尽到合理的注意义务来避免事故的发生而有过错,则被告违反了义务这一点能够成立。这种注意义务,我们可以说它是"合理的注意""一般的注意"或者"适当的注意";以上的各种说法我们都能在以前的判例中找到。然而无论采取哪种说法,有一点是不变的:理性人会为自己的行为或者其邻居的行为设置一个标准,只有当某人的行为低于这个行为标准因而受到理性人的谴责时,他才违反了法定的义务。而在我看来,在本案中被上诉人的主张很难得到支持。在我看来,一个考虑到了事故发生概率的理性人,既不会觉得有必要去放弃这块土地作为球场的用途,也不会去加高球场周围栅栏的高度。他只会做本案中上诉人所做的事——那就是什么也不做。当这种极不可能发生的事故确实发生了,而且他人确实因此遭受了伤害时,就算此时肇事者对受害人的安慰仅仅是"人对来自社会的风险是无法避免的",我也只能默不作声,因为肇事者这么做是否正当和他是否应该承担法律责任,是毫无关系的两件事。

我同样赞同各位大法官的意见:如果被上诉人不能在"过失"这个诉由上胜诉,他也不能在任何其他的诉由上胜诉。

17. Bolam v Friern Hospital Management Committee [1957] 1 WLR 582

Queen's Bench Division, High Court, United Kingdom

MCNAIR J.

Members of the jury, ... it is right that I should say this, that you must look at this case in its proper perspective. You have been told by Dr. Page that he had only seen one acetabular fracture in 50,000 cases, involving a quarter of a million treatments, and it is clear, is it not, that the particular injury which produced these disastrous results in the plaintiff is one of extreme rarity. Another fact which I think it is right that you should bear in mind is this, that whereas some years ago when a patient went into a mental institution afflicted with mental illness, suffering from one of the most terrible ills from which a man can suffer, he had very little hope of recovery — in most cases he could only expect to be carefully and kindly treated until in due course merciful death released him from his sufferings — today, according to the evidence, the position is entirely changed. The evidence shows that today a man who enters one of these institutions suffering from particular types of mental disorder has a real chance of recovery. Dr. Marshall told you that in his view that change was due almost entirely to the introduction of physical methods of treatment of mental illness, and of those physical methods the electric convulsive therapy (E.C.T) which you have been considering during the last few days is the most important. When you approach this case and consider whether it has been proved against this hospital that negligence was committed, you have to consider that against that background, and bearing in mind the enormous benefits which are conferred upon unfortunate men and women by this form of treatment.

Another general comment which I would make is this: on the evidence it is clear, is it not, that the use of E.C.T. is a progressive science. You have had it traced for you historically over the quite few years in which it has been used in this country, and you may think on the evidence that even today there is no standard settled technique upon all points, to which all competent doctors will agree. The doctors called before you have mentioned in turn different variants of the technique they use. Some use restraining sheets, some use relaxants, some use manual control; but the final question you have got to make up your minds about is this, whether Dr. Allfrey, following upon the practice he had learnt at Friern and following upon the technique which he had shown to him by Dr. Bastarrechea, was negligent in failing to use relaxant drugs or, if he decided not to use relaxant drugs, that he was negligent in failing to exercise any manual control over the patient beyond merely arranging for his shoulders to be held, the chin supported, a gag used, and a pillow put under his back. No one suggests that there was any negligence in the diagnosis or in the decision to use E.C.T. Furthermore, no one suggests that Dr. Allfrey or anyone at the hospital was in any way indifferent to the care of their patients. The only question is really a question of professional skill.

Before I turn to that, I must tell you what in law we mean by "negligence." In the ordinary

17. Bolam v Friern Hospital Management Committee [1957] 1 WLR 582

联合王国高等法院王座分庭

Mcnair 法官主笔：

各位陪审员，……我有必要提醒大家，应从正确的角度看待本案。Page 医生已经告诉诸位，在 25 万起诊断中，他发现髋臼骨折的概率是五万分之一；同时，原告所遭受到的这种灾难性的伤害是及其罕见的。我觉得还应当提醒诸位的是，若干年前当患有人类所能罹患的最严重的精神疾病的病人走进精神病院时，他康复的希望是极其渺茫的——在大部分情况下，病人所能期望的不过是被用心、善良地照顾，直到大限来临死神帮他解脱。而从今天的证据来看，情况完全变了。证据表明，今天，因为罹患某种精神疾病而进入精神病院的病人是完全有希望康复的。Marshall 医生已经告诉诸位这种变化完全是因为物理治疗方法的应用；在这些物理治疗方法中，很多人认为电抽搐疗法（简称 ECT）是近些年来最重要的。当诸位考虑本案中医院的过错是否得到了证明时，诸位应将上述背景事实纳入考量因素，并应考虑到这种疗法给那些不幸的男人和女人所到来的巨大的益处。

还有一点我要跟大家交代：证据表明 ECT 的使用是一个很明显的科学进步。我们已经回顾了最近几年本国适用 ECT 的历史，诸位可能会发现，证据表明，即便是今天依然不存在所有合格医生都同意的关于所有要点的技术标准。出庭作证的各位医生们已经向诸位依次提及了他们所适用的不同的技术。他们有的用的是约束带，有的用的是松弛剂，还有的用的是手动控制的方法。然而诸位需要回答的关键问题是，Allfrey 医生，根据他在 Friern 所学到的操作流程和 Bastarrechea 医生所展示给他的技术，没有使用松弛剂是否属于过失，在实施人工控制的过程中仅仅按住了病人的肩膀、仅仅撑起了她的下巴、仅仅塞住了他的嘴巴、仅仅在他的背后放了一个枕头是否属于过失。至于在诊断中决定使用 ECT 属于过失这一点，则没有任何人提出。同样也没有人提出 Allfrey 医生或者医院中的任何其他人对于病人的照顾有任何不尽心。因此本案唯一的焦点是一个关于职业技术的问题。

在我们讨论这一点之前，我有必要向诸位介绍一下什么是法律上的"过失"。在普通的不涉及任何专业技术的案件中，法律上的过失是指未做出相

case which does not involve any special skill, negligence in law means a failure to do some act which a reasonable man in the circumstances would do, or the doing of some act which a reasonable man in the circumstances would not do; and if that failure or the doing of that act results in injury, then there is a cause of action. How do you test whether this act or failure is negligent? In an ordinary case it is generally said you judge it by the action of the man in the street. He is the ordinary man. In one case it has been said you judge it by the conduct of the man on the top of a Clapham omnibus. He is the ordinary man. But where you get a situation which involves the use of some special skill or competence, then the test as to whether there has been negligence or not is not the test of the man on the top of a Clapham omnibus, because he has not got this special skill. The test is the standard of the ordinary skilled man exercising and professing to have that special skill. A man need not possess the highest expert skill; it is well established law that it is sufficient if he exercises the ordinary skill of an ordinary competent man exercising that particular art. I do not think that I quarrel much with any of the submissions in law which have been put before you by counsel. Mr. Fox-Andrews put it in this way, that in the case of a medical man, negligence means failure to act in accordance with the standards of reasonably competent medical men at the time. That is a perfectly accurate statement, as long as it is remembered that there may be one or more perfectly proper standards; and if he conforms with one of those proper standards, then he is not negligent. Mr. Fox-Andrews also was quite right, in my judgment, in saying that a mere personal belief that a particular technique is best is no defence unless that belief is based on reasonable grounds. That again is unexceptionable. But the emphasis which is laid by the defence is on this aspect of negligence, that the real question you have to make up your minds about on each of the three major topics is whether the defendants, in acting in the way they did, were acting in accordance with a practice of competent respected professional opinion. Mr. Stirling submitted that if you are satisfied that they were acting in accordance with a practice of a competent body of professional opinion, then it would be wrong for you to hold that negligence was established. In a recent Scottish case, *Hunter v. Hanley*, Lord President Clyde said:

> "In the realm of diagnosis and treatment there is ample scope for genuine difference of opinion and one man clearly is not negligent merely because his conclusion differs from that of other professional men, nor because he has displayed less skill or knowledge than others would have shown. The true test for establishing negligence in diagnosis or treatment on the part of a doctor is whether he has been proved to be guilty of such failure as no doctor of ordinary skill would be guilty of, if acting with ordinary care."

If that statement of the true test is qualified by the words "in all the circumstances," Mr. Fox-

应情况下理性人会做的事，或者做出了在相应的情况下理性人不会做的事；若该不作为或者作为导致了损害，则受害人就有了起诉的基础。那么我们如何判断一个作为或者不作为是否构成过失呢？在日常案件中，一般人认为我们是按照大街上的人的行为标准——这个人就是一般理性人。在一个案件中，法官认为应该按照在一辆 Clapham 的公交车上的人的行为标准——这个公交车上的人就是一般理性人。然而，当我们面临的问题涉及专业技能，我们就不能用 Clapham 的公交车上的人作为判断过失的标准了，因为他并不具备相应的技能。这里的判断标准是一般的通过练习和执业而获得该技能的人。我们并不要求一个人必须拥有最高等级的专家技能；实定法上只要他运用的技能达到了一个从事相关执业的一般的合格的人所运用的技能的程度即可。我不认为我对律师向诸位提交的任何法律意见书有什么意见。Fox-Andrews 先生认为，对于医生来说，过失意味着未能按照当时一般的合格的医生所遵守的标准从事医疗活动。这个表述是完全正确的，只要不忘记一点：所谓的合格的标准是有很多的，而只要当事人按照其中的一种行事，他就不属于过失。在我看来 Fox-Andrews 先生的另一个观点也是对的：个人的内心确信某个技术是最好的，除非这种确信是建立在合理的基础上的，否则其并不能作为很好的抗辩事由。这点也是无懈可击的。然而，这种抗辩事由的重点其实是在"过失"的这样一个方面：对于本案中的三个主要论题，其实最关键的需要诸位决定的是，各位被告人的行为是否符合一个合格的受人尊敬的专业意见的惯例。Stirling 先生认为，如果诸位同意相关的医生是按照一个合格的专业意见团体的惯例来行事的，同时又认可了他们有过失的意见，那么诸位就是在自相矛盾了。在一起最近的苏格兰判例 *Hunter v Hanley* 中，苏格兰最高民事法院院长 Clyde 说：

> 在诊断和治疗的领域，人们对很多问题都有不同的意见。因此不能仅仅因为一个人的结论和其他的专业人士不一样，或者仅仅因为他的技能或知识看起来比别人的更少，而得出他具有过失这种结论。在诊断和治疗领域判断过失的真正标准是，证明一个医生犯了任何其他的拥有一般程度的技能的医生只要尽到了一般的注意义务都不会犯的错误。

如果在上述的真正标准之中加上"在任何情况下"的限定语，Fox-Andrews 先生应该不会说这个说法所表达出来的观念与英格兰法相抵牾。其实，

Andrews would not seek to say that that expression of opinion does not accord with the English law. It is just a question of expression. I myself would prefer to put it this way, that he is not guilty of negligence if he has acted in accordance with a practice accepted as proper by a responsible body of medical men skilled in that particular art. I do not think there is much difference in sense. It is just a different way of expressing the same thought. Putting it the other way round, a man is not negligent, if he is acting in accordance with such a practice, merely because there is a body of opinion who would take a contrary view. At the same time, that does not mean that a medical man can obstinately and pig-headedly carry on with some old technique if it has been proved to be contrary to what is really substantially the whole of informed medical opinion. Otherwise you might get men today saying:

> "I do not believe in anaesthetics. I do not believe in antiseptics. I am going to continue to do my surgery in the way it was done in the eighteenth century."

That clearly would be wrong.

这不过是一个用语的问题。就我个人而言，我更喜欢这种说法："如果一个医生是按照一个负责任的有技术的医生团体所接受的做法来行事的，那么他便没有过失。"我认为我的说法和上面的说法其实在意思上没有太大差别，我们只是用了不同的说法来表达同样的思想。反过来说，一个人不会仅仅因为有一个团体持有相反的意见就被判定为具有过失。当然，我们不是说如果已经证明这种技术是为整个医学界所反对的，一个人仍有权利固执己见地使用某些过时的技术。否则，我们就会听到今天有人会这么说：

  我不相信麻醉，我不相信消毒剂。我会继续按照18世纪的手术方式来做手术。

这显然是错误的。

Chapter 3. Defenses

Section 1. Defences in Intentional Torts
A. Consent

18. O'Brien v. Cunard Steamship Co., 154 Mass. 272, 28 N.E. 266 (1891)

Supreme Judicial Court of Massachusetts, United States

Knowlton, J.

This case presents the question of whether there was any evidence to warrant the jury in finding that the defendant, by any of its servants or agents, committed a battery on the plaintiff.... To sustain this count, which was for an alleged battery, the plaintiff relied on the fact that the surgeon who was employed by the defendant vaccinated her on shipboard, while she was on her passage from Queenstown to Boston. On this branch of the case the question is whether there was any evidence that the surgeon used force upon the plaintiff against her will. In determining whether the act was lawful or unlawful, the surgeon's conduct must be considered in connection with the circumstances. If the plaintiff's behavior was such as to indicate consent on her part, he was justified in his act, whatever her unexpressed feelings may have been. In determining whether she consented, he could be guided only by her overt acts and the manifestations of her feelings. It is undisputed that at Boston there are strict quarantine regulations in regard to the examination of immigrants, to see that they are protected from small-pox by vaccination, and that only those persons who hold a certificate from the medical officer of the steamship, stating that they are so protected, are permitted to land without detention in quarantine or vaccination by the port physician. It appears that the defendant is accustomed to have its surgeons vaccinate all immigrants who desire it, and who are not protected by previous vaccination, and give them a certificate which is accepted at quarantine as evidence of their protection. Notices of the regulations at quarantine, and of the willingness of the ship's medical officer to vaccinate such as needed vaccination, were posted about the ship, in various languages, and on the day when the operation was performed the surgeon had a right to presume that she and the other women who were vaccinated understood the importance and purpose of vaccination for those who bore no marks to show that they were protected. By the plaintiff's testimony, which in this particular is undisputed, it appears that about

第三章 抗辩事由

第一节 故意侵权责任中的抗辩事由

一、同意

18. O'Brien v. Cunard Steamship Co., 154 Mass. 272, 28 N.E. 266 (1891)

美国马萨诸塞州最高法院

Knowlton 法官主笔：

本案提出了一个问题，即是否有证据确保陪审团查明，被告通过其雇员或代理人，向原告实施殴击行为……为支撑该声称为殴击的诉因，其依据的事实是被告雇佣的外科医生在原告从 Queenstown 到 Boston 的途中，在船上对她进行了预防接种。本案在这一点上的分歧在于，是否有证据证明医生违背原告的同意对其实施了强制。在确定医生的行为是否合法时，必须结合当时的环境进行考察。如果原告的行为显示出原告的同意，那么医生的行为便具有合理性，无论原告有无公开表达的感觉如何。而确定原告是否同意，医生只有通过原告公开的行为和感觉的表现形式来判断。无可争辩的是，Boston 对移民的检查中有严格的检疫规定，目的在于确定移民是否接种过天花疫苗，只有那些具有船上医务人员开具的证明他们已经接种过天花疫苗接种证明书的移民，才不会被扣留接受检疫或由港口医生接种而顺利上岸。被告似乎已经习惯于要求他的外科医生为所有过去没有接受过而且希望得到预防接种的移民进行免疫接种，并且为他们开具检疫部门接受的证明他们已经受过接种保护的证明书。检疫部门的通知以及船上的医务人员愿意为需要的人群提供免疫接种的说明，以多种语言张贴在轮船的各个角落，而且从实施接种的第一天起，医生便有权认为原告和其他接受接种的妇女已经理解对于那些没有接种记号以证明她们具有免疫力的人而言，免疫接种的重要性和目的是什么。在原告的证词中，这一细节是不存在争议的，但是约两百名妇女被集中在下面，

two hundred women passengers were assembled below, and she understood from conversation with them that they were to be vaccinated; that she stood about fifteen feet from the surgeon, and saw them form in a line and pass in turn before him; that he "examined their arms, and, passing some of them by, proceeded to vaccinate those that had no mark"; that she did not hear him say anything to any of them; that upon being passed by they each received a card and went on deck; that when her turn came she showed him her arm, and he looked at it and said there was no mark, and that she should be vaccinated; that she told him she had been vaccinated before and it left no mark; "that he then said nothing, that he should vaccinate her again"; that she held up her arm to be vaccinated; that no one touched her; that she did not tell him that she did not want to be vaccinated; and that she took the ticket which he gave her certifying that he had vaccinated her, and used it at quarantine. She was one of a large number of women who were vaccinated on that occasion, without, so far as appears, a word of objection from any of them. They all indicated by their conduct that they desired to avail themselves of the provisions made for their benefit. There was nothing in the conduct of the plaintiff to indicate to the surgeon that she did not wish to obtain a card which would save her from detention at quarantine, and to be vaccinated, if necessary, for that purpose. Viewing his conduct in the light of the circumstances, it was lawful; and there was no evidence tending to show that it was not. The ruling of the court on this part of the case was correct....

19. Barton v. Bee Line, Inc., 238 App. Div. 501, 265 N.Y.S. 284 (1933)

Appellate Division, Supreme Court of New York, United States

Lazansky, J.

Plaintiff appeals from an order setting aside the verdict of a jury in her favor and ordering a new trial. Plaintiff, who was fifteen years of age at the time, claimed that while a passenger of the defendant, a common carrier, she was forcibly raped by defendant's chauffeur. The chauffeur testified that she consented to their relations. It was conceded that if the chauffeur assaulted plaintiff while a passenger, defendant became liable in damages for failure to perform its duty as a common carrier to its passenger. The jury was charged that plaintiff was entitled to recover even if she consented, although consent might be considered in mitigation of damages. She had a verdict of $3,000. The court set the verdict aside on the ground that if plaintiff consented the verdict was excessive, while if she was outraged the verdict was inadequate. The court is not disposed to interfere with this exercise of discretion. The determination of the trial court was warranted for another reason which may be considered, since the verdict was set aside upon the other grounds set forth in section 549 of the Civil Practice Act as well as upon the ground that it was excessive.

It was error for the trial court to have instructed the jury that plaintiff was entitled to a

原告是从与其他妇女的交谈中才得知她们将接受免疫接种的；她站的位置离医生有 15 英尺远，她看到所有妇女排成一行，在医生面前一个一个地通过；医生"检查她们的胳膊，让一些人通过，然后在那些没有接种记号的人身上实施注射"；她没有听到医生对这些人讲的话；在医生面前通过的人都会得到一个卡片，然后回到甲板上；轮到她的时候，她把胳膊给医生看，医生说胳膊上没有接种记号，说她应该接受接种；然后她告诉医生她曾经接受过接种，但没有留下记号；"医生什么也没有说，他应该对她再次接种"；她举起胳膊接受了注射；没有人碰到她；她没有告诉医生她不想接受接种注射；她拿走了医生交给她的证明她已经接受过注射的卡片，并在检疫部门出示了该卡片。她是当时那种情况下接受接种注射的大批妇女中的其中一名，至少从表面上看，这些妇女都没有表达一个字的反对意见。她们的行为都显示出她们愿意接受这项有利于她们的服务。在医生看来，原告的行为丝毫没有显示出她不想接受那张可以使她免于被检疫扣留的卡片，不想为此而拒绝注射。从当时的情况来考察医生的行为，该行为是合法的；而且没有证据证明医生的行为不具有合法性。法院在本案中就这一部分的裁决是正确的……

19. Barton v. Bee Line, Inc., 238 App. Div. 501, 265 N.Y.S. 284 (1933)

美国纽约州最高法院上诉庭

Lazansky 法官主笔：

针对一项撤销有利于原告的陪审团裁断，并要求对案件重审的法庭命令，原告提起上诉。原告当时 15 岁，声称当时她是被告公共承运者的一名乘客，她被被告的司机强奸了。司机在证词中说原告同意与他发生关系。已经确认的是，如果司机向作为乘客的原告实施了侵犯，那么被告便因没有履行作为公共承运者对乘客的义务而需要承担损害责任。陪审团被指示即使原告同意，也有权获得赔偿，尽管同意会在损害赔偿金的减少中被考虑。陪审团裁断给原告 3 000 美元。法院没有接受陪审团的裁决，其理由是，如果原告表示了同意，那么裁断便超额了，而如果原告是被强奸的，这个赔偿额又是不够的。本法院并不打算介入裁量权的行使。初审法院的决定是合法的，这是因为另一个值得考虑的原因，即裁决被撤销是出于《民事诉讼法》第 549 条的规定，同时也出于损害赔偿金超额的考虑。

verdict even if she consented to consort with the chauffeur. By the last paragraph of subdivision 5 of section 2010 of the Penal Law it is provided: "A person who perpetrates an act of sexual intercourse with a female, not his wife, under the age of eighteen years, under circumstances not amounting to rape in the first degree, is guilty of rape in the second degree, and punishable with imprisonment for not more than ten years." Under this subdivision a crime is committed even if the female consents. The effect of the charge of the court was that the provisions of the act are made the basis of a civil liability. The age limitation has been changed from time to time. At first it was ten years, then sixteen, now eighteen. There can be no doubt that the purpose of the legislative enactments was and is to protect the virtue of females and to save society from the ills of promiscuous intercourse. A female over eighteen who is ravished has a cause of action against her assailant. Should a consenting female under the age of eighteen have a cause of action if she has full understanding of the nature of her act? It is one thing to say that society will protect itself by punishing those who consort with females under the age of consent; it is another to hold that, knowing the nature of her act, such female shall be rewarded for her indiscretion. Surely public policy—to serve which the statute was adopted—will not be vindicated by recompensing her for willing participation in that against which the law sought to protect her. The very object of the statute will be frustrated if by a material return for her fall "we should unwarily put it in the power of the female sex to become seducers in their turn." (Smith v. Richards, 29 Conn. 232.) Instead of incapacity to consent being a shield to save, it might be a sword to desecrate. The court is of the opinion that a female under the age of eighteen has no cause of action against a male with whom she willingly consorts, if she knows the nature and quality of her act....

Order setting aside verdict in favor of plaintiff unanimously affirmed, with costs.

20. Bang v. Charles T. Miller Hospital, 251 Minn. 427, 88 N.W.2d 186 (1958)

Supreme Court of Minnesota, United States

Gallagher, J.

Appeal from an order of the district court denying plaintiffs' alternative motion to vacate the dismissal of their action against Frederic E. B. Foley, herein referred to as defendant, or for a new trial.

This was an action for damages for alleged…unauthorized operation by the defendant on his patient, Helmer Bang, referred to herein as plaintiff. The latter contends that the question as to whether he expressly or impliedly consented to the operating procedures involved was one of fact for the jury. At the close of plaintiffs' case, the defendant moved for a directed verdict upon the grounds that plaintiffs had failed to prove any actionable negligence or any cause of action against him. This motion…was granted. A similar motion was granted with respect to the other defendant,

即使原告同意与司机厮混，初审法院指示陪审团作出有利于原告的裁断也是错误的。作为州法的《刑法》第2010条第5款最后一段指出："与自己妻子之外的18岁以下的女性发生性关系的人，在不足以达到第一级强奸罪的情况下，犯有第二级强奸罪，应该判处10年以下的监禁。"在该款规定下，即使女性同意，行为人也犯了罪。法院指示的效果在于，这些法律条文成为民事责任的基础。年龄的限制更改了许多次。一开始是10岁，然后改为16岁，现在是18岁。毫无疑问，相关法律的立法目的在于保护女性，防止社会出现滥交的罪恶。被强奸的18岁以上的女性对于施暴者享有诉因。如果一个18岁以下的女性完全理解自己行为的本质，她是否享有诉因呢？社会通过惩罚那些与同意年龄以下的女性发生性关系的男性的方式来保护女性，这是一回事；知道自己的行为本质是什么的女性从自己的轻率行为中得到了满足，这又是另一回事。当然，公共政策——制定法律为其服务——的正当性不需要通过赔偿那些参与违反旨在保护自己的法律的女性来维护。如果通过物质来回报她的堕落，"我们一不小心让女性反过来变成了勾引者"（Smith v. Richards, 29 Conn. 232），那么法律的目标将会落空。不具有同意能力非但不是一个保护盾牌，反而成为亵渎的武器。法院认为，18岁以下的女性如果知道自己行为的本质和性质，对她自愿与之发生性关系的男性没有诉因……

撤销有利于原告的裁决的指示得到了一致维持，由败诉方承担费用。

20. Bang v. Charles T. Miller Hospital, 251 Minn. 427, 88 N.W.2d 186 (1958)

美国明尼苏达州最高法院

Gallagher 法官主笔：

联邦地区法院拒绝原告要求撤销驳回对被告 Frederic E. B. Foley 的诉讼或要求重审的申请，因此而提起上诉。

本案是一起关于……被告未经允许便在其病人 Helmer Bang（以下称之为"原告"）身上实施手术的损害赔偿案件。原告主张，他是否明示地（expressly）或默示地（impliedly）同意实施本案涉及的手术，是一个程序上由陪审团决定的事实。在案件的最后，被告提出了指示裁断申请，理由是原告没有证明被告存在可诉的过失或任何针对他的诉因。该申请……被准许了。法院也准许了本案中的另一个被告——Charles T. Miller 医院的指示裁断申请，但是该诉

Charles T. Miller Hospital, but that action is not questioned on appeal.

The sole issue raised by the plaintiff on appeal is: Should the question of whether or not there was an...unauthorized operation have been submitted to the jury as a fact issue?...

...Plaintiff consulted with the defendant on April 6, 1953, at the latter's office in St. Paul. The defendant testified that at that time the patient complained of diminished size and force of the urinary stream and increased frequency of urination. He said that the plaintiff described various urinary symptoms and that a rectal examination of the prostate was performed. Not being certain at that time of the exact nature of the plaintiff's ailment, the defendant informed plaintiff that he wished to make a cystoscopic examination the following day and suggested that plaintiff be admitted to the Miller Hospital in St. Paul for further investigation, which was done. He said that he informed his patient "that the purpose of his going into the hospital was for further investigation with a view to making a prostate operation if the further examination showed that that was indicated."

The important question for determination of the matter presently before us is whether the evidence presented a fact question for the jury as to whether plaintiff consented to the severance of his spermatic cords when he submitted to the operation. Defendant testified on cross-examination under the rules that he did not tell plaintiff at the time of the office visit, April 6, that any examination defendant had made or was going to make had anything to do with the spermatic cords, nor did he recall explaining to his patient what a prostate-gland operation involved. He also said that plaintiff's life was in no immediate danger because of his condition on that day.

He was further questioned:

Q: Did you tell him in your office that if the later examination in the hospital the following day indicated prostate trouble it would be necessary for you as part of your operation to cut his spermatic cords?

A: I am not certain that particular detail of the operation was explained to him.

Q: Dr. Foley, is it not true that the only thing mentioned to Mr. Bang in your office was that a further examination was needed in order to confirm your diagnosis so that you would know what you were going to do next?

A: That is correct.

On the following day the operation was performed. When defendant was asked as to the procedure used, he replied:

A: ...the cysto-urethroscopic examination was made; following that I went

讼在上诉中没有被提出异议。

原告在上诉中提到的唯一问题是：未经允许进行手术这个事实是否应该提交陪审团决定？……

……原告于 1953 年 4 月 6 日在被告位于 St. Paul 的办公室咨询了被告。被告在证词中说，当时病人向他抱怨自己的小便量减少，力度不够，小便次数越来越多。他说原告形容了小便的多种症状，而且对前列腺进行过直肠检查。由于被告当时对原告到底得了什么病不太确定，于是告知原告他希望第二天对原告做一个膀胱内窥镜检查，并建议原告住进位于 St. Paul 的 Miller 医院接受进一步的检查，事实上，原告也是这样做的。被告说他告诉他的病人，"住院的目的是为了做进一步的检查以便进行前列腺手术，如果进一步的检查显示有必要这样做的话"。

我们现在面临要确定的一个问题是，证据是否向陪审团呈现了一个事实，即原告在接受手术的时候是否同意切断自己的输精管。被告在依据规则的交叉询问中作证说，4 月 6 日原告访问他的办公室时他没有告诉原告他已经完成的、或即将开始的检查与原告的输精管有什么联系，同时被告也没有向其病人解释手术会影响到前列腺的哪些部分。被告还说，根据原告当天的身体状况，他当时并没有紧急的生命危险。

被告被进一步询问：

问：在你的办公室里，你有没有告诉他，如果第二天医院的检查显示他的前列腺有问题，作为手术的一部分，你应该切除他的输精管？

答：我不确定是否向他说明了手术的这个细节问题。

问：Foley 医生，在你的办公室里，你向 Bang 先生提起过的唯一的事情是，他需要作进一步检查以确定你的诊断，你好清楚下一步应该做些什么。不是这样的吗？

答：是这样的。

第二天进行了手术。在被问到采用了哪些程序时，被告回答：

答：……做了膀胱尿道镜检查；之后我走到手术台的一头，告诉 Bang 先生检查的结果，而且告诉他我认为应该做一个经尿道前列腺切除

over to the head of the table and talked to Mr. Bang, told him what the findings were, and that in my opinion the transurethral prostatic resection should be done and I had his consent that we proceed with that operation.

Q: Did you at that time as I understand it now ask him for his consent?

A: Yes....

Q: ...did you at the time you talked to Mr. Bang on the table tell him anything about what you were going to do about his spermatic cords?

A: I do not recall definitely whether that particular detail of the operation was discussed with Mr. Bang or not.

The patient recalled the start of the operation and, when questioned on direct examination, stated:

Q: Did he at any time before the operation began tell you that he cut your spermatic cords?

A: No.

Q: Did he at any time before the operation began tell you that it was necessary to cut your cords?

A: No.

When being questioned on cross-examination with reference to consent, the plaintiff was asked:

Q: And you certainly did consent, didn't you, Mr. Bang, to Dr. Foley doing anything to correct your trouble which in his medical knowledge he felt should be corrected?

A: Not anything he wanted to, no.

Q: Did you put any limitation on his job as a surgeon?

A: No.

Q: When he said, if I find anything that needs correction I will do it at the same time and you said that was all right, that was all of the conversation there was, wasn't it?

A: That was all of the conversation there was.

It is plaintiff's claim that he thought he was discussing his bladder because he understood from his Austin physicians something about burning out the ulcers if there were any ulcers in there.

手术，我们进行那个手术得到了他的同意。

  问：根据我现在的理解，你当时有没有征求他的同意？

  答：有的。

  问：……你在手术台对 Bang 先生说话的时候，你有没有告诉他你们会对他的输精管怎么处理？

  答：我确实想不起有没有和 Bang 先生讨论那个手术的细节信息。

病人回忆了手术一开始的情况，在接受直接询问时说道：

  问：在手术开始之前，他有没有告诉你他会切断你的输精管？

  答：没有。

  问：在手术开始之前，他有没有告诉你有必要切断你的输精管？

  答：没有。

在交叉询问中提到同意问题时，原告被问到：

  问：Bang 先生，你确实作出了同意，难道不是吗？让 Foley 医生采取措施依据他的医疗知识认为应该治好的你的疾病？

  答：并不是任何他想做的事情，没有。

  问：你是否对他作为外科医生的工作进行了任何限制？

  答：没有。

  问：当他说，如果我发现了任何需要治疗的情况，我会同时处理，而你说"好的"，这是你们对话的全部内容，不是吗？

  答：这是当时的全部对话。

  原告声称，他认为他是在谈论他的膀胱，因为他在 Austin 的医生那里得知，如果膀胱出现溃疡，那么就必须把溃疡处理干净。但是，他也承认被告没有对他说起过溃疡。原告也承认他并不想告诉医生该做些什么；说他相信医生；说他并不希望告诉医生该怎么做手术。他说他希望医生能够实施治愈他的病

He admitted, however, that defendant said nothing to him about ulcers. Plaintiff also admitted that he did not expect to tell the doctor what to do; that he had faith in him; and that he did not expect to tell him how to perform the operation. He said that he expected the doctor would operate to do what was necessary to right and cure his condition. He testified that he did not ask the doctor what he intended to do and left it up to him to do the right thing.

…It is our opinion that under the record here the question as to whether plaintiff consented to the severance of his spermatic cords was a fact question for the jury and that it was error for the trial court to dismiss the action.…

While we have no desire to hamper the medical profession in the outstanding progress it has made and continues to make in connection with the study and solution of health and disease problems, it is our opinion that a reasonable rule is that, where a physician or surgeon can ascertain in advance of an operation alternative situations and no immediate emergency exists, a patient should be informed of the alternative possibilities and given a chance to decide before the doctor proceeds with the operation. By that we mean that, in a situation such as the case before us where no immediate emergency exists, a patient should be informed before the operation that if his spermatic cords were severed it would result in his sterilization, but on the other hand if this were not done there would be a possibility of an infection which could result in serious consequences. Under such conditions the patient would at least have the opportunity of deciding whether he wanted to take the chance of a possible infection if the operation was performed in one manner or to become sterile if performed in another.

Reversed and a new trial granted.

21. Kennedy v. Parrott, 243 N.C. 355, 90 S.E.2d 754 (1956)

Supreme Court of North Carolina, United States

Civil action to recover damages for personal injuries resulting from an alleged unauthorized operation performed by the defendant, a surgeon.

The plaintiff consulted the defendant as a surgeon. He diagnosed her ailment as appendicitis and recommended an operation to which she agreed. During the operation the doctor discovered some enlarged cysts on her left ovary, and he punctured them. After the operation the plaintiff developed phlebitis in her leg. She testified that Doctor Parrott told her "that while he was puncturing this cyst in my left ovary that he had cut a blood vessel and caused me to have phlebitis and that those blood clots were what was causing the trouble." She also testified that defendant told Dr. Tyndall, who was called in to examine her for her leg condition, "that while he was operating he punctured some cysts on my ovaries, and while puncturing the cyst on my left ovary he cut a blood vessel which caused me to bleed," to which Dr. Tyndall said, "Fountain, you have played hell."

情的必要手术。他声明，他并没有告诉医生自己想做什么，全部由医生来决定怎么做才是正确的。

……我们的意见是，依据这里的案卷，原告是否同意切断自己的输精管的问题是应该由陪审团查明的事实，初审法院驳回诉讼的做法存在错误……

尽管我们不希望阻碍医学行业的发展，医学行业在研究与健康和疾病相关的解决方案上取得了瞩目的进步，而且还将继续发展，但是我们认为合理的规则应该是，在内科医生或外科医生在手术之前便已经对手术的替代情况十分确定，而且没有紧急情况时，医生应该将这种替代可能性告知病人，并且在手术实施之前给予病人决定的机会。我们的意思是，在某种情况下，如本案没有涉及紧急事件的这种情况，在手术实施之前，应该告知病人，如果切断他的输精管，他将失去生育能力，但是另一方面，如果不切断输精管，便有可能出现感染，从而造成严重的后果。在这样的情况下，病人至少有机会进行选择：这样动手术，可以碰运气不发生感染；或者那样动手术，然后失去生育能力。

撤销判决并发回重审。

21. Kennedy v. Parrott, 243 N.C. 355, 90 S.E.2d 754 (1956)

美国北卡罗来纳州最高法院

指控被告医生未经允许实施手术造成人身伤害，要求对该人身伤害进行赔偿的民事诉讼。

原告咨询了作为外科医生的被告。医生诊断原告得的是阑尾炎，并建议她接受手术，原告同意了医生的建议。在手术过程中，医生发现原告左边卵巢有一些大的囊肿，于是医生刺破了囊肿。手术之后，原告的腿上出现了静脉炎。原告作证说，Parrott 医生告诉她"在刺破左卵巢的时候，他切到了一根血管，导致我出现了静脉炎，并告诉我正是这些血块造成了麻烦"。原告还作证说，被告告诉被叫来检查她腿部的 Tyndall 医生，"在他刺破我卵巢的一些囊肿时，正在刺破左卵巢的囊肿时，他切到了血管，造成了我流血"。对此，Tyndall 医生说："Fountain，你闯祸了。"

The defendant recommended that the plaintiff go to Duke Hospital, and there is evidence he promised he would pay the bill. She also saw Dr. I. Ridgeway Trimble at Johns Hopkins, Baltimore. Dr. Trimble operated on her left leg and side "to try to correct the damage that was done."

Plaintiff had to undergo considerable pain and suffering on account of the phlebitis....

At the conclusion of the testimony, the court, on motion of the defendant, entered judgment of involuntary nonsuit. Plaintiff excepted and appealed.

Barnhill, C.J.

On the other hand, if her cause of action is for damages for personal injuries proximately resulting from a trespass on her person, as she now asserts, and such operation was neither expressly nor impliedly authorized, she is entitled at least to nominal damages....

Prior to the advent of the modern hospital and before anesthesia had appeared on the horizon of the medical world, the courts formulated and applied a rule in respect to operations which may now be justly considered unreasonable and unrealistic. During the period when our common law was being formulated and applied, even a major operation was performed in the home of the patient, and the patient ordinarily was conscious, so that the physician could consult him in respect to conditions which required or made advisable an extension of the operation. And even if the shock of the operation rendered the patient unconscious, immediate members of his family were usually available. Hence the courts formulated the rule that any extension of the operation by the physician without the consent of the patient or someone authorized to speak for him constituted a battery or trespass upon the person of the patient for which the physician was liable in damages.

However, now that hospitals are available to most people in need of major surgery; anesthesia is in common use; operations are performed in the operating rooms of such hospitals while the patient is under the influence of an anesthetic; the surgeon is bedecked with operating gown, mask, and gloves; and the attending relatives, if any, are in some other part of the hospital, sometimes many floors away, the law is in a state of flux. More and more courts are beginning to realize that ordinarily a surgeon is employed to remedy conditions without any express limitation on his authority in respect thereto, and that in view of these conditions which make consent impractical, it is unreasonable to hold the physician to the exact operation—particularly when it is internal—that his preliminary examination indicated was necessary. We know that now complete diagnosis of an internal ailment is not effectuated until after the patient is under the influence of the anesthetic and the incision has been made.

These courts act upon the concept that the philosophy of the law is embodied in the ancient Latin maxim: Ratio est legis anima; mutata legis ratione mutatur et lex. Reason is the soul of the law; the reason of the law being changed, the law is also changed.

Some of the courts which realize that in view of modern conditions there should be some

被告建议原告到Duke医院去，而且有证据显示他允诺支付原告的医药费。原告还去了位于Baltimore的Johns Hopkins医院的I. Ridgeway Trimble医生那里。Trimble医生为她的左腿和左肋动了手术，"为的是纠正已经造成的损害"。

由于静脉炎，原告不得不忍受巨大的疼痛和痛苦……

根据对证词的推断，法院应被告的申请，判决强制终结诉讼（involuntary nonsuit）。原告提出异议，提起上诉。

Barnhill大法官主笔：

另一方面，如果原告的诉因，如她所声称的，是获得她受到的人身侵害直接造成的人身伤害的赔偿，而且该手术既没有得到明示的或默示的授权，那么她有权至少获得名义损害赔偿金……

在现代医院出现之前和在医学世界还没有麻醉技术的时候，法院制定并采用了一种关于手术问题的规则，这些规则在现在被认为是不合理的和不现实的。在我们的普通法被制定并运用起来的时期，一个较大的手术甚至也是在病人家里完成的。而且病人通常是清醒的，所以医生可以就某些情况征求病人的意见，这些情况要么需要做进一步的手术，要么促使医生建议病人做进一步的手术。即使病人因害怕手术而昏迷过去，他的近亲属或家人也在身边。因此，法院制定了一条规则，即如果医生在没有征得病人或受托为病人表达意思的人的允许的情况下擅自对手术进行了扩展，那么便构成了殴击或对病人的人身侵害，医生需要承担赔偿责任。

然而，现在多数人需要做较大的手术时都可以到医院去；麻醉的使用也很普遍；手术是在这些医院的手术室进行的，而病人都接受了麻醉；医生都穿着手术服，戴着口罩和手套；而如果有亲属在场，他们也等待在医院的另一边，有时和手术室隔了好几层楼，因此法律便处在不断变动的状态之中。越来越多的法院开始认识到，病人通常请医生对某种病情进行治疗，对医生的权限并没有明确的限制，考虑到这些病情使病人要表达同意变得不切实际，因此认为医生必须单纯地实施应对他最早诊断出来的病情的某个手术——特别是体内手术——这样的认识是不合理的。我们知道，现在，在病人被麻醉、开刀之前，对内部疾病进行全面的诊断是不可能的。

这些法院在履行着一个古代拉丁格言中所体现出的法律哲学思想：理性是法律的灵魂；法律理性改变，法律亦随之改变。

一些法院虽然认为，鉴于现代的条件，对严格的普通法规则也应该进行一些调整，但是认为仍然应该将医生未经病人同意便擅自扩展手术的权利限

modification of the strict common law rule still limit the rights of surgeons to extend an operation without the express consent of the patient to cases where an emergency arises calling for immediate action for the preservation of the life or health of the patient, and it is impracticable to obtain his consent or the consent of someone authorized to speak for him.

Other courts, though adhering to the fetish of consent, express or implied, realize "that the law should encourage self-reliant surgeons to whom patients may safely entrust their bodies, and not men who may be tempted to shirk from duty for fear of a law suit." They recognize that "the law does not insist that a surgeon shall perform every operation according to plans and specifications approved in advance by the patient and carefully tucked away in his office-safe for courtroom purposes."…

In major internal operations, both the patient and the surgeon know that the exact condition of the patient cannot be finally and definitely diagnosed until after the patient is completely anesthetized and the incision has been made. In such case the consent—in the absence of proof to the contrary—will be construed as general in nature and the surgeon may extend the operation to remedy any abnormal or diseased condition in the area of the original incision whenever he, in the exercise of his sound professional judgment, determines that correct surgical procedure dictates and requires such an extension of the operation originally contemplated. This rule applies when the patient is at the time incapable of giving consent, and no one with authority to consent for him is immediately available.

In short, where an internal operation is indicated, a surgeon may lawfully perform, and it is his duty to perform, such operation as good surgery demands, even when it means an extension of the operation further than was originally contemplated, and for so doing he is not to be held in damages as for an unauthorized operation.

"Where one has voluntarily submitted himself to a physician or surgeon for diagnosis and treatment of an ailment it, in the absence of evidence to the contrary, will be presumed that what the doctor did was either expressly or by implication authorized to be done."

Unexpected things which arise in the course of an operation and incidental thereto must generally at least be met according to the best judgment and skill of the surgeon. And ordinarily a surgeon is justified in believing that his patient has assented to such operation as approved surgery demands to relieve the affliction with which he is suffering.

Here plaintiff submitted her body to the care of the defendant for an appendectomy. When the defendant made the necessary incision he discovered some enlarged follicle cysts on her ovaries. He, as a skilled surgeon, knew that when a cyst on an ovary grows beyond the normal size, it may continue to grow until it is large enough to hold six to eight quarts of liquid and become dangerous by reason of its size. The plaintiff does not say that the defendant exercised bad judgment or that the extended operation was not dictated by sound surgical procedure. She now asserts only that it

制在一些场合内,在这些场合中出现了一些必须采取紧急措施以挽救病人的生命或健康的情况,而获取病人的同意或受托为病人表达意思的人的同意是不现实的。

其他法院,尽管坚持对同意的迷恋,但是也明示或暗示地认识到"法律应该鼓励那些病人将自己的身体安全地托付给具有自主精神的医生,而不应鼓励那些因为害怕引来官司而犹豫的医生"。他们认识到"法律并不一定坚决主张医生实施每一个手术时都必须按照计划或病人提前的嘱托来进行,为了避免在法庭相见,便小心地躲在办公室里不出来。"……

对于较大的内部手术来说,病人和医生都知道,在病人被完全麻醉和开刀之前,病人的确切情况是无法得到最后确诊的。在这样的情况下,可以将同意——在没有相反证据时——理解为一般性规则,而当医生通过自己合理的专业判断确定矫正手术需要且必须对事先设想的手术进行扩展时,可以在已有手术切口处扩展手术以矫正异常或病变情况。这条规则适用于病人不具备表达同意的能力,而且不能马上找到受托为病人表达同意的人的情形。

简而言之,只要出现了需要实施内部手术的迹象时,那么医生可以合法地实施,并且也有责任按照好的外科手术所要求的那样实施该手术,哪怕这样意味着需要对先前设想的手术进行扩展,医生不需要为实施了未经授权的手术承担损害赔偿责任。

"当某人自愿将自己托付给内科医生或外科医生以便对某一疾病进行诊断或治疗时,在没有相反证据时,可以认为医生的行为是得到了明示或暗示的授权"。

如果在手术的过程中出现了意想不到的情况和偶然事故,那么至少应该依据医生的最佳判断和技术对该情况进行处理。通常情况下,医生可以证明相信他的病人已经赞同实施该手术是正当的,因为被认可的外科手术旨在减轻病人正在遭受的痛苦。

这里,原告将自己的身体托付给被告实施阑尾切除手术。当被告切开原告的身体时发现她的卵巢上有一些大的囊肿。他作为一个熟练的外科医生,知道当卵巢上的囊肿长到超过正常程度时,可能会继续生长,直到大到可以容纳 6 到 8 夸脱的液体,这样的囊肿由于太大而非常危险。原告并没有说被告的判断错误,或扩展手术没有依据合理的外科程序。原告现在指控的只是该手术没有得到她的授权,而且她也不能出示手术造成的具体的伤害或损失。

was unauthorized, and she makes no real showing of resulting injury or damage.

In this connection it is not amiss to note that the expert witnesses testified that the puncture of the cysts was in accord with sound surgical procedure, and that if they had performed the appendectomy they would have also punctured any enlarged cysts found on the ovaries. "That is the accepted practice in the course of general surgery."

What was the surgeon to do when he found abnormal cysts on the ovaries of plaintiff that were potentially dangerous? Was it his duty to leave her unconscious on the operating table, doff his operating habiliments, and go forth to find someone with authority to consent to the extended operation, and then return, go through the process of disinfecting, don again his operating habiliments, and then puncture the cysts; or was he compelled, against his best judgment, to close the incision and then, after plaintiff had fully recovered from the effects of the anesthesia, inform her as to what he had found and advise her that these cysts might cause her serious trouble in the future? The operation was simple, the incision had been made, the potential danger was evident to a skilled surgeon. Reason and sound common sense dictated that he should do just what he did do. So all the expert witnesses testified.

Therefore, we are constrained to hold that the plaintiff's testimony fails to make out a… case for a jury on the theory she brings her appeal to this Court. The judgment entered in the court below is affirmed.

22. Hackbart v. Cincinnati Bengals, Inc., 601 F.2d 516 (10th Cir. 1979)

Tenth Circuit, Court of Appeals, United States

Doyle, Circuit Judge.

The question in this case is whether in a regular season professional football game an injury which is inflicted by one professional football player on an opposing player can give rise to liability in tort where the injury was inflicted by the intentional striking of a blow during the game.

The injury occurred in the course of a game between the Denver Broncos and the Cincinnati Bengals, which game was being played in Denver in 1973. The Broncos' defensive back, Dale Hackbart, was the recipient of the injury and the Bengals' offensive back, Charles "Booby" Clark, inflicted the blow which produced it.

By agreement the liability question was determined by the United States District Court for the District of Colorado without a jury. The judge resolved the liability issue in favor of the Cincinnati team and Charles Clark. Consistent with this result, final judgment was entered for Cincinnati and the appeal challenges this judgment. In essence the trial court's reasons for rejecting plaintiff's claim were that professional football is a species of warfare and that so much physical force is tolerated and the magnitude of the force exerted is so great that it renders injuries not actionable in

就此而论，注意到这样一点是十分正确的，即专家证人在证词中指出，刺破囊肿符合合理的外科程序，而且如果他们在阑尾手术中发现病人卵巢上有扩大的囊肿，他们也会将其刺破。"这是普通外科手术中被接受的做法"。

如果医生发现原告卵巢上存在有潜在危险的异常囊肿，那么医生应该怎么办呢？他是不是应该让病人不省人事地躺在手术台上，然后脱掉自己的手术服，找到可以授权他扩展手术的人并征求他的同意，然后再回去完成一套消毒程序，穿上他的手术服，最后刺破囊肿；或者他是否应该不顾自己正确的判断，不得已地缝合手术切口，等到原告完全从麻醉中清醒过来，再告诉她他发现的情况，并劝告她这些囊肿今后可能会引起严重的问题？手术很简单，切口已经打开，而且对于熟练的医生而言潜在的危险是再明显不过的了。理智和合理的常识决定了医生会这样做。所有专家证人都对此予以了证实。

因此，我们不得不认为，原告上诉时向法院提出的证词中没有证明……殴击案的成立。下级法院作出的判决被维持。

22. Hackbart v. Cincinnati Bengals, Inc., 601 F.2d 516 (10th Cir. 1979)

美国联邦上诉法院第十巡回法庭

Doyle 巡回法院法官主笔：

本案涉及的问题是，在职业橄榄球赛的常规赛季，一名职业橄榄球运动员在对方球员身上造成的伤害的行为是否构成了侵权责任，而该伤害由比赛中的一个故意殴打引发。

伤害发生于1973年在 Denver 举行的丹佛野马队和辛辛那提猛虎队之间的橄榄球比赛进行过程中。野马队的防守后卫 Dale Hackbart 是受害人，猛虎队的攻击后卫 Charles "Booby（傻瓜）" Clark 是打击的实施者。

经双方协商，责任的认定问题在不使用陪审团的情况下由科罗拉多州辖区联邦地区法院判定。法官在责任问题上作出了有利于辛辛那提猛虎队和 Charles Clark 的认定。与这一认定结果一致的是，作出的最终判决有利于辛辛那提猛虎队，而原告上诉要求推翻该判决。初审法院驳回原告的赔偿请求，其根本理由是职业橄榄球赛是具有竞争冲突性的一种运动类型，其间产生的身体冲撞是可以容忍的，而冲撞的力量非常之大，以至于由此造成的伤害不具有可诉性；故意殴击行为也不属于司法程序的范围。

court; that even intentional batteries are beyond the scope of the judicial process.

Clark was an offensive back and just before the injury he had run a pass pattern to the right side of the Denver Broncos' end zone. The injury flowed indirectly from this play. The pass was intercepted by Billy Thompson, a Denver free safety, who returned it to mid-field. The subject injury occurred as an aftermath of the pass play. As a consequence of the interception, the roles of Hackbart and Clark suddenly changed. Hackbart, who had been defending, instantaneously became an offensive player. Clark, on the other hand, became a defensive player. Acting as an offensive player, Hackbart attempted to block Clark by throwing his body in front of him. He thereafter remained on the ground. He turned, and with one knee on the ground, watched the play following the interception.

The trial court's finding was that Charles Clark, "acting out of anger and frustration, but without specific intent to injure…stepped forward and struck a blow with his right forearm to the back of the kneeling plaintiff's head and neck with sufficient force to cause both players to fall forward to the ground." Both players, without complaining to the officials or to one another, returned to their respective sidelines since the ball had changed hands and the offensive and defensive teams of each had been substituted. Clark testified at trial that his frustration was brought about by the fact that his team was losing the game.

Due to the failure of the officials to view the incident, a foul was not called. However, the game film showed very clearly what had occurred. Plaintiff did not at the time report the happening to his coaches or to anyone else during the game. However, because of the pain which he experienced he was unable to play golf the next day. He did not seek medical attention, but the continued pain caused him to report this fact and the incident to the Bronco trainer who gave him treatment. Apparently he played on the specialty teams for two successive Sundays, but after that the Broncos released him on waivers. (He was in his thirteenth year as a player.) He sought medical help and it was then that it was discovered by the physician that he had a serious neck fracture injury.

Despite the fact that the defendant Charles Clark admitted that the blow which had been struck was not accidental, that it was intentionally administered, the trial court ruled as a matter of law that the game of professional football is basically a business which is violent in nature, and that the available sanctions are imposition of penalties and expulsion from the game. Notice was taken of the fact that many fouls are overlooked; that the game is played in an emotional and noisy environment; and that incidents such as that here complained of are not unusual.

The trial court spoke as well of the unreasonableness of applying the laws and rules which are part of injury law to the game of professional football, noting the unreasonableness of holding that one player has a duty of care for the safety of others. He also talked about the concept of assumption of risk and contributory fault as applying and concluded that Hackbart had to recognize

Clark 是一名攻击后卫，在原告受伤之前，他把球传入了丹佛野马队的球门区右侧。这个举动间接造成了 Hackbart 受伤。丹佛野马队的自由后卫 Bill Thompson 截断了这次传球，然后将球重新传入球场中央部分。传球行为造成了原告受伤。由于 Thompson 的拦截，Hackbart 和 Clark 的角色突然间发生了改变。原来处于进攻位置的 Hackbart 一瞬间变为了防守队员。而另一方面，Clark 成为了进攻队员。作为防守队员，Hackbart 想用身体挡住 Clark。因此他站在场上不动。他转过身来，一条腿跪在地上，注视着截球行动之后的事态发展。

初审法院查明的事实是，Charles Clark"出于愤怒和沮丧，但没有具体地实施伤害的意图……上前一步，将右前臂打在了跪在地上的原告的后脑勺和后颈部，力量之大，以至于两个人都摔倒在了地上"。两名球员都没有向裁判或对方抱怨，回到他们各自的边线上，因为控球方已经发生改变，所以防守方和进攻方也相互交换。Clark 在证词中说，他感到很沮丧，因为他的球队即将输掉比赛。

由于裁判没有看到这个事件，因此没有吹犯规。但是比赛回放录像清楚地显示了事情的全貌。原告当时并没有向教练或场上队员报告事情经过。然而，伤痛使他第二天无法打高尔夫球。他并没有进行治疗，但是持续不断的疼痛促使他将情况和事件报告给了为他进行治疗的野马队的教练。很明显，他连续两个周日都为专业队比赛，但是在那之后，野马队根据弃权证书（waivers）解雇了他（他已经打了13年的球）。他开始接受治疗，就是那时医生才发现他的脖子有严重的骨折现象。

虽然被告 Charles Clark 承认他的殴打行为不是意外，是故意实施的，但是初审法院仍然认为作为一个法律问题，职业橄榄球比赛根本上来说是一个暴力的行业，其制裁方式为施加罚球或驱逐。同时也注意到的事实有：许多犯规行为没有被发现；比赛是在情绪化和嘈杂的环境下进行的；诸如这里申诉的事故并不少见。

初审法院的法官还提到，将伤害法的一部分的法律和规则运用到职业橄榄球比赛当中是不合理的，特别提到一位球员对其他球员的安全负有注意义务是不合理的。他同时还谈到了可以运用到的自甘风险（assumption of risk）和助成过错（contributory fault）的概念，认定 Hackbart 必须认识到他已经接受了他可能因这种行为而受伤的风险……

that he accepted the risk that he would be injured by such an act....

The evidence at the trial uniformly supported the proposition that the intentional striking of a player in the head from the rear is not an accepted part of either the playing rules or the general customs of the game of professional football. The trial court, however, believed that the unusual nature of the case called for the consideration of underlying policy which it defined as common law principles which have evolved as a result of the case to case process and which necessarily affect behavior in various contexts. From these considerations the belief was expressed that even intentional injuries incurred in football games should be outside the framework of the law. The court recognized that the potential threat of legal liability has a significant deterrent effect, and further said that private civil actions constitute an important mechanism for societal control of human conduct. Due to the increase in severity of human conflicts, a need existed to expand the body of governing law more rapidly and with more certainty, but that this had to be accomplished by legislation and administrative regulation. The judge compared football to coal mining and railroading insofar as all are inherently hazardous. Judge Matsch said that in the case of football it was questionable whether social values would be improved by limiting the violence. Thus the district court's assumption was that Clark had inflicted an intentional blow which would ordinarily generate civil liability and which might bring about a criminal sanction as well, but that since it had occurred in the course of a football game, it should not be subject to the restraints of the law; that if it were it would place unreasonable impediments and restraints on the activity. The judge also pointed out that courts are ill-suited to decide the different social questions and to administer conflicts on what is much like a battlefield where the restraints of civilization have been left on the sidelines....

Plaintiff, of course, maintains that tort law applicable to the injury in this case applies on the football field as well as in other places. On the other hand, plaintiff does not rely on the theory of negligence being applicable. This is in recognition of the fact that subjecting another to unreasonable risk of harm, the essence of negligence, is inherent in the game of football, for admittedly it is violent. Plaintiff maintains that in the area of contributory fault, a vacuum exists in relationship to intentional infliction of injury. Since negligence does not apply, contributory negligence is inapplicable. Intentional or reckless contributory fault could theoretically at least apply to infliction of injuries in reckless disregard of the rights of others. This has some similarity to contributory negligence and undoubtedly it would apply if the evidence would justify it. But it is highly questionable whether a professional football player consents or submits to injuries caused by conduct not within the rules, and there is no evidence which we have seen which shows this. However, the trial court did not consider this question and we are not deciding it.

Contrary to the position of the court then, there are no principles of law which allow a court to rule out certain tortious conduct by reason of general roughness of the game or difficulty of

初审中，各项证据都一致支持一种说法，即从背后故意击打一名球员的头部既不能被比赛规则所接受，而且也不是职业橄榄球赛的常见做法。但是，初审法院认为，案件的性质不寻常，需要考虑被法院认定为普通法准则背后的法律目的，这些普通法准则伴随着一个一个案件的审理而不断的演变，在不同情况下影响着人们的行为。有了这样的认识，法院认为，尽管橄榄球比赛中出现了故意伤害，但是也不应归属于法律的框架。法院认识到，法律责任存在的潜在威胁可以产生重大的阻吓作用，而且还指出，个人的民事诉讼构成了控制人们行为的重要机制。由于人类冲突变得逐渐严重，有必要以更快更确定的方式对适用的法律进行扩展，但是这一点必须通过立法和行政法规来完成。法官将橄榄球比赛与采矿以及铁路建设进行比较，它们都具有固有的危险性。Matsch 法官认为，在橄榄球赛案件中，通过限制暴力能否提高社会价值是值得怀疑的。因此，联邦地区法院的假定是，Clark 实施的故意殴打通常会使其承担民事责任，同时还有可能带来刑事制裁，但是由于该行为发生在橄榄球场内，因此不应该受到法律的限制；如果受到法律限制，那么橄榄球运动便会受到无理的阻碍和限制。法官同时还指出，法院不适合决定不同的社会问题，也不适合决定那些类似战场上发生的冲突，在这些场合下文明的制约已经被束之高阁……

当然，原告认为可适用于本案中的伤害行为的侵权法就像适用于其他场合一样，也适用于橄榄球场。另一方面，原告没有将过失责任规则作为适用规则。这是因为过失的根本问题在于将另一方置于不合理的受伤风险之下，而这正是橄榄球赛所固有的特征，因为众所周知，橄榄球赛是暴力的。原告主张，在助成过失领域，存在与故意伤害相关联的真空地带。由于过失责任规则不适用，助成过失规则便也不适用。故意或放任助成过失至少在理论上可以适用于放任地漠视他人权利而导致损害的情形。这与助成过失有一些相似之处，而且无疑在证据充分的情况下可以适用。但是对在一名职业橄榄球运动员同意或准许规则之外的行为造成的伤害，这是非常值得质疑的，而且我们也没有看到任何证据证明这一点。然而，初审法院没有考虑这个问题，我们也不作考虑。

与法院的立场相反，没有法律规则允许法院以比赛的粗暴性和审理存在难度为由便排除了特定侵权行为。

administering it.

Indeed, the evidence shows that there are rules of the game which prohibit the intentional striking of blows. Thus, Article 1, Item 1, Subsection C, provides that:

> All players are prohibited from striking on the head, face or neck with the heel, back or side of the hand, wrist, forearm, elbow or clasped hands.

Thus the very conduct which was present here is expressly prohibited by the rule which is quoted above.

The general customs of football do not approve the intentional punching or striking of others. That this is prohibited was supported by the testimony of all of the witnesses. They testified that the intentional striking of a player in the face or from the rear is prohibited by the playing rules as well as the general customs of the game. Punching or hitting with the arms is prohibited. Undoubtedly these restraints are intended to establish reasonable boundaries so that one football player cannot intentionally inflict a serious injury on another. Therefore, the notion is not correct that all reason has been abandoned, whereby the only possible remedy for the person who has been the victim of an unlawful blow is retaliation....

In sum, having concluded that the trial court did not limit the case to a trial of the evidence bearing on defendant's liability but rather determined that as a matter of social policy the game was so violent and unlawful that valid lines could not be drawn, we take the view that this was not a proper issue for determination and that plaintiff was entitled to have the case tried on an assessment of his rights and whether they had been violated.

The trial court has heard the evidence and has made findings. The findings of fact based on the evidence presented are not an issue on this appeal. Thus, it would not seem that the court would have to repeat the areas of evidence that have already been fully considered. The need is for a reconsideration of that evidence in the light of that which is taken up by this court in its opinion. We are not to be understood as limiting the trial court's consideration of supplemental evidence if it deems it necessary.

The cause is reversed and remanded for a new trial in accordance with the foregoing views.

23. Chatterton v Gerson [1981] QB 432

Queen's Bench Division, High Court, United Kingdom

BRISTOW J

Trespass to the person and consent

It is clear law that in any context in which consent of the injured party is a defence to what

实际上,有证据显示,比赛的一些规则禁止故意的击打行为。因此,比赛规则第 1 条第 1 款第 C 项规定:

> 禁止所有球员以脚后跟、手背或手的侧部、手腕、前臂、肘或双手相互紧握的方式击打另一方的头部、面部或颈部。

因此,本案涉及的行为是上诉规则所明文禁止的。

橄榄球赛的一般习惯做法并不准许对他人的故意冲击或击打行为。所有的证人都证明了该行为是被禁止的。他们作证说,对一名球员的面部或从后面进行击打是被比赛规则所禁止的,也被比赛的一般习惯所禁止。用手臂进行冲击或击打是被禁止的。毫无疑问,这些限制的目的在于建立一些合理的界线,使一名橄榄球运动员不能对另一名球员实施严重的伤害行为。因此,认为所有的理性都被抛弃了,非法击打行为的受害人能够采取的唯一补救方法便是报复的认识是错误的……

总而言之,我们的结论是,初审法院没有将案件限制在审理证明被告应承担责任的证据上,而是作为一个社会政策问题,认为该项比赛是极为暴力和不合法的,以至于不能对其进行有效的界定,我们认为这样的判断并不适当,原告有权获得对其案件中的权利进行评估,请求审理其权利是否被侵犯。

初审法院对证据进行了听证,并且作出了裁决。以证据为基础的对事实的裁决不属于上诉范围。鉴于此,法院不必重复已经得到充分研究的证据问题。需要重新考虑的是该法院判决意见书依据的证据。我们的意见不应被认为是对初审法院认定的必要的补充证据的限制。

案件被推翻并发回依照上述意见重审。

23. Chatterton v Gerson [1981] QB 432

联合王国高等法院王座分庭

Bristow 法官主笔:

人身侵害和受害人同意

受害人的同意要能阻却一个行为成为犯罪行为或者侵权行为的话,这种同意必须是真实的,这一点在法律上是很清楚的。比如,如果一个女性因为对方

would otherwise be a crime or a civil wrong, the consent must be real. Where for example a woman's consent to sexual intercourse is obtained by fraud, her apparent consent is no defence to a charge of rape. It is not difficult to state the principle or to appreciate its good sense. As so often, the problem lies in its application.

No English authority was cited before me of the application of the principle in the context of consent to the interference with bodily integrity by medical or surgical treatment. In *Reibl v. Hughes* (1978) 89 D.L.R. (3d) 112, which was an action based on negligence by failure to inform the patient of the risk in surgery involving the carotid artery, the Ontario Court of Appeal said that the trial judge was wrong in injecting the issue, "Was it a battery?" into the case pleaded and presented in negligence. The majority of the court, having referred to the United States cases on what is there called the "doctrine of informed consent," decided that the action of "battery" seemed quite inappropriate to cases in which the doctor has acted in good faith, and in the interests of the patient, but in doing so has been negligent in failing to disclose a risk inherent in the recommended treatment. They reversed the finding of battery. I am told that that decision is now under appeal.

In Stoffberg v. Elliott [1923] C.P.D. 148, Watermeyer J., in his summing up to the jury in an action of assault in this context, directed them that consent to such surgical and medical treatment as the doctors might think necessary is not to be implied simply from the fact of going to hospital. There it was admitted that express consent to the operation should have been obtained, but was not, due to oversight.

In my judgment what the court has to do in each case is to look at all the circumstances and say "Was there a real consent?" I think justice requires that in order to vitiate the reality of consent there must be a greater failure of communication between doctor and patient than that involved in a breach of duty if the claim is based on negligence. When the claim is based on negligence the plaintiff must prove not only the breach of duty to inform, but that had the duty not been broken she would not have chosen to have the operation. Where the claim is based on trespass to the person, once it is shown that the consent is unreal, then what the plaintiff would have decided if she had been giventhe information which would have prevented vitiation of the reality of her consent is irrelevant.

In my judgment once the patient is informed in broad terms of the nature of the procedure which is intended, and gives her consent, that consent is real, and the cause of the action on which to base a claim for failure to go into risks and implications is negligence, not trespass. Of course if information is withheld in bad faith, the consent will be vitiated by fraud. Of course if by some accident, as in a case in the 1940's in the Salford Hundred Court where a boy was admitted to hospital for tonsilectomyand due to administrative error was circumcised instead, trespass would be the appropriate cause of action against the doctor, though he was as much the victim of the error as the boy. But in my judgment it would be very much against the interests of justice if actions

欺诈而同意了性行为，她表面上的同意就不能阻却对强奸的指控。阐述这个原则或者理解它的积极意义不是什么难事。常常遇到的问题是如何适用这个原则。

我并没有看到有英格兰的判例说明在医疗诊断和外科手术干涉了身体完整性的情形下，这种原则应该怎么适用。*Reibl v Hughes*（1978）89 D.L.R.（3d）112 案中，医生因为过失而没有告知病人颈动脉手术的风险，病人因此提起了过失之诉；安大略上诉法院表示，一审法院在过失之诉中，错误地引入了"这构不构成殴击（battery）"的问题。在参考了美国法上所谓的"告知后同意理论"，大多数的法官都认为，在这个案件中医生是善意且为了病人的利益在行事，只是因为过失而没有将其所建议的治疗方案的风险告知病人；因此就认为这构成"殴击"，实在是太不恰当了。上诉法院因此推翻了对"殴击"的认定。我听说现在这个二审判决被上诉了。

在南非案件 *Stoffberg v Elliott* [1923] C.P.D. 148 中，Watermeyer 法官以"威吓之诉"的名义召集了陪审团，引导他们并不能仅仅因为病人去了医院这事，就推断病人同意了医生认为必要的手术或者治疗措施。这里认定，病人对手术明确的同意，应当需要事先获得，但是因为医生的过失而没有获得。

在我看来，法院在这些案件中能做的，是考察所有的情况，并问问自己："受害人真的同意了吗？"我认为根据正义的要求，要否认受害人的同意的真实性，则医生和病人之间的缺乏沟通应该严重于过失之诉中用来判断医生是否违反了义务的缺乏沟通。在过失之诉中，原告除了要证明医生违反了告知义务，还需要证明如果医生没有违反告知义务，原告是不会选择做手术的。而当提起的是人身侵害之诉时，只要证明了病人的同意是不真实的即可，至于原告如果被告知了相关的信息还会作出何种选择，这时能不能避免他的同意被否定，则是无关的情节了。

在我看来，只要病人大体上被告知了将要进行的手术的性质和程序，且病人作出了同意，那么这种同意就是真实的。这时如果因为医生没有告知风险和后果而提起诉讼，诉由就只能是过失，而不是人身侵害了。当然，如果医生是恶意不告知相关信息的，那么病人的同意可以因为受欺诈而被否定。当然，在某些案件中，比如 1940 年代 Salford Hundred 法院判决的一个案件中，一个男孩到医院做扁桃体切除术，但是却因为管理错误而被割掉了包皮，这类案件中对医生提起人身侵害之诉就是恰当的了，虽然医生和男孩一样其实也是这个错误的受害者。但是在我看来，如果那些真的是基于医生没有适当履行其告知义务而提起的诉讼却去适用人身侵害的诉由，这将极大地损害司

which are really based on a failure by the doctor to perform his duty adequately to inform were pleaded in trespass.

24. Balmain New Ferry Co Ltd v Robertson (1906) 4 CLR 379

High Court of Australia, British Australia (as it then was)

Griffith C.J.

This agreement involves, in my opinion, an implied promise by the plaintiff that he would not ask for egress by land except on payment of one penny, and, further, a consent on his part that the defendants should be entitled to prevent him from departing in that way until he paid the penny.

O'Connor J.

… But the abridgment of a man's liberty is not under all circumstances actionable. He may enter into a contract which necessarily involves the surrender of a portion of his liberty for a certain period, and if the act complained of is nothing more than a restraint in accordance with that surrender he cannot complain. Nor can he, without the assent of the other party, by electing to put an end to the contract become entitled at once, unconditionally and irrespective of the other party's rights, to regain his liberty as if he had never surrendered it. A familiar instance of such a contract is that between a passenger and the railway company which undertakes to carry him on a journey. If the passenger suddenly during the journey decided to abandon it and to leave the train at the next station, being one at which the train was not timed to stop, he clearly would not be entitled to have the train stopped at that station. However much he might object, the railway company could lawfully carry him on to the next stopping place of that particular train. In such a case the passenger's liberty would be for a certain period restrained, but the restraint would not be actionable, because it is an implied term of such a contract that the passenger will permit the restraint of his liberty so far as may be necessary for the performance by the company of the contract of carriage according to the time table of that train. Or a person may conditionally, by his own act, place himself in such a position that he cannot complain of a certain restraint of his liberty. Take an illustration which was used in the course of the argument. Assume that the turnstiles on the company's wharf completely closed the opening between the bulkheads, that they were worked on the penny in the slot system, and would not open except when a penny dropped in the slot operated the mechanism. If under these circumstances the plaintiff, having opened the entry turnstile by his penny and entered the wharf, changed his mind about crossing in the company's steamers, and wished to return at once to the street, could he claim that he was not bound to use the ordinary means of opening the exit turnstile by dropping in his penny, but was entitled to break his way through it, or to demand from the company's officers that they should specially unlock the apparatus to enable him to pass out? If, under the circumstances, the officers refused

法公正的价值。

24. Balmain New Ferry Co Ltd v Robertson (1906) 4 CLR 379

澳大利亚高等法院，英属澳大利亚（当时澳大利亚属于英国）

Griffith 首席法官主笔：

在我看来，根据合同，原告默示地承诺除非他支付了一便士，他不会要求从陆路离开码头；此外原告还默示地同意，除非他支付了这一便士，被告有权阻止他从陆路离开码头。

O'Connor 法官主笔：

……然而，并非所有情况下，一个人的自由被限制了，他就可以因此而起诉。他完全可能参与订立了某个合同，根据这个合同他必须在一定的时间段内放弃一部分自由；如果别人据此限制了他的自由，他并不能因此而起诉。在没有另外一方同意的情况下，他也不能仅仅因为解除了合同，就可以无条件地、枉顾对方权利地，如同没有签订合同一样重新获得已经放弃的自由。旅客和铁路公司的合同就是这样一个例子。铁路公司承诺运输旅客。如果旅客突然在旅途中突然决定不再继续他的旅程，并希望在下一站下车，而下一站并不是计划的停靠站，他当然无权在那一站下车。无论他有多不愿意，铁路公司都可以合法地将他带到火车预定停靠的下一站。在这种情况下，旅客的自由在特定的时间段内就被限制了，且旅客还并不能因为这种限制就起诉铁路公司，因为他在合同里默示了他是允许铁路公司限制其自由的，只要这种限制是铁路公司按照火车的时间表履行运输合同所必须的。一个人也可能在某些条件下，通过自己的行为，让其处于一种不能因为自己的某些自由被限制而抱怨的状态。以双方辩论时用到的例子为例。假设运输公司码头上的旋转门开在海墙上，门上有个投币装置，只有当投币孔中有一枚硬币投入运行时才能打开。在这种情况下，假设原告投入一便士硬币打开了旋转门，进入了码头，然后改变了注意，不想乘坐轮船公司的船了，想回到街上；这时他能够宣布他不必通过投币打开旋转门这种常规方式出去，而是可以直接强行从门里挤过去，或者宣布公司的职员应该为他专门把门打开让他通过吗？在这种情况下，如果公司职员拒绝了他的请求，难道可以说公司就要为此承担非法拘禁的责任？表

to comply with his request, could it possibly be contended that the company would be liable to an action for false imprisonment? *Primâ facie*, no doubt, any restraint of a person's liberty without his consent is actionable. But, when the restraint is referable to the terms on which the person entered the premises in which he complains he was imprisoned, we must examine those terms before we can determine whether there has been an imprisonment which is actionable. The fallacy in the plaintiff's legal position lies in the assumption that, immediately he abandoned the contract to be carried to Balmain by the company's steamer, he was in the same position as if the wharf was one to which the public had free right of access, that, finding his exit barred by the turnstiles, he was entitled either to squeeze past them, or to demand from the company's officers that they should be specially released to let him through. Whether that assumption is or is not justifiable depends upon the terms on which the plaintiff was permitted to enter the wharf. In ascertaining those terms it must be remembered that the wharf was not a place to which the public had free right of access. If it had been so no one could legally place upon the wharf any bar or obstruction to the free entry or exit of any member of the public. But it was not a public place in that sense. It was private property. No one had a right to enter there without the company's permission, and they could impose on the members of the public any terms they thought fit as a condition of entering or leaving the premises. What were the terms on which the plaintiff entered the company's wharf? There was no express contract, and the terms must therefore be implied from the circumstances. In dealing with the circumstances I leave the question of the notice board out of consideration. In my view, it is immaterial whether the company did what was reasonable to direct public attention to the notice, or whether the plaintiff ever read it until his attention was called to it by the officer at the turnstile. But as to the material facts from which the contract must be implied there is no dispute. The plaintiff was aware that the only entrance to and exit from the wharf on the land side was through the turnstiles, and that, to quote his evidence, "When the turnstile was not released there was a complete barrier stretching across the whole entrance," in other words, entrance to and exit from the wharf were completely barred except when by the action of the officer in charge the turnstile was released. He also knew that the turnstiles were so constructed as to admit only persons entering the wharf through the entry turnstile, and only persons leaving the wharf through the exit turnstile, that the passing through of every passenger was automatically registered by the turnstile, and that the automatic register was a check on the cash taken by the officer. He himself in speaking to one of the officers said, "If it is the question of putting out the tally of your turnstiles I can squeeze through there," referring to the eight and a-half inch space before mentioned. Having travelled on many occasions backward and forward by the company's boats, and, as he says, paid his fare to the officers at the turnstiles, he must have been aware that the company's method of conducting their business was to release the turnstiles only on payment of a penny, and that in every case where there was a departure from that method "the tally of the turnstile," as he terms it,

面上看，任何未经一个人同意的对其人身自由的限制都是可诉的。然而，如果一个人是根据某种约定进入一块土地，而他的自由可能会被限制的，如果他这时起诉说他的人身自由在这块土地上被限制了，我们就必须先考察下这个约定的条款是什么，才能决定原告是否能因为其人身自由被限制提起诉讼。原告的主张的错误在于，他假设在他放弃乘坐运输公司的船去 Balmain 之后，便有权把码头当作公众可以随便进出的地方；当发现出口旋转门时，他便有权要么硬挤过去，要么要求公司的职员打开旋转门让他出去。原告的这种假设有没有道理，取决于据以进入码头的条款的内容。我们要考察这些条款之前，必须先明确一点，那就是码头并不是公众可以随意进出之地。如果公众有权随意进出码头，那么任何人都无权设置任何障碍来阻止公众的进出。问题是码头并不是这样一个公共设施。它是私有财产。除非获得运输公司的允许，没有人有权进入码头；而运输公司也有权制定任何其认为合理的条款，作为进出码头的条件。那么原告是依据什么条款进入码头的呢？合同里面没有明文规定这个问题；因此需要从相关的情况推断出一个默示条款。在讨论相关情况时，我不会考虑布告牌上的内容。在我看来，公司用了什么合理的手段让公众注意到布告牌，或者原告在旋转门前被职员要求看布告牌之前他有没有阅读上面的内容，都是无关紧要的情节。但是对于那些可以据以推断合同的默示条款的重要事实，则是没有争议的。原告知道从陆路进出码头的唯一通道只有旋转门；这点可以由他自己的证词证明"旋转门未开时，整个的入口被完全堵住了"；换言之，码头的入口和出口都被完全堵住了，除非执勤的公司职员把旋转门打开。他同样知道旋转门之所以这样设计，是为了让人们只能从入口旋转门进入码头，从出口旋转门离开码头；他同样知道，每个进出旋转门的乘客都会被自动记录，这种自动记录是通过在他支付给职员的现金上做记号来实现的。他自己就曾对一名职员说："如果你在乎的是统计有多少人用过这个旋转门的问题，我可以从那里挤出去。"他所说的那里是我之前提到的一个八英寸半的缝隙。他乘坐过很多次这个公司的船了，而且如他所说，也每次都在旋转门前向职员支付了费用。因此他肯定知道这个公司的盈利模式就是只有支付一便士才能打开旋转门；而且知道每当有人从旋转门进出的时，如他所说，"职员就会统计一下有人用过了这个旋转门"。

would be thrown out.

Such being the condition of the company's premises, and such being their method of carrying on their business, the plaintiff paid his penny to the officer and went through the entry turnstile on to the wharf. The first question is, what is the contract to be implied from the plaintiff's payment at and passing through the turnstiles under these circumstances? It is that in consideration of that payment the company undertook to carry him as a passenger to Balmain by any of their ferry boats from that wharf. That is the only contract which could be implied from those circumstances, and the plaintiff was permitted to enter the wharf for the purpose of that contract being performed. It is not denied that the company were ready to perform their part, but the plaintiff, as far as one party can do so, rescinded the contract and determined to go back from the wharf to the street. What then were his rights? They were, in my opinion, no more and no less than they would have been if he had landed from his own boat at the company's wharf. He was on private property. He had not been forced or entrapped there. He had entered it of his own free will and with the knowledge that the only exit on the land side was through the turnstile, operated as a part of the company's system of collecting fares in the manner I have mentioned. If he wished to use the turnstile as a means of exit he could only do so on complying with the usual conditions on which the company opened them. The company were lawfully entitled to impose the condition of a penny payment on all who used the turnstiles, whether they had travelled by the company's steamers or not, and they were under no obligation to make an exception in the plaintiff's favour. The company, therefore, being lawfully entitled to impose that condition, and the plaintiff being free to pass out through the turnstile at any time on complying with it, he had only himself to blame for his detention, and there was no imprisonment of which he could legally complain.

B. Self-Defence, Defence of Others, and Defence of Property

25. Courvoisier v. Raymond, 23 Colo. 113, 47 P. 284 (1896)

Supreme Court of Colorado, United States

Edwin S. Raymond, appellee, as plaintiff below, complains of Auguste Courvoisier, appellant, and alleges that on the 12th day of June, a.d. 1892, plaintiff was a regularly appointed and duly qualified acting special policeman in and for the city of Denver; that while engaged in the discharge of his duties as such special policeman, the defendant shot him in the abdomen, thereby causing a serious and painful wound; that in so doing the defendant acted wilfully, knowingly and maliciously, and without any reasonable cause....

The defendant, answering the complaint, denies each allegation thereof, and, in addition to such denials, pleads five separate defenses. These defenses are all in effect a justification by reason of unavoidable necessity. A trial resulted in a verdict and judgment for plaintiff for the sum of

这就是码头的情况，这就是公司盈利的模式，原告也是向职员支付了一便士才通过旋转门进入的码头。我们要问的第一个问题是原告支付费用后通过旋转门进入码头这件事，能推断出什么样的默示合同？这个默示的合同就是，作为他支付的费用的对价，公司承诺用客船将他作为旅客从码头运送到 Balmain。这是唯一的能从相关的情况中推断出来的合同，而原告之所以被允许进入码头，是为了让被告能履行这个合同。我们不能否认公司是愿意履行它的义务的；是原告解除了合同（他有权这么做），并决定离开码头回到街上去的。那么此时他有什么权利呢？他的权利在我看来，就和他乘坐自己的船，并在码头靠岸时是一样的。他现在在私有的地产上。他并非是被强迫带到这的，也不是被欺骗来到这儿的。他进入这里是出于他的自由意志，并且他知道唯一的从陆路离开的出口是那些旋转门，而如前所述这些旋转门是公司收费的方式。他要使用这些旋转门作为离开的方式的话，他只能遵守一般情况下公司打开这些门的条件。公司完全有权要求那些使用这些门的人支付一便士，无论这些人是否乘坐了公司的船。而且公司没有义务去为原告搞特殊。因此，公司可以合法地实施上述的条件，而原告也有权在遵守这些条件的情况下在任何时间自由地通过这些旋转门；他之所以被留置在了码头，完全是他自己的原因；没有任何人对他拘禁，他也不能合法地起诉任何人。

二、自卫、防卫他人和防卫财产

25. Courvoisier v. Raymond, 23 Colo. 113, 47 P. 284 (1896)

美国科罗拉多州最高法院

被上诉人 Edwin S. Raymond 是下文中的原告，控诉人（即上诉人）Auguste Courvoisier 指控如下：1892 年 6 月 12 日，原告在 Denver 市生活和工作，他是一名被正式任命的完全合格的代理特别警察；在履行这种特别警察的职责时，被告开枪打中了他的腹部，造成原告严重受伤，疼痛不已；被告的行为是蓄意的、有意识的和恶意的，没有任何合理的原因……

被告在回应原告的控诉时，不仅否认了上诉指控，还提出了五个抗辩事由。这些抗辩事由实际上基于不可避免的必要性来证明其正当性。初审最终由陪审团作出裁决，判决原告获得 3 143 美元的赔偿。为了推翻该判决，该案上诉

three thousand, one hundred and forty-three (3,143) dollars. To reverse this judgment, the cause is brought here by appeal.

Chief Justice Hayt delivered the opinion of the court.

It is admitted or proven beyond controversy that appellee received a gunshot wound at the hands of the appellant at the time and place designated in the complaint, and that as the result of such wound the appellee was seriously injured. It is further shown that the shooting occurred under the following circumstances:

That Mr. Courvoisier, on the night in question, was asleep in his bed in the second story of a brick building, situate at the corner of South Broadway and Dakota streets in South Denver; that he occupied a portion of the lower floor of this building as a jewelry store. He was aroused from his bed shortly after midnight by parties shaking or trying to open the door of the jewelry store. These parties, when asked by him as to what they wanted, insisted upon being admitted, and upon his refusal to comply with this request, they used profane and abusive epithets toward him. Being unable to gain admission, they broke some signs upon the front of the building, and then entered the building by another entrance, and passing upstairs commenced knocking upon the door of a room where defendant's sister was sleeping. Courvoisier partly dressed himself, and, taking his revolver, went upstairs and expelled the intruders from the building. In doing this he passed downstairs and out on the sidewalk as far as the entrance to his store, which was at the corner of the building. The parties expelled from the building, upon reaching the rear of the store, were joined by two or three others. In order to frighten these parties away, the defendant fired a shot in the air, but instead of retreating they passed around to the street in front, throwing stones and brickbats at the defendant, whereupon he fired a second and perhaps a third shot. The first shot fired attracted the attention of plaintiff Raymond and two deputy sheriffs, who were at the Tramway depot, across the street. These officers started toward Mr. Courvoisier, who still continued to shoot, but two of them stopped when they reached the men in the street, for the purpose of arresting them, Mr. Raymond alone proceeding towards the defendant, calling out to him that he was an officer and to stop shooting. Although the night was dark, the street was well lighted by electricity, and when the officer approached him defendant shaded his eyes, and, taking deliberate aim, fired, causing the injury complained of.

The plaintiff's theory of the case is that he was a duly authorized police officer, and in the discharge of his duties at the time; that the defendant was committing a breach of the peace, and that the defendant, knowing him to be a police officer, recklessly fired the shot in question.

The defendant claims that the plaintiff was approaching him at the time in a threatening attitude, and that the surrounding circumstances were such as to cause a reasonable man to believe that his life was in danger, and that it was necessary to shoot in self-defense, and that defendant did so believe at the time of firing the shot....

至上诉法院。

Hayt 首席大法官表达了法院的意见。

被上诉人在控诉所提到的时间和地点被上诉人用枪打伤，该枪伤造成被上诉人的严重伤害，这一点已经得到了承认或证明，不存在争议。可以进一步认为枪击事件发生的情况如下：

Courvoisier 先生在事发当晚正在一座砖制大楼的二楼床上睡觉，该大楼位于 South Denver 镇的 South Broadway 和 Dakota 街交叉的街角；他占用了一楼的一部分开了间珠宝店。午夜刚过，他被一群人惊醒，这些人摇晃珠宝店的门想打开它。Courvoisier 问他们要干什么，这些人坚持说他们得到了允许可以进入店内，在拒绝了他们的要求之后，他们开始用侮辱性的语言辱骂他。没有得到他的允许，他们便砸坏了大楼前面的一些标牌，并从另一个入口进入楼内，上楼之后开始踢打被告正在睡觉的姐姐的房间门。Courvoisier 套上衣裤，拿起他的左轮手枪，上楼赶走了这些闯入大楼的不速之客。为了赶走他们，他下楼一直走到人行道上位于大楼角落处的珠宝店入口处。这群被赶出来的人还没有来到珠宝店后面，又有两三个人加入了他们。为了吓跑这些人，被告向天空开了一枪，结果他们不但没有被吓跑，反而绕到前面来，向被告扔石头和砖块，这时被告开了第二枪，可能还有第三枪。第一枪便引起了原告 Raymond 和两名协警的注意，当时他们正在街对面的 Tramway 仓库。警官们朝着继续开枪的 Courvoisier 跑去，在跑到街上这些人跟前时，其中两名警官为了抓捕他们停了下来，只有 Raymond 一个人向被告跑去，喊自己是警察，要求被告停止射击。虽然夜很黑，但是街上灯光却很亮，在警察跑到被告跟前时，被告用手挡住眼镜，故意瞄准、开枪，造成了诉讼中提到的原告损害。

原告在本案中的主张是，他是一名得到正式授权的警察，当时正在履行他的职责；被告的行为打破了平静，被告在知道他是警察的情况下，鲁莽地开了本案争议的那一枪。

被告声称原告当时是带着威胁性的态度向他跑来的，当时周围的环境会造成一个理性人认为他的生命处于危险之中，有必要开枪以自卫，被告在开枪时确实也是这样认为的……

The next error assigned relates to the instructions given by the court to the jury and to those requested by the defendant and refused by the court. The second instruction given by the court was clearly erroneous. The instruction is as follows: "The court instructs you that if you believe from the evidence, that, at the time the defendant shot the plaintiff, the plaintiff was not assaulting the defendant, then your verdict should be for the plaintiff."

The vice of this instruction is that it excluded from the jury a full consideration of the justification claimed by the defendant. The evidence for the plaintiff tends to show that the shooting, if not malicious, was wanton and reckless, but the evidence for the defendant tends to show that the circumstances surrounding him at the time of the shooting were such as to lead a reasonable man to believe that his life was in danger, or that he was in danger of receiving great bodily harm at the hands of the plaintiff, and the defendant testified that he did so believe.

He swears that his house was invaded shortly after midnight by two men, whom he supposed to be burglars; that when ejected, they were joined on the outside by three or four others; that the crowd so formed assaulted him with stones and other missiles, when, to frighten them away, he shot into the air; that instead of going away someone approached him from the direction of the crowd; that he supposed this person to be one of the rioters, and did not ascertain that it was the plaintiff until after the shooting. He says that he had had no previous acquaintance with plaintiff; that he did not know that he was a police officer, or that there were any police officers in the town of South Denver; that he heard nothing said at the time by the plaintiff or anyone else that caused him to think the plaintiff was an officer; that his eyesight was greatly impaired, so that he was obliged to use glasses, and that he was without glasses at the time of the shooting, and for this reason could not see distinctly. He then adds: "I saw a man come away from the bunch of men and come up towards me, and as I looked around I saw this man put his hand to his hip pocket. I didn't think I had time to jump aside, and therefore turned around and fired at him. I had no doubts but it was somebody that had come to rob me, because some weeks before Mr. Wilson's store was robbed. It is next door to mine."

By this evidence two phases of the transaction are presented for consideration: *First,* was the plaintiff assaulting the defendant at the time plaintiff was shot? *Second,* if not, was there sufficient evidence of justification for the consideration of the jury? The first question was properly submitted, but the second was excluded by the instruction under review. The defendant's justification did not rest entirely upon the proof of assault by the plaintiff. A riot was in progress, and the defendant swears that he was attacked with missiles, hit with stones, brickbats, etc.; that he shot plaintiff, supposing him to be one of the rioters. We must assume these facts as established in reviewing the instruction, as we cannot say what the jury might have found had this evidence been submitted to them under a proper charge.

By the second instruction the conduct of those who started the fracas was eliminated from

下一个陈述的错误与法院向陪审团作出的指示和那些由被告申请并被法院拒绝的指示有关。法院作出的第二个指示存在明显的错误。该指示如下："法院指示你们，如果你们根据证据认为在被告开枪射击原告时，原告并没有在侵害被告，那么你们的裁断应该对原告有利。"

这条指示的问题在于它排除了陪审团充分考虑被告提出的理由。对原告有利的证据倾向于证明对原告的射击即使不存在恶意，也是肆意和鲁莽的，但是对被告有利的证据倾向于证明被告当时所处的环境会促使一个理性人认为他的生命处于危险之中，或者他可能受到来自原告的严重的身体伤害，而且被告也作证他确实这样认为。

他发誓，在刚过午夜之时，两名男子闯入了他的房子，他认为这些人是盗贼；在被驱除出去之后，房外又有三到四个人加入了他们；形成的人群向他投掷石块和其他投掷物，为了吓跑他们，他向天空开了枪；这些人不但没有走开，有人反而从人群那个方向向他走来；他以为这个人也是暴徒中间的一员，在开枪之后才确定那个人正是原告。他说他以前从未见过原告；不知道他是一名警察，也不知道 South Denver 镇有警察；他没有听见原告或其他人说一些让他认为他们是警察的话；他的视力非常不好，必须戴眼镜，但是在开枪时他并没有戴眼镜，所以看得不是非常分明。他补充道："我看见这个人从一群人中间朝我走过来，我四处看了看，我看见这个人将他的手放入了他屁股裤兜里。我觉得我没有时间闪到一边，所以转过身去向他开了枪。我毫不怀疑这个人是来抢劫我的，因为几个星期以前 Wilson 先生的商店就被抢了。就在我隔壁。"

根据这个证据，有两个方面的因素需要考虑：第一，原告在被枪击中时是否正在威吓被告？第二，如果没有，那么是否有足够的正当性证据支持陪审团的意见？第一个问题被适当地提交了，但是被审查的指示却将第二个问题排除在外。被告的正当性并没有完全建立在被原告威吓的证明之上。暴行在继续，被告发誓他遭到了投掷物的攻击，如石头和砖块等，他以为原告是暴徒中的一员，因此开枪打中了原告。我们在对指示进行审查时，必须假定这些事实已经被确定，因为我们无法得知当这些证据被以合适的方式指示给陪审团时他们会从中发现什么。

通过第二个指示，发起闹事的人的行为便不再是陪审团考虑的对象。如果陪审团依据证据，相信一个人像原告一样向被告走来，那么被告射击一个

the consideration of the jury. If the jury believed from the evidence that the defendant would have been justified in shooting one of the rioters had such person advanced towards him as did the plaintiff, then it became important to determine whether the defendant mistook plaintiff for one of the rioters, and if such a mistake was in fact made, was it excusable in the light of all the circumstances leading up to and surrounding the commission of the act? If these issues had been resolved by the jury in favor of the defendant, he would have been entitled to a judgment....

Where a defendant in a civil action like the one before us attempts to justify on a plea of necessary self-defense, he must satisfy the jury not only that he acted honestly in using force, but that his fears were reasonable under the circumstances; and also as to the reasonableness of the means made use of. In this case perhaps the verdict would not have been different had the jury been properly instructed, but it might have been, and therefore the judgment must be reversed.

Reversed.

26. Katko v. Briney, 183 N.W.2d 657 (Iowa 1971)

Supreme Court of Iowa, United States

Moore, C.J.

...Plaintiff's action is for damages resulting from serious injury caused by a shot from a 20-gauge spring shotgun set by defendants in a bedroom of an old farm house which had been uninhabited for several years. Plaintiff and his companion, Marvin McDonough, had broken and entered the house to find and steal old bottles and dated fruit jars which they considered antiques.

At defendants' request plaintiff's action was tried to a jury consisting of residents of the community where defendants' property was located. The jury returned a verdict for plaintiff and against defendants for $20,000 actual and $10,000 punitive damages.

After careful consideration of defendants' motions for judgment notwithstanding the verdict and for new trial, the experienced and capable trial judge overruled them and entered judgment on the verdict. Thus we have this appeal by defendants....

Most of the facts are not disputed. In 1957 defendant Bertha L. Briney inherited her parents' farmland in Mahaska and Monroe Counties. Included was an 80-acre tract in southwest Mahaska County where her grandparents and parents had lived. No one occupied the house thereafter. Her husband, Edward, attempted to care for the land. He kept no farm machinery thereon. The outbuildings became dilapidated.

For about 10 years, 1957 to 1967, there occurred a series of trespassing and housebreaking events with loss of some household items, the breaking of windows and "messing up of the property in general." The latest occurred June 8, 1967, prior to the event on July 16, 1967 herein involved.

暴徒的行为是合理的,那么确认被告是否将原告误认为一名暴徒便非常重要,如果被告确实误解了,那么导致并围绕这种行为的环境是否可以使被告的行为得到原谅?如果陪审团以对被告有利的方式解答了这些问题,那么被告有权赢得判决……

在像我们面前的这场民事诉讼中,如果被告要基于必要的自卫行为这一辩护理由证明其正当性,那么他不仅必须说服陪审团他确实使用了武力,但是在那种环境下他的恐惧是合理的;同时还要说明他所采取的手段具有合理性。在本案中,如果陪审团得到了适当的指示,裁决可能不会有所不同,但是也有可能不同,因此必须撤销判决。

撤销判决。

26. Katko v. Briney, 183 N.W.2d 657 (Iowa 1971)

美国爱荷华州最高法院

Moore 大法官主笔:

……在一个多年无人居住的农场旧房子的卧室中,原告被一把 20 口径的弹簧手枪击中并造成重伤,原告因此提起诉讼。原告及其同伴 Marvin McDonough 闯入了这个旧房子寻找一些他们认为是古董的旧瓶子和陈旧的水果罐。

依据被告的要求,原告的诉讼被提交给由被告房屋地的社区居民组成的陪审团审理。陪审团作出了有利于原告的裁断,要求被告向原告赔偿 2 万美元的实际损害赔偿金和 1 万美元的惩罚性赔偿。

在仔细考虑了被告提出的与陪审团裁断相反的判决和重新审理的申请之后,经验丰富且能力超群的初审法官驳回了被告的申请,依据陪审团的裁断作出了判决。因此被告上诉到本院……

大多数事实都不存在争议。1957 年,被告 Bertha L. Briney 继承了她父母在 Mahaska 县和 Monroe 县的农场。其中包括位于 Mahaska 县西南地区的一块 80 英亩的土地,她的祖父母和父母曾经在那里居住。自那以后没有人再到那里居住过。她的丈夫 Edward 试图照料这片土地。在上面没有安置任何的机械设备。那里的附属建筑已经荒废。

从 1957 年到 1967 年的 10 年间,发生了一系列的非法入侵和入室盗窃事件,一些家庭用品丢失,窗户被打碎,"大体上财产被弄得一团糟"。最近一次盗窃事件发生在 1967 年 6 月 8 日,就在本案涉及事件发生的 1967 年 7 月 16 日之前。

Defendants through the years boarded up the windows and doors in an attempt to stop the intrusions. They had posted "no trespass" signs on the land several years before 1967. The nearest one was 35 feet from the house. On June 11, 1967 defendants set "a shotgun trap" in the north bedroom. After Mr. Briney cleaned and oiled his 20-gauge shotgun, the power of which he was well aware, defendants took it to the old house where they secured it to an iron bed with the barrel pointed at the bedroom door. It was rigged with wire from the doorknob to the gun's trigger so it would fire when the door was opened. Briney first pointed the gun so an intruder would be hit in the stomach but at Mrs. Briney's suggestion it was lowered to hit the legs. He admitted he did so "because I was mad and tired of being tormented" but "he did not intend to injure anyone." He gave no explanation of why he used a loaded shell and set it to hit a person already in the house. Tin was nailed over the bedroom window. The spring gun could not be seen from the outside. No warning of its presence was posted.

Plaintiff lived with his wife and worked regularly as a gasoline station attendant in Eddyville, seven miles from the old house. He had observed it for several years while hunting in the area and considered it as being abandoned. He knew it had been uninhabited. In 1967 the area around the house was covered with high weeds. Prior to July 16, 1967 plaintiff and McDonough had been to the premises and found several old bottles and fruit jars which they took and added to their collection of antiques. On the latter date about 9:30 p.m. they made a second trip to the Briney property. They entered the house by removing a board from a porch window which was without glass. While McDonough was looking around the kitchen area plaintiff went to another part of the house. As he started to open the north bedroom door the shotgun went off striking him in the right leg above the ankle bone. Much of his leg, including part of the tibia, was blown away. Only by McDonough's assistance was plaintiff able to get out of the house and after crawling some distance was put in his vehicle and rushed to a doctor and then to a hospital. He remained in the hospital 40 days....

There was undenied medical testimony plaintiff had a permanent deformity, a loss of tissue, and a shortening of the leg.

The record discloses plaintiff to trial time had incurred $710 medical expense, $2056.85 for hospital service, $61.80 for orthopedic service and $750 as loss of earnings. In addition thereto the trial court submitted to the jury the question of damages for pain and suffering and for future disability.

Plaintiff testified he knew he had no right to break and enter the house with intent to steal bottles and fruit jars therefrom. He further testified he had entered a plea of guilty to larceny in the nighttime of property of less than $20 value from a private building. He stated he had been fined $50 and costs and paroled during good behavior from a 60-day jail sentence. Other than minor traffic charges this was plaintiff's first brush with the law. On this civil case appeal it is not our

多年来，被告一直试图通过将窗户和门用木板封住来阻止被侵入。他们在1967年之前便在这片土地上竖起了"禁止侵入"的牌子。最近的一块牌子离房屋只有35英尺。1967年6月11日，被告在北边的卧室里设下了"猎枪陷阱"。Briney先生擦干净了他的20口径猎枪，并上了油，他对这把枪的威力十分清楚，随后被告将枪拿到了旧房子，他们把枪架在一张铁床上，将枪管对准卧室的门。他们在门把手和枪的扳机之间连接了一根铁丝，当门被打开时，枪便会开火。Briney先将枪对准了可能伤到闯入者腹部的地方，但是在Briney太太的建议下，他们把瞄准位置降到了可能打到闯入者腿部的位置。他承认他这样做的原因是"我气疯了，不想再被折磨"，但是"他并没有想伤害任何人"。他没有解释为什么他会把枪上膛，用它来射击已经在屋子里的人。卧室窗户上钉满了锡皮。从外面看不到这只弹簧枪，也没有关于其存在的警告。

原告与他的妻子住在一起，在Eddyville的一个加油站当全职的服务员，该加油站离旧房子有7英里远。他在附近打猎时观察了这个房子很多年，认为该房子已经被废弃。他知道里面没有人居住。1967年，房子周围长满了杂草。1967年7月16日之前，原告和McDonough曾经到过该房屋，找到了一些旧瓶子和水果罐，他们将这些东西拿回家，和他们收集的古董放在了一起。在案发当天，大约晚上9∶30，他们再次来到了Briney的房子。他们拿开了门廊处没有玻璃的窗户上的木板，进入了房间。McDonough在厨房四处寻找的时候，原告来到了房子的另外一头。当他推开北侧卧室门的时候，扳动了猎枪的扳机，子弹打在了他右腿膝盖以上的部位。他的腿的大部分，包括一部分胫骨都被炸掉了。在McDonough的帮助下，原告才离开了房子，爬行了一段之后才坐上了他的汽车急忙去看大夫，然后被送入了医院。他在医院待了40天……

医学证明确定原告将落下永久性的残疾，组织缺损和伤腿变短。

案卷显示，原告到审理时为止已经用去了710美元的医疗费用、2 056.85美元的医院服务费用、61.80美元的外科整形费用和750美元的误工费。除此之外，初审法院还向陪审团提交了关于痛苦和精神损失以及未来残疾的赔偿问题。

原告作证说他知道他没有权利闯入他人的房屋去偷瓶子和水果罐。他还作证说已经作出了晚上从私人房屋内偷盗不足20美元财产的偷盗罪认罪答辩（plea of guilty）。他说他已经被罚款50美元和其他费用，并被判入狱60天，但因表现良好而获得假释（parole）。除了一些小的交通罚款之外，这是原告的第一次违法行为。在作为民事上诉案的本案中，我们没有特权去审视针对

prerogative to review the disposition made of the criminal charge against him.

The main thrust of defendants' defense in the trial court and on this appeal is that "the law permits use of a spring gun in a dwelling or warehouse for the purpose of preventing the unlawful entry of a burglar or thief." They repeated this contention in their exceptions to the trial court's instructions 2, 5, and 6. They took no exception to the trial court's statement of the issues or to other instructions.

In the statement of issues the trial court stated plaintiff and his companion committed a felony when they broke and entered defendants' house. In instruction 2 the court referred to the early case history of the use of spring guns and stated under the law their use was prohibited except to prevent the commission of felonies of violence and where human life is in danger. The instruction included a statement breaking and entering is not a felony of violence.

Instruction 5 stated: "You are hereby instructed that one may use reasonable force in the protection of his property, but such right is subject to the qualification that one may not use such means of force as will take human life or inflict great bodily injury. Such is the rule even though the injured party is a trespasser and is in violation of the law himself."

Instruction 6 stated: "An owner of premises is prohibited from willfully or intentionally injuring a trespasser by means of force that either takes life or inflicts great bodily injury; and therefore a person owning a premise is prohibited from setting out 'spring guns' and like dangerous devices which will likely take life or inflict great bodily injury, for the purpose of harming trespassers. The fact that the trespasser may be acting in violation of the law does not change the rule. The only time when such conduct of setting a 'spring gun' or a like dangerous device is justified would be when the trespasser was committing a felony of violence or a felony punishable by death, or where the trespasser was endangering human life by his act."

Instruction 7, to which defendants made no objection or exception, stated: "To entitle the plaintiff to recover for compensatory damages, the burden of proof is upon him to establish by a preponderance of the evidence each and all of the following propositions:

> "1. That defendants erected a shotgun trap in a vacant house on land owned by defendant, Bertha L. Briney, on or about June 11, 1967, which fact was known only by them, to protect household goods from trespassers and thieves.
>
> "2. That the force used by defendants was in excess of that force reasonably necessary and which persons are entitled to use in the protection of their property.
>
> "3. That plaintiff was injured and damaged and the amount thereof.
>
> "4. That plaintiff's injuries and damages resulted directly from the discharge of the shotgun trap which was set and used by defendants."

他刑事指控的判决。

在初审法院和上诉中,被告辩护的要点是"法律允许在住宅或仓库使用弹簧枪防止强盗和小偷的非法进入"。他们在反驳初审法院的第2、5、6条指示时不断重复这一论点。而对初审法院陈述的争议点或作出的其他指示没有进行反驳。

初审法院在陈述争议点时指出,原告和他的同伴在闯入被告的房屋时犯了重罪(felony)。在第2条指示中,法院参考了早期使用弹簧枪的案件,指出法律禁止使用弹簧枪,除非为了防止暴力重罪和个人生命受到威胁。该条指示还指出,破窗而入不算暴力重罪。

第5条指示指出:"特指示如下,人们可以采用合理的武力来保护他们的财产,但是该权利不适用于那些使人致死或造成严重身体伤害的手段作为武力的情况。即使受伤一方是侵入者并且自身正在违反法律,该规定也一样适用。"

第6条指示指出:"禁止建筑物的所有者蓄意或故意采用使人致死或造成严重身体伤害的武力去伤害侵入者;因此,建筑物的所有者不得设置可能使人致死或造成严重身体伤害的'弹簧枪'或类似的危险装置去伤害侵入者。如果侵入者的行为本身是违法行为也不能改变该规则。只有当侵入者正在实施暴力的或可判处死刑的重罪,或者侵入者的行为威胁到了他的生命,这时设置'猎枪'或类似的危险装置才具有正当理由。"

被告对第7条指示没有表示反对或反驳,这条指示指出,如果原告要取得获得损害赔偿的权利,那么原告就负有确定以下各条件和全部陈述的优势证据举证义务:

 1. 被告大约于1967年6月11日在被告 Bertha L. Briney 所有的一栋空房子内设置了一个猎枪陷阱,事实上只有被告自己知道这一陷阱,目的是为了防止侵入者和小偷盗取房屋内的东西。
 2. 被告使用的武力超过了合理的必要性和人们在保护他们的财产时有权使用的武力。
 3. 原告受到了伤害,并蒙受了相关数额的损失。
 4. 原告受到的伤害和损失由被告设置并使用的猎枪陷阱直接造成。

压倒性的权威观点,包括教科书和判例法,都支持初审法院作出的关于

The overwhelming weight of authority, both textbook and case law, supports the trial court's statement of the applicable principles of law.

Prosser on Torts, Third Edition, pages 116-118, states:

> "...the law has always placed a higher value upon human safety than upon mere rights in property, it is the accepted rule that there is no privilege to use any force calculated to cause death or serious bodily injury to repel the threat to land or chattels, unless there is also such a threat to the defendant's personal safety as to justify a self-defense....Spring guns and other man-killing devices are not justifiable against a mere trespasser, or even a petty thief. They are privileged only against those upon whom the landowner, if he were present in person would be free to inflict injury of the same kind."...

In Hooker v. Miller, 37 Iowa 613, we held defendant vineyard owner liable for damages resulting from a spring gun shot although plaintiff was a trespasser and there to steal grapes. At pages 614, 615, this statement is made: "This court has held that a mere trespass against property other than a dwelling is not a sufficient justification to authorize the use of a deadly weapon by the owner in its defense; and that if death results in such a case it will be murder, though the killing be actually necessary to prevent the trespass. The State v. Vance, 17 Iowa 138." At page 617 this court said: "Trespassers and other inconsiderable violators of the law are not to be visited by barbarous punishments or prevented by inhuman inflictions of bodily injuries."

The facts in Allison v. Fiscus, 156 Ohio 120, 100 N.E.2d 237, 44 A.L.R.2d 369, decided in 1951, are very similar to the case at bar. There plaintiff's right to damages was recognized for injuries received when he feloniously broke a door latch and started to enter defendant's warehouse with intent to steal. As he entered a trap of two sticks of dynamite buried under the doorway by defendant owner was set off and plaintiff seriously injured. The court held the question whether a particular trap was justified as a use of reasonable and necessary force against a trespasser engaged in the commission of a felony should have been submitted to the jury. The Ohio Supreme Court recognized plaintiff's right to recover punitive or exemplary damages in addition to compensatory damages....

In Wisconsin, Oregon and England the use of spring guns and similar devices is specifically made unlawful by statute. 44 A.L.R., section 3, pages 386, 388.

The legal principles stated by the trial court in instructions 2, 5, and 6 are well established and supported by the authorities cited and quoted supra. There is no merit in defendants' objections and exceptions thereto. Defendants' various motions based on the same reasons stated in exceptions to instructions were properly overruled....

适用法律原则的陈述。

《Prosser 论侵权法》（Prosser on Torts），第三版，第 116—118 页写道：

> ……法律总是将人的安全置于高于单纯财产权的地位之上，一个普遍接受的规则是，为了阻止对土地或动产构成的威胁，人们没有权利采用那些可以造成人员死亡或严重的身体伤害的武力，除非这种危险同时威胁到了被告的人身安全而证明自卫措施是正当的……对于单纯的侵入者或其他小贼，使用弹簧枪和其他杀人装置是不正当的。只有当土地所有人作为个人（面临窃贼）有权对侵害者造成同样伤害的情形中，才能够被特免。……

在 Hooker v. Miller, 37 Iowa 613 案中，虽然原告是闯入者并且是为了偷葡萄，但是我们仍然认为作为葡萄园所有者的被告应该为弹簧枪造成的损害承担赔偿责任。在（该案判决书）第 614 页和第 615 页作出了这样的陈述："本院认为单纯地侵入被告的不动产而非住宅并非足够的正当化理由来授权财产所有人使用致命武器进行防卫；如果导致本案中原告死亡，那么这便是谋杀，哪怕杀人对于防止侵入行为存在实际的必要性。(The State v. Vance, 17 Iowa 138.)"在(Hooker 案)案卷第 617 页，该法院指出："侵入者和其他微不足道的违法者不应受到野蛮的惩罚或以非人道的被造成人身伤害的方式被制止。"

1951 年判决的 Allison v. Fiscus, 156 Ohio 120, 100 N.E.2d 237, 44 A.L.R.2d 369 案中的事实和正在审理的本案非常相似。原告因为他在凶恶地打破了被告的仓库门闩后，企图进去实施盗窃时受到的伤害要求赔偿的权利得到了认可。他进入仓库时，仓库所有人即被埋在门口的两根炸药被引爆，造成原告的严重伤害。为了防止正在实施重罪行为的侵入者，将某种陷阱作为合理且必要的预防手段是否具有合理性，法院认为这个问题应该提交陪审团。俄亥俄州高等法院认可原告除了应获得损害赔偿外，还应该获得被告的惩罚性赔偿……

在威斯康星州、俄勒冈州和英格兰，法律规定使用弹簧枪和类似的装置都是违法的。(44 A.L.R., 第 3 条, 第 386 页和第 388 页。)

初审法院在第 2、5、6 条指示中陈述的法律原则均被较为充分地确立，且得到了上文引用和引证法源的支持。被告的反对和反驳没有法律依据。被告在反驳指示中依据同样理由提出的申请被完全驳回……

Study and careful consideration of defendants' contentions on appeal reveal no reversible error.

Affirmed.

All Justices concur except Larson, J., who dissents.

Larson, J.

I respectfully dissent, first, because the majority wrongfully assumes that by installing a spring gun in the bedroom of their unoccupied house the defendants intended to shoot any intruder who attempted to enter the room. Under the record presented here, that was a fact question. Unless it is held that these property owners are liable for any injury to an intruder from such a device regardless of the intent with which it is installed, liability under these pleadings must rest upon two definite issues of fact, i.e., did the defendants intend to shoot the invader, and if so, did they employ unnecessary and unreasonable force against him?

It is my feeling that the majority oversimplifies the impact of this case on the law, not only in this but other jurisdictions, and that it has not thought through all the ramifications of this holding.

There being no statutory provisions governing the right of an owner to defend his property by the use of a spring gun or other like device, or of a criminal invader to recover punitive damages when injured by such an instrumentality while breaking into the building of another, our interest and attention are directed to what should be the court determination of public policy in these matters. On both issues we are faced with a case of first impression. We should accept the task and clearly establish the law in this jurisdiction hereafter. I would hold there is no absolute liability for injury to a criminal intruder by setting up such a device on his property, and unless done with an intent to kill or seriously injure the intruder, I would absolve the owner from liability other than for negligence. I would also hold the court had no jurisdiction to allow punitive damages when the intruder was engaged in a serious criminal offense such as breaking and entering with intent to steal.

It appears to me that the learned trial court was and the majority is now confused as to the basis of liability under the circumstances revealed. Certainly, the trial court's instructions did nothing to clarify the law in this jurisdiction for the jury. Timely objections to Instructions Nos. 2, 5, and 6 were made by the defendants, and thereafter the court should have been aware of the questions of liability left unresolved, i.e., whether in this jurisdiction we by judicial declaration bar the use in an unoccupied building of spring guns or other devices capable of inflicting serious injury or death on an intruder regardless of the intent with which they are installed, or whether such an intent is a vital element which must be proven in order to establish liability for an injury inflicted upon a criminal invader.

Although the court told the jury the plaintiff had the burden to prove "That the force used by defendants was in excess of that force reasonably necessary and which persons are entitled to use

经过对被告上述论点进行研究和仔细考虑，没有发现可被推翻的错误。
维持原判。

除 Larson 法官反对之外，其他所有法官赞同判决。

Larson 法官主笔：

我谦恭地[①]反对如下：首先，由于多数意见错误地认为被告在自己没有居住的房屋内的卧室中安装弹簧枪的目的，就是意图射击试图进入房间的任何闯入者。基于我们面前的案卷，这是一个事实问题。除非认为无论安装这些设备的意图如何，这些财产的所有人都应该为装置造成的闯入者损害负责，否则这些起诉状涉及的责任便必须依据两个明确的事实问题，即被告是否意图射击闯入者，如果是，那么他们是否针对闯入者采取了不必要和不合理的武力？

我感觉，多数意见过于简单地考虑了本案对法律造成的影响，不光在本法域如此，在其他法域也是如此，也没有对该裁决产生的各种后果得出结论。

法律条文没有规定所有者有权使用弹簧枪或其他装置保护自己的财产，也没有规定犯罪的闯入者在闯入这些别人建筑物时被这些装置伤害后有权获得惩罚性赔偿，我们的兴趣和注意力被引导到了这些问题中作为公共政策的法院判决上。在事实和法律两方面，我们都以第一印象在面对这个案件。我们应该接受这个任务，并在这个法域清晰地确立起法律规则。我认为，在自己的财产上设置这种装置造成违法闯入者受伤不应该承担绝对责任，除非这样做的目的是为了杀死或严重伤害闯入者，即应当预料到会有损害结果而没预料到或者预料到了而轻信能够避免。我还认为，在闯入者以盗窃为目的闯入或进入房屋从事严重刑事犯罪行为的情形下，该法院没有实施准许惩罚性赔偿的裁判权。

在我看来，精通法律的初审法院和多数意见现在对于展现出的情境背后的责任基础感到迷惑。的确，初审法院的指示并没有向陪审团说明本法域的法律。被告及时地反对了第 2、5、6 条指示，在那之后该法院本应该注意到那些尚未解决的责任问题，即在本法域，我们是否通过司法判决禁止在无人居住的建筑物内使用弹簧枪或其他可造成闯入者严重受伤或死亡的装置，无论设置这些装置的意图如何；或者这种意图是否是一个关键要素，必须通过证明才能确定造成违法闯入者伤害的责任。

虽然法院告诉陪审团，原告负有证明"被告使用的武力超过了合理的必

---

① 这是表示反对意见的法官的用语习惯，并无特别的意义。——译者注

in the protection of their property," it utterly failed to tell the jury it could find the installation was not made with the intent or purpose of striking or injuring the plaintiff. There was considerable evidence to that effect. As I shall point out, both defendants stated the installation was made for the purpose of scaring or frightening away any intruder, not to seriously injure him. It may be that the evidence would support a finding of an intent to injure the intruder, but obviously that important issue was never adequately or clearly submitted to the jury.

Unless, then, we hold for the first time that liability for death or injury in such cases is absolute, the matter should be remanded for a jury determination of defendants' intent in installing the device under instructions usually given to a jury on the issue of intent....

If, after proper instructions, the finder of fact determines that the gun was set with an intent and purpose to kill or inflict great bodily injury on an intruder, then and only then may it be said liability is established unless the property so protected is shown to be an occupied dwelling house. Of course, under this concept, if the finder of fact determines the gun set in an unoccupied house was intended to do no more than to frighten the intruder or sting him a bit, no liability would be incurred under such pleadings as are now presented. If such a concept of the law were adopted in Iowa, we would have here a question for the fact-finder or jury as to whether the gun was willfully and intentionally set so as to seriously injure the thief or merely scare him away.

I feel the better rule is that an owner of buildings housing valuable property may employ the use of spring guns or other devices intended to repel but not seriously injure an intruder who enters his secured premises with or without a criminal intent, but I do not advocate its general use, for there may also be liability for negligent installation of such a device. What I mean to say is that under such circumstances as we have here the issue as to whether the set was with an intent to seriously injure or kill an intruder is a question of fact that should be left to the jury under proper instructions, and that the mere setting of such a device with a resultant serious injury should not as a matter of law establish liability.

In the case of a mere trespass able authorities have reasoned that absolute liability may rightfully be fixed on the landowner for injuries to the trespasser because very little damage could be inflicted upon the property owner and the danger is great that a child or other innocent trespasser might be seriously injured by the device. In such matters they say no privilege to set up the device should be recognized by the courts regardless of the owner's intent. I agree.

On the other hand, where the intruder may pose a danger to the inhabitants of a dwelling, the privilege of using such a device to repel has been recognized by most authorities, and the mere setting thereof in the dwelling has not been held to create liability for an injury as a matter of law. In such cases intent and the reasonableness of the force would seem relevant to liability.

Although I am aware of the often-repeated statement that personal rights are more important than property rights, where the owner has stored his valuables representing his life's accumulations,

要性和人们在保护他们的财产时有权使用的武力"的举证义务,但是却完全没有告诉陪审团,可以查明被告设置该装置的意图或目的不是为了攻击或伤害原告。有值得重视的证据指向这一点。正如我将指出的那样,两个被告都表示设置猎枪的目的是想吓跑闯入者,而不是严重地伤害他。证据也有可能支持认为被告具有伤害闯入者的意图的结论,但是显然,这个重要的问题从来没有被充分地或清晰地提交给陪审团。

那么除非我们破天荒地认为本案中被告对死亡或伤害负有的责任是绝对的,否则就应该将该案发回重审,以通常针对意图问题向陪审团发出的指示,交由陪审团确定被告在设置装置时的意图……

在作出恰当的指示后,如果事实认定者确定被告设置猎枪存在杀死闯入者或造成闯入者严重身体伤害的意图或目的,那么这时,也只有在这时能确定被告的责任,除非证明被保护的财产是居住的住所。当然,在这样的观念下,如果事实认定者确定在无人居住的房屋内设置猎枪的目的不外乎只是为了吓跑闯入者,或刺激他一下,那么基于我们面前的起诉状,被告无需承担责任。如果爱荷华州采纳了这种法律观念,那么我们要向事实认定者或者陪审团提出这样的问题:被告是否蓄意并故意地设置了猎枪?其目的在于严重伤害盗贼还是仅仅想吓跑他?

我认为好一点的规则是,存有贵重财产的房屋的所有者可以采用弹簧枪或其他装置阻止而不是严重伤害进入其保护领地的闯入者,无论该闯入者是否具有犯罪的意图,但是我并不倡导普遍适用该规则,因为安装这些装置的过失行为也可能导致行为人承担责任。我想说的是,在我们现在遇到的这种情境下,设置这些装置的意图是否是为了严重伤害或杀死闯入者,这个事实问题应该依据适当的指示由陪审团来确定,仅仅因为设置这些装置造成了严重伤害不应该作为法律问题而确定责任。

在单纯的侵入案件中,有力的法源(able authorities)认为,房主因为对侵入者造成了伤害而承担绝对责任是正当的,因为财产所有者遭受的损失可能很小,而儿童或其他无辜的侵入者可能因为这些装置而受到严重的伤害。在这些问题上,他们说无论财产所有者的意图是什么,他们设置这些装置都不能获得特免。我同意。

另一方面,当闯入者对住宅里的居住者构成威胁时,使用这些装置阻止闯入者可以获得特免,这点被主流法源所认可,而在住宅内单纯地设置这些装置不会作为法律问题对造成的伤害承担责任。在这些案件中,使用武力的意图和合理性似乎和责任相关。

his livelihood business, his tools and implements, and his treasured antiques as appears in the case at bar, and where the evidence is sufficient to sustain a finding that the installation was intended only as a warning to ward off thieves and criminals, I can see no compelling reason why the use of such a device alone would create liability as a matter of law....

In the case at bar, as I have pointed out, there is a sharp conflict in the evidence. The physical facts and certain admissions as to how the gun was aimed would tend to support a finding of intent to injure, while the direct testimony of both defendants was that the gun was placed so it would "hit the floor eventually" and that it was set "low so it couldn't kill anybody." Mr. Briney testified, "My purpose in setting up the gun was not to injure somebody. I thought more or less that the gun would be at a distance of where anyone would grab the door, it would scare them," and in setting the angle of the gun to hit the lower part of the door, he said, "I didn't think it would go through quite that hard."

If the law in this jurisdiction permits, which I think it does, an explanation of the setting of a spring gun to repel invaders of certain private property, then the intent with which the set is made is a vital element in the liability issue.

In view of the failure to distinguish and clearly give the jury the basis upon which it should determine that liability issue, I would reverse and remand the entire case for a new trial....

Being convinced that there was reversible error in the court's instructions, that the issue of intent in placing the spring gun was not clearly presented to the jury...I would reverse and remand the matter for a new trial....

27. Ashley and Another v Chief Constable of Sussex [2008] UKHL 25, [2008] 1 AC 962

House of Lords, United Kingdom

LORD SCOTT

Issue 1: the self-defence criteria

In para 37 of his judgment Sir Anthony Clarke MR identified three possible approaches to the criteria requisite for a successful plea of self-defence, namely, (1) the necessity to take action in response to an attack, or imminent attack, must be judged on the assumption that the facts were as the defendant honestly believed them to be, whether or not he was mistaken and, if he made a mistake of fact, whether or not it was reasonable for him to have done so (solution 1); (2) the necessity to take action in response to an attack or imminent attack must be judged on the facts as the defendant honestly believed them to be, whether or not he was mistaken, but, if he made a mistake of fact, he can rely on that fact only if the mistake was a reasonable one for him to have made (solution 2); (3) in order to establish the relevant necessity the defendant must establish that there was in fact an imminent and real risk of attack (solution 3). It was common ground that, in

尽管我注意到人们经常说人身权比财产权更重要,但是当所有者将那些代表他一生的财富积累、他赖以生活的营业、他的工具和装备,以及他的宝贝古董存储起来,就像本案中我们看到的这样,而且证据也足以证明他设置猎枪的意图只是为了警告盗贼和其他犯罪分子不要进入时,作为法律问题,我不认为有任何具有说服力的理由认为仅仅使用了这些装置便需要承担责任……

在本案中,正如我所指出的,证据中存在明显的矛盾。客观事实以及关于枪的瞄准位置的特定承认都足以支持伤害的意图,而两位被告的直接证词则是,枪放置的位置使其"最终将打到地上",而且枪瞄准的位置"很低以避免伤到人"。Briney 先生作证说:"我设置枪的目的不是为了伤到任何人。我多多少少认为枪的位置和人们打开门的位置之间还有一段距离,它会吓到他们。"将枪的角度设得很低以便枪只能打到门的下部,他说:"我没想到会造成如此严重的后果。"

如果本法域的法律允许,而我认为确实允许,对为赶跑那些侵犯私人财产的闯入者而设置弹簧枪的做法进行解释,那么设置弹簧枪的意图在确认责任问题上就显得非常重要。

鉴于法院没有区别并清楚地向陪审团提供确定责任问题依据的基础,我希望撤销判决,将整个案件发回重审……

基于对法院的指示存在可被推翻的错误的确信,即关于设置弹簧枪的意图问题没有清楚地提交给陪审团……我希望撤销判决,发回重审……

27. Ashley and Another v Chief Constable of Sussex [2008] UKHL 25, [2008] 1 AC 962

联合王国上议院

Scott 大法官主笔:

第一个争议焦点:正当防卫的标准

在其判决的第 37 段,掌卷法官 Anthony Clarke 爵士列举了三种关于正当防卫要件的观点。第一,对于正在发生的攻击或者可能的攻击作出回击是否必要,我们在判断这个问题的时候应该假设事实就像被告所真诚地以为的那样,无论他的认识是正确的还是错误的;如果他确实对事实认识有错误,那么不需要判断他是不是有合理的理由这么认为(第一种观点)。第二,对于正在发生的攻击或者可能的攻击作出回击是否必要,我们在判断这个问题的时候应该按照被告所真诚地以为的事实来判断,无论他的认识是正确还是错误,然而如果他的认识是错误的,那么只有在他是出于合理的原因作出这种

addition, based on whatever belief the defendant is entitled to rely on, the defendant must, in a civil action, satisfy the court that it was reasonable for him to have taken the action he did. Of the three solutions the Court of Appeal held that solution 2 was the correct one. On this appeal the chief constable has contended, as he did below, that solution 1 is the correct one. The claimants have not cross-appealed in order to contend that solution 3 should be preferred.

It was held in *R v Williams (Gladstone)* [1987] 3 All ER 411 and is now accepted that, for the purposes of the criminal law, solution 1 is the correct one. "Even if the jury come to the conclusion that the mistake was an unreasonable one, if the defendant may genuinely have been labouring under it, he is entitled to rely on it": per Lord Lane CJ, at p 415. (See also *Beckford v The Queen* [1988] AC 130, 142–145.) The chief constable has submitted that, for civil law purposes too, solution 1 should be the preferred solution. It is urged upon your Lordships that the criteria for self-defence in civil law should be the same as in criminal law. In my opinion, however, this plea for consistency between the criminal law and the civil law lacks cogency for the ends to be served by the two systems are very different. One of the main functions of the criminal law is to identify, and provide punitive sanctions for, behaviour that is categorised as criminal because it is damaging to the good order of society. It is fundamental to criminal law and procedure that everyone charged with criminal behaviour should be presumed innocent until proven guilty and that, as a general rule, no one should be punished for a crime that he or she did not intend to commit or be punished for the consequences of an honest mistake. There are of course exceptions to these principles but they explain, in my opinion, why a person who honestly believes that he is in danger of an imminent deadly attack and responds violently in order to protect himself from that attack should be able to plead self-defence as an answer to a criminal charge of assault, or indeed murder, whether or not he had been mistaken in his belief and whether or not his mistake had been, objectively speaking, a reasonable one for him to have made. As has often been observed, however, the greater the unreasonableness of the belief the more unlikely it may be that the belief was honestly held.

The function of the civil law of tort is different. Its main function is to identify and protect the rights that every person is entitled to assert against, and require to be respected by, others. The rights of one person, however, often run counter to the rights of others and the civil law, in particular the law of tort, must then strike a balance between the conflicting rights. Thus, for instance, the right of freedom of expression may conflict with the right of others not to be defamed. The rules and principles of the tort of defamation must strike the balance. The right not to be physically harmed by the actions of another may conflict with the rights of other people to engage in activities involving the possibility of accidentally causing harm. The balance between these conflicting rights must be struck by the rules and principles of the tort of negligence. As to assault and battery and self-defence, every person has the right in principle not to be subjected to physical harm by the intentional actions of another person. But every person has the right also to

错误判断时，他才可以依据他所以为的事实来主张正当防卫（第二种观点）。第三，要证明其回击行为的必要性，被告必须证明他确实有危险受到攻击，且这种危险是急迫且真实的（第三种观点）。无论选择上述哪一种观点，还有一个共同要件，那就是被告在民事诉讼中，需要让法院相信，他所采取的手段是合理的。在上述三种观点中，上诉法院认为第二种观点是正确的。在本院的这轮上诉中，警察局长认为上述第一种观点是正确的。而原告则并未交叉上诉以主张第三种观点才是应该被选择的。

R v Williams（*Gladstone*）[1987] 3 All ER 411 案确定了现在公认的观点：在刑法领域，观点一是正确的。"即使陪审团认为被告所犯的错误是不合理的，如果被告确实是真正地因为这个错误才做出相应的行为，则被告有权据此主张正当防卫。" Lane 首席大法官在 415 页说道［另参见 *Beckford v The Queen*（1988）AC 130, 第 142 到 145 页。］警察局长主张，对于民事诉讼，观点一同样应该被选择。他对诸位大法官说，民法和刑法上的正当防卫的标准应该是一样的。然而在我来，这种要求民法和刑法具有一致性的观点是没有什么说服力的，因为两种法律要实现的目的都不一样。刑法的功能之一是确定哪些行为属于犯罪，并对其加以惩罚，因为这些行为损害了良好的公共秩序。刑法和刑事诉讼法上，极其重要的一点是任何一个犯罪嫌疑人都应该被假定为无罪，直到证明其有罪；而作为一般的规则，没有人应该因为他并不希望实施的罪行而受到惩罚，也不应该因为无心之过产生的后果而受到惩罚。以上的这些原则当然有例外，但是这些原则在我看来，解释了为什么当一个人真诚地相信他有受到急迫且致命的攻击的危险，为了自保而回应暴力时，这个人是有权以正当防卫来作为故意伤害甚至故意杀人这样的刑事指控的抗辩事由的，无论他是不是曲解了事实，也无论他的这种曲解客观来看是不是合理的。当然，通常情况下，一个人所相信的事情越不合理，则越说明他的这种相信其实并不是真诚的。

而民事侵权法的功能则不同。它的主要功能是确认并保护每个人都享有的维护自身与他人相对的权利和要求得到他人尊重的权利。然而，一个人的权利常常会和他人的权利相冲突，因此，民法，特别是侵权法，就需要在互相冲突的权利之间找到一个平衡点。比如说，言论自由的权利有时候会和不被他人诽谤的权利冲突。诽谤之诉的规则和原则因此就需要找到一个平衡点。不受身体侵害的权利可能会和他人拥有的"从事可能会造成伤害的活动的权利"相冲突。这两种互相冲突的权利则应该由过失之诉的规则和原则来给出平衡点。至于涉及威吓、攻击和自卫时，则每个人都有权保证其身体不受到

protect himself by using reasonable force to repel an attack or to prevent an imminent attack. The rules and principles defining what does constitute legitimate self-defence must strike the balance between these conflicting rights. The balance struck is serving a quite different purpose from that served by the criminal law when answering the question whether the infliction of physical injury on another in consequence of a mistaken belief by the assailant of a need for self-defence should be categorised as a criminal offence and attract penal sanctions. To hold, in a civil case, that a mistaken and unreasonably held belief by A that he was about to be attacked by B justified a pre-emptive attack in believed self-defence by A on B would, in my opinion, constitute a wholly unacceptable striking of the balance. It is one thing to say that if A's mistaken belief was honestly held he should not be punished by the criminal law. It would be quite another to say that A's unreasonably held mistaken belief would be sufficient to justify the law in setting aside B's right not to be subjected to physical violence by A. I would have no hesitation whatever in holding that for civil law purposes an excuse of self-defence based on non existent facts that are honestly but unreasonably believed to exist must fail. This is the conclusion to which the Court of Appeal came in preferring solution 2.

  I have found it helpful to consider also the somewhat analogous defence of consent. Consent is, within limits, a defence to a criminal charge of assault. It is relevant in physical contact games but is also frequently put forward as a defence where allegations of sexual assault, whether of rape or less serious varieties, are made. If the consent relied on had not been given but was honestly believed by the assailant to have been given, the accused would be entitled, as I understand it, to an acquittal. An honest belief that could not be rebutted by the prosecution would suffice. But why should that suffice in a tort claim based upon the sexual assault? It would surely not be a defence in a case where the victim of the assault had neither expressly nor impliedly consented to what the assailant had done for the assailant to say that he had honestly albeit mistakenly thought that she had, unless, at the very least, the mistake had been a reasonable one for him to have made in all the circumstances. So, too, with self-defence.

  I would, therefore, dismiss the chief constable's appeal against the Court of Appeal's adoption of solution 2. It has not been contended on behalf of the Ashleys that solution 3 might be the correct solution in a civil case but, speaking for myself, I think that that solution would have a good deal to be said for it, as appears to have been the view also of Sir Anthony Clarke In *Ashley and Another v Chief Constable of Sussex*, MR [2007] 1 WLR 398, paras 63–78. I would start with the principle that every person is prima facie entitled not to be the object of physical harm intentionally inflicted by another. If consent to the infliction of the injury has not been given and cannot be implied why should it be a defence in a tort claim for the assailant to say that although his belief that his victim had consented was a mistaken one none the less it had been a reasonable one for him to make? Why, for civil law purposes, should not a person who proposes to make

他人故意行为的侵害。然而每个人也同样有权为了自保而使用合理的暴力去反抗他人的攻击或者避免将要发生的攻击。正当防卫的规则和原则就必须在上述这两种互相冲突的权利之间寻找平衡点。在侵权法中寻找的平衡点，其目的和刑法中寻找的平衡点目的是不一样的。刑法这么做的目的是回答这样一个问题：当一个人错误地以为他需要正当防卫时，他对他人人身造成的伤害是否应该被视为犯罪行为，而他是否应该因此受到刑事制裁？在民事诉讼中，如果我们认为只要 A 认为他要被 B 攻击，即便这种想法是错误且不恰当地，它也能正当化 A 基于他的假想防卫而对 B 做出的先发制人的攻击；那么我们就给出了一个非常不可接受的平衡点。A 错误但是真诚的看法可以让他免受刑事处罚，这是一回事；A 不恰当的错误看法能不能让法律无视 B 不受到 A 的身体暴力的权利，则是另一回事。我毫不犹豫地认为，在民法上，基于并不存在的事实主张正当防卫，即便一个人是真诚地相信这些虚假的事实，但如果这种相信是不合理的，那么这种主张是必然要失败的。这也是上诉法院的结论，他们选择了以上第二种观点。

　　我觉得我们可以来类比一下"受害人同意"这个抗辩事由。受害人同意在一定程度上是可以作为故意伤害这样的刑事指控的抗辩事由的。在有肢体接触的运动中，这种抗辩事由是有意义的；除此之外，这种抗辩事由也经常在有关性侵害的犯罪指控中提出，可能是强奸，也可能是更轻微的指控。如果事实上，受害人并没有同意，但是攻击者确实真诚地以为受害人同意了，那么在我看来他应当被无罪释放。只要检察机关没有办法否认攻击者是真诚地这么以为，"受害人同意"的抗辩就足够成立了。然而仅仅是"真诚地以为"就足够在依据性侵害提起的侵权之诉中，成立"受害人同意"的抗辩了吗？当性侵案的受害人并没有明示或者默示地给出同意时，仅仅因为性侵者说他错误但真诚地以为她同意了，性侵者的抗辩是不能成立的，除非，最起码，他犯的这种错误在任何情况下都是合理的。这种推理也适用于提出"正当防卫"的场合。

　　综上所述，我驳回警察局局长因为上诉法院采信了第二种观点而提起的上诉。Ashley 等人一方并没有主张上述第三种观点才是民事案件中应当采用的标准，然而我自己认为这种观点有很多值得称赞之处，这好像也是掌卷法官 Anthony Clarke 爵士的观点。[参见 *Ashley and Another v Chief Constable of Sussex* （2007）1 WLR 398, 第 63 至 78 段。] 我立论的起点是，初步地看，任何人都有权不受到他人故意的身体伤害。如果受害人并没有明示或默示地同意愿意遭受伤害，为什么攻击者能够以"他以为受害人同意了一事虽属错误，然而他的错误确实真诚的"的情节作为抗辩？在民法意义上，为什么一个希望和

physical advances of a sexual nature to another be expected first to make sure that the advances will be welcome? Similarly, where there is in fact no risk or imminent danger from which the assailant needs to protect himself, I find it difficult to see on what basis the right of the victim not to be subjected to physical violence can be set at naught on the ground of mistake made by the assailant, whether or not reasonably made. If A assaults B in the mistaken belief that it is necessary to do so in order to protect himself from an imminent attack by B, or in the mistaken belief that B has consented to what is done, it seems to me necessary to enquire about the source of the mistake. If the mistake were attributable in some degree to something said or done by B or to anything for which B was responsible, then it seems to me that the rules relating to contributory fault can come into play and provide a just result. If the mistake were attributable in some degree to something said to A by a third party, particularly if the third party owed a duty to take care that information he gave was accurate, the rules relating to contributions by joint or concurrent tortfeasors might come into play. But I am not persuaded that a mistaken belief in the existence of non-existent facts that if true might have justified the assault complained of should be capable, even if reasonably held, of constituting a complete defence to the tort of assault. However, and in my view, unfortunately, solution 3 has not been contended for on this appeal, its pros and cons have not been the subject of argument, and your Lordships cannot, therefore, conclude that it is the correct solution. But I would, for my part, regard the point as remaining open.

...

LORD NEUBERGER

Thirdly, there is the argument that the inflictor of an alleged battery has to go further than the Court of Appeal held, and show that he was in fact under imminent threat of attack. The point appears to me to be difficult, and the authorities are not entirely clear on the point: see Sir Anthony Clarke MR's analysis, in paras 63 to 78. Like him, I think that the balance of authority favours the conclusion that a defendant does not have to go that far, although the point is plainly open for reconsideration in your Lordships' House.

There are powerful arguments both ways. It is easy to conceive of circumstances where it would be inevitable that either the inflictor or the victim would have a thoroughly understandable sense of great grievance if, as the case may be, there was or was not a valid claim for damages for the infliction of severe violence in circumstances where the inflictor reasonably, but wrongly, believed he was under imminent threat of attack. As the Ashleys have not challenged the Court of Appeal's conclusion on this issue, it appears to me that in this case it should be left open in your Lordships' House.

Fourthly, if a reasonable but mistaken belief will do, other questions may need to be considered. One such question is whether, when seeking to justify the reasonableness of his belief, a defendant can rely on factors which were not the claimant's responsibility. There is obviously

他人有性行为的人不被要求先确定他的性行为是对方所乐于接受的？同样的，如果事实上并不存在针对攻击者的急迫的危险，而使他并不需要保护自己时，那么仅仅因为攻击者错误地以为有这种危险（无论这种错误是合理的还是不合理的），我认为都很难支持此时应该无视受害人所具有的不受到人身暴力的权利。若 A 因为错误地以为他有被 B 攻击的急迫的危险，为了自保而攻击了 B；或者错误地以为 B 同意他这么做，在我看来我们应该考察一下这种错误的来源是什么。如果这种错误在某种程度上可以归因于 B 的语言或行为，那么在我看来适用与有过失的规则就会得到公正的结果。如果这种错误在某种程度上可归因于某个第三人对 A 说的话，特别是如果此时这个第三人负有责任保证他的话语的准确，那么我们就应该适用有关共同侵权或者多人侵权的规则。但我不相信，如果错误地相信不存在的事实（如果这些事实是正确的，那么就可以证明被诉的人身攻击是正当的），就能够构成对人身攻击侵权行为的完全抗辩，即使这种抗辩是合理的。在我看来非常遗憾的是，原告并没有在本次的上诉中主张应该适用上述第三种观点，这种观点是好是坏不属于争论的对象，因此诸位大法官并不能判决第三种观点是正确的观点。但是就我而言，我会将这一点视为未决的问题。

……

Neuberger 大法官主笔：

第三，有人主张殴击之诉中的攻击者需要证明的比上诉法院要求的还多，要证明他确实受到了急迫的被攻击的威胁。这个问题对我来说是比较困难的，各个判例对此也并不是特别清楚：参见掌卷法官 Anthony Clarke 爵士的分析，在第 63—78 页。跟他一样，我也认为在比较分析了判例之后，得出的结论是应该倾向于认为被告不需证明那么多东西，虽然这个问题现在并没有定论，之后诸位大法官完全可以再作考虑。

对于这个问题，其实正反两方面都有比较有力的论证。我们可以想象有一种情况，在这种情况下，攻击者错误地相信他受到急迫的攻击的威胁，但是他的错误确实是因合理的理由产生的；此时，允许受害者因为其遭受的严重暴力而请求损害赔偿，则会让攻击者产生可以理解的严重的不满；而不允许受害者请求损害赔偿，则会让受害人产生可以理解的严重的不满。由于 Ashley 等人并没有对上诉法院针对这个问题的结论提出上诉，在我看来这对诸位大法官来说是一个未决的以后可以再讨论的问题。

第四，假设我们认同，就算侵权人对事实的认识是错误的，但只要他犯这种错误有合理的原因，那么就能成立正当防卫的抗辩，我们依然面临其他的一些问题需要考虑。其中的一个问题就是，为了证明其错误有合理的原因，

a strong argument for saying that a defendant can rely on such factors. Otherwise, one would be getting close to holding that the belief must be correct. Further, it could lead to difficulties if one had to decide whether the claimant was responsible for the defendant's belief, especially if only some of the factors which influenced the defendant could be taken into account. However, it can also be said to be unfair on the claimant if matters for which he had no responsibility can serve to justify the reasonableness of the defendant's mistaken belief. The answer may ultimately depend on whether one judges the issue of reasonableness from the claimant's point of view or from that of the defendant.

C. Necessity

28. Ploof v. Putnam, 81 Vt. 471, 71 A. 188 (1908)

Supreme Court of Vermont, United States

Munson, J.

It is alleged as the ground of recovery that on the 13th day of November, 1904, the defendant was the owner of a certain island in Lake Champlain, and of a certain dock attached thereto, which island and dock were then in charge of the defendant's servant; that the plaintiff was then possessed of and sailing upon said lake a certain loaded sloop, on which were the plaintiff and his wife and two minor children; that there then arose a sudden and violent tempest, whereby the sloop and the property and persons therein were placed in great danger of destruction; that to save these from destruction or injury the plaintiff was compelled to, and did, moor the sloop to defendant's dock; that the defendant by his servant unmoored the sloop, whereupon it was driven upon the shore by the tempest, without the plaintiff's fault; and that the sloop and its contents were thereby destroyed, and the plaintiff and his wife and children cast into the lake and upon the shore, receiving injuries.

This claim is set forth in two counts; one in trespass, charging that the defendant by his servant with force and arms wilfully and designedly unmoored the sloop; the other in case, alleging that it was the duty of the defendant by his servant to permit the plaintiff to moor his sloop to the dock, and to permit it to remain so moored during the continuance of the tempest, but that the defendant by his servant, in disregard of this duty, negligently, carelessly and wrongfully unmoored the sloop. Both counts are demurred to generally.

There are many cases in the books which hold that necessity, and an inability to control movements inaugurated in the proper exercise of a strict right, will justify entries upon land and interferences with personal property that would otherwise have been trespasses....

A traveller on a highway, who finds it obstructed from a sudden and temporary cause, may pass upon the adjoining land without becoming a trespasser, because of the necessity.

被告是否能依赖那些和原告无关的因素。很显然,被告可以依赖这些因素的观点是很有道理的。要不然,这就几乎等同于认为侵权人所以为的事实必须是真的发生了,才成立正当防卫。另外,如果我们需要关心原告对于被告的错误是否应该负责,就会造成如果有多个因素都影响了被告而作出错误判断,却只能将其中一部分纳入考量因素的结果,而这会造成很大的问题。然而,从原告的角度说,如果他不能负责的事情可以用来证明被告错误的正当性,那对原告来说也是很不公平的。对于这个问题到底要怎么回答,最终取决于我们是从原告还是从被告的角度来看待"什么是合理的错误"这个问题。

三、紧急避险

28. Ploof v. Putnam, 81 Vt. 471, 71 A. 188 (1908)

美国佛蒙特州最高法院

Munson 法官主笔:

1904 年 11 月 13 日,被告是 Champlain 湖中一个小岛及其码头的所有者,当时被告的仆人负责管理小岛和码头。原告当时拥有一条载满了人的单桅帆船在上述湖泊中行驶,小船上坐着原告、原告的妻子和两个未成年的孩子。当时湖面上突然出现了强烈的风暴,小船和小船上的财产和人员都面临毁灭的威胁。为了避免财产受到毁灭和人员伤亡,原告不得不将小船系在了被告的码头上,被告让他的仆人解开了小船,小船在风暴的推动下被冲到了岸上,原告不存在过错;小船和小船上的物品因此被全部毁掉,原告及其妻子和孩子被抛到湖中,冲到岸上,因此而受伤。原告提起赔偿诉讼。

该主张中陈述了两项诉因:一条是侵害,指控被告通过其仆人以暴力蓄意解开了小船;另一条是间接侵害,指控被告通过其仆人有义务允许原告将小船固定在码头上,并且在暴风雨仍在继续的情况下允许其一直留在码头上,但是被告通过其仆人全然不顾这项义务,过失地、不负责任地并且错误地解开了小船。被告对这两条指控都提出了一般性的异议。

本判例集中的多个案例都表明,进入别人的私人土地本来是构成非法侵入的,但若是行为人遇到紧急状态,或者为了要实施某项绝对权利而不得不这么做时,就不再是非法侵入了。

一个行驶在高速公路上的旅行者发现突如其来的暂时性障碍阻断了他的道路,可以穿过邻近的土地而不会成为侵入者,其理由就是紧急避险。

进入土地去拯救处在丢失或被水、火摧毁危险之中的物品的行为不是侵

An entry upon land to save goods which are in danger of being lost or destroyed by water or fire is not a trespass. In Proctor v. Adams, 113 Mass. 376, 18 Am. Rep. 500, the defendant went upon the plaintiff's beach for the purpose of saving and restoring to the lawful owner a boat which had been driven ashore and was in danger of being carried off by the sea; and it was held no trespass.

This doctrine of necessity applies with special force to the preservation of human life. One assaulted and in peril of his life may run through the close of another to escape from his assailant. One may sacrifice the personal property of another to save his life or the lives of his fellows. In Mouse's Case, 12 Co. 63, the defendant was sued for taking and carrying away the plaintiff's casket and its contents. It appeared that the ferryman of Gravesend took forty-seven passengers into his barge to pass to London, among whom were the plaintiff and defendant; and the barge being upon the water a great tempest happened, and a strong wind, so that the barge and all the passengers were in danger of being lost if certain ponderous things were not cast out, and the defendant thereupon cast out the plaintiff's casket. It was resolved that in case of necessity, to save the lives of the passengers, it was lawful for the defendant, being a passenger, to cast the plaintiff's casket out of the barge; that if the ferryman surcharge the barge the owner shall have his remedy upon the surcharge against the ferryman, but that if there be no surcharge, and the danger accrue only by the act of God, as by tempest, without fault of the ferryman, every one ought to bear his loss, to safeguard the life of a man.

It is clear that an entry upon the land of another may be justified by necessity, and that the declaration before us discloses a necessity for mooring the sloop. But the defendant questions the sufficiency of the counts because they do not negative the existence of natural objects to which the plaintiff could have moored with equal safety. The allegations are, in substance, that the stress of a sudden and violent tempest compelled the plaintiff to moor to defendant's dock to save his sloop and the people in it. The averment of necessity is complete, for it covers not only the necessity of mooring, but the necessity of mooring to the dock; and the details of the situation which created this necessity, whatever the legal requirements regarding them, are matters of proof and need not be alleged. It is certain that the rule suggested cannot be held applicable irrespective of circumstance, and the question must be left for adjudication upon proceedings had with reference to the evidence or the charge....

Judgment affirmed and cause remanded.

29. In Re F (Mental Patient: Sterilisation) [1990] 2 AC 1

House of Lords, United Kingdom

LORD GOFF

Upon what principle can medical treatment be justified when given without consent? We are

犯行为。在 Proctor v. Adams（113 Mass. 376, 18 Am. Rep. 500）案中，被告作为小船的合法所有者进入原告沙滩的目的是为了拯救和修理小船，小船被冲到了岸上，有可能被海浪卷走。被告的行为不构成侵害。

紧急避险适用于拯救人的生命而具有特殊法律效力。一个人被攻击，生命处在危险之中，他可能跑过他人的封闭场以逃避袭击他的人。一个人可能牺牲他人的个人财产来保护自己的生命或同伴的生命。在 Mouse 案（12 Co. 63）中，被告因拿走了原告的珠宝箱及其里面的东西而被起诉。情况是 Gravesend 的摆渡船夫在他的船上载了47名乘客摆渡到伦敦去，其中两名乘客就是原告和被告。船在下水之后遇上了强烈的风暴，除非抛弃一些沉重的物品，否则船只和所有的乘客都有可能掉入海里，因此被告便扔掉了原告的珠宝箱。法院认定，在紧急避险的情况下，为了拯救乘客的生命，作为其中一名乘客的被告将原告的珠宝箱扔出船外的做法是合法的；如果船夫对其收取了附加费用，那么货物的所有者便应该向船夫提出补救要求，但是如果船夫没有收取附加费用，造成危险的原因是不可抗力（Act of God），即暴风雨，而船夫没有过错，那么每一个人都应该对其自身的损失承担责任，以保护每一个人的生命。

显然，基于紧急避险，一个人进入另一个人的土地可以是具有正当性的，而我们面前的陈述说明了停泊小船是为了紧急避险。但是被告对原告指控的充分性提出了质疑，因为这条理由并没有排除另一种可能性的存在，即原告将船固定在自然物体上也能够获得同样的安全。实质上，原告的指控是，出于突如其来的强烈风暴的压力，为了拯救自己的小船和船上的人，原告不得不将船停靠在了被告的码头上。关于紧急避险的主张是完整的，因为它不但涵盖了停靠的必要性，而且包括了停靠在码头上的必要性；而造成这种紧急避险的情形的细节信息，无论法律对其提出了怎样的要求，都是证明问题而不需要声明。可以确定的是，上文提到的规则肯定不会在任何情况下都适用，该问题应该经过初审程序、考量证据或者指示确定……

维持原判，案件发回重审。

29. In Re F (Mental Patient: Sterilisation) [1990] 2 AC 1

联合王国上议院

Goff 大法官主笔：

在没有征得病人同意的情况下，即对其进行医疗治疗，在某种原则规定

searching for a principle upon which, in limited circumstances, recognition may be given to a need, in the interests of the patient, that treatment should be given to him in circumstances where he is (temporarily or permanently) disabled from consenting to it. It is this criterion of a need which points to the principle of necessity as providing justification.

That there exists in the common law a principle of necessity which may justify action which would otherwise be unlawful is not in doubt. But historically the principle has been seen to be restricted to two groups of cases, which have been called cases of public necessity and cases of private necessity. The former occurred when a man interfered with another man's property in the public interest - for example (in the days before we could dial 999 for the fire brigade) the destruction of another man's house to prevent the spread of a catastrophic fire, as indeed occurred in the Great Fire of London in 1666. The latter cases occurred when a man interfered with another's property to save his own person or property from imminent danger - for example, when he entered upon his neighbour's land without his consent, in order to prevent the spread of fire onto his own land.

There is, however, a third group of cases, which is also properly described as founded upon the principle of necessity and which is more pertinent to the resolution of the problem in the present case. These cases are concerned with action taken as a matter of necessity to assist another person without his consent. To give a simple example, a man who seizes another and forcibly drags him from the path of an oncoming vehicle, thereby saving him from injury or even death, commits no wrong. But there are many emanations of this principle, to be found scattered through the books. These are concerned not only with the preservation of the life or health of the assisted person, but also with the preservation of his property (sometimes an animal, sometimes an ordinary chattel) and even to certain conduct on his behalf in the administration of his affairs. Where there is a pre-existing relationship between the parties, the intervenor is usually said to act as an agent of necessity on behalf of the principal in whose interests he acts, and his action can often, with not too much artificiality, be referred to the pre-existing relationship between them. Whether the intervenor may be entitled either to reimbursement or to remuneration raises separate questions which are not relevant in the present case.

We are concerned here with action taken to preserve the life, health or well-being of another who is unable to consent to it. Such action is sometimes said to be justified as arising from an emergency; in Prosser and Keeton, Hornbook on Torts, 5th ed. (1984), p. 117, the action is said to be privileged by the emergency. Doubtless, in the case of a person of sound mind, there will ordinarily have to be an emergency before such action taken without consent can be lawful; for otherwise there would be an opportunity to communicate with the assisted person and to seek his consent. But this is not always so; and indeed the historical origins of the principle of necessity do not point to emergency as such as providing the criterion of lawful intervention without consent.

的情况下是正当的；那么是什么情况呢？我们就是要找到这样一种原则：根据这种原则，在限定的情况下，在病人无法对治疗作出同意时（无论是临时的还是永久的），医生可以根据病人的利益，确认他需要接受治疗。这种病人接受治疗的需求，就引出了我们现在要讨论的，作为正当化事由的紧急避险。

普通法上存在紧急避险原则，能够让不合法的行为变得合法，这应该是不用怀疑的。但是在历史上这种原则只能在两种情况的案件下适用：公益的紧急避险和私益的紧急避险。前者是指一个人为了公共利益而妨碍他人的财产——比如1666年伦敦大火时，毁掉他人的房子来避免大火的蔓延（那时候可不能打999叫消防队）。后者则是指一个人为了挽救他自己的人身或者财产免受急迫的危险，而妨害他人的财产——比如一个人为了避免大火蔓延到自己的土地上而未经许可进入邻居的土地。

然而，其实还有第三种类型的案件也可以说是建立在紧急避险原则之上的；这种类型的紧急避险对于解决本案的问题来说，更具有相关性。这种类型的案件下，一个人出于必要的原因在未征得另一个人同意的情况下，对其实施了帮助行为。比如，一个人抓住另一个人然后用力地把他拉离车辆行驶的路线，因此拯救了后者使其免于受伤或者死亡，这时前者的行为就不属于侵权行为。这种原则的具体类型散见于各种书籍之中。它们不仅涉及为保护受救助者的生命或健康的情形，还涉及为保护其财产的情形（有时是动物，有时是普通动产），甚至涉及代其管理事务的行为。如果在双方当事人之间存在在先关系，则通常称介入者是为了本人利益行事的本人的紧急代理人；将介入者的行为和在先关系联系到一起，也不会让我们觉得是刻意的解释。至于介入者是否有权请求补偿金，则是另一个问题，和本案无关。

在本案中，我们面临的是一个为了保护他人的生命、健康或者幸福，而他人却没有办法先对这个行为表示同意的行为。人们有时认为，这种情形的正当性事由是事出紧急。在 Prosser and Keeton 所著的《侵权法入门》（*Hornbook on Torts*）第五版（1984）的第117页中，这种行为被特别许可的原因被解释为事出紧急。毋庸置疑，当一个人头脑清醒的时候，一般来说只有事出紧急、未经受助人允许的行为才是合法的；否则完全可以先和受助人沟通并取得其同意。然而这并不绝对，其实从历史的源头来看，紧急避险原则并非是以事出紧急来作为判断未经他人同意而妨害他人情形是否合法的依据的。罗马法上的无因管理理论，其之所以允许管理人去管理他人的事务，与其说是因为事出紧急，不

The old Roman doctrine of negotiorum gestio presupposed not so much an emergency as a prolonged absence of the dominus from home as justifying intervention by the gestor to administer his affairs. The most ancient group of cases in the common law, concerned with action taken by the master of a ship in distant parts in the interests of the shipowner, likewise found its origin in the difficulty of communication with the owner over a prolonged period of time - a difficulty overcome today by modern means of communication. In those cases, it was said that there had to be an emergency before the master could act as agent of necessity; though the emergency could well be of some duration. But when a person is rendered incapable of communication either permanently or over a considerable period of time (through illness or accident or mental disorder), it would be an unusual use of language to describe the case as one of "permanent emergency" - if indeed such a state of affairs can properly be said to exist. In truth, the relevance of an emergency is that it may give rise to a necessity to act in the interests of the assisted person, without first obtaining his consent. Emergency is however not the criterion or even a pre-requisite; it is simply a frequent origin of the necessity which impels intervention. The principle is one of necessity, not of emergency.

We can derive some guidance as to the nature of the principle of necessity from the cases on agency of necessity in mercantile law. ...From them can be derived the basic requirements, applicable in these cases of necessity, that, to fall within the principle, not only (1) must there be a necessity to act when it is not practicable to communicate with the assisted person, but also (2) the action taken must be such as a reasonable person would in all the circumstances take, acting in the best interests of the assisted person.

On this statement of principle, I wish to observe that officious intervention cannot be justified by the principle of necessity. So intervention cannot be justified when another more appropriate person is available and willing to act; nor can it be justified when it is contrary to the known wishes of the assisted person, to the extent that he is capable of rationally forming such a wish. On the second limb of the principle, the introduction of the standard of a reasonable man should not in the present context be regarded as materially different from that of Sir Montague Smith's "wise and prudent man," because a reasonable man would, in the time available to him, proceed with wisdom and prudence before taking action in relation to another man's person or property without his consent. I shall have more to say on this point later. Subject to that, I hesitate at present to indulge in any greater refinement of the principle, being well aware of many problems which may arise in its application - problems which it is not necessary, for present purposes, to examine. But as a general rule, if the above criteria are fulfilled, interference with the assisted person's person or property (as the case may be) will not be unlawful. Take the example of a railway accident, in which injured passengers are trapped in the wreckage. It is this principle which may render lawful the actions of other citizens - railway staff, passengers or outsiders - who rush to give aid and

如说是因为被管理人长期离家。而在普通法上，最早的这类案件则涉及航行到遥远的地方的船长为了船主的利益为其行事的情形。普通法上的案件的起源，也是因为要与主人联络需要很长的时间，因而联络很困难。这种困难在今天已经被现代化的通讯手段克服了。在这类案件中，据说船长之所以能当紧急代理人，是因为事出紧急；而这种紧急状况可能会持续很长时间。当一个人不能和受助者沟通，无论是永久的还是持续很长时间（比如因病或者因为事故或者因为精神错乱），我们一般都用"永久性的紧急情况"来描述这种状况，如果确实有这种情况存在的话。其实，紧急状况之所以和紧急避险有关，是因为紧急状态确实导致了为受助者的利益行事而不先取得其同意的必要性。然而，紧急状况并不是紧急避险的要件；紧急状况仅仅是必要状况产生的惯常原因之一。这个原则本身强调的是必要性，而不是紧急性。

我们可以以商法上相关的紧急代理制的案例为参考，来探究紧急避险原则的性质……从这些判例中，我们可以找到一些适用这些判例的要件，即要构成紧急避险的话，不但必须要有与受助人沟通不可行又必须采取行为的必要性，而且所采取的行为必须是理性人在任何情况下都会采取的行动，并以受助人的最佳利益为出发点。

介绍完了这个原则，我想表达的是多管闲事地介入他人生活并不能用紧急避险来抗辩。因此，如果有介入者以外的更合适的人存在且愿意介入时，介入者的介入就不能用紧急避险做抗辩事由了。同样不能用紧急避险做抗辩事由的情形，还有当介入人的行为违反受助人可知的意志时，当然受助人要有能力形成理性的意志。而对于这个原则的第二个要件涉及的"理性人标准"，在本案的语境之下，不应该和 Montague Smith 爵士所说的"睿智而谨慎的人"有什么区别，因为理性人在处理涉及他人的人身或者财产的事务时，如果不经同意就代为处理相关事务，是一定会先在他所能支配的时间内睿智而谨慎地考虑的。之后我会再回过头来谈谈这个问题。我就说这么多了，不会再详细阐释这个原则了；虽然我知道这个原则在适用的时候会产生很多问题，但是这些问题并不需要在本案中来探讨。然而总体来说，一旦满足了以上的条件，那么去干涉受助人的人身或者财产（看具体案件是人身或者财产）就不会是违法的了。以火车事故为例，假设受伤的乘客们被困在了火车残骸之中，这时，紧急避险原则就会让其他公民（比如火车员工、其他乘客或者局外人）冲向受害者为其提供帮助和慰藉的行为变得合法：比如为昏迷的乘客截肢以

comfort to the victims: the surgeon who amputates the limb of an unconscious passenger to free him from the wreckage; the ambulance man who conveys him to hospital; the doctors and nurses who treat him and care for him while he is still unconscious. Take the example of an elderly person who suffers a stroke which renders him incapable of speech or movement. It is by virtue of this principle that the doctor who treats him, the nurse who cares for him, even the relative or friend or neighbour who comes in to look after him, will commit no wrong when he or she touches his body.

The two examples I have given illustrate, in the one case, an emergency, and in the other, a permanent or semi-permanent state of affairs. Another example of the latter kind is that of a mentally disordered person who is disabled from giving consent. I can see no good reason why the principle of necessity should not be applicable in his case as it is in the case of the victim of a stroke. Furthermore, in the case of a mentally disordered person, as in the case of a stroke victim, the permanent state of affairs calls for a wider range of care than may be requisite in an emergency which arises from accidental injury. When the state of affairs is permanent, or semi-permanent, action properly taken to preserve the life, health or well-being of the assisted person may well transcend such measures as surgical operation or substantial medical treatment and may extend to include such humdrum matters as routine medical or dental treatment, even simple care such as dressing and undressing and putting to bed.

The distinction I have drawn between cases of emergency, and cases where the state of affairs is (more or less) permanent, is relevant in another respect. We are here concerned with medical treatment, and I limit myself to cases of that kind. Where, for example, a surgeon performs an operation without his consent on a patient temporarily rendered unconscious in an accident, he should do no more than is reasonably required, in the best interests of the patient, before he recovers consciousness. I can see no practical difficulty arising from this requirement, which derives from the fact that the patient is expected before long to regain consciousness and can then be consulted about longer term measures. The point has however arisen in a more acute form where a surgeon, in the course of an operation, discovers some other condition which, in his opinion, requires operative treatment for which he has not received the patient's consent. In what circumstances he should operate forthwith, and in what circumstances he should postpone the further treatment until he has received the patient's consent, is a difficult matter which has troubled the Canadian Courts (see *Marshall v. Curry* [1933] 3 DLR 260, and *Murray v. McMurchy* [1949] 2 DLR 442), but which it is not necessary for your Lordships to consider in the present case.

But where the state of affairs is permanent or semi-permanent, as may be so in the case of a mentally disordered person, there is no point in waiting to obtain the patient's consent. The need to care for him is obvious; and the doctor must then act in the best interests of his patient, just as if he had received his patient's consent so to do. Were this not so, much useful treatment and care could, in theory at least, be denied to the unfortunate.

使其能够从废墟中被解救出来的外科医生，救护车上把他送到医院的救护员，在他依然昏迷的时候治疗并照顾他的医生和护士。再比如老人突然中风，因此无法说话也无法行动了。也是因为紧急避险原则，因此治疗他的医生、照顾他的护士，甚至来看望他的亲友，便不会因接触了他的身体而构成侵权行为了。

我举的这两个例子，一个是紧急情况，另一个则是永久或者半永久状态。后者这种类型的例子还有精神错乱而无法作出同意之人。既然在中风病人的例子中，紧急避险原则可以适用，我找不到理由不在精神错乱的人这个例子中也适用这个原则。此外，在精神错乱之人和中风病人这两个例子中，这种永久的状态都需要比意外伤害造成的紧急情况更广泛的照料行为。在永久状态或者半永久状态的情况下，用以挽救受助者的生命、健康或者福祉的行为，可能会达到外科手术或者重大的医疗措施这样的程度，也可能会包括一些日常的事务，比如常规的医疗或者牙科检查，甚至可能包括很简单的护理活动，比如帮助受助者穿衣脱衣、帮助其上床等。

我之所以区别紧急状态的情况和（或多或少是）永久状态的情况，还在另一个层面上有意义。本案涉及的是医疗活动，我也因此将我的论述局限于医疗案件。对于一个因为事故而暂时昏迷的病人，医生未经其同意为他做手术的话，只能做那些为了他的利益必须在他苏醒前做的部分。这样的要求不会带来什么问题，因为预期病人将很快康复的话，可以直接询问他对后续的长期治疗有什么想法。然而如果医生在做手术的时候发现了某些其他的疾病也需要做手术，但是却没有获得病人的同意，则问题就会变得很尖锐了。在哪些情况下他应该继续，在哪些情况下他应该中止接下来的手术以等待病人的同意，这是一个加拿大法院所面临的很困难的问题。[参见 *Marshall v Curry*（1933）3 DLR 260；*Murray v. McMurchy*（1949）2 DLR 442。]但就本案而言，诸位大法官并不需要讨论这个问题。

然而在病人的状态是永久的或者半永久的情况下，比如精神错乱病人的例子中，介入者是没有必要去等待病人的同意的。病人需要帮助这一点是很明显的，因此医生应该为了病人的最大利益去行事，就如同他已经获得了病人的同意那样。如果我们不赞同此时医生有权这么做，至少在理论上，那个不幸的病人将无法获得有益的治疗和照顾。

Section 2. Defences in Negligence

A. Contributory and Comparative negligence

30. Butterfield v Forrester (1809) 11 East 60, 103 ER 926

Court of King's Bench, United Kingdom

This was an action on the case for obstructing a highway, by means of which obstruction the plaintiff, who was riding along the road, was thrown down with his horse, and injured, &c. At the trial before Bayley J. at Derby, it appeared that the defendant, for the purpose of making some repairs to his house, which was close by the road side at one end of the town, had put up a pole across this part of the road, a free passage being left by another branch or street in the same direction. That the plaintiff left a public house not far distant from the place in question at 8 o'clock in the evening in August, when they were just beginning to light candles, but while there was light enough left to discern the obstruction at 100 yards distance: and the witness, who proved this, said that if the plaintiff had not been riding very hard he might have observed and avoided it: the plaintiff however, who was riding violently, did not observe it, but rode against it, and fell with his horse and was much hurt in consequence of the accident; and there was no evidence of his being intoxicated at the time. On this evidence Bayley J. directed the jury, that if a person riding with reasonable and ordinary care could have seen and avoided the obstruction; and if they were satisfied that the plaintiff was riding along the street extremely hard, and without ordinary care, they should find a verdict for the defendant: which they accordingly did....

Lord Ellenborough, C.J.

A party is not to cast himself upon an obstruction which has been made by the fault of another, and avail himself of it, if he do not himself use common and ordinary caution to be in the right. In cases of persons riding upon what is considered to be the wrong side of the road, that would not authorise another purposely to ride up against them. One person being in fault will not dispense with another's using ordinary care for himself. Two things must concur to support this action, an obstruction in the road by the fault of the defendant, and no want of ordinary care to avoid it on the part of the plaintiff.

Per Curiam. Rule refused.

31. Davies v Mann (1842) 10 M & W 546, 152 ER 588

Court of Exchequer, United Kingdom

At the trial, before Erskine, J., at the last Summer Assizes for the county of Worcester, it appeared that the plaintiff, having fettered the fore feet of an ass belonging to him, turned it into

第二节 过失侵权责任中的抗辩事由
一、与有过失与比较过失

30. Butterfield v Forrester (1809) 11 East 60, 103 ER 926

联合王国王座法院

这是一起由公路障碍引发的诉讼,由于路上的障碍,骑马的原告从马上摔下来并受伤,以及由此引发了其他后果。从 Bayley 法官在 Derby 对案件进行的初审来看,被告的房屋位于紧邻路旁的小镇一头,为了对其房屋进行一定的维修,在路的这一侧横跨了一根杆子,同一方向的路上还有另一条通道可供通过。原告于 8 月份的一个晚上 8 点离开了距事发地不远处的一个公共房屋,当时光线足以看清 100 码之外的障碍物。目击者证实,如果原告骑马的速度没有那么快,那么他可以看见并躲开障碍物。然而,原告驾马疾驰,并没有看见障碍物,反而向其冲了过去,最后和马一起摔倒并受伤,没有证据显示原告当时醉酒骑马。根据这一证据,Bayley 法官指示陪审团,如果一个人在骑马的时候尽到合理的一般性注意,那么他可以看到并避免障碍物;如果陪审团也同意原告沿着道路骑马的速度过快,没有尽到一般的注意义务,那么他们应该作出对被告有利的裁断:陪审团确实作出了对被告有利的裁断……

Ellenborough 首席大法官主笔:

如果一个人自己不尽到普通且一般性注意义务以保护自己的安全,那么这个人就不能指责他人因过错而设置障碍物,并且利用该障碍物。如果有人沿着错误的方向骑马,另一人也无权故意径直撞向他们。一个人有过错并不意味着另一个人无需为自己尽到一般性的注意义务。必须同时发生两件事情才能支持本诉讼,即被告因过错而在道路中设置障碍物,原告缺少避开障碍物的一般注意。

本院全体法官同意。裁定驳回。

31. Davies v Mann (1842) 10 M & W 546, 152 ER 588

联合王国财税法院

Erskine 法官主持的 Worcester 县巡回审判夏季开庭期的最后一次初审显示,原告将自己驴子的前蹄锁起来之后,将其放在了公共道路上,事发时驴

a public highway, and at the time in question the ass was grazing on the off side of a road about eight yards wide, when the defendant's wagon, with a team of three horses, coming down a slight descent, at what the witness termed a smartish pace, ran against the ass, knocked it down, and the wheels passing over it, it died soon after. The ass was fettered at the time, and it was proved that the driver of the wagon was some little distance behind the horses. The learned Judge told the jury, that though the act of the plaintiff, in leaving the donkey on the highway so fettered as to prevent his getting out of the way of carriages travelling along it, might be illegal, still, if the proximate cause of the injury was attributable to the want of proper conduct on the part of the driver of the wagon, the action was maintainable against the defendant; and his Lordship directed them, if they thought that the accident might have been avoided by the exercise of ordinary care on the part of the driver, to find for the plaintiff. The jury found their verdict for the plaintiff, damages 40s.

...

Lord Abinger, C.B.

I am of opinion that there ought to be no new trial in this case. The defendant has not denied that the ass was lawfully in the highway, and therefore we must assume it to have been lawfully there; but even were it otherwise, it would have made no difference, for as the defendant might, by proper care, have avoided injuring the animal, and did not, he is liable for the consequences of his negligence, though the animal may have been improperly there.

Parke, B.

This subject was fully considered by this Court in the case of Bridge v. The Grand Junction Railway Company, (3 M. & W. 246), where, as appears to me, the correct rule is laid down concerning negligence, namely, that the negligence which is to preclude a plaintiff from recovering in an action of this nature, must be such as that he could, by ordinary care, have avoided the consequences of the defendant's negligence. I am reported to have said in that case, and I believe quite correctly, that "the rule of law is laid down with perfect correctness in the case of *Butterfield v. Forrester*, that, although there might have been negligence on the part of the plaintiff, yet unless he might, by the exercise of ordinary care, have avoided the consequences of the defendant's negligence, he is entitled to recover; if by ordinary care he might have avoided them, he is the author of his own wrong." In that case of *Bridge v. Grand Junction Railway Company*, there was a plea imputing negligence on both sides; here it is otherwise; and the Judge simply told the jury, that the mere fact of negligence on the part of the plaintiff in leaving his donkey on the public highway, was no answer to the action, unless the donkey's being there was the immediate cause of the injury; and that, if they were of opinion that it was caused by the fault of the defendant's servant in driving too fast or, which is the same thing, at a smartish pace, the mere fact of putting the ass upon the road would not bar the plaintiff of his action. All that is perfectly correct; for although the ass may have been wrongfully there, still the defendant was bound to go along the road at such a pace as

子正在路旁 8 码宽的地方吃草，这时被告的马车由三匹马拉着，沿着缓坡走了过来，目击者说当时马车迈着"敏捷的步伐"，撞倒了驴子，车轮碾过驴子，导致驴子很快死亡。当时驴子被锁链锁起来了，而且有证据证明马车车夫在马匹之后有一定的距离。博学的法官在了解情况之后告诉陪审团，尽管原告将驴子放在公路上并且锁起来使驴子无法避开沿途过往的车辆的行为，可能是违法的，但是如果造成损害的直接原因是马车车夫未采取适当的行为，那么针对被告的诉讼可以被维持。尊贵的法官指示他们，如果他们认为马车车夫只要尽到一般的注意义务便可以避免事故的发生，那么陪审团就应该作出有利于原告的裁断。陪审团作出了有利于原告的裁断，损害赔偿金为 40 先令。

……

财税法院 Abinger 首席法官主笔：

我认为不应该对本案进行重审。驴子合法地出现在公路上，对此被告并没有否认，因此我们必须认为这一点是合法的。但是即使不合法，也不会有什么区别，因为被告可以通过适当的注意避免伤害到驴子，但是被告没有尽到注意义务，他应该为其过失造成的后果承担责任，尽管驴子出现在道路上可能是不适当的。

财税法院 Parke 法官主笔：

本院在 *Bridge v. The Grand Junction Railway Company* 案中已经对这个问题进行了充分的考虑。在那个案件中，在我看来，已经确立了有关过失的正确规则，即导致原告无法得到赔偿的过失在本质上必须是：通过一般的注意便可以避免被被告过失造成的后果所伤害。我相信在那个案件中我表达的观点相当正确，"在 *Butterfield v. Forrester* 案中，法律规则已经得到了完美正确的确定，尽管原告可能存在过失，但是除非原告在尽到了一般注意义务之后可以避免被告过失所造成的后果，否则原告都有权获得赔偿。如果通过一般注意原告便可以避免后果的发生，那么原告便是自己遭受的不法行为的始作俑者"。在 *Bridge v. The Grand Junction Railway Company* 案中，双方都提出了对方存在过失的辩解。这里的情况则不同。法官只是告诉陪审团，原告将驴子放在公共道路上的做法存在过失，这一事实并不是诉讼的最终判决，除非驴子存在于公路上的事实直接造成了损害的发生；如果陪审团认为造成损害的原因是被告的佣人驾车速度过快，即与"敏捷的步伐"是一回事，那么将驴子放在公路上的事实并不能阻却原告赢得该诉讼。一切完全正确，因为尽管驴子不应该出现在公路上，被告一定也应该以可能避免损害的速度沿路行驶。

would be likely to prevent mischief. Were this not so, a man might justify the driving over goods left on a public highway, or even over a man lying asleep there, or the purposely running against a carriage going on the wrong side of the road.

GURNEY, B., and EOLFE, B., concurred. Rule refused.

32. Knight v. Jewett, 3 Cal. 4th 296, 834 P.2d 696, 11 Cal. Rptr. 2d 2 (1992)

Supreme Court of California, United States

George, Justice.

A number of appellate decisions, focusing on the language in *Li* indicating that assumption of risk is in reality a form of contributory negligence "where a plaintiff unreasonably undertakes to encounter a specific known risk imposed by a defendant's negligence" (13 Cal. 3d at p. 824, 119 Cal. Rptr. 858, 532 P.2d 1226), have concluded that *Li* properly should be interpreted as drawing a distinction between those assumption of risk cases in which a plaintiff "unreasonably" encounters a known risk imposed by a defendant's negligence and those assumption of risk cases in which a plaintiff "reasonably" encounters a known risk imposed by a defendant's negligence. These decisions interpret *Li* as subsuming into the comparative fault scheme those cases in which the plaintiff acts unreasonably in encountering a specific known risk, but retaining the assumption of risk doctrine as a complete bar to recovery in those cases in which the plaintiff acts reasonably in encountering such a risk. Although aware of the apparent anomaly of a rule under which a plaintiff who acts reasonably is completely barred from recovery while a plaintiff who acts unreasonably only has his or her recovery reduced, these decisions nonetheless have concluded that this distinction and consequence were intended by the *Li* court.

In our view, these decisions—regardless whether they reached the correct result on the facts at issue—have misinterpreted *Li* by suggesting that our decision contemplated less favorable legal treatment for a plaintiff who reasonably encounters a known risk than for a plaintiff who unreasonably encounters such a risk. Although the relevant passage in *Li* indicates that the assumption of risk doctrine would be merged into the comparative fault scheme in instances in which a plaintiff " 'unreasonably undertakes to encounter a specific known risk imposed by a defendant's negligence' " (13 Cal. 3d at p. 824, 119 Cal. Rptr. 858, 532 P.2d 1226), nothing in this passage suggests that the assumption of risk doctrine should survive as a total bar to the plaintiff's recovery whenever a plaintiff acts reasonably in encountering such a risk. Instead, this portion of our opinion expressly contrasts the category of assumption of risk cases which " 'involve contributory negligence' " (and which therefore should be merged into the comparative fault scheme) with those assumption of risk cases which involve " 'a reduction of defendant's duty of care.' " (Id. at p. 825, 119 Cal. Rptr. 858, 532 P.2d 1226).

如果不是这样，那么一个人可能会证明其碾过公路上放置的物品，或者甚至碾过睡在那里的一个人，或者故意撞上另一辆沿着道路以相反方向行驶的车辆是正当的。

财税法院 Gurney 法官和财税法院 Eolfe 法官赞成，裁定驳回。

32. Knight v. Jewett, 3 Cal. 4th 296, 834 P.2d 696, 11 Cal. Rptr. 2d 2 (1992)

美国加利福尼亚州最高法院

George 法官主笔：

不少上诉法院的判决关注 Li 案中的用语显示出的自甘风险在事实上是一种助成过失，"原告不合理地主动承担了由被告过失带来的某种具体风险"（13 Cal. 3d at p. 824, 119 Cal. Rptr. 858, 532 P.2d 1226）。这些上诉判决认定，可以认为 Li 案应该被解读为对两种自甘风险作出了区分，即原告"不合理地"遭遇了因被告过失带来的已知风险，和原告"合理地"承担了因被告过失带来的已知风险。这些判决对 Li 案的解读是，Li 案将原告不合理地承担了某种已知的风险的案件融入了比较过失体系中，保留了原告合理地承担了这些风险作为完全阻却原告获得赔偿的事由。虽然这些判决也意识到了该规则存在明显的异常结果，即实施合理行为的原告被完全阻却获得赔偿，而实施不合理行为的原告却仅仅是减少他/她的赔偿，尽管如此，这些判决认为这正是 Li 案中法院意图得到的区别和结果。

在我们看来，这些判决——无论它们是否根据关键问题的事实得出了正确的结论——都误读了 Li 案，认为我们的判决较之那些合理遭遇已知风险的原告法律救济而言，对那些不合理遭遇风险的原告法律待遇更低。虽然 Li 案中相关的文句指出当原告"不合理地自愿遭遇由被告过失引起的某种已知风险时，自甘风险原则将会被并入比较过错体系"（13 Cal. 3d at p. 824, 119 Cal. Rptr. 858, 532 P.2d 1226），但是该文句中并未指出只要原告合理地遭遇了这种风险，那么自甘风险原理就会成为原告获得赔偿的阻却事由。相反，我们这部分的意见明显地将两类自甘风险案件进行了对比，一类案件"涉及与有过失"（因此应该并入到比较过错体系），而另一类自甘风险的案件则涉及"被告未完全尽到注意义务"（Id. at p. 825, 119 Cal. Rptr. 858, 532 P.2d 1226）。

的确，特别是将上文提到的 Li 案相关文句（13 Cal. 3d at pp. 824–825, 119

Indeed, particularly when the relevant passage in *Li*, supra, 13 Cal. 3d at pp. 824-825, 119 Cal. Rptr. 858, 532 P.2d 1226, is read as a whole *and in conjunction with the authorities it cites*, we believe it becomes clear that the distinction in assumption of risk cases to which the *Li* court referred in this passage was not a distinction between instances in which a plaintiff unreasonably encounters a known risk imposed by a defendant's negligence and instances in which a plaintiff reasonably encounters such a risk. Rather, the distinction to which the *Li* court referred was between (1) those instances in which the assumption of risk doctrine embodies a legal conclusion that there is "no duty" on the part of the defendant to protect the plaintiff from a particular risk—the category of assumption of risk that the legal commentators generally refer to as "primary assumption of risk"—and (2) those instances in which the defendant does owe a duty of care to the plaintiff but the plaintiff knowingly encounters a risk of injury caused by the defendant's breach of that duty—what most commentators have termed "secondary assumption of risk." Properly interpreted, the relevant passage in *Li* provides that the category of assumption of risk cases that is not merged into the comparative negligence system and in which the plaintiff's recovery continues to be completely barred involves those cases in which the defendant's conduct did not breach a legal duty of care to the plaintiff, i.e., "primary assumption of risk" cases, whereas cases involving "secondary assumption of risk" properly are merged into the comprehensive comparative fault system adopted in *Li*....

An amicus curiae in the companion case has questioned, on a separate ground, the duty approach to the post-*Li* assumption of risk doctrine, suggesting that if a plaintiff's action may go forward whenever a defendant's breach of duty has played some role, however minor, in a plaintiff's injury, a plaintiff who voluntarily engages in a highly dangerous sport—for example, skydiving or mountain climbing—will escape *any* responsibility for the injury so long as a jury finds that the plaintiff was not "unreasonable" in engaging in the sport. This argument rests on the premise that, under comparative fault principles, a jury may assign some portion of the responsibility for an injury to a plaintiff only if the jury finds that the plaintiff acted *unreasonably*, but not if the jury finds that the plaintiff knowingly and voluntarily, but reasonably, chose to engage in a dangerous activity. Amicus curiae contends that such a rule frequently would permit voluntary risk takers to avoid all responsibility for their own actions, and would impose an improper and undue burden on other participants.

Although we agree with the general thesis of amicus curiae's argument that persons generally should bear personal responsibility for their own actions, the suggestion that a duty approach to the doctrine of assumption of risk is inconsistent with this thesis rests on a mistaken premise. Past California cases have made it clear that the "comparative fault" doctrine is a flexible, commonsense concept, under which a jury properly may consider and evaluate the relative responsibility of various parties for an injury (whether their responsibility for the injury rests on negligence, strict liability, or other theories of responsibility), in order to arrive at an "equitable apportionment or allocation of loss."

Accordingly, contrary to amicus curiae's assumption, we believe that under California's

Cal. Rptr. 858, 532 P.2d 1226.）作为整体并且结合其引用的法源进行阅读时，我们认为很明显，Li 案审理法院在这段文句中所提到的自甘风险案件的区别并非以下两种案件的区别——即原告不合理地遭遇了由被告过失引发的已知风险和原告合理地遭遇了这种风险。相反，Li 案中法院提到的区别在于下面的两种情况：（1）自甘风险原理体现了一种法律观点，即被告"没有义务"保护原告免于遭受某种风险——这种类型的自甘风险通常被法律评论者称为"初级自甘风险"。（2）被告确实对原告负有注意义务，但是原告在知情的情况下遭遇了由被告违背义务引发的损害风险——多数评论者称之为"次级自甘风险"。对 Li 案的相关文句的合理解读认为，这种类型的自甘风险案件无法并入比较过失体系，在这类案件中原告的赔偿请求仍然会被完全阻却，这类案件包括被告的行为并没有违反对原告应尽的法律义务，即"初级自甘风险"案件，而涉及"次级自甘风险"的案件则可以很好地并入 Li 案所采纳的全面的比较过错体系之中……

一位法庭顾问在同类案件中根据不同的依据提出了以下疑问，Li 案之后的自甘风险原理提到的义务问题显示，如果原告实施了行为，但是只要被告违背义务，无论被告的行为对原告的损害起到了多么小的促成作用，原告自愿参加了高度危险的体育活动——如高空跳伞或登山——那么只要陪审团认定原告并非"不合理地"参与了该项运动，原告也不需要为损害承担责任。这一观点存在的前提条件是，根据比较过错原理，只有当陪审团认定原告的行为具有不合理性时，原告才需要为自己促成的那部分损害承担有责性，但是如果陪审团认定原告选择参与危险活动的行为是一种知情和自愿的行为，但却具有合理性，那么原告不需要承担责任。法庭顾问认为这种规则经常会促使自愿承担风险的人避免为自己的行为承担责任，而给活动的其他参与者带来不合理且不适当的负担。

虽然我们同意法庭顾问提出的一般性论点，即人们往往需要为自己的行为承担个人责任，但是认为自甘风险的义务处理方式与法庭顾问的论点不一致的认识是建立在错误的前提之上的。以往的加州案例已经明确地说明，比较过错原理是一种灵活的、常识性的概念，根据这一原理，陪审团可以适当地对造成损害的各方的相对有责性进行考虑和评估（无论他们造成损害的原因是过失、严格责任，还是其他责任理论），这样才能实现"损失的平等分担或分摊"。

comparative fault doctrine, a jury in a "secondary assumption of risk" case would be entitled to take into consideration a plaintiff's voluntary action in choosing to engage in an unusually risky sport, whether or not the plaintiff's decision to encounter the risk should be characterized as unreasonable, in determining whether the plaintiff properly should bear some share of responsibility for the injuries he or she suffered. Thus, in a case in which an injury has been caused by both a defendant's breach of a legal duty to the plaintiff and the plaintiff's voluntary decision to engage in an unusually risky sport, application of comparative fault principles will not operate to relieve either individual of responsibility for his or her actions, but rather will ensure that neither party will escape such responsibility....

Accordingly, in determining the propriety of the trial court's grant of summary judgment in favor of the defendant in this case, our inquiry does not turn on the reasonableness or unreasonableness of plaintiff's conduct in choosing to subject herself to the risks of touch football or in continuing to participate in the game after she became aware of defendant's allegedly rough play. Nor do we focus upon whether there is a factual dispute with regard to whether plaintiff subjectively knew of, and voluntarily chose to encounter, the risk of defendant's conduct, or impliedly consented to relieve or excuse defendant from any duty of care to her. Instead, our resolution of this issue turns on whether, in light of the nature of the sporting activity in which defendant and plaintiff were engaged, defendant's conduct breached a legal duty of care to plaintiff. We now turn to that question.

...

... We conclude that a participant in an active sport breaches a legal duty of care to other participants—i.e., engages in conduct that properly may subject him or her to financial liability—only if the participant intentionally injures another player or engages in conduct that is so reckless as to be totally outside the range of the ordinary activity involved in the sport....

Therefore, we conclude that defendant's conduct in the course of the touch football game did not breach any legal duty of care owed to plaintiff. Accordingly, this case falls within the primary assumption of risk doctrine, and thus the trial court properly granted summary judgment in favor of defendant. Because plaintiff's action is barred under the primary assumption of risk doctrine, comparative fault principles do not come into play. The judgment of the Court of Appeal, upholding the summary judgment entered by the trial court, is affirmed.

33. Jones v Livox Quarries [1952] 2 QB 608

Court of Appeal, United Kingdom

DENNING L.J.

The facts are simple. The plaintiff rode on the towbar of a vehicle, which was a careless

因此，和法庭顾问的臆断相反，我们认为根据加州比较过错原理，"次级自甘风险"案件中的陪审团有权考虑原告选择参与异常危险体育活动的自愿行为，无论原告遭遇风险的决定是否具有合理性，这样陪审团才可以确定原告是否应该为自己遭受的损害承担自己份额的责任。因此，在一个案件中，如果造成损害的原因有两个——被告未尽到对原告应尽的法律义务以及原告自愿决定参与异常危险的体育活动，那么适用比较过错原理将不会减轻任何个体应为他/她的行为承担的责任，相反会确认双方都不会免除该有责性……

因此，当我们考虑这个案件中的初审法院作出有利于被告的简易判决是否合理时，我们并不研究原告的下列行为是否合理：原告选择承担触身式橄榄球的风险，或者原告在意识到被告的粗暴比赛方式后仍然选择继续参与比赛。我们也不关注是否存在下列事实性争论——有关原告主观上知道并且自愿选择承受被告行为引发的风险，或者原告默许被告可以不完全尽到或者完全不必尽到对自己的注意义务。相反，我们对这个问题的解决方案在于，鉴于被告和原告参与的体育运动的危险性，被告的行为是否违反了对原告应尽的法定注意义务。我们现在转到这个问题上。

……

……我们认为，只有在参与体育活动者故意伤害另一名球员，或者实施了完全超出该体育活动一般行为类型的不计后果的行为，才违反了对其他参与者应尽的法定注意义务——即，参与活动可能使他/她承担经济上的赔偿责任……

鉴于此，我们认为在触身式橄榄球比赛的过程当中，被告的行为并没有违反对原告应尽的法定义务。因此，本案符合初级自甘风险原理，进而初审法院合理地作出了对被告有利的简易判决。由于根据初级自甘风险原理，原告的赔偿请求被阻却，因此不得适用比较过错原理。维持上诉法院的判决，即支持初审法院作出的简易判决。

33. Jones v Livox Quarries [1952] 2 QB 608

联合王国上诉法院

丹宁勋爵主笔：

本案案情很简单。原告坐在拖拉机的拖曳杆上，这是一个很冒失的行为，

thing to do because of the danger that he might fall off. Later, whilst the vehicle was almost stationary, another vehicle negligently ran into him from the back as he stood on the towbar, and he was crushed between the two vehicles. The question is whether he was guilty of contributory negligence such as to reduce his damages. ...

Although contributory negligence does not depend on a duty of care, it does depend on foreseeability. Just as actionable negligence requires the foreseeability of harm to others, so contributory negligence requires the foreseeability of harm to oneself. A person is guilty of contributory negligence if he ought reasonably to have foreseen that, if he did not act as a reasonable, prudent man, he might be hurt himself; and in his reckonings he must take into account the possibility of others being careless.

Once negligence is proved, then no matter whether it is actionable negligence or contributory negligence, the person who is guilty of it must bear his proper share of responsibility for the consequences. The consequences do not depend on foreseeability, but on causation. The question in every case is: What faults were there which caused the damage? Was his fault one of them? The necessity of causation is shown by the word "result" in section 1 (1) of the Act of 1945, and it was accepted by this court in *Davies v. Swan Motor Co. (Swansea) Ld.*

There is no clear guidance to be found in the books about causation. All that can be said is that causes are different from the circumstances in which, or on which, they operate. The line between the two depends on the facts of each case. It is a matter of common sense more than anything else. In the present case, as the argument of Mr. Arthian Davies proceeded, it seemed to me that he sought to make foreseeability the decisive test of causation. He relied on the trial judge's statement that a man who rode on the towbar of the traxcavator "ran the risk of being thrown off and no other risk." That is, I think, equivalent to saying that such a man could reasonably foresee that he might be thrown off the traxcavator, but not that he might be crushed between it and another vehicle.

In my opinion, however, foreseeability is not the decisive test of causation. It is often a relevant factor, but it is not decisive. Even though the plaintiff did not foresee the possibility of being crushed, nevertheless in the ordinary plain common sense of this business the injury suffered by the plaintiff was due in part to the fact that he chose to ride on the towbar to lunch instead of walking down on his feet. If he had been thrown off in the collision, Mr. Arthian Davies admits that his injury would be partly due to his own negligence in riding on the towbar; but he says that, because he was crushed, and not thrown off, his injury is in no way due to it. That is too fine a distinction for me. I cannot believe that that purely fortuitous circumstance can make all the difference to the case. As Scrutton L.J. said in *In re Polemis and Another and Furness, Withy & Co. Ld.*: "Once the act is negligent, the fact that its exact operation was not foreseen is immaterial."

In order to illustrate this question of causation, I may say that if the plaintiff, whilst he was riding on the towbar, had been hit in the eye by a shot from a negligent sportsman, I should have

因为他面临被甩下去的危险。过了一会儿，拖拉机基本上停稳了，另一辆车过失地从后面撞向了站在拖曳杆上的原告，他因此被夹在了两辆车之间。这里的问题是他是否构成与有过失，因而应该减少其应得的赔偿金……

虽然与有过失并不以存在注意义务为要件，但是却以可预见性为要件。如同作为诉由的过失以"可预见到自己的行为会对他人造成损害"为要件一样，与有过失以"可预见到自己的行为会对自己造成损害"为要件。一个人具有与有过失，即他应该合理地预见到，如果他不像理性而谨慎的人那样行事，他就可能伤害到自己，而且他应该把"他人是有可能草率行事的"这一点纳入考量因素。

但是在证明了过失之后，无论是作为诉由的过失还是与有过失，过失之人都应该承担根据过失的后果而确定的责任份额。这时过失的后果不再取决于可预见性，而是取决于因果性。所有的案件中都要问的问题是，到底是哪些过错造成了损害？这个过错属于上述的过错吗？因果关系的必要体现在1945年《法律改革法（与有过失）》的第1条第1款使用的"导致"一词，该种观点也被本院在 *Davies v Swan Motor Co.（Swansea）Ld* 案中接受。

到底什么是因果关系，去翻书找答案是没用的。我们唯一能说的是，原因不同于"原因所运行的环境"。要区别二者，需要考察不同案件的不同事实。完成这个工作更多依靠的应该是常识。本案中，Arthian Davies 先生在我看来是想用可预见性作为判断因果关系的决定性标准。他的观点是建立在一审法官的表述上的。一审法官说，坐在拖拉机的拖曳杆上会面临"被甩出去的危险，但不会有其他危险"。这在我看来等于是说，一个人可以合理地预见到他可能被从拖拉机上甩出去，但是他不能预见到他会被另一辆车撞到。

然而在我看来，可预见性并不是判断因果关系的决定性的标准。可预见性经常是一个相关的考量因素，但是绝不是决定性的因素。就算原告不能预见到他会被车撞，但日常的经验告诉我们，他受的伤害部分原因是由于他坐在拖曳杆上去吃午餐而不是走着去。如果他在碰撞之时被甩了出去，那么 Arthian Davies 先生承认他的伤部分是由于自己过失地坐在拖曳杆上造成的，然而他说因为他是被撞到的，而不是被甩出去的，所以他否认自己受伤也有自己的过失。在我看来，这种区别太微小了。我无法相信完全随机的这种区别能在后果上造成多大的不同。正如 Scrutton 上诉法院法官在 *In re Polemis and Another and Furness, Withy & Co. Ld.* 一案中说的那样："只要认定了一个行为是过失的，行为人没有预见到这个行为具体的造成损害的机制这一点就不重要了。"

为了阐明关于因果关系的问题，我举个例子，比如如果原告站在拖曳杆上，这时一个射击运动员过失地开枪击中了他的眼睛。这时，我就会说原告的过失

thought that the plaintiff's negligence would in no way be a cause of his injury. It would only be the circumstance in which the cause operated. It would only be part of the history. But I cannot say that in the present case. The man's negligence here was so much mixed up with his injury that it cannot be dismissed as mere history. His dangerous position on the vehicle was one of the causes of his damage just as it was in *Davies v. Swan Motor Co. (Swansea) Ld.*

The present case is good illustration of the practical effect of the Act of 1945. In the course of the argument my Lord suggested that before the Act of 1945 he would have regarded this case as one where the plaintiff should recover in full. That would be because the negligence of the dumper driver would then have been regarded as the predominant cause. Now, since the Act, we have regard to all the causes, and one of them undoubtedly was the plaintiff's negligence in riding on the towbar of the traxcavator. His share in the responsibility was not great - the trial judge assessed it at one-fifth - but, nevertheless, it was his share, and he must bear it himself.

We were referred by Mr. Arthian Davies to the Canadian case of *McLaughlin v. Long*. In that case a boy riding on the running-board of a car was flung off when the car crashed owing to the driver's negligence. The boy recovered full damages without any reduction. The case seems to have proceeded on the ground that the boy was on the car with the tacit consent of the driver and was not guilty of contributory negligence. I confess that I do not follow this. If people choose to ride in a dangerous position, surely it is their own fault, even if the driver acquiesces in it. If the boy was guilty of contributory negligence, I should have thought it plain that his negligence was one of the causes of his injury, though the driver's negligence was, of course, the principal cause. The explanation of the decision may be that in 1926 the doctrine of last opportunity was still influential in Canada, as, indeed, it was here at that time. But it is so no longer, at any rate not here.

It all comes to this: If a man carelessly rides on a vehicle in a dangerous position, and subsequently there is a collision in which his injuries are made worse by reason of his position than they otherwise would have been, then his damage is partly the result of his own fault, and the damages recoverable by him fall to be reduced accordingly.

34. Froom v Butcher [1976] QB 286

Court of Appeal, United Kingdom

LORD DENNING

Contributory negligence

Negligence depends on a breach of duty, whereas contributory negligence does not. Negligence is a man's carelessness in breach of duty to *others*. Contributory negligence is a man's carelessness in looking after *his own* safety. He is guilty of *contributory* negligence if he ought reasonably to have foreseen that, if he did not act as a reasonable prudent man, he might be hurt

和他受到的伤害之间没有一丝一毫的因果关系。他的过失这时就只是原因起作用的环境。他的过失只是历史的一部分。但是在本案中我就不能这么说。这里原告的过失和他所受的伤害之间的联系太紧密了,我们没有办法认为他的过失仅仅是伤害发生的历史环境。他站在拖拉机上的危险位置一事,就是他受损害的原因之一,如同 *Davies v Swan Motor Co.*(*Swansea*)*Ld* 案那样。

本案很能说明 1945 年法的效果是什么。大法官认为在 1945 年法颁布之前,他会认为本案的原告可以获得全额赔偿。那是因为运渣车司机的过失在当时被认为是造成损害的主要原因。在 1945 年法颁布之后,我们要考虑造成损害的所有原因,而原告过失地站在拖拉机的拖曳杆上,毫无疑问是原因之一。他的责任份额倒是不大,一审法官确定他的份额是五分之一。然而,这确实是他的份额,他必须自己承受这部分损失。

Arthian Davies 先生引用了一个加拿大判例 *McLaughlin v Long*。在该案中,一个男孩站在汽车的侧面脚踏板上,因为司机过失,车翻了,男孩儿也被甩了出去。本案的男孩就获得了没有减少的全额赔偿。本案判决的依据似乎是说男孩站在脚踏板上是获得了司机的默认许可的,因此不属于与有过失。恕我直言,我无法同意该案的观点。如果一个人要站在危险的地方,那当然是他自己的过错,即便司机默认了这种行为。如果我们确认了男孩的行为属于与有过失,那么他的过失当然是造成他伤害的数个原因中的一个,虽然司机的过失当然是损害的主要原因。该案这么判决可能可以这么解释,就是 1926 年的时候在加拿大,最后机会理论还有很大的影响力,当时在我们这里也是这样。然而,如今在我们这里,这个理论不再适用了。

因此结论如下:如果一个人草率地站在车辆的危险位置,而且之后又因为车辆与其他车辆的碰撞而受伤,且他的伤因为自己所处的危险位置而比不处在那种位置时更严重,那么他的伤部分是由于他自己的过错造成的,他能获得的损害赔偿金也应该相应地有所减少。

34. Froom v Butcher [1976] QB 286

联合王国上诉法院

丹宁勋爵主笔:

与有过失

过失是指违反某种义务,而与有过失则不是这样。过失是指一个人因为其粗心大意而违反对他人的义务。而与有过失是指一个人因为粗心大意而没有保证自己的安全。如果一个人应该合理地预见到,如果他不像理性人那样

himself: see *Jones v. Livox Quarries Ltd.* [1952] 2 Q.B. 608. Before 1945 a plaintiff, who was guilty of contributory negligence, was disentitled from recovering anything if his own negligence was one of the substantial causes of the injury: see *Swadling v. Cooper* [1931] A.C. 1. Since 1945 he is no longer defeated altogether. He gets reduced damages: see *Davies v. Swan Motor Co. (Swansea) Ltd.* [1949] 2 K.B. 291.

The present law is contained in section 1 (1) of the Law Reform (Contributory Negligence) Act 1945, which provides:

> "When any person suffers damage as the result partly of his own fault and partly of the fault of any other person or persons, a claim in respect of that damage shall not be defeated by reason of the fault of the person suffering the damage, but the damages recoverable in respect thereof shall be reduced to such extent as the court thinks just and equitable having regard to the claimant's share in the responsibility for the damage."

Section 4 provides:

> "'fault' means negligence, breach of statutory duty or other act or omission which gives rise to a liability in tort or would, apart from this Act, give rise to the defence of contributory negligence."

Those provisions must be borne in mind as we take our consideration further.

The cause of the damage

In these seat belt cases, the injured plaintiff is in no way to blame for the accident itself. Sometimes he is an innocent passenger sitting beside a negligent driver who goes off the road. At other times he is an innocent driver of one car which is run into by the bad driving of another car which pulls out on to its wrong side of the road. It may well be asked: why should the injured plaintiff have his damages reduced? The accident was solely caused by the negligent driving of the defendant. Sometimes outrageously bad driving. It should not lie in his mouth to say: "You ought to have been wearing a seat belt." That point of view was strongly expressed in *Smith v. Blackburn (Note)* [1974] R.T.R. 533, 536 by O'Connor J.:

> "... the idea that the insurers of a grossly negligent driver should be relieved in any degree from paying what is proper compensation for injuries is an idea that offends ordinary decency. Until I am forced to do so by higher authority I will not so rule."

行事，他就可能受伤，（而他又没有这样行事，因此而受伤了），那么他的行为就属于与有过失。[参见 Jones v Livox Quarries Ltd.（1952）2 QB 608。] 1945 年之前，如果自己的疏忽是造成伤害的实质原因之一，那么与有过失的原告是不能获得任何赔偿的。[参见 Swadling v Cooper（1931）AC 1] 1945 年之后，他的请求权不会再彻底地消灭了，只是他所得的损害赔偿金会减少。[参见 Davies v Swan Motor Co（Swansea）Ltd（1949）2 KB 291。]

以上的规定载于 1945 年《法律改革法（与有过失）》的第 1 条第 1 款中，规定如下：

> 对受害人的损害，受害人自身和侵权人都有过错的，不因受害人的过错而使其无法获得赔偿。但该赔偿的数额将根据法院依据公正之考量，根据原告对损害发生的责任份额，被相应减少。

该法第 4 条规定：

> "过错"是指过失、违反成文法上之义务，或任何能导致侵权责任的作为或者不作为，以及没有本法时亦可成立与有过失抗辩的前述事项。

我们之后的论述将以上述法条作为基础展开。

损害的原因

在这些涉及受害人没有系安全带的案件中，受伤的原告对于车祸本身的发生是没有任何可指责之处的。有的案件中他只是坐在过失的司机旁边的无辜乘客，是司机把车开出公路的。另一些案件中原告则只是个无辜的司机，是另一个人乱开，把车开到错误的车道，从而撞上了原告的车。我们可能会问：凭什么要减少受伤的原告的损害赔偿金？车祸完全是由过失驾驶的被告产生的。有时候被告的车开得实在是太差了。他没有资格去说："你应该系安全带的。"这种观点在 Smith v Blackburn（Note）[1974] R.T.R. 533, 536 案中，O'Connor 法官表达得很清楚：

> 严重过失的司机的承保人可以在任何意义上不履行应该对伤者承担的合理的赔偿义务，这样的想法违反一般道德。除非能找到约束我的更高的判例，否则我是不会这样判决的。

I do not think that is the correct approach. The question is not what was the cause of the accident. It is rather what was the cause of the damage. In most accidents on the road the bad driving, which causes the accident, also causes the ensuing damage. But in seat belt cases the cause of the accident is one thing. The cause of the damage is another. The *accident* is caused by the bad driving. The *damage* is caused in part by the bad driving of the defendant, and in part by the failure of the plaintiff to wear a seat belt. If the plaintiff was to blame in not wearing a seat belt, the damage is in part the result of his own fault. He must bear some share in the responsibility for the damage: and his damages fall to be reduced to such extent as the court thinks just and equitable. In Admiralty the courts used to look to the causes of the *damage* : see The Margaret (1881) 6 P.D. 76 . In a leading case in this court, under the Act of 1945, we looked to the cause of the *damage:* see *Davies v. Swan Motor Co. (Swansea) Ltd.* [1949] 2 K.B. 291, 326. In the crash helmet cases this court also looked at the causes of the damage: see *O'Connell v. Jackson* [1972] 1 Q.B. 270. So also we should in seat belt cases.

The share of responsibility

Whenever there is an accident, the negligent driver must bear by far the greater share of responsibility. It was his negligence which caused the accident. It also was a prime cause of the whole of the damage. But in so far as the damage might have been avoided or lessened by wearing a seat belt, the injured person must bear some share. But how much should this be? Is it proper to inquire whether the driver was grossly negligent or only slightly negligent? or whether the failure to wear a seat belt was entirely inexcusable or almost forgivable? If such an inquiry could easily be undertaken, it might be as well to do it. In *Davies v. Swan Motor Co. (Swansea) Ltd.* [1949] 2 K.B. 291, 326, the court said that consideration should be given not only to the causative potency of a particular factor, but also its blameworthiness. But we live in a practical world. In most of these cases the liability of the driver is admitted, the failure to wear a seat belt is admitted, the only question is: what damages should be payable? This question should not be prolonged by an expensive inquiry into the degree of blameworthiness on either side, which would be hotly disputed. Suffice it to assess a share of responsibility which will be just and equitable in the great majority of cases.

Sometimes the evidence will show that the failure made no difference. The damage would have been the same, even if a seat belt had been worn. In such case the damages should not be reduced at all. At other times the evidence will show that the failure made all the difference. The damage would have been prevented altogether if a seat belt had been worn. In such cases I would suggest that the damages should be reduced by 25 per cent. But often enough the evidence will only show that the failure made a considerable difference. Some injuries to the head, for instance, would have been a good deal less severe if a seat belt had been worn, but there would still have been some injury to the head. In such case I would suggest that the damages attributable to the

这种想法在我看来是错误的。这里的关键问题不在于事故的原因是什么。而是损害的原因是什么。大多数差劲的驾驶不但导致了车祸的发生，而且导致了损害的发生。然而在受害人不系安全带的案件中，车祸的发生原因是一回事，损害的发生原因却是另一回事。车祸确实是因为不良驾驶引起的，但是损害却是部分因为不良驾驶引起的，而另一部分是由原告不系安全带引起的。如果原告没有系安全带，那么损害在一部分意义上是由他自己的过错造成的。他对于损害应当承担一定份额的责任，他能获得的损害赔偿金因此应当由法院按照公正原则，降低到一定的程度。在海商案件中，法院会去考察损害的原因。[参见 *The Margaret*（1881）6 PD 76] 在本院判决的一起著名的，适用上述 1945 年法的判例中，我们考察了损害的原因。[参见 *Davies v Swan Motor Co*（*Swansea*）*Ltd*（1949）2 KB 291, 326] 在涉及头盔的案件中，也考察了损害的原因。[参见 *O'Connell v Jackson*（1972）1 Q.B. 270] 因此在涉及没有系安全带的案件时，我们也应该考察损害的原因是什么。

责任的份额

目前为止只要有车祸发生，过失的司机一定会承担更多的责任。因为是他的过失引发了车祸。他的过失也是损害的主要原因。然而因为损害是可以通过受害人系安全带来避免或者减轻的，受害人也因此应该承担一定的份额。然而这种份额应该是多少呢？我们关心司机到底是重过失还是轻过失是否恰当呢？没有系安全带是完全不可原谅的吗？或者是可以完全原谅的吗？如果可以很容易地进行这样的调查，那么最好还是这样做。在 *Davies v. Swan Motor Co.*（*Swansea*）*Ltd.* 案中，法院认为对于一个因素不仅应该考察它的原因力，还应该考察它的可谴责性。然而我们是生活在真实世界上的。在大多数情况下是已经确定司机该承担责任，也确定了受害人没有系安全带。唯一的问题是：应该判决多少数额的损害赔偿金？解决这个问题，不应当麻烦到要去讨论双方的可谴责性，这将会引起激烈的争论。对大多数的案件来说，评估一下双方的责任份额就已经足够达到公正的要求了。

有时候证据会显示系不系安全带对于损害后果来说没有区别。即使受害人系了安全带，还是会发生同样的损害。在这种情况下，损害赔偿金就不应该减少。在其他时候证据可能会显示系不系安全带很有关系。如果受害人系了安全带，那么损害会完全得到避免。在这种情况下，我认为损害赔偿金应该减少 25%。然而大多数情况下，证据只能证明系不系安全带对结果有很大的影响。比如如果系了安全带，头部的某些损伤会轻微很多，然而头部是依然会有损伤的。在这种情况下，我认为因为没有系安全带，损害赔偿金应该

failure to wear a seat belt should be reduced by 15 per cent.

Conclusion

Everyone knows, or ought to know, that when he goes out in a car he should fasten the seat belt. It is so well known that it goes without saying, not only for the driver, but also the passenger. If either the driver or the passenger fails to wear it and an accident happens - and the injuries would have been prevented or lessened if he had worn it - then his damages should be reduced. Under the Highway Code a driver may have a duty to invite his passenger to fasten his seat belt: but adult passengers possessed of their faculties should not need telling what to do. If such passengers do not fasten their seat belts, their own lack of care for their own safety may be the cause of their injuries. In the present case the injuries to the head and chest would have been prevented by the wearing of a seat belt and the damages on that account might be reduced by 25 per cent. The finger would have been broken any way and the damages for it not reduced at all. Overall the judge suggested 20 per cent. and the plaintiff has made no objection to it. So I would not interfere. I would allow the appeal and reduce the damages by £100.

B. Assumption of Risk (*Volenti non fit injuria*)

35. Meistrich v. Casino Arena Attractions, Inc., 31 N.J. 44, 155 A.2d 90 (1959)

Supreme Court of New Jersey, United States

Weintraub, C.J. Plaintiff was injured by a fall while ice-skating on a rink operated by defendant. The jury found for defendant. The Appellate Division reversed, 54 N.J. Super. 25 (1959), and we granted defendant's petition for certification. 29 N.J. 582 (1959)....

The Appellate Division found error in the charge of assumption of the risk. It also concluded there was no evidence of contributory negligence and hence that issue should not have been submitted to the jury.

Defendant urges there was no negligence and therefore the alleged errors were harmless. We think there was sufficient proof to take the case to the jury. There was evidence that defendant departed from the usual procedure in preparing the ice, with the result that it became too hard and hence too slippery for the patron of average ability using skates sharpened for the usual surface....

We however agree with defendant that the issue of contributory negligence was properly left to the trier of the facts. Plaintiff had noted that his skates slipped on turns. A jury could permissibly find he carelessly contributed to his injury when, with that knowledge, he remained on the ice and skated cross-hand with another.

The remaining question is whether the trial court's charge with respect to assumption of risk

减少 15%。

结论

众所周知,开车出门应该系安全带。这件事应该人人都知道,因而对司机和乘客来说都是不言而喻的。若司乘人员在没有系安全带时车祸发生了,而如果系了安全带能避免或者减少伤害的程度,那么损害赔偿金应该减少。根据《公路法典》,司机倒是有义务提醒乘客系安全带。然而成年乘客如果有健全的判断能力的话并不需要别人告诉他这么做。如果这样的乘客没有系安全带,那么他对自己的安全的粗心大意很可能是他受伤的原因。在本案中,头部和胸部的伤害可以由系安全带来避免,因此损害赔偿金应该减少 25%。手指折断则一定会发生,因此损害赔偿金并不能减少。总体来说,我认为损害赔偿金应该减少 20%,原告对此没有异议。我也就不会介入这点。我同意上诉并将损害赔偿金减少 100 英镑。

二、自甘风险

35. Meistrich v. Casino Arena Attractions, Inc., 31 N.J. 44, 155 A.2d 90 (1959)

美国新泽西州最高法院

Weintraub 大法官主笔:原告在被告经营的滑冰场滑冰时被坠落物打伤。陪审团作出了有利于被告的裁断。上诉分庭撤销了初审法院的判决 [54 N.J. Super. 25 (1959)],我们准许了被告提请审查的申诉 [29 N.J. 582 (1959)] ……

上诉分庭认为初审法院有关自甘风险的判决存在错误。上诉分庭还认为没有证据证明原告存在与有过失,因此不应该将该问题提交陪审团裁断。

被告极力声称自己没有过失,因此所谓的错误是无害的。我们认为有充分的证据将案件提交给陪审团裁断。有证据证明,被告并没有遵循常规的制冰程序,结果冰面变得过于坚硬,以至于滑冰技术一般的客户如果穿着锋利程度匹配常规冰面的冰刀鞋则很容易滑倒在冰面上……

然而,我们认同被告的观点,即与有过失的问题应该交由事实认定者来裁断。原告提到他的冰鞋在转弯时打滑。陪审团可以被允许认定原告的疏忽促成了自己受伤,因为在知道打滑之后,他仍然呆在冰上,并与另一名滑冰者交叉拉手滑冰。

剩下的问题是,初审法院有关自甘风险的判决是否错误……

was erroneous....

The Appellate Division...found the trial court failed to differentiate between assumption of risk and contributory negligence. The Appellate Division added:

> We note that contributory negligence involves some breach of duty on the part of the plaintiff. His actions are such as to constitute a failure to use such care for his safety as the ordinarily prudent man in similar circumstances would use. On the other hand, assumption of risk may involve no fault or negligence, but rather entails the undertaking of a risk or a known danger. Hendrikson v. Koppers Co., Inc., 11 N.J. 600, 607 (1953).

As we read the charge, the trial court expressed essentially the same thought, i.e., that assumption of risk may be found if plaintiff knew or reasonably should have known of the risk, notwithstanding that a reasonably prudent man would have continued in the face of the risk. We think an instruction to that effect is erroneous in the respect hereinafter delineated. The error is traceable to confusion in the opinions in our State.

Assumption of risk is a term of several meanings. For present purposes, we may place to one side certain situations which sometimes are brought within the sweeping term but which are readily differentiated from the troublesome area. Specifically we place beyond present discussion the problem raised by an express contract not to sue for injury or loss which may thereafter be occasioned by the covenantee's negligence, and also situations in which actual consent exists, as, for example, participation in a contact sport.

We here speak solely of the area in which injury or damage was neither intended nor expressly contracted to be non-actionable. In this area, assumption of risk has two distinct meanings. In one sense (sometimes called its "primary" sense), it is an alternate expression for the proposition that defendant was not negligent, i.e., either owed no duty or did not breach the duty owed. In its other sense (sometimes called "secondary"), assumption of risk is an affirmative defense to an established breach of duty. In its primary sense, it is accurate to say plaintiff assumed the risk whether or not he was "at fault," for the truth thereby expressed in alternate terminology is that defendant was not negligent. But in its secondary sense, i.e., as an affirmative defense to an established breach of defendant's duty, it is incorrect to say plaintiff assumed the risk whether or not he was at fault....

Hence we think it clear that assumption of risk in its secondary sense is a mere phase of contributory negligence, the total issue being whether a reasonably prudent man in the exercise of due care (a) would have incurred the known risk and (b) if he would, whether such a person in the light of all of the circumstances including the appreciated risk would have conducted himself in the

上诉分庭……发现初审法院未能区分自甘风险和与有过失。上诉分庭补充道：

> 我们注意到与有过失涉及原告对义务的某种违反。原告的行为构成了未能像一般理性的人在类似的情况下一样，为保障自己的安全而尽到注意义务。另一方面，自甘风险不涉及过错或过失，而是原告需要承担风险或已知危险。[Hendrikson v. Koppers Co., Inc., 11 N.J. 600, 607 (1953)。]

正如我们在判决中所看到的，初审法院表达了完全一样的想法，即如果原告知道或者有理由应该知道风险的存在，但是理性而谨慎的人面对风险不会继续行动下去，那么便可以认定为原告自甘风险。我们认为初审法院为此作出的指示存在错误，下文详述。错误起源于本州判决意见中存在的混淆情况。

自甘风险一词有多个含义。为了说明当前这个案件，我们单独列出了一些情况，这些情况可以用一般性语言加以说明，但是完全区别于一些棘手的领域。具体来讲，我们在本讨论之外提出了两种情况：不予起诉的明示合同问题，订约方的过失可能在合同签订之后造成损害或损失；另一种情况是当事人表明了合意的情况，例如当事人参加身体接触性体育运动。

我们这里只谈一个方面，即损害或损失既不是故意的，明示合同又没有规定是不能起诉的。在这一领域中，自甘风险有两个不同的含义。第一个含义（有时也被称为"初级"含义），这是对被告无过失——既不负有义务又未违背应尽的义务——的另外一种表达方式。另一个含义（有时也被称为"次级"含义）是，自甘风险是针对已被确定的违背义务的情况的积极性抗辩。根据自甘风险的初级含义，可以说原告无论存在过错与否，原告都是自甘风险，因为以另一种术语表达出的真实意思是被告没有过失。但是根据其次级含义，即针对已被证实的违背义务的情况的积极性抗辩，则不能说无论原告是否存在过错都自担了风险……

因此，我们认为自甘风险的次级含义只是与有过失的一个方面而已，全部问题在于一个理性且谨慎的人在尽到了适当的注意之后：（1）是否会招惹已知的风险；（2）如果会，那么鉴于包括已知风险在内的各种情况，他是否会采取和原告一样的行为方式。

manner in which plaintiff acted.

Thus in the area under discussion there are but two basic issues: (1) defendant's negligence, and (2) plaintiff's contributory negligence. In view of the considerations discussed above, it has been urged that assumption of risk in both its primary and secondary senses serves merely to confuse and should be eliminated....

In short, each case must be analyzed to determine whether the pivotal question goes to defendant's negligence or to plaintiff's contributory negligence. If the former, then what has been called assumption of risk is only a denial of breach of duty and the burden of proof is plaintiff's. If on the other hand assumption of risk is advanced to defeat a recovery despite a demonstrated breach of defendant's duty, then it constitutes the affirmative defense of contributory negligence and the burden of proof is upon defendant.

With the modification expressed above, the judgment of the Appellate Division is affirmed.

For modification—Chief Justice Weintraub, and Justices Burling, Jacobs, Francis and Proctor—5.

Opposed—None.

36. Morris v Murray [1991] 2 QB 6

Court of Appeal, United Kingdom

After drinking alcohol during the whole of the afternoon, the plaintiff and his friend decided to go on a flight in the friend's light aircraft. The plaintiff drove the car which took them to the airfield and he helped to start and refuel the aircraft, which was piloted by the friend. Shortly after take off the aircraft crashed, killing the pilot and severely injuring the plaintiff. In an action against the pilot's personal representatives for personal injuries, the judge [of the Queen's Bench Division], in giving judgment for the plaintiff, held that the defendants had succeeded on their plea of contributory negligence but not their alternative plea of volenti non fit injuria.

On the defendants' appeal:

FOX L.J.

The reasoning of Asquith J. was that a person who voluntarily travels as a passenger with a driver who is known to the passenger to have driven negligently in the past cannot properly be regarded as volens to future acts of negligence by the driver. Should it then make any difference that the driver is likely to drive negligently on the material occasion, not because he is shown to have driven negligently in the past, but because he is known by the plaintiff to be under the influence of drink? Asquith J. thought not and held that the plaintiff by embarking in the car, or re-entering it, with the knowledge that through drink the driver had materially reduced his capacity for driving safely, did not implicitly consent to or absolve the driver from liability for any

因此，在我们讨论的领域中只有两个基本的问题：（1）被告的过失；（2）原告的与有过失。鉴于我们上文讨论到的各种考虑，有人提出无论是初级层次的自甘风险还是次级层次的自甘风险，这一概念都只会造成混淆，因此应该予以抛弃……

简而言之，应该对每个案件进行分析，以确定关键问题在于被告的过失还是原告的与有过失。如果是被告的过失，那么所谓的自甘风险不过是否定了违背义务以及原告承担举证责任而已。如果是原告的与有过失，那么即使证明被告违背义务，自甘风险也足以使原告不能获得赔偿，因此自甘风险构成了与有过失的积极性抗辩，而被告负有举证责任。

在上述修改的基础上，上诉分庭的判决被维持。

赞成修改——Weintraub 大法官和 Burling 法官、Jacobs 法官、Francis 法官、Proctor 法官——5 票。

反对——无。

36. Morris v Murray [1991] 2 QB 6

联合王国上诉法院

喝了一下午酒之后，原告和朋友决定乘坐朋友的轻型飞机去兜风。原告开车将二人带到机场，并帮助发动了飞机，还帮助给飞机加了油。飞机则是由朋友驾驶。起飞之后不就，飞机就坠机了。飞行员死亡，原告则受了重伤。原告因其所受之人身损害起诉飞行员的代理人，［王座分院的］法官判决支持了原告，其承认被告提出的与有过失的抗辩是成立的，却否定了他提出的另一个抗辩自甘风险。

被告因此上诉。

Fox 上诉法院法官主笔：

Asquith 法官认为，即使乘客在知道之前司机开车不认真的情况下自愿地乘坐了他的车，也不能就据此认为他对司机的过失行为属于自甘风险。而如果在案发时乘客知道司机很可能无法认真开车，但是并不是因为他之前表现出来的过失，而是因为他喝了酒，那么此时的结果是否应该有所不同呢？Asquith 法官认为结果并无不同。他认为仅仅因为原告上了被告的车，或者再一次上了被告的车，且知道被告因为喝了酒所以安全驾驶的能力严重下降，并不能认定原告默示地同意了被告之后实施的可能造成她伤害的过失行为，

subsequent negligence on his part whereby she might suffer harm. Having reached that conclusion, Asquith J., however, continued, at p. 518:

> "There may be cases in which the drunkenness of the driver at the material time is so extreme and so glaring that to accept a lift from him is like engaging in an intrinsically and obviously dangerous occupation, intermeddling with an unexploded bomb or walking on the edge of an unfenced cliff. It is not necessary to decide whether in such a case the maxim 'volenti non fit injuria' would apply, for in the present case I find as a fact that the driver's degree of intoxication fell short of this degree."

The question before us, I think, is whether, as a matter of law, there are such cases as Asquith J. refers to and, if so, whether this present case is one of them. As to the first of these questions there is a fundamental issue whether the volenti doctrine applies to the tort of negligence at all. In *Wooldridge v. Sumner* [1963] 2 Q.B. 43, 69 Diplock L.J. said:

> "In my view, the maxim in the absence of expressed contract has no application to negligence simpliciter where the duty of care is based solely upon proximity or 'neighbourship' in the Atkinian sense. The maxim in English law presupposes a tortious act by the defendant. The consent that is relevant is not consent to the risk of injury but consent to the lack of reasonable care that may produce that risk . . . and requires on the part of the plaintiff at the time at which he gives his consent full knowledge of the nature and extent of the risk that he ran."

Asquith J. himself raised the same question in *Dann v. Hamilton* [1939] 1 K.B. 509, 516-517. He drew a distinction between two kinds of case. First, where a dangerous physical condition has been brought about by the negligence of the defendant and, after it has arisen, the plaintiff fully appreciating its dangerous character elects to assume the risk. In that sort of case Asquith J. regarded the volenti maxim as capable of applying. That, however, is not this case. Diplock L.J. indeed would not have regarded the maxim as truly applicable and was of the opinion that the correct test of liability of the person creating the risk was whether it was reasonably foreseeable by him that the plaintiff would so act in relation to it as to endanger himself, which is the principle of the "rescue" cases. The second class of case is where the act of the plaintiff relied on as a consent precedes and is claimed to licence in advance a possible subsequent act of negligence. *Dann v. Hamilton* itself was an instance of that class in which Asquith J. held on the facts the maxim not to be applicable. But as I have indicated he left open the question of extreme cases.

. . .

也没有因此就免除被告的相应责任。在得出这个结论之后，Asquith 法官却这么说（518 页）：

> 在某些情况下，司机在案发时不是一般的醉，而且醉得太明显了，因而上他的车简直就像是在从事本质上明显很危险的工作；像是在摆弄未爆炸的炸弹；像是在没有栅栏的悬崖边行走。这类情况下自甘风险理论是否应该适用，在这里我就不作讨论了，因为在本案中我认定司机酒醉的程度还没有那么严重。

我认为我们需要解决的法律上的争议焦点就是，是否真的存在 Asquith 法官所说的那种类型的情况；而如果存在，那么本案属不属于这种类型的情况。对于第一个问题，需要先解决一个基本的争议焦点：自甘风险理论是否适用于过失之诉？在 *Wooldridge v Sumner* [1963] 2 Q.B. 43, 69 案中，Diplock 上诉法院法官说到：

> 我认为，在没有明确约定的情况下，如果其中的注意义务仅仅是产生于 Atkin 大法官所说的那种意义上的"邻近性"或者"邻近关系"，自甘风险理论是绝对不能适用到过失之诉中的。自甘风险理论的适用前提是假定被告实施了侵权行为。这里有意义的是，受害人的同意不是对受伤的同意，而是对"被告人不尽合理的注意义务因此可能会导致风险一事"的同意，这里的同意还需要原告在他作出同意之时对可能产生的风险的性质和程度有清晰的认识。

Asquith 法官自己在 *Dann v Hamilton* 案中也提出了这个问题。他区分了两种情形。第一种类型的情形是被告的过失导致了一种非常危险的状况，原告在这之后明知其危险还依然选择承受这种风险。在这种情形中，Asquith 法官认为自甘风险理论是能够适用的。这不属于他面临的这个案件的情况。如果是 Diplock 上诉法院法官的话，可能不会觉得自甘风险可以在这里适用。他的观点应该是，要判断一个造成了危险的人的责任，应该看他是否能合理地预见原告面临这种风险时会不会做出让自己陷入危险的事，这就是"拯救"原则。第二种类型的情形是据以认定为原告同意表示的行为，发生的时间早于后续的被告的过失行为，且这个同意行为被宣称为对后续过失行为的授权。*Dann v Hamilton* 案本身属于这种类型，Asquith 法官认定这种类型下自甘风险理论并不适用。然而正如我刚才所说的，对于极端的情况应该怎么处理，他没有给出意见。

……

In general, I think that the volenti doctrine can apply to the tort of negligence, though it must depend upon the extent of the risk, the passenger's knowledge of it and what can be inferred as to his acceptance of it. The passenger cannot be volens (in the absence of some form of express disclaimer) in respect of acts of negligence which he had no reason to anticipate and he must be free from compulsion.

…

If the plaintiff had himself been sober on the afternoon of the flight it seems to me that, by agreeing to be flown by Mr. Murray, he must be taken to have accepted fully the risk of serious injury. The danger was both obvious and great. He could not possibly have supposed that Mr. Murray, who had been drinking all the afternoon, was capable of discharging a normal duty of care. But as he himself had been drinking, can it be assumed that he was capable of appreciating the risks? The matter was not very deeply examined at the trial, but he was certainly not "blind drunk." In cross-examination, he agreed with the description "merry." He was capable of driving a car from the Blue Boar to the airfield; and he did so for the purpose of going on a flight with Mr. Murray. He helped to start the aircraft and fuel it. Immediately before take off he asked Mr. Murray whether he should not "radio in" - a sensible inquiry. None of this suggests that his faculties were so muddled that he was incapable of appreciating obvious risks. Moreover, he gave no specific evidence to the effect, "I was really too drunk to know what I was doing." Nor did anyone else give such evidence about him. …

In my opinion, on the evidence the plaintiff knew that he was going on a flight; he knew that he was going to be piloted by Mr. Murray; and he knew that Mr. Murray had been drinking heavily that afternoon. The plaintiff's actions that afternoon, from leaving the Blue Boar to the take off, suggest that he was capable of understanding what he was doing. There is no clear evidence to the contrary. I think he knew what he was doing and was capable of appreciating the risks. I do not overlook that the plaintiff's evidence was that, if he had been sober, he would not have gone on the flight. That is no doubt so but it does not establish that he was in fact incapable of understanding what he was doing that afternoon. If he was capable of understanding what he was doing, then the fact is that he knowingly and willingly embarked on a flight with a drunken pilot. The flight served no useful purpose at all; there was no need or compulsion to join it. It was just entertainment. The plaintiff co-operated fully in the joint activity and did what he could to assist it. He agreed in evidence that he was anxious to start the engine and to fly. A clearer source of great danger could hardly be imagined. The sort of errors of judgment which an intoxicated pilot may make are likely to have a distastrous result. The high probability was that Mr. Murray was simply not fit to fly an aircraft. Nothing that happened on the flight itself suggests otherwise, from the take off downwind to the violence of the manoeuvres of the plane in flight.

The situation seems to me to come exactly within Asquith J.'s example of the case where

总体说来，我认为自甘风险的理论可以适用到过失之诉中。但是要适用这个理论应当考虑风险的大小、乘客对风险大小的认知，以及那些可以被认为构成他接受这个风险的事实。如果乘客并不能预见到行为人的过失，那么我们不能说乘客对于行为人的过失属于自甘风险（除非存在某种形式的书面的免责声明）；另外，乘客的自甘风险决定也不能是被迫作出的。

……

如果原告在飞行的那个下午是清醒的，那在我看来，他允许 Murray 来驾驶飞机就说明了他完全接受了严重受伤的风险。这里涉及的危险非常明显，程度也很深。他不可能在 Murray 先生喝了一下午酒的情况下，觉得他有能力履行正常的注意义务。但是原告自己也喝了酒，那么我们能认为他能理解这种风险吗？在一审过程中，对这个问题虽然没有很深入的讨论，但是很显然他并不属于那种烂醉如泥的状态。在交叉询问环节，他承认自己只是"微醺"。他有能力从 Blue Boar 把车开到机场，而且他这么做的目的是要去坐 Murray 先生驾驶的飞机。他帮着把飞机启动，还给飞机加了油。在即将起飞之前他还问了问 Murray 先生是不是要打开无线电——这是很明智的询问。以上这些事实共同说明，他的神志并没有不清到无法识别显而易见的危险的程度。另外，他自己也没能就"我已经醉到不知道自己在做什么了"这件事，提供任何详细的证据。别人也没有提出可以证明他当时状况的证据……

在我看来，现有的证据证明原告知道他要坐飞机上天；他知道是 Murray 先生在开飞机；他也知道 Murray 先生当天下午喝了很多酒。原告当天下午从离开 Blue Boar 到起飞之间的行为表明他有能力理解他自己在做什么。没有明确的证据证明相反的事实。我相信他知道自己在做什么，也能理解风险。我并没有忽视原告证明了如果他当时是清醒的，他是不会坐那架飞机的。毫无疑问这确实是事实，但这个事实不能说明他没有能力理解他当天下午在干什么。既然他有能力理解自己在干什么，那么事实就是他在明知飞行员喝醉了的情况下，自愿地乘坐了这个飞行员驾驶的飞机。这次飞行没有任何意义，他没有任何必要去乘坐这架飞机，也没有任何人强迫他。他们这么做仅仅是为了娱乐。原告在这个共同活动中倾力合作，做到了他能尽力协助的事情。他也同意证据证明了他当时非常急切地想要启动引擎，非常急切地想要起飞。我们很难想象有什么比这更危险的了。喝醉了的飞行员可能会犯很多判断错误，这非常可能导致灾难性的后果。Murray 先生有极大的可能根本就不适合驾驶一架飞机。然而从顺风起飞到飞机在飞行中剧烈的操纵，飞行过程中发生的任何事情本身都不能说明这一点。

这种情形在我看来完全符合 Asquith 法官所举的这个例子：

"the drunkenness of the driver at the material time is so extreme and so glaring that to accept a lift from him is like engaging in an intrinsically and obviously dangerous occupation."

I think that in embarking upon the flight the plaintiff had implicitly waived his rights in the event of injury consequent on Mr. Murray's failure to fly with reasonable care. ...

Considerations of policy do not lead me to any different conclusion. Volenti as a defence has, perhaps, been in retreat during this century - certainly in relation to master and servant cases. It might be said that the merits could be adequately dealt with by the application of the contributory negligence rules. The judge held that the plaintiff was only 20 per cent to blame (which seems to me to be too low) but if that were increased to 50 per cent, so that the plaintiff's damages were reduced by half, both sides would be substantially penalised for their conduct. It seems to me, however, that the wild irresponsibility of the venture is such that the law should not intervene to award damages and should leave the loss where it falls. Flying is intrinsically dangerous and flying with a drunken pilot is great folly. The situation is very different from what has arisen in motoring cases.

I should mention that the defence of volenti has been abrogated in relation to passengers in motor vehicles covered by comprehensive insurance: section 148 of the Road Traffic Act 1972 . It is not suggested, however, that there is any similar enactment relating to aircraft and applicable to this case.

...

STOCKER L.J.

Where a plaintiff is aware that his driver is to some extent intoxicated his responsibility can be reflected by an apportionment on the basis of contributory negligence. Whether such a course is appropriate or whether the volenti maxim applies depends upon the facts of each case. In particular, it is relevant to consider the degree of intoxication and the nature of the act to be performed by the driver. In motoring cases it may well be that an apportionment on the basis of contributory negligence will usually be the appropriate course but in my view to pilot an aircraft requires a far higher standard of skill and care than driving a motor car and the effect of intoxication becomes all the more important. It seems to me from the authorities cited that this is the approach which the courts ought to apply to this problem: how intoxicated was the driver? How obvious was this to the plaintiff, the extent of the potential risk if he voluntarily accepted the offer of carriage?

In the light of these observations I turn next to the crucial issue in this case. Did the plaintiff voluntarily accept the risk of injury and Mr. Murray's likely breach of duty in negligence with full knowledge of the facts?

I therefore first consider the position on the basis that the plaintiff himself was sober, or at

司机在案发时不是一般的醉,而且醉得太明显了;因而上他的车简直就像是在从事本质上明显很危险的工作。

我认为,原告从登机那一刻起,就默示地放弃了自己因为 Murray 先生未能尽到足够的注意义务而受伤时本来能行使的权利。

政策考量也并不会让我得出不同的结论。自甘风险作为抗辩事由,在 21 世纪已经式微了——尤其是在雇佣关系中。有人也许会说自甘风险的功能可以由与有过失规则来代替。本案中一审法官认定原告的过错只有 20%(在我看来这样认定太低了)。然而如果原告的过错被提升到 50%,这样原告获得的损害赔偿金就将降到一半,这样双方都因为各自的行为受到了足够的惩罚。然而在我看来,双方的冒险实在是太不负责任了,法律根本就不应该介入,不应该判决任何赔偿金,应该让损失停留在发生处。飞行是本质上就危险的活动。让一个醉鬼来驾驶更简直是在玩儿命。这种情况和那些由车辆驾驶引发的案件完全不同。

需要注意的是,在乘客乘坐的车是上了综合意外险的情况下,自甘风险这一抗辩事由已经被 1972 年《道路交通法》第 148 条废除了。然而,这并不意味着在航空器领域也有类似的法律,更不用说这样的法律能适用到本案中。

……

Stocker 上诉法院法官:

如果原告知道司机在某种程度上已经喝醉了,那么他就可能要根据与有过失原则分担一定份额的责任。是适用与有过失原则还是适用自甘风险理论,取决于每个案件的具体情况。我们特别需要考察的,是司机醉酒的程度,以及司机的行为性质。在涉及机动车驾驶的案件中,我认为根据与有过失原则分担责任可能是比较正确的做法。然而在我看来如果是驾驶飞机的话,那么技能要求和注意力要求都比驾驶汽车高多了,这样,飞行员醉酒这个情节就重要得多。根据判例,我认为法院要解决这个问题需要关注下面的问题:司机醉酒的程度有多大;司机醉酒的程度对原告来说有多明显;如果原告自愿地接受了同乘的要求,那么潜在的风险是多大。

根据以上观点,我下面将要讨论本案最关键的争议焦点:原告是否自愿地接受了受伤的风险,是否自愿地接受了 Murray 先生很可能会过失地违反他的义务,他接受这一切时是否知道全部的事实?

我理论的基础是原告是清醒的这一事实,或者至少他没有醉到无法辨别

least not so intoxicated as the result of alcohol as to be incapable of assessing the risk. I would unhesitatingly answer this question "Yes." The facts were as follows.

1. Mr. Murray had consumed at least the equivalent of 17 whiskies and when absorption rate is considered over the period of time involved must, in fact, have consumed rather more.

2. The plaintiff was drinking with him over several hours and knew how much Mr. Murray had had to drink.

3. The risk of accident was manifest to any sober person when the activity to be carried out involved flying an aircraft. The risk was far greater than driving a car in a similar condition of insobriety. The plaintiff had flown with Mr. Murray before; he co-operated and, indeed, encouraged Mr. Murray throughout; he drove him to the airfield and filled the aircraft with aviation spirit. The purpose of going to the airfield can only have been to fly in the aircraft. That Mr. Murray was in fact incapable of flying the aircraft is demonstrated by a number of factors. First, he took off downwind and uphill - a highly dangerous manoeuvre - and in fact only just managed to get airborne shortly before the end of the runway. The evidence suggests that the aircraft was out of control virtually at all times therafter.

4. The plaintiff not only accepted the offer of being taken for a joy ride in the aircraft but actively sought it. Discussion as to this possibility had taken place at the first public house, the Red Lion in Harlow, and again at the Blue Boar when Mr. Murray was present. Without the plaintiff's co-operation the flight in the aircraft could never have taken place at all since Mr. Murray had no motor car and Mr. Moran was disqualified from driving.

Thus, on the basis that the plaintiff himself was capable of appreciating the full nature and extent of the risk and voluntarily accepted it, I would have no doubt whatever that this maxim would have applied to defeat his claim. If this was not a case of volenti non fit injuria I find it very difficult to envisage circumstances in which that can ever be the case. However, the position is that the plaintiff himself must have consumed an amount of drink not dissimilar to that consumed by Mr. Murray and, therefore, the question falls to be considered whether or not his own condition was such as to render him incapable of fully appreciating the nature and extent of the risk and of voluntarily accepting it.

It was submitted to this court that the proper test of this, that is to say, the plaintiff's appreciation of the risk and his consent to it, was an objective one. ... I do not, for my part, go so far as to say that the test is an objective one (though if it is not, a paradoxical situation arises that the plaintiff's claim could be defeated by the application of the maxim if he was sober, but he could recover damages if he was drunk), but unless there is specific evidence either from the plaintiff himself or from some other source that the plaintiff was in fact so intoxicated that he was incapable of appreciating the nature and extent of the risk and did not in fact appreciate it, and thus did not consent to it, it seems to me that the court is bound to judge the matter in the light of the

风险的程度。对以上的问题，我将毫不犹豫地回答："是的。"以下是所发生的事实。

1. Murray 先生至少喝了相当于 17 杯威士忌的量，考虑到相关时间段内的吸收率，他其实只会喝得更多。

2. 原告和他一起喝了几个小时，因此原告知道 Murray 先生喝了酒。

3. 对于任何清醒的人来说，驾驶飞机这种活动出事的风险都是显而易见的。原告之前曾经和 Murray 先生一起飞行过；他协助甚至一直在鼓励 Murray 先生去做这件事；他开车载 Murray 先生到了机场，并为飞机加满航空燃油。去机场的唯一目的只可能是开飞机。Murray 先生当时不能驾驶飞机这件事，已经通过很多因素表现出来了。首先，他在顺风和上坡的情况下起飞——这是一个非常危险的动作——实际上，只是在跑道快结束的时候才勉强升空。有证据表明那架飞机此后几乎一直处于失控状态。

4. 原告并不是仅仅接受了坐飞机兜风的邀请，他是主动请求别人载他兜风的。在第一家酒吧，Red Lion in Harlow，他们就已经在讨论坐飞机兜风的可能了，在 Blue Boar 他们又讨论了第二次，这次 Murray 先生在场了。如果没有原告的协助，飞机是飞不起来的，因为 Murray 先生没有汽车，而 Moran 先生的驾驶执照则被吊销了。

综上，因为原告自己完全有能力评估风险的性质和程度，却还是接受了风险，所以我坚决支持适用自甘风险原则来否定他的赔偿请求。如果本案的情况都不属于自甘风险，我实在想不出还有什么其他情况能属于自甘风险。然而，由于原告自己喝得并不比 Murray 先生少，所以要回答他是否是自甘风险，需要先考虑他当时的状况是否已经让他无法完全评估风险的性质和程度了，以及他当时是否自愿地接受了这种风险。

有人对本庭说，要正确回答这个问题，换言之，回答原告是否有能力评估风险，以及是否对此给出了有效的同意这个问题，需要客观的标准……我没有极端到敢说需要的标准确实是客观的（然而，如果这个标准不是客观的会产生一个矛盾的问题，那就是如果被告是清醒的，自甘风险理论将否定他的请求，而如果他是酒醉状态，则可以获得损害赔偿），除非原告本人或其他来源给出了特别的证据，证明原告酒醉的程度让他无法评估风险的程度和性质，且没有成功评估风险，因此并没有同意风险。在我看来，法院应当依据呈现在其面前的证据来判决案件。

evidence which is put before it for consideration.

In this case the plaintiff did not say, "I did not appreciate the risk as I was too drunk." What he did say was that, looking back on it, he would not have gone on the flight had he not been drunk. This is a wholly different proposition. The evidence seems to me to establish that the plaintiff was not so drunk as to be incapable of appreciating the risk or knowing really the state of intoxication of Mr. Murray. The factors which tend to this conclusion seem to me to be that he himself drove the car to the aerodrome with no other object than that of going on a flight with Mr. Murray; he himself assisted to start the engine by swinging the propeller and filling the aircraft with petrol; and he queried with Mr. Murray whether he should "radio in" to control. I do not feel that he could have done these things if he was in any way seriously incapacitated by alcohol or unaware of knowing just what it was he was doing. He must have known a number of facts such as the amount of drink Mr. Murray had taken and the risks in general terms at least of flying in an aircraft. He was not himself so drunk as to be in a state of incomprehension. He himself assented to the proposition that he was "merry." In my view, therefore, there was no evidence before the judge, even if the matter had been fully canvassed, which could have justified the proposition that the plaintiff's own condition was such as to render him incapable of appreciating the nature of the risk and its extent or indeed that he did in fact fail to appreciate the nature and extent of such risk. ...

To accept a flight in an aircraft piloted by a pilot who had had any significant amount of drink, let alone the amount which manifestly Mr. Murray had had, was to engage in an intrinsically and obviously dangerous occupation. For these reasons, in my judgment the judge ought to have found that the plaintiff's claim should be rejected on the basis of the application of the maxim volenti non fit injuria.

在本案中，原告并未说："我因为太醉了因此无法评估风险。"我们回过头来看，他说的其实是，如果他没有喝酒，他是不会上这架飞机的。这其实是两个完全不同的命题。证据显示，原告并没有醉到无法评估风险，也没有醉到无法辨别 Murray 先生喝醉的程度。得出这个结论的因素包括：他是自己驾车到的机场，且唯一的目的是要 Murray 先生载他上天；他通过旋转螺旋桨的方式帮助启动了引擎，还给飞机加满了油；他还询问了 Murray 先生是否应该"接入无线电"以便控制飞机。我不认为，如果他的能力真的因为醉酒而被严重削弱了，或者已经完全不知道自己在做什么了，他还能做到这些。他肯定知道许多事实，比如：Murray 先生喝了多少，以及至少在一般情况下乘坐飞机上天的风险。他自己并没有喝到人事不省的程度。他承认他当时的状态是"微醺"。因此，在我看来，即使我们彻查此事，也并没有任何证据能证明原告当时的状态使得他无法评估风险的性质和程度，也无法证明他当时没有正确评估风险……

乘坐一个喝了很多酒的飞行员驾驶的飞机，属于显而易见的存在固有危险的活动，更别说喝到 Murray 先生当时的那种程度了。综上所述，在我看来一审法官应当认定原告的请求因为自甘风险理论而被驳回。

Chapter 4. Causations

Section 1. Causation: Factual or Legal

37. Hoyt v. Jeffers, 30 Mich. 181 (1874)

Supreme Court of Michigan, United States

Christiancy, J.

...The chimney was a square brick chimney, originally about seventy feet high, but in the spring of 1870 about twelve or twelve and one-half feet were added to the height; but neither before nor after the addition did it have any spark-catcher on it, nor what is called a butterfly valve, with wire netting, nor a hole behind the boiler for the sparks to fall into, so far as the evidence shows. The Sherman House was situated about two hundred and thirty-three feet to the northeast of the mill, and on the other side of the street from it.

There was evidence on the part of the plaintiff relating to the particular time of the fire, which tended to show that the plaintiff's buildings were set on fire and burned by a spark from the mill chimney, though the spark was not seen to fall, or the fire to start from there. But this evidence was greatly strengthened by, and to some extent consisted of, a large amount of testimony showing the action and operation of the chimney in throwing such sparks, endangering and setting fire to property, for a long time previous, and up to the time of the fire, and how the mill had been run, and what measures had been taken or omitted by those running the mill, to avoid such danger to surrounding property, a change made in the height of the chimney, and whether, and how far, that change affected the action of the chimney by increasing or diminishing the escape of, and danger from sparks or cinders.

The evidence on the part of the plaintiff (some of which was received under objection, which will be noticed hereafter) tended to show, *first,* as to the habit of the chimney to throw sparks and the danger to surrounding property:—that from 1862 down to and after the time of this fire, sparks of fire and burning cinders or fragments of fire were frequently and quite generally emitted from the chimney when the mill was running, and carried to considerable distance (as far, and often farther than the Sherman House), falling to the ground and on buildings and sidewalks while still on fire, and sometimes setting fire to buildings and other wooden material they fell upon; that when

第四章　因果关系

第一节　事实因果关系或法律因果关系

37. Hoyt v. Jeffers, 30 Mich. 181 (1874)

美国密歇根州最高法院

Christiancy 法官主笔：

……烟囱呈方形，由砖砌成，原来的高度为70英尺，但是在1870年的春天，烟囱又被加高了12到12.5英寸。但是就证据提供的信息来看，在加高之前和之后烟囱上都没有安装灭火集尘器，也没有安装有金属网的被称为蝶形阀的装置，锅炉的后面也没有一个让火星掉入的洞。Sherman House 旅馆位于锯木厂东北方向的233英里处，和它隔街而望。

原告提供的证据特别提到了火灾的时间，意图证明原告的房屋着火是由锯木厂烟囱中溅出的火星引起的，尽管没有人看到火星溅落，也没有人看到火星是从那里冒出来的。但是许多证人的证词都显示这是非常有可能的。这些证词证明：在发生火灾之前的很长时期里，烟囱在锯木厂运行和操作时会抛出一些这种火星，威胁到财产安全并使其起火，以及锯木厂是如何经营的；在经营过程中为了避免对周围的财产造成危害采取或未采取哪些措施，如增加烟囱的高度，以及改进措施是否对烟囱的活动产生了影响、如何影响使其增加或消除了火星或煤渣被溅出的可能。

原告出示的证据（一些是在被告反对下被接受的，我们后文中会提到）意图显示，首先，关于烟囱抛出火星给周围财产造成危险的习性——从1862年到火灾之时和火灾之后，在锯木厂工作的时候，火星和燃烧的煤渣或碎片时常频繁地从烟囱中飞出，而且飞到很远的距离（经常比 Sherman House 所处的位置还远），落到地上或建筑物或人行道上时仍然没有熄灭，而且经常造成建筑物和其他木质材料着火。如果风从西南方向来（尤其是风力较强的时候），而锯木厂又在工作，人们会经常看到燃烧的火星从烟囱中飞出，落在

the wind was from the southwest (especially if strong), and the mill was running, live sparks were frequently seen to fly from the chimney and fall around the Sherman House and near to and upon other buildings, on sidewalks and the yards in and near the same direction; that in 1862 sparks from the chimney were seen to fall and set fire to sawdust near this house; that in 1863 or 1864, and again in 1869, this same Sherman House took fire on the outer south side, when the wind was in the southwest, and mill running, and sparks coming from that direction; that sparks were seen to fall on the sidewalk and set it on fire at one time; that sparks had been picked up on the platform of the Sherman House; that on one occasion clothes were set on fire when out drying on the line near the premises, and that clothes on the line drying in this neighborhood had holes burned in them, and were covered with black, dead sparks, and blackened, and that furniture set out at a cabinet shop about the same distance was rendered smutty in the same way; and that several houses near the Sherman House, and some further off, had to keep their windows shut to avoid injury of this kind to clothes, etc., inside, when the mill was running and the wind coming from the mill; that in 1873, after this fire, the Garvey House, somewhat near the mill, was set on fire under circumstances indicating that it came from such sparks; that fire had caught in several buildings similarly situated, and that all caught on the side towards the mill, and as far as known, when the mill was running, and the wind in the southwest, etc.

  The first set of errors assigned are based upon exceptions to the admission of evidence tending to show how this chimney had been in the habit of throwing sparks, and setting fire to buildings, etc., for several years previous to the burning of this hotel. The court upon the objection of the defendant, refused to receive evidence extending back over so long a period, except upon the understanding and with the undertaking, on the part of the plaintiff, to follow it up with evidence to show that it was then in the same condition as at the time of the fire; and the plaintiff did produce a large amount of evidence tending to show this, and that the mode of using the mill, the throwing of sparks from the chimney, and the danger to other property in the vicinity, continued substantially the same, from the earliest period to which this evidence referred, down to the time of this fire, and that the raising of the chimney about twelve feet, in the spring prior to the fire, did not appreciably diminish the emission of sparks, or the danger therefrom.

  Now, as the evidence of the burning of the plaintiff's property complained of, need not and did not consist of direct evidence, that in that particular instance a particular spark was seen to come from the mill, traced by the same eye through the air and seen to light upon the side of the house and set it on fire, but the plaintiff must be at liberty to show, as he did, circumstances tending to prove that the property was set on fire in this way on the occasion alluded to, I can see no sound reason why he should not be at liberty to show any circumstances fairly tending to prove, or calculated to produce a reasonable belief, that this fire originated in this way on the occasion in question. On principle, I think all such testimony is admissible, and its force or weight to be estimated by the jury. It does not, as is here objected, raise a multitude of distinct issues,

Sherman House 周围和其他建筑物及其附近的地方，以及同一方向附近的人行道和院子里。1862 年，有人看见从烟囱中飞出的火星落在了该旅馆附近的锯木屑堆里，并点燃了锯木屑。1863 年或 1864 年，就是这家旅馆的南侧外面失火，当时正在刮西南风，而锯木厂也在工作，火星来自于那个方向。同样的事件在 1869 年再次重演，有人看见火星落在了人行道上并一度使其着火，火星还落在了 Sherman House 的平台上，曾经在旅馆附近区域挂在绳子上晾晒的衣服也被点着，在这片居住区晾晒的衣服都有烧破的痕迹，衣服上有一层黑糊糊的火星熄灭时的灰尘。同样距离远的橱柜店里陈列的家具上也有一层黑色的煤灰。在锯木厂工作而且有风从锯木厂方向刮过来时，Sherman House 附近的以及更远的许多房子不得不关上窗户，以便使衣服等财物不受到这样的损坏。1873 年，在 Sherman House 火灾之后，锯木厂附近的 Garvey House 也发生了火灾，当时的情况显示火灾由这些火星引起。差不多距离的几个建筑物都发生了火灾，发生火灾的都是面向锯木厂的一侧，而且据已知的情况来看，当时锯木厂都在运行，而且风向为西南风，等等。

第一组陈述的错误在于对证据采信的异议，而该证据意图证明在旅馆发生火灾之前的几年中，这个烟囱习惯性地喷出火星，造成建筑物等的失火。在被告的反对之下，法院拒绝采信时间跨度如此之长的证据，除非基于默契并作出保证，原告一方更进一步地举证证明当时的情况与发生火灾时的情况完全一样；而原告确实也出示了大量证据来证明这一点，并且证明从该证据涉及的最早时期开始直到火灾时为止，锯木厂的运行模式、烟囱里喷出的火星，以及对邻近建筑物构成的威胁都没有发生变化，而且在发生火灾之前的那个春天将烟囱加高 12 英尺并没有明显消除火星的排放，也没有消除相应的危险。

现在，指控原告房屋被烧毁的证据不必包括也没有包括证明有人现场亲眼见证了某个火星从锯木厂飞出，以及见到该火星在空中飞舞直到点燃了原告的一侧房屋，最终导致该房屋被烧毁的直接证据，但是原告必须被允许去证明，在上文提及的情况中，该环境下房屋可以这种方式被点燃，而且他也这么做了。我看不到任何合理理由，为何原告不被允许去证明任何清楚地倾向于证明或预计可以使人合理相信发生火灾的情况，就是本案涉及的情况。原则上，我认为所有这类证词都是可以被采信的，其说服力和有效性应该由陪审团来评估。正如这里所反对的，它并没有引发大量截然不同的问题，和其他所有的间接证据案件一样，存在大量的案件情节。为了说明，而且这里

any more than in all other cases of circumstantial evidence, where the circumstances are equally numerous. And to show, as was done here, that while the mill and chimney, and the mode of using them, remained the same in all essential respects, the wind in the same direction, and the other surrounding circumstances the same, sparks had been seen to issue from this chimney in large quantities, watched, and seen to fall upon buildings or sidewalks, or other wood material, and to set them on fire, and all the other facts which the evidence given tended to show, as already stated, would strongly tend to produce a reasonable belief of the particular fact of the burning being from this cause on the occasion in question. I therefore see no error in the admission of this evidence.

Upon the same principle, I think the evidence of the Garvey House taking fire, in May, 1873 (though after the burning of plaintiff's building) was admissible, together with all the circumstances tending to show that it was set on fire by sparks from this chimney....

I see no error in the record, and the judgment should be affirmed, with costs.

The other justices concurred.

38. Smith v. Rapid Transit Inc., 317 Mass. 469, 58 N.E.2d 754 (1945)

Supreme Judicial Court of Massachusetts, United States

Spalding, J.

The decisive question in this case is whether there was evidence for the jury that the plaintiff was injured by a bus of the defendant that was operated by one of its employees in the course of his employment. If there was, the defendant concedes that the evidence warranted the submission to the jury of the question of the operator's negligence in the management of the bus. The case is here on the plaintiff's exception to the direction of a verdict for the defendant.

These facts could have been found: While the plaintiff at about 1:00 a.m. on February 6, 1941, was driving an automobile on Main Street, Winthrop, in an easterly direction toward Winthrop Highlands, she observed a bus coming toward her which she described as a "great big, long, wide affair." The bus, which was proceeding at about forty miles an hour, "forced her to turn to the right," and her automobile collided with a "parked car." The plaintiff was coming from Dorchester. The department of public utilities had issued a certificate of public convenience or necessity to the defendant for three routes in Winthrop, one of which included Main Street, and this was in effect in February, 1941. "There was another bus line in operation in Winthrop at that time but not on Main Street." According to the defendant's time-table, buses were scheduled to leave Winthrop Highlands for Maverick Square via Main Street at 12:10 a.m., 12:45 a.m., 1:15 a.m., and 2:15 a.m. The running time for this trip at that time of night was thirty minutes.

The direction of a verdict for the defendant was right. The ownership of the bus was a matter of conjecture. While the defendant had the sole franchise for operating a bus line on Main

也已经说明，锯木厂和烟囱及其使用模式在所有的重要方面都是一样的，风向也一样，其他周围的环境也相同，有人看见大量火星从烟囱冒出，并且看到火星落到建筑物和人行道上或其他木质材料上，使其被点燃，证据显示的所有其他事实都如以上陈述的那样，使人非常合理地相信，即火灾发生的原因是本案涉及的情况。因此我认为采信该证据没有错误。

根据同样的理由，我认为 1873 年 5 月 Garvey House 失火（尽管发生在原告房屋被烧之后）的证据是可以被采信的，同时被采信的还有其他各种可以证明引起火灾的原因是来自烟囱的火星的情况……

我没发现案件卷宗的错误，我认为本庭应维持原判，由败诉方承担诉讼费用。其他法官赞同。

38. Smith v. Rapid Transit Inc., 317 Mass. 469, 58 N.E.2d 754 (1945)

美国马萨诸塞州最高法院

Spalding 法官主笔：

本案中的关键问题在于，向陪审团提供的证据是否能证明被告的一名员工在工作期间驾驶一辆公共汽车导致原告受伤。如果有这样的证据，那么被告承认该证据足以保证可以将公交车经营过程中经营者是否存在过失行为的问题提交给陪审团来判断。该案是原告针对对被告有利的指示裁断而提出的异议。

可以认定如下事实问题：1941 年 2 月 6 日凌晨 1 点，当原告驾驶汽车在 Winthrop 的 Main Street 街上向东朝 Winthrop Highlands 行驶时，她看到一辆公交车朝她驶来，她对公交车的形容为"一个非常巨大的，又长又宽的家伙"。公交车的行进时速达到了每小时 40 英里，"使她不得不向右转弯"，她的汽车撞上了一辆"停在路边的车辆"。原告从 Dorchester 来。公共事业局向被告颁发了一个公共事业运营证，使其在 Winthrop 经营三条路线，其中一条包括 Main Street 街，而该执照正好是 1941 年 2 月生效。"当时 Winthrop 还有另外一条公交线路，但是不经过 Main Street 街"。根据被告的时刻表，公交车离开 Winthrop Highlands 经过 Main Street 街前往 Maverick Square 的时间为凌晨 12 时 10 分、12 时 45 分、1 时 15 分和 2 时 15 分。当时晚上该路线的运行时间为 30 分钟。

对被告有利的裁断指引是正确的。公交车的所有权是一个推测问题。尽管被告拥有在 Winthrop 的 Main Street 街上经营公交线路的独家特许经营权，

Street, Winthrop, this did not preclude private or chartered buses from using this street; the bus in question could very well have been one operated by someone other than the defendant. It was said in Sargent v. Massachusetts Accident Co., 307 Mass. 246, at page 250, that it is "not enough that mathematically the chances somewhat favor a proposition to be proved; for example, the fact that colored automobiles made in the current year outnumber black ones would not warrant a finding that an undescribed automobile of the current year is colored and not black, nor would the fact that only a minority of men die of cancer warrant a finding that a particular man did not die of cancer." The most that can be said of the evidence in the instant case is that perhaps the mathematical chances somewhat favor the proposition that a bus of the defendant caused the accident. This was not enough. A "proposition is proved by a preponderance of the evidence if it is made to appear more likely or probable in the sense that actual belief in its truth, derived from the evidence, exists in the mind or minds of the tribunal notwithstanding any doubts that may still linger there." Sargent v. Massachusetts Accident Co., 307 Mass. 246, at page 250....

Exceptions overruled.

39. Summers v. Tice, 33 Cal. 2d 80, 199 P.2d 1 (1948)

Supreme Court of California, United States

Carter, J.

Each of the two defendants appeals from a judgment against them in an action for personal injuries. Pursuant to stipulation the appeals have been consolidated.

Plaintiff's action was against both defendants for an injury to his right eye and face as the result of being struck by birdshot discharged from a shotgun. The case was tried by the court without a jury and the court found that on November 20, 1945, plaintiff and the two defendants were hunting quail on the open range. Each of the defendants was armed with a 12-gauge shotgun loaded with shells containing 7½ size shot. Prior to going hunting plaintiff discussed the hunting procedure with defendants, indicating that they were to exercise care when shooting and to "keep in line." In the course of hunting plaintiff proceeded up a hill, thus placing the hunters at the points of a triangle. The view of defendants with reference to plaintiff was unobstructed and they knew his location. Defendant Tice flushed a quail which rose in flight to a 10-foot elevation and flew between plaintiff and defendants. Both defendants shot at the quail, shooting in the plaintiff's direction. At that time defendants were 75 yards from plaintiff. One shot struck plaintiff in his eye and another in his upper lip. Finally it was found by the court that as the direct result of the shooting by defendants the shots struck plaintiff as above mentioned and the defendants were negligent in so shooting and plaintiff was not contributorily negligent....

The problem presented in this case is whether the judgment against both defendants may

但是这并不排除其他私人的或特许的公交车经过这条街道。本案中的公交车有可能是由被告之外的其他所有者运营的。在 Sargent v. Massachusetts Accident Co. 案判决书的第 250 页中，提到"数学概率对于某个需要证明的主张是不充分的；例如，本年度生产的彩色汽车的数量超过了黑色汽车的数量，并不能说明本年度的一辆未被描述的汽车的颜色是彩色而不是黑色的；仅有少数人死于癌症这一事实，不能说明某个人不是死于癌症"。本案中的证据最多说明，数学概率在一定程度上支持了被告的公交车导致了交通事故的主张。这是不充分的。"庭审人员仍可能存有疑问，根据优势证据规则，如果证据能够证明某个主张相比其相反的主张更可能，即根据证据法官虽然可能心存疑惑但是依然相信了这样的主张，则这个证明得到了证明"。[参见 Sargent v. Massachusetts Accident Co., 307 Mass. 246, at page 250]

异议被驳回。

39. Summers v. Tice, 33 Cal. 2d 80, 199 P.2d 1 (1948)

美国加利福尼亚州最高法院

Carter 法官主笔：

在一起人身伤害案中，法院作出对两名被告不利的判决，他们分别因此提起上诉。根据诉讼协议，两个上诉合并进行。

原告的右眼和脸部因为被鸟枪发出的小子弹伤到，原告因此向两名被告均提起了起诉。案件的初审没有经过陪审团。法院查明，在 1945 年 11 月 20 日，原告和两名被告在一个开放的空地上捕猎鹌鹑。两名被告都配备了一只装有 NO. 7/$\frac{1}{2}$ 号子弹弹珠的 12 发容量的鸟枪。在打猎之前，原告便与被告讨论了打猎的程序问题，指出他们应该谨慎行事以"保持步调一致"。在打猎的过程中，原告上了山，这时三名猎人的位置构成了一个三角形。被告关于原告的认识没有任何障碍，他们知道他的位置。被告 Tice 使得一只鹌鹑受到惊吓而飞到了 10 英尺的高度，飞到了原告和两名被告之间的位置。两名被告都向鹌鹑开枪，开枪的方向朝着原告。当时，被告与原告的距离有 75 码。一枪打到了原告的眼睛，另一枪打到了他的上嘴唇。最后，法院认定被告射击行为导致的直接结果是，原告受到了上述伤害，被告在这样射击时存在过失，而不是与有过失……

这个案件中的问题是，对被告不利的判决是否可以站得住脚。被告提出，由于他们并未实施共同行为而不是共同侵权行为人，因此不该承担连带

stand. It is argued by defendants that they are not joint tort feasors, and thus jointly and severally liable, as they were not acting in concert, and that there is not sufficient evidence to show which defendant was guilty of the negligence which caused the injuries—the shooting by Tice or that by Simonson....

Considering this argument, we believe it is clear that the court sufficiently found on the issue that defendants were jointly liable and that thus the negligence of both was the cause of the injury or to that legal effect. It found that both defendants were negligent and "That as a direct and proximate result of the shots fired by *defendants, and each of them*, a birdshot pellet was caused to and did lodge in plaintiff's right eye and that another birdshot pellet was caused to and did lodge in plaintiff's upper lip."…Implicit in such finding is the assumption that the court was unable to ascertain whether the shots were from the gun of one defendant or the other or one shot from each of them. The one shot that entered plaintiff's eye was the major factor in assessing damages and that shot could not have come from the gun of both defendants. It was from one or the other only....

...Dean Wigmore has this to say: "When two or more persons by their acts are possibly the sole cause of a harm, or when two or more acts of the same person are possibly the sole cause, and the plaintiff has introduced evidence that the one of the two persons, or the one of the same person's two acts, is culpable, then the defendant has the burden of proving that the other person, or his other act, was the sole cause of the harm....The real reason for the rule that each joint tortfeasor is responsible for the whole damage is the practical unfairness of denying the injured person redress simply because he cannot prove how much damage each did, when it is certain that between them they did all; let them be the ones to apportion it among themselves. Since, then, the difficulty of proof is the reason, the rule should apply whenever the harm has plural causes, and not merely when they acted in conscious concert...." (Wigmore, Select Cases on the Law of Torts, §153.)...

When we consider the relative position of the parties and the results that would flow if plaintiff was required to pin the injury on one of the defendants only, a requirement that the burden of proof on that subject be shifted to defendants becomes manifest. They are both wrong doers—both negligent toward plaintiff. They brought about a situation where the negligence of one of them injured the plaintiff, hence it should rest with them each to absolve himself if he can. The injured party has been placed by defendants in the unfair position of pointing to which defendant caused the harm. If one can escape the other may also and plaintiff is remediless. Ordinarily defendants are in a far better position to offer evidence to determine which one caused the injury....

Cases are cited for the proposition that where two or more tort feasors acting independently of each other cause an injury to plaintiff, they are not joint tort feasors and plaintiff must establish the portion of the damage caused by each, even though it is impossible to prove the portion of the injury caused by each. In view of the foregoing discussion it is apparent that defendants in cases

责任,而且也没有足够证据证明哪一名被告因过失导致了伤害——由 Tice 或 Simonson 开枪……

考虑该主张,我们认为,很明显,法院充分认定了被告负有共同责任,因此双方的过失是造成原告受伤或该法律效果的原因。法院认定被告双方都存在过失,"作为被告开枪行为的直接的和间接的结果,一颗猎枪弹珠射入了原告的右眼,另一颗猎枪弹珠射中了原告的上嘴唇"……在这个认定结果中有一个假设没有说明,即法院无法确定这两枪是发射自同一名被告,还是两名被告各发了一枪。射中原告眼睛的那一枪是评估损害程度的主要因素,而这一枪不可能来自两名被告。如果它不来自于其中一名被告,便来自于另一名被告……

……Wigmore 院长这样说道:"当两个或两个以上的人的行为有可能是造成伤害的唯一原因,或者当同一人的两个或两个以上的行为是唯一原因,而原告有证据证明两人之中的其中一人,或一人的两个行为中的其中一个行为存在过失,那么被告负有证明另一名行为人或他的另一个行为是造成伤害的唯一原因的举证责任……受害人无法证明每个行为人或行为人的每个行为具体造成了多大的损害,但对于损害是来自两个行为人或其行为却非常确定,因为这个原因而否定受害人应获得的赔偿在实践中是有失公平的,这是每个共同侵权行为人对整个损害负有责任这条原则的真实理由,应该让行为人自己在他们之间对责任进行分配。其次,由于举证困难,因此当出现多个原因致害情况,而不仅仅是行为人有意识地共同行动时,便应该应用这条原则……"[Wigmore,《侵权法案例精选》(Select Cases on the Law of Torts, §153)]……

当我们思考各方的相对地位,以及如果要求原告将损害锁定在其中一名被告身上可能产生的结果,那么很明显的是,该问题的举证责任便转向了被告。被告都是不法行为人——都对原告存在过失。他们导致了一种情况,即他们中的一方伤害了原告,因此应该由他们自己每个人来免除自己的责任,如果他们能做到的话。如果要求受害方指出哪名被告造成了损害,那么被告便将受害方置于不公平的地位。如果一方能够逃避责任,那么另一方也可以,结果是原告得不到赔偿。通常情况下,被告的地位更便于提供证据证明哪一方造成了伤害……

为了证明该观点引用的一些案例中,当两名或两名以上的侵权行为人的单独行动造成了原告的伤害、他们不是共同侵权行为人时,原告必须确认两名行为人各自造成了多少损失,即使要证明行为人各自造成伤害的比例是多少是不可能的。根据上述讨论的内容,和本案类似的案例中的被告可能受到

like the present one may be treated as liable on the same basis as joint tortfeasors, and hence the last-cited cases are distinguishable inasmuch as they involve independent tort feasors.

In addition to that, however, it should be pointed out that the same reasons of policy and justice shift the burden to each of defendants to absolve himself if he can—relieving the wronged person of the duty of apportioning the injury to a particular defendant, apply here where we are concerned with whether plaintiff is required to supply evidence for the apportionment of damages. If defendants are independent tort feasors and thus each liable for the damage caused by him alone, and, at least, where the matter of apportionment is incapable of proof, the innocent wronged party should not be deprived of his right to redress. The wrong doers should be left to work out between themselves any apportionment. Some of the cited cases refer to the difficulty of apportioning the burden of damages between the independent tort feasors, and say that where factually a correct division cannot be made, the trier of fact may make it the best it can, which would be more or less a guess, stressing the factor that the wrongdoers are not in a position to complain of uncertainty....

The judgment is affirmed.

40. Ybarra v. Spangard, 25 Cal. 2d 486, 154 P.2d 687 (1944)

Supreme Court of California, United States

Gibson, C.J.

This is an action for damages for personal injuries alleged to have been inflicted on plaintiff by defendants during the course of a surgical operation. The trial court entered judgments of nonsuit as to all defendants and plaintiff appealed.

On October 28, 1939, plaintiff consulted defendant Dr. Tilley, who diagnosed his ailment as appendicitis, and made arrangements for an appendectomy to be performed by defendant Dr. Spangard at a hospital owned and managed by defendant Dr. Swift. Plaintiff entered the hospital, was given a hypodermic injection, slept, and later was awakened by Doctors Tilley and Spangard and wheeled into the operating room by a nurse whom he believed to be defendant Gisler, an employee of Dr. Swift. Defendant Dr. Reser, the anesthetist, also an employee of Dr. Swift, adjusted plaintiff for the operation, pulling his body to the head of the operating table and, according to plaintiff's testimony, laying him back against two hard objects at the top of his shoulders, about an inch below his neck. Dr. Reser then administered the anesthetic and plaintiff lost consciousness. When he awoke early the following morning he was in his hospital room attended by defendant Thompson, the special nurse, and another nurse, who was not made a defendant.

Plaintiff testified that prior to the operation he had never had any pain in, or injury to, his right arm or shoulder, but that when he awakened he felt a sharp pain about half way between the neck and the point of the right shoulder. He complained to the nurse, and then to Dr. Tilley, who gave

和共同侵权行为人同样的对待，由于这些案例涉及单独的多个侵权行为人，因此引用的最后一个案例是显然不同的。

不仅如此，需要指出的是，出于法律目的和公平性的同样原因，免除自己责任的负担也移转到他们这一方，如果他们能够做到的话——免除了受害人将伤害分配到某一被告身上的义务，这里我们关注的是是否要求原告提供分配损失的证据。如果被告是独立的侵权行为人而只需要对自己所造成的损害承担责任，而且至少是在缺乏证据支持责任分配的情况下，那么不应该剥夺无辜受害人获得赔偿的权利。应该让过错方自己协商如何分配责任。一些引用的案例提到在独立的侵权行为人之间分配损失存在困难，而且指出正确划分责任并不现实，事实认定者可能会尽全力划分责任，但这也是他们的猜测，强调了一个要素，即不法行为人并没有对这种不确定性进行申辩的权利……

维持原判。

40. Ybarra v. Spangard, 25 Cal. 2d 486, 154 P.2d 687 (1944)

美国加利福尼亚州最高法院

Gibson 大法官主笔：

这是一起损害赔偿案，原告因在外科手术过程中受到被告实施的伤害而提起人身伤害诉讼。初审法院作出了驳回起诉的裁决，所有被告和原告都进行了上诉。

1939 年 10 月 28 日，原告咨询被告 Tilley 医生，Tilley 医生诊断原告患了阑尾炎，并且安排被告 Spangard 医生为其实施阑尾切除手术，Spangard 医生是另一被告 Swift 医生所有并经营的一家医院的医生。原告进入医院，然后接受了皮下注射睡了过去，之后又被 Tilley 医生和 Spangard 医生叫醒，并且由护士推进了手术室，原告认为被告 Gisler 护士，是 Swift 医生雇佣的一名员工。被告 Reser 医生是麻醉师，也是 Swift 医生雇佣的员工，他负责调整原告的位置以进行手术。根据原告的证词，他将原告的身体拖到手术台的一头，然后在他的肩头抵上两个硬物，大约在脖子以下 1 英寸的位置。Reser 医生随后实施了麻醉，原告失去了意识。第二天早晨原告醒来时躺在医院的病房中，照顾他的是医院的专设护士被告 Thompson 和另一名护士，后者没有成为被告。

原告在证词中说，在手术之前，他的右臂或右肩从未出现过疼痛或伤口，但是当他醒来时，他感到脖子到右肩的中间部位强烈疼痛。他先告诉了护士，

him diathermy treatments while he remained in the hospital. The pain did not cease, but spread down to the lower part of his arm, and after his release from the hospital the condition grew worse. He was unable to rotate or lift his arm, and developed paralysis and atrophy of the muscles around the shoulder. He received further treatments from Dr. Tilley until March, 1940, and then returned to work, wearing his arm in a splint on the advice of Dr. Spangard.

Plaintiff also consulted Dr. Wilfred Sterling Clark, who had X-ray pictures taken which showed an area of diminished sensation below the shoulder and atrophy and wasting away of the muscles around the shoulder. In the opinion of Dr. Clark, plaintiff's condition was due to trauma or injury by pressure or strain, applied between his right shoulder and neck.

Plaintiff was also examined by Dr. Fernando Garduno, who expressed the opinion that plaintiff's injury was a paralysis of traumatic origin, not arising from pathological causes, and not systemic, and that the injury resulted in atrophy, loss of use and restriction of motion of the right arm and shoulder.

…

The present case is of a type which comes within the reason and spirit of the doctrine more fully than any other. The passenger sitting awake in a railroad car at the time of a collision, the pedestrian walking along the street and struck by a falling object or the debris of an explosion, are surely not more entitled to an explanation than the unconscious patient on the operating table. Viewed from this aspect, it is difficult to see how the doctrine can, with any justification, be so restricted in its statement as to become inapplicable to a patient who submits himself to the care and custody of doctors and nurses, is rendered unconscious, and receives some injury from instrumentalities used in his treatment. Without the aid of the doctrine a patient who received permanent injuries of a serious character, obviously the result of someone's negligence, would be entirely unable to recover unless the doctors and nurses in attendance voluntarily chose to disclose the identity of the negligent person and the facts establishing liability. If this were the state of the law of negligence, the courts, to avoid gross injustice, would be forced to invoke the principles of absolute liability, irrespective of negligence, in actions by persons suffering injuries during the course of treatment under anesthesia. But we think this juncture has not yet been reached, and that the doctrine…is properly applicable to the case before us.…

The argument of defendants is simply that plaintiff has not shown an injury caused by an instrumentality under a defendant's control, because he has not shown which of the several instrumentalities that he came in contact with while in the hospital caused the injury; and he has not shown that any one defendant or his servants had exclusive control over any particular instrumentality. Defendants assert that some of them were not the employees of other defendants, that some did not stand in any permanent relationship from which liability in tort would follow, and that in view of the nature of the injury, the number of defendants and the different functions

然后告诉了 Tilley 医生。Tilley 医生在他住院期间为他进行了热透疗法。疼痛非但没有减轻，反而扩散到手臂的下部，出院之后情况变得更加糟糕。他无法转动或抬起手臂，肩膀周围的肌肉出现了麻痹和微缩症状。他在 Tilley 医生那里接受了进一步的治疗，直到 1940 年 3 月重新开始上班时，在 Spangard 医生的建议下，他的手臂戴上了夹板。

原告还咨询了 Wilfred Sterling Clark 医生，他为原告照的 X 光片显示，肩以下的部位出现了知觉减弱、肩周围的肌肉有麻痹和消瘦的情况。Clark 医生认为，原告的病情是由右肩和颈部之间受到的压力或拉力造成的外伤或损伤引起的。

为原告进行检查的还有 Fernando Garduno 医生，他也认为原告的损伤是外伤引起的麻痹，而非病理上的原因，不是组织性的，该损伤造成的结果是右臂和右肩出现麻痹、功能丧失和活动受限。

……

本案是对法律学说的逻辑和精神的无与伦比的体现。有轨电车碰撞时清醒坐在车上的乘客和走在大街上被掉下的物体或爆炸物碎片砸到的行人无疑都不比手术台上昏迷不醒的病人更有解释的能力。病人将自己托付给医生和护士照料和看护，自身处于无意识的状况，在治疗过程中又受到了治疗手段引起的伤害，从这个方面来看，无论具有怎样的合理性，该法律学说都不能因为受制于其表述方式，而无法运用到病人身上。病人受到了永久性的严重伤害，该伤害显然是某人的过失行为造成的，但是如果没有该法律学说的帮助，除非参与治疗的医生和护士自愿揭露过失者的身份以及构成责任的相关事实，否则病人也完全无法获得赔偿。如果这是过失法的状态，法院为了避免严重的不公平，将不得不对在涉及治疗过程中处于麻醉状态的病人的诉讼中，不考虑过失、援引绝对责任原则。但是我们认为该案尚未达到（援引绝对责任原则）的程度，该法律学说……可以合适地适用于我们面前的这个案件……

被告的主张较为简单，即原告并没有证明被告所控制的治疗手段引起的伤害，因为他没有证明在住院期间所接触到的所有治疗手段中哪种治疗手段造成了伤害，而且他也没有证明某被告或看护者是否对某项特殊的治疗手段单独负责。被告声称，一些被告并非其他被告的雇员，因此并非处于因永久性工作关系而可能承担侵权责任的地位。即使有侵权责任，鉴于伤害的性质、被告的数量以及被告所发挥的不同作用，也不应该让他们所

performed by each, they could not all be liable for the wrong, if any.

We have no doubt that in a modern hospital a patient is quite likely to come under the care of a number of persons in different types of contractual and other relationships with each other. For example, in the present case it appears that Doctors Swift, Spangard and Tilley were physicians or surgeons commonly placed in the legal category of independent contractors; and Dr. Reser, the anesthetist, and defendant Thompson, the special nurse, were employees of Dr. Swift and not of the other doctors. But we do not believe that either the number or relationship of the defendants alone determines whether the jury may draw an inference of negligence. Every defendant in whose custody the plaintiff was placed for any period was bound to exercise ordinary care to see that no unnecessary harm came to him and each would be liable for failure in this regard. Any defendant who negligently injured him, and any defendant charged with his care who so neglected him as to allow injury to occur, would be liable. The defendant employers would be liable for the neglect of their employees; and the doctor in charge of the operation would be liable for the negligence of those who became his temporary servants for the purpose of assisting in the operation....

It may appear at the trial that, consistent with the principles outlined above, one or more defendants will be found liable and others absolved, but this should not preclude the application of the doctrine. The control, at one time or another, of one or more of the various agencies or instrumentalities which might have harmed the plaintiff was in the hands of every defendant or of his employees or temporary servants. This, we think, places upon them the burden of initial explanation. Plaintiff was rendered unconscious for the purpose of undergoing surgical treatment by the defendants; it is manifestly unreasonable for them to insist that he identify any one of them as the person who did the alleged negligent act....

The judgment is reversed.

41. Barnett v Chelsea and Kensington Hospital Management Committee [1969] 1 QB 428

Queen's Bench Division, High Court, United Kingdom

At a hospital casualty department, provided and run by the defendants, three fellow night-watchmen presented themselves, complaining to a nurse on duty that they had been vomiting for three hours after drinking tea. The nurse reported their complaints by telephone to the duty medical casualty officer, who thereupon instructed her to tell the men to go home to bed and call in their own doctors. That she did. The men then left, and, about five hours later, one of them died from poisoning by arsenic which had been introduced into the tea; he might have died from the poisoning even if he had been admitted to the hospital wards and treated with all care five hours before his death.

NIELD J.

At the outset of my judgment in this case I propose to indicate the general conclusions which

有人都为之负责。

在现代医院中，病人很有可能受到多人的照料，这些人之间存在多种类型的合同关系或其他关系，对于这点我们并不怀疑。例如，在本案中，看起来 Swift 医生、Spangard 医生和 Tilley 医生是内科医生或外科医生，他们通常在法律上属于独立承揽人；麻醉师 Reser 医生和被告专设护士 Thompson 是 Swift 医生的雇员，而不是其他医生的雇员。但是我们不认为仅仅依据被告的数量和被告之间的关系就可以确定陪审团是否可以得出过失推论。在任何一段时间内对原告进行看护的每一个被告都必须实施普通的注意，以确保原告不会受到不必要的伤害，因此每名被告都必须为没能做到这点而负责。任何因过失而伤害到原告的被告，任何负责照顾原告但因为过失导致原告受到伤害的被告，都应该承担责任。雇主被告应该为其雇员的过失承担责任；负责手术的医生应该对在手术中提供帮助的临时雇员的过失承担责任……

在初审中，一名或多名被告被认为需要承担责任，而其他人则被宣布免除责任，似乎与上文所列出的原则相一致，但是也不应该排除该法律学说的运用。可能导致原告伤害的各种方式或手段中的一种或者多种，曾经控制在每一名被告、其员工或其临时雇员的手中。我们认为，这就使得被告负有初步解释责任。为了接受被告实施的外科治疗手段，原告处于无意识状态，要求原告指明实施该过失行为的人是谁，这显然是不合理的……

判决被撤销。

41. Barnett v Chelsea and Kensington Hospital Management Committee [1969] 1 QB 428

联合王国高等法院王座分庭

三位守夜人来到被告运营的医院的急诊室，告知值班护士他们三人自从三小时前喝了茶之后就呕吐不止。值班护士将该三人的描述告知了值班医生，后者则告诉护士让三位病人回家去，躺在床上，并给他们自己的医生打电话。值班护士照做了。三人遂离开。五个小时后，其中一位因为茶中的砒霜而中毒死亡。然而，即便他死前五小时的时候被允许住院，且也获得了相应的诊治，他还是有可能死亡。

Nield 法官主笔：

开宗明义，我将发表我的最终结论，那就是原告 Bessie Irene Barnett

I have reached. ... My conclusions are: that the plaintiff, Mrs. Bessie Irene Barnett, has failed to establish, on the balance of probabilities, that the death of the deceased, William Patrick Barnett, resulted from the negligence of the defendants, the Chelsea and Kensington Hospital Management Committee, my view being that had all care been taken, still the deceased must have died. But my further conclusions are that the defendants' casualty officer was negligent in failing to see and examine the deceased, and that, had he done so, his duty would have been to admit the deceased to the ward and to have treated him or caused him to be treated.

The plaintiff is the widow of the deceased, who died on January 1, 1966, from arsenical poisoning, and she is also the administratrix of his estate. She claims damages on behalf of herself and two of her children as dependants of the deceased and also on behalf of his estate. The defendants were at all material times responsible for the management of St. Stephen's Hospital, Chelsea.

...

It remains to consider whether it is shown that the deceased's death was caused by that negligence or whether, as the defendants have said, the deceased must have died in any event. In his concluding submission Mr. Pain submitted that the casualty officer should have examined the deceased and had he done so he would have caused tests to be made which would have indicated the treatment required and that, since the defendants were at fault in these respects, therefore the onus of proof passed to the defendants to show that the appropriate treatment would have failed, and authorities were cited to me. I find myself unable to accept that argument, and I am of the view that the onus of proof remains upon the plaintiff, and I have in mind (without quoting it) the decision cited by Mr. Wilmers in *Bonnington Castings Ltd. v. Wardlaw*. However, were it otherwise and the onus did pass to the defendants, then I would find that they have discharged it, as I would proceed to show.

There has been put before me a timetable which I think is of much importance. The deceased attended at the casualty department at five or 10 minutes past eight in the morning. If the casualty officer had got up and dressed and come to see the three men and examined them and decided to admit them, the deceased (and Dr. Lockett agreed with this) could not have been in bed in a ward before 11 a.m. I accept Dr. Goulding's evidence that an intravenous drip would not have been set up before 12 noon, and if potassium loss was suspected it could not have been discovered until 12.30 p.m. Dr. Lockett, dealing with this, said: "If this man had not been treated until after 12 noon the chances of survival were not good."

Without going in detail into the considerable volume of technical evidence which has been put before me, it seems to me to be the case that when death results from arsenical poisoning it is brought about by two conditions; on the one hand dehydration and on the other disturbance of the enzyme processes. If the principal condition is one of enzyme disturbance - as I am of the view it

夫人并未证明 William Patrick Barnett 先生的死亡是因为被告（Chelsea and Kensington 医院管理委员会）的过失而引起的，这一结论的可能性比相反的结论的可能性要大。我的观点是，即便被告尽到了相应的注意义务，原告的死亡依然是不可避免的。我需要指出的是，就被告所雇佣的值班医生没有接诊死者这一点而言，是有过失的。如果他当时接诊了，他有义务让死者住院，并给他诊断或者请别人给他诊断。

原告是在 1966 年 1 月 1 日死于砒霜中毒的死者的遗孀，同时她也是死者的财产管理人。她以自己的名义、死者的被扶养人（两个孩子）的名义和死者的财产管理人的名义起诉。被告则在所有时间都负责经营管理切尔西的 St. Stephen's 医院。

……

（被告诚然确实是有过失的，然而）我们依然需要考察死者的死亡到底是由该过失引起的呢，还是如被告所说，死者无论如何都会死。Pain 先生在其总结陈词中主张值班医生应该接诊死者，对其做相应的检查，并给他提供需要的治疗。由于值班医生没有这么做，因而是有过失的，因此应该由被告来承担证明即使采取了恰当的措施被告也会死亡这一事实的举证责任。为证明他的观点，他给我引用了许多的判例。然而我很难接受这一观点。我认为举证责任依然应该由原告来承担，因为我似乎记得 Wilmers 先生在 *Bonnington Castings Ltd. v Wardlaw* 一案中所引用的判例就是这种主张。然而，即便我同意此时举证责任应该转移给被告，我依然认为被告已经完成了他的举证责任。下面我将解释为什么我这么认为。

我收到了一份很重要的时间表。（根据这份时间表）死者在早上的 8 点过 5 分或者 10 分到达急诊科。如果当时急诊科医生已经起床、穿好衣服并接诊了三位患者，在诊断了他们三人后同意接收他们，那么死者将可以在 11 点前躺在病床上（Lockett 医生同意这个观点）。我同意 Goulding 医生的证词，他认为静脉注射在中午 12 点前是不可能准备好的，而在 12 点半之前，也是不可能发现钾流失的。Lockett 医生针对此事则说：“如果此人没有在 12 点之前获得治疗，那么他存活的概率是很渺茫的。”

我面前有海量的技术性证据，我不打算详细地叙述它们。然而在我看来当一个人死于砒霜中毒时，其实是两个症状在作祟：失水和酶催化失常。

was here - then the only method of treatment which is likely to succeed is the use of the specific antidote which is commonly called B.A.L. Dr. Goulding said in the course of his evidence:

> "The only way to deal with this is to use the specific B.A.L. I see no reasonable prospect of the deceased being given B.A.L. before the time at which he died" - and at a later point in his evidence - "I feel that even if fluid loss had been discovered death would have been caused by the enzyme disturbance. Death might have occurred later."

I regard that evidence as very moderate, and it might be a true assessment of the situation to say that there was no chance of B.A.L. being administered before the death of the deceased.

For those reasons, I find that the plaintiff has failed to establish, on the balance of probabilities, that the defendants' negligence caused the death of the deceased.

42. Gregg v Scott [2005] UKHL 2, [2005] 2 AC 176

House of Lords, United Kingdom

LORD NICHOLLS (dissenting opinion)

My Lords, this appeal raises a question which has divided courts and commentators throughout the common law world. The division derives essentially from different perceptions of what constitutes injustice in a common form type of medical negligence case. Some believe a remedy is essential and that a principled ground for providing an appropriate remedy can be found. Others are not persuaded. I am in the former camp.

This is the type of case under consideration. A patient is suffering from cancer. His prospects are uncertain. He has a 45% chance of recovery. Unfortunately his doctor negligently misdiagnoses his condition as benign. So the necessary treatment is delayed for months. As a result the patient's prospects of recovery become nil or almost nil. Has the patient a claim for damages against the doctor? No, the House was told. The patient could recover damages if his initial prospects of recovery had been more than 50%. But because they were less than 50% he can recover nothing.

This surely cannot be the state of the law today. It would be irrational and indefensible. The loss of a 45% prospect of recovery is just as much a real loss for a patient as the loss of a 55% prospect of recovery. In both cases the doctor was in breach of his duty to his patient. In both cases the patient was worse off. He lost something of importance and value. But, it is said, in one case the patient has a remedy, in the other he does not.

This would make no sort of sense. It would mean that in the 45% case the doctor's duty would be hollow. The duty would be empty of content. For the reasons which follow I reject

而主要的症状其实是酶催化失常，而这种症状只能通过使用一种特殊的解毒剂——二巯丙醇来治疗。Goulding 医生在提供的证词中说道：

> 患者唯一能获救的可能是获得二巯丙醇的治疗。然而我认为死者在其死亡前获得二巯丙醇的可能非常渺茫。在其证据的后段部分他说："我认为即使医生发现了体液流失，患者还是会因为酶催化反应失常而死。当然，死亡的时间可能会延后。"

我认为上述的证据是可以接受的。因此，考察当时的情况后，应该可以说死者在其死亡前是不可能获得二巯丙醇的治疗的。

综上所述，我认为原告并未证明"被告的过失是死者死亡的原因"比"被告的过失不是死者死亡的原因"有更大的可能性。

42. Gregg v Scott [2005] UKHL 2, [2005] 2 AC 176

联合王国上议院

Nicholls 大法官（反对意见）

各位大法官，本案的焦点是一个普通法世界中法官们和评注者们争论不休的问题。他们的争议在于，在一般的医疗过失案件中，什么样的情形下相关医生才应该被非难。有人认为患者获得救济是很重要的，且我们可以找到提供适当救济的原则基础。有人则不这么认为。而我属于前者的阵营。

本案中需要考虑的是如下这个问题。一位病人得了癌症，他的前景不明，有 45% 的概率康复。然而他的医生由于过失，误诊其为良性。由此，必要的治疗措施耽搁了数月。这样，被告康复的概率锐减为零或者接近零。此时，患者是否有权对医生请求损害赔偿？按照上议院之前的说法，结论是否定的。在患者最初康复的概率大于 50% 的情况下，他才有权获得损害赔偿。而由于本案中他康复的概率是小于 50% 的，他什么赔偿都得不到。

这种说法显然不是我们今天的法律状态。这种说法是不合理的，是站不住脚的。患者丧失了 45% 的康复概率，和他丧失了 55% 的康复概率，对他来说都是一样的真实的损失。在这两种情况下医生都违反了他对患者的义务。在这两种情况下患者的境况都变得更糟了。患者都丧失了某些重要而有价值的东西。然而，以前的说法居然认为，只有在后一种情况下患者才能获得救济，在前一种情况下，他不能获得救济。

这种说法毫无道理。如果这种说法站得住脚，那么意味着在患者有 45% 的康复概率的情况下，医生居然什么义务都没有。因此根据以上的推理，我

this suggested distinction. The common law does not compel courts to proceed in such an unreal fashion. I would hold that a patient has a right to a remedy as much where his prospects of recovery were less than 50-50 as where they exceeded 50-50. Perforce the reasoning is lengthy, in parts intricate, because this is a difficult area of the law.

The present case

First I must mention the salient facts of this appeal. These are not quite so straightforward or extreme as in the example just given. At the risk of over-simplification they can be summarised as follows. The defendant Dr Scott negligently diagnosed as innocuous a lump under the left arm of the claimant Mr Malcolm Gregg when in fact it was cancerous (non-Hodgkin's lymphoma). This led to nine months' delay in Mr Gregg receiving treatment. During this period his condition deteriorated by the disease spreading elsewhere. The deterioration in Mr Gregg's condition reduced his prospects of disease-free survival for 10 years from 42%, when he first consulted Dr Scott, to 25% at the date of the trial. The judge found that, if treated promptly, Mr Gregg's initial treatment would probably have achieved remission without an immediate need for high dose chemotherapy. Prompt treatment would, at least initially, have prevented the cancer spreading to the left pectoral region.

However, the judge found also that, although Mr Gregg's condition deteriorated and in consequence his prospects were reduced in this way, a better outcome was never a probability. It was not possible to conclude on the balance of probability that, in the absence of the negligence, Mr Gregg's medical condition would have been better or that he would have avoided any particular treatment. Before the negligence Mr Gregg had a less than evens chance (45%) of avoiding the deterioration in his condition which ultimately occurred. The delay did not extinguish this chance but reduced it by roughly half. The judge assessed this reduction at 20%. That was the extent to which the negligence reduced Mr Gregg's prospects of avoiding the deterioration in his condition which ultimately occurred. The facts can be found more fully stated in the judgments of the Court of Appeal and in the speech of my noble and learned, friend Lord Phillips of Worth Matravers MR.

On these findings the trial judge, Judge Inglis, dismissed the claim. He considered he was driven to this conclusion by the reasoning of your Lordships' House in *Hotson v East Berkshire Area Health Authority* [1987] AC 750. The Court of Appeal [2002] EWCA Civ 1471 ... by a majority (Simon Brown and Mance LJJ, Latham LJ dissenting) dismissed Mr Gregg's appeal.

...

Medical negligence

Against this background I turn to the primary question raised by this appeal: how should the loss suffered by a patient in Mr Gregg's position be identified? The defendant says "loss" is confined to an *outcome* which is shown, on balance of probability, to be worse than it otherwise would have been. Mr Gregg must prove that, on balance of probability, his medical condition

反对这种根据患者的康复概率进行的区分。普通法不会要求法院根据这么没有道理的机制来作出判决。我认为，不论一个患者康复的概率是不是大于一半，他都是有权利获得救济的。当然，本案的论证将是冗长甚至琐碎的，因为本案属于一个法律上非常复杂的领域。

本案案情

首先让我来介绍一下本案中重要的事实。与我刚才所举的例子相比，本案的事实没那么直接，也没那么简单。冒着过分简化的风险，我将本案案情总结如下。被告 Scott 医生因为过失而将原告 Malcolm Gregg 先生左臂下方的一个实际上癌变了的肿块（非霍奇金淋巴瘤）误诊为良性。因为这个误诊，Gregg 先生耽误了九个月才获得相应的治疗。在这九个月期间，他的状况因为癌症的扩散而恶化了。因此，他无病生存十年的可能性，由他向 Scott 医生求诊时的 42%，降到了本案一审时的 25%。一审法官认定，如果 Gregg 先生当时获得了正确的治疗，那么他应该有所缓解，也并不需要马上接受高剂量的化疗。恰当的治疗至少在开始的阶段，是可以阻止癌症扩散到其左胸部的。

然而，一审法官同样认定，Gregg 先生状况确实恶化了，也因此导致其康复的可能性减少，他的情况好转其实相当不可能。没有办法认为，在不存在医疗过失的情况下，Gregg 先生的医疗状况变好或者他可以避免后续发生的治疗措施的可能性大于相反的可能性。在医疗过失发生之前，Gregg 先生只有一半不到（45%）的可能性能够避免其状况如现实发生的那样恶化。因为医疗过失而导致的耽搁治疗并没有完全消灭这种可能性，而只是使这种可能性降低了一半。一审法官认为康复的可能性降到了 20%。医疗过失大概就是在这个程度上降低了 Gregg 先生避免其状况恶化的可能性，而最终其状况确实恶化了。上述事实在上诉法院的判决书中和我那高贵而博学的朋友 Phillips 大法官的意见中，可以找到更详细的描述。

根据上述对事实的认定，一审法官 Linglis 驳回了原告的诉讼请求。他的结论是建立在上议院所判决的 *Hotson v East Berkshire Area Health Authority* [1987] AC 750 一案的法理上的。上诉法院在其主要意见书［（2002）EWCA Civ 1471；Simon Brown 和 Mance 上诉法院法官认同，Latham 上诉法院法官有不同意见］中则驳回了 Gregg 先生的上诉。

……

医疗过失

在这样的背景下我要讨论本案主要的争议焦点：我们如何来确定像 Gregg 先生这种境遇下的病人的损失？按照被告的说法，损失只包括那种在概率平衡下判断出的比没有发生事故时更坏的"结果"。Gregg 先生必须证明，按照

after the negligence was worse than it would have been in the absence of the negligence. Mr Gregg says his "loss" includes proved diminution in the *prospects* of a favourable outcome. Dr Scott's negligence deprived him of a worthwhile chance that his medical condition would not have deteriorated as it did.

...

Given this uncertainty of outcome, the appropriate characterisation of a patient's loss in this type of case must surely be that it comprises the loss of the chance of a favourable outcome, rather than the loss of the outcome itself. Justice so requires, because this matches medical reality. This recognises what in practice a patient had before the doctor's negligence occurred. It recognises what in practice the patient lost by reason of that negligence. The doctor's negligence diminished the patient's prospects of recovery. And this analysis of a patient's loss accords with the purpose of the legal duty of which the doctor was in breach. In short, the purpose of the duty is to promote the patient's*prospects* of recovery by exercising due skill and care in diagnosing and treating the patient's condition.

This approach also achieves a basic objective of the law of tort. The common law imposes duties and seeks to provide appropriate remedies in the event of a breach of duty. If negligent diagnosis or treatment diminishes a patient's prospects of recovery, a law which does not recognise this as a wrong calling for redress would be seriously deficient today. In respect of the doctors' breach of duty the law would not have provided an appropriate remedy. Of course, losing a chance of saving a leg is not the same as losing a leg: see Tony Weir, *Tort Law* (2002), p 76. But that is not a reason for declining to value the chance for whose loss the doctor was directly responsible. The law would rightly be open to reproach were it to provide a remedy if what is lost by a professional adviser's negligence is a financial opportunity or chance but refuse a remedy where what is lost by a doctor's negligence is the chance of health or even life itself. Justice requires that in the latter case as much as the former the loss of a chance should constitute actionable damage.

...

Identifying a lost chance in medical negligence cases

I come next to a further twist in the story. It concerns an additional complication. It is a difficult part of this appeal. With "loss of chance" cases such as *Chaplin v Hicks* [1911] 2 KB 786 identifying the "chance" the claimant lost is straightforward enough. The position of the claimant in the *Chaplin* case, had there been no wrong, could not be decided satisfactorily because no one could know what would have been the outcome of the beauty contest if the claimant had appeared at the interview. It was this uncertainty which made it appropriate to treat her loss of a chance as itself actionable damage. Otherwise she would have had no remedy. The chance she lost was the opportunity to attend and be considered at the interview. Thus, in this type of case the claimant's *actual* position at the time of the negligence, proved on balance of probability if

概率平衡的方法,他的医疗状况因为医疗过失而变得比没有过失的时候更坏了。Gregg 先生则主张"损失"应当包括他所丧失的经过证明的能够获得一种更好的结果的可能性。Scott 医生的过失使得他丧失了"情况不会恶化"这样一种宝贵的可能性。

......

鉴于这种情况下结果的不确定性,合理地判断病人损失的方式,当然应包括该病人所丧失的获得一种更好的结果的机会。损失不能仅包括这种更好的结果本身的丧失。正义如此要求,因为只有这样才符合医疗界的真实情况。这种方式考虑到了病人在医疗过失发生之前的状况,也考虑到了他因为该过失所丧失的东西。医生的过失减少了病人康复的希望。另外,我们这种分析病人损失的方法也符合医生所违反的法定义务的目的。简而言之,这种义务的目的是要求医生通过其所投入的诊断并治疗病人的技能和心血,来增加病人康复的可能性。

我们的这种判断损失的方式同样符合侵权法的基本目标。侵权法对一些人施加义务,并在他们违反这些义务时给予受害人救济。如果过失的诊断或者治疗减少了病人康复的希望,而法律却并不把这种过失视为一种需要救济的侵权行为,那么这样的法律在今天便是有严重缺陷的。如果是这样,那么在涉及医生违反其法定义务的情况时,法律便无法为受害人提供合理的救济措施。当然,我们并不是说丧失保住一条腿的可能性和丧失这条腿本身是一回事。[参见 Tony Weir,《侵权法》(2002),第 76 页。]然而,这并不意味着我们要否认医生应该负责的那种被减少的机会是有价值的。如果法律承认专业的建议者的过失使得受害人丧失了某种财产机会时,受害人应该获得救济,但却否认,医生的过失使康复或者生存的机会丧失时,受害者可以获得救济,这样的法律是会遭到大家的抨击的。正义的观念要求后者与前者一样,都属于可诉的损失。

......

在医疗过失案件中确定损失的机会

有个比较复杂的问题可能会反转我们从刚才到现在的分析,这个问题也是本案中一个讨论起来非常困难的部分。像 *Chaplin v Hicks* [1911] 2 KB 786 这样的涉及"机会损失"的案件,判断原告到底损失了什么机会是非常直截了当的事情。假设侵权行为不存在,此时 Chaplin 案的原告到底会处于什么样的状态,我们很难得出满意的结论,因为谁也不知道,如果原告参加了面试,在之后的选美比赛中她将获得什么名次。由于存在这样的一种不确定性,我们可以说此时她所丧失的机会是一种可诉的损失。如果不这么处理,她就没有办法获得任何救济了。由于她(以及所代表的这种类型的原告)丧失的其

disputed, is not determinative of the crucial *hypothetical* fact: what would have been the claimant's position in the absence of the wrong?

The position with medical negligence claims is different. The patient's actual condition at the time of the negligence will often be determinative of the answer to the crucially important hypothetical question of what would have been the claimant's position in the absence of the negligence. *Hotson v. East Berkshire Area Heath Authority* is an instance of this. The relevant factual question concerning Stephen Hotson's condition immediately prior to the negligence was whether his fall from the tree had left sufficient blood vessels intact to keep his left femoral epiphysis alive. The answer to this question of actual fact ipso facto provided the answer to the vital hypothetical question: would avascular necrosis have been avoided if Stephen Hotson's leg had been treated promptly? The answer to the first question necessarily provided the answer to the second question, because the second question is no more than a mirror image of the first. Built into the formulation of the first question was the answer to the second question.

This is not always so. Many cases are not so straightforward. Sometimes it is not possible to frame factual questions about a patient's condition which are (a) susceptible of sure answer and also (b) determinative of the outcome for the patient. As already noted, limitations on scientific and medical knowledge do not always permit this to be done. There are too many uncertainties involved in this field.

The present case is a good example. Identifying the nature and extent of Mr Gregg's cancer at the time of the mistaken diagnosis (the first question), so far as this could be achieved with reasonable certainty, did not provide a simple answer to what would have been the outcome had he been treated promptly (the second question). There were several possible outcomes. Recourse to past experience in other cases, that is statistics, personalised so far as possible, was the best that could be done. These statistics expressed the various possible outcomes in percentage terms of likelihood.

Thus, for present purposes medical negligence cases fall into one or other of two categories depending on whether a patient's condition at the time of the negligence does or does not give rise to significant medical uncertainty on what the outcome would have been in the absence of negligence. The Hotson case was in one category. There was no significant uncertainty about what would have happened to Stephen Hotson's leg if treated promptly, once his condition at the time of the negligence has been determined on the usual probability basis. The present case is in the other category. Identifying Mr Gregg's condition when he first visited Dr Scott did not provide an answer to the crucial question of what would have happened if there had been no negligence. There was considerable medical uncertainty about what the outcome would have been had Mr Gregg received appropriate treatment nine months earlier.

......

实是一个参加面试的机会，所以在这种类型的案件中，原告在被告的过失发生时到底处于一个什么样的实际的状况，其实对下面这个假设的事实没有什么意义（即便在有争议的情况下，原告已经通过"可能性平衡"的方式证明了其主张）：如果侵权行为没有发生，原告的境遇如何？

然而在医疗过失案件中，则是另外一种情况。原告在医疗过失发生时实际上的状况，对回答那个非常重要的假设性问题来说，是非常关键的：如果医疗过失没发生，原告的境遇是什么样的？*Hotson v East Berkshire Area Heath Authority* 一案就是例子。有关 Stephen Hotson 在医疗事故发生之前的状况的争议是：当他从树上掉下来之后，到底有没有足够多的完好的血管来保证其股骨头骺不会坏死？对于这个真实发生了的事实的回答，决定了一个非常重要的假设性问题的答案：如果 Stephen Hotson 的左腿得到了恰当的治疗，那么可不可以避免该腿的缺血性坏死？上述第一个问题的答案显然也决定了第二个问题的答案，而第二个问题显然不过是第一个问题的镜像问题。对第一个问题怎么回答一经确定，我们就已经知道了第二个问题的答案。

然而并不是在所有情况下都是这样。很多情形并没有那么直截了当。很多时候，关于病人的状况这一事实：① 很难有确切的答案；② 很难确定其是否对病人的最终结果起决定性作用。如前所述，科学和医疗知识的局限性阻碍了对上面两个方面的事实的完全的认识。在这个领域，有太多不确定性了。

本案就是一个很好的例子。Gregg 先生所患癌症的性质和程度，即便能够在一定程度上确定（第一个问题），也并没有很好地回答"如果他得到了正确的治疗，他的结果会是如何"（第二个问题）。他的结果依然有很多可能性。我们能做的最多不过是诉诸过去的经验（即诉诸统计学），然后尽可能用在他这个个案上。然而这些数据只能告诉我们，每种的可能性会有多大概率。

综上所述，就本案的目的而言，医疗过失案件属于这两种类型的哪一种，取决于在医疗过失发生之前，病人的状况和（如果没有发生医疗过失时）其最终的结果之间的关系是否足够不确定。Hotson 案属于一种类型。在该案中，只要我们按照通常的概率平衡法确定了 Stephen Hotson 在医疗过失案刚发生之前的状况，我们可以确切地知道"他的腿如果得到了及时治疗会发生什么"这个问题的答案。而本案则属于另一种类型。在本案中，明确了 Gregg 先生在向 Scott 医生求诊时的状况，并不足以回答"如果没有医疗过失，那么会发生什么"这样一个重要的问题。"如果 Gregg 先生在九个月前获得了恰当的治疗，他的结局如何"这个问题的答案实在是太不确定了。

……

The way ahead must surely be to recognise that where a patient is suffering from illness or injury and his prospects of recovery are attended with a significant degree of medical uncertainty, and he suffers a significant diminution of his prospects of recovery by reason of medical negligence whether of diagnosis or treatment, that diminution constitutes actionable damage. This is so whether the patient's prospects immediately before the negligence exceeded or fell short of 50%. "Medical uncertainty" is uncertainty inherent in the patient's condition, uncertainty which medical opinion cannot resolve. This is to be contrasted with uncertainties arising solely from differences of view expressed by witnesses. Evidential uncertainties of this character should be resolved in the usual way.

...

LORD HOFFMAN

Loss of a chance

The alternative submission was that reduction in the prospect of a favourable outcome ("loss of a chance") should be a recoverable head of damage. There are certainly cases in which it is. *Chaplin v Hicks* [1911] 2 KB 786 is a well known example. The question is whether the principle of that case can apply to a case of clinical negligence such as this.

The answer can be derived from three cases in the House of Lords: *Hotson v East Berkshire Area Health Authority* [1987] AC 750, *Wilsher v Essex Area Health Authority* [1988] AC 1074 and Fairchild v Glenhaven Funeral Services Ltd [2003] 1 AC 32 .

In Hotson's case the claimant was a boy who broke his hip when he fell out of a tree. The hospital negligently failed to diagnose the fracture for five days. The hip joint was irreparably damaged by the loss of blood supply to its cartilage. The judge found that the rupture of the blood vessels caused by the fall had probably made the damage inevitable but there was a 25% chance that enough had remained intact to save the joint if the fracture had been diagnosed at the time. He and the Court of Appeal awarded the claimant damages for loss of the 25% chance of a favourable outcome.

The House of Lords unanimously reversed this decision. They said that the claimant had not lost a chance because, on the finding of fact, nothing could have been done to save the joint. The outcome had been determined by what happened when he fell out of the tree. Either he had enough surviving blood vessels or he did not. That question had to be decided on a balance of probability and had been decided adversely to the claimant.

In Wilsher's case a junior doctor in a special care baby unit negligently put a catheter in the wrong place so that a monitor failed to register that a premature baby was receiving too much oxygen. The baby suffered rentrolental fibroplasia ("RLF"), a condition of the eyes which resulted in blindness. The excessive oxygen was a possible cause of the condition and had increased the chances that it would develop but there were other possible causes: statistics showed a correlation

我们的选择因此当然就是要确认：当一个病人的康复前景不确定时，如果因为诊断或者治疗过失，他康复的概率有很大程度地会减少，那么这种减少就构成可诉的损失。这种减少是可诉的，不论在医疗过失发生前，病人康复的概率是大于还是小于50%。"医疗不确定性"属于病人的状况本身所固有的不确定性，医生的意见并不能消灭这种不确定性。这种不确定性要和那种因为不同的证人作出了不同的证词而产生的不确定性区分开来。证据的不确定性，要靠常规的手段来解决。

……

Hoffman 大法官主笔：
机会损失

原告的另一项主张则是：一种良好的结果发生的可能性如果减少了，则属于可以请求损害赔偿的损失。毫无疑问，我们能找到支持这种主张的判例。*Chaplin v Hicks* [1911] 2 KB 786 就是一个很好的例子。然而，在这里，我们的问题在于，前述这个案子确定的原则能不能适用于如同本案这样的医疗过失类案件。

有三个上议院的判例可以回答这个问题：*Hotson v East Berkshire Area Health Authority* [1987] AC 750, *Wilsher v Essex Area Health Authority* [1988] AC 1074 以及 *Fairchild v Glenhaven Funeral Services Ltd* [2003] 1 AC 32。

在 Hotson 一案中，原告男孩从树上摔下来，摔伤了他的臀部。医院因为过失，在五日内都没有诊断出他的骨折。因为软骨未能得到供血，其髋关节不可逆地坏死了。一审法官认定，原告摔伤导致的血管损伤很可能使得最后的髋关节坏死不可避免，然而如果他的骨折当时被诊断了出来，那么有25%的概率，他剩下的完好的血管是可以挽救他的关节的。一审法官和上诉法院都判决原告可以因其丧失了25%的康复机会而获得损害赔偿。

上议院全员一致地推翻了这个判决。他们表示，根据一审法院认定的事实，原告的髋关节是不可能挽救的。这一结果自其从树上摔下时既已确定。（对于法院来说）原告要么还剩下足够的完好的血管，要么没有。这个问题需要用"概率平衡法"确定，而根据该法确定的结果是对原告不利的。

在 Wilsher 一案中，一位特殊婴儿病房中的实习医生因为过失把导管安在了错误的地方，因此监视器未能发现一个早产儿的吸氧量太多了。这个早产儿因此罹患了晶体后纤维增生症（RLF），可能致盲。过度吸氧可能是该病的一个原因并且也增加了它产生的概率，然而也有其他的可能性：统计数据显示，Wilsher 家的早产儿所患有的其他病症和 RLF 之间有相关性。然而这些病症和

between RLF and various conditions present in the Wilsher baby. But the causal mechanism linking them to RLF was unknown.

The Court of Appeal awarded damages for the reduction in the chance of a favourable outcome. Again this was reversed by the House of Lords. The baby's RLF was caused by lack of oxygen or by something else or a combination of causes. The defendant was liable only if the lack of oxygen caused or substantially contributed to the injury. That had to be proved on a balance of probability.

In Fairchild's case, the claimant had contracted mesothelioma by exposure to asbestos. The medical evidence was that the condition was probably the result of a cell mutation caused by a single fibre. The claimant had worked with asbestos for more than one employer and could not prove whose fibre had caused his disease. The Court of Appeal said that the cause of the disease was not indeterminate. It had either been caused by the defendant's fibre or it had not. It was for the claimant to prove causation on a balance of probability. The House of Lords accepted that the disease had a determinate cause in one fibre or other but constructed a special rule imposing liability for conduct which only increased the chances of the employee contracting the disease. That rule was restrictively defined in terms which make it inapplicable in this case.

What these cases show is that, as Helen Reece points out in an illuminating article "Losses of Chances in the Law" (1996) 59 MLR 188 , the law regards the world as in principle bound by laws of causality. Everything has a determinate cause, even if we do not know what it is. The blood-starved hip joint in Hotson's case, the blindness in Wilsher's case, the mesothelioma in Fairchild's case; each had its cause and it was for the plaintiff to prove that it was an act or omission for which the defendant was responsible. The narrow terms of the exception made to this principle in Fairchild's case only serves to emphasise the strength of the rule. The fact that proof is rendered difficult or impossible because no examination was made at the time, as in Hotson's case, or because medical science cannot provide the answer, as in Wilsher's case, makes no difference. There is no inherent uncertainty about what caused something to happen in the past or about whether something which happened in the past will cause something to happen in the future. Everything is determined by causality. What we lack is knowledge and the law deals with lack of knowledge by the concept of the burden of proof.

Similarly in the present case, the progress of Mr Gregg's disease had a determinate cause. It may have been inherent in his genetic make-up at the time when he saw Dr Scott, as Hotson's fate was determined by what happened to his thigh when he fell out of the tree. Or it may, as Mance LJ suggests, have been affected by subsequent events and behaviour for which Dr Scott was not responsible. Medical science does not enable us to say. But the outcome was not random; it was governed by laws of causality and, in the absence of a special rule as in Fairchild's case, inability to establish that delay in diagnosis caused the reduction in expectation in life cannot be remedied

RLF 之间是否有因果关系，则是未知的。

上诉法院因为原告丧失了获得康复的机会而判决给予其损害赔偿。然而上议院再次推翻了这种类型的判决。该早产儿所患的 RLF 可能是由缺氧引起的，可能是由其他原因引起的，也可能是多种原因混合引起的。而被告只有在该病症是由缺氧引起的，或者缺氧是促成损害的重要原因时，才应该承担责任。而这应该按照"概率平衡法"来证明。

在 Fairchild 一案中，原告诉称其由于长期接触石棉网而罹患间质瘤。医疗证据显示，该病症很可能是由于纤维导致的细胞变异。原告曾经为多个雇主工作，因而并不能证明到底是哪个雇主的纤维导致了他所罹患的疾病。上诉法院认为，该疾病的成因不可能处于不定状态：该疾病要么是由原告的纤维造成的，要么不是。疾病和纤维之间的因果关系，应该由原告按照"概率平衡法"来证明。上议院同意，该疾病一定是由某个确定的纤维造成的。然而上议院同样设立了一项特别的规则，根据该规则，如果某个雇主的行为增加了员工罹患疾病的可能性，那么该雇主也是需要承担责任的。该规则的措辞非常严格，因此使得该规则并不能在本案中适用。

正如 Hellen Reece 在其著名的论文《机会损失》（1996）59 MLR 188 中提到的那样，上述判例说明，在法律看来，世界是被因果律支配的。万事万物都有确定的原因，即使我们并不知道这个原因是什么。Hotson 案中缺血的髋关节，Wilsher 案中原告的致盲，以及 Fairchild 案中的间质瘤，这些案件都是存在原因的，而证明该原因是被告的作为或者不作为造成的，则属于原告的举证责任。Fairchild 一案中所确定的对上述原则的例外，其措辞是非常严格的，这其实正说明了该原则是多么得有力。Hotson 案中，因为没有及时地检查，相关的证明变得非常困难甚至不可能。在 Wilsher 案中，医疗科学尚不能对涉案争议提供确切的答案。然而，即便这样，也不能说上述原则就不适用了。过去某事件的成因是什么或者过去某事件是否可能导致未来某事件，对于这样的问题，其实并没有固有的不确定性。万事万物都由因果律来调整。我们只是没有相关的知识罢了。而在没有相关知识的时候，我们的法律是通过举证责任的制度来分配不利后果的。

同样的，在本案中，一定有某个确定的原因导致了 Gregg 先生所患疾病的发展。也许这个原因是他在向 Scott 医生求诊时他自己的基因组合，就如同 Hotson 的命运在其从树上跌下时即已确定一样。也许这个结果，如 Mance 上诉法院法官的意见，是由于之后的和 Scott 医生无关的事件或者行为造成的。现有的医疗科学不能回答造成这个结果原因到底是什么。然而，有一点是肯定的，那就是 Gregg 先生的结果一定不是随机产生的；这个结果的产生一定是服从于因果律的。在 Fairchild 案所确定的例外不能适用的情况下，如果原告未能证明诊断的迟延和预期生存可能的降低有因果关系，我们不能因此说

by treating the outcome as having been somehow indeterminate.

...

...In the present case it is urged that Mr Gregg has suffered a wrong and ought to have a remedy. Living for more than ten years is something of great value to him and he should be compensated for the possibility that the delay in diagnosis may have reduced his chances of doing so. In effect, the appellant submits that the exceptional rule in Fairchild's case should be generalised and damages awarded in all cases in which the defendant may have caused an injury and has increased the likelihood of the injury being suffered. In the present case, it is alleged that Dr Scott may have caused a reduction in Mr Gregg's expectation of life and that he increased the likelihood that his life would be shortened by the disease.

It should first be noted that adopting such a rule would involve abandoning a good deal of authority. The rule which the House is asked to adopt is the very rule which it rejected in *Wilsher's case* [1988] AC 1074. Yet Wilsher's case was expressly approved by the House in Fairchild's case [2003] 1 AC 32. *Hotson's case* [1987] AC 750 too would have to be overruled. Furthermore, the House would be dismantling all the qualifications and restrictions with which it so recently hedged the Fairchild exception. There seem to me to be no new arguments or change of circumstances which could justify such a radical departure from precedent.

Control mechanisms

The appellant suggests that the expansion of liability could be held in reasonable bounds by confining it to cases in which the claimant had suffered an injury. In this case, the spread of the cancer before the eventual diagnosis was something which would not have happened if it had been promptly diagnosed and amounted to an injury caused by the defendant. It is true that this is not the injury for which the claimant is suing. His claim is for loss of the prospect of survival for more than 10 years. And the judge's finding was that he had not established that the spread of the cancer was causally connected with the reduction in his expectation of life. But the appellant submits that his injury can be used as what Professor Jane Stapleton called a "hook" on which to hang a claim for damage which it did not actually cause: see (2003) 119 LQR 388, 423.

An artificial limitation of this kind seems to me to be lacking in principle. It resembles the "control mechanisms" which disfigure the law of liability for psychiatric injury. And once one treats an "injury" as a condition for imposing liability for some other kind of damage, one is involved in definitional problems about what counts as an injury. Presumably the internal bleeding suffered by the boy Hotson was an injury which would have qualified him to sue for the loss of a chance of saving his hip joint. What about baby Wilsher? The doctor's negligence resulted in his having excessively oxygenated blood, which is potentially toxic: see [1987] QB 730, 764-766. Was this an injury? The boundaries of the concept would be a fertile source of litigation.

Similar comments may be made about another proposed control mechanism, which is to

导致原告现状的原因在某种程度是不确定的,原告可以获得救济。
......

......本案中,有人宣称,因为 Gregg 先生遭到了侵权行为的损害,所以他应当获得救济。能多活十多年,这对他来说是很有价值的,因此当诊断延误减少了他能多活十多年的可能性时,他就应当就这种可能性的减少而获得赔偿。其实,上诉人所主张的是将 Fairchild v Glenhaven Funeral services Ltd. 一案中所确定的例外一般化:即只要被告的行为可能导致损害结果或者增加损害结果发生的可能性,就同意原告的损害赔偿请求。在本案中,原告主张 Scott 医生的行为可能导致了 Gregg 先生预期寿命的减少,增加了疾病缩短其寿命的可能性。

我们首先需要注意的是,如果我们接受了原告所提出的这种规则,则意味着我们要否定一系列的判例。原告要求上议院接受的这个规则,正是上议院在 Wilsher v Essex Area Health Authority [1988] AC 1074 一案中明确否定了的。而上议院在 Fairchild v Glenhaven Funeral services Ltd. [2003] 1 AC 32 案中是明确确认了 Wilsher 案的判例的。同样需要推翻的,还有 Hotson v East Berkshine Area Health Authority [1987] AC 750 案的判例。另外,上议院需要将其最近为 Fairchild v Glenhaven Funeral services Ltd. 一案所确立的例外所构建的适用条件和限制全部推翻。在我看来,并没有什么新的论证或者情势变更,足以支撑这样极端的对先例的背离。

控制机制

上诉人建议,可以将赔偿责任的扩大限制在索赔人遭受人身伤害的情况下,从而将其限制在合理的范围内。本案中,在最终确诊之前,癌症已经扩散了,而如果受害人得到了正确的诊治,这种扩散本可以避免。这种癌症的扩散就属于被告所造成的一种人身伤害。诚然,本案中,原告并非为了人身伤害请求损害赔偿。他的请求是为了所丧失的十多年的预期寿命。然而,虽然一审法官认定了原告并未成功地证明癌症的扩散和其预期寿命的减少之间有因果联系,但是上诉人认为他所遭受的人身伤害可以被用来当作 Jane Stapleton 教授所说的一个"钩子",然后将其损害赔偿的请求挂在这个钩子上。他所请求的损害并非一定是这里的人身伤害所导致的〔参见(2003)119 LQR 388, 423。〕

在我看来,这样的限制责任范围的方法是武断的,因而并不存在既有的法律原则。这种限制责任的方法很像所谓的把精神损害赔偿规则变得面目全非的"控制机制"。如果我们一旦将人身伤害作为被告承担损害赔偿责任的构成要件,我们就面临如何定义人身伤害的问题。我们大概可以无争议地认为小男孩 Hotson 所受的内伤属于人身伤害,因而他可以据此就其所丧失的髋关节的康复机会提起损害赔偿之诉。然而小宝宝 Wilsher 呢?因为医生的过失,他的血液中融入了太多的氧气,这也很可能是有毒的。〔参见(1987)QB 730, 764-766。〕那么这时他有没有受到人身伤害?人身伤害的边界到底在

confine the principle to cases in which inability to prove causation is a result of lack of medical knowledge of the causal mechanism (as in Wilsher's case) rather than lack of knowledge of the facts (as in Hotson's case). Again, the distinction is not based upon principle or even expediency. Proof of causation was just as difficult for Hotson as it was for Wilsher. It could be said that the need to prove causation was more unfair on Hotson, since the reason why he could not prove whether he had enough blood vessels after the fall was because the hospital had negligently failed to examine him.

In Fairchild's case [2003] 1 AC 32, 68, Lord Nicholls of Birkenhead said of new departures in the law:

> "To be acceptable the law must be coherent. It must be principled. The basis on which one case, or one type of case, is distinguished from another should be transparent and capable of identification. When a decision departs from principles normally applied, the basis for doing so must be rational and justifiable if the decision is to avoid the reproach that hard cases make bad law."

I respectfully agree. And in my opinion, the various control mechanisms proposed to confine liability for loss of a chance within artificial limits do not pass this test. But a wholesale adoption of possible rather than probable causation as the criterion of liability would be so radical a change in our law as to amount to a legislative act. It would have enormous consequences for insurance companies and the National Health Service. In company with my noble and learned friends, Lord Phillips of Worth Matravers and Baroness Hale of Richmond, I think that any such change should be left to Parliament.

…

BARONESS HALE

The loss of a chance argument

The second, and more radical, way of redefining the claimant's damage is in terms of the loss of a chance. Put this way, his claim is not for the loss of an outcome, in this case the cure of his disease, which he would have enjoyed but for the negligence. His claim is for the reduced chance of achieving that outcome. As Jane Stapleton explained (by reference to the argument accepted by the Court of Appeal in *Hotson v East Berkshire Area Health Authority* [1987] AC 750) in "The Gist of Negligence" (1988) 104 LQR 389, 391-392:

> "Clearly, if the gist of the complaint were traditionally formulated in terms of contraction of necrosis, the plaintiff would fail to establish the requisite causal link on the balance of probability. The novelty of the case was that the plaintiff attempted

哪里，这一问题将引起大量的诉讼。

有人又评论说，我们可以用另一种控制规则：我们可以只接受那种因果关系不清楚的案件（如 *Wilsher v Essex Area Health Authority* 案），而不接受那种事实不清楚的案件（如 *Hotson v East Berkshine Area Health Authority* 案）。然而，这种区别并非基于法律的一般原则，甚至并不属于便宜行事。在 Hotson 案和 Wilsher 案中，证明因果关系是一样困难的。我们甚至可以说，要求 Hotson 去证明因果关系是不公平的，因为他之所以无法证明他在摔下树之后是否还剩下足够的血管，完全是因为当时医院疏忽而没有及时对他做检查。

在 *Fairchild v Glenhaven Funeral services Ltd.* [2003] 1 AC 32, 68 案中，伯肯黑德的 Nicholls 大法官评论了对法律的偏离：

> 法律若要被接受，则其内部必须自洽。法律必须是能根据原则推出结论的。一个案件或者一类案件之所以区别于其他案件，其所依赖的理由必须是清楚而明确的。在判决中如果我们没有适用基本原则，一定是因为某些理性而正当的原因，否则我们就会受到这样的批判："难办的案件引出了坏法律。"

我恭敬地同意他的意见。在我看来，上述的各种限制机会损失责任的控制标准，并不符合上面这段话所提出的准则。在作为责任承担依据中，用百分比的因果关系来替代"根据概率平衡法下的举证责任来确定的或有或无的因果关系"，属于过于激进的变化，激进得属于立法行为了。如果这样做，那么保险公司和国家医保系统都会受到巨大的冲击。因此，我和我高贵而博学的朋友 Phillips 大法官和 Hale 大法官，都认为是否采取这种变化应该由议会来作出决定。

……

Hale 大法官主笔：
对机会损失的论证

第二种也是更激进的一种做法，是用原告所丧失的机会作为其损失。这样，他就并不是因为某种结果的丧失——在本案中即是他因为医疗过失而丧失的疾病痊愈这种结果——去起诉的。相反，他所起诉的是获得某种结果的可能性的减损。正如 Jane Stapleton 在《过失的主旨》[（1988）104 LQR 389, 391–392] 一文中所解释的（他提到在 *Hotson v East Berkshire Area Health Authority* 一案中，上诉法院所接受的一种论证）：

> 显然，如果原告是以其罹患坏疽为由起诉的，则其很难在概率平衡法下证明所需要的因果关系。本案的新颖之处在于，为了避免这种结果，原

to circumvent this result by choosing to formulate the gist of his action, not in terms of the necrosis outcome, but in terms of the lost chance of avoiding that outcome. In other words, although the plaintiff fails to establish causation on the balance of probabilities to one formulation of the damage forming the gist, he seeks to succeed in doing so to an alternative formulation based on loss of a chance. Importantly, the Hotson argument retains the traditional form of the causation test …"

In that case, the claimant had actually suffered the adverse outcome, avascular necrosis. The risk of suffering that outcome as a result of falling from the tree was 75%. The defendant's negligent failure to detect the injury to his hip took away the remaining 25% chance of avoiding it. Clearly he could not prove that the negligence had caused the outcome. It was more likely than not that it had made no difference. But might he have proved that it was more likely than not that the negligence had reduced his chance of avoiding that outcome?

The House of Lords treated this as a case in which the die was already cast by the time the claimant got to the hospital (or at least the claimant could not prove otherwise). The defendant had not even caused the loss of the chance of saving the situation, because by the time the claimant got to them there was no chance. The coin had already been tossed, and had come down heads or tails. But there must be many cases in which that is not so. The coin is in the air. The claimant does have a chance of a favourable outcome which chance is wiped out or significantly reduced by the negligence. The coin is whipped out of the air before it has been able to land.

This is, therefore, a new case, not covered precisely by previous authority. The appellant himself describes his argument as the "policy approach". He recognises that it is a question of legal policy whether the law should be developed as he argues it should be. The wide version of the argument would allow recovery for any reduction in the chance of a better physical outcome, or any increase in the chance of an adverse physical outcome, even if this cannot be linked to any physiological changes caused by the defendant. A defendant who has negligently increased the risk that the claimant will suffer harm in future (for example from exposure to asbestos or cigarette smoke) would be liable even though no harm had yet been suffered. This would be difficult to reconcile with our once and for all approach to establishing liability and assessing damage. Unless damages were limited to a modest sum for anxiety and distress about the future, sensible quantification would have to "wait and see". The narrower version of the argument would require that there be some physiological change caused by the defendant's negligence, bringing with it a reduced prospect of a favourable outcome.

…

Almost any claim for loss of an outcome could be reformulated as a claim for loss of a chance of that outcome. The implications of retaining them both as alternatives would be substantial. That

告并非以其罹患坏疽这个结果来起诉的,而是以其所丧失的避免该结果的机会来起诉的。换言之,虽然原告并未按照概率平衡法证明医疗过失和一种损害赔偿请求下的因果关系,他却成功地证明了另一种基于机会损失的赔偿请求下的因果关系。很重要的一点是,Hotson 的论证甚至还保留了传统的因果关系的判断方法。

在该案中,原告确实遭受到了一种不利的结果:缺血性坏死。在原告从树上摔下来后,他罹患这种疾病的概率是 75%。然而,被告因为过失未能检测出原告髋关节受到的损失,剥夺了他最后 25% 的避免这种结果的希望。显然,原告是不可能证明被告的过失导致了这种结果。非常可能的是,无论有没有被告的过失,结果都不会变。然而,他是否证明了另一个问题呢,即被告的过失减少了他避免那种结果的可能性?

对于本案,上议院认为在原告进入医院那一刻起,"骰子就已经掷下了"(至少原告不能证明骰子没有掷下)。甚至并非被告导致了其获救可能性的减少,因为他进入医院的时候就已经没有机会了。这里,硬币已经投下,是正面还是反面早已确定。然而,肯定有很多情况并不是这样:此时,硬币尚在空中。此时的原告是本有可能获得更好的结果的,而这种结果的可能性被被告的过失消灭了,或者严重地减少了。这时的硬币在落地前就被毁掉了。

这样说来,本案就是一个新案件,一个并不属于先前判例调整范围的新案件。上诉人自己,将其论证方式描述为"政策方法"。他看出来这里的焦点是个法律政策的问题:法律是否应该朝着他所主张的那个方向发展?他的主张的广义版是,即使原告身上没有发现任何被告导致的生理变化,只要原告获得更好的健康结果的可能性变小了,或者只要原告遭受更坏的健康结果的可能性变大了,就应当允许原告获得赔偿。如果被告因为过失增加了原告未来受到伤害的风险(比如让其暴露在石棉下或者香烟的烟雾中),他就需要承担责任,即使现在原告还未受到任伤害。这种主张和我们现有的确定责任和赔偿的方式很难调和。除了对未来的焦虑或者痛苦的少量赔偿,合理的做法是"等等再看"。原告的主张的狭义版是,被告应该因为其过失造成了原告的某种生理性变化,这种变化使得一种更好的结果发生的可能性变小了。

……

任何针对丧失了某个结果的诉讼,其实都可以转换为一个针对丧失了获得这个结果的机会的诉讼。如果我们把这两种诉讼的可能性都保留,则会有

is, the claimant still has the prospect of 100% recovery if he can show that it is more likely than not that the doctor's negligence caused the adverse outcome. But if he cannot show that, he also has the prospect of lesser recovery for loss of a chance. If (for the reasons given earlier) it would in practice always be tempting to conclude that the doctor's negligence had affected his chances to some extent, the claimant would almost always get something. It would be a "heads you lose everything, tails I win something" situation. But why should the defendant not also be able to redefine the gist of the action if it suits him better?

The appellant in this case accepts that the proportionate recovery effect must cut both ways. If the claim is characterised as loss of a chance, those with a better than evens chance would still only get a proportion of the full value of their claim. But I do not think that he accepts that the same would apply in cases where the claim is characterised as loss of an outcome. In that case there is no basis for calculating the odds. If the two are alternatives available in every case, the defendant will almost always be liable for something. He will have lost the benefit of the 50% chance that causation cannot be proved. But if the two approaches cannot sensibly live together, the claimants who currently obtain full recovery on an adverse outcome basis might in future only achieve a proportionate recovery. This would surely be a case of two steps forward, three steps back for the great majority of straightforward personal injury cases. In either event, the expert evidence would have to be far more complex than it is at present. Negotiations and trials would be a great deal more difficult. Recovery would be much less predictable both for claimants and for defendants' liability insurers. There is no reason in principle why the change in approach should be limited to medical negligence. Whether or not the policy choice is between retaining the present definition of personal injury in outcome terms and redefining it in loss of opportunity terms, introducing the latter would cause far more problems in the general run of personal injury claims than the policy benefits are worth.

Much of the discussion in the cases and literature has centred round cases where the adverse outcome has already happened. The patient has lost his leg. Did the doctor's negligence cause him to lose the leg? If not, did it reduce the chances of saving the leg? But in this case the most serious of the adverse outcomes has not yet happened, and (it is to be hoped) may never happen. The approach to causation should be the same for both past and future events. What, if anything, has the doctor's negligence caused in this case? We certainly do not know whether it has caused this outcome, because happily Mr Gregg has survived each of the significant milestones along the way. Can we even say that it reduced the chances of a successful outcome, given that Mr Gregg has turned out to be one of the successful minority at each milestone? This is quite different from the situation in Hotson's case, where the avascular necrosis had already happened, or in Rufo v Hosking, where the fractures had already happened. Mr Gregg faced a risk of an adverse outcome which happily has not so far materialised, serious though the effects of his illness, treatment and

很大的影响。原告如果能证明，医生的过失导致了不好的结果的可能性比没有导致的可能性要大，则原告依然能获得百分之百的赔偿。但是如果他不能证明这一点，他依然可以拥有因为机会损失而获得的更小赔偿。如果正如我之前给出的原因，在实践中我们总是会倾向认为医生的过失在某种程度上影响了病人获得康复的机会，因此原告只要起诉就会得到一些东西。这种情况就像"正面你输完，背面我赢一点"。然而，凭什么被告不能更改诉讼理由，使得结果对他更好一些呢？

上诉人承认它所主张的这种按比例补偿法的效果是一柄双刃剑。如果原告是基于机会损失提起的诉讼，那么即便原告的机会是大于一半的，他也只能获得全部金额的一定比例的赔偿。然而，我并不认为他会承认当原告是基于结果损失而起诉时，结果会是一样的。在这种情况下，不具备计算概率的依据。如果在每个案件中，原告都可以选择基于哪种理由提起诉讼，被告将会永远要承担一定的责任。被告将失去占一半情况的原告无法证明因果关系的情形的好处。而如果我们认为这两种方式并不能理性地共存，则现在能基于坏结果而获得全额赔偿的原告，未来可能就只能获得一定比例的赔偿。这种结果对于大部分直截了当的人身伤害案件，是进两步退三步的。无论两种起诉理由能不能共存，专家证据都会变得比现在复杂得多。谈判庭审会变得比现在困难得多。而且原则上没有理由认为这种起诉理由的变化应该被仅仅局限于医疗过失类的案件。无论是不是要在现有的依据结果定义的人身伤害和将人身伤害重新定义为基于机会损失的两种政策之间选择，将后者引入法律，对大多数的人身伤害案件，都是弊大于利的。

现有的大多数的判例和文献都是围绕那种不利结果已经发生的情形。比如病人失去了他的腿。我们先判断，是医生的过失导致他失去了腿吗？如果不是，我们再判断医生的过失导致他保住腿的概率减少了吗？然而在本案中，最严重的不利结果还没有发生，而且可能永远不会发生（我们希望如此）。我们判断因果关系的方法，对于过去和未来的事件，应该是一样的。在本案中，如果医生的过失确实导致了一些东西，那到底是导致的什么呢？我们显然不知道是不是医生的过失导致了现在的结果，因为很幸运 Gregg 先生在每个关键的环节都挺了过来。鉴于 Cregg 先生属于那个在每个环节都挺了过来的少数幸运儿，我们甚至很难说是医生的过失减少了其获得痊愈的可能性。这确实跟 *Hotson v East Berkshine Area Health Authority* 案不一样，因为该案中缺血性坏死已经发生了；也与 *Rufo v Hosking* 不一样，因为该案中骨折已经发生了。

prognosis have been. The complexities of attempting to introduce liability for the loss of a chance of a more favourable outcome in personal injury claims have driven me, not without regret, to conclude that it should not be done.

43. Bonnington Castings Ltd v Wardlaw [1956] AC 613

House of Lords, United Kingdom

APPEAL from the First Division of the Court of Session.

The facts, stated by Lord Reid, were as follows: The respondent was employed by the appellants for eight years in the dressing shop of their foundry in Leith, and while employed there he contracted the disease of pneumoconiosis by inhaling air which contained minute particles of silica. He ceased work on May 12, 1950.

The appellants produce steel castings. These are made by pouring molten metal into moulds which consist of sand with a very high silica content. When the casting has cooled it is freed from sand, so far as possible, and then annealed. The annealed casting has a certain amount of the sand adhering to it or burnt into it and the surface of the casting is somewhat irregular. It is then necessary to remove these irregularities and smooth the surface of the casting, and in the course of doing this any adhering sand is also removed. This is done in the dressing shop by three types of machine. In two of these machines, floor grinders and swing grinders, the means employed are grinding wheels made of carborundum, and in the third a hammer or chisel is driven by compressed air so that it delivers some 1,800 blows per minute. There are several of each type of machine in the dressing shop and all of them produce dust, part of which is silica from the sand which they remove. The particles of this sand are originally sufficiently large not to be dangerous, because it is only exceedingly small particles of silica which can produce the disease - particles which are quite invisible except through a powerful microscope. But either in the annealing process or by the working of these machines or at both stages (the evidence on this is inconclusive) a number of the original particles are broken up and the dust produced by all of these machines contains a certain proportion of the dangerous minute particles of silica.

Most of the dust from the grinders can be sucked into ducts or pipes, but during the time when the respondent contracted his disease there was no known means of preventing the dust from the pneumatic hammers from escaping into the air, and it is now admitted that no form of mask or respirator had then been invented which was effective to protect those exposed to the dust.

Throughout his eight years in the appellants' service the respondent operated one of these pneumatic hammers and he admits that he cannot complain in so far as his disease was caused by the dust from his own or any of the other pneumatic hammers. As there was no known means of collecting or neutralizing this dust, and as it is not alleged that these machines ought not to have

无论其疾病的状况、疾病的治疗和预测的结果是多么严重，Gregg 先生面临的不利后果都很幸运地还没有发生。如果我们要在人身侵害的诉讼中，尝试引入一种针对更好结果的丧失的责任，那么我们会把事情变得很复杂。因此，我不无遗憾地认为，我们不应该这么做。

43. Bonnington Castings Ltd v Wardlaw [1956] AC 613

联合王国上议院

由苏格兰高等民事法院第一分院上诉至本院。

如 Reid 大法官所言，本案事实如下：被上诉人为诸上诉人的雇员。被上诉人在诸上诉人位于 Leith 的铸造厂的装配车间工作了八年。在工作期间，其因为吸入含有硅微粒的空气而染上了尘肺病。因此于 1950 年 5 月 12 日停止了工作。

诸上诉人以铸造钢铸件为业。要制作钢铸件，需要将融化的金属倒进模具中，而这些模具是由沙子做成，含有非常高浓度的硅。当这些钢铸件冷却之后，需要尽可能地除去其上的沙子，之后进行退火程序。完成了退火程序的钢铸件可能依然附着了一定数量的沙子，这些沙子也可能经过燃烧而和钢铸件融为了一体，因此这些钢铸件的表面总是或多或少有些不平。所以，有必要磨去钢铸件表面的这些不平之处，而在这个过程中，也能去掉那些残留吸附在其表面的沙子。这道工序是在装配车间的三种机器上完成的。在地板打磨机和旋启式打磨机这两种机器上，用的是由碳化硅制成的砂轮；第三种机器则使用压缩空气驱动的锤子和凿子，它们每分钟要敲击钢铸件 1 800 下。在装配车间，每种机器都有数台，所有的机器都会扬起尘埃，这些尘埃的部分成分则是被除去的沙子中的硅。这些砂砾本来是足够大的，并不危险，因为只有特别细微，细微到显微镜的尺度的硅粒才会致病。然而或许在退火工序中，或许在这些机器的工序中，或者二者都有（证据不充足），机器砸碎了原始的大颗粒，生成的沙尘都含有一定比例的危险的硅微粒。

研磨机所生成的砂砾，大部分可以被水槽或者管道吸收。然而在被上诉人患病之时，并不存在已知的可以避免气动锤子带来的沙子进入空气的方法。现在大家也承认那时并不存在一种口罩或者面具能够有效地保护那些暴露在这种沙子中的人。

在为诸位上诉人工作的八年间，被上诉人一直在操作一台气动锤子，他承认他并不清楚他所患的疾病是他自己的锤子产生的尘埃还是别的锤子产生的尘埃造成的。由于并无收集或者移除这些尘埃的已知手段，也由于被上诉人并未

been used, there was no breach of duty on the part of the appellants in allowing this dust to escape into the air. The respondent makes no complaint with regard to the floor grinders, because the dust extracting plant for them was apparently effective so far as that was possible, and it seems that any noxious dust which escaped from these grinders was of negligible amount. But the respondent alleged, and it is admitted, that a considerable quantity of dust escaped into the air of the workshop from the swing grinders, because the dust-extraction plant for these grinders was not kept free from obstruction as it should have been. It frequently became choked and ineffective.

LORD REID

It would seem obvious in principle that a pursuer or plaintiff must prove not only negligence or breach of duty but also that such fault caused or materially contributed to his injury, and there is ample authority for that proposition both in Scotland and in England. I can find neither reason nor authority for the rule being different where there is breach of a statutory duty. The fact that Parliament imposes a duty for the protection of employees has been held to entitle an employee to sue if he is injured as a result of a breach of that duty, but it would be going a great deal farther to hold that it can be inferred from the enactment of a duty that Parliament intended that any employee suffering injury can sue his employer merely because there was a breach of duty and it is shown to be possible that his injury may have been caused by it. In my judgment, the employee must in all cases prove his case by the ordinary standard of proof in civil actions: he must make it appear at least that on a balance of probabilities the breach of duty caused or materially contributed to his injury.

...

The medical evidence was that pneumoconiosis is caused by a gradual accumulation in the lungs of minute particles of silica inhaled over a period of years. That means, I think, that the disease is caused by the whole of the noxious material inhaled and, if that material comes from two sources, it cannot be wholly attributed to material from one source or the other. I am in agreement with much of the Lord President's opinion in this case, but I cannot agree that the question is: which was the most probable source of the respondent's disease, the dust from the pneumatic hammers or the dust from the swing grinders? It appears to me that the source of his disease was the dust from both sources, and the real question is whether the dust from the swing grinders materially contributed to the disease. What is a material contribution must be a question of degree. A contribution which comes within the exception de minimis non curat lex is not material, but I think that any contribution which does not fall within that exception must be material. I do not see how there can be something too large to come within the de minimis principle but yet too small to be material.

...

I think that the position can be shortly stated in this way. It may be that, of the noxious dust in

主张不该使用这些机器,就尘埃进入空气而言,上诉人并未违反其义务。被上诉人并未就地板研磨机提起诉讼,因为这些机器的除尘装置显然是有效的(如果客观上这些装置是可能起作用的话),而如果有任何有害尘埃从研磨机中释放出来,其数量都是可忽略不计的。但是被上诉人主张,后来也经确认,旋转式研磨机确实释放了客观数量的尘埃进入空气,因为这种研磨机的除尘装置并未保持其应有的清除障碍物的功能,反而经常卡住而不起作用。

Reid 大法官主笔:

显而易见,根据原则,原告不但有责任证明被告的过失或者违反义务,而且有责任证明是被告的过错导致了他的损害,这点在苏格兰和英格兰都有足够多的判例支持。当被告违反成文法规定的义务时,我不认为有任何理由或者判例支持我们适用不同的规则。议会之所以要创设保护雇员的义务,是为了让雇员在因为雇主违反该义务而使其遭受伤害时,有起诉的依据。然而,如果我们因此就认为,议会创设这种义务是为了让雇员在只要雇主违反了义务而有可能导致了其所遭受的损害时,就可以起诉雇主,就有点过了。在我看来,雇员要胜诉,在任何情况下都必须满足一般民事诉讼规则下的举证责任:他必须证明,至少在概率平衡法下,被告所违反的义务导致了其所遭受的损害,或者对其所遭受的损害的产生有实质性的作用。

……

医疗证据显示,尘肺病是由多年吸入带有硅微粒的空气而导致硅微粒在肺中积累造成的。我认为这就意味着原告的病是由所有的被吸入的有害物质造成的;而如果有害物质来自两个来源,那么我们就不能说原告的病只是由来自这个或者那个的有害物质造成的。就本案而言,我认同苏格兰最高民事法院院长大部分的观点,除了一点:使被上诉人所患的疾病的有害物质,最可能的来源是什么?是气动锤子还是旋转式研磨机?在我看来,二者都是被上诉人所患疾病的来源。因此本案的真正的问题是来自旋转式研磨机的尘埃是否对于疾病的产生有实质性的作用。何为实质性的作用是一个度的问题。如果某个因素属于"法律不究细故"这个谚语所规定的例外情况,那么它就对结果的产生没有实质性的作用;反之,如果不属于这个谚语所规定的那种例外情况,则当然产生了实质性的作用。我不能理解怎么可能有某种因素,显著到不适用上述例外,然而却又细微到没有对结果产生实质性作用。

……

我的观点可以简要地总结如下。空气中的有害尘埃可以说大部分都来自

the general atmosphere of the shop, more came from the pneumatic hammers than from the swing grinders, but I think it is sufficiently proved that the dust from the grinders made a substantial contribution. The respondent, however, did not only inhale the general atmosphere of the shop: when he was working his hammer his face was directly over it and it must often have happened that dust from his hammer substantially increased the concentration of noxious dust in the air which he inhaled. It is therefore probable that much the greater proportion of the noxious dust which he inhaled over the whole period came from the hammers. But, on the other hand, some certainly came from the swing grinders, and I cannot avoid the conclusion that the proportion which came from the swing grinders was not negligible. He was inhaling the general atmosphere all the time, and there is no evidence to show that his hammer gave off noxious dust so frequently or that the concentration of noxious dust above it when it was producing dust was so much greater than the concentration in the general atmosphere, that that special concentration of dust could be said to be substantially the sole cause of his disease.

…In my opinion, it is proved not only that the swing grinders may well have contributed but that they did in fact contribute a quota of silica dust which was not negligible to the pursuer's lungs and therefore did help to produce the disease. That is sufficient to establish liability against the appellants, and I am therefore of opinion that this appeal should be dismissed.

44. Fairchild v Glenhaven Funeral Services Ltd [2002] UKHL 22, [2003] 1 AC 32

House of Lords, United Kingdom

LORD BINGHAM

My Lords, on 16 May 2002 it was announced that these three appeals would be allowed. I now give my reasons for reaching that decision.

The essential question underlying the appeals may be accurately expressed in this way. If (1) C was employed at different times and for differing periods by both A and B, and (2) A and B were both subject to a duty to take reasonable care or to take all practicable measures to prevent C inhaling asbestos dust because of the known risk that asbestos dust (if inhaled) might cause a mesothelioma, and (3) both A and B were in breach of that duty in relation to C during the periods of C's employment by each of them with the result that during both periods C inhaled excessive quantities of asbestosaa c dust, and (4) C is found to be suffering from a mesothelioma, and (5) any cause of C's mesothelioma other than the inhalation of asbestos dust at work can be effectively discounted, but (6) C cannot (because of the current limits of human science) prove, on the balance of probabilities, that his mesothelioma was the result of his inhaling asbestos dust during his employment by A or during his employment by B or during his employment by A and B taken together, is C entitled to recover damages against either A or B or against both A and B? To this

气动锤子,少部分来自旋转式研磨机。然而我认为这已经足以证明研磨机对尘埃的产生有实质性的作用。除了被上诉人呼吸了车间里的空气一事,我们须注意到在用锤子工作的时候,他的脸是直接对着这个锤子的,因此锤子产生的尘埃一定实质性地增加了他呼吸的空气中有害物质的浓度。因此,在他的整个工作期间,他所呼吸的大部分有害尘埃非常有可能是来自锤子的。然而,从另一方面来讲,肯定有部分的尘埃是来自旋转式研磨机的,而我也很难反对这么一个结论:有害尘埃来自旋转式研磨机的部分是不可忽略的。被上诉人一直在呼吸车间里的空气,而我们并没有证据去证明锤子产生的有害尘埃足够频繁,或者锤子在产生有害尘埃时所积累的有害尘埃的浓度比车间空气中整体的浓度要高得多,而锤子产生的尘埃聚积是他的疾病产生的几乎唯一的原因。

……在我看来,被上诉人已经证明含硅尘埃中不可忽视的比例是由旋转式研磨机产生的,而这个比例对于被上诉人的肺来说,确实足以导致疾病。证明了这个就足以请求几位上诉人承担责任了,因此我认为上诉应该被驳回。

44. Fairchild v Glenhaven Funeral Services Ltd [2002] UKHL 22, [2003] 1 AC 32

联合王国上议院

Bingham 大法官主笔:

各位大法官,2002 年 5 月 16 日,我们支持了三起案件的上诉。下面我将给出我们作出如此决定的理由。

该三起案件中最关键的问题可以表述如下,如果:(1)C 在不同的时间受雇于 A 和 B。(2)A 和 B 都应当对 C 尽到合理的注意义务,或者说都需要采取一切可行的措施以防止 C 吸入石棉;因为某种未知的原因,吸入石棉可能会导致间质瘤。(3)A 和 B 都在雇佣 C 的期间违反了其义务,以致 C 吸入了大量含有石棉的尘埃。(4)C 被发现罹患了间质瘤。(5)除在工作中吸入了石棉这个理由以外,其他的理由都可以被有效地排除。然而(6)C 因为现代人体科学的局限,无法根据概率平衡法证明他所患的间质瘤到底是因为他在为 A 工作时吸入的,还是为 B 工作时吸入的,还是跟二者都有关系。此时 C 是否有权单独向 A,或者单独向 B,或者向 A 和 B 二人共同请求损害赔偿?上诉法院(Brooke,Latham 和 Kay 上诉法院法官)在一份推翻了原审判决的

question (not formulated in these terms) the Court of Appeal (Brooke, Latham and Kay LJJ), in a reserved judgment of the court reported at [2002] 1 WLR 1052 , gave a negative answer. It did so because, applying the conventional "but for" test of tortious liability, it could not be held that C had proved against A that his mesothelioma would probably not have occurred but for the breach of duty by A, nor against B that his mesothelioma would probably not have occurred but for the breach of duty by B, nor against A and B that his mesothelioma would probably not have occurred but for the breach of duty by both A and B together. So C failed against both A and B. The crucial issue on appeal is whether, in the special circumstances of such a case, principle, authority or policy requires or justifies a modified approach to proof of causation.

It is common ground that in each of the three cases under appeal conditions numbered (1) to (5) above effectively obtained. ...

...

...It is not known what level of exposure to asbestos dust and fibre can be tolerated without significant risk of developing a mesothelioma, but it is known that those living in urban environments (although without occupational exposure) inhale large numbers of asbestos fibres without developing a mesothelioma. It is accepted that the risk of developing a mesothelioma increases in proportion to the quantity of asbestos dust and fibres inhaled: the greater the quantity of dust and fibre inhaled, the greater the risk. But the condition may be caused by a single fibre, or a few fibres, or many fibres: medical opinion holds none of these possibilities to be more probable than any other, and the condition once caused is not aggravated by further exposure. So if C is employed successively by A and B and is exposed to asbestos dust and fibres during each employment and develops a mesothelioma, the very strong probability is that this will have been caused by inhalation of asbestos dust containing fibres. But C could have inhaled a single fibre giving rise to his condition during employment by A, in which case his exposure by B will have had no effect on his condition; or he could have inhaled a single fibre giving rise to his condition during his employment by B, in which case his exposure by A will have had no effect on his condition; or he could have inhaled fibres during his employment by A and B which together gave rise to his condition; but medical science cannot support the suggestion that any of these possibilities is to be regarded as more probable than any other. There is no way of identifying, even on a balance of probabilities, the source of the fibre or fibres which initiated the genetic process which culminated in the malignant tumour. It is on this rock of uncertainty, reflecting the point to which medical science has so far advanced, that the three claims were rejected by the Court of Appeal and by two of the three trial judges.

Principle

...In the generality of personal injury actions, it is of course true that the claimant is required to discharge the burden of showing that the breach of which he complains caused the damage for

判决书中［案号（2002）1 WLR 1052］对此的回答（他们的判决中问题并不是如这里这样描述的）是否定的。他们这么做的原因，是因为他们对此适用了传统侵权法的必要条件理论。按照这种理论，C 没有证明如果不是因为 A 违反义务，他的间质瘤就不会发生；他也没有证明如果不是因为 B 违反义务，他的间质瘤就不会发生；他同样也没有证明如果不是因为 A 和 B 都违反了的义务，他的间质瘤就不会发生。因此，他针对 A 和 B 的诉讼都无法获得成功。这里，我们面临的最重要的焦点问题是，在这种案件的特殊情况下，原则、判例和政策是否要求，或者是否支持我们改变现有的判断因果关系的方法。

上述的三个案件的共同点是，上述条件（1）到（5）都已经满足了……
……

……我们并不知道，多大程度上暴露于含有石棉的尘埃或者石棉纤维会显著增加罹患间质瘤的风险，我们知道的是生活在一般城市环境里的人都会吸入大量的石棉纤维，但是并不会罹患间质瘤（除了那些在工作环境中暴露于石棉的人外）。公认的事实是罹患间质瘤的风险随着吸入的石棉尘埃和石棉纤维的数量的增加而增加：吸入的尘埃和纤维越多，越有可能罹患这种疾病。然而，这种疾病可能是由一根石棉纤维造成的，也可能是几根石棉纤维造成的，还可能是大量的石棉纤维造成的：按照医学观点，这几种可能性差不多，并且一旦罹患了这种疾病，继续暴露在石棉环境中并不会加重病情。这样，如果 C 依次受雇于 A 和 B，两者的工作环境都存在石棉尘埃和石棉纤维，且 C 最终罹患了间质瘤，那么他的病最有可能是因为他吸入了含有石棉纤维的尘埃引起的。但是 C 可能是在为 A 工作的期间，因为仅仅吸入了一根石棉纤维就得病了，这种情况下他在为 B 工作的期间所接触到的石棉就对他患病一事没有影响。他也可能是在为 B 工作的期间，因为仅仅吸入了一根石棉纤维就得病了，这种情况下他在为 A 工作的期间所接触到的石棉就对他患病一事没有影响。也有可能他的病是在为 A 和 B 工作期间吸入的石棉所共同造成的。然而，医疗科学并不能回答上述哪种可能比其他的可能更具有可能性。即便是基于概率平衡法，人们也很难确定到底是哪个纤维开启了最终导致恶性肿瘤产生的基因突变的进程。正是因为这一医疗科学局限产生的不确定性，上述三起案件中，原告的请求都被上诉法院拒绝了，其中两起案件中，原告的请求被一审法官拒绝了。

原则

……在一般的人身侵害案件中，原告当然应该承担证明以下事实的义务：被告因为违反原告所主张成立的某个义务，导致了原告所主张应该予以赔偿的

which he claims and to do so by showing that but for the breach he would not have suffered the damage.

The issue in these appeals does not concern the general validity and applicability of that requirement, which is not in question, but is whether in special circumstances such as those in these cases there should be any variation or relaxation of it. The overall object of tort law is to define cases in which the law may justly hold one party liable to compensate another. Are these such cases? A and B owed C a duty to protect C against a risk of a particular and very serious kind. They failed to perform that duty. As a result the risk eventuated and C suffered the very harm against which it was the duty of A and B to protect him. Had there been only one tortfeasor, C would have been entitled to recover, but because the duty owed to him was broken by two tortfeasors and not only one, he is held to be entitled to recover against neither, because of his inability to prove what is scientifically unprovable. If the mechanical application of generally accepted rules leads to such a result, there must be room to question the appropriateness of such an approach in such a case.

…

Policy

…The crux of cases such as the present, if the appellants' argument is upheld, is that an employer may be held liable for damage he has not caused. The risk is the greater where all the employers potentially liable are not before the court. This is so on the facts of each of the three appeals before the House, and is always likely to be so given the long latency of this condition and the likelihood that some employers potentially liable will have gone out of business or disappeared during that period. It can properly be said to be unjust to impose liability on a party who has not been shown, even on a balance of probabilities, to have caused the damage complained of. On the other hand, there is a strong policy argument in favour of compensating those who have suffered grave harm, at the expense of their employers who owed them a duty to protect them against that very harm and failed to do so, when the harm can only have been caused by breach of that duty and when science does not permit the victim accurately to attribute, as between several employers, the precise responsibility for the harm he has suffered. I am of opinion that such injustice as may be involved in imposing liability on a duty-breaking employer in these circumstances is heavily outweighed by the injustice of denying redress to a victim. Were the law otherwise, an employer exposing his employee to asbestos dust could obtain complete immunity against mesothelioma (but not asbestosis) claims by employing only those who had previously been exposed to excessive quantities of asbestos dust. Such a result would reflect no credit on the law.…

Conclusion

To the question posed in paragraph 2 of this opinion I would answer that where conditions (1)-(6) are satisfied C is entitled to recover against both A and B. That conclusion is in my opinion consistent with principle, and also with authority (properly understood). Where those conditions

损失。要完成这个证明责任,需要证明,若非被告违反义务,原告并不会遭受损失。

上述三起上诉案件中,这一要求在一般条件下的有效性和可适用性,不是争议焦点。争议焦点是,在上述案件涉及的那种特殊情况下,这种一般情况下的要求是不是应该得到某种变更或者软化。总体来说,侵权法的功能是在诸多案件中划定一定的范围,在这个范围内法律可以正当地要求一方对另一方承担损害赔偿责任。那么这三起案件属于这样的范围吗? A 和 B 都对 C 承担了保护其不受某种严重风险侵害的责任,然而最终,这种风险背后的事故确实发生了,C 也受到了 A 和 B 有义务防止的事故的侵害。如果仅有一个侵权人,C 毋庸置疑有权请求损害赔偿;然而,当有两个侵权人违反了对他的义务时,他却不能请求任何一个人赔偿了,因为他无法证明在科学上无法证明的事实。如果机械地适用一般规则会导致这样的一种结果,我们有必要质疑在这种情况下适用一般规则的正当性。

……

政策

……上述案件在目前的关键问题是,如果上诉人的主张得到了支持,那么雇主可能会因为并非其造成的损害而承担责任。另一个更大的风险是,并非是所有的可能应当承担责任的雇主都会出现在法庭上。上述三起上议院所审理的案件都属于这种情况,而且这种情况很可能是常态,因为间质瘤有很长的潜伏期,因此很可能潜在的应该承担责任的雇主早在这个潜伏期内就倒闭或者歇业了。要求一个没有被证明,即便是在概率平衡法下证明,确实造成损害的人承担责任,的确可以说是不公平的。然而从另一个角度来说,确实存在一个非常有利的法政策观点来支持某些损害的受害人的赔偿请求,这种赔偿请求有损他们的雇主的利益。这些雇主对受害人承担保护他们免受某种损害的义务,然而他们没有尽到这种义务,这种损害只可能因为他们的未尽义务而起,但是受害人又因为科学水平的限制,没有办法精确地在多个雇主之间找到那个确实应该负责的人。我认为,要求所有在这种情况下的违反了义务的雇主承担责任,可能是不公平的,然而这种不公平是远远轻于另一种不公平的:即不给受害人提供救济的不公平。如果法律拒绝在这种情况下要求雇主承担责任,那么要求其员工暴露于石棉尘埃下的雇主就可以完全豁免于涉及间质瘤的诉讼(不是豁免于涉及石棉的诉讼)。他们可以只雇佣那些曾经已经大量暴露于石棉尘埃下的人。这种结果将表明,法律没有任何信用……

结论

对本意见书第二段中的问题,我作出以下回答:当条件(1)到(6)都满足时,C 有权请求 A 和 B 共同对其赔偿。我的这个结论是符合现有的原则,也是符

are satisfied, it seems to me just and in accordance with common sense to treat the conduct of A and B in exposing C to a risk to which he should not have been exposed as making a material contribution to the contracting by C of a condition against which it was the duty of A and B to protect him. I consider that this conclusion is fortified by the wider jurisprudence reviewed above. Policy considerations weigh in favour of such a conclusion. It is a conclusion which follows even if either A or B is not before the court. It was not suggested in argument that C's entitlement against either A or B should be for any sum less than the full compensation to which C is entitled, although A and B could of course seek contribution against each other or any other employer liable in respect of the same damage in the ordinary way. No argument on apportionment was addressed to the House. I would in conclusion emphasise that my opinion is directed to cases in which each of the conditions specified in (1)-(6) of paragraph 2 above is satisfied and to no other case. It would be unrealistic to suppose that the principle here affirmed will not over time be the subject of incremental and analogical development. Cases seeking to develop the principle must be decided when and as they arise. For the present, I think it unwise to decide more than is necessary to resolve these three appeals which, for all the foregoing reasons, I concluded should be allowed.

Section 2. Concurrent and Sccessive Causation

45. Dillon v. Twin State Gas & Electric Co., 85 N.H. 449, 163 A. 111 (1932)

Supreme Court of New Hampshire, United States

The defendant maintained wires to carry electric current over a public bridge in Berlin.

The decedent age 14 and other boys had been accustomed for a number of years to play on the bridge in the daytime, habitually climbing the sloping girders to the horizontal ones, on which they walked and sat and from which they sometimes dived into the river. No current passed through the wires in the daytime except by chance.

The decedent while sitting on a horizontal girder at a point where the wires from the post to the lamp were in front of him or at his side and while facing outwards from the side of the bridge, leaned over, lost his balance, instinctively threw out his arm and took hold of one of the wires with his right hand to save himself from falling. The wires happened to be charged with a high voltage current at the time and he was electrocuted.

Further facts appear in the opinion.

Transferred…on the defendant's exception to the denial of its motion for a directed verdict.

Allen, J.

…The circumstances of the decedent's death give rise to an unusual issue of its cause. In leaning over from the girder and losing his balance he was entitled to no protection from the

合判例的（当然要作正确解读才行）。当上述条件都满足时，我认为，A 和 B 让 C 暴露在一个他不该暴露的风险下，对 C 罹患一个 A 和 B 有义务保护他不会罹患的疾病这件事，是有实质性的作用的。我这么想完全符合正义的要求，也符合一般常识的要求。我的这个结论也得到了上面引用的法理的支持。政策考量也支持这个结论。这个结论是正确的，即便在 A 和 B 没有出现在法庭上的场合。C 对 A 或者 B 的求偿金额也不应低于他所应当获得的全部赔偿金额，这不妨碍 A 或者 B 采取通常的手段向另一方或者其他应该对同一损害承担责任的雇主追偿。对各责任人之间的内部责任分配问题，上议院无需答复。我想总结强调一下，我的意见是针对那些满足第二段中条件（1）到条件（6）的案件的，不是针对任何其他案件的。我们在本案中确定的原则永远不会随着时间的推移成为渐进的和类推的发展，这是不现实的，但要发展这个原则，应该等到相应的案件发生时，通过判决这些案件来发展它。就当下而言，我认为我们如果要就解决这三个案件以外的目的提出其他的主张是不明智的。基于上述理由，我认为对该三起案件的上诉应予支持。

第二节 并发因果关系和继发因果关系

45. Dillon v. Twin State Gas & Electric Co., 85 N.H. 449, 163 A. 111 (1932)

美国新罕布什尔州最高法院

被告从事一条电线的维护工作，该电线跨过一座公共大桥输送电流。

死者 14 岁，和其他男孩多年来已经惯于白天在桥上玩耍，他们习惯性地从斜梁爬到横梁上，在横梁上行走、坐下，有时还从那里跳入河中。除了偶然情况之外，白天从未有电流通过电线。

死者坐在横梁上时，灯柱到路灯的电线正好在他所在位置的面前或者旁边。他面朝桥外，探出身子时失去了平衡。他本能地伸出手臂，用右手抓住了一根电线以使自己不会摔下去。在他触电身亡时，电线刚好有高压电通过。

事实情况详情见于法院意见书。

被告提出的指示裁断申请被拒绝，被告对此提出异议……案件被移送。

Allen 法官主笔：

……死者的死亡环境引发了一个不寻常的起因问题。死者从桥梁上俯身并失去平衡，没有理由从被告那里获得保护而确保不摔倒。被告唯一的责任

defendant to keep from falling. Its only liability was in exposing him to the danger of charged wires. If but for the current in the wires he would have fallen down on the floor of the bridge or into the river, he would without doubt have been either killed or seriously injured. Although he died from electrocution, yet if by reason of his preceding loss of balance he was bound to fall except for the intervention of the current, he either did not have long to live or was to be maimed. In such an outcome of his loss of balance the defendant deprived him, not of a life of normal expectancy, but of one too short to be given pecuniary allowance, in one alternative, and not of normal, but of limited, earning capacity, in the other.

If it were found that he would have thus fallen with death probably resulting, the defendant would not be liable unless for conscious suffering found to have been sustained from the shock. In that situation his life or earning capacity had no value. To constitute actionable negligence there must be damage, and damage is limited to those elements the statute prescribes.

If it should be found that but for the current he would have fallen with serious injury, then the loss of life or earning capacity resulting from the electrocution would be measured by its value in such injured condition. Evidence that he would be crippled would be taken into account in the same manner as though he had already been crippled.

His probable future but for the current thus bears on liability as well as damages. Whether the shock from the current threw him back on the girder or whether he would have recovered his balance, with or without the aid of the wire he took hold of if it had not been charged, are issues of fact, as to which the evidence as it stands may lead to different conclusions.

Exception overruled.

46. Kingston v. Chicago & N.W. Ry.Co., 191 Wis. 610, 211 N.W. 913 (1927)

Supreme Court of Wisconsin, United States

Owen, J.

…We…have this situation: A fire was set by sparks emitted from defendant's locomotive. This fire, according to the finding of the jury, constituted a proximate cause of the destruction of plaintiff's property. This finding we find to be well supported by the evidence. We have the northwest fire, of unknown origin. This fire, according to the finding of the jury, also constituted a proximate cause of the destruction of the plaintiff's property. This finding we also find to be well supported by the evidence. We have a union of these two fires 940 feet north of plaintiff's property, from which point the united fire bore down upon and destroyed the property. We therefore have two separate, independent, and distinct agencies, each of which constituted the proximate cause of plaintiff's damage, and either of which, in the absence of the other, would have accomplished such result.

It is settled in the law of negligence that any one of two or more joint tortfeasors, or one of

是不应该使死者面临通电线路的危险。如果不是因为电线中的电流，死者可能会跌倒在桥面上或河中，毫无疑问，死者要么会丧生，要么严重受伤。尽管死者死于触电，但是如果他之前失去了平衡，他肯定会跌倒，只是电流使他未能跌下，他要么丧生，要么落下残疾。作为失去平衡的结果，被告并没有夺走他的正常寿命，只是剥夺了一个短暂得不足以获得经济收入的生命，即没有夺走他正常的工作能力，而是夺走了他有限的工作能力。

如果调查发现死者跌落后可能死亡，那么被告将不需要承担责任，除非发现死者因为受到电击而在意识清醒的情况下遭受了痛苦。在那样的情况下，他的生命或工作便没有价值。要构成可以起诉的过失就必须要有损害，而损害的认定要限于法令规定的要素中。

如果发现若非有电流，死者跌落后会受到重伤，那么由于触电而失去的生命或生产能力将由跌落受伤造成的最终价值来衡量。如果有证据证明他的腿会受伤，那么尽管他的腿已经受伤，也应该考虑这些证据。

如果没有该电流，他还会有未来，所以本案才涉及责任和损害赔偿。无论是电击的力量会不会将他击回桥梁上，还是他有没有抓住未通电的电线来重新恢复了平衡，这些都是事实问题，它们所显示的证据会引出不同的结论。

异议被推翻。

46. Kingston v. Chicago & N.W. Ry.Co., 191 Wis. 610, 211 N.W. 913 (1927)

美国威斯康星州最高法院

Owen 法官主笔：

……我们……面对的情况是这样的：一场大火由被告火车头溅出的火星引起。根据陪审团调查的结果，这场大火成为毁灭原告房产的近因。我们认为这一结论具有充分的证据支持。我们知道西北方向有不明原因的大火。根据陪审团的调查，这场大火同样也构成了毁灭原告房产的近因。我们认为这一结论也具有充分的证据支持。两场大火在距离原告房产北方 940 英尺的地点结合在了一起，从这一点开始，大火向南压进，摧毁了原告的房产。因此，我们看到的是两个单独的、相互独立的、不同的原因行为，每一个都构成了原告损失的近因，如果离开了其中任何一个原因行为，另一个原因行为也会产生这样的结果。

如果两名或多名共同侵权行为人中的任何一方，或两名或多名不法行为人

two or more wrongdoers whose concurring acts of negligence result in injury, are each individually responsible for the entire damage resulting from their joint or concurrent acts of negligence. This rule also obtains "where two causes, each attributable to the negligence of a responsible person, concur in producing an injury to another, either of which causes would produce it regardless of the other,…because, whether the concurrence be intentional, actual, or constructive, each wrongdoer, in effect, adopts the conduct of his co-actor, and for the further reason that it is impossible to apportion the damage or to say that either perpetrated any distinct injury that can be separated from the whole. The whole loss must necessarily be considered and treated as an entirety." Cook v. M., St. P. & S.S.M.R. Co., 98 Wis. 624 (74 N.W. 561), at p. 642.…

From our present consideration of the subject we are not disposed to criticise the doctrine which exempts from liability a wrongdoer who sets a fire which unites with a fire originating from natural causes, such as lightning, not attributable to any human agency, resulting in damage. It is also conceivable that a fire so set might unite with a fire of so much greater proportions, such as a raging forest fire, as to be enveloped or swallowed up by the greater holocaust, and its identity destroyed, so that the greater fire could be said to be an intervening or superseding cause. But we have no such situation here. These fires were of comparatively equal rank. If there was any difference in their magnitude or threatening aspect, the record indicates that the northeast fire was the larger fire and was really regarded as the menacing agency. At any rate there is no intimation or suggestion that the northeast fire was enveloped and swallowed up by the northwest fire. We will err on the side of the defendant if we regard the two fires as of equal rank.

According to well settled principles of negligence, it is undoubted that if the proof disclosed the origin of the northwest fire, even though its origin be attributed to a third person, the railroad company, as the originator of the northeast fire, would be liable for the entire damage. There is no reason to believe that the northwest fire originated from any other than human agency. It was a small fire. It had traveled over a limited area. It had been in existence but for a day. For a time it was thought to have been extinguished. It was not in the nature of a raging forest fire. The record discloses nothing of natural phenomena which could have given rise to the fire. It is morally certain that it was set by some human agency.

Now the question is whether the railroad company, which is found to have been responsible for the origin of the northeast fire, escapes liability because the origin of the northwest fire is not identified, although there is no reason to believe that it had any other than human origin. An affirmative answer to that question would certainly make a wrongdoer a favorite of the law at the expense of an innocent sufferer. The injustice of such a doctrine sufficiently impeaches the logic upon which it is founded. Where one who has suffered damage by fire proves the origin of a fire and the course of that fire up to the point of the destruction of his property, one has certainly established liability on the part of the originator of the fire. Granting that the union of that fire with

中的任何一方同时实施了过失行为并造成了损害，那么每一方都需要对他们的共同或并存的过失行为造成的整个损害承担责任，这在关于过失的法律规定中已经有了定论。该规则还适用于"当两个原因中的每个原因都促成了责任人的过失行为，两个原因同时发生造成了他人的损害，那么无论另一个原因的情况如何，两个原因都成为造成损害的原因……因为无论同时发生的两个原因是故意的、现实的还是推定的，事实上每个不法行为人都采取了其共同行为人的行为，更因为对损害进行分摊是不可能的，换句话说，其中一方造成的损害具有独特性，以至于可以从整体损害中分离出来，这是不可能的。有必要将整个损失作为一个整体来考虑和处理"。［Cook v. M., St. P. & S. S. M. R. Co., 98 Wis. 624（74 N.W. 561），at p. 642。］……

　　其中一场大火由自然原因引起，如闪电，并非人为所致，造成了损害，而不法行为人引发的大火与前者相结合，从我们现在关于这个案件的考虑出发，我们不愿对免除不法行为人责任的法律学说进行批评。还可以想象的是，这样引发的大火还可以与更大范围的大火相结合，如肆虐的森林大火，它自身都可能被包围或被更大的灾难所吞没，其本身被完全毁灭，这样联合之后的大火可以被认为是介入原因或替代原因。但是现在的情况并非如此。两场大火的大小都差不多。如果两场大火在规模和威胁程度方面存在差别的话，案卷显示东北方面的大火规模更大，实际上被认为是具有威胁性的原因行为。无论如何，没有迹象显示或暗示东北方向的大火被西北方向的大火包围和吞并。如果我们将两场大火视为同等规模的话，那么我们便过于偏袒被告。

　　根据已成定论的过失责任原则，毫无疑问，如果有证据证明西北方向的大火源自何处，哪怕大火由第三方引发，铁路公司作为东北大火的始作俑者也应该对整个损失承担责任。没有任何理由使我们相信西北大火不是由人为因素引起。那是一场小火灾，只影响到了有限的区域，其持续的时间只有一天。曾经人们还以为火已经被扑灭。这场火灾完全算不上是肆虐的森林大火。案卷显示，自然现象不可能引发这场火灾。通常可以肯定的是它是由某种人为原因引起的。

　　现在的问题是，尽管没有理由认为西北大火不是人为引起，但是西北大火的起因仍没有被查明，那么引起东北大火的铁路公司是否能够免于承担责任。如果回答"是"，那么不法行为人在法律上的获利将建立在无辜受害人损失的基础上。这种法律学说体现出不公正性，过度破坏了该法律学说存在的逻辑基础。当遭受火灾损失的一方证明了火灾的起因以及火灾如何发展到足以摧毁其财产的程度时，那么他已经证明了引发火灾的人需要承担责任。

another of natural origin, or with another of much greater proportions, is available as a defense, the burden is on the defendant to show that by reason of such union with a fire of such character the fire set by him was not the proximate cause of the damage. No principle of justice requires that the plaintiff be placed under the burden of specifically identifying the origin of both fires in order to recover the damages for which either or both fires are responsible....

...There being no attempt on the part of the defendant to prove that the northwest fire was due to an irresponsible origin, that is, an origin not attributable to a human being, and the evidence in the case affording no reason to believe that it had an origin not attributable to a human being, and it appearing that the northeast fire, for the origin of which the defendant is responsible, was a proximate cause of plaintiff's loss, the defendant is responsible for the entire amount of that loss. While under some circumstances a wrongdoer is not responsible for damage which would have occurred in the absence of his wrongful act, even though such wrongful act was a proximate cause of the accident, that doctrine does not obtain "where two causes, each attributable to the negligence of a responsible person, concur in producing an injury to another, either of which causes would produce it regardless of the other." This is because "it is impossible to apportion the damage or to say that either perpetrated any distinct injury that can be separated from the whole," and to permit each of two wrongdoers to plead the wrong of the other as a defense to his own wrongdoing would permit both wrongdoers to escape and penalize the innocent party who has been damaged by their wrongful acts.

The fact that the northeast fire was set by the railroad company, which fire was a proximate cause of plaintiff's damage, is sufficient to affirm the judgment. This conclusion renders it unnecessary to consider other grounds of liability stressed in respondent's brief.

By the Court. Judgment affirmed.

47. Baker v Willoughby [1970] AC 467

House of Lords, United Kingdom

LORD REID.

My Lords, the appellant was knocked down by the respondent's car about the middle of a straight road crossing Mitcham Common. The road is 33 feet wide at this point and there was a 40 m.p.h. limit in operation. There was not much traffic, the time being Saturday morning. The trial judge held both parties to blame and apportioned 75 per cent. liability to the respondent. The Court of Appeal altered this and held each 50 per cent. liable. The first question in the case is whether the Court of Appeal were right in so doing. ... In my opinion it is quite possible that the motorist may be very much more to blame than the pedestrian. and in the present case I can see no reason to disagree with the trial judge's assessment. I would therefore restore the trial judge on this issue.

即使能够以这场火灾与其他自然原因引发的火灾相互结合,或者和其他更大规模的火灾相互结合作为辩护理由。但是被告也负有举证责任,即需要证明即使与具有这些特征的大火结合,被告引起的大火也不是造成损害的近因。没有任何正义的原则规定原告必须先证明引发两场大火的原因是什么,然后才能获得两场大火造成的损失的救济……

……被告方也不需要证明引发西北大火的原因不具有可责性,也就是说,非人为因素引起,而且本案中的证据也没有提供任何理由使人相信火灾原因与人为因素无关,此外,被告引起的东北大火是造成原告损失的近因,那么被告也需要对全部损失承担责任。尽管在一些情况下,不法行为人对损失不需要承担责任,因为即使其不法行为没有实施也会发生损失,尽管这种不法行为是事故产生的近因,而该法律学说也不适用于"当两个原因中的每个原因都促成了责任人的过失,两个原因同时发生造成了他人的损害,那么无论另一个原因的情况如何,两个原因都成为造成损害的原因"的情况。这是因为,"对损害进行分摊,或者换句话说,其中一方造成的可区别出的损害可以从整体损害中分离出来,是不可能的"。允许不法行为人双方各自以对方的不法行为开脱自己不法行为,会使不法行为人双方逃避责任,而蒙受了他们不法行为造成损失的无辜受害人的利益将受到侵犯。

东北大火由铁路公司引起,是造成原告损失的近因,这个事实足以维持原判。这一结论使得我们没有必要考虑被告辩护状中提到的其他责任基础。

本院维持原判。

47. Baker v Willoughby [1970] AC 467

联合王国上议院

Reid 大法官主笔:

各位大法官,上诉人在一条横贯 Mitcham Common 的公路的中间被被上诉人的车撞倒了。在发生事故的地点,路宽 33 英尺,且有 40 英里每小时的限速。当时此处车辆不多,且处于星期六的早上。一审法官认定双方都有过错,而被上诉人应当承担 75% 的责任份额。上诉法院则将各自的责任份额都定在了 50%。本案的第一个焦点问题是上诉法院这么做是否正确。……在我看来,车辆驾驶者极有可能比行人更具有可归责性,因此在本案中我没有理由反对一审法官的判断。因此,在这个问题上,我将恢复一审法官的认定。

The second question is more difficult. It relates to the proper measure of damages. The car accident occurred on September 12, 1964. The trial took place on February 26, 1968. But meanwhile on November 29, 1967, the appellant had sustained a further injury and the question is whether or to what extent the damages which would otherwise have been awarded in respect of the car accident must be reduced by reason of the occurrence of this second injury.

There is no doubt that it is proper to lead evidence at the trial as to any events or developments between the date of the accident and the date of the trial which are relevant for the proper assessment of damages. The plaintiff may have died (*Williamson v. John I. Thorneycroft & Co. Ltd.* [1940] 2 K.B. 658): or the needs of the widow (*Curwen v. James* [1963] 1 W.L.R. 748) or of the children (*Mead v. Clarke, Chapman & Co. Ltd.* [1956] 1 W.L.R. 76) may have become less because of her remarriage. and it is always proper to take account of developments with regard to the injuries which were caused by the defendant's tort: those developments may show that any assessment of damages that might have been made shortly after the accident can now be seen to be either too small or too large. The question here is how far it is proper to take into account the effects of a second injury which was in no way connected with the first.

As a result of the car accident the appellant sustained fairly severe injury to his left leg and ankle, with the result that his ankle was stiff and his condition might get worse. So he suffered pain, loss of such amenities of life as depend on ability to move freely and a certain loss of earning capacity. The trial judge did not deal with these matters separately. He assessed the whole damage at £1,600 and making allowance for the appellant's contributory negligence awarded £1,200 with minor special damage.

After the accident the appellant tried various kinds of work, finding some too heavy by reason of his partial incapacity. In November 1967 he was engaged in sorting scrap metal and while he was alone one day two men came in, demanded money, and, when they did not get it, one of them shot at him. The shot inflicted such serious injuries to his already damaged leg that it had to be amputated. Apparently he made a fairly good recovery but his disability is now rather greater than it would have been if he had not suffered this second injury. He now has an artificial limb whereas he would have had a stiff leg.

The appellant argues that the loss which he suffered from the car accident has not been diminished by his second injury. He still suffers the same kind of loss of the amenities of life and he still suffers from reduced capacity to earn though these may have been to some extent increased. and he will still suffer these losses for as long as he would have done because it is not said that the second injury curtailed his expectation of life.

The respondent on the other hand argues that the second injury removed the very limb from which the earlier disability had stemmed, and that therefore no loss suffered thereafter can be attributed to the respondent's negligence. He says that the second injury submerged or obliterated

第二个问题则复杂得多。它涉及我们如何计算损害赔偿金的问题。车祸发生在 1964 年 9 月 12 日。庭审发生在 1968 年 2 月 26 日。然而在 1967 年 11 月 29 日，上诉人却遭受了另一次伤害。这样，争议焦点就是：因为车祸而产生的损害赔偿金是否应该因为第二次受伤的产生而减少？如果是，那么减少多少？

我们允许双方在庭审中出示任何证据去证明事故发生到庭审开始之间这一段时间发生的任何事件或者事态的发展，为了更好地评估损害赔偿金额，这一点是毋庸置疑的。这个期间内，原告可能死亡［*Williamson v John I. Thorneycroft & Co. Ltd.*（1940）2 K.B. 658］，或者遗孀［*Curwen v James*（1963） 1 W.L.R. 748］或子女的必需品因为遗孀的再婚而减少［*Mead v Clarke, Chapman & Co. Ltd.*（1956）1 W.L.R. 76］。同样，我们也要考虑在这个期间内被告所造成的损害的发展情况：这种发展可能显示在事故发生之后很短时间即做出的对损害赔偿金额的评估，可能太少或者太多了。本案中的问题是，在多大程度上，我们应该考虑与第一次受伤无关的第二次受伤的影响。

车祸严重地伤害了上诉人的左腿和左脚踝。他的脚踝因此变得僵硬，情况可能还会恶化。他因此遭受了痛苦，失去了生命中许多依赖于自由移动的美好事物，也失去了一定的挣钱能力。一审法院没有分别评估这些事项，而是给出了一个总体的损害的金额：1 600 英镑。而考虑到上诉人也有过失这一事实，判决上诉人可以获得 1 200 英镑的赔偿以及一些细小的特别事项的赔偿。

在车祸之后，上诉人尝试了多种工作。因为他身体的部分残疾，这些工作中的有些部分对他来说太沉重了。在 1967 年 11 月，他在从事为废旧金属分类的工作。有一天，他只有独自一人在时，两个人闯了进来，向他索要金钱；因为没能如愿，其中一个人枪击了他。枪伤使得他本已残疾的左腿雪上加霜，最终只能截肢。显然，他康复得还不错，但是如果没有第二次受伤的话，他的残疾状况也许要比现在好得多。他那原本僵直的左腿，现在是一只义肢。

上诉人主张，他第二次遭受的伤害并没有减少他车祸受到的伤害。他和之前一样依然不能享受生命的美好，他挣钱的能力依然减少了，甚至因为后来这次事故减少得更多了，他承受这一切的时间依然是那么长，因为第二次受伤并没有缩短他的预期寿命。

被上诉人一方则主张，第二次受伤使得上诉人的左腿被截肢，导致了原先可以避免的残疾。因此，自那时起他所遭受的损失就不能归咎于被上诉人的过失了。他主张第二次的伤害掩盖并消灭了第一次伤害的效果，这之后的

the effect of the first and that all loss thereafter must be attributed to the second injury. The trial judge rejected this argument which he said was more ingenious than attractive. But it was accepted by the Court of Appeal.

The respondent's argument was succinctly put to your Lordships by his counsel. He could not run before the second injury: he cannot run now. But the cause is now quite different. The former cause was an injured leg but now he has no leg and the former cause can no longer operate. His counsel was inclined to agree that if the first injury had caused some neurosis or other mental disability, that disability might be regarded as still flowing from the first accident: even if it had been increased by the second accident the respondent might still have to pay for that part which he caused. I agree with that and I think that any distinction between a neurosis and a physical injury depends on a wrong view of what is the proper subject for compensation. A man is not compensated for the physical injury: he is compensated for the loss which he suffers as a result of that injury. His loss is not in having a stiff leg: it is in his inability to lead a full life, his inability to enjoy those amenities which depend on freedom of movement and his inability to earn as much as he used to earn or could have earned if there had been no accident. In this case the second injury did not diminish any of these. So why should it be regarded as having obliterated or superseded them?

If it were the case that in the eye of the law an effect could only have one cause then the respondent might be right. It is always necessary to prove that any loss for which damages can be given was caused by the defendant's negligent act. But it is a commonplace that the law regards many events as having two causes: that happens whenever there is contributory negligence for then the law says that the injury was caused both by the negligence of the defendant and by the negligence of the plaintiff. and generally it does not matter which negligence occurred first in point of time.

…

…exemplify the general rule that a wrongdoer must take the plaintiff (or his property) as he finds him: that may be to his advantage or disadvantage. In the present case the robber is not responsible or liable for the damage caused by the respondent: he would only have to pay for additional loss to the appellant by reason of his now having an artificial limb instead of a stiff leg.

…

If the later injury suffered before the date of the trial either reduces the disabilities from the injury for which the defendant is liable, or shortens the period during which they will be suffered by the plaintiff, then the defendant will have to pay less damages. But if the later injuries merely become a concurrent cause of the disabilities caused by the injury inflicted by the defendant, then in my view they cannot diminish the damages. Suppose that the plaintiff has to spend a month in bed before the trial because of some illness unconnected with the original injury, the defendant

所有的损失因此都应该归于第二次伤害。一审法官认为这种论证非常精巧，但是却并没有买账。然而这种论证却得到了上诉法院的支持。

现在，被上诉人的律师将其观点呈现在诸位大法官面前。原告在第二次事故之前无法奔跑；他现在依然无法奔跑。然而不能奔跑的原因却大不一样。之前那是因为他的腿受伤了，而现在他根本就没腿了，因此之前的原因就不再是原因了。被上诉人的律师倾向于同意，如果第一次的伤害导致了原告患上某些神经性疾病或者其他的精神残障，这种残障还可以依然算作第一次事故的结果：即便第二次事故增加了这种残障，被上诉人依然应该为他所导致的那一部分承担赔偿责任。这一点我倒是同意的。但是我认为去区分神经性的伤害和身体的伤害，其实是弄错了到底什么是赔偿的目标。一个人并非因为他遭受了身体损害而获得赔偿：他是因为身体损害所带来的那些损失而获得的赔偿。他的损失并非是一只僵直的左腿：他的损失是他无法再过正常的生活，是无法再享受那些依赖于自由行动的美好事物，是无法再挣以前挣的数额或者在没有事故时可能挣的数额。在这个意义上，第二次伤害其实并没有减损任何这些问题，遑论消除或者了替代了它们？

如果法律对于一个后果只允许存在一个原因，那么被上诉人就是对的。任何的损失，如果要获得赔偿，都需要证明该损失是由被告的过失行为引起的。然而，很多事件都有两个原因，这在法律上是很常见的：在与有过失的场合就是这样，这时法律认为损害是由原被告的过失共同导致的，而且通常法律不关心谁的过失在先。

……

……例证了一项一般规则：侵权人应该让原告（或他的财产）回到侵权发生时的状态：这可能对原告有利，也可能不利。在本案中，歹徒并不对被上诉人造成的损害负责：他只需要就上诉人因为多了一条假腿（而不再是一条僵直的腿）而产生的额外损失承担赔偿责任。

……

如果第二次伤害在庭审之前减少了原告残疾（被告应该负责）的程度，或者缩短了原告需要承受残疾的时间，被告确实可以减少其赔偿金额。然而，如果第二次伤害仅仅是原告承受的、被告导致的残疾的共同原因，那么在我看来就不能减少被告应该赔偿的数额。假设原告在庭审前因为某种和最初的伤害无关的原因而需要卧床一个月，被告不能因此就说他不需要为那一个月付钱：在那个月里，最初的伤害和新的疾病都是原告不能工作的共同原因，

cannot say that he does not have to pay anything in respect of that month: during that month the original injuries and the new illness are concurrent causes of his inability to work and that does not reduce the damages.

LORD PEARSON

The second question is, as my noble and learned friend has said, more difficult. There is a plausible argument for the defendant on the following lines. The original accident, for which the defendant is liable, inflicted on the plaintiff a permanently injured left ankle, which caused pain from time to time, diminished his mobility and so reduced his earning capacity, and was likely to lead to severe arthritis. The proper figure of damages for those consequences of the accident, as assessed by the judge before making his apportionment, was £1,600. That was the proper figure for those consequences if they were likely to endure for a normal period and run a normal course. But the supervening event, when the robbers shot the plaintiff in his left leg, necessitated an amputation of the left leg above the knee. The consequences of the original accident therefore have ceased. He no longer suffers pain in his left ankle, because there no longer is a left ankle. He will never have the arthritis. There is no longer any loss of mobility through stiffness or weakness of the left ankle, because it is no longer there. The injury to the left ankle, resulting from the original accident, is not still operating as one of two concurrent causes both producing discomfort and disability. It is not operating at all nor causing anything. The present state of disablement, with the stump and the artificial leg on the left side, was caused wholly by the supervening event and not at all by the original accident. Thus the consequences of the original accident have been submerged and obliterated by the greater consequences of the supervening event.

That is the argument, and it is formidable. But it must not be allowed to succeed, because it produces manifest injustice. The supervening event has not made the plaintiff less lame nor less disabled nor less deprived of amenities. It has not shortened the period over which he will be suffering. It has made him more lame, more disabled, more deprived of amenities. He should not have less damages through being worse off than might have been expected.

The nature of the injustice becomes apparent if the supervening event is treated as a tort (as indeed it was) and if one envisages the plaintiff suing the robbers who shot him. They would be entitled, as the saying is, to "take the plaintiff as they find him." *(Performance Cars Ltd. v. Abraham* [1962] 1 Q.B. 33) They have not injured and disabled a previously fit and able-bodied man. They have only made an already lame and disabled man more lame and more disabled. Take, for example, the reduction of earnings. The original accident reduced his earnings from £x per week to £y per week, and the supervening event further reduced them from £y per week to £z per week. If the defendant's argument is correct, there is, as Mr. Griffiths has pointed out, a gap. The plaintiff recovers from the defendant the £x-y not for the whole period of the remainder of his working life, but only for the short period up to the date of the supervening event. The robbers are

但这并不能减少被告的赔偿金额。

Pearson 大法官主笔：

如我那高贵而博学的朋友所言，第二个问题更加困难。下面有这么一种站在被告这边的论证。被告应该承担引发责任的最初的事故——使原告的脚踝永久地受伤了，使他时常感到疼痛，减损了他行动的能力，因此减少了他挣钱的能力，还可能让他罹患关节炎。一审法官就上述后果所确定的赔偿金额，在不考虑与有过失的情况下，是 1 600 英镑。这个金额对上述的后果来说，是正确的，但是这仅仅是在这些后果将持续正常的时间，且按照正常方向发展的情况下。然而，当后续时间发生时，当歹徒枪击了原告的左腿时，原告左腿的脚踝以上的部分都需要截肢。这样，最初的事故造成的后果其实都消失了。原告不再因为他的左脚踝而伤痛，因为他根本就没有左脚踝了。他也不会再得关节炎了。他也不会再因为他的左脚踝的僵硬而虚弱、减损行动能力，因为左脚踝根本就不存在。他因为最初的事故而遭受的左脚踝上的伤，并不是导致其痛苦和残疾的两个共同原因之一。这个伤根本不再是任何事情的原因了。原告现在的残疾的状态，他的左腿处的残肢和义肢，完全是由后续事件导致的，而完全不是由最初的事故导致的。这样，最初的事故的后果因为后续事件的出现，而被掩盖和消灭了。

论证就是这样，非常精彩。但是这种论证不能成立，因为它带来了肉眼可见的不公。后续事件并没有减轻原告瘸腿的程度，没有减轻其残疾的程度，更没有减少其美好生活被剥夺的程度。后续事件也并没有缩短原告需要忍受这一切的时间。后续事件使得原告变得更瘸了，变得更残疾了，剥夺了更多他生活中的美好事物。总不能因为他变得比预期更差了而说他损失得更少了吧？

如果我们把后续事件当作是一个侵权行为（它也确实是），然后想象一下原告起诉了枪击他的两个歹徒，那么我们能显而易见地看出被告的论证的不公正之处。这两名歹徒只需要"把原告带回到他们伤害他的时候"。[*Performance Cars Ltd. v Abraham*（1962）1 Q.B. 33.] 这两名歹徒并没有伤害并致残一名之前是健康而正常的人。他们只是让一位之前已经瘸腿且残疾的人更加得瘸腿和残疾了。我们以原告所丧失的收入为例。最初的事故让他的收入由每周 X 英镑降为了每周 Y 英镑，后续则将其收入由每周 Y 英镑降到了 Z 英镑。如果我们赞同了被告的论证，那么正如 Griffiths 先生指出的那样，会产生一个问题：原告从被告处获得的 X-Y 英镑的补偿将不再是针对他的整个剩下的工作年龄，而是到后续事件发生之前这个很短的时间。而这两名歹

liable only for the £y-z from the date of the supervening event onwards. In the Court of Appeal an ingenious attempt was made to fill the gap by holding that the damages recoverable from the later tortfeasors (the robbers) would include a novel head of damage, viz., the diminution of the plaintiff's damages recoverable from the original tortfeasor (the defendant). I doubt whether that would be an admissible head of damage: it looks too remote. In any case it would not help the plaintiff, if the later tortfeasors could not be found or were indigent and uninsured. These later tortfeasors cannot have been insured in respect of the robbery which they committed.

 I think a solution of the theoretical problem can be found in cases such as this by taking a comprehensive and unitary view of the damage caused by the original accident. Itemization of the damages by dividing them into heads and sub-heads is often convenient, but is not essential. In the end judgment is given for a single lump sum of damages and not for a total of items set out under heads and sub-heads. The original accident caused what may be called a "devaluation" of the plaintiff, in the sense that it produced a general reduction of his capacity to do things, to earn money and to enjoy life. For that devaluation the original tortfeasor should be and remain responsible to the full extent, unless before the assessment of the damages something has happened which either diminishes the devaluation (e.g. if there is an unexpected recovery from some of the adverse effects of the accident) or by shortening the expectation of life diminishes the period over which the plaintiff will suffer from the devaluation. If the supervening event is a tort, the second tortfeasor should be responsible for the additional devaluation caused by him.

徒仅仅对后续事故发生之后的 Y-Z 英镑的损失负责。上诉法院发明了一个聪明的方法来解决这个问题：他们指出原告可以向后来的侵权人（就是两位歹徒）请求赔偿的事项多一项，即原告向最初的侵权人（被告）的赔偿金额因为后续时间而减少的部分。而我则怀疑这种事项是否应该作为可以赔偿的事项：这里的因果关系太遥远了。而且，这种方法并不能在任何意义上帮到原告。后面的侵权人确实不可能有保险，因为没有人会去为抢劫投保。

我觉得从全面而统一的角度来考察最初的事故所带来的损害能够解决这类案件中的理论问题。将原告所受的损害分解为一项一项的赔偿项目，在很多时候是很方便的做法，然而这并不是必须的。最终，判决书是给出了一个总体的赔偿数额，而不是先认定一系列的赔偿项目再求和。最初的事故在某种意义上造成了原告的"贬值"，这里所谓"贬值"的意思是事故减少了他做事情的能力、挣钱的能力和享受生活的能力。最初事故的侵权人对于这种贬值，应该一直承担全部责任，除非在评估损害赔偿金额之前，有别的什么事减少了这种贬值（比如原告奇迹般地居然从事故带来的某些副作用中康复了）或者通过缩短原告的预期生存时间而减少了原告承受这种贬值的时长。而若后续的事件也是个侵权行为，那么第二个侵权人则要为受害人承受的额外的贬值部分承担责任。

Chapter 5. Trespass to Land and Nuisance

Section 1. Trespass to Land and Nuisance in US Cases

48. Peters v. Archambault, 361 Mass. 91, 278 N.E.2d 729 (1972)

Supreme Judicial Court of Massachusetts, United States

Cutter, Justice.

The plaintiffs by this bill seek to compel the defendants (the Archambaults) to remove a portion of the Archambault house which encroaches on the plaintiffs' land in Marshfield. The plaintiffs and the Archambaults own adjoining ocean-front lots. Both lots are registered (G.L. c. 185). Neither certificate of title shows the Archambault lot to have any rights in the plaintiffs' lot.

The Archambaults' predecessor in title obtained a building permit in 1946 and built a house partly on their own lot and partly on the plaintiffs' lot, of which the total area is about 4,900 square feet. Each lot had a frontage of only fifty feet on the adjacent way. The encroachment contains 465 square feet, and the building extends fifteen feet, three inches, onto the plaintiffs' lot, to a depth of thirty-one feet, four inches. The trial judge found that it will be expensive to remove the encroaching portion of the Archambaults' building. He ruled (correctly, so far as appears from his subsidiary findings and from the small portion of the evidence which has been reported) that there had been established no estoppel of, or laches on the part of, the plaintiffs in seeking to have the encroachment removed. It appears from the evidence that the Archambaults bought their lot from one vendor and the plaintiffs on June 14, 1966, bought their lot from another vendor. The judge found no evidence of any permission by the owners of the plaintiffs' lot for the encroachment. The encroachment was discovered in July 14, 1966, when the plaintiffs had a survey of their land made.

A final decree ordered the removal of the encroachment. The Archambaults appealed. The judge adopted as his report of material facts the findings already summarized.

1. In Massachusetts a landowner is ordinarily entitled to mandatory equitable relief to compel removal of a structure significantly encroaching on his land, even though the encroachment was unintentional or negligent and the cost of removal is substantial in comparison to any injury suffered by the owner of the lot upon which the encroachment has taken place. ...In rare cases, referred to in our decisions as "exceptional," ...courts of equity have refused to grant a mandatory

第五章 侵入土地与妨害

第一节 美国法上的侵入土地与妨害

48. Peters v. Archambault, 361 Mass. 91, 278 N.E.2d 729 (1972)

美国马萨诸塞州最高法院

Cutter 法官主笔：

原告通过本起诉状试图迫使被告（Archambault 一家）将侵占了原告 Marshfield 处土地的 Archambault 家的部分房屋拆除。原告和 Archambault 家各自拥有一块相邻的海边土地。两块土地都得到了注册（《马萨诸塞州一般法》第 185 章）。原告和被告的产权证书都没有显示 Archambault 家的土地在原告土地上拥有任何权利。

Archambault 一家的前手产权人于 1946 年获得了建筑许可证，修建了一幢房子，房子的一部分位于自己的土地，另一部分在原告土地上，房屋总面积为 4 900 平方英尺。两块土地只有 50 英尺位于邻近道路的街面。被告侵占的土地面积为 465 平方英尺，房屋有 15 英尺 3 英寸延伸到了原告的土地上，深度为 31 英尺 4 英寸。初审法官认为将 Archambault 家房屋侵占了原告土地的那部分拆除非常昂贵。他判决（至少从他的辅助性裁决和已报告的一小部分证据可以看出，裁决是正确的）原告要求侵占其土地的建筑物拆除不具有不容否认性或迟误性。证据显示，Archambault 家从一名卖家手中购得土地，原告于 1966 年 6 月 14 日从另一名卖家那里购得土地。法官认为没有证据证明原告土地的原所有人对侵占予以过同意。1966 年 7 月 14 日，原告在对自己的土地进行测量时发现了侵占情况。

最终判决要求被告拆除侵占土地上的建筑物。Archambault 一家提出了上诉。法官采纳了裁决已经概括的关键事实报告。

1. 在马萨诸塞州，土地所有者通常可以获得强制衡平法救济，要求严重侵占其土地的建筑物从其土地上拆除，哪怕侵占为非故意行为或过失行为，即使拆除的费用远远超过了侵占发生时土地所有人所遭受的损失……在很少的情况下，衡平法院不会准予命令性强制令，只允许原告获得损害救济，在

injunction and have left the plaintiff to his remedy of damages, "where the unlawful encroachment has been made innocently, and the cost of removal by the defendant would be greatly disproportionate to the injury to the plaintiff from its continuation, or where the substantial rights of the owner may be protected without recourse to an injunction, or where an injunction would be oppressive and inequitable."...

2. We here are considering the remedies to be applied with respect to registered land. Such land is protected to a greater extent than other land from unrecorded and unregistered liens, prescriptive rights, encumbrances, and other burdens. ... Adverse possession (c. 185, §53) does not run against such land....

3. The present record discloses no circumstances which would justify denial of a mandatory injunction for removal of an encroachment taking away over nine per cent (465/4900) of the plaintiffs' lot....The invasion of the plaintiffs' lot is substantial and not de minimis. Photographs and maps in evidence, portraying the encroachment, show that the intrusion of the Archambaults' building on the plaintiffs' small lot greatly increases the congestion of that lot. The plaintiffs were entitled to receive whatever was shown by the land registration certificate as belonging to their grantor, unencumbered by any unregistered prescriptive easement or encroachment....

Decree affirmed with costs of appeal.

Tauro, Chief Justice (dissenting.)

The plaintiffs and defendants are owners of adjoining lots, with dwellings, both registered under G.L. c. 185. The defendants acquired title to their lot on June 18, 1954, and the plaintiffs acquired their title on June 14, 1966. The plaintiffs seek removal of a portion of the defendants' dwelling which encroaches on their land. This encroachment existed in full view from June, 1946, when the defendants' predecessor in title erected the dwelling, until July 14, 1966, when the plaintiffs had their property surveyed for the purpose of erecting a retaining wall. During this period, neither the plaintiffs' predecessor in title nor the plaintiffs raised any objection to the location of the defendants' dwelling. It is reasonable to infer that prior to taking title, the plaintiffs viewed the property. Thus they had actual notice of the location of the defendants' dwelling and its relative position to their own dwelling.

The plaintiffs do not seek money damages but rather a decree for the removal of the encroachment on their land which, in effect, would result in the destruction of the defendants' dwelling. The Superior Court made, and the majority today affirm, such a decree. I cannot agree with the opinion of the majority that, in the property exercise of the court's discretion, " the present record discloses no circumstances which would justify denial of a mandatory injunction" compelling the removal of the encroaching structure. To the contrary, I believe that the record before us sets forth unusual circumstances which would justify this court in denying a mandatory injunction and leaving the plaintiffs to seek their remedy at law from damages. Moreover,

我们的决定中称之为"例外"……"当非法侵占行为的发生出于无辜,而被告拆除侵占的费用与原告受到的损失严重不成比例,或者当土地所有人的实质性权利在没有禁止令的情况下可以得到保护,或者当禁止令是苛刻的或不公正之时"……

2. 我们这里考虑关于注册土地如何适用救济的问题。和其他土地相比,这种土地在未登记和未注册留置权、依时效而取得的权利、土地负担以及其他义务方面,受到了更多的保护……反向占有(第185章第53条)不针对这种土地……

3. 对于原告土地被侵占的比例达到9%以上(465/4900)的情况,现有的案卷并没有揭示任何情况,可以证明拒绝发出命令性拆除强制令的正当性……对原告土地的侵犯是实质性的,而并非琐事。证明侵占事实的照片和地图证据都表明 Archambault 家在原告小小土地上的那部分房屋极大地加剧了那一地区的拥挤程度。原告有权接受产权证上所标明的其让渡人所有的一切,不受任何未经注册的时效地役权或侵占行为所妨碍……

维持原判,包括上诉费用。

Tauro 法官(反对)主笔:

原告和被告为相邻两块土地的所有人,土地上都有住房,都基于《马萨诸塞州一般法》第185章注册过。被告于1954年6月18日获得其土地权利,原告于1966年6月14日获得他们的土地权利。原告要求被告将侵占了其土地的那部分住房拆除。从被告的前手产权人于1946年6月修建住房开始,一直到1966年7月14日,原告为了修建一个护墙而勘测土地,侵占事实一直被人们所知。在此期间,无论是原告的前手产权人还是原告,都没有对被告住房的位置提出过任何的反对意见。因此,他们事实上是注意到了被告住房的位置以及该住房相对于自己住房的位置。

原告并未提出金钱补偿,但是却要求法院作出被告从被侵占的土地上拆除房屋的裁决,而拆除实际上将导致被告住房的毁坏。高等法院以及今天的多数意见都赞同了该裁决。就法院在财产问题上行使的裁量权,我不能同意多数意见,即"现有的案卷并没有揭示任何情况,可以证明拒绝发出命令性强制令的正当性"以强制要求拆除侵占建筑。相反,我相信我们所面对的案卷展现了一个不同寻常的情况,使法院能够拒绝发出命令性强制令,从而使原告依据损害赔偿法寻求救济。不仅如此,在本案这种情况下发出禁止令救

the granting of injunctive relief in the circumstances of this case would be "oppressive and inequitable."

To conclude, as does the majority opinion, that this court must grant a mandatory injunction because the facts in the instant case do not precisely fit the factual pattern adjudged to be "exceptional" in prior Massachusetts cases is illogical and untenable. Courts, especially courts of equity, should not be restricted to so fossilized a concept of what the law is or should be. The cause of justice deserves a better fate....

As stated above, the defendants occupied their dwelling for over twelve years peacefully and without complaint prior to the present lawsuit. They bought their property in June, 1954, apparently without knowledge that, in 1946, their predecessor in title had mistakenly built partially upon an adjoining lot. The defendants' house was in plain view when the plaintiffs acquired title to the adjoining lot in June, 1966. It seems likely that, before the plaintiffs took title, they viewed the property and were aware of the location of the defendants' house and its proximity (by approximately six feet) to the house they might purchase. It is reasonable to infer, either that they inquired and were told that the space between the dwellings marked the property line, or that they made this assumption. The plaintiffs have disclosed that they discovered the encroachment one month after taking title as the result of a survey undertaken by them for the purpose of constructing a retaining wall. Apparently there was nothing about the defendants' dwelling which was offensive to the plaintiffs or even aroused their suspicions at the time of purchase. It appears therefore that the plaintiffs were satisfied with their purchase and the proximity of the defendants' dwelling to their own until the survey and that, but for the fortuity of the survey, the encroachment might have continued undiscovered indefinitely as it had during the entire period 1946 to 1966.

The discovery of the encroachment in these circumstances is best characterized as an unexpected windfall rather than an intentional injury. The defendants are innocent of any wrongdoing and are at most guilty of unknowingly continuing a longstanding encroachment. Nor can it be said that the defendants have deprived the plaintiffs of something which they believed they were entitled to at the time of their purchase. On the contrary, the plaintiffs could only have believed that they were acquiring exactly what they contemplated when they inspected the property. Subsequently, by virtue of the survey which they had made, the plaintiffs discovered they had purchased more than they had bargained for. At the same time, the defendants learned that what they had purchased in 1954 was less than they had bargained for. These circumstances should not pass unnoticed.

Moreover, removal would be a severe burden upon the defendant. As the trial judge indicated, it would "cost a lot of money, and involve a lot of inconvenience, and… reduce…the property value to a great extent." The judge does not appear to have considered whether removal might require the razing of a substantial portion of the defendants' house, but from the exhibits, we

济将是"苛刻的或不公正的"。

  总之，如多数意见那样，如果最终认为法院必须发出命令性强制令，因为当前案件中的事实并不完全符合马萨诸塞州以往案件中被裁定为"例外"的事实类型，那么这种做法是不合逻辑的，是站不住脚的。法院，特别是衡平法院，不应该在法律是什么或应该是什么的问题上如此的顽固守旧。正义的事业需要一个更好的结果……

  正如上面所谈到的，被告在他们的住房相安无事地已经居住了12年，在本案之前未收到任何的抱怨。他们于1954年6月购买了该不动产，显然对于其前手产权人在1946年误将一部分住房修建在了邻居的土地上毫不知情。当原告于1966年6月获得了土地的产权时，被告房屋的情况是众所周知的。在原告获得土地产权之前，他们就对不动产进行了审查，并且意识到被告房屋的位置以及该房屋靠近（大约6英尺）他们可能购买的房屋，这是有可能的。有理由推断，他们要么对此进行了询问，得到的回答是两个房屋之间的地方就是两块土地的分界线，要么他们是自己这样认为的。原告提出，在获得土地所有权的一个月之后，他们为了修建一堵护墙而勘测了土地，那时才发现被告房屋侵占了自己的土地。显然，在原告购买土地时，被告的住房并未对原告构成侵犯，或者甚至引起他们的怀疑。因此，直到他们进行了勘测，似乎原告之前对自己购买的土地以及被告住房与他们的毗邻关系都非常满意，要不是因为偶然的勘测，侵占事实可能会像1946年至1966年间一样永远不为人所知。

  在这些情况下发现的侵占事实应该被形容为意外所得，而非故意侵害。被告就构成任何不法行为来说都是无辜的，最多也就是在不知情的情况下继续了长期以来的侵占而有所愧疚。也不能说在原告购买财产时，被告剥夺了本属于原告的东西。相反，原告可能只是在检查土地时认为他们购买了预期中的土地。因此，由于原告所做的勘测，原告发现他们购买的土地超过了他们预料的那块土地。同时，被告发现他们于1954年购买的土地比预料的土地小。这些情况都不得不考虑。

  不仅如此，拆除对于被告来讲将是一个沉重的负担。正如初审法官指出的，"需要大量的钱财，带来极大的不便，并且……很大程度上降低……财产的价值"。法官似乎并未考虑拆除是否需要将被告在原告土地上的那部分房产夷为平地，但是从提交给法院的证据来看，我们不能不注意到这种可能性。法

should not be unaware of this possibility. The judge made no finding of irreparable injury to the plaintiffs. Under the other facts which he did find, however, I conclude to the contrary that the injury to the plaintiffs, if any, is not of great significance compared with the defendants' loss and that money damages should be sufficient remedy.

In the totality of circumstances, I conclude that equity does not, in the exercise of our sound discretion, require us to grant injunctive relief. Removal imposes upon the defendants substantial cost and inconvenience which are entirely disproportionate to the injury to the plaintiffs. Where, as here, it appears that the plaintiffs were content with the status quo until fortuitous discovery of the encroachment, it would be oppressive and inequitable for this court to grant a mandatory injunction against the defendants who have acted in good faith, albeit their predecessor in title made a mistake which remained undiscovered for some twenty years. Hardship alone is of course not a ground for denial of injunctive relief …, but this court should take relative hardship into account, if, as in the instant case, the owner of the encroaching structure is not guilty of an intentional trespass.… Here, it appears not only that the defendants have always acted in good faith but that the initial trespass was committed many years before they acquired title to their lot.…

If we were to refuse injunctive relief, common sense suggests that, in all probability, this dispute would be settled eventually without the need for the destruction of the defendants' dwelling. This could be accomplished through an agreement by the plaintiffs to voluntarily relocate their boundary line in return for payment by the defendants of any amount negotiated between them. The parties would then have their certificates of title reformed to reflect the agreement. In the alternative, the plaintiffs could bring an action at law and the court would make an impartial assessment of damages. The placing of the potent weapon of injunctive relief in the hands of the plaintiffs is hardly conducive to a fair and just settlement.…I would dismiss the bill and relegate the plaintiffs to their remedy at law.

49. Davis v. Georgia-Pacific Corp., 251 Or. 239, 445 P.2d 481 (1968)

Supreme Court of Oregon, United States

Holman, J.

Plaintiff Veva Davis owns a residence in the city of Toledo. Subsequent to her occupation of the premises defendant commenced the operation of a pulp and paper plant in close proximity thereto. The plaintiffs, Mrs. Davis and her husband, testified the premises was rendered uninhabitable by the operation of defendant's plant because of the emanation therefrom of vibrations, offensive odors, fumes, gases, smoke and particulates which damaged the residence and plant life. Plaintiffs secured a judgment against defendant for both compensatory and punitive damages for trespass. Defendant appealed.

官并未发现原告受到了不可挽回的损害。但是，根据他发现的其他事实，我反而认为原告如果受到损害，其损害程度也远远不及被告的损失，经济上的赔偿应该足以实现救济。

综观各种情况，我认为，在行使了合理的裁量权之后，公正性并不要求我们给予强制令救济。拆除将会给被告带来巨大的损失和不便，远远超过了原告受到的损害。正如这个案件一样，在原告意外发现侵占事实存在之前，原告对现状都非常满意，因此法院向被告发出命令性强制令的做法是苛刻的和不公正的，因为被告一直表现得很诚实，虽然其前手产权人犯了错误而且这个错误20年来都不为人们所发现。仅有困难当然还不足以成为拒绝强制令救济的根据……但是正如本案一样，侵占建筑物的所有人并无故意侵入行为，那么法院应该将相对困难考虑在内……这里，看得出来被告不但一直表现得很诚实，而且最初的侵入行为发生的时间也在被告购买土地的很多年之前……

如果我们拒绝了禁止令救济，常识告诉我们，这场争端很可能在不需要毁坏被告住房的情况下得到解决。可以通过协议，原告自愿重新划定他们的界线，而作为回报，被告向原告支付双方达成的数额的补偿。然后双方可以根据协议修改他们各自的产权证。或者，原告可以依据法律提起诉讼，而法院将对双方的损失做出不偏不倚的评估。原告手中的禁止令救济是有效的武器，但却不利于公正公平地解决问题……我拒绝接受该起诉状，要求原告根据法律获得救济。

49. Davis v. Georgia-Pacific Corp., 251 Or. 239, 445 P.2d 481 (1968)

美国俄勒冈州最高法院

Holman 法官主笔：

原告 Veva Davis 在 Toledo 市拥有一处住所。就在她搬进该住房之后，被告在其附近开办了一家造纸厂。原告 Davis 太太及其丈夫在证词中指出，从造纸厂传出来的振动、臭味、烟尘、气体、烟雾和颗粒损害了住房和植物，使得他们的住所已经变得无法再居住下去。原告获得被告为侵入行为支付损害赔偿和惩罚性赔偿的判决。被告提起了上诉。

Defendant's first four assignments of error relate to the admission of evidence and an instruction to the jury which allowed the jury to consider whether the intrusion of fumes, gases, and odors upon the property in question constituted a trespass. Defendant contends such intrusions constitute a nuisance rather than a trespass because there was no direct physical invasion of the property. The traditional concept that a trespass must be a direct intrusion by a tangible and visible object…has been abandoned in this state. In Martin et ux v. Reynolds Metals Co., 221 Or. 86, 342 P.2d 790 (1960), we decided that the deposit of airborne particulates upon another's land constituted a trespass even though the particulates were so small as to be invisible in the atmosphere.…Error was not committed by allowing the jury to consider an intrusion of fumes, gases, smoke and odors as a trespass.

The next five assignments of error relate to the refusal of the trial court to admit evidence and give instructions relevant to weighing the utility of defendant's conduct of its business and its efforts to prevent harm, against the seriousness of the harm, if any, suffered by plaintiffs. Traditionally, such a weighing process by the jury is one which is permitted in nuisance cases but not in those of trespass. In a trespass case the social value of defendant's conduct, its efforts to prevent the harm and other circumstances that tend to justify an intrusion cannot be considered by the trier of the facts.

This does not mean, however, that a weighing process does not take place when a court decides whether a particular kind of an intrusion, if found by the jury to exist, is of such a nature that it should be classified as a trespass. …The decision of courts that the normal operation of airplanes high in a property's airspace does not constitute a trespass. A similar kind of weighing process takes place when a court decides whether a trespass is privileged. Such classifications however, are ones that are made by courts and not by juries. If the jury finds that an intrusion occurred which is of a kind that courts hold to be an unprivileged trespass, strict liability results. The jury is not allowed to consider the utility of the use to which defendant is putting his land or his efforts to prevent harm to plaintiff in deciding plaintiff's recovery. Therefore, it was proper in this case for the trial court not to allow the jury to consider the evidence and instructions in question in deciding whether defendant should be responsible for *compensatory* damages.

We wish to make clear that no conclusion should be drawn from the above language that such a weighing process is inappropriate in a court's consideration whether an injunction should issue to restrain a continuing unprivileged trespass or whether a plaintiff should be left to his remedy at law for damages.…

We have found no prejudicial error relevant to…compensatory damages. Therefore, the judgment for compensatory damages is affirmed…and that for punitive damages is set aside…

被告提出的第一组四个错误陈述是关于证据的采纳以及对陪审团的指示，后者允许陪审团考虑进入原告住房的烟尘、气体和臭味是否构成了侵入。被告认为进入的这些物质构成了妨害而非侵入，因为并不存在对房产的直接物质性侵犯。本州已经放弃了传统的概念，即侵入必须是有形的可见物质的直接进入。在 Martin et ux v. Reynolds Metals Co., 221 Or. 86, 342 P.2d 790（1960）案中，我们认定，尽管空气传播的颗粒在空气之中几乎不被人们所看见，但是这些颗粒在他人土地上沉积下来也构成了侵入……允许陪审团将烟尘、气体、烟雾和臭味的进入认定为侵入，这并不构成法院的错误。

被告接下来指出的五个错误陈述，涉及初审法院拒绝采纳证据并且拒绝作出指示以对被告商业行为的效用及其为避免损害而作出的努力，与原告受到的损害的严重程度进行衡量。传统上，陪审团作出的这种衡量出现在妨害案件中，而不是侵入案件。在侵入案件中，事实判断者不考虑被告行为的社会价值、其为避免损害而作出的努力，以及其他可能证实进入行为合理性的情形。

然而，这并不意味着如果陪审团发现确实存在某种类型的闯入事实，而且当法院在决定这类闯入是否应该被归入侵入类型时，没有出现衡量过程。法院认定正常操作的飞机高高地飞在原告房产的上空，并不构成侵入。当法院决定一个侵入行为是否得到特免时，也会有类似的衡量过程。然而，这种分类是由法院而非陪审团来完成的。如果陪审团认定发生的进入行为也属于法院判定的那种非特免的侵入行为，那么被告就要承担严格责任。陪审团不能在决定原告的救济方式时考虑被告为避免对原告造成损害在土地利用或付出努力方面的效用。因此，在本案中，适当的做法是，初审法院不允许陪审团在决定被告是否应该承担损害赔偿责任时考虑证据或相关的指示。

我们希望明确一点，即根据上述内容，不应得出结论，认为法院在考量是否应该发出禁止令以制止持续性的非特免侵入行为，或者是否应该让原告依据法律获得损害赔偿，法院的这种衡量过程是不适当的……

我们没有发现与损害赔偿……相关的偏见性错误。因此，维持损害赔偿的原判……至于惩罚性赔偿，本庭不予支持……

50. Jost v. Dairyland Power Cooperative, 45 Wis. 2d 164, 172 N.W.2d 647 (1969)

Supreme Court of Wisconsin, United States

The action is one for damages for injury to crops and loss of market value of farm lands. The plaintiffs are farmers living within, or near, the city limits of Alma, Wisconsin. Their farms are located on the bluffs overlooking the Mississippi River. In 1947 the Dairyland Power Cooperative erected a coal burning electric generating plant at Alma. It is the contention of the farmers that consumption of high-sulfur-content coal at this plant has increased from 300 tons per day in 1948 to 1,670 tons per day in 1967. There was testimony that the 1967 coal consumption resulted in discharging approximately 90 tons of sulphur-dioxide gas into the atmosphere each day. There was substantial evidence to show that the sulphur-dioxide gas, under certain atmospheric conditions, settled on the fields, causing a whitening of the alfalfa leaves and a dropping off of some of the vegetation. There was also testimony to show that the sulphur compounds resulting from the industrial pollution killed pine trees, caused screens to rust through rapidly, and made flower raising difficult or impossible. There was some testimony to show that some of the sulphur came from locomotives or from river barges, but there was testimony that the power plant was the source of most of the contamination. Defendant's witness, a farmer who was "hit" less frequently by the sulphurous fumes, estimated his crop damage at 5 percent. There was also evidence of damage to apple trees, sumac, and wild grape, in addition to the alfalfa damage.

Each of the plaintiff farmers testified that his land had diminished in value as the result of the continuing crop loss....

The trial judge...entered judgment upon the verdict for the plaintiffs. Defendant has appealed from the whole of the judgment, and plaintiffs have filed for a review of the judgment which sustained the jury's finding in regard to loss of market value.

Heffernan, J.

Defendant strenuously argues that it was prejudiced by the court's refusal to permit certain testimony, particularly testimony that tended to show that defendant had used due care in the construction and operation of its plant, and to show that the social and economic utility of the Alma plant outweighed the gravity of damage to the plaintiffs.

Defendant's contention that the evidence should have been admitted rests on two theories; one, that due care, if shown, defeats a claim for nuisance, and, two, that, if the social utility of the offending industry substantially outweighs the gravity of the harm, the plaintiffs cannot recover damages.

We can agree with neither proposition....

In any event it is apparent that a continued invasion of a plaintiff's interests by non-negligent

50. Jost v. Dairyland Power Cooperative, 45 Wis. 2d 164, 172 N.W.2d 647 (1969)

美国威斯康星州最高法院

这是一起由于农作物受损和农田市场价值下降而提起的损害赔偿诉讼。原告是一群农民，居住在威斯康星州 Alma 市边界及其附近地区。他们的农场位于密西西比河旁耸立的峭壁上。1947 年，Dairyland Power Cooperative 在 Alma 修建了一个火力发电厂。农民认为，该工厂消耗的高浓度硫煤矿从 1948 年的每天 300 吨提高到了 1967 年的每天 1 670 吨。证词证明，1967 年消耗的煤矿造成工厂每天向空气中排放约 90 吨的二氧化硫气体。有充分的证据证明，在特定空气状况下，二氧化硫气体会沉积到地面，导致苜蓿叶变白，其他植物的叶片脱落。还有证词证明，工业污染生产出的硫化合物会导致松树死亡，大棚遮挡物很快被锈穿导致难以或无法培养花卉。一些证词认为，一些硫化物来自火车机车或河流上的船只，但是也有证词认为，发电厂是造成绝大多数污染的主要来源。被告的一名证人是受到硫磺废气"影响"较少的农民，他估计自己的农作物损失了 5%。同时还有证据证明，除了苜蓿的损失之外，苹果树、漆树和野葡萄也都受到了损害。

所有原告农民都证明由于农作物不断受到损失，他们的土地价值已经贬值……

初审法院……根据对原告有利的陪审团裁断作出了判决。被告对整个判决提起了上诉，而原告则要求对判决进行重新审理，因为该判决维持了陪审团关于市场价值贬损方面的事实认定。

Heffernan 法官主笔：

被告极力争辩，认为法院拒绝采纳某些证词的做法存在偏见，特别是关于被告在修建和经营发电厂时尽到了合理的注意义务的证词，以及关于 Alma 发电厂的社会和经济效用超过了原告损失的严重程度的证词。

被告认为，应该基于两个理论来采纳证据：第一，如果被告证明了合理注意，那么就可以否决被告构成妨害的主张；第二，如果造成不便的工厂在社会效用上超过了损害的严重程度，那么原告便不应该获得损害赔偿。

我们不能同意任何一个观点……

无论如何，显然，在行为人知道会造成什么性质的损害时，这种无过失的行为持续侵犯原告权益，已经构成了故意侵权，而且实施的伤害行为不存

conduct, when the actor knows of the nature of the injury inflicted, is an intentional tort, and the fact the hurt is administered non-negligently is not a defense to liability.

It is thus apparent that the facts tending to show freedom from negligence would not have constituted a defense to plaintiffs' nuisance action. It was therefore proper that such evidence was excluded (the nominal character of plaintiffs' proof as to negligence has been commented on above).

While there are some jurisdictions that permit the balancing of the utility of the offending conduct against the gravity of the injury inflicted, it is clear that the rule, permitting such balancing, is not approved in Wisconsin where the action is for damages....

We therefore conclude that the court properly excluded all evidence that tended to show the utility of the Dairyland Cooperative's enterprise. Whether its economic or social importance dwarfed the claim of a small farmer is of no consequence in this lawsuit. It will not be said that, because a great and socially useful enterprise will be liable in damages, an injury small by comparison should go unredressed. We know of no acceptable rule of jurisprudence that permits those who are engaged in important and desirable enterprises to injure with impunity those who are engaged in enterprises of lesser economic significance. Even the government or other entities, including public utilities, endowed with the power of eminent domain—the power to take private property in order to devote it to a purpose beneficial to the public good—are obliged to pay a fair market value for what is taken or damaged. To contend that a public utility, in the pursuit of its praiseworthy and legitimate enterprise, can, in effect, deprive others of the full use of their property without compensation, poses a theory unknown to the law of Wisconsin, and in our opinion would constitute the taking of property without due process of law....

Judgment affirmed in part and reversed in part consistent with this opinion.

51. Spur Industries, Inc. v. Del E. Webb Development Co., 108 Ariz. 178, 494 P.2d 700 (1972)

Supreme Court of Arizona, United States

Cameron, Vice C.J.

From a judgment permanently enjoining the defendant, Spur Industries, Inc., from operating a cattle feedlot near the plaintiff Del. E. Webb Development Company's Sun City, Spur appeals, Webb cross-appeals. Although numerous issues are raised, we feel that it is necessary to answer only two questions. They are:

1. Where the operation of a business, such as a cattle feedlot is lawful in the first instance, but becomes a nuisance by reason of a nearby residential area, may the feedlot operation be enjoined in an action brought by the developer of the residential area?

2. Assuming that the nuisance may be enjoined, may the developer of a completely new town or

在过失,这不能成为免于承担责任的抗辩理由。

因此,明显可以看出,旨在证明被告不存在过失的事实证据不能构成对原告妨害诉讼的抗辩理由。因此,排除这些证据的做法是适当的(原告关于过失的证据是有名无实的,上文已经对其进行了评价)。

尽管有法域允许在冒犯性行为的效用和该行为造成的损害的严重程度之间进行权衡,但是此损害赔偿诉讼所在的威斯康星州明确禁止进行这样的权衡……

因此我们认为,法院排除了所有旨在证明 Dairyland Cooperative 企业效用的证据是适当的。被告的经济或社会重要性使得农民的主张成立显得渺小,这和该诉讼无关。不应该这样说,即由于对具有巨大社会效用的事业需要承担损害责任,那么相比之下微不足道的损害就不应该得到赔偿。我们知道,任何法学规则都不允许从事重要的有利事业的人在伤害了那些从事经济意义相对较低的人之后,不受到惩罚。即使是被赋予了国家征用权——为了将私人财产投入到有利于公共利益的目的而获得该财产的权力——的政府或其他实体,包括公共事业机构,也有责任对被拿走或损害的财产的公平市场价值进行赔付。认为公共事业单位在追求值得人们颂扬的合法事业时可以剥夺他人充分使用其财产的权利,而不需要进行任何赔偿,威斯康星州的法律从来没有认可过这样的理论,而且在我们看来构成了未经正当程序剥夺财产……

判决的一部分得到了维持,另一部分根据本意见被撤销。

51. Spur Industries, Inc. v. Del E. Webb Development Co., 108 Ariz. 178, 494 P.2d 700 (1972)

美国亚利桑那州最高法院

Cameron 助理大法官主笔:

初审法院判决永久性地禁止被告 Spur Industries, Inc. 在原告 Del. E. Webb 开发公司的太阳城附近经营养牛场。Spur 提起上诉,Del Webb 提起交叉上诉。虽然引发了很多问题,但是我们认为只需要回答两个问题。这两个问题是:

1. 虽然类似于养牛场这样的商业活动在一开始是合法的,但是后来由于距离居住区太近而构成了妨害,那么居住区开发商是否可以提起诉讼要求禁止养牛场的经营活动?

2. 假设可以禁止妨害行为,由于开发商修建了居住区而导致养牛场不得不搬离或停止经营活动,那么在过去的农业地区修建新城镇或市区的开发商

urban area in a previously agricultural area be required to indemnify the operator of the feedlot who must move or cease operation because of the presence of the residential area created by the developer?

Del Webb's suit complained that the Spur feeding operation was a public nuisance because of the flies and the odor which were drifting or being blown by the prevailing south to north wind over the southern portion of Sun City. At the time of the suit, Spur was feeding between 20,000 and 30,000 head of cattle, and the facts amply support the finding of the trial court that the feed pens had become a nuisance to the people who resided in the southern part of Del Webb's development. The testimony indicated that cattle in a commercial feedlot will produce 35 to 40 pounds of wet manure per day, per head, or over a million pounds of wet manure per day for 30,000 head of cattle, and that despite the admittedly good feedlot management and good housekeeping practices by Spur, the resulting odor and flies produced an annoying if not unhealthy situation as far as the senior citizens of southern Sun City were concerned. There is no doubt that some of the citizens of Sun City were unable to enjoy the outdoor living which Del Webb had advertised and that Del Webb was faced with sales resistance from prospective purchasers as well as strong and persistent complaints from the people who had purchased homes in that area....

May Spur Be Enjoined? ...

It is clear that as to the citizens of Sun City, the operation of Spur's feedlot was both a public and a private nuisance. They could have successfully maintained an action to abate the nuisance. Del Webb, having shown a special injury in the loss of sales, had standing to bring suit to enjoin the nuisance. The judgment of the trial court permanently enjoining the operation of the feedlot is affirmed.

Must Del Webb Indemnify Spur?

A suit to enjoin a nuisance sounds in equity and the courts have long recognized a special responsibility to the public when acting as a court of equity....

In addition to protecting the public interest, however, courts of equity are concerned with protecting the operator of a lawful, albeit noxious, business from the result of a knowing and willful encroachment by others near his business.

In the so-called "coming to the nuisance" cases, the courts have held that the residential landowner may not have relief if he knowingly came into a neighborhood reserved for industrial or agricultural endeavors and has been damaged thereby....Were Webb the only party injured, we would feel justified in holding that the doctrine of "coming to the nuisance" would have been a bar to the relief asked by Webb, and, on the other hand, had Spur located the feedlot near the outskirts of a city and had the city grown toward the feedlot, Spur would have to suffer the cost of abating the nuisance as to those people locating within the growth pattern of the expanding city:

"The case affords, perhaps, an example where a business established at a place remote from population is gradually surrounded and becomes part of a populous center, so that a business which formerly was not an interference with the rights of others has become so by the encroachment of

51. Spur Industries, Inc. v. Del E. Webb Development Co., 108 Ariz. 178, 494 P.2d 700 (1972)

是否应该对养牛场的经营者进行补偿呢？

Del Webb 在诉讼中指控 Spur 的饲养业务构成了公共妨害，因为盛行的南风将苍蝇和臭气刮到太阳城南部地区。到诉讼时，Spur 已经饲养了 2 万到 3 万头牛，事实充分支持了初审法院的认定，即养牛场已经对居住在 Del Webb 开发区南部的人们构成了妨害。证词显示，商业养牛场饲养每头牛每天产生 35 到 40 磅的粪便，3 万头牛每天产生的粪便高达 100 万磅。即使 Spur 对饲养场进行了良好的管理，进行了仔细的清扫，造成的臭气和苍蝇对于太阳城南部的老年居民来说就算不损害健康也令人烦恼。毫无疑问，太阳城的一些居民不但无法享受 Del Webb 所宣传的户外生活，而且 Del Webb 还面临未来消费者的抵制，以及已经在这一地区购买房产的人们没完没了的强烈抗议……

Spur 的行为是否应该被禁止？……

显然，对于太阳城的居民来说，Spur 经营的养牛场既构成了公共妨害又构成了私人妨害。他们可以提起诉讼要求减轻妨害。Del Webb 证明了销售受到的特殊损害，坚持提起诉讼要求对妨害予以禁止。初审法院做出的要求永久禁止经营养牛场的判决得到了支持。

Del Webb 是否必须对 Spur 进行补偿？

在衡平法上可以提起禁止妨害的诉讼，而法院长期以来都认识到在扮演衡平法院角色时自己对公众肩负的特殊责任……

不过，除了保护公共利益，衡平法院还要考虑对合法但有害的企业经营者提供保护，以免遭到邻近其企业的他人明知和蓄意的侵占。

在所谓的"自找妨害"案件中，法院认为，居住区所有人如果明知邻近的土地会用于工业或农业用途，而且会因此而受到损害，那么他就不应该获得救济……如果 Webb 是唯一受到损害的一方，那么我们有理由认为"自找妨害"原理将成为 Webb 获得救济的障碍；另一方面，如果 Spur 将养牛场建立在城市的周边地区，随着城市向养牛场地区扩张，那么养牛场对城市扩张范围内居住的人们构成了妨害，而 Spur 应该承受减轻妨害而带来的损失：

"修建在远离人群的地区的企业渐渐被包围，最后成为人口聚居区的中心，导致过去对他人权利不构成干扰的企业随着人口的包围而干扰到了他人的利益，这个案件也许提供了这样的例子……"［City of Ft. Smith v. Western Hide & Fur Co., 153 Ark. 99, 103, 239 S.W. 724, 726（1922）.］

the population...." *City of Ft. Smith v. Western Hide & Fur Co.,* 153 Ark. 99, 103, 239 S.W. 724, 726 (1922).

We agree, however, with the Massachusetts court that:

"The law of nuisance affords no rigid rule to be applied in all instances. It is elastic. It undertakes to require only that which is fair and reasonable under all the circumstances. In a commonwealth like this, which depends for its material prosperity so largely on the continued growth and enlargement of manufacturing of diverse varieties, 'extreme rights' cannot be enforced...." *Stevens v. Rockport Granite Co.,* 216 Mass. 486, 488, 104 N.E. 371, 373 (1914).

There was no indication in the instant case at the time Spur and its predecessors located in western Maricopa County that a new city would spring up, full-blown, alongside the feeding operation and that the developer of that city would ask the court to order Spur to move because of the new city. Spur is required to move not because of any wrongdoing on the part of Spur, but because of a proper and legitimate regard of the courts for the rights and interests of the public.

Del Webb, on the other hand, is entitled to the relief prayed for (a permanent injunction), not because Webb is blameless, but because of the damage to the people who have been encouraged to purchase homes in Sun City. It does not equitably or legally follow, however, that Webb being entitled to the injunction, is then free of any liability to Spur if Webb has in fact been the cause of the damage Spur has sustained. It does not seem harsh to require a developer, who has taken advantage of the lesser land values in a rural area as well as the availability of large tracts of land on which to build and develop a new town or city in the area, to indemnify those who are forced to leave as a result.

Having brought people to the nuisance to the foreseeable detriment of Spur, Webb must indemnify Spur for a reasonable amount of the cost of moving or shutting down. It should be noted that this relief to Spur is limited to a case wherein a developer has, with foreseeability, brought into a previously agricultural or industrial area the population which makes necessary the granting of an injunction against a lawful business and for which the business has no adequate relief.

It is therefore the decision of this court that the matter be remanded to the trial court for a hearing upon the damages sustained by the defendant Spur as a reasonable and direct result of the granting of the permanent injunction. Since the result of the appeal may appear novel and both sides have obtained a measure of relief, it is ordered that each side will bear its own costs.

Affirmed in part, reversed in part, and remanded for further proceedings consistent with this opinion.

Hays, C.J., Struckmeyer and Lockwood, JJ., and Udall, Retired Justice.

然而，我们赞同马萨诸塞州法院的看法：

"妨害法并没有提供适用于各种情况的刚性规则，而是有弹性的。妨害法只对各种情况下的公平性和合理性提出了要求。在这样的一个各州联盟里，其繁荣的物质条件极大取决于各种产品制造业的不断增长和扩大，不应该强行执行'极端权利'……"［Stevens v. Rockport Granite Co., 216 Mass. 486, 488, 104 N.E. 371, 373（1914）.］

在这个案件中并没有迹象显示，在 Spur 及其前手设置在 Maricopa 县西部时，一个新的城市会伴随养牛场的经营突然出现、迅速长大，城市的开发商因为新城市的出现而要求法院命令 Spur 搬离。要求 Spur 搬离，并不是因为其存在任何的不法行为，而是因为法院合理合法地考虑到了公众的权利和利益。

另一方面，Del Webb 有权获得它所寻求的救济（一项永久性禁止令），并不是因为 Webb 自身毫无可责难之处，而是因为被鼓励在太阳城购买房产的人们受到了损失。然而，由此而认为如果事实上 Webb 是导致 Spur 承受损失的原因，但是因为 Webb 有权获得禁止令，所以不需要对 Spur 承担任何责任，这既不公平又不合法。利用郊区相对便宜的地价和大量可以获得的土地在这一地区修建和开发新城镇，要求开发商对最后被迫离开该地区的当事人进行补偿，这样的做法看起来并不苛刻。

由于 Webb 引导人们受到妨害，并由此对 Spur 造成了可预见的损害，所以 Webb 必须对 Spur 的搬离或关闭支付合理金额的补偿。应该注意到的是，对 Spur 的救济仅限于此类案件，即开发商在可以预见的情况下将人口引入到过去的农业用地或工业用地上，由于这些人口的原因，有必要对一个合法的企业发出禁止令，而且该企业没有获得足够的救济。

因此，本法院作出判决，将本案发回初审法院，就因永久性禁止令合理而直接地给 Spur 造成的损害问题举行听证。由于上诉的结果可能看起来比较新颖，双方都获得了救济措施，所以判决双方各自承担自己的费用。

判决部分得到维持，部分被撤销，根据本意见书对案件进行重审。

Hays 大法官和 Struckmeyer 法官、Lockwood 法官以及 Udall 退休法官赞同。

Section 2. Trespass to Land and Nuisance in English Cases

52. Graham v Peat (1801) 1 East 244, 102 ER 95

Court of King's Bench, United Kingdom

Lord Kenyon C.J. There is no doubt butthat the plaintiff's possession in this case was sufficient to maintain trespass against a wrong-doer; and if he could not have maintained an ejectment upon such a demise, it is because that is a fictitious remedy founded upon title. Any possession is a legal possession against a wrong-doer. Suppose a burglary committed in the dwelling-house of such an one, must it not be laid to be his dwelling-house notwithstanding the defect of his title under that statute.

53. Smith v Stone (1647) Sty 65, 82 ER 533

Court of King's Bench, United Kingdom

Smith brought an action of trespasse against Stone, the defendant pleads this special plea in justification, viz. that he was carried upon the land of the plaintiff by force, and violence of others, and was not there voluntarily, which is the same trespasse, for which the plaintiff brings his action. The plaintiff demurs to this plea: in this case Roll Iustice said, that it is the trespass of the party that carried the defendant upon the land, and not the trespasse of the defendant: as he that drives my cattel into another mans land is the trespassor against him, and not I who am owner of the cattel.

54. Cambridge Water Co Ltd v Eastern Counties Leather plc [1994] 2 AC 264

House of Lords, United Kingdom

LORD GOFF

...

Foreseeability of damage in nuisance

It is against this background that it is necessary to consider the question whether foreseeability of harm of the relevant type is an essential element of liability either in nuisance or under the rule in Rylands v. Fletcher . I shall take first the case of nuisance. In the present case, as I have said, this is not strictly speaking a live issue. Even so, I propose briefly to address it, as part of the analysis of the background to the present case.

It is, of course, axiomatic that in this field we must be on our guard, when considering liability for damages in nuisance, not to draw inapposite conclusions from cases concerned only

第二节 英国法上的侵入土地与妨害

52. Graham v Peat (1801) 1 East 244, 102 ER 95

联合王国王座法院

Kenyon 首席大法官：毫无疑问，本案中原告对房屋的占有本身，即足以支持对任何一个侵入者的"非法侵入之诉"；如果说原告不能依据租约而驱逐侵入之人，这只是因为"驱逐侵入之人"是基于所有权的救济方式，通常并不能用来救济无所有权之人。对于非法侵入者来说，任何的占有皆是合法的占有。假如有人在这样一个所有权有瑕疵人的住宅里行窃，即使后者的所有权有法律上的缺陷，难道不应该把该房屋当作他的住宅吗？

53. Smith v Stone (1647) Sty 65, 82 ER 533

联合王国王座法院

Smith 以入侵之诉起诉 Stone。被告人 Stone 则作出"情有可原"的特殊答辩：他辩称其侵入原告所有之土地，并非出于本意，而是第三人实施暴力之结果；该实施暴力之人，才应该向原告承担非法侵入之诉意义上的责任。原告对被告的答辩进行了抗辩。本案中，Roll 法官认为，本案中应承担侵入责任之人，为将被告带到原告土地上之人，而非被告本人。正如赶着我的牛到他人的土地上之人，才是入侵他人土地之人，而不能说这个入侵之人是我这个牛的主人。

54. Cambridge Water Co Ltd v Eastern Counties Leather plc [1994] 2 AC 264

联合王国上议院

Goff 大法官
……

妨害之诉中的"损害的可预见性"

根据以上的事实，我们有必要先讨论下对损害的可预见性是否是"妨害之诉"或者在"Rylands v. Fletcher"案中所确立的规则下所必需的要件。我将先讨论"妨害之诉"。在本案中，如我所言，严格来说这其实并不是一个很需要讨论的问题。然而，为了能够分析本案的背景，我觉得还是有必要简单提两句。

不言而喻，当涉及妨害之诉的损害赔偿时，我们需要特别注意不要依

with a claim for an injunction. This is because, where an injunction is claimed, its purpose is to restrain further action by the defendant which may interfere with the plaintiff's enjoyment of his land, and ex hypothesi the defendant must be aware, if and when an injunction is granted, that such interference may be caused by the act which he is restrained from committing. It follows that these cases provide no guidance on the question whether foreseeability of harm of the relevant type is a prerequisite of the recovery of damages for causing such harm to the plaintiff. In the present case, we are not concerned with liability in damages in respect of a nuisance which has arisen through natural causes, or by the act of a person for whose actions the defendant is not responsible, in which cases the applicable principles in nuisance have become closely associated with those applicable in negligence: see *Sedleigh-Denfield v. O'Callaghan* [1940] A.C. 880 and *Goldman v. Hargrave* [1967] 1 A.C. 645. We are concerned with the liability of a person where a nuisance has been created by one for whose actions he is responsible. Here, as I have said, it is still the law that the fact that the defendant has taken all reasonable care will not of itself exonerate him from liability, the relevant control mechanism being found within the principle of reasonable user. But it by no means follows that the defendant should be held liable for damage of a type which he could not reasonably foresee; and the development of the law of negligence in the past 60 years points strongly towards a requirement that such foreseeability should be a prerequisite of liability in damages for nuisance, as it is of liability in negligence. For if a plaintiff is in ordinary circumstances only able to claim damages in respect of personal injuries where he can prove such foreseeability on the part of the defendant, it is difficult to see why, in common justice, he should be in a stronger position to claim damages for interference with the enjoyment of his land where the defendant was unable to foresee such damage. Moreover, this appears to have been the conclusion of the Privy Council in *Overseas Tankship (U.K.) Ltd. v. Miller Steamship Co. Pty. (The Wagon Mound (No. 2))* [1967] 1 A.C. 617. The facts of the case are too well known to require repetition, but they gave rise to a claim for damages arising from a public nuisance caused by a spillage of oil in Sydney Harbour. Lord Reid, who delivered the advice of the Privy Council, considered that, in the class of nuisance which included the case before the Board, foreseeability is an essential element in determining liability. He then continued, at p. 640:

> "It could not be right to discriminate between different cases of nuisance so as to make foreseeability a necessary element in determining damages in those cases where it is a necessary element in determining liability, but not in others. So the choice is between it being a necessary element in all cases of nuisance or in none. In their Lordships' judgment the similarities between nuisance and other forms of tort to which *The Wagon Mound (No. 1)* applies far outweigh any differences, and they must therefore hold that the judgment appealed from is wrong on this branch of the case.

据那些以禁止令为诉讼目的的判例而得出不恰当的结论。这是因为原告请求禁止令的目的是为了阻止未来被告的那些妨碍原告用益土地的行为。在这种情况下，我们可以理所当然地推测在禁止令被准许时，被告是应该对其被禁止令所禁止的行为给他人造成的妨害知情的。因此，这些类型的判例对损害的可预见性是否是原告获得损害赔偿的要件这一问题，是没有什么用处的。在本案中，我们需要讨论的损害赔偿责任并非产生于自然原因造成的妨害，也并非产生于被告对行为无法控制之人的行为，在这两种情况下，适用于妨害之诉的原则和适用于过失之诉的原则是非常类似的：参见 *Sedleigh-Denfield v O'Callaghan* [1940] A.C. 880 和 *Goldman v Hargrave* [1967] 1A.C. 645。我们需要讨论的损害赔偿责任是产生于那种被告可以控制的人的行为导致的妨害。在本案中如同我前面所述，法律依然规定，被告已经尽到了所有应尽的注意义务这一事实本身，并不能使他免除相应的责任（相关的控制机制属于"合理的使用者"原则的调整范围）。然而，这并不意味着被告应该对其不能预见的损害类型承担责任。最近六十年间"过失之诉"的发展强烈地表明可预见性是"妨害之诉"中损害赔偿责任的必要条件，如同它也是"过失之诉"的必要条件一样。我们这么说是因为，如果在一般条件下，一个原告仅仅只有在能够证明被告对损害可预见的情况下，才能主张对其人身伤害的赔偿，那么我们很难同意，一般正义允许一个妨害之诉的原告有更强的地位，这种地位居然允许他在被告不能预见其行为会妨碍到原告对土地的用益的情况下，就需要承担相应的损害赔偿责任。我们的这种观点似乎也是枢密院在 *Overseas Tankship（U.K.）Ltd. v Miller Steamship Co. Pty.（The Wagon Mound（No. 2））* [1967] 1 A.C. 617 一案中所表达的观点。本案的事实为大众所熟知，因此本来并无需赘述。大致来说，本案中原告以被告在悉尼湾中的泄漏原油构成公共妨害为由，请求其承担损害赔偿责任。以 Reid 大法官为代表的枢密院认为：在包括该案在内的"妨害之诉"这一类型的案件中，可预见性都是确定责任的必要条件。在判决的第 640 页，他继续说道：

> 把"妨害之诉"分为以可预见性为损害赔偿要件之诉和不以之为要件之诉的做法是错误的。因此，我们要么把它作为一切妨害之诉的要件，要么不认为它是任何妨害之诉的要件。诸位大法官认为，妨害之诉和 *The Wagon Mound (No. 1)* 这个判例所调整的那些侵权的诉由之间的相似性是远远大于不同点的，因此原判决在这一点上是错误的。如果被上

It is not sufficient that the injury suffered by the respondents' vessels was the direct result of the nuisance if that injury was in the relevant sense unforeseeable."

It is widely accepted that this conclusion, although not essential to the decision of the particular case, has nevertheless settled the law to the effect that foreseeability of harm is indeed a prerequisite of the recovery of damages in private nuisance, as in the case of public nuisance. I refer in particular to the opinion expressed by Professor Fleming in Fleming on the Law of Torts, 8th ed. (1992), pp. 443-444. It is unnecessary in the present case to consider the precise nature of this principle; but it appears from Lord Reid's statement of the law that he regarded it essentially as one relating to remoteness of damage.

55. Sedleigh-Denfield v O'Callaghan [1940] AC 880

House of Lords, United Kingdom

APPEAL from the Court of Appeal.

The appellant, the plaintiff in the action, was the owner and occupier of a house at Mill Hill. At the upper end of its garden was a ditch, and beyond the ditch a bank with trees upon it, the land beyond the ditch and bank belonging to the respondents. To the west of the respondents' plot was a block of flats called "Holcombe Court." Before 1934 the ditch, as an open course, continued along the northern edge of Holcombe Court to a roadway running from north to south on the western side of Holcombe Court. In 1934 the then owners of Holcombe Court made an agreement with the Middlesex County Council by which the latter undertook to substitute a pipe or culvert in the line of the ditch. The county council made the culvert and covered the top of it with earth. To prevent the possibility of wood or leaves blocking the opening of the fifteen-inch pipe, it would have been proper practice to fix a grid or grating in the ditch a little way from the opening of the pipe, inasmuch as there were trees in the hedge, and sticks and leaves would be apt to fall into the ditch. The county council recognized the necessity for a grating, and provided one, but their workmen, instead of fixing it in the ditch a foot or two from the opening of the pipe or culvert, where it would intercept leaves and other refuse, placed it on the top of the culvert, where it was useless. The mouth of the culvert was on the respondents' land. Till April, 1937, the respondents' servants periodically cleaned out the ditch, but on April 20 of that year there was a very heavy rainstorm, the culvert became blocked with refuse, and the appellant's premises were flooded by water coming down the ditch, which could not get away through the fifteen-inch pipe, and in respect of this the appellant, who suffered substantial damage, sued the respondents. It was given in evidence that a grating or grid placed properly in the ditch would have intercepted debris, rubbish or foreign matter, and would have prevented such a blockage of the flow of water as caused the

诉人的损失并不在上诉人的预见范围内的话，仅仅因为其船只遭受的损害是上诉人的妨害行为的直接后果这一点，并不足以支撑被上诉人的诉讼请求。

上述的结论虽然在该案的判决中并非是重要的部分，但是却在此意义上确定了相应的规则：可预见性是私有妨害和公共妨害中共同的损害赔偿的要件。我特别提议去参考 Fleming 教授在其著作《Fleming 谈侵权法》（1992 年第八版，第 443—444 页）一书中的观点。对于本案来说，上述原则的确切性质并非关键问题；从 Reid 大法官关于法律问题的阐释中，我们似乎可以看到，他认为这个原则本质上是与损害程度有关的法律意义上的问题。

55. Sedleigh-Denfield v O'Callaghan [1940] AC 880

联合王国上议院

从上诉法院上诉。

上诉人（原审原告）是一栋在 Mill Hill 的房屋的所有者和使用者。在这栋房屋的花园的外面是一条壕沟，壕沟外面是一片堤岸，上面有树；壕沟和堤岸外面的土地属于被上诉人（原审被告）。被上诉人的土地西边有一片叫做"Holcombe Court"的公寓楼。1934 年之前，这条壕沟是没有加盖的，它沿着 Holcombe Court 北部边沿一直延伸到 Holcombe Court 西边的一条南北向的公路。1934 年，当时 Holcombe Court 的业主和 Middlesex 县议会达成协议，后者承诺在壕沟里修一条涵洞。县议会修建了涵洞后把它埋在了土里。为了避免木材和树叶堵塞这条 15 英寸口径管子的排水口，正确的做法本应是在离排水口不远的地方给涵洞装上除渣网，因为树篱的枝叶会掉到沟里。县议会意识到了对除渣网的需求，也确实提供了一个。但是雇的工人没有把除渣网装在壕沟里离涵洞的排污口一两英尺的地方（只有装在这里才能拦截树叶或其他垃圾），而是把它装在了涵洞口上，这样除渣网就起不到作用了。涵洞的排污口在被上诉人的土地上。直到 1937 年 4 月，被告的仆人都会时不时清理壕沟，但是在那年的 4 月 29 日刮了一场大风暴，涵洞被垃圾堵住了，积水无法从 15 英寸口径的管道排出，因此从壕沟里漫了出来淹了原告的土地。上诉人为此遭受了严重的损失，因此起诉了被上诉人。有证据证明如果在壕沟里正确安装了除渣网，那么它是能够拦截垃圾和异物的，因此能够避免水流堵

ditch to overflow. This evidence was accepted by the trial judge, who came to the conclusion that the ditch, unprotected by any grid or grating, was of the nature of a nuisance, giving the appellant, on damage being proved, a prima facie right to recover damages. But the respondents raised the defence that they never consented to the making of the culvert, and were, in fact, ignorant of its existence, evidence which Branson J. accepted. It appeared, however, that some one on behalf of the respondents had cleaned out the ditch twice a year, and in view of that their Lordships took the view that before the flooding complained of the respondents must be taken to have had knowledge of the existence of the unguarded culvert, and the damage which had been caused.

...

LORD ATKIN

In this state of the facts the legal position is not I think difficult to discover. For the purpose of ascertaining whether as here the plaintiff can establish a private nuisance I think that nuisance is sufficiently defined as a wrongful interference with another's enjoyment of his land or premises by the use of land or premises either occupied or in some cases owned by oneself. The occupier or owner is not an insurer; there must be something more than the mere harm done to the neighbour's property to make the party responsible. Deliberate act or negligence is not an essential ingredient but some degree of personal responsibility is required, which is connoted in my definition by the word "use." This conception is implicit in all the decisions which impose liability only where the defendant has "caused or continued" the nuisance. We may eliminate in this case "caused." What is the meaning of "continued"? In the context in which it is used "continued" must indicate mere passive continuance. If a man uses on premises something which he found there, and which itself causes a nuisance by noise, vibration, smell or fumes, he is himself in continuing to bring into existence the noise, vibration, etc., causing a nuisance. Continuing in this sense and causing are the same thing. It seems to me clear that if a man permits an offensive thing on his premises to continue to offend, that is, if he knows that it is operating offensively, is able to prevent it, and omits to prevent it, he is permitting the nuisance to continue; in other words he is continuing it. The liability of an occupier has been carried so far that it appears to have been decided that, if he comes to occupy, say as tenant, premises upon which a cause of nuisance exists, caused by a previous occupier, he is responsible even though he does not know that either the cause or the result is in existence.

...

In the present case, however, there is as I have said sufficient proof of the knowledge of the defendants both of the cause and its probable effect. What is the legal result of the original cause being due to the act of a trespasser? In my opinion the defendants clearly continued the nuisance for they come clearly within the terms I have mentioned above, they knew the danger, they were able to prevent it and they omitted to prevent it.

塞造成的积水泛滥。一审法官采信了这些证据，得出结论：这条壕沟因为没有安装起到保护作用的除渣网，具有"妨害"的性质，因此判决原告在证明了自己的损失的情况下有权获得损害赔偿。被上诉人抗辩称他们从未同意修建这条涵洞，而且其实他们都不知道 Branson 法官所采信的证据的存在。然而为被上诉人工作的人好像每年要清理这条壕沟两次，由此上议院认定在洪水泛滥之前被上诉人是一定知道这条地下壕沟的存在的，也是知道曾经已经造成了的损失的。

……

Atkin 大法官

对于这样的事实应该如何判决不是一个很难回答的问题。为了判断本案中的原告是否能够提起私有妨害之诉，我认为妨害一词的定义应该是"通过使用自己所有或占有的土地非法妨碍他人对土地的使用"。由于土地的占有人或者所有人并不是保险人，因此他的邻居不能仅仅因为后者的土地被前者损害就提起诉讼，必须有其他的情节才行。这里并不是一定要求前者有故意或者过失的行为，但是至少需要前者有一定程度的介入行为，这种介入行为对应我对妨害下的定义中的"使用"一词。这个概念在所有的判决支持被告责任成立的妨害之诉的案件中都有体现，而被告的责任的前提则是其"造成或者维持了妨害"。本案不属于"造成"的类型。那么"维持"是什么意思？这个表达所指的"维持"中有"被动的持续"即可。如果一个人在他的土地上使用某种东西，这个东西发出的噪音、产生的震动、发出的气味或者烟雾构成某种妨害，那么他就是在维持这些构成妨害的噪音或者震动。在这个意义上，"维持"和"造成"是一回事。在我看来如果一个人允许某种讨厌的东西在他的土地上持续地冒犯他人，且在他能够制止这个东西的前提下没有这么做，他就是在允许妨害持续，换言之他就是在维持妨害。土地占有人的责任是很大的，好像很多法官会判决如果妨害的原因一个人在占有土地的时候（比如作为承租人）已经存在了，即使这个妨害是前任占有人造成的，这个后占有人也应该承担责任，即便他并不知道妨害的存在或者其结果的存在。

……

然而在本案中，如前所述有足够的证据证明被告知道妨害的产生原因和知道其可能的后果。妨害最初是由侵入者的行为造成的这一点，在法律上有什么意义呢？在我看来被告确实维持了妨害，因为他们的行为完全符合我以上描述的情形，他们知道危险的存在，他们有能力避免它，但是他们没有避免它。

…

LORD WRIGHT

If it were merely a question of the physical conditions no one would doubt that a case of private nuisance was established. The interposition of the pipe as the means of carrying the water from the ditch in place of the former open watercourse was not in itself objectionable. The trouble was that no protecting grid was put in place, and there was nothing to prevent the pipe getting choked. There was thus the risk of a flood, which might spread, as in fact happened, to the appellant's premises, causing damage which in the actual result was considerable.

…

But where, as here, a plaintiff is damaged by his land being flooded, the facts bring it well within the sphere of nuisance. Such a case has a certain similarity with those to which the rule of *Rylands v. Fletcher* applies, but there are obvious differences in substance. There are indeed well marked differences between the two juristic concepts. This case has therefore properly been treated as a case of nuisance. It has affinity also with a claim for negligence, because the trouble arose from the negligent fitting of the grid. But the gist of the present action is the unreasonable and unjustified interference by the defendant in the user of his land with the plaintiff's right to enjoy his property. Negligence, moreover, is not a necessary condition of a claim for nuisance. What is done may be done deliberately, and in good faith and in a genuine belief that it is justified. Negligence here is not an independent cause of action but is ancillary to the actual cause of action, which is nuisance.

…

In these cases the plaintiff failed because he did not establish that the defendant either knew or ought to have known. In the present case it is in my opinion clear on the facts stated by my noble and learned friend Lord Maugham that the respondents, by their servant, knew or at least ought to have known of the nuisance. On the law, as I have accepted it, the respondents' responsibility would seem to follow.

…

LORD ROMER

In these circumstances the question to be decided is whether the respondents can be held liable for the damage caused to the appellant by the floods that took place in April and in November 1937, which were without question due to the accumulation in the culvert of rubbish that would not have been there had a proper grid been provided in the respondents' ditch.

My Lords, I should have thought that, consistently with well-established principles of law, this question only permitted of an answer in the affirmative. An owner or occupier of land must so use it that he does not thereby substantially interfere with the comfortable enjoyment of their land by his neighbours. The user of the ditch by the construction of the culvert was not, indeed, a user

……

Wright 大法官主笔：

如果争议焦点只是关于地形条件的话，没有人会怀疑本案成立"私有妨害之诉"。加装水管以替代之前的露天水渠作为从壕沟里排水的方法，这本身无可指摘。之所以会有问题，是因为保护性的除渣网没有安装到位，因而无法防止管道被堵塞。因此会有洪水的风险；而洪水也确实发生了，它淹没了上诉人的土地，造成了严重的损害。

……

但是正如本案这样，原告因为其土地被淹而受损，由此本案应属于妨害之诉。本案和 Rylands v Fletcher 案所适用的规则相比有一些共同点，但是在内容上显然也有不同点。事实上这两个法律概念之间有明显的区别。因此本案被视为妨害之诉是恰当的。本案的案情也和过失之诉很类似，因为损害的产生是有人因为过失没有安装好除渣网。但是本案中原告选择起诉的依据却是被告不合理也不正当地妨碍了原告对其土地的用益。而过失却并不是妨害之诉的要件。被告的所作所为完全可能是有意的善意，而且是真的相信他的所作所为是正当的。被告的过失在这里并不是一个独立的诉由，而是附属于真正的诉由"妨害"。

……

在那些案件中，原告之所以会失败是因为其未能证明被告知道或者应该知道（妨害的存在）。在本案中，我认为我高贵而博学的朋友 Mangham 大法官所陈述的事实已经很清楚了，被上诉人通过其仆人知道或者应该知道妨害的存在。我认为被上诉人因此应该承担法律上的责任。

……

Romer 大法官主笔：

在这种情况下需要判断的问题是被上诉人是否应该因为在 1937 年 4 月发生的洪水而对原告的损失承担责任。洪水的发生无疑是因为涵洞中淤积了垃圾。如果当时被上诉人的壕沟里面正确地装了除渣网就不会淤积垃圾。

诸位大法官，根据既定的法律原则，我只能认为这个问题的答案是肯定的。一块土地的使用人或者占有人对自己土地的使用，必须以不会严重影响其邻居用益其土地为前提。在壕沟里面修涵洞的并不是被上诉人而是侵入者。但是被上诉人在此之后继续使用涵洞来为其附近的土地排水，而并未采取措

of their land by the respondents at all. It was the act of a trespasser. But the respondents continued thereafter to use the ditch for the purpose of draining their adjoining fields without taking steps to ensure that the water did not accumulate therein and as a consequence flood the appellant's premises. Such steps were well within their power. All that it was necessary to do was to provide a grid that would prevent the rubbish that fell into the ditch from passing into the culvert. In these circumstances it seems to me that they committed a nuisance upon their land for which they must be held responsible.

...

LORD PORTER

It is clear that an occupier may be liable though he (1.) is wholly blameless, (2.) is not only ignorant of the existence of the nuisance but also without means of detecting it, and (3.) entered into occupation after the nuisance had come into existence: see Broder v. Saillard.

Such a liability is, I think, inconsistent with the contention that the occupier is not liable for the acts of a trespasser of which he has knowledge, though possibly it might be contended that he is responsible for the acts of his predecessor in title but not for those of a trespasser. However this may be, the true view is, I think, that the occupier of land is liable for a nuisance existing on his property to the extent that he can reasonably abate it, even though he neither created it nor received any benefit from it. It is enough if he permitted it to continue after he knew or ought to have known of its existence. To this extent, but to no greater extent, he must be proved to have adopted the act of the creator of the nuisance.

Finally, however, it is said that the respondents knew, it is true, of the absence of a grid in front of the pipe, but did not know and had no reason for suspecting that any trouble would ensue. Therefore it was contended that they had no knowledge of the nuisance and indeed that no nuisance existed, only the potentiality of a nuisance, i.e., the possibility that the pipe might become blocked and cause a flood on the appellant's land. In a sense this is true, the nuisance is not the existence of the pipe unprotected by a grid but the flooding of the appellant's garden - flooding which might be repeated at any time of severe rain.

The respondents, however, ought, I think, as reasonable persons to have recognized the probability, or at least the possibility of a flood occurring. Even if it were conceded that the appellant might in the light of such cases as *Lemmon v. Webb* have entered the respondents' lands after notice and placed the grid in its proper place, he was not obliged to do so. As was pointed out in *Lagan Navigation Co. v. Lambeg Bleaching, &c., Co., Ld.*, the abatement of a nuisance by a private individual is a remedy which the law does not favour. Moreover, in the present case the evidence shows that the appellant had no knowledge of or reason to suspect the existence of any trouble owing to the pipe. But the respondents had, as I have indicated, or ought to have had knowledge of the danger, and could have prevented the danger if they had acted reasonably. For

施来避免积水，避免因此淹到上诉人的土地。这些避免措施是他们完全能够做的。他们只需装一个除渣网来避免垃圾掉入壕沟进而掉入涵洞。这种情况下，我认为他们就在其土地上实施了妨害的行为因此应当承担责任。

……

Porter 大法官主笔：

有一点非常清楚，土地的占有人即便有下列情形，依然要承担责任：（1）他没有一点可谴责性；（2）他不但不知道妨害的存在，而且没有手段来发现妨害的存在；（3）他是在妨害产生之后才占有土地的（参见 Broder v Saillard 案）。

我认为在这种责任下是不能说因为占有人不知情，他就不该为侵入者的行为负责；虽然有人可能会说占有人只该为有权占有的前任的行为负责，而不为侵入者的行为负责，但是无论这样的说法对不对，我认为正确的观点应该是土地的占有人应该为存在于他的土地上且他可以合理地减轻的妨害负责，即便并不是他造成的妨害，他也没有从妨害中获得什么好处。（他要承担责任）需要的仅仅是他在知道或者应当知道妨害存在后同意妨害继续。在这种程度上，也仅仅在这种程度上，原告需要证明被告接受了妨害制造者的行为。

但是最后，被上诉人指出他虽然知道管道前头没有装好除渣网，但是他并不知道或者没有理由知道这会带来麻烦。因此他并不知道妨害的存在，妨害也并不存在，存在的只是妨害的可能性，即管道可能堵塞以淹没上诉人的土地。在某种意义上这是对的，妨害并不是没有用除渣网保护的管道，而是在下大雨时随时产生的淹没上诉人花园的积水。

然而我认为被上诉人作为理性人应该对积水泛滥的可能性有所了解。即便我们承认，上诉人可以在给出通知之后自己到被上诉人的土地上安装除渣网，就像是 Lemmon v Webb 一类的案件那样，他并不必须这么做。如 Lagan Navigation Co. v Lambeg Bleaching, &c., Co., Ld. 案所示，由私人来减少妨害并不是法律所赞成的解决方案。另外，在本案中的证据证明上诉人并不知道也不应该知道问题出在管子上。但是，正如我所指出的，被上诉人是知道或者应该知道危险的存在的，而且他们通过采取合理的手段是完全能够避免这种危险的。因此，我认为他们应当承担责任——不是因为他们的过失（虽然他们确实可能有过失），而是因为妨害的存在，因为他们虽然知道可能导致妨

this I think they were liable - not because they were negligent, though it may be that they were, but for nuisance because with knowledge that a state of things existed which might at any time give rise to a nuisance they took no steps to remedy that state of affairs.

The appellant is in my opinion entitled to succeed.

56. Hunter v Canary Wharf Ltd [1997] AC 655

House of Lords, United Kingdom

LORD GOFF

My Lords, there are before your Lordships' House appeals in two actions, which raise fundamental questions relating to the law of private nuisance.

In the first action, Hunter v. Canary Wharf Ltd. , the appellant plaintiffs claim damages in respect of interference with the television reception at their homes. This, they claim, was caused by the construction of the Canary Wharf Tower, which was built on land developed by the defendants. The tower is nearly 250 metres (about 800 feet) high and over 50 metres square. The source of television transmissions in the area is a B.B.C. transmitter at Crystal Palace; and the plaintiffs claim that, because of its size and the metal in its surface (it has stainless steel cladding and metallised windows), it has caused interference with the television signals from Crystal Palace. The plaintiffs all lived at the material time in an area on the Isle of Dogs affected by the interference, which has been called "the shadow area." They claim that the interference began in 1989, during the construction of the tower. A relay transmitter was then built to overcome the problem of interference in the shadow area. This came into operation in April 1991, and it is claimed that the aerials at the plaintiffs' homes were adjusted or replaced between July 1991 and April 1992 to achieve satisfactory reception. The plaintiffs claim damages in respect of the interference with their television reception during the intervening period. Their claim was framed in nuisance and in negligence, though their claim in negligence has since been abandoned.

In the second action, Hunter v. London Docklands Development Corporation , the respondent plaintiffs claim damages in respect of damage caused by what they claim to be excessive amounts of dust created by the construction by the defendants of a road 1,800 metres in length, known as the Limehouse Link Road, which was constructed by the defendants between November 1989 and May 1993. The plaintiffs are residents in the affected area, and they advanced their claims in negligence and nuisance and under the rule in *Rylands v. Fletcher* (1868) L.R. 3 H.L. 330, though this last head of claim has been abandoned.

In both actions, Judge Fox-Andrews Q.C. made orders for the trial of a number of preliminary issues of law. Of the issues of law in the first action, two have survived to reach your Lordships' House, viz. (1) whether interference with television reception is capable of constituting an

害的情形但是却并没有对其采取任何措施。

我认为上诉人应该胜诉。

56. Hunter v Canary Wharf Ltd [1997] AC 655

联合王国上议院

Goff 大法官主笔：

诸位上议院的大法官，这里需要审理的是两件上诉案，二者都涉及某些有关"私有妨害"的基本问题。

在第一起案件（*Hunter v Canary Wharf Ltd.*）中，上诉人（原审原告）以被告干扰其家中的电视信号为由，请求损害赔偿。上诉人诉称，被告在其土地上修建 Canary Wharf 塔是其电视信号受阻的原因。该塔高 250 米（约 800 英尺），宽超过 50 米。系争区域的电视信号由 BBC 公司在 Crystal Palace 的发射机发射。原告诉称，由于该塔的高度及其表面使用的金属材质（该塔喷镀了不锈钢，并安装了钢化玻璃），Crystal Palace 的信号受到了干扰。所有的原告都在相应的时间居住在受到干扰的 Isle of Dogs，此时此区域被很多人称为"阴影之地"。原告诉称对信号的干扰开始于 1989 年，并与该塔的修建"相伴"始终。后来，为了解决信号干扰的问题，有人修建了一个信号中继器。这个信号中继器在 1991 年 4 月投入使用。原告诉称，他们在 1991 年 7 月到 1992 年 4 月间，为了获得满意的信号，调整或者更换了家里的电视天线。原告依据在这段过程中所遭受到的信号干扰为由，请求损害赔偿。原告的诉由开始是妨害和过失，后来他们放弃了后者。

在第二起案件（*Hunter v London Docklands Development Corporation*）中，被上诉人（原审原告）以被告在修建一条 1800 米长的道路（即 Limehouse Link Road，由被告修建于 1989 年 11 月和 1993 年 5 月之间）时产生了过量的尘土为由，请求损害赔偿。原告们是受到修路时尘土影响的地区的居民。他们的诉由是三项：过失、妨害，以及 *Rylands v Fletcher*（1868）L.R. 3 H.L. 330 一案所确定的规则，他们后来放弃了第三项诉由。

在这两起案件中，巡回法官 Fox-Andrews 御用大律师决定先审理一系列的先决法律问题。在第一起案件涉及的问题中，有两个问题最终需要各位大法官来决定，即：第一，电视信号被干扰是否属于妨害；第二，若某人要提起私有妨害之诉，他是否需要对系争地产享有某种利益，如果答案是肯定的，

actionable nuisance, and (2) whether it is necessary to have an interest in property to claim in private nuisance and, if so, what interest in property will satisfy this requirement. In the second action, the only issue to reach your Lordships' House is the latter of these two issues.

The preliminary issues in the two actions were considered by Judge Havery Q.C. at separate hearings. In respect of the two issues in the first action, he held (1) that interference with television reception is capable of constituting an actionable nuisance, but (2) that a right of exclusive possession of land is necessary to entitle a person to sue in private nuisance. He later held that his answer on the second issue was applicable in the case of the same issue in the second action. The Court of Appeal, ante, pp. 662G et seq., reversed the decision of Judge Havery on both issues, holding (1) that the creation or presence of a building in the line of sight between a television transmitter and other properties is not actionable as an interference with the use and enjoyment of land, but (2) that occupation of property as a home provided a sufficiently substantial link to enable the occupier to sue in private nuisance. The plaintiffs in the first action now appeal to your Lordships' House against the first of these answers, and the defendants in both actions appeal or cross-appeal against the second.

…

The question therefore arises whether your Lordships should be persuaded to depart from established principle, and recognise such a right in others who are no more than mere licensees on the land. At the heart of this question lies a more fundamental question, which relates to the scope of the law of private nuisance. Here I wish to draw attention to the fact that although, in the past, damages for personal injury have been recovered at least in actions of public nuisance, there is now developing a school of thought that the appropriate remedy for such claims as these should lie in our now fully developed law of negligence, and that personal injury claims should be altogether excluded from the domain of nuisance. The most forthright proponent of this approach has been Professor Newark, in his article "The Boundaries of Nuisance,"65 L.Q.R. 480 from which I have already quoted. Furthermore, it is now being suggested that claims in respect of physical damage to the land should also be excluded from private nuisance: see, e.g., the article by Mr. Conor Gearty on "The Place of Private Nuisance in a Modern Law of Torts" [1989] C.L.J. 214 . In any event, it is right for present purposes to regard the typical cases of private nuisance as being those concerned with interference with the enjoyment of land and, as such, generally actionable only by a person with a right in the land. Characteristic examples of cases of this kind are those concerned with noise, vibrations, noxious smells and the like. The two appeals with which your Lordships are here concerned arise from actions of this character.

For private nuisances of this kind, the primary remedy is in most cases an injunction, which is sought to bring the nuisance to an end, and in most cases should swiftly achieve that objective. The right to bring such proceedings is, as the law stands, ordinarily vested in the person who has

那么需要什么样的利益才能满足要求。第二起案件中需要诸位大法官来审理的问题只有一个,该问题和第一起案件的第二个问题相同。

巡回法官 Havery 御用大律师在不同的听证会上,审理了这两起案件中的先决问题。对于第一起案件,他认为:首先,干扰电视信号属于可诉的妨害;其次,提起私有妨害之诉之人需要对涉案土地享有独占权。最后,他表示他对第一起案件第二个问题的观点,同样适用于第二起案件中的类似问题。上诉法院撤销了 Havery 法官对于这两个问题的判决,他们认为:首先,在电视信号发射机和他人的地产之间、目视距离内修建或持有建筑,不属于可诉的对他人地产用益的妨害;其次,若某人以居住目的,占有一块地产,该人即与该地有足够的"实质联系",他因此足以提起私有妨害之诉。第一起案件中的原告向诸位大法官就第一个问题提起上诉;两起原告中的被告则就第二个问题提起上诉。

……

这样看来,需要请诸位大法官决定的问题是我们是否应该背离既定的原则,以承认那不过是一块土地上的"被许可进入者"的权利。这个问题的更基本的实质其实是,"私有妨害"法的调整范围到底多大。这里我觉得有必要提醒一下各位:虽然在过去,要救济人身损害至少可以用"公共妨害"这一诉由,但是如今却有一种学说认为,鉴于"过失"这一诉由在今天已经发展非常充分了,人身伤害应该完全由"过失"这一诉由来救济,而不应该由"妨害"来调整。这种观点最坚定的支持者之一是 Newark 教授,他的《妨害的边界》一文(载于 65 L.Q.R. 480)前已引述。就解决本案的问题来说,我们所说的私有妨害通常是指由对土地享有某种权利之人提起的,旨在解决妨碍土地用益的情形。典型的例子是噪音、震动、有毒气味之类的。诸位大法官面对的这两宗上诉案件即属于此类情形。

对于此类的"私有妨害",在多数情况下主要的救济措施是禁止令,一般来说禁止令足以很快地实现排除妨害这一目标。这样,提起诉讼的权利就一般由对土地享有完全的占有权之人行使。当然,如果有权提起诉讼之人愿意,也可以与制造妨害之人达成协议:这种协议或者允许妨害制造者在一段时间内继续其妨害行为(当然一般是在支付一定补偿金的情况

exclusive possession of the land. He or she is the person who will sue, if it is necessary to do so. Moreover he or she can, if thought appropriate, reach an agreement with the person creating the nuisance, either that it may continue for a certain period of time, possibly on the payment of a sum of money, or that it shall cease, again perhaps on certain terms including the time within which the cessation will take place. The former may well occur when an agreement is reached between neighbours about the circumstances in which one of them may carry out major repairs to his house which may affect the other's enjoyment of his property. An agreement of this kind was expressly contemplated by Fletcher Moulton L.J. in his judgment in *Malone v. Laskey* [1907] 2 K.B. 141, 153. But the efficacy of arrangements such as these depends upon the existence of an identifiable person with whom the creator of the nuisance can deal for this purpose. If anybody who lived in the relevant property as a home had the right to sue, sensible arrangements such as these might in some cases no longer be practicable.

Moreover, any such departure from the established law on this subject, such as that adopted by the Court of Appeal in the present case, faces the problem of defining the category of persons who would have the right to sue. The Court of Appeal adopted the not easily identifiable category of those who have a "substantial link" with the land, regarding a person who occupied the premises "as a home" as having a sufficient link for this purpose. But who is to be included in this category? It was plainly intended to include husbands and wives, or partners, and their children, and even other relatives living with them. But is the category also to include the lodger upstairs, or the au pair girl or resident nurse caring for an invalid who makes her home in the house while she works there? If the latter, it seems strange that the category should not extend to include places where people work as well as places where they live, where nuisances such as noise can be just as unpleasant or distracting. In any event, the extension of the tort in this way would transform it from a tort to land into a tort to the person, in which damages could be recovered in respect of something less serious than personal injury and the criteria for liability were founded not upon negligence but upon striking a balance between the interests of neighbours in the use of their land. This is, in my opinion, not an acceptable way in which to develop the law.

It was suggested in the course of argument that at least the spouse of a husband or wife who, for example as freeholder or tenant, had exclusive possession of the matrimonial home should be entitled to sue in private nuisance. For the purposes of this submission, your Lordships were referred to the relevant legislation, notably the Matrimonial Homes Act 1983 and the Family Law Act 1996. I do not however consider it necessary to go through the statutory provisions. As I understand the position, it is as follows. If under the relevant legislation a spouse becomes entitled to possession of the matrimonial home or part of it, there is no reason why he or she should not be able to sue in private nuisance in the ordinary way. But I do not see how a spouse who has no interest in the matrimonial home has, simply by virtue of his or her cohabiting in the

下），或者要求妨害制造者马上停止妨害（当然一般也会附有规定妨害必须完全停止的时间的条款）。签订前一种协议的情况一般是某人为了维修自己的房屋可能会影响其邻居对其财产的用益。Fletcher Moulton 上诉法院法官在 *Malone v Laskey* [1907] 2 K.B. 141, 153 一案中即讨论了这种情况。然而能签订此类协议的前提是妨害的制造者知道跟谁签订协议。如果所有住在同一地产上的人都有权起诉，那么签订这种类型的协议就不再具有可行性了。

另外，像上诉法院就本案的这种偏离实在法的做法，会面临一个定义谁是有权起诉之人的问题。上诉法院认为所有的与系争土地有"实质联系"之人都可以起诉，而所谓的"实质联系"是指一个人以系争的地产作为其住所。然而，这个"与土地具有实质联系之人"到底包括多大的一个群体呢？很明显，这个标准肯定是要包括土地独占权人的配偶、他们的同居伴侣、他们的子女，以及和他们共同生活之人。然而这个标准是否也要包括租客、换工住宿女孩或者在主人家照顾瘫痪病人的住家护士呢？如果上述之人也包括的话，那么就没有理由不把可以提起诉讼之人扩大到所有的在系争地产上工作并居住的人，因为他们和前述人员一样都遭受到了妨害。如果我们允许这种扩张"妨害"诉由范围的调整，那么它很可能就会从一个针对土地的诉由变成一个针对人身的诉由。在这种诉由下，就算受害人遭受到的损害比"人身损害"更轻，他也可以得到赔偿；并且此时归责的出发点不再是加害人的过失，而是邻居之间的利益平衡。在我看来，这并不是值得我们接受的一种发展法律规范的方法。

各位大法官还指出，如果一个人的配偶对婚姻居所有独占权（作为所有权人或者承租人），那么这个配偶至少应该有权依据"私有妨害"来起诉。为了支撑这种观点，各位大法官提到了一系列规范性文件，比如《1983 年婚姻居所法》和《1996 年家庭法》。然而，我觉得我们没有必要去翻看这些文件，因为下面的这些理由：如果一个配偶因为相关的规范性文件而对婚姻居所的全部或者部分享有独占权，那么我们自然没有理由不允许他正常地行使独占权人可以行使的"私有妨害"之诉的诉权。然而，如果一个人对婚姻居所其实并没有类似的利益，那么仅仅因为他住在婚姻居所里面且其配偶是系争地产的所有权人或者承租人，就允许他行使私有妨害之诉的诉权是不恰当的。我这么说是因为上述的配偶其实和其他类型的同居者，如子女或者祖父

matrimonial home with his or her wife or husband whose freehold or leasehold property it is, a right to sue. No distinction can sensibly be drawn between such spouses and other cohabitees in the home, such as children, or grandparents. Nor do I see any great disadvantage flowing from this state of affairs. If a nuisance should occur, then the spouse who has an interest in the property can bring the necessary proceedings to bring the nuisance to an end, and can recover any damages in respect of the discomfort or inconvenience caused by the nuisance. Even if he or she is away from home, nowadays the necessary authority to commence proceedings for an injunction can usually be obtained by telephone. Moreover, if the other spouse suffers personal injury, including injury to health, he or she may, like anybody else, be able to recover damages in negligence. The only disadvantage is that the other spouse cannot bring an independent action in private nuisance for damages for discomfort or inconvenience.

...

LORD LLOYD

If the occupier of land suffers personal injury as a result of inhaling the smoke, he may have a cause of action in negligence. But he does not have a cause of action in nuisance for his *personal* injury, nor for interference with his *personal* enjoyment. It follows that the quantum of damages in private nuisance does not depend on the number of those enjoying the land in question. It also follows that the only persons entitled to sue for loss in amenity value of the land are the owner or the occupier with the right to exclusive possession.

...

LORD HOFFMAN

Up to about 20 years ago, no one would have had the slightest doubt about who could sue. Nuisance is a tort against land, including interests in land such as easements and profits. A plaintiff must therefore have an interest in the land affected by the nuisance. ... But the concept of nuisance as a tort against land has recently been questioned by the decision of the Court of Appeal in *Khorasandjian v. Bush* [1993] Q.B. 727.

...

This reasoning, which is echoed in some academic writing and the Canadian case of Motherwell v. Motherwell 73 D.L.R. (3d) 62 , which the Court of Appeal followed, is based upon a fundamental mistake about the remedy which the tort of nuisance provides. It arises, I think, out of a misapplication of an important distinction drawn by Lord Westbury L.C. in *St. Helen's Smelting Co. v. Tipping* (1865) 11 H.L.Cas. 642. In that case, the plaintiff bought a 1,300 acre estate in Lancashire. He complained that his hedges, trees and shrubs were being damaged by pollution from the defendants' copper-smelting works a mile and a half away. The defendants said that the area was full of factories and chemical works and that if the plaintiff was entitled to complain, industry would be brought to a halt.

母没有本质区别。我这么说还有一个原因，那就是现行法的规定其实并不会产生什么严重的弊端。如果一个配偶对系争地产存在相应的利益，那么他自然可以按照现行法提起"私有妨害"之诉，或者通过禁止令来排除妨害，或者获得损害赔偿以弥补其遭受的不适。现在这个时代就算这个配偶不在家，他也可以打个电话来完成相应的程序来申请禁止令。而如果一个配偶遭受了人身损害（比如其健康权被侵害），那么他自然可以像任何别人一样提起"过失之诉"。唯一可能存在的问题是这个配偶此时没办法提起独立的私有妨害之诉来申请损害赔偿，以弥补其遭受的不适。

......

Lloyd 大法官主笔：

若一块土地的占有者因为吸入烟尘而遭受人身损害，他可以提起过失之诉。然而他却不能因为人身损害或者"对人身性的用益权的妨害"提起妨害之诉。因此，私有妨害之诉中的赔偿额，显然并不取决于有多少人在使用一块土地。因此，能因为土地休憩价值减少而提起诉讼之人，只是该土地的所有权人或者其他的有独占权之人。

......

Hoffman 大法官主笔：

二十年前，谁能提起妨害之诉是毫无疑问的。妨害之诉是对土地的诉讼，为的是保护土地上的利益，如地役权和孳息。因此，该诉的原告必须拥有一项被妨害所影响的对土地的权益。然而，*Khorasandjian v Bush* [1993] Q.B. 727 一案的上诉法院对这种把妨害之诉视为对土地的诉讼的观点有所质疑。

......

这种观点反映在某些学术作品和一个加拿大的判例 *Motherwell v. Motherwell* 73 D.L.R.（3d）62（该判例为上诉法院所遵循）中。然而，它们对妨害之诉所提供的救济的理解，犯有根本的错误。在我看来，这种错误的原因是他们误解了 Westbury 大法官在 *St. Helen's Smelting Co. v Tipping*（1865）11 H.L.Cas. 642 一案中所做出的对妨害的一个重要划分。在这个案件中，原告在兰开夏购买了 1300 英亩的土地。原告诉称他的各种树木，因一英里半外被告的炼铜厂所排放的污染，而遭到了损害。被告辩称，涉案区域内遍布各种工厂，若类似原告这样的人都有权起诉，那么工厂就会被迫停业。

......

St. Helen's Smelting Co. v Tipping 是一个里程碑式的判决。这个判决

…

St. Helen's Smelting Co. v. Tipping was a landmark case. It drew the line beyond which rural and landed England did not have to accept external costs imposed upon it by industrial pollution. But there has been, I think, some inclination to treat it as having divided nuisance into two torts, one of causing "material injury to the property," such as flooding or depositing poisonous substances on crops, and the other of causing "sensible personal discomfort" such as excessive noise or smells. In cases in the first category, there has never been any doubt that the remedy, whether by way of injunction or damages, is for causing damage to the land. It is plain that in such a case only a person with an interest in the land can sue. But there has been a tendency to regard cases in the second category as actions in respect of the discomfort or even personal injury which the plaintiff has suffered or is likely to suffer. On this view, the plaintiff's interest in the land becomes no more than a qualifying condition or springboard which entitles him to sue for injury to himself.

If this were the case, the need for the plaintiff to have an interest in land would indeed be hard to justify. The passage I have quoted from Dillon L.J. (*Khorasandjian v. Bush* [1993] Q.B. 727, 734) is an eloquent statement of the reasons. But the premise is quite mistaken. In the case of nuisances "productive of sensible personal discomfort," the action is not for causing discomfort to the person but, as in the case of the first category, for causing injury to the land. True it is that the land has not suffered "sensible" injury, but its utility has been diminished by the existence of the nuisance. It is for an unlawful threat to the utility of his land that the possessor or occupier is entitled to an injunction and it is for the diminution in such utility that he is entitled to compensation.

…

There may of course be cases in which, in addition to damages for injury to his land, the owner or occupier is able to recover damages for consequential loss. He will, for example, be entitled to loss of profits which are the result of inability to use the land for the purposes of his business. Or if the land is flooded, he may also be able to recover damages for chattels or livestock lost as a result. But inconvenience, annoyance or even illness suffered by persons on land as a result of smells or dust are not damage consequential upon the injury to the land. It is rather the other way about: the injury to the amenity of the land consists in the fact that the persons upon it are liable to suffer inconvenience, annoyance or illness.

It follows that damages for nuisance recoverable by the possessor or occupier may be affected by the size, commodiousness and value of his property but cannot be increased merely because more people are in occupation and therefore suffer greater collective discomfort. If more than one person has an interest in the property, the damages will have to be divided among them. If there are joint owners, they will be jointly entitled to the damages. If there is a reversioner and

划了一条红线，在这条红线内英国的乡绅们可以免受工业污染所带来的额外代价。然而，我发现有人会把这个判决的意思解读成要把"妨害"分成两种：一种是那些"对土地本身产生的物质性损害"，如水淹或者在庄嫁上投放有毒物质；另一种是那些"对人的感官造成的不适"，如过度的噪音或者气味。对于第一种妨害，毫无疑问，救济措施——无论是禁止令还是损害赔偿——都是针对土地本身的。很明显，此时能够提起诉讼的只有对土地有某种利益之人。问题是，现在好像有一种倾向，认为对第二种类型的妨害提起的诉讼是针对原告所遭受的或者可能遭受的不适或者人身损害。在这种观点之下，原告对于土地的利益不过是一个让他能够起诉的适格条件或者借口。

如果我们认同这种说法，那么我们就很难明白为什么原告需要对土地有某种利益才能起诉。我所引用的 Dillon 上诉法院法官的话就非常清楚地阐明了这点。然而，他的话犯了一个前提性的错误：即便我们面临的妨害是那种"对人的感官造成的不适"的类型，我们的诉讼所针对的也并不是对人造成的不适，而是对土地的损害。诚然在这种情况下，土地不可能遭受感官性的损害，然而此时土地的效用因为妨害的存在而被打了折扣。因此，土地的占有者之所以能申请禁止令，是因为对土地的效用受到减损的危险；土地的占有者之所以能请求损害赔偿，是因为对土地的效用已经实际地减损了。

……

除了对土地的直接损害，土地的所有者或者占有者当然有时也可以请求对间接损害进行赔偿，比如因土地无法使用而导致营业收入的减少，或者当土地被水淹时的牲畜损失。然而，人在一块土地上所遭受的，因为气味或尘土而产生的不便、不适甚至伤害绝不是对这块土地的损害。恰恰相反，这种损害不如说是一块土地不可避免地会给进入它的人带来不便、不适或者伤害。

对妨害的赔偿金额取决于所涉及的土地的面积和价值的大小，但这个金额绝不可能仅仅因为住在上面的人更多因而遭受到了更多的不适就有所提高。若不止一人对一块土地有利益，那么赔偿金需要在他们之间分配。如果是共有人，那么他们共有赔偿金，如果是复归权人且其复归权因为被妨害而遭到了永久性的损害，那么该复归权人根据他所享有的利益可以请求相应的赔偿金。然而绝不能仅仅因为土地上的利益被分割了，更不能仅仅因为住在一块土地上的人数增加了，就增加赔偿金的数额。

the nuisance has caused damage of a permanent character which affects the reversion, he will be entitled to damages according to his interest. But the damages cannot be increased by the fact that the interests in the land are divided; still less according to the number of persons residing on the premises.

...

Once it is understood that nuisances "productive of sensible personal discomfort" (*St. Helen's Smelting Co. v. Tipping,* 11 H.L.Cas. 642, 650) do not constitute a separate tort of causing discomfort to people but are merely part of a single tort of causing injury to land, the rule that the plaintiff must have an interest in the land falls into place as logical and, indeed, inevitable.

Is there any reason of policy why the rule should be abandoned? Once nuisance has escaped the bounds of being a tort against land, there seems no logic in compromise limitations, such as that proposed by the Court of Appeal in this case, requiring the plaintiff to have been residing on land as his or her home. This was recognised by the Court of Appeal in *Khorasandjian v. Bush* [1993] Q.B. 727 where the injunction applied whether the plaintiff was at home or not. There is a good deal in this case and other writings about the need for the law to adapt to modern social conditions. But the development of the common law should be rational and coherent. It should not distort its principles and create anomalies merely as an expedient to fill a gap.

...

So far as the claim is for personal injury, it seems to me that the only appropriate cause of action is negligence. It would be anomalous if the rules for recovery of damages under this head were different according as to whether, for example, the plaintiff was at home or at work. It is true, as I have said, that the law of negligence gives no remedy for discomfort or distress which does not result in bodily or psychiatric illness. But this is a matter of general policy and I can see no logic in making an exception for cases in which the discomfort or distress was suffered at home rather than somewhere else.

Finally there is the position of spouses. It is said to be contrary to modern ways of thinking that a wife should not be able to sue for interference with the enjoyment of the matrimonial home merely because she has no proprietary right in the property. To some extent, this argument is based upon the fallacy which I have already discussed, namely that the action in nuisance lies for inconvenience or annoyance caused to people who happen to be in possession or occupation of land. But so far as it is thought desirable that the wife should be able to sue for injury to a proprietary or possessory interest in the home, the answer in my view lies in the law of property, not the law of tort. The courts today will readily assume that a wife has acquired a beneficial interest in the matrimonial home. If so, she will be entitled to sue for damage to that interest. On the other hand, if she has no such interest, I think it would be wrong to create a quasi-proprietary interest only for the purposes of giving her locus standi to sue for nuisance. What would she be

……

现在我们知道了"对人的感官造成的不适"的那类妨害（*St. Helen's Smelting Co. v Tipping,* 11 H.L.Cas. 642, 650）并不构成一类单独的对人的侵权诉因，而仅仅是对土地的侵权的一种。因此，原告必须在土地上有利益这一规则逻辑上讲，自然成立。

那么有没有什么政策的原因让我们要放弃这个规则呢？如果妨碍不再仅仅是一种对土地的侵权，那么我们就没有什么理由要对它的适用范围进行任何限制，比如像本案中的上诉法院要求原告需要在涉及的土地上设定居所这样的限制。在 *Khorasandjian v Bush* [1993] Q.B. 727 一案中，上诉法院就持有这种不需对原告的范围进行限制的观点：本案中上诉法院认为无论原告是否在家，都有权申请禁止令。这个案件和其他一系列的文献都在强调法律适应现代社会情况的必要性。然而，普通法的发展应该是理性而自洽的，不能仅仅因为需要填补法律漏洞就扭曲普通法的原则或者创造新的特例。

……

鉴于本案中原告的请求是损害赔偿，我认为唯一合适的诉由是"过失"。如果是按照过失来判决的话，那么我们根据原告是以涉案土地为居所还是工作场所，而对他的诉讼请求有不同的意见，就极不恰当了。诚然，正如我之前所言，如果原告并没有遭受身体或者精神上的病害，仅仅是遭受了不适或者痛苦，过失之诉并不能给其以救济。然而，这种救济的缺失是基于政策的考量。我认为没有任何理由仅仅因为原告遭受到的不适或者痛苦是在其家中发生的而不是其他地方发生的，就对其网开一面放弃这种政策考量。

最后我们要讨论一下配偶在妨害之诉中的地位。或许有人认为，仅仅因为一个妻子对其婚姻居所不享有财产性权利就不允许她就在这里受到的妨害向法院起诉，这是与现代的思考方式相冲突的。这种说法其实在某种程度上是基于我已经讨论过的一种谬误：即妨害之诉救济的是土地的占有人在这块土地上遭受到的不便或者烦恼。有人认为应该允许该妻子以某种对共同居所的财产性利益而起诉。我认为，这个说法其实反映了这是一个财产法问题而不是侵权法问题。现在的法院常常认为妻子可以在婚姻居所上获得一种"受益的利益"。如果确实是这样，那么该妻子就可以基于这个"受益的利益"被损害这一事实提起诉讼。相反，如果我们不给她这种利益，那么仅仅为了给她一种临时的提起妨害之诉的诉讼资格而给她创设一种准财产性权益，就是错误的。此时，她起诉是为了什么呢？Brennan 先生（原告的代理人），援引了《1983 年婚姻居所法》，该法对那种对婚姻居所本身并无财产权利的配偶，赋予了某种权利。然而，该法条的效果其实是，根据离婚时法院的命令，一个配偶可以对其婚姻居所获得独占权。如果一个配偶确实获得这种独占权，

suing for? Mr. Brennan, who appeared for the plaintiffs, drew our attention to the rights conferred upon a wife with no proprietary interest by the Matrimonial Homes Act 1983. The effect of these provisions is that a spouse may, by virtue of an order of the court upon a break-up of the marriage, become entitled to exclusive possession of the home. If so, she will become entitled to sue for nuisance. Until then, her interest is analogous to a contingent reversion. It cannot be affected by a nuisance which merely damages the amenity of the property while she has no right to possession.

...

LORD COOKE

Private nuisance is commonly said to be an interference with the enjoyment of land and to be actionable by an occupier. But "occupier" is an expression of varying meanings, as a perusal of legal dictionaries shows. ... Where interference with an amenity of a home is in issue there is no a priori reason why the expression should not include, and it appears natural that it should include, anyone living there who has been exercising a continuing right to enjoyment of that amenity. ... A temporary visitor, however, someone who is "merely present in the house" (a phrase used by Fletcher Moulton L.J. in *Malone v. Laskey* [1907] 2 K.B. 141, 154), would not enjoy occupancy of sufficiently substantial nature.

Malone v. Laskey, a case of personal injury from a falling bracket rather than an interference with amenities, is not directly in point, but it is to be noted that the wife of the subtenant's manager, who had been permitted by the subtenant to live in the premises with her husband, was dismissed by Sir Gorell Barnes P., at p. 151, as a person who had "no right of occupation in the proper sense of the term" and by Fletcher Moulton L.J. as being "merely present." My Lords, whatever the acceptability of those descriptions 90 years ago, I can only agree with the Appellate Division of the Alberta Supreme Court in Motherwell v. Motherwell, at p. 77, that they are "rather light treatment of a wife, at least in today's society where she is no longer considered subservient to her husband." Current statutes give effect to current perceptions by according spouses a special status in respect of the matrimonial home, as by enabling the court to make orders regarding occupation (see in England the Family Law Act 1996, sections 30 and 31). Although such provisions and orders thereunder do not of themselves confer proprietary rights, they support in relation to amenities the force and common sense of the words of Clement J.A. in Motherwell v. Motherwell, at p. 78:

> "Here we have a wife harassed in the matrimonial home. She has a status, a right to live there with her husband and children. I find it absurd to say that her occupancy of the matrimonial home is insufficient to found an action in nuisance."

As between spouses and de facto partners the question whether contributions in money or services give a proprietary equitable interest in a matrimonial home is a notoriously difficult one

那么她自然是可以提起妨害之诉的。然而在这之前,她的利益类似于一个"或有复归权"。此时,如果她对土地并无其他类型的占有权,那么她的这种利益就不会仅仅因为土地休憩价值的减损而受到损害。

……

Cooke 大法官主笔:

私有妨害通常是指对土地用益价值的妨碍,通常土地的"占用者"可以提出这种诉讼。然而,查诸各种法律词典,"占用者"一词具有多种含义。……当发生了房屋的休憩价值被妨碍的事件时,我们可以理所当然地认为这个词包括任何在该房屋上行使不间断休憩权之人。……然而,临时的房客,或者说一个"仅仅存在于房屋中的人"〔Fletcher Moulton 上诉法院法官在 *Malone v Laskey*(1907)2 K.B. 141, 154 一案中适用这个表述〕,就因为不具有足够的实质的特征,而不属于这里所说的"占用者"。

Malone v Laskey 一案涉及的是因为脱落的支架造成的人身伤害,而非对土地的妨害,因此与本案并无直接相关性。然而,这个案件中有一点还是需要注意的,那就是本案中次承租人的经理获得了次承租人的允许,与丈夫同住在涉案地产上。首席法官 Gorell Barnes 爵士就认为此时的这个经理并不具有"正确意义的占有权";Fletcher Moulton 上诉法院法官则认为她"仅仅是出现在涉案地产上"的人。诸位大法官,无论上述说法在 90 年前是如何适当,但是在今天我只能同意阿尔伯塔高等法院上诉庭在 *Motherwell v. Motherwell*(第 77 页)中的观点,"这是对一个妻子的轻视,至少在今天这个妻子不再从属于丈夫的时代是种轻视"。我们的这种观点,也得到了当代的法律的支持:根据相关法条,法院有权作出有关居住权的决定,以此授予一个配偶一定的对婚姻居所的特殊地位(参见英格兰的《1996 年家庭法》第 30 条和第 31 条)。虽然上述的法条本身并没有直接授予配偶以财产权,但是这些法条却能够用来支持 Clement J.A 在 *Motherwell v Motherwell* 一案中就休憩权所发表的言论(第 78 页):

> 本案中的妻子在婚姻居所中受到了骚扰。她有(对于该居所特殊的)地位,有权和她的丈夫、孩子住在这里。因此,在我看来,那种认为她对婚姻居所的居住权并不足以支撑她提起妨害之诉的看法,是荒谬的。

对于配偶和事实伴侣,投入金钱或者劳务是否能够给其婚姻居所上的衡平法上的财产利益,是一个在今天看来非常困难的问题,困扰了整个普通法世界。因此,我们在考虑妨害之诉时,最好不要涉及这个复杂的枝节问题。

孩子对于居所的地位则是另一回事,而且可能更复杂。然而,经过考虑,

today, wrestled with throughout the common law world. Nuisance actions would seem better left free of the complication of this side issue.

The status of children living at home is different and perhaps more problematical but, on consideration, I am persuaded by the majority of the Court of Appeal in *Khorasandjian v. Bush* [1993] Q.B. 727 and the weight of North American jurisprudence to the view that they, too, should be entitled to relief for substantial and unlawful interference with the amenities of their home.

...

My Lords, there is a maxim *communis error facit jus (common error makes law)*. I have collected the foregoing references not to invoke it, however, but to suggest respectfully that on this hitherto unsettled issue the general trend of leading scholarly opinion need not be condemned as erroneous. Although hitherto the law of England on the point has not been settled by your Lordships' House, it is agreed on all hands that some link with the land is necessary for standing to sue in private nuisance. The precise nature of that link remains to be defined, partly because of the ambiguity of "occupy" and its derivatives. In ordinary usage the verb can certainly include "reside in," which is indeed the first meaning given in the *Concise Oxford Dictionary* .

In logic more than one answer can be given. Logically it is possible to say that the right to sue for interference with the amenities of a home should be confined to those with proprietary interests and licensees with exclusive possession. No less logically the right can be accorded to all who live in the home. Which test should be adopted, that is to say which should be the governing principle, is a question of the policy of the law. It is a question not capable of being answered by analysis alone. All that analysis can do is expose the alternatives. Decisions such as *Malone v. Laskey* [1907] 2 K.B. 141 do not attempt that kind of analysis, and in refraining from recognising that value judgments are involved they compare less than favourably with the approach of the present-day Court of Appealin Khorasandjian and this case. The reason why I prefer the alternative advocated with unwonted vigour of expression by the doyen of living tort writers is that it gives better effect to widespread conceptions concerning the home and family.

Of course in this field as in most others there will be borderline cases and anomalies wherever the lines are drawn. Thus there are, for instance, the lodger and, as some of your Lordships note, the au pair girl (although she may not figure among the present plaintiffs). It would seem weak, though, to refrain from laying down a just rule for spouses and children on the ground that it is not easy to know where to draw the lines regarding other persons. Without being wedded to this solution, I am not persuaded that there is sufficient justification for disturbing the conclusion adopted by Pill L.J. with the concurrence of Neill and Waite L.JJ. Occupation of the property as a home is, to me, an acceptable criterion, consistent with the traditional concern for the sanctity of family life and the Englishman's home - which need not in this context include his workplace. As already mentioned, it is consistent also with international standards.

我赞同 *Khorasandjian v Bush* [1993] Q.B. 727 一案中上诉法院的多数意见；这种意见也是北美的通说：孩子也应该有权获得一定的救济措施，以解决严重且违法的对他们的居所的休憩价值的妨碍。

……

诸位大法官，法谚有云："众人之误，则成法律。"当然，我引述前面的内容并不是为了提出这句谚语。我的目的是想提醒诸位，对于我们目前面临的这个未决的疑问，学界的主流观点不能被随意地视为错误。虽然到目前为止，诸位尚未有机会对英格兰法律如何处理这个问题作出决定，但是，几乎所有人都认同只要一个人和一块土地有某种联系，他就有权提起私有妨害之诉。当然，这个联系具体是什么是需要讨论的，部分原因是因为"占据"一词及其派生词所具有的歧义。在日常用语中，这个词当然包括"居住在"这一意思，这个义项是《牛津简明词典》对这个词的第一解释。

然而在逻辑上，对于这个问题众说纷纭，都不能算错。那种认为要提起对房屋的休憩价值的妨碍，需要对涉案地产具有财产性利益，或者具有独占权的观点，可以说是合乎逻辑的。然而，那种认为这种诉权应该被任何居住在这里的人所享有的观点，也是合乎逻辑的。那么我们应该采纳何种标准，或者说适用哪一种原则呢？这其实是一个法政策的问题。要解决这个问题不能只靠分析。分析所能做的是列出所有的可能性。*Malone v Laskey* [1907] 2 K.B. 141 一类的判决也并没有做这样的分析。这一类的判决没有做任何的价值判断，而是不得不参考现今上诉法院在 Khorasandjian 和本案中所采纳的那种方法。我是更赞同侵权法学者们那激情洋溢的话语的，因为他们的观点更加考虑到了人民群众所广泛接受的对于住宅和家庭的观点。

当然，如同在任何其他领域，在本案涉及的这个领域内，只要我们划出一条有权提起诉讼之人的线，那么必然会面临临界案件的问题。比如在涉及寄宿者或者某些大法官提到的换工住宿女孩（虽然这些人并不是本案的被告）时。然而，如果仅仅因为我们很难清楚地知道如何划出一条线来确定能够起诉之人，就去否认配偶和子女属于这个范围的话，那就有些错误了。我不会得出这样错误的结论，因为我不认为我们有足够的理由来偏离 Pill 上诉法院法官作出的结论（Neill 和 Waite 法官复议）。对我来说，是否以居住为目的占据一块地产，是一个可以接受的判断谁可以起诉的标准。这个标准符合我们英国人对家庭和居所的神圣性的重视，而工作场所则缺乏这种神圣性。同时如我前面所说，这也符合国际标准。

其他的同居家庭成员，包括同居者和寄宿者，在某些特定的情况下可以被认为是在涉案土地上设定了住所，因此在这些情况下也可以就那些对他依

Other resident members of the family, including such de facto partners and lodgers as may on the particular facts fairly be considered as having a home in the premises, could therefore be allowed standing to complain of truly serious interference with the domestic amenities lawfully enjoyed by them. By contrast, the policy of the law need not extend to giving a remedy in nuisance to non-resident employees in commercial premises. The employer is responsible for their welfare. On this part of the case I have only to add that normally there should not be any difficulty about sensible compromises with the author of the nuisance. Members of a household impliedly authorise the householder to represent them in such matters.

…

LORD HOPE

There is no reported case where an easement against the interruption of the receipt of radio or television signals has yet been recognised. The closest analogy is with uninterrupted prospect, which cannot be acquired by prescription, but only by agreement or by express grant. Unless restricted by covenant the owner is entitled to put up whatever he chooses on his own land, even though his neighbour's view is interrupted. The interruption of view will carry with it various consequences. It may reduce amenity generally, or it may impede more particular things such as the transmission of visual signals to the land from other properties. That may be highly inconvenient and it may even diminish the value of the land which is affected. But the proprietor of the affected land has nevertheless no actionable ground of complaint. He must make other arrangements if he wishes to continue to receive these signals on his own property. Radio and television signals seem to me to fall into the same general category. They may come from various directions over a wide area as they cross the developer's property. They may be of various frequencies, more or less capable of interruption by tall or metal-clad structures. Their passage from one point to another is invisible. It would be difficult, if not impossible, for the developer to become aware of their existence before he puts up the new building. If he were to be restricted by an easement from putting up a building which interfered with these signals, he might not be able to put up any substantial structures at all. The interference with his freedom would be substantial. I do not think that it would be consistent with principle for such a wide and novel restriction to be recognised. If that is so for easements, then the same result must follow so far as a remedy in nuisance is concerned.

…

法享有的休憩权的严重妨害提起诉讼。相反地，法政策无须将这一救济措施扩展到商业楼宇内的非居住雇员。此时，应该是他们的雇主来考虑到他们的福祉。我需要强调一点，那就是在允许居住者们提起诉讼，并不会妨碍与妨害的制造者达成合理的妥协。家庭成员实质上默示地委托了他们的户主来代表他们去达成这样的妥协。

……

Hope 大法官主笔：

目前为止我们尚未发现涉及旨在保证广播或者电视信号接收的地役权的案件。跟这种情况最类似的，是那种旨在保证自己土地上视野不被遮挡的地役权。这种地役权不可能是法定的，只可能是约定的。因此，一块土地的主人除非受到某种合约的限制，他有权在他的土地上建造任何东西，即便这样做会阻挡他邻居的视野。邻居的视野被阻挡了，可能会导致多种结果。这种阻挡可能在概括意义上减少一块土地的休憩价值；它也可能阻碍某些东西从其他土地上来到涉案土地上，比如阻碍电视信号。这样的阻碍很可能会给土地的利用者带来极大的不便，甚至严重减少土地的价值。然而，受害土地的所有权人从来就没有任何针对这类妨害的适格的诉由。如果他希望能继续接收电视信号，他只能去想其他办法。本案涉及的广播或者电视信号被阻碍就应该属于这类情况。这些信号可能是从一片广阔的区域，从各种不同的方向经过被告开发商的土地的。它们可能具有不同的频率，因此具有不同的被表面镀了金属的高层建筑所阻挡的可能。它们从一地到另一地的轨迹是肉眼不可见的。因此，要让这些开发商在修建建筑之前，提前知道信号的存在，即便不是不可能，也是很困难的。如果开发商受到某种禁止他修建能阻挡信号的建筑的地役权的限制，那么他可能不能修建任何的建筑。这种对开发商的自由的限制，是非常严重的。我认为，承认这种范围过大的新型限制将会与法律的一般原则相抵触。如果对于地役权来说是如此，那么对于与之相关的妨害救济来说亦如是。

……

Chapter 6. Strict Liability

Section 1. Common Starting Point: Rylands v Fletcher

57. Fletcher v Rylands (1865–66) LR 1 Ex 265

Court of Exchequer Chamber, United Kingdom

BLACKBURN J.

This was a special case stated by an arbitrator, under an order of nisi prius, in which the question for the Court is stated to be, whether the plaintiff is entitled to recover any, and, if any, what damages from the defendants, by reason of the matters thereinbefore stated.

In the Court of Exchequer, the Chief Baron and Martin, B., were of opinion that the plaintiff was not entitled to recover at all, Bramwell, B., being of a different opinion. The judgment in the Exchequer was consequently given for the defendants, in conformity with the opinion of the majority of the court. The only question argued before us was, whether this judgment was right, nothing being said about the measure of damages in case the plaintiff should be held entitled to recover. We have come to the conclusion that the opinion of Bramwell, B., was right, and that the answer to the question should be that the plaintiff was entitled to recover damages from the defendants, by reason of the matters stated in the case, and consequently, that the judgment below should be reversed, but we cannot at present say to what damages the plaintiff is entitled.

It appears from the statement in the case, that the plaintiff was damaged by his property being flooded by water, which, without any fault on his part, broke out of a reservoir constructed on the defendants' land by the defendants' orders, and maintained by the defendants.

It appears from the statement in the case that the coal under the defendants' land had, at some remote period, been worked out; but this was unknown at the time when the defendants gave directions to erect the reservoir, and the water in the reservoir would not have escaped from the defendants' land, and no mischief would have been done to the plaintiff, but for this latent defect in the defendants' subsoil. And it further appears, that the defendants selected competent engineers and contractors to make their reservoir, and themselves personally continued in total ignorance of what we have called the latent defect in the subsoil; but that these persons employed by them in the course of the work became aware of the existence of the ancient shafts filled up with soil, though

第六章 严格责任

第一节 共同的起点：Rylands v Fletcher 案

57. Fletcher v Rylands (1865—66) LR 1 Ex 265

联合王国财政署内室法庭

Blackburn 法官主笔：

基于初审法院的法庭命令，仲裁员进行了特别案情陈述，提交给本法官的问题是，原告是否有权获得赔偿，如果有，那么根据陈述中提到的原因，应该从被告处获得多少赔偿。

在财税上诉法院，财税法院首席法官和财税法院 Martin 法官认为，原告根本不应该获得赔偿，财税法院 Bramwell 法官提出了不同意见。财税法院之后作出了与法院的多数意见一致的有利于被告的判决。我们面前讨论的唯一问题是这个判决是否正确，不涉及如果认定原告有权获得赔偿应如何衡量损失的问题。我们认为，财税法院 Bramwell 法官的意见是正确的，并且问题的答案是，根据案件陈述的理由，原告有权从被告处获得损害赔偿，因此应该撤销下级法院的判决，但是目前我们不能就原告有权获得多少赔偿发表意见。

案件陈述显示，原告由于洪水原因遭受了财产损失，原告一方对洪水的暴发不存在任何过错。暴发洪水的水库由被告授意修建在被告的土地上，并由被告维护。

案件陈述显示，被告土地下面的煤炭在很久以前就被消耗殆尽，但是被告在指示修建水库的时候对此并不知情，如果不是因为被告水库的天然地基存在缺陷，水库的水不会从被告土地上泄漏出去，原告是不会受到损害的。陈述进一步显示，被告选择了有资质的工程师和承包商来修建水库，他们对于我们所谓的天然地基的潜在缺陷也完全不知情，但是他们雇佣的人员在作业过程中注意到有一些填满了泥土的古老通风井，但是他们并不知道，或者

they did not know or suspect that they were shafts communicating with old workings.

It is found that the defendants, personally, were free from all blame, but that in fact proper care and skill was not used by the persons employed by them, to provide for the sufficiency of the reservoir with reference to these shafts. The consequence was, that the reservoir when filled with water burst into the shafts, the water flowed down through them into the old workings, and thence into the plaintiff's mine, and there did the mischief.

The plaintiff, though free from all blame on his part, must bear the loss, unless he can establish that it was the consequence of some default for which the defendants are responsible. The question of law therefore arises, what is the obligation which the law casts on a person who, like the defendants, lawfully brings on his land something which, though harmless whilst it remains there, will naturally do mischief if it escapes out of his land. It is agreed on all hands that he must take care to keep in that which he has brought on the land and keeps there, in order that it may not escape and damage his neighbours, but the question arises whether the duty which the law casts upon him, under such circumstances, is an absolute duty to keep it in at his peril, or is, as the majority of the Court of Exchequer have thought, merely a duty to take all reasonable and prudent precautions, in order to keep it in, but no more. If the first be the law, the person who has brought on his land and kept there something dangerous, and failed to keep it in, is responsible for all the natural consequences of its escape. If the second be the limit of his duty, he would not be answerable except on proof of negligence, and consequently would not be answerable for escape arising from any latent defect which ordinary prudence and skill could not detect.

Supposing the second to be the correct view of the law, a further question arises subsidiary to the first, viz., whether the defendants are not so far identified with the contractors whom they employed, as to be responsible for the consequences of their want of care and skill in making the reservoir in fact insufficient with reference to the old shafts, or the existence of which they were aware, though they had not ascertained where the shafts went to.

We think that the true rule of law is, that the person who for his own purposes brings on his lands and collects and keeps there anything likely to do mischief if it escapes, must keep it in at his peril, and, if he does not do so, is prima facie answerable for all the damage which is the natural consequence of its escape. He can excuse himself by showing that the escape was owing to the plaintiff's default; or perhaps that the escape was the consequence of vis major, or the act of God; but as nothing of this sort exists here, it is unnecessary to inquire what excuse would be sufficient. The general rule, as above stated, seems on principle just. The person whose grass or corn is eaten down by the escaping cattle of his neighbour, or whose mine is flooded by the water from his neighbour's reservoir, or whose cellar is invaded by the filth of his neighbour's privy, or whose habitation is made unhealthy by the fumes and noisome vapours of his neighbour's alkali works, is damnified without any fault of his own; and it seems but reasonable and just that the neighbour,

怀疑这些通风井连接着古老的矿井。

可以认定被告个人不存在可责难之处，但是事实上，考虑到这些通风井，被告雇佣的人员未能尽到适当的注意义务并采取合适的技术确保水库合格。后果是，当水库注满水时，水便冲入了通风井，然后向下进入古老的矿井，进而进入了原告的煤矿，最终造成了损害。

尽管原告自身并不存在任何可责难之处，但是必须承担损失，除非原告能够证明是由于被告未履行某种义务而造成了这样的结果。由此而出现了法律问题，即如果像被告一样的某个人合法地将某种物品带入了自己的土地，这个物品留在被告土地上时是无害的，但是如果脱离了被告的土地便会造成损害，那么法律要求这个人承担怎样的义务呢？他必须注意保管该物品，并使该物品留在自己的土地上，以便确保该物品不会脱离自己的土地损害到自己的邻居，这个问题在各个方面都达成了一致意见。但是带来的问题是，法律要求他承担的义务是否是绝对义务，即在这样的情况下，他必须自负后果地将物品留在自己的土地内；还是像财税上诉法院多数意见提出的那样，只是有义务采取所有合理且慎重的预防措施将物品留在自己的土地内，仅此而已。如果前者是法律义务，那么将危险物品带入自己的土地，但却没有能够看管好该物品的人应该对物品脱离土地造成的所有自然结果承担责任。如果他的义务仅限于后者，那么除非有证据证明他存在过失，否则他不需要承担责任。因此，对于采取一般谨慎态度和技术所不能察觉到的潜在缺陷而造成的损失，他不需要承担责任。

假设后者是正确的法律意见，那么又会进一步出现仅次于第一个问题的另一个问题，即尽管不确定通风井的走向，但是考虑到古老通风井或者意识到这些通风井的存在之后，承包商没有尽到注意义务并发挥专业技术，造成水库事实上不合格，对于这样的结果，被告及其雇佣的承包商是否并不应在一定程度上被视为一体？

我们认为真正的法律规则是，如果一个人为了自己的目的将某物品带入自己的土地，聚集并保管这种一旦脱离这片土地便会造成损害的物品，那么他必须自负后果地将该物品留在自己的土地上，如果他没有能够做到这点，那么就足以推断他要为物品脱离土地而自然而然造成的后果承担所有损害赔偿责任。要免除自己的责任，他可以证明物品脱离自己的土地是由于原告未履行义务；或者证明物品之所以脱离土地是由于不可抗力或者天灾。但是如果没有这两种原因的存在，那么便没有必要探讨何种理由是充足的。正如上文陈述的，一般性规则似乎是一种原则性的正义。一个人的草或玉米被邻居出逃的牛吃光了，或者他的煤矿被邻居水库泄漏出的水淹没了，或者他的地窖被邻居的户外厕所污染，或者他的住房因邻居的制碱厂排放的废气和有毒

who has brought something on his own property which was not naturally there, harmless to others so long as it is confined to his own property, but which he knows to be mischievous if it gets on his neighbour's, should be obliged to make good the damage which ensues if he does not succeed in confining it to his own property. But for his act in bringing it there no mischief could have accrued, and it seems but just that he should at his peril keep it there so that no mischief may accrue, or answer for the natural and anticipated consequences. And upon authority, this we think is established to be the law whether the things so brought be beasts, or water, or filth, or stenches.

The case that has most commonly occurred, and which is most frequently to be found in the books, is as to the obligation of the owner of cattle which he has brought on his land, to prevent their escaping and doing mischief. The law as to them seems to be perfectly settled from early times; the owner must keep them in at his peril, or he will be answerable for the natural consequences of their escape; that is with regard to tame beasts, for the grass they eat and trample upon, though not for any injury to the person of others, for our ancestors have settled that it is not the general nature of horses to kick, or bulls to gore; but if the owner knows that the beast has a vicious propensity to attack man, he will be answerable for that too....

… But it was further said by Martin, B., that when damage is done to personal property, or even to the person, by collision, either upon land or at sea, there must be negligence in the party doing the damage to render him legally responsible; and this is no doubt true, and as was pointed out by Mr. Mellish during his argument before us, this is not confined to cases of collision, for there are many cases in which proof of negligence is essential, as for instance, where an unruly horse gets on the footpath of a public street and kills a passenger; or where a person in a dock is struck by the falling of a bale of cotton which the defendant's servants are lowering; and many other similar cases may be found. But we think these cases distinguishable from the present. Traffic on the highways, whether by land or sea, cannot be conducted without exposing those whose persons or property are near it to some inevitable risk; and that being so, those who go on the highway, or have their property adjacent to it, may well be held to do so subject to their taking upon themselves the risk of injury from that inevitable danger; and persons who by the license of the owner pass near to warehouses where goods are being raised or lowered, certainly do so subject to the inevitable risk of accident. In neither case, therefore, can they recover without proof of want of care or skill occasioning the accident; and it is believed that all the cases in which inevitable accident has been held an excuse for what prima facie was a trespass, can be explained on the same principle, viz., that the circumstances were such as to shew that the plaintiff had taken that risk upon himself. But there is no ground for saying that the plaintiff here took upon himself any risk arising from the uses to which the defendants should choose to apply their land. He neither knew what these might be, nor could he in any way control the defendants, or hinder their building what reservoirs they liked, and storing up in them what water they pleased, so long as the defendants

水蒸气而不利于身体健康,那么他在自身不存在任何过失的情况下受到了损害;那个邻居将原本并不存在于自己土地上的物品带入自己的土地,该物品只有当留在这片土地上时才不具有危害性,但是他知道一旦该物品跑到邻居的土地上便会造成损害,那么如果他没有能够在自己的土地上好好保管该物品而造成了损害,他有义务来弥补损害。如果不是因为他的行为将该物品带到这里,那么就不会发生损害,为了保证不会发生损害他应该自负后果地确保该物品留在自己的土地上,或者为自然而然发生的结果以及预料到的结果承担赔偿责任,这样的做法看起来的确是公平的。依据法源,无论被带入土地的是动物、水、垃圾还是臭气,我们认为这都应该被确定为法律。

最常见的案件,同时也是书本中最容易找到的案件就是牛群所有人在将牛群带入自己的土地之后避免牛群逃跑造成损害的义务。关于这些案件的法律似乎在很早以前便已经确定。所有人必须自负后果地看管牛群,否则他就必须对牛群逃跑造成的自然后果承担责任。对于被驯服的动物,这是针对被它们吃掉和践踏的草地,而不适用于造成人身损害,因为我们的祖先已经发现,从本性来看,马一般不会踢人,牛一般不会顶人;但是如果动物的所有人知道这种动物具有伤人的凶恶本性,那么他也应该为人身损害承担责任……

……财税法院 Martin 法官进一步指出,当陆上或海上撞击造成私人财产损失,或者甚至是人身伤害,那么造成损害的一方必定存在过失,他因此需要承担法律责任,这是毫无疑问的,正如 Mellish 先生和我们现在主张的一样,这不应该仅限于撞击案件,因为在许多案件中证明过失的证据是至关重要的。例如,不受约束的马闯入公共人行道造成行人死亡;或者被告的雇工在降下一包棉花时砸到了一名站在甲板上的人,还可以找到很多类似的案件。但是我们认为这些案件与我们现在这个案件都不一样。公共交通,无论是陆地上还是海上,都不可避免地使附近的人或财产面临风险,正是因为这样的原因,那些选择公路交通的人,或者将自己的财产置于公路附近的人,便自然而然地使自己面临不可避免的危险;而那些得到所有人许可路过正在起吊或降下货物的仓库的人,肯定面临不可避免的事故风险。因此,在这两种案例中,他们如果不能证明引起事故是因为缺乏注意或技术,那么他们都不得获得赔偿。对于被推断为侵入行为但却以发生了不可避免的事故作为开脱理由的所有案件,都可以用同样的原理来解释,即这是一种原告自己承担了风险的情况。但是并没有依据认为,对于被告选择如何使用自己土地造成的任何风险,原告都需要自己承担。只要被告成功地避免导入自己土地的水影响到原告的财产,原告既不知道土地的用途是什么,又无法控制被告的行为,或者阻止被告按照自己喜欢的方式修建水库并依据自己的喜好储存什么样的水。

succeeded in preventing the water which they there brought from interfering with the plaintiff's property.

The view which we take of the first point renders it unnecessary to consider whether the defendants would or would not be responsible for the want of care and skill in the persons employed by them, under the circumstances stated in the case.

We are of the opinion that the plaintiff is entitled to recover, but as we have not heard any argument as to the amount, we are not able to give judgment for what damages. The parties probably will empower their counsel to agree on the amount of damages; should they differ on the principle, the case may be mentioned again.

Judgment for the plaintiff.

58. Rylands v Fletcher (1868) L.R. 3 H.L. 330

House of Lords, United Kingdom

The Lord Chancellor (Lord Cairns):...My lords, the principles on which this case must be determined appear to me to be extremely simple. The Defendants, treating them as the owners or occupiers of the close on which the reservoir was constructed, might lawfully have used that close for any purpose for which it might in the ordinary course of the enjoyment of land be used; and if, in what I may term the natural use of that land, there had been any accumulation of water, either on the surface or underground, and if, by the operation of the laws of nature, that accumulation of water had passed off into the close occupied by the Plaintiff, the Plaintiff could not have complained....

On the other hand if the Defendants, not stopping at the natural use of their close, had desired to use it for any purpose which I may term a nonnatural use, for the purpose of introducing into the close that which in its natural condition was not in or upon it, for the purpose of introducing water either above or below ground in quantities and in a manner not the result of any work or operation on or under the land,—and if in the consequence of their doing so, or in consequence of any imperfection in the mode of their doing so, the water came to escape and to pass off into the close of the Plaintiff, then it appears to me that that which the Defendants were doing they were doing at their own peril; and, if in the course of their doing it, the evil arose to which I have referred, the evil, namely, of the escape of the water and its passing away to the close of the Plaintiff and injuring the Plaintiff, then for the consequence of that, in my opinion, the Defendants would be liable....

My Lords, these simple principles, if they are well founded, as it appears to me they are, really dispose of this case....

Judgment of the Court of Exchequer Chamber affirmed.

我们关于第一点的观点使得我们没有必要考虑,在案件所陈述的情况下,被告是否应该因为被雇佣人缺乏注意和技能承担责任。

我们认为原告有权获得赔偿,但是由于我们没有审理任何关于赔偿金额的主张,因此我们无法对赔偿金额作出判决。双方当事人可以授权他们的辩护律师就赔偿金额达成一致;如果他们在原则上存在分歧,那么可以再次提起诉讼。

原告胜诉。

58. Rylands v Fletcher (1868) L.R. 3 H.L. 330

联合王国上议院

Cairns 首席大法官主笔:……法官阁下,判决该案依据的原理在我看来非常简单。将被告当作那片建有水库的圈地的所有人或占有人,被告可以合法地将该圈地以土地用益的通常方式用于任何目的。在我称之为自然地使用土地的情况下,如果根据自然规律在土地的表面或地下聚集了水,而且随着水量的聚集,水冲破圈地冲入了原告占有的圈地之内,那么原告不得提起控诉……

另一方面,如果被告不仅限于圈地的自然使用,还希望用于我称之为非自然使用的目的,在圈地内引入在原本自然条件下并不存在的事物,以便引入地面水或地下水,而地面或地下作业或操作都不可能以如此方式达到如此多的水量——而如果水从被告的圈地上泄漏出去并涌入了原告的圈地,造成这样的后果可能是被告正常工作的结果,或者可能是被告在操作时存在纰漏,那么在我看来被告必须为他们正在做的事自负后果。如果在被告如此使用土地的过程之中,出现了我所说的灾害,即水从被告的圈地上泄漏出去并进入了原告的圈地,造成原告的损害,那么我认为,被告应该对这样的后果承担责任……

法官阁下,这些简单的原理,如果其具有良好的基础,正如对我来说它们的确如此一样,则能够真正地处理这个案件……

维持财政署内室法庭的判决。

Section 2. Development in US Law: Abnormally Dangerous Activities

59. Turner v. Big Lake Oil Co., 128 Tex. 155, 96 S.W.2d 221 (1936)

Supreme Court of Texas, United States

Mr. Chief Justice Cureton delivered the opinion of the court.

The primary question for determination here is whether or not the defendants in error, without negligence on their part, may be held liable in damages for the destruction or injury to property occasioned by the escape of salt water from ponds constructed and used by them in the operation of their oil wells....

The defendants in error in the operation of certain oil wells in Reagan County constructed large artificial earthen ponds or pools into which they ran the polluted waters from the wells. On the occasion complained of, water escaped from one or more of these ponds, and, passing over the grass lands of the plaintiffs in error, injured the turf, and after entering Garrison draw flowed down the same into Centralia draw. In Garrison draw there were natural water holes, which supplied water for the livestock of plaintiffs in error. The pond, or ponds, of water from which the salt water escaped were, we judge from the map, some six miles from the stockwater holes to which we refer. The plaintiffs in error brought suit, basing their action on alleged neglect on the part of the defendants in error in permitting the levees and dams, etc., of their artificial ponds to break and overflow the land of plaintiffs in error, and thereby pollute the waters to which we have above referred and injure the turf in the pasture of plaintiffs in error. The question was submitted to a jury on special issues, and the jury answered that the defendants in error did permit salt water to overflow from their salt ponds and lakes down Garrison draw and on to the land of the plaintiffs in error. *However, the jury acquitted the defendants in error of negligence in the premises....*

The immediate question presented is whether or not defendants in error are to be held liable as insurers, or whether the cause of action against them must be predicated upon negligence. We believe the question is one of first impression in this Court, and so we shall endeavor to discuss it in a manner in keeping with its importance.

Upon both reason and authority we believe that the conclusion of the Court of Civil Appeals that negligence is a prerequisite to recovery in a case of this character is a correct one. There is some difference of opinion on the subject in American jurisprudence brought about by differing views as to the correctness or applicability of the decision of the English courts in Rylands v. Fletcher, L.R. 3 H.L. 330....

In Rylands v. Fletcher the Court predicated the absolute liability of the defendants on the proposition that the use of land for the artificial storage of water was not a natural use, and that, therefore, the land owner was bound at his peril to keep the waters on his own land. This basis of

第二节　美国法上的发展：异常危险活动

59. Turner v. Big Lake Oil Co., 128 Tex. 155, 96 S.W.2d 221 (1936)

美国得克萨斯州最高法院

Cureton 大法官宣布了法庭意见。

被上诉人在油田作业过程中修建并使用了池塘，从池塘中泄漏出去的盐水毁灭或损害了上诉人的财产。这里要确定的主要问题是，被上诉人在不存在过失的情况下，是否需要对损失承担赔偿责任……

被上诉人在 Reagan 县经营一些油井，他们修建了大型的人工土质池塘或蓄水池，将来自油井的污水排入池塘。在控诉的案件中，一个或多个池塘泄漏出的污水流过了上诉人的草地，损害了草皮，进入了 Garrison 取水点之后流入了 Centralia 取水点。在 Garrison 取水点中，有许多天然出水孔，为上诉人的牲畜提供饮水。我们从地图上可以看出，泄漏盐水的池塘离我们提到的牲畜饮水孔大约有 6 英里。上诉人提起了诉讼，指控被上诉人任由人工池塘的堤坝和水坝决口，淹没了上诉人的土地，然后污染了上文中提到的水源，损害了上诉人牧场的草皮，因此被上诉人存在过失。这一问题被提交给特别问题陪审团，陪审团回复称，被上诉人确实任由盐水从盐池中溢出并流入 Garrison 取水点，进入了上诉人的土地。然而，*陪审团裁断被上诉人不存在过失*……

紧接着出现的问题是，被上诉人是否应该作为保险人承担责任，或者针对被上诉人的诉因是否必须建立在过失的基础上。我们认为这个问题对本院而言是无先例可循的，我们将尽力以确保其重要性的方式来讨论这个案件。

民事上诉法院认为在这类案件中，过失是获得赔偿的前提条件。依据理性和法源，我们认为该结论是正确的。美国法学界关于这个问题存在一些不同的意见，主要是对英国法院在 *Rylands v Fletcher*, (1868) L.R. 3 H.L. 330 案中作出的判决的正确性或者可适用性存在分歧……

在 *Rylands v Fletcher* 案中，法院认定被告应该承担严格责任，其依据的观点是将土地用于建造人工储水设施并非自然用途，因此土地所有人（即被告）有义务自负后果地确保水留在自己的土地上。英国法院认定这个规则的基础取决于那里的气候条件。英国是个多雨的国家，由于有持续的河流和充足的降雨，如果是出于一般性的或普遍性的目的，人们没有必要储存水。在

the English rule is to be found in the meteorological conditions which obtain there. England is a pluvial country, where constant streams and abundant rains make the storage of water unnecessary for ordinary or general purposes. When the Court said in Rylands v. Fletcher that the use of land for storage of water was an unnatural use, it meant such use was not a general or an ordinary one; not one within the contemplation of the parties to the original grant of the land involved, nor of the grantor and grantees of adjacent lands, but was a special or extraordinary use, and for that reason applied the rule of absolute liability. This conclusion is supported by the fact that those jurisdictions which adhere to the rule in Rylands v. Fletcher do not apply that rule to dams or reservoirs constructed in rivers and streams, which they say is a natural use, but apply the principle of negligence. In other words, the impounding of water in streamways, being an obvious and natural use, was necessarily within the contemplation of the parties to the original and adjacent grants, and damages must be predicated upon negligent use of a granted right and power; while things not within the contemplation of the parties to the original grants, such as unnatural uses of the land, the land owner may do only at his peril. As to what use of land is or may be a natural use, one within the contemplation of the parties to the original grant of land, necessarily depends upon the attendant circumstances and conditions which obtain in the territory of the original grants, or the initial terms of those grants.

In Texas we have conditions very different from those which obtain in England. A large portion of Texas is an arid or semi-arid region. West of the 98th meridian of longitude, where the rainfall is approximately 30 inches, the rainfall decreases until finally, in the extreme western part of the State, it is only about 10 inches. This land of decreasing rainfall is the great ranch or livestock region of the State, water for which is stored in thousands of ponds, tanks, and lakes on the surface of the ground. The country is almost without streams; and without the storage of water from rainfall in basins constructed for the purpose, or to hold waters pumped from the earth, the great livestock industry of West Texas must perish. No such condition obtains in England. With us the storage of water is a natural or necessary and common use of the land, necessarily within the contemplation of the State and its grantees when grants were made, and obviously the rule announced in Rylands v. Fletcher, predicated upon different conditions, can have no application here.

Again, in England there are no oil wells, no necessity for using surface storage facilities for impounding and evaporating salt waters therefrom. In Texas the situation is different. Texas has many great oil fields, tens of thousands of wells in almost every part of the State. Producing oil is one of our major industries. One of the by-products of oil production is salt water, which must be disposed of without injury to property or the pollution of streams. The construction of basins or ponds to hold this salt water is a necessary part of the oil business. In Texas much of our land was granted without mineral reservation to the State, and where minerals were reserved, provision

Rylands v Fletcher 案中，当法院提出将土地用于储存水时，那就意味着这种用途不是一般性的或普遍性用途，这并未在最初被授予的涉诉土地一方预料之中，也未在相邻土地的出让人和受让人的预料之中，而是一种特殊的或者说是异常的使用方式，因此应该适用绝对责任。这一结论还得到了以下事实的支持，即那些遵循 *Rylands v Fletcher* 案的法域并没有将这条规则运用到在河流和溪流上修建水坝或水库的情况中，他们认为修建水坝或水库是一种自然用途，只适用过失责任原则。换句话说，在河流水道中蓄水显然是一种自然用途，必然是在最初被授予土地和邻近土地的各方预料之中，那么损害赔偿就必须建立在行使受让权利和权力时存在过失的基础之上。而对于未在最初被授予权利时各方预料之内的事物，如以非自然的方式使用土地，土地的所有者需要对土地的使用自负后果。如何使用土地才是或者可能是自然使用，才在最初被授予土地时的各方预料之中，基本取决于最初被授予土地时所伴随的环境和条件，或者那些授予时的最初条款。

  得克萨斯州的情况与英国的情况有很大的不同。得克萨斯州的大部分地区都是干旱或者半干旱地区。在西经98度以西的地区，年降水大约只有30英寸，降水量向西不断减少，到达得克萨斯州最西的地区时年降水量只有10英寸了。这片降水量逐渐减少的地区正是全州最大的农场或牧场的所在地，牲畜的饮用水都储存在成千上万个地面池塘、蓄水池和湖泊中。农村地区几乎没有溪流，如果不修建蓄水用的凹地以储存降雨，或者储存抽取的地下水，那么得克萨斯州西部规模巨大的牲畜饲养业就将消亡。英国不存在这样的现象。对于我们来说，储存水是自然或合理使用土地的一种方式，十分常见，这是在出让土地时出让方与州政府的预料之中的，显然，*Rylands v Fletcher* 案中宣布的规则依据的是不同的情况，不能应用到这里。

  再者，英国没有油井，因此没有必要修建地表存储设施来储存和蒸发油井流出来的盐水。在得克萨斯州，情况是不一样的。得克萨斯州有许多大型油田，全州几乎每一个地区都有成千上万个油井。石油生产是我们的一个支柱行业。石油生产过程中的一个副产品便是盐水，而处理盐水不得损害财产或者污染河流。修建储存这些盐水的池塘或水池是石油工业的一个必要组成部分。在得克萨斯州，多数土地在出让时都没有附加州政府的矿藏保留，如果矿藏由州政府保留，那么就会制定租赁和经营的相关规定。因而，可以确定，关于这种出让和租赁活动，州政府与所有的受让人和矿藏承租人都已经考虑

has usually been made for leasing and operating. It follows, therefore, that as to these grants and leases the right to mine in the usual and appropriate way, as, for example, by the construction and maintenance of salt water pools such as here involved, incident to the production of oil, were contemplated by the State and all its grantees and mineral lessees, that being a use of the surface incident and necessary to the right to produce oil....

The judgments of the Court of Civil Appeals and of the District Court are affirmed.

60. Siegler v. Kuhlman, 81 Wash. 2d 448, 502 P.2d 1181 (1972)

Supreme Court of Washington, United States

Hale, J.

Seventeen-year-old Carol J. House died in the flames of a gasoline explosion when her car encountered a pool of thousands of gallons of spilled gasoline. She was driving home from her after-school job in the early evening of November 22, 1967, along Capitol Lake Drive in Olympia; it was dark but dry; her car's headlamps were burning. There was a slight impact with some object, a muffled explosion, and then searing flames from gasoline pouring out of an overturned trailer tank engulfed her car. The result of the explosion is clear, but the real cause of what happened will remain something of an eternal mystery.

In the Court of Appeals, the principal claim of error was directed to the trial court's refusal to give an instruction on res ipsa loquitur, and we think that claim of error well taken. Our reasons for ruling that an instruction on res ipsa loquitur should have been given and that an inference of negligence could have been drawn from the event are found, we believe, in our statements on the subject.... We think, therefore, that plaintiff was entitled to an instruction permitting the jury to infer negligence from the occurrence.

But there exists here an even more impelling basis for liability in this case than its derivation by allowable inference of fact under the res ipsa loquitur doctrine, and that is the proposition of strict liability arising as a matter of law from all of the circumstances of the event.

Strict liability is not a novel concept; it is at least as old as Fletcher v. Rylands, L.R. 1 Ex. 265, 278 (1866), *aff'd,* House of Lords, 3 H.L. 330 (1868)....The basic principles supporting the *Fletcher* doctrine, we think, control the transportation of gasoline as freight along the public highways the same as it does the impounding of waters and for largely the same reasons.

In many respects, hauling gasoline as freight is no more unusual, but more dangerous, than collecting water. When gasoline is carried as cargo—as distinguished from fuel for the carrier vehicle—it takes on uniquely hazardous characteristics, as does water impounded in large quantities. Dangerous in itself, gasoline develops even greater potential for harm when carried as freight—extraordinary dangers deriving from sheer quantity, bulk and weight, which enormously

到了以常规的适当方式利用矿产权,如这里涉及的修建和维护盐水池属于石油生产过程中的附带事件,也是利用地表时的附带事件,对石油生产权是必要的……

维持民事上诉法院和联邦地区法院的判决。

60. Siegler v. Kuhlman, 81 Wash. 2d 448, 502 P.2d 1181 (1972)

美国华盛顿州最高法院

Hale 法官主笔:

17 岁的 Carol J. House 开车时遇到了洒了一地的几千加仑的汽油,汽油发生了爆炸,Carol 死于爆炸。1967 年 11 月 22 日的傍晚,她在课余打工结束之后沿着 Olympia 的 Capitol Lake 公路开车回家。天色已晚,但空气很干燥。她打开了车头灯。她的车轻轻撞上了一个物体,发生了低沉的爆炸,然后从一辆翻倒在地的油罐拖车冒出来的灼热大火吞灭了她的汽车。爆炸的结果非常清楚,但是引起爆炸的真正原因却成为了永远的谜。

在上诉法院,错误的主张主要是针对初审法院拒绝作出事实自证的指示,我们认为初审存在错误。我们认为法院应该作出事实自证的指示,从事实可以推断过失,我们相信,该事实存在于这个问题的陈述中……因此,我们认为原告有权获得法院作出的要求陪审团从发生的事实推断过失的指示。

依据事实自证法律学说对事实进行推断会出现偏差,但是在这个案件中,在责任基础问题上还有一个比偏差更紧迫的问题,即根据事件发生时的所有情况,提出作为法律问题的严格责任的观点。

严格责任并非一个新奇的概念;严格责任至少和 *Fletcher v Rylands*, L.R. 1 Ex. 265, 278 (1866), *aff'd*, House of Lords, 3 H.L. 330 (1868) 案一样古老……我们认为,基于同样的理由,支持 Fletcher 案的基础原则不仅适用于蓄水,也同样适用于沿着公共公路运输汽油的问题。

在许多方面,将汽油作为货物来拖运并不比运水更为少见,只是更加危险。当汽油作为货物被运输时,与运输车上的燃料汽油不同,汽油便具有了特别危险的特性,就像水被大量储存是一样的。汽油自身具有危险性,当它被运输时便具有了更大的潜在致害性——数量、体积和重量使其危险特质翻倍,具有了特别巨大的危险性。汽油的装载量、体积和数量以及沿着高速公路运动具有危险性,这是为什么要采用上文 *Fletcher v Rylands* 案的规则

multiply its hazardous properties. And the very hazards inhering from the size of the load, its bulk or quantity and its movement along the highways presents another reason for application of the Fletcher v. Rylands, supra, rule not present in the impounding of large quantities of water—the likely destruction of cogent evidence from which negligence or want of it may be proved or disapproved. It is quite probable that the most important ingredients of proof will be lost in a gasoline explosion and fire. Gasoline is always dangerous whether kept in large or small quantities because of its volatility, inflammability and explosiveness. But when several thousand gallons of it are allowed to spill across a public highway—that is, if, while in transit as freight, it is not kept impounded—the hazards to third persons are so great as to be almost beyond calculation. As a consequence of its escape from impoundment and subsequent explosion and ignition, the evidence in a very high percentage of instances will be destroyed, and the reason for and causes contributing to its escape will quite likely be lost in the searing flames and explosions....

Thus, the reasons for applying a rule of strict liability obtain in this case. We have a situation where a highly flammable, volatile and explosive substance is being carried at a comparatively high rate of speed, in great and dangerous quantities as cargo upon the public highways, subject to all of the hazards of high-speed traffic, multiplied by the great dangers inherent in the volatile and explosive nature of the substance, and multiplied again by the quantity and size of the load. Then we have the added dangers of ignition and explosion generated when a load of this size, that is, about 5,000 gallons of gasoline, breaks its container and, cascading from it, spreads over the highway so as to release an invisible but highly volatile and explosive vapor above it....

The rule of strict liability, when applied to an abnormally dangerous activity, as stated in the Restatement (Second) of Torts §519 (Tent. Draft No. 10, 1964), was adopted as the rule of decision in this state in Pacific Northwest Bell Tel. Co. v. Port of Seattle, 80 Wash. 2d 59, 64, 491 P.2d 1037, 1039-1040 (1971), as follows:

> (1) One who carries on an abnormally dangerous activity is subject to liability for harm to the person, land or chattels of another resulting from the activity, although he has exercised the utmost care to prevent such harm.
>
> (2) Such strict liability is limited to the kind of harm, the risk of which makes the activity abnormally dangerous.

As to what constitutes an abnormal activity, section 520 states:

> In determining whether an activity is abnormally dangerous, the following factors are to be considered:
>
> (a) Whether the activity involves a high degree of risk of some harm to the

的另一个原因。这一原因在大量储水的情况之中不适用——即有可能毁掉可以认定或推翻过失或无过失的强有力证据。有可能最重要的证据要素已经毁灭在了汽油爆炸和大火之中。由于汽油具有挥发性、易燃性和爆炸性，无论量多量少，汽油都是危险的。但是，如果几千加仑的汽油洒在公共高速公路上——也就是作为货物被运输时没有被聚集在一起——那么第三人面临的危险将大得无法估量。汽油从储存容器中溢出，然后爆炸并引起大火，极有可能证据已经不复存在，证明为什么汽油会溢出，以及是什么原因导致了汽油溢出的证据很有可能已经消失在了熊熊燃烧的大火和爆炸之中……

  因此，在这个案件中有理由运用严格责任规则。我们看到的情况是，数量巨大而危险的具有挥发性的易燃易爆物质，在高速公路上作为货物以较高的速度被运输。本来高速行驶便具有危险性，现在加上被运送物质本身具有非常危险的挥发性和易爆炸性，同时汽油的运载数量和体积更加加大了其危险性。因此，当装载的 5000 加仑汽油冲破了储存容器，倾泄到地上，在高速公路上四处流淌，释放出虽然看不见但是却具有高度挥发性和易爆性的气体，那么汽油被点燃并引爆的风险便大大增加了……

  《侵权法重述·第二次》（1964 年暂行草案第 10 号）第 519 条对严格责任规则运用到异常危险的活动中的情况进行了规定，在本州的 Pacific Northwest Bell Tel. Co. v. Port of Seattle, 80 Wash. 2d 59, 64 491 P.2d 1037, 1039-1040（1971）案的法院判决中被采纳：

  （1）从事异常危险活动的人应该对该活动对他人的人身、土地或动产造成的损害承担责任，尽管他为避免造成这种损害已经尽到了最大注意。

  （2）这种严格责任只限于损害的可能性使得活动异常危险的损害类型。

第 520 条对异常危险活动的构成进行了界定：

  为了确定一项活动是否是异常危险的，将考虑以下因素：

  （a）该行为是否涉及对他人人身、土地或动产造成某种损害的高度风险；

  （b）因该危险导致的伤害严重性是否可能会是极大的；

person, land or chattels of others;

(b) Whether the gravity of the harm which may result from it is likely to be great;

(c) Whether the risk cannot be eliminated by the exercise of reasonable care;

(d) Whether the activity is not a matter of common usage;

(e) Whether the activity is inappropriate to the place where it is carried on; and

(f) The value of the activity to the community.

…Transporting gasoline as freight by truck along the public highways and streets is obviously an activity involving a high degree of risk; it is a risk of great harm and injury; it creates dangers that cannot be eliminated by the exercise of reasonable care. That gasoline cannot be practicably transported except upon the public highways does not decrease the abnormally high risk arising from its transportation. Nor will the exercise of due and reasonable care assure protection to the public from the disastrous consequences of concealed or latent mechanical or metallurgical defects in the carrier's equipment, from the negligence of third parties, from latent defects in the highways and streets, and from all of the other hazards not generally disclosed or guarded against by reasonable care, prudence and foresight. Hauling gasoline in great quantities as freight, we think, is an activity that calls for the application of principles of strict liability.

The case is therefore reversed and remanded to the trial court for trial to the jury on the sole issue of damages.

Hamilton, C.J., Finley, Rosellini, and Hunter, JJ., and Ryan, J. Pro Tem., concur.

Rosellini, J. (concurring). I agree with the majority that the transporting of highly volatile and flammable substances upon the public highways in commercial quantities and for commercial purposes is an activity which carries with it such a great risk of harm to defenseless users of the highway, if it is not kept contained, that the common-law principles of strict liability should apply. In my opinion, a good reason to apply these principles, which is not mentioned in the majority opinion, is that the commercial transporter can spread the loss among his customers—who benefit from this extrahazardous use of the highways. Also, if the defect which caused the substance to escape was one of manufacture, the owner is in the best position to hold the manufacturer to account.

I think the opinion should make clear, however, that the owner of the vehicle will be held strictly liable only for damages caused when the flammable or explosive substance is allowed to escape without the apparent intervention of any outside force beyond the control of the manufacturer, the owner, or the operator of the vehicle hauling it. I do not think the majority means to suggest that if another vehicle, negligently driven, collided with the truck in question, the truck owner would be held liable for the damage. But where, as here, there was no outside force which （c）是否无法通过尽到合理注意消除该危险；

（d）该活动是否不属于通常习惯事宜；

（e）该活动对于从事该活动的地点是否是不适当的；以及

（f）该活动对公共福祉的价值。

……利用卡车沿公共高速公路将汽油作为货物来运输显然是一种具有高度风险的活动；该活动具有引起巨大损害和伤害的风险；通过尽到合理的注意义务仍然无法消除活动带来的危险。除了通过公共高速公路运输之外，其他运输方式都不具有可行性，并没有降低运输本身带来的异常巨大的风险。尽到充分合理的注意义务并不能保护公众免于遭受灾难性的后果，如运输者交通工具隐藏的或潜在的机械缺陷或冶炼缺陷、第三方的过失、高速公路或街道上潜在的缺陷，以及即使进行了合理的注意、谨慎和深谋远虑往往也无法发现或预防的其他危险。我们认为，将汽油作为货物大量运输是一种需要适用严格责任的活动。

因此，撤销判决，案件发回初审法院重审，陪审团仅对损害赔偿金问题进行裁断。

Hamilton 大法官和 Finley 法官、Rosellini 法官、Hunter 法官，以及 Ryan 临时法官，赞同。

Rosellini 法官（协同意见）：

我同意多数意见，即为商业目的并以商业化的数量在公共高速公路上运输高挥发性和易燃性物质，如果没有对其进行储存的话，是一种给其他毫无防备的高速公路使用者造成巨大风险的活动，应该运用普通法的严格责任原则。在我看来，虽然多数意见没有提到，但是运用该原则还有一个很好的理由，即商业运输者可以将损失分摊到消费者头上——消费者从这种高速公路的异常危险的使用方式上受益。同时，如果汽油泄漏是由制造商引起的，那么卡车的所有人是要求制造商承担责任的最佳人选。

然而，我认为意见书应该明确写明，只有在没有超出制造商、机动车所有人，或运输货物的机动车司机控制之外的明显外来因素的干扰之下出现的易燃物或易爆物溢出，机动车所有人才对这些物质造成的损失承担严格责任。我不认为多数意见意味着，如果另一辆机动车由于驾驶过失撞上了本案的卡车，卡车所有人需要对损失承担责任。但是正如本案的情况一样，如果没有外来因素导致拖车脱离了卡车，那么应该适用严格责任规则……

Hamilton 大法官和 Finley 法官、Ryan 临时法官赞同 Rosellini 法官的协同

caused the trailer to become detached from the truck, the rule of strict liability should apply....

Hamilton, C.J., Finley, J., and Ryan, J. Pro Tem., concur with Rosellini, J.

...

61. PSI Energy, Inc. v. Roberts, 829 N.E.2d 943 (Ind. 2005)

Supreme Court of Indiana, United States

Boehm, Justice...The "inherently dangerous" exception is normally associated with strict liability and does not require negligence on the part of the contractor....It imposes liability for activities that are dangerous by nature, not merely because they are carried out in a risky manner. For example, if the enterprise hires an independent contractor to dust crops with poison, it is liable for damage to neighbors' crops without regard to negligence....

Roberts asserts that asbestos itself is intrinsically dangerous and "any work that causes inherently dangerous fibers to enter the breathing space of humans is intrinsically dangerous work." He points to Covalt v. Carey Canada, Inc., 543 N.E.2d 382 (Ind. 1989), in which this Court described asbestos fibers as "an inherently dangerous substance...a toxic foreign substance...an inherently dangerous product...and a hazardous foreign substance." Id. at 384-86. Roberts asserts that there is nothing that can make asbestos fibers safe. PSI responds that although asbestos may be an inherently dangerous substance, it does not follow that working with material containing asbestos is intrinsically dangerous work. PSI asserts that the evidence at trial demonstrates that the dangers of working with asbestos could have been minimized if Roberts had taken proper precautions....

We agree that working with asbestos can be perilous, but that is not enough to render it intrinsically dangerous as that term is used to establish liability for actions of an independent contractor. For example in McDaniel v. Business Investment Group, Ltd., 709 N.E.2d 17 (Ind. Ct. App. 1999) *trans. denied*, an employee working on a sewer line in a 9 foot deep trench was killed when the sides of the trench caved in. The Indiana Court of Appeals held that trenching is not intrinsically dangerous work because "although it can be dangerous, the use of proper procedures...renders the work relatively safe." Id. at 21...Therefore, we conclude that working with asbestos is not intrinsically dangerous such that anyone hiring a contractor to address it incurs strict liability for injuries sustained from exposure to it....We also recognize, as the dissent points out, that the consequences of mesothelioma can be horrific. But that does not render asbestos intrinsically dangerous. The same is true of electricity and a number of other substances that, if mishandled, can be dangerous....

Shepard, C.J., and Sullivan, J., concur.

Dickson, J., concurs in result and dissents with separate opinion in which Rucker, J., concurs.

意见。
……

61. PSI Energy, Inc. v. Roberts, 829 N.E.2d 943 (Ind. 2005)

美国印第安纳州最高法院

Boehm 法官……"固有危险"的例外通常和严格责任有关，不需要承包商存在过失……如果活动在本质上就是危险的，那么行为人就应当承担责任，并不需要其以危险的方式开展活动。例如，如果一家公司雇用了一名独立承揽人向农作物喷洒毒药，那么不必考虑该公司是否存在过失，都应该为邻居的粮食损失承担责任……

Roberts 强调，石棉本身就具有固有危险性，"导致具有固有危险性的纤维进入人体呼吸系统的任何工作就是固有危险工作"。他提出在 Covalt v. Carey Canada, Inc., 543 N.E.2d 382（Ind. 1989）案中，法院对石棉纤维的描述是"固有危险的物质……有毒的外来物质……固有危险的产品……危险的外来物质"。（Id. at 384-86.）Roberts 断言，无论如何都不可能使石棉纤维变得安全。PSI 的回应是，尽管石棉可能是一种固有危险的物质，但是不能由此认定工作时接触到含有石棉的材料具有固有危险性。PSI 认为，初审中的证据显示，如果 Roberts 采取了适当的预防措施，那么可以将工作时石棉造成的危险降至最小……

我们同意工作时接触石棉是危险的，但是仅凭这点还不足以认定工作具有固有危险性，这一术语是用于说明为独立承揽人的行为承担责任。例如，在 McDaniel v. Business Investment Group, Ltd., 709 N.E.2d 17（Ind. Ct. App. 1999）trans. denied 案中，一名员工在污水管道地下 9 英尺深的沟渠中工作时，沟渠的两侧发生了垮塌，致使原告死亡。印第安纳州上诉法院认为挖渠工作本身并不是固有危险的工作，因为"尽管是危险的，但是如果采取了适当的措施……工作仍然相对安全"。（Id. at 21）……因此，我们认为在工作中接触石棉具有的固有危险性还不至于造成聘请承包人处理石棉的人为承包人接触石棉受到的伤害承担严格责任……我们还认识到，正如反对意见指出的，间质瘤的后果是可怕的。但是间质瘤也不能证明石棉具有固有危险性。这和电以及许多其他物质的道理是一样的，如果处理不当也很危险……

Shepard 大法官和 Sullivan 法官赞同。

Dickson 赞同判决结果，但撰写了独立的反对意见，并得到了 Rucker 法官的赞同。

Dickson, Justice, concurring in result and dissenting. I concur with the majority's affirmance of the trial court judgment. But I dissent from the majority's general discussion regarding the responsibility of a principal or landowner for injuries suffered by workers employed by an independent contractor hired by the landowner or principal. In an apparent effort to provide protection for landowners and other entities that employ independent contractors to eliminate or ameliorate dangerous conditions, the Court's opinion, in my judgment, goes too far....

The Court concludes that "working with asbestos is not intrinsically dangerous such that anyone hiring a contractor to address it incurs strict liability for injuries sustained from exposure to it." Id. at 955. I strongly disagree with this assertion, believing that asbestos is precisely the sort of danger to which the intrinsically dangerous exception should apply.

This principle is expressed in Restatement of Torts, Second §427A: "One who employs an independent contractor to do work which the employer knows or has reason to know to involve an abnormally dangerous activity, is subject to liability to the same extent as the contractor for physical harm to others caused by the activity." The underlying purpose of this rule is that:

> One who employs an independent contractor to do work which the employer knows or has reason to know to involve an abnormally dangerous activity cannot be permitted to escape the responsibility for the abnormal danger created by the activity which he has set in motion, and so cannot delegate the responsibility for harm resulting to others to the contractor.

Comment b to §427A. The illustrations following §427 refer to injuries resulting from the non-negligent escape of lions and urban blasting operations as examples of abnormally dangerous activities....

Dr. David Mares, who diagnosed the plaintiff's peritoneal mesothelioma, stated that, without a doubt, "it was caused by asbestos exposure." Trans. at 1208. Dr. Mares also provided vivid testimony describing the disease's deadly nature. He declared that malignant mesothelioma is a fatal disease process. "It is not curable." Trans. at 1196. The time from the date of diagnosis to the date of death in a person with malignant peritoneal mesothelioma is usually "a year or less." Trans. at 1206....

Dr. Mares pointed out that Mr. Roberts's pain will be "uncontrollable" and "unbearable" and that the "best medications will not provide pain relief." Trans. at 1220.

Describing the nature of mesothelioma, pathologist Arnold R. Brody, Ph.D., explained: "Our peritoneal cavity is where some of our organs are, like the stomach and the liver and the spleen sit in the peritoneal cavity. And that is lined by a single layer of cells, the mesothelium....And when there is cancer of those cells, those mesothelial cells, it is mesothelioma." Trans. at 1383. Professor

Dickson 法官主笔：

赞同判决结果并提出反对意见。我同意多数意见对初审法院判决的维持。但是关于土地所有人或委托人聘请的独立承揽人雇佣的工人遭受的损害，土地所有人或委托人需要承担责任的问题，我不同意多数意见的一般性讨论。这显然是想努力保护那些为了消除或改善危险环境而雇佣独立承揽人的土地所有人或其他实体，但是在我看来，法院的意见书已经走得太远了……

法院认为"在工作中接触石棉具有的固有危险性还不至于造成聘请承包人处理石棉的人为承包人接触石棉受到的伤害承担严格责任"。（Id. at 955.）我强烈反对这一论断，我认为石棉正是应该适用于固有危险例外的一种危险物质。

《侵权法重述·第二次》第427A条对该原则这样规定："雇主知道或有理由知道某工作涉及异常危险的活动，雇佣独立承揽人从事该工作，那么对于承揽人因活动给他人造成的物质损害，雇主需要承担同样范围的责任。"这个规定所隐含的目的是：

雇主知道或有理由知道某工作涉及异常危险的活动，雇佣独立承揽人从事该工作，那么对于雇主发起的活动带来的异常危险，雇主不得逃脱责任，因此对于承包人在从事该工作时给他人造成的损害，雇主也必须承担责任。

第427A条，评论b。第427条之后的范例列举了一些异常危险活动的例子，如无过失行为造成狮子逃跑引起的损害；在市区进行爆炸工作造成的损害……

David Mares 医生对原告的腹膜间质瘤进行了诊断，指出，毫无疑问，"是因为接触石棉引起的"。（Trans.① at 1208.）Mares 医生还提供了生动的证词，描述了该疾病的致命性本质。他断言，恶性间质瘤是一种致命性疾病过程，"无法医治"。Trans. at 1196. 患有恶性腹膜间质瘤的患者从诊断发现之日到病人死亡之日，通常"是一年或者更短"。（Trans. at 1206）……

Mares 医生指出，Roberts 先生的疼痛将"无法控制""无法忍受""最好的药物没有止痛作用"。（Trans. at 1220.）

病理学家 Arnold R. Brody 医生对间质瘤的特征进行了描述，说道："在我们的腹腔里有各种器官，如胃、肝和脾等都在腹腔内。它们之间的分隔线是一层细胞，也就是间皮……当这些细胞，也就是间皮细胞中出现了癌细胞，那么就出现了间质瘤。"（Trans. at 1383.）Brody 教授说："每一种类型的石

---

① 译者注："trans."或者"Tr."，是 transcript 的缩写，是指庭审记录或者证言笔录。

Brody stated, "All of the asbestos fiber types can cause mesothelioma…they all are perfectly good carcinogens." Trans. at 1384. He observed that no safe level of asbestos exposure has ever been established and that "there is no level below which we know it to be absolutely safe and will not cause mesothelioma." Trans. at 1429.

One of the more insidious aspects of this fatal disease is the fact that its symptoms suddenly appear often decades after a worker is exposed to asbestos. Regarding this latency period between the exposure to asbestos and the first appearance of symptoms of malignant mesotheliomas, Dr. Brody testified that the probability for the latency period to be less than 10 years is about zero; for latency periods of 10 to 14 years about 0.5%; for 15 to 19 years, still just about 3%; and for 20 years or more, 96%. Dr. Brody agreed with an estimate that the average period in these cases from initial exposure to death is about 32 years. Trans. at 1480-82.

The Court specifically notes the testimony of Dr. Michael Ellenbecker emphasizing that "when we're talking about mesothelioma, I think it's difficult to do any activities with asbestos where you completely eliminate the hazard." Op. at 954, quoting Tr. at 2538. Asked whether there is any safe level of exposure to asbestos in the context of the risk of developing mesothelioma, Dr. Eugene Mark answered, "I don't think there is any safe level." Tr. at 2021. Likewise, Dr. Edwin Holstein testified that there is no recognized safe level of exposure to asbestos insulation such that no mesothelioma would occur in insulation workers. He explained, "There may be such a level at very, very, very low levels, but we don't know what it is. What we do know is that even very small exposures have caused mesothelioma in some people." Tr. at 1559. In fact, the Court itself acknowledges that "it is clear that working with any level of asbestos can be associated with mesothelioma." Op. at 956.

Thus we see that asbestos workers are extraordinarily susceptible to this insidious and virulent disease that will usually go undetected for decades but then suddenly erupt with devastating and almost inevitably fatal consequences. Elimination of this enormous risk is virtually impossible because it requires preventing every possibility of asbestos workers inhaling any asbestos fibers.

Conceding that working with asbestos can be perilous, the Court nevertheless concludes that the work does not qualify for the intrinsically dangerous exception to the rule of subcontractor nonliability because, although dangerous, "proper precautions can minimize the risk of injury." Id. at 955….

An intrinsically dangerous activity, also referred to as an "abnormally dangerous activity" in the Restatement of Torts, Second §520…requires the full inability to eliminate the risk, not merely to significantly reduce it. In my view, this is preferable to the prevailing Indiana appellate view that prohibits resort to the intrinsically dangerous exception wherever risks can be 'significantly reduced,' rather than requiring that they be eliminated.

Even applying the view that the intrinsically dangerous exception is applicable where risks

棉纤维都会引起间质瘤……它们都具有强致癌性。"（Trans. at 1384.）他指出，还没有确认接触多少石棉是在安全范围之内的，"我们不知道不会导致间质瘤的绝对安全水平是多少"。（Trans. at 1429.）

这种致命性疾病更可怕的方面是，工人在接触到石棉之后的几十年后才突然出现症状。关于接触石棉到间质瘤早期症状出现中间的潜伏期，Brody 医生在证词中说，潜伏期的时间少于 10 年的可能性大约为零；10 年到 14 年的可能性为 0.5%；15 年到 19 年的可能性也只有 3%；超过 20 年的可能性为 96%。Brody 医生同意，在这些病例中，从接触石棉到死亡的平均期限为 32 年。（Trans. at 1480-82.）

法院特别注意到 Michael Ellenbecker 医生的证词，他强调说："当我们谈到间质瘤时，我认为在与石棉接触的活动中，很难做到完全消除危险。"（Op.[①] at 954, quoting Tr. at 2538.）当问到患间质瘤风险的问题，是否存在一个接触石棉的安全水平时，Eugene Mark 医生回答说："我认为不存在任何的安全度。"（Tr. at 2021.）同样的，Edwin Holstein 医生作证说，还没有发现石棉绝缘材料的任何安全接触程度不会造成绝缘工人患上间质瘤。他解释说："如果有，那么这种水平是非常非常得低，但是我们不知道有多低。我们所知的是，即使非常少地接触到了石棉，也导致一些人患上了间质瘤。"（Tr. at 1559.）事实上，法院自己也认识到，"显然，工作时接触到任何水平的石棉都会导致间质瘤"。（Op. at 956.）

因此，我们看到石棉工人非常容易受到这种可怕的致命性疾病的影响，这种疾病往往在几十年内都不为人们所发觉，然后突然暴发，造成灾难性的几乎无法避免的致命后果。消除这种令人生畏的风险完全不可能，因为这样就要求对石棉工人吸入任何石棉纤维的每个可能性进行预防。

法院承认工作时接触石棉是致命的，但是最终还是认为这种工作仍然不符合不为次承揽人承担责任的规则——固有危险活动例外，因为尽管工作存在危险，但是"采取适当的预防措施可以将损害风险降低到最小"。（Id. at 955）……

固有危险活动，在《侵权法重述·第二次》第 520 条中也被称为"异常危险活动"……要求完全无法消除风险，而不仅仅是无法明显地降低风险。在我看来，这比印第安纳州上诉法院的主流意见更合适，即当可以"明显地降低"而不是要求消除风险时，不得例外适用固有危险活动。

---

① "Op."，是 "opinion" 的缩写，是指法庭意见。——译者注

either cannot be eliminated, or significantly reduced by due precaution, it appears clear that the risk of contracting mesothelioma demands that working with asbestos still be deemed intrinsically dangerous. As noted above, the Restatement cites the escape of lions and urban blasting as examples of abnormally dangerous activities. Obviously, such risks can be somewhat reduced with due precaution, but they cannot be eliminated or even significantly reduced. So it is with asbestos.

The Court today asserts only that "precautions could have minimized Roberts's exposure to asbestos" to justify its conclusion that "working with asbestos is not intrinsically dangerous." Op. at 955. But minimizing is not enough. Not only must due precautions have "minimized" the risk; they must have been able to eliminate or significantly reduce it. The risk of asbestos workers contracting mesothelioma cannot be eliminated nor significantly reduced. It is the quintessential example of an intrinsically dangerous activity....

Rucker, J., concurs.

Section 3. Development in English Law: Escape of Dangerous Things in the Course of Non-natural Use of Land

62. Cambridge Water Co Ltd v Eastern Counties Leather Plc [1994] 2 AC 264

House of Lords, United Kingdom

LORD GOFF

Nuisance and the rule in Rylands v. Fletcher

As I have already recorded, there was no appeal by C.W.C. to the Court of Appeal against the judge's conclusion in nuisance. The question of E.C.L.'s liability in nuisance has really only arisen again because the Court of Appeal allowed C.W.C.'s appeal on the ground that E.C.L. was liable on the basis of strict liability in nuisance on the principle laid down, as they saw it, in *Ballard v. Tomlinson*. Since, for the reasons I have given, that case does not give rise to any principle of law independent of the ordinary law of nuisance or the rule in Rylands v. Fletcher, L.R. 3 H.L. 330, the strict position now is that C.W.C., having abandoned its claim in nuisance, can only uphold the decision of the Court of Appeal on the basis of the rule in *Rylands v. Fletcher*. However, one important submission advanced by E.C.L. before the Appellate Committee was that strict liability for an escape only arises under that rule where the defendant knows or reasonably ought to have foreseen, when collecting the relevant things on his land, that those things might, if they escaped, cause damage of the relevant kind. Since there is a close relationship between nuisance and the rule in *Rylands v. Fletcher*, I myself find it very difficult to form an opinion as to the validity of that submission without first considering whether foreseeability of such damage is an essential element in the law of nuisance. For that reason, therefore, I do not feel able altogether to ignore the latter

即使采用了这种观点,即当采取了适当的预防措施仍无法消除或明显降低风险时应适用固有危险活动的例外,但是似乎患间质瘤的风险决定了在工作时接触石棉仍然具有固有危险性。正如上文所提到的,《重述》引用了狮子逃跑和在市区爆炸的例子来说明异常危险活动。显然,这些风险都可以采取适当的预防措施被降低,但是却无法被完全消除或者甚至明显降低。石棉也是如此。

今天,法院只确定了"预防措施可能将 Roberts 接触到的石棉数量降低到最低",以这个理由来说明"工作接触石棉不具有固有危险性"的看法。(Op. at 955.)但是仅仅是降到最低还不够。适当的预防措施不但必须将"风险"降至最低,而且还要消除风险或明显的降低风险。石棉工人患间质瘤的风险无法消除或明显降低,这正是固有危险活动的一个最典型的例子。

Rucker 法官赞同。

第三节 英国法上的发展:在土地非自然利用中溢出的危险物

62. Cambridge Water Co Ltd v Eastern Counties Leather Plc [1994] 2 AC 264

联合王国上议院

Goff 大法官主笔:

妨害之诉与"Rylands v. Fletcher 一案所确立的规则"

如前所述,CWC 公司向上诉法院提起的上诉中,并未质疑原审法院关于妨害之诉的判决结论。之所以 ECL 公司的责任依然需要讨论,是因为上诉法院以 ECL 公司需要承担严格责任为理由,受理了 CWC 公司的上诉。根据上诉法院的理解,这种严格责任是建立在妨害之诉上的,其依据是 *Ballard v Tomlinson* 一案所确立的原则。然而就如我之前所述,相比较于一般的妨害之诉,或者相比较于 *Rylands v Fletcher*,L.R. 3 H.L. 330 一案所确立的规则,*Ballard v Tomlinson* 一案所确定的原则并无太多的特殊性。因此,从严格意义上讲,CWC 公司只能在 *Rylands v Fletcher* 一案所确立的规则的基础上支持上诉法院的判决,因为该公司已经放弃了针对妨害之诉的主张。然而,鉴于 ECL 公司对本上诉委员会所提出的其中一项重要的主张是"当被告在其土地上存放某物品时,若要求其对该物品的泄漏承担严格责任,应以被告明知或者可预见该排放物会造成相应损害为前提";又鉴于妨害之诉和 *Rylands v Fletcher* 一案所确立的规则有紧密的联系,我认为很有必要先讨论一下"可预见性"是否是妨害之诉的构成要件这个问题,否则我就很难去判断 ECL 公司

question simply because it was no longer pursued by C.W.C. before the Court of Appeal.

In order to consider the question in the present case in its proper legal context, it is desirable to look at the nature of liability in a case such as the present in relation both to the law of nuisance and the rule in *Rylands v. Fletcher*, and for that purpose to consider the relationship between the two heads of liability.

I begin with the law of nuisance. Our modern understanding of the nature and scope of the law of nuisance was much enhanced by Professor Newark's seminal article on "The Boundaries of Nuisance" (1949) 65 L.Q.R. 480. The article is avowedly a historical analysis, in that it traces the nature of the tort of nuisance to its origins, and demonstrates how the original view of nuisance as a tort to land (or more accurately, to accommodate interference with servitudes, a tort directed against the plaintiff's enjoyment of rights over land) became distorted as the tort was extended to embrace claims for personal injuries, even where the plaintiff's injury did not occur while using land in his occupation. In Professor Newark's opinion (p. 487), this development produced adverse effects, viz., that liability which should have arisen only under the law of negligence was allowed under the law of nuisance which historically was a tort of strict liability; and that there was a tendency for "cross-infection to take place, and notions of negligence began to make an appearance in the realm of nuisance proper." But in addition, Professor Newark considered, at pp. 487-488, it contributed to a misappreciation of the decision in *Rylands v. Fletcher*:

> "This case is generally regarded as an important landmark - indeed, a turning point - in the law of tort; but an examination of the judgments shows that those who decided it were quite unconscious of any revolutionary or reactionary principles implicit in the decision. They thought of it as calling for no more than a restatement of settled principles, and Lord Cairns went so far as to describe those principles as 'extremely simple.' and in fact the main principle involved was extremely simple, being no more than the principle that negligence is not an element in the tort of nuisance. It is true that Blackburn J. in his great judgment in the Exchequer Chamber never once used the word 'nuisance,' but three times he cited the case of fumes escaping from an alkali works - a clear case of nuisance - as an instance of liability under the rule which he was laying down. Equally it is true that in 1866 there were a number of cases in the reports suggesting that persons who controlled dangerous things were under a strict duty to take care, but as none of these cases had anything to do with nuisance Blackburn J. did not refer to them.
>
> "But the profession as a whole, whose conceptions of the boundaries of nuisance were now becoming fogged, failed to see in *Rylands v. Fletcher* a simple case of nuisance. They regarded it as an exceptional case - and the Rule in *Rylands*

的这项主张是否正确。我们不能仅仅因为"前述问题并非属于CWC公司对上诉法院的提出的上诉内容"这一理由,就忽略这个问题。

为了能够在正确的法律语境下探讨上述的这个问题,我们有必要先探究一下在本案这样的案件中,分别在妨害之诉和 Rylands v Fletcher 所确立的规则下,被告有什么样的责任。而为了这个目的,我们又有必要先考察一下这两个诉由之间到底有什么关系。

我们先来看妨害之诉。现代人对妨害之诉的性质和范围的理解,在很大程度上是受益于 Newark 教授著名的论文《妨害之诉的边界》〔(1949)65 L.Q.R. 480〕。该论文在性质上属于历史分析:该文梳理了妨害之诉的来源,并指出"妨害之诉是对土地之诉"这样一种最初的观念(更确切地说,妨害之诉是为了救济地役权,因此妨害之诉最初是用来保护原告对土地的使用权的)已经渐渐被扭曲,因为妨害之诉也渐渐被用来救济人身损害,即使原告的损害并非在其占用土地的期间发生。在 Newark 教授看来(第487页),妨害之诉的这种发展产生了一些不利的效果:一来,某些只有满足过失之诉的被告才会承担责任的情形,变得可以由妨害之诉来调整了,而在历史上妨害之诉的归责原则为严格责任;二来,人们开始趋向于"混淆这两种诉由,其效果就是在确实需要提起妨害之诉的场合,人们却开始关注过失这一概念"。此外,Newark 教授还认为,妨害之诉的这种发展加剧了人们对 Rylands v Fletcher 一案的误解(第487到第488页):

> 人们往往认为本案是一个里程碑式的判例,甚至是一个侵权法上的转折点;然而如果我们仔细阅读判决书,我们就会发现该案的法官并不觉得自己的判决书中有提出了什么"革命性的"或者"反动的"的原则。该案的法官觉得自己不过是重申了某些既定的原则,Cairns 大法官甚至认为这些原则"极其简单"。确实,本案中涉及的主要的原则确实极其简单,不过是"过失并非妨害之诉的构成要件"。诚然,Blackburn 法官在为财税法院所起草的判决中并未用到"妨害"一词,然而他却有三次提到了从制碱厂中泄漏的烟雾,并认为这属于依照他所确定的规则被告应该承担责任的情形,而这很明显是属于妨害之诉的情形。同样,在1866年,其实有好几个判例都认为危险物品的控制者要承担严格责任意义上的注意义务,但是因为它们都并不涉及妨害之诉,所以 Blackburn 法官并没有引用它们。

> 然而实务界对妨害之诉的界限的看法已经变得模糊了,因此他们并

v. Fletcher as a generalisation of exceptional cases, where liability was to be strict on account of 'the magnitude of danger, coupled with the difficulty of proving negligence,' [Pollock, Law of Torts, 14th ed. (1939), p. 386] rather than on account of the nature of the plaintiff's interest which was invaded. They therefore jumped rashly to two conclusions: firstly, that the Rule in *Rylands v. Fletcher* could be extended beyond the case of neighbouring occupiers; and secondly, that the Rule could be used to afford a remedy in cases of personal injury. Both these conclusions were stoutly denied by Lord Macmillan in *Read v. Lyons* [1947] A.C. 156, but it remains to be seen whether the House of Lords will support his opinion when the precise point comes up for decision."

We are not concerned in the present case with the problem of personal injuries, but we are concerned with the scope of liability in nuisance and in *Rylands v. Fletcher*. In my opinion it is right to take as our starting point the fact that, as Professor Newark considered, *Rylands v. Fletcher* was indeed not regarded by Blackburn J. as a revolutionary decision: see, e.g., his observations in *Ross v. Fedden* (1872) 26 L.T. 966 , 968. He believed himself not to be creating new law, but to be stating existing law, on the basis of existing authority; and, as is apparent from his judgment, he was concerned in particular with the situation where the defendant collects things upon his land which are likely to do mischief if they escape, in which event the defendant will be strictly liable for damage resulting from any such escape. It follows that the essential basis of liability was the collection by the defendant of such things upon his land; and the consequence was a strict liability in the event of damage caused by their escape, even if the escape was an isolated event. Seen in its context, there is no reason to suppose that Blackburn J. intended to create a liability any more strict than that created by the law of nuisance; but even so he must have intended that, in the circumstances specified by him, there should be liability for damage resulting from an isolated escape.

Of course, although liability for nuisance has generally been regarded as strict, at least in the case of a defendant who has been responsible for the creation of a nuisance, even so that liability has been kept under control by the principle of reasonable user - the principle of give and take as between neighbouring occupiers of land, under which "those acts necessary for the common and ordinary use and occupation of land and houses may be done, if conveniently done, without subjecting those who do them to an action:" see *Bamford v. Turnley* (1862) 3 B. & S. 62, 83, *per* Bramwell B. The effect is that, if the user is reasonable, the defendant will not be liable for consequent harm to his neighbour's enjoyment of his land; but if the user is not reasonable, the defendant will be liable, even though he may have exercised reasonable care and skill to avoid it. Strikingly, a comparable principle has developed which limits liability under the rule in Rylands v.

不认为 *Rylands v Fletcher* 只是一个简单的妨害之诉。他们认为该案是一种特殊类型的案件，而该案中所总结出的规则其实是对许多的这种特殊类型案件的抽象。他们认为此时，被告人要承担严格责任，是基于"危险大小和证明过失的困难"这样的原因 [Pollock,《侵权法》，第 14 版（1939 年），第 386 页]，而不是基于原告所受到损害的性质。他们由此武断地得出了两个结论：首先，*Rylands v Fletcher* 一案的规则可以适用到相邻的土地占有者以外的情形；其次，该案的规则可以用来救济人身损害。Macmillan 大法官在 *Read v Lyons* [1947] A.C. 156 一案中已经坚决地否定了这两个结论；而上议院的观点则要到需要其判决的问题出现时才能知道。

本案中并不涉及人身损害，我们需要关注的仅仅是在妨害之诉和 *Rylands v Fletcher* 中责任的范围。在我看来，Newark 教授的这个观点应该是我们讨论的起点：Blackburn 法官自己并没有把 *Rylands v Fletcher* 看做革命性的判决 [参见他在 *Ross v Fedden*（1872）26 L.T. 966, 968 一案中的观点]。他觉得他自己并没有创造新法律，不过是在重申既存的法律，援引既存的法律渊源；而且很明显，他最重视的是这么一个观点——"被告人如果在其土地上存放某种物质，这种物质若泄漏很可能会造成损害，那么此时被告人应对损害结果承担严格责任"。这样说来，此时责任的基础是"被告人在其土地上存放有害物质"；其结果是即使该物质的泄漏只是一个孤立的事件，被告人也要对泄漏物质所造成的损害承担严格责任。这么看来，我们没有理由认为 Blackburn 法官意图创造一种比妨害之诉更加严格的责任；然而即使是这样，Blackburn 法官一定认同，在他所描述的情况下，即使有害物质的泄漏仅仅是孤立事件，被告人也应当承担责任。

虽然我们说妨害之诉之下的责任是严格责任（至少当被告人对这种妨害的产生负有责任时），但是即使如此，其责任仍受到"合理使用者原则"的限制：这种原则要求邻近土地的占有者要互相妥协，因此"对于那些通常的、为了公共利益的、且为了使用或者占有土地和房屋而必须的使用方式，如果这种使用方式是正常进行的，那么就不会使得使用人遭受诉讼的风险"[参见 *Bamford v Turnley*（1862）3 B. & S. 62, 83, 财税法院 Bramwell 法官的话]，其责任的效果却是这样的：当土地的使用人以合理的方式使用土地时，其并不会为对邻居的土地用益造成的损害承担责任；只有当其适用的方式不合理

Fletcher. This is the principle of natural use of the land. I shall have to consider the principle at a later stage in this judgment. The most authoritative statement of the principle is now to be found in the advice of the Privy Council delivered by Lord Moulton in *Rickards v. Lothian* [1913] A.C. 263, 280, when he said of the rule in *Rylands v. Fletcher*:

> "It is not every use to which land is put that brings into play that principle. It must be some special use bringing with it increased danger to others, and must not merely be the ordinary use of the land or such a use as is proper for the general benefit of the community."

It is not necessary for me to identify precise differences which may be drawn between this principle, and the principle of reasonable user as applied in the law of nuisance. It is enough for present purposes that I should draw attention to a similarity of function. The effect of this principle is that, where it applies, there will be no liability under the rule in *Rylands v. Fletcher*; but that where it does not apply, i.e. where there is a non-natural use, the defendant will be liable for harm caused to the plaintiff by the escape, notwithstanding that he has exercised all reasonable care and skill to prevent the escape from occurring.

63. Transco Plc v Stockport Metropolitan Borough Council [2003] UKHL 61, [2004] 2 AC 1

House of Lords, United Kingdom

LORD BINGHAM

It has from the beginning been a necessary condition of liability under the rule in *Rylands v Fletcher* that the thing which the defendant has brought on his land should be "something which ... will naturally do mischief if it escape out of his land" (LR 1 Ex 265, 279 per Blackburn J), "something dangerous ...", "anything likely to do mischief if it escapes", "something ... harmless to others so long as it is confined to his own property, but which he knows to be mischievous if it gets on his neighbour's" (p 280), "anything which, if it should escape, may cause damage to his neighbour" (LR 3 HL 330, 340, per Lord Cranworth). The practical problem is of course to decide whether in any given case the thing which has escaped satisfies this mischief or danger test, a problem exacerbated by the fact that many things not ordinarily regarded as sources of mischief or danger may none the less be capable of proving to be such if they escape. I do not think this condition can be viewed in complete isolation from the non-natural user condition to which I shall shortly turn, but I think the cases decided by the House give a valuable pointer. In *Rylands v Fletcher* itself the courts were dealing with what Lord Cranworth (LR 3 HL 330, 342) called "a large accumulated mass of water" stored up in a reservoir, and I have touched on the historical

时，被告人才会承担责任，此时他的责任并不会因为他已经尽到了合理的注意义务和适用了合理的技术来避免损失就被排除。显然，我们可以由此得出一个能限制 Rylands v Fletcher 一案确立的被告所承担的责任的原则。这个原则就是"自然使用土地原则"。在本判决的后续部分我将再来讨论这个原则。现在，我将援引对这个原则最权威的陈述，该陈述是由 Moulton 大法官为枢密院在 Rickards v Lothian [1913] A.C. 263, 280 一案的判决中所作出的。在此处，他提到了 Rylands v Fletcher 一案所确立的规则：

> 并非所有的对土地的使用方式都会导致"自然使用土地原则"的适用。要适用该原则一定符合下列情形：对土地的使用会增加对他人的危险，且该使用方式并非一般人日常对土地的使用方式，且该使用方式并不会增进公共福祉。

"自然使用土地原则"和妨害之诉中的"合理使用者原则"到底有什么精确的区别，在这里我就不细说了。就本案的目的而言，我只需要指出我们的注意力应当放在这两个原则所承担的类似的功能上。"自然使用土地原则"的效果是，如果该原则适用了，那么被告就不承担 Rylands v Fletcher 一案意义上的责任；而当该原则不适用时，即被告对土地的使用方式是非自然时，那么被告就需要对因为其土地上所泄漏之物对原告造成的损害承担责任，即便被告已经尽到了所有适当的注意义务并用到了所有适当的技术来避免这种泄漏的发生。

63. Transco Plc v Stockport Metropolitan Borough Council [2003] UKHL 61, [2004] 2 AC 1

联合王国上议院

Bingham 大法官主笔：
自 Rylands v Fletcher 一案诞生起，根据该案所确定的责任必须满足这样的条件：被告将某种物品放置在了他的土地上，而该物品"在泄漏时会自然地造成损害"（LR 1 Ex 265, 279 per Blackburn J），"是危险的……"；"是任何会在泄漏时造成损害之物"；"在被限制在（侵权人）自己的土地上时是无害的……只要（侵权人）知道一旦该物品泄漏则会损害其邻居"（p 280），"是任何一旦泄漏就会对邻居造成损害之物"（LR 3 HL 330, 340, per Lord Cranworth）。在实践中，最重要的问题是判断在某个特定的情况下，当有东西从一块土地逃逸时，此物是否满足上述的"危害或危险测试"。这个问题的判断并不容易，特别是当我们考虑到很多情况下某些物品在通常看来并不会致害，也并不危险，然而当它们泄漏时，

context of the decision in paragraph 3(3) above. *Rainham Chemical Works* [1921] 2 AC 465, 471, involved the storage of chemicals, for the purpose of making munitions, which "exploded with terrific violence". In *Attorney General v Cory Bros & Co Ltd* [1921] 1 AC 521, 525, 530, 534, 536, the landslide in question was of what counsel described as an "enormous mass of rubbish", some 500,000 tons of mineral waste tipped on a steep hillside. In *Cambridge Water* [1994] 2 AC 264 the industrial solvents being used by the tannery were bound to cause mischief in the event, unforeseen on the facts, that they percolated down to the water table. These cases are in sharp contrast with those arising out of escape from a domestic water supply (such as *Carstairs v Taylor* (1871) LR 6 Ex 217, *Ross v Fedden* (1872) 26 LT 966 or *Anderson v Oppenheimer* (1880) 5 QBD 602) which, although decided on other grounds, would seem to me to fail the mischief or danger test. Bearing in mind the historical origin of the rule, and also that its effect is to impose liability in the absence of negligence for an isolated occurrence, I do not think the mischief or danger test should be at all easily satisfied. It must be shown that the defendant has done something which he recognised, or judged by the standards appropriate at the relevant place and time, he ought reasonably to have recognised, as giving rise to an exceptionally high risk of danger or mischief if there should be an escape, however unlikely an escape may have been thought to be.

No ingredient of *Rylands v Fletcher* liability has provoked more discussion than the requirement of Blackburn J (LR 1 Ex 265, 280) that the thing brought on to the defendant's land should be something "not naturally there", an expression elaborated by Lord Cairns (LR 3 HL 330, 339) when he referred to the putting of land to a "non-natural use": see Stallybrass, "Dangerous Things and the Non-Natural User of Land" (1929) 3 CLJ 376-397; Goodhart, "Liability for Things Naturally on the Land" (1932) 4 CLJ 13-33; Newark, "Non-Natural User and Rylands v Fletcher" (1961) 24 MLR 557-571; Williams, "Non-Natural Use of Land" [1973] CLJ 310-322; Weir, " *Rylands v Fletcher* Reconsidered" [1994] CLJ 216. Read literally, the expressions used by Blackburn J and Lord Cairns might be thought to exclude nothing which has reached the land otherwise than through operation of the laws of nature. But such an interpretation has been fairly described as "redolent of a different age" (*Cambridge Water [1994] 2 AC 264*, 308), and in *Read v J Lyons & Co Ltd* [1947] AC 156, 169, 176, 187 and *Cambridge Water*, at p 308, the House gave its imprimatur to Lord Moulton's statement, giving the advice of the Privy Council in *Rickards v Lothian [1913] AC 263*, 280:

> "It is not every use to which land is put that brings into play that principle. It must be some special use bringing with it increased danger to others, and must not merely be the ordinary use of the land or such a use as is proper for the general benefit of the community."

却可以造成实实在在的危害。在我看来，我们刚说到的这个条件是不能完全脱离"非自然使用者"这个条件来考察的。对于"非自然使用者"这个条件，我待会儿会再回过头来讨论，不过现在我觉得我们应该先来看看上议院作出的一些判例，这些判例可能给我们提供有价值的指引。在 Rylands v Fletcher 这一案件中，法院所面临的是 Cranworth 大法官（LR 3 HL 330, 342）说的，存储于水库中的"超大量的水"（本案的历史情况我已经在上文第三段第三小段中介绍了）。而 Rainham Chemical Works [1921] 2 AC 465, 471 一案涉及的是作为炸药原料的化学品的存储，而后来这些原料"猛烈地爆炸"了。在 Attorney General v Cory Bros & Co Ltd [1921] 1 AC 521, 525, 530, 534, 536 一案中，根据一方律师的描述，"巨量的垃圾"——5000 吨煤渣从山上滑了下来。在 Cambridge Water [1994] 2 AC 264 一案中，制鞋厂所使用的化工溶剂只要渗透到地下水中，是必然会造成损害的，虽然案发时这一事实尚不为人所知。以上这些案件和那种家庭用水溢出造成的损害相比，是大有不同的［比如 Carstairs v Taylor（1871）LR 6 Ex 217, Ross v Fedden（1872）26 LT 966 or Anderson v Oppenheimer（1880）5 QBD 602］。这种涉及家庭用水的案件在我看来是很难满足我们刚才说的"危害或危险测试"的，当然这些案件也并不是根据这个标准来判决的。如果我们考虑一下 Fletcher 案的起源和效果，该案是为了在无法证明被告人存在过失且事故只发生过一次时，确定被告人的责任，那么我们可以想到，这个"危害或危险测试"并不是那么容易满足的。要满足这个测试，原告需要证明被告知道或者依据相关的时间和地点上适当的标准应该知道，他所存储在他的土地上之物，如果泄漏了，是会造成严重的危险或者危害的，即使这种泄漏是非常不可能的。

Rylands v Fletcher 责任的要件中，最有争议的是 Blackburn 法官（LR 1 Ex 265, 280）提出的要件：即致害物应该是由被告所搬运到其土地上的，且该物并非"自然地在那儿"。这个标准，经 Cairns 大法官阐释为（LR 3 HL 330, 339）"土地被用作非自然的用途"［参见 Stallybrass, "Dangerous Things and the Non-Natural User of Land"（1929）3 CLJ 376-397; Goodhart, "Liability for Things Naturally on the Land"（1932）4 CLJ 13-33; Newark, "Non-Natural User and Rylands v Fletcher"（1961）24 MLR 557-571; Williams, "Non-Natural Use of Land"（1973）CLJ 310-322; Weir, " Rylands v Fletcher Reconsidered"（1994）CLJ 216.］如果从字面上理解，按照 Blackburn 法官和 Cairns 大法官的标准，能够确定责任的致害物，仅仅只包括那些通过自然力而到达加害人的土地上的东西。然而，这种狭义的解释已经被很公正地描述为"旧时代的孑遗"［Cambridge Water（1994）2 AC 264, 308］。而在 Read v J Lyons & Co Ltd [1947] AC 156, 169, 176, 187 和 Cambridge Water（第 308 页）中，上议院支持了 Moulton's 大法官代表枢密院所给出的意见。该意见是针对 Rickards v Lothian [1913] AC 263, 280 —

I think it clear that ordinary user is a preferable test to natural user, making it clear that the rule in *Rylands v Fletcher* is engaged only where the defendant's use is shown to be extraordinary and unusual. This is not a test to be inflexibly applied: a use may be extraordinary and unusual at one time or in one place but not so at another time or in another place (although I would question whether, even in wartime, the manufacture of explosives could ever be regarded as an ordinary user of land, as contemplated by Viscount Simon, Lord Macmillan, Lord Porter and Lord Uthwatt in *Read v J Lyons & Co Ltd* [1947] AC 156, 169-170, 174, 176-177, 186-187). I also doubt whether a test of reasonable user is helpful, since a user may well be quite out of the ordinary but not unreasonable, as was that of *Rylands* , *Rainham Chemical Works* or the tannery in *Cambridge Water*. Again, as it seems to me, the question is whether the defendant has done something which he recognises, or ought to recognise, as being quite out of the ordinary in the place and at the time when he does it. In answering that question, I respectfully think that little help is gained (and unnecessary confusion perhaps caused) by considering whether the use is proper for the general benefit of the community. In *Rickards v Lothian* itself, the claim arose because the outflow from a wash-basin on the top floor of premises was maliciously blocked and the tap left running, with the result that damage was caused to stock on a floor below: not surprisingly, the provision of a domestic water supply to the premises was held to be a wholly ordinary use of the land. An occupier of land who can show that another occupier of land has brought or kept on his land an exceptionally dangerous or mischievous thing in extraordinary or unusual circumstances is in my opinion entitled to recover compensation from that occupier for any damage caused to his property interest by the escape of that thing, subject to defences of Act of God or of a stranger, without the need to prove negligence.

...

LORD HOFFMAN

It remains, however, if not to rationalise the law of England, at least to introduce greater certainty into the concept of natural user which is in issue in this case. In order to do so, I think it must be frankly acknowledged that little assistance can be obtained from the kinds of user which Lord Cairns must be assumed to have regarded as "non-natural" in *Rylands v Fletcher* itself. They are, as Lord Goff of Chieveley said in the *Cambridge Water case* [1994] 2 AC 264, 308, "redolent of a different age". So nothing can be made of the anomaly that one of the illustrations of the rule given by Blackburn J is cattle trespass. Whatever Blackburn J and Lord Cairns may have meant by "natural", the law was set on a different course by the opinion of Lord Moulton in *Rickards v Lothian* [1913] AC 263 and the question of what is a natural use of land or, (the converse) a use creating an increased risk, must be judged by contemporary standards.

Two features of contemporary society seem to me to be relevant. First, the extension of statutory regulation to a number of activities, such as discharge of water (section 209 of the Water

案的：

> 并非所有对土地的使用都适用"自然使用土地原则"。要适用该原则必须符合下列特殊使用的情形：对土地的使用会增加对他人的危险，且该使用方式并非一般人日常对土地的使用方式，且该使用方式并不会增进公共福祉。

在我看来，这里的"通常的使用者"的标准是比刚才说的"自然的使用者"测试更好的判断标准。因为前者表明，*Rylands v Fletcher* 的规则旨在能证明被告人对其土地的使用是"非同寻常"时才能适用。"通常的使用者"这个标准也并非是一成不变的：在此时此地，一种对土地的使用方式可能是非同寻常的，而在彼时彼地，则不一定［虽然我怀疑即便在战争时期，制造炸药也不属于对土地的通常用途，如 Simon 子爵、Macmillan 大法官、Porter 大法官和 Uthwatt 大法官在 *Read v J Lyons & Co Ltd*（1947）AC 156, 169-170, 174, 176-177, 186-187 中所想的那样］。另外，我怀疑合理使用者这个标准的用处，因为对土地的使用方式可能非常不"通常"，但是却非常合理，正如 *Rylands*、*Rainham Chemical Works* 和 *Cambridge Water* 一案中的制鞋厂的例子。还有，就回答被告人是否知道或者应当知道他对土地的使用方式是"非常规的"这个问题来看，我确实觉得考虑这种使用方式是否能增进公共福祉是毫无意义的（也许还会造成不必要的混淆）。在 *Rickards v Lothian* 一案中，争议的起因是楼上水池的自来水龙头没有关且水池被堵住了，导致水漫出来淹了楼下：不出意外，给住处通自来水自然是不属于"非常规的"使用土地的方式。综上，在我看来，一块土地的占有人如果能证明另一块土地的占有人，在其土地上存储了特别危险的致害物，且这种存储属于非常规的情况，那么前者有权就致害物泄漏对其土地造成的损害，向后者提出损害赔偿；这种请求无须证明后者的过失，而后者的抗辩事由只能是不可抗力或第三人行为。

……

Hoffman 大法官主笔：

我们如果无法进一步合理化英国的法律，也至少需要明晰本案争议中涉及的"自然使用者"这个概念。我们必须要承认，Cairns 大法官所认为的，在 *Rylands v Fletcher* 一案判决中列举的那些"非自然的对土地的使用方式"，就上述目标而言，是几乎没有什么用处的。按照 Chieveley 大法官在 *Cambridge Water case* [1994] 2 AC 264, 308 一案中的说法，他们不过是"旧时代的孑遗"。而 Blackburn 大法官为解释 *Fletcher* 一案的规则而举的饲养动物入侵的例子，也同样对于解释什么是"非正常的使用"毫无意义。Blackburn

Industry Act 1991) pollution by the escape of waste (section 73(6) of the Environmental Protection Act 1990) and radioactive matter (section 7 of the Nuclear Installations Act 1965). It may have to be considered whether these and similar provisions create an exhaustive code of liability for a particular form of escape which excludes the rule in *Rylands v Fletcher*.

Secondly, so far as the rule does have a residuary role to play, it must be borne in mind that it is concerned only with damage to property and that insurance against various forms of damage to property is extremely common. A useful guide in deciding whether the risk has been created by a "non-natural" user of land is therefore to ask whether the damage which eventuated was something against which the occupier could reasonably be expected to have insured himself. Property insurance is relatively cheap and accessible; in my opinion people should be encouraged to insure their own property rather than seek to transfer the risk to others by means of litigation, with the heavy transactional costs which that involves. The present substantial litigation over £100,000 should be a warning to anyone seeking to rely on an esoteric cause of action to shift a commonplace insured risk.

In the present case, I am willing to assume that if the risk arose from a "non-natural user" of the council's land, all the other elements of the tort were satisfied. Transco complains of expense having to be undertaken to avoid damage to its gas pipe; I am willing to assume that if damage to the pipe would have been actionable, the expense incurred in avoiding that damage would have been recoverable. I also willing to assume that Transco's easement which entitled it to maintain its pipe in the embankment and receive support from the soil was a sufficient proprietary interest to enable it to sue in nuisance and therefore, by analogy, under the rule in *Rylands v Fletcher*. Although the council, as owner of Hollow End Towers, was no doubt under a statutory duty to provide its occupiers with water, it had no statutory duty or authority to build that particular tower block and it is therefore not suggested that the pipe was laid pursuant to statutory powers so as to exclude the rule. So the question is whether the risk came within the rule.

The damage which eventuated was subsidence beneath a gas main: a form of risk against which no rational owner of a gas main would fail to insure. The casualty was caused by the escape of water from the council's land. But the source was a perfectly normal item of plumbing. The pipe was, it is true, considerably larger than the ordinary domestic size. But it was smaller than a water main. It was installed to serve the occupiers of the council's high rise flats; not strictly speaking a commercial purpose, but not a private one either.

In my opinion the Court of Appeal was right to say that it was not a "non-natural" user of land. I am influenced by two matters. First, there is no evidence that it created a greater risk than is normally associated with domestic or commercial plumbing. True, the pipe was larger. But whether that involved greater risk depends upon its specification. One cannot simply assume that the larger the pipe, the greater the risk of fracture or the greater the quantity of water likely to be

法官和 Cairns 大法官对于什么是"自然的使用"方式，有他们自己的理解，然而无论他们到底有什么意见，Moulton 大法官在 *Rickards v Lothian* [1913] AC 263 一案中已经改变了实在法的轨迹。那么关于何为对土地的自然使用方式，或者相反，何为对土地的可能增加他人风险的使用方式，则是一个需要用现代标准来衡量的问题。

就这个问题而言，我们需要讨论两个现代社会的特征。其一，我们制定了许多成文法来调整许多事项，如排水（1991 年《水工业法》第 209 条）、废物泄漏所致污染（1990年《环境保护法》第 73 条第 6 款）以及放射性物质（1965 年《核设施法》第 7 条）。我们必须考虑，这些成文法和类似的规定所确立的针对某种致害物泄漏的成文法上的责任，是否意味着 *Rylands v Fletcher* 所确立的规则会被排除适用。

其二，即便 *Rylands v Fletcher* 的规则还有适用的余地，我们需要注意它也仅仅只能调整对土地的侵害案件；而在现代社会中，对土地的各种侵害进行保险是非常普遍的现象。这样，在我们讨论某种风险是否是由"非自然的"土地使用者造成时，一个很有用的思路是去讨论这种风险是否是受害土地的占有者可以合理地预见并自己去通过保险来规避的。财产保险是很便宜的，也是很容易买到的。在我看来，我们应当鼓励人们自己对其财产保险，而不是通过有巨额交易成本的诉讼来转移风险。诉讼标的涉及 10 万英镑的本案，应该成为一个警示，警告每一个希望通过晦涩的诉讼来转嫁常见风险之人。

就本案而言，我认为除了市政厅对其土地的使用是"非自然的"这个要件外，其他的要件原告都已经满足了。Transco 请求赔偿为避免对其燃气管道的损害而必须支出的费用。如果对燃气管道的损害是可诉的，那么同样为避免这种损害而支出的费用也是可诉的。同样，Transco 的地役权——该地役权使得其可以在涉案地块上维护其管道并使其管道获得来自土地的支撑——也是足以使其有资格提起"妨害之诉"的财产性权利。而类推可知，这也是使其有资格在 *Rylands v Fletcher* 的规则下提起诉讼的财产性权利。虽然市政厅作为 Hollow End 塔的所有权人，根据成文法是有义务为土地上的居民提供自来水的，但是它却并无法定的义务或者职权去建设这个特定的塔；因此我们不能说市政厅是根据成文法上的权力来铺设涉案的水管的，也因此可以排除适用 Fletcher 的规则。这样，我们的核心问题就是，本案中涉及的风险，是否属于 Fletcher 规则所要求的那种风险。

本案涉及的损害是由煤气总管下面的土地的塌陷造成的：这种类型的风险是任何理性的煤气总管的所有人都会自己去投保的。诚然损害是由市政厅的土地上泄漏的水造成的；然而水源却是一种非常常见的水泵。涉案的水管却是比通常的家用水管要大，然而却小于总水管。这里，水管是为了市政厅

discharged. I agree with my noble and learned friend, Lord Bingham of Cornhill, that the criterion of exceptional risk must be taken seriously and creates a high threshold for a claimant to surmount. Secondly, I think that the risk of damage to property caused by leaking water is one against which most people can and do commonly insure. This is, as I have said, particularly true of Transco, which can be expected to have insured against any form of damage to its pipe. It would be a very strange result if Transco were entitled to recover against the council when it would not have been entitled to recover against the water authority for similar damage emanating from its high-pressure main.

...

LORD SCOTT

The House held, in the *Cambridge Water Co* case, that the use of land for the storage of chemicals in substantial quantities could not be described as a "natural or ordinary" use of land so as to exclude the application of the *Rylands v Fletcher* rule (p 309) but held, also, that, as in nuisance cases, foreseeability of the damage was a prerequisite of liability. The House thereby added to the two conditions formulated in *Read v Lyons* a third condition on which liability under the rule in *Rylands v Fletcher* would depend.

Just as in *Cambridge Water* the House found it impossible to regard the storage of chemicals in substantial quantities as a natural or ordinary use of land so, in the present case, it is in my opinion equally impossible to regard the supply by the council of water to the block of flats as anything other than a natural or ordinary use.

Indeed, the council was under a statutory obligation to provide a suitable supply of water for domestic purposes to the occupiers of the 66 flats. Nobody has suggested that the means by which the council did so could have been satisfactorily achieved by some other practicable method which would have carried with it a lesser risk of serious flood.

There is no doubt that the rule in *Rylands v Fletcher* can be excluded by statute. In Green v Chelsea Waterworks Co (1894) 70 LT 547 a water main belonging to a waterworks company, which had been authorised by Parliament to lay the main, burst. There had been no negligence on the part of the waterworks company. The claimants' premises were flooded but the waterworks company was held to have no liability. The case was applied in this House in *Longhurst v Metropolitan Water Board* [1948] 2 All ER 834, a case in which water had leaked from a main and disturbed paving stones in the highway. The water board had had no knowledge of or reason to suspect any danger to the public at the place in question. The House, affirming the Court of Appeal, held that since the board was acting under statutory authority in maintaining the main, they were not liable in the absence of negligence. And more recently, Lord Wilberforce in *Allen v Gulf Oil Refining Ltd* [1981] AC 1001, 1011 reaffirmed the point. He said:

所有的高层公寓的住客所铺设的，这严格来说虽不是商业目的，但也并不是私人目的。

我认为上诉法院关于被告对土地的使用并非"非自然的"的观点，是正确的。我得出这个结论是基于两点事实。其一，本案中水管的铺设并没有造成比一般的家用商用水泵更高的风险。诚然，本案中的水管更大。然而这是否意味着它会造成更大的风险，则取决于水管的规格。我们不能说因为水管更大，所以它爆管的风险就更高或者（一旦爆管则）会泄漏更多的水。我同意我高贵而博学的朋友 Bingham 大法官的意见，即我们应该慎重对待"特别的风险"这一要件，应该就此对原告提出高要求。其二，我认为水泄漏对其财产造成的这种风险，属于大多数人都会自己去投保的类型。对 Transco 而言，尤其是这样，他应该对任何对其燃气管可能造成的风险进行投保。当水政部门的高压主水管爆管时，Transco 是不能获得赔偿的；那么如果我们允许他向市政厅取得赔偿，就会非常奇怪。

……

Scott 大法官主笔：

上议院在 *Cambridge Water Co* 一案中指出在涉案土地上存储大量的化学物质并不属于"非自然或非常规的"对土地的使用方式，因此应当排除适用 *Rylands v Fletcher* 案的规则（p309）；上议院还认为，如同"妨害之诉"，对损害的可预见性也是 Flecher 规则下的一个要件。这样，对于 *Rylands v Fletcher* 的要件，上议院就在 *Read v Lyons* 案所确定的两个要件的基础上，增加了第三个要件。

正如在 *Cambridge Water* 一案中上议院认为我们不能将存储大量的化学物质视为对土地的自然而日常的使用方式一样，在本案中，我们同样不能否认，市政厅对涉案公寓的供水，是完全自然而日常的对其土地的使用方式。

市政厅其实负有一种法定的对 66 栋公寓楼的住客供水的义务。没人能证明市政厅有其他的、可行的，且使爆管风险更小的手段来履行这个义务。

没人能否认 *Ryland v. Fletcher* 的规则可以被成文法排除适用。在 *Green v Chelsea Waterworks Co*（1894）70 LT 547 一案中，一家自来水公司的总水管爆管了，这个总水管是议会授权铺设的。自来水公司对爆管是没有任何过失的。原告的住宅因此被淹没了，但是自来水公司却并未承担任何责任。在 *Longhurst v Metropolitan Water Board* [1948] 2 All ER 834 一案中，上议院也作出了同样的判决：该案中，主水管漏水，并因此破坏了公路上的石块路面。水政部门对爆管会给当地公众带来的危险并无所知，也并无理由怀疑这样的危险确实存在。上议院支持了上诉法院的判决，指出因为水政部门是在成文法的义务之下去管理水管的，因此如果不能证明其有过错，是不用承担责任的。

"It is now well settled that where Parliament by express direction or by necessary implication has authorised the construction and use of an undertaking or works, that carries with it an authority to do what is authorised with immunity from any action based on nuisance. The right of action is taken away ... To this there is made the qualification, or condition, that the statutory powers are exercised without 'negligence'—that word here being used in a special sense so as to require the undertaker, as a condition of obtaining immunity from action, to carry out the work and conduct the operation with all reasonable regard and care for the interests of other persons."

These principles regarding statutory authority and immunity from action are not directly applicable in the present case. There was no specific statutory authority for the council to build the block of flats. But it had a statutory function in regard to housing and the building of the block of flats was in discharge of that statutory function. There was no specific statutory authority for the council to lay the supply pipe where it did in order to provide a water supply to the block of flats. But it did have a statutory duty by some suitable means or other to provide a supply of water for domestic purposes to the flats and no one has suggested that the laying of the supply pipe was not a proper discharge of that duty. In these circumstances the remarks of Lord Wilberforce, although not directly applicable, are in my opinion highly relevant to the question whether the laying and maintaining by the council of the supply pipe was, for *Rylands v Fletcher* purposes, a "natural" or "ordinary" use of its land so as to exempt it from liability resulting therefrom in the absence of negligence.

Before answering that question it is, I think, worth reflecting on why it is that an activity authorised, or required, by statute to be carried on will not, in the absence of negligence, expose the actor to strict liability in nuisance or under the rule in *Rylands v Fletcher*. The reason, in my opinion, is that members of the public are expected to put up with any adverse side-effects of such an activity provided always that it is carried on with due care. The use of the land for carrying on the activity cannot be characterised as unreasonable if it has been authorised or required by statute. Viewed against the fact of the statutory authority, the user is a natural and ordinary use of the land. This approach applies in my opinion, to the present case. The council had no alternative, given its statutory obligations to the occupiers of the flats, but to lay on a water supply. Strict liability cannot be attached to it for having done so.

最近，Wilberforce 大法官在 *Allen v Gulf Oil Refining Ltd* [1981] AC 1001, 1011 一案中重申了这一观点。他说：

> 如果议会明示或者暗示地许可了一项工程的建设或者使用，那么从事议会许可的这项工作之人不应承担"妨害之诉"下的责任。这个观点应该没有什么争议。原告的诉权在此时被剥夺是有条件的，即行为人实施其在成文法下的权利时，是没有"过失"的。"过失"一词在这里有一种特殊的含义，即为了豁免他人的"妨害之诉"，行为人从事他的工作时，应对他人的利益尽到合理的注意义务。

上述涉及成文法授权和豁免责任的原则，并不能在本案中直接适用。没有明确的成文法授权市政厅修建这些公寓楼。然而市政厅确实承担一项成文法授予的建设住宅的职责，而修建这些公寓楼就是在履行这项成文法授予职责。同样并无明确的成文法授权市政厅为这些公寓楼铺设水管。然而，它确实承担一种成文法的职责，去采取这样或那样的适当措施为这些公寓提供家庭用水；而铺设本案中的水管是恰当履行这种职责的做法。在这样的情况下，Wilberforce 大法官的观点虽然并不能直接适用，但是在我看来对回答以下这个问题非常相关：即市政厅铺设和管理这些水管，是否属于能够使它在除了有过错的情况下免除那种对土地的"自然的"或"通常的"使用方式的所有责任。

在回答这些问题之前，我认为我们有必要先思考一下为什么根据成文法的许可或者要求而为某行为之人，只要没有过失，就不用承担妨害之诉和在 *Rylands v Fletcher* 规则下的责任。在我看来，其理由在于，在这类行为的行为人尽到了注意义务的情况下，社会的成员应当容忍其行为所造成的副作用。当成文法许可或者要求了某种事项，为了实现这种事项而对土地的使用就不能被视为不合理的。当存在成文法授权的情况下，土地的使用者对土地的使用便是自然而通常的。对于其向公寓住户所负担的成文法义务，市政厅并无供水以外的其他途径来履行该义务。而在履行该义务时，市政厅则不应当承受严格责任。

Chapter 7. Products Liability

Section 1. US Law: A Three-fold Taxonomy of Defect

64. MacPherson v. Buick Motor Co., 217 N.Y. 382, 111 N.E. 1050 (1916)

Court of Appeals of New York, United States

Cardozo, J. The defendant is a manufacturer of automobiles. It sold an automobile to a retail dealer. The retail dealer resold to the plaintiff. While the plaintiff was in the car, it suddenly collapsed. He was thrown out and injured. One of the wheels was made of defective wood, and its spokes crumbled into fragments. The wheel was not made by the defendant; it was bought from another manufacturer. There is evidence, however, that its defects could have been discovered by reasonable inspection, and that inspection was omitted. There is no claim that the defendant knew of the defect and willfully concealed it....The charge is one, not of fraud, but of negligence. The question to be determined is whether the defendant owed a duty of care and vigilance to any one but the immediate purchaser.

...

We hold, then, that the principle of Thomas v. Winchester is not limited to poisons, explosives, and things of like nature, to things which in their normal operation are implements of destruction. If the nature of a thing is such that it is reasonably certain to place life and limb in peril when negligently made, it is then a thing of danger. Its nature gives warning of the consequences to be expected. If to the element of danger there is added knowledge that the thing will be used by persons other than the purchaser, and used without new tests, then, irrespective of contract, the manufacturer of this thing of danger is under a duty to make it carefully. That is as far as we are required to go for the decision of this case. There must be knowledge of a danger, not merely possible, but probable. It is *possible* to use almost anything in a way that will make it dangerous if defective. That is not enough to charge the manufacturer with a duty independent of his contract. Whether a given thing is dangerous may be sometimes a question for the court and sometimes a question for the jury. There must also be knowledge that in the usual course of events the danger will be shared by others than the buyer. Such knowledge may often be inferred from the nature of the transaction. But it is possible that even knowledge of the danger and of the use will not always

第七章　产品责任

第一节　美国法：缺陷三分法

64. MacPherson v. Buick Motor Co., 217 N.Y. 382, 111 N.E. 1050 (1916)

美国纽约上诉法院

Cardozo 法官主笔：

被告是一家汽车制造者，向零售经销商出售汽车。经销商再将汽车卖给原告。当原告驾驶汽车时，汽车突然散架了。原告被扔出汽车，受了伤。汽车的一个车轮是由有缺陷的木头制造的，而轮辐则碎成了残片。车轮并不由被告生产；被告是从另一名制造者那里购买的车轮。然而，有证据证明，如果经过合理的检测，可以发现车轮的缺陷，但检测过程被省掉了。原告没有提出被告知道缺陷而故意隐瞒了缺陷……指控内容为过失，而不是欺诈。要确定的问题是，除了直接购买人，被告是否尽到注意和警惕义务。

……

我们认为，Thomas v. Winchester 案的原则并不仅限于毒药、爆炸物和类似的物品，也不仅限于正常操作都会引起毁灭性后果的物品。如果一个物品的性质决定了一旦出现过失，生命和健康必定受到威胁，那么这个物品便是危险物品。该物品的性质使得对后果作出警告是被期待的。如果已经知道该物品会被购买者之外的其他人，在对其危险特性没有经过重新测试的情况下使用，无论是否存在合同，该危险物品的制造者都有义务仔细的制造该物品。这是在这个案件中我们要作出决定前必须明确的。使用者必须被告知危险，不但是可能的，而且是很可能的。如果存在缺陷，那么对任何物品进行使用都可能是以一种导致其变得危险的方式。这对于要求制造者承担独立于合同的义务是不够的。一个物品是否危险这个问题，有时需要法院来决定，有时需要陪审团来决定。同时还必须知道，根据事情通常的发展进程，危险会涉及购买者以外的人。通过交易的本质可以推断出这点。但是，仅仅知道危险

be enough. The proximity or remoteness of the relation is a factor to be considered. We are dealing now with the liability of the manufacturer of the finished product, who puts it on the market to be used without inspection by his customers. If he is negligent, where danger is to be foreseen, a liability will follow. We are not required at this time to say that it is legitimate to go back of the manufacturer of the finished product and hold the manufacturers of the component parts. To make their negligence a cause of imminent danger, an independent cause must often intervene; the manufacturer of the finished product must also fail in *his* duty of inspection. It may be that in those circumstances the negligence of the earlier members of the series is too remote to constitute, as to the ultimate user, an actionable wrong. We leave that question open. We shall have to deal with it when it arises. The difficulty which it suggests is not present in this case. There is here no break in the chain of cause and effect. In such circumstances, the presence of a known danger, attendant upon a known use, makes vigilance a duty. We have put aside the notion that the duty to safeguard life and limb, when the consequences of negligence may be foreseen, grows out of the contract and nothing else. We have put the source of the obligation where it ought to be. We have put its source in the law.

From this survey of the decisions, there thus emerges a definition of the duty of a manufacturer which enables us to measure this defendant's liability. Beyond all question, the nature of an automobile gives warning of probable danger if its construction is defective. This automobile was designed to go fifty miles an hour. Unless its wheels were sound and strong, injury was almost certain. It was as much a thing of danger as a defective engine for a railroad. The defendant knew the danger. It knew also that the car would be used by persons other than the buyer. This was apparent from its size; there were seats for three persons. It was apparent also from the fact that the buyer was a dealer in cars, who bought to resell. The maker of this car supplied it for the use of purchasers from the dealer just as plainly as the contractor in Devlin v. Smith supplied the scaffold for use by the servants of the owner. The dealer was indeed the one person of whom it might be said with some approach to certainty that by him the car would not be used. Yet the defendant would have us say that he was the one person whom it was under a legal duty to protect. The law does not lead us to so inconsequent a conclusion. Precedents drawn from the days of travel by stage coach do not fit the conditions of travel to-day. The principle that the danger must be imminent does not change, but the things subject to the principle do change. They are whatever the needs of life in a developing civilization require them to be....

We think the defendant was not absolved from a duty of inspection because it bought the wheels from a reputable manufacturer. It was not merely a dealer in automobiles. It was a manufacturer of automobiles. It was responsible for the finished product. It was not at liberty to put the finished product on the market without subjecting the component parts to ordinary and simple tests. Under the charge of the trial judge nothing more was required of it. The obligation to inspect

和使用仍然有可能是不够的，还应该考虑联系的远近问题。我们现在应对的是成品的制造者的责任问题，制造者将产品放在市场上，消费者在使用该产品时并没有进行检验。如果制造者对可以预见的危险存在过失，他就应该承担责任。这个时候，我们并不必认为探明成品制造者的究竟，要求零部件制造者承担责任的做法是合法的。他们的过失要构成紧急的危险，还必须存在独立的介入原因：成品制造者还必须没有尽到其检验的义务。可能在那种情况下，早期加工程序的过失对最终使用者来说，由于其太过遥远还不足以构成可以被起诉的过错。我们先不讨论这个问题。在出现了这个问题时我们再来研究它。在这个案件中并没有出现这样的难题。这里，因果关系之间并没有出现断裂。在这种情况下，已知的危险，加上已知的使用活动，使警惕成为了一种义务。我们先将这一观点放在一边，即当可以预见到过失产生的后果时，保护人的生命和身体安全的义务起源于合同而不是别的什么。我们已经将义务的起源置于它应该在的地方。我们认为它的起源是法律。

对这些法院判决进行了回顾后，会出现一个有关制造者义务的定义，这使我们能够衡量被告的责任。毫无疑问，如果汽车的制造存在缺陷，汽车的特性就对可能的危险提出了警告。该汽车被设计成可以每小时行进50英里。除非汽车的车轮非常稳定和牢固，否则伤害在所难免。与有危险与缺陷的火车头对铁路造成的危险相当。被告对危险是知情的。被告也知道除了购买人之外还有其他人会使用该汽车。从汽车的大小就很容易看出这点，并且车上设计了三个座位。同时，购买人是一个汽车经销商，他买车的目的是为了再出售，从这一情况也很容易看出。汽车的制造者将汽车提供给从经销商手中购买汽车的买家使用，这一事实和 Devlin v. Smith 案中的承包人将脚手架提供给所有人的雇员使用是一样清晰明白的。从经销商身上几乎就可以很肯定地判断他并非汽车的使用者。但是，被告可能要我们认为他是受到法律保护的人。法律并没有引导我们做出如此不切题的结论。过去搭乘公共马车出行带给我们的先例，并不符合今天的出行方式。危险必须具有紧急性，这一原则并没有改变，但是该原则指导下的情况已经发生了改变。在一个发展中的文明社会中，生活的需求要求它们改变，它们就会发生改变……

我们认为，不能因为被告从一家声誉良好的制造者那里购买了车轮，就会免除被告实施检测的义务。被告不仅是一个汽车经销商，他还是汽车的制造者。他对成品汽车负有责任。在没有对零部件进行常规和简单的测试之前，他不得随意地将成品汽车放在市场上销售。在初审判决的指控下，这一点是

must vary with the nature of the thing to be inspected. The more probable the danger, the greater the need of caution....

Hiscock, Chase and Cuddeback, JJ., concur with Cardozo, J., and Hogan, J., concurs in result; Willard Bartlett, Ch. J., reads dissenting opinion; Pound, J., not voting.

Judgment affirmed.

65. Vandermark v. Ford Motor Co., 391 P.2d 168 (Cal. 1964)

Supreme Court of California, United States

Traynor, Justice.

In October 1958 plaintiff Chester Vandermark bought a new Ford automobile from defendant Lorimer Diesel Engine Company, an authorized Ford dealer doing business as Maywood Bell Ford. About six weeks later, while driving on the San Bernardino Freeway, he lost control of the car. It went off the highway to the right and collided with a light post. He and his sister, plaintiff Mary Tresham, suffered serious injuries. They brought this action for damages against Maywood Bell Ford and the Ford Motor Company, which manufactured and assembled the car. They pleaded causes of action for breach of warranty and negligence. The trial court granted Ford's motion for a nonsuit on all causes of action and directed a verdict in favor of Maywood Bell on the warranty causes of action. The jury returned a verdict for Maywood Bell on the negligence causes of action, and the trial court entered judgment on the verdict. Plaintiffs appeal.

Vandermark had driven the car approximately 1500 miles before the accident. He used it primarily in town, but drove it on two occasions from his home in Huntington Park to Joshua Tree in San Bernardino County. He testified that the car operated normally before the accident except once when he was driving home from Joshua Tree. He was in the left-hand west-bound lane of the San Bernardino Freeway when traffic ahead slowed. He applied the brakes and the car "started to make a little dive to the right and continued on across the two lanes of traffic till she hit the shoulder. Whatever it was then let go and I was able to then pull her back into the road." He drove home without further difficulty, but before using the car again, he took it to Maywood Bell for the regular 1000-mile new car servicing. He testified that he described the freeway incident to Maywood Bell's service attendant, but Maywood Bell's records do not indicate that any complaint was made.

After the car was serviced, Vandermark drove it in town on short trips totaling approximately 300 miles. He and his sister then set out on another trip to Joshua Tree. He testified that while driving in the right-hand lane of the freeway at about 45 to 50 miles per hour, "the car started to make a little shimmy or weave and started pulling to the right....I tried to pull back, but it didn't seem to come, so I applied my brakes gently to see if I could straighten her up, but I couldn't

最为重要的。检测的义务必须随着检测对象特性的变化而发生变化。危险性越大的部件,越需要谨慎检测……

Hiscock 法官、Chase 法官和 Cuddeback 法官赞同 Cardozo 法官的意见,Hogan 法官赞同判决结果;Willard Bartlett 大法官发表了反对意见;Pound 法官没有参与表决。

维持原判。

65. Vandermark v. Ford Motor Co., 391 P.2d 168 (Cal. 1964)

美国加利福尼亚州最高法院

Traynor 法官主笔:

1958 年 10 月,原告 Chester Vandermark 从被告 Lorimer Diesel Engine 公司那里购买了一辆新的福特汽车,Lorimer Diesel Engine 公司是经授权销售福特汽车的经销商,销售店的名称为 Maywood Bell Ford。大约 6 周之后,当他驾驶汽车行驶在 San Bernardino 的高速公路上时,他的汽车失去了控制。汽车向右开出了高速公路,撞上了一根路灯杆。原告及其妹妹,同时也是原告 Mary Tresham 受伤严重。他们向 Maywood Bell Ford 和生产、装配汽车的福特汽车公司提起了诉讼,要求其进行损害赔偿。他们提出的诉因是被告违背了保证,并且存在过失。初审法院批准了福特公司提出的驳回所有诉因的申请,并指示陪审团在保证诉因上作出对 Maywood Bell 有利的裁断。陪审团在过失诉因的基础上作出了有利于 Maywood Bell 的裁断,初审法院依据裁断作出了判决。原告提起了上诉。

在发生事故之前,Vandermark 的汽车已经行驶了大约 1500 英里。他多数时候是在镇里驾驶汽车,但是有两次驾车从 Huntington Park 的家中前往 San Bernardino 县的 Joshua Tree。他作证说,在事故发生之前汽车工作正常,除了有一次他从 Joshua Tree 驾车回家时。当时他正行驶在 San Bernardino 的高速公路西向的左手车道,前方的交通堵塞使他的车速慢了下来。他踩了刹车,汽车"开始有些向右偏移,穿过了两根车道,直到撞上路肩。无论当时汽车怎么开,我还是能将它开回路上"。他驾车回家时没有出现其他问题,但是在再次使用汽车之前,他将车开到 Maywood Bell 那里接受新车的 1000 英里常规保养。他作证说,他将高速公路上发生的事故告诉给了 Maywood Bell 的维修人员,但是 Maywood Bell 的记录上并没有显示他有任何的投诉。

在接受了保养之后,Vandermark 在镇内开过两次车,行程一共约 300 英里。然后,他和他的妹妹再次前往 Joshua Tree。他作证说,当时他们以 45 到

seem to pull on the brakes and she wouldn't come back, and all of a sudden this pole was in front of me and we smashed into it." Plaintiff Tresham testified to a substantially similar version of the accident. A witness for plaintiffs, who was driving about 200 feet behind them, testified that plaintiff's car was in the right-hand lane when he saw its taillights come on. The car started to swerve and finally skidded into the light post. An investigating officer testified that there were skid marks leading from the highway to the car.

Plaintiffs called an expert on the operation of hydraulic automobile brakes. In answer to hypothetical questions based on evidence in the record and his own knowledge of the braking system of the car, the expert testified as to the cause of the accident. It was his opinion that the brakes applied themselves owing to a failure of the piston in the master cylinder to retract far enough when the brake pedal was released to uncover a bypass port through which hydraulic fluid should have been able to escape into a reservoir above the master cylinder. Failure of the piston to uncover the bypass port led to a closed system and a partial application of the brakes, which in turn led to heating that expanded the brake fluid until the brakes applied themselves with such force that Vandermark lost control of the car. The expert also testified that the failure of the piston to retract sufficiently to uncover the bypass port could have been caused by dirt in the master cylinder, a defective or wrong-sized part, distortion of the fire wall, or improper assembly or adjustment. The trial court struck the testimony of the possible causes to the failure of the piston to retract, on the ground that there was no direct evidence that any one or more of the causes existed, and it rejected plaintiffs' offer to prove that all of the possible causes were attributable to defendants. These rulings were erroneous, for plaintiffs were entitled to establish the existence of a defect and defendants' responsibility therefor by circumstantial evidence, particularly when, as in this case, the damage to the car in the collision precluded determining whether or not the master cylinder assembly had been properly installed and adjusted before the accident.

Accordingly, for the purposes of reviewing the nonsuit in favor of Ford and the directed verdict in favor of Maywood Bell on the warranty causes of action, it must be taken as established that when the car was delivered to Vandermark, the master cylinder assembly had a defect that caused the accident. Moreover, since it could reasonably be inferred from the description of the braking system in evidence and the offer of proof of all possible causes of defects that the defect was owing to negligence in design, manufacture, assembly, or adjustment, it must be taken as established that the defect was caused by some such negligence.

Ford contends, however, that it may not be held liable for negligence in manufacturing the car or strictly liable in tort for placing it on the market without proof that the car was defective when Ford relinquished control over it. Ford points out that in this case the car passed through two other authorized Ford dealers before it was sold to Maywood Bell and that Maywood Bell removed the power steering unit before selling the car to Vandermark.

50英里的时速在高速公路的右车道行驶,"车有些轻微的摇动或晃动,然后向右偏移……我试图纠正车的方向,但是似乎无法做到。所以我轻轻地踩刹车看我能否将车调整过来,但是我踩不动刹车,车也调整不过来。突然我们面前出现了一根电杆,然后我们撞了上去"。原告 Tresham 在证词中对事故的描述基本上和这个差不多。原告的目击证人当时在原告身后 200 英尺的地方,其作证说,原告的车行驶在右车道上,他看见原告汽车的尾灯亮了起来。汽车开始转向,最终撞向了路灯杆。调查人员作证说,在高速公路和汽车之间有刹车的痕迹。

原告邀请了汽车液压制动操作方面的专家证人。在根据案卷和自己关于汽车制动系统的知识回答假定问题时,专家对导致事故的原因作证并认为,放开刹车板以打开旁路口,可以使液压液体进入主汽缸上部的贮液器,但由于主汽缸中的活塞没有收回足够的距离,因此刹车出现了自己制动的情况。活塞没有打开旁路口导致系统未开放,刹车无法完全制动,这又反过来导致刹车液加热膨胀,直到刹车自己制动,制动的力量之大,造成 Vandermark 失去了对汽车的控制。专家还作证说,导致活塞无法收回足够的距离以打开旁路口的原因有多种,可能是主汽缸中的灰尘,也可能是部件有缺陷或大小不合适,或者隔火墙变形,或者组装或调试时操作不当。初审法院没有采纳造成活塞无法收回的几种可能原因,理由是没有直接证据证明有一个或多个原因造成了这一结果,初审法院还驳回了原告提出的证明所有原因都应该归咎于被告的意见。初审法院的裁决存在错误,因为原告有权通过间接证据调换语序,特别是在这个案件中,汽车受到的损失排除了事故前主汽缸体是否得到适当的安装或调试的问题,证明汽车存在缺陷,以及被告在这个问题上负有责任。

因此,出于重新审视对福特公司有利的诉讼驳回以及保证诉因上对 Maywood Bell 有利的裁断的目的,可以确认当汽车交付给 Vandermark 时,主汽缸体存在缺陷,而且该缺陷导致了事故。此外,从对制动系统的描述以及所有可能的缺陷原因的证据中可以合理推断,造成缺陷的原因是设计、制造、组装或调试过程中存在过失,因此可以确定缺陷是由过失引起的。

然而,福特公司提出,如果没有证据证明福特公司在放弃对汽车的控制之时汽车便存在缺陷,就不应该为汽车制造过程中的过失负责,也不应该为在市场中投放汽车承担严格责任。福特公司还指出,在这个案件中,汽车经过了两个福特公司经销商之手,然后才卖给了 Maywood Bell,而 Maywood Bell 在将车卖给 Vandermark 之前,取下了动力方向盘系统。

In Greenman v. Yuba Power Products, Inc., 59 Cal.2d 57, 62, 27 Cal. Rptr. 697, 700, 377 P.2d 897, 900, we held that "A manufacturer is strictly liable in tort when an article he places on the market, knowing that it is to be used without inspection for defects, proves to have a defect that causes injury to a human being." Since the liability is strict it encompasses defects regardless of their source, and therefore a manufacturer of a completed product cannot escape liability by tracing the defect to a component part supplied by another. (Goldberg v. Kollman Instrument Corp., 12 N.Y.2d 432, 437, 240 N.Y.S.2d 592, 191 N.E.2d 81.) Moreover, even before such strict liability was recognized, the manufacturer of a completed product was subject to vicarious liability for the negligence of his suppliers or subcontractors that resulted in defects in the completed product. (Dow v. Holly Manufacturing Co., 49 Cal.2d 720, 726-727, 321 P.2d 736; Ford Motor Co. v. Mathis, 5 Cir., 322 F.2d 267, 273; Boeing Airplane Co. v. Brown, 9 Cir., 291 F.2d 310, 313; see Rest., Torts, §400.) These rules focus responsibility for defects, whether negligently or nonnegligently caused, on the manufacturer of the completed product, and they apply regardless of what part of the manufacturing process the manufacturer chooses to delegate to third parties. It appears in the present case that Ford delegates the final steps in that process to its authorized dealers. It does not deliver cars to its dealers that are ready to be driven away by the ultimate purchasers but relies on its dealers to make the final inspections, corrections, and adjustments necessary to make the cars ready for use. Since Ford, as the manufacturer of the completed product, cannot delegate its duty to have its cars delivered to the ultimate purchaser free from dangerous defects, it cannot escape liability on the ground that the defect in Vandermark's car may have been caused by something one of its authorized dealers did or failed to do.

Since plaintiffs introduced or offered substantial evidence that they were injured as a result of a defect that was present in the car when Ford's authorized dealer delivered it to Vandermark, the trial court erred in granting a nonsuit on the causes of action by which plaintiff sought to establish that Ford was strictly liable to them. Since plaintiffs also introduced or offered substantial evidence that the defect was caused by some negligent conduct for which Ford was responsible, the trial court also erred in granting a nonsuit on the causes of action by which plaintiffs sought to establish that Ford was liable for negligence.

Plaintiffs contend that Maywood Bell is also strictly liable in tort for the injuries caused by the defect in the car and that therefore the trial court erred in directing a verdict for Maywood Bell on the warranty causes of action. Maywood Bell contends that the rule of strict liability in the Greenman case applies only to actions against manufacturers brought by injured parties with whom the manufacturers did not deal....

Retailers like manufacturers are engaged in the business of distributing goods to the public. They are an integral part of the overall producing and marketing enterprise that should bear the cost of injuries resulting from defective products. (See Greenman v. Yuba Power Products, Inc.,

在 Greenman v. Yuba Power Products, Inc., 59 Cal.2d 57, 62, 27 Cal. Rptr. 697, 700, 377 P.2d 897, 900 案中，我们认为："当制造者将产品放入市场，并且知道人们在使用该产品时不会检测其是否存在缺陷，而该产品被证明是存在会导致人身伤害的缺陷时，该制造者应该承担严格责任。"既然责任是严格的，它就包括了所有缺陷，无论缺陷来自哪里，因此成品制造者不得通过追踪缺陷部件来自哪个供应商的方式来逃避责任。（Goldberg v. Kollman Instrument Corp., 12 N.Y.2d 432, 437, 240 N.Y.S.2d 592, 191 N.E.2d 81.）此外，在严格责任被认可之前，成品制造者也应该为导致成品出现缺陷的供应商或次级承包商的过失承担替代责任。（Dow v. Holly Manufacturing Co., 49 Cal.2d 720, 726–727, 321 P.2d 736; Ford Motor Co. v. Mathis, 5 Cir., 322 F.2d 267, 273; Boeing Airplane Co. v. Brown, 9 Cir., 291 F.2d 310, 313; Rest., Torts, § 400.）这些规则关注的焦点都是成品制造者的缺陷责任，无论缺陷是由过失还是非过失因素引起，无论制造者选择将制造过程的哪一部分委托给第三方。在这个案件中，看得出来福特公司将最后一部分委托给了授权经销商。福特公司交付给经销商的汽车并不是可以让最终购买者立即开走的汽车，而依靠经销商对汽车进行最后的检测、矫正和调试之后才能使用汽车。将毫无危险缺陷的汽车交付给最终购买者，这是作为成品制造者的福特公司无法委托给他人的义务，因此福特公司不能因为其授权经销商之一做了或者没做什么而可能导致 Vandermark 汽车的缺陷，而免除其自身的责任。

由于原告提供了实质性的证据证明，在福特公司的授权经销商将汽车交付给 Vandermark 后，汽车的缺陷造成了他们的损害，原告希望通过该诉因证明福特公司应该对他们承担严格责任，因此初审法院批准对该诉因的诉讼驳回申请的做法存在错误。由于原告还提供了实质性的证据证明造成缺陷的原因是福特公司方面的过失行为，原告希望通过该诉因证明福特公司应该承担过失责任，因此初审法院批准对该诉因的诉讼驳回申请的做法存在错误。

原告提出，Maywood Bell 也应该为汽车缺陷造成的损害承担严格的侵权责任，因此初审法院在保证诉因上对指示陪审团作出有利于 Maywood Bell 的裁断是错误的。Maywood Bell 提出 Greenman 案中的严格责任规则，只适用于受伤当事人针对没有和受伤当事人发生交易行为的制造者而提出的诉讼……

零售商和制造者一样从事的是向公众出售商品的商业活动。他们是整个生产和销售事业中不可或缺的一部分，而生产和销售事业应该承担缺陷产品造成的损害成本（参见 Greenman v. Yuba Power Products, Inc., 59 Cal.2d 57, 63,

59 Cal.2d 57, 63, 27 Cal. Rptr. 697, 377 P.2d 897.) In some cases the retailer may be the only member of that enterprise reasonably available to the injured plaintiff. In other cases the retailer himself may play a substantial part in insuring that the product is safe or may be in a position to exert pressure on the manufacturer to that end; the retailer's strict liability thus serves as an added incentive to safety. Strict liability on the manufacturer and retailer alike affords maximum protection to the injured plaintiff and works no injustice to the defendants, for they can adjust the costs of such protection between them in the course of their continuing business relationship. Accordingly, as a retailer engaged in the business of distributing goods to the public, Maywood Bell is strictly liable in tort for personal injuries caused by defects in cars sold by it....

Although plaintiffs sought to impose strict liability on Maywood Bell on the theory of sales-act warranties, they pleaded and introduced substantial evidence of all of the facts necessary to establish strict liability in tort. Accordingly, the trial court erred in directing a verdict for Maywood Bell on the so-called warranty causes of action....

The judgment of nonsuit in favor of Ford Motor Company is reversed. The judgment in favor of Maywood Bell Ford on the negligence causes of action is affirmed and in all other respects the judgment in favor of Maywood Bell Ford is reversed.

Gibson, C.J., and Schauer, Mccomb, Peters, Tobriner and Peek, JJ., concur.

66. Sheckells v. AGV Corp., 987 F.2d 1532 (11th Cir. 1993)

Eleventh Circuit, Court of Appeals, United States

Birch, Circuit Judge.

Plaintiff Charles Sheckells ("Sheckells"), the natural father and guardian of John Sheckells, an incapacitated adult, appeals from the grant of summary judgment in favor of AGV, a defendant in the underlying product liability action. The grant of summary judgment in favor of AGV is Affirmed in Part and Reversed in Part.

I. Background

John Sheckells was injured when he lost control of his motorcycle after striking debris in the road. At the time of the accident, he was wearing a helmet manufactured by AGV. On behalf of his son, Sheckells filed suit against AGV alleging that the helmet was defectively designed and manufactured and that the defendants failed to warn that the helmet would not afford any significant protection from certain reasonably foreseeable impacts. On appeal, Sheckells has abandoned his theory of defective design and appeals the judgment only upon the failure to warn theory.

When purchased, the helmet contained a warning label affixed to the inside of the helmet, stating in substance that "some reasonably foreseeable impacts may exceed this helmet's capability

27 Cal. Rptr. 697, 377 P.2d 897 案）。在一些情况下，零售商可能是这个事业中可以接触到受伤原告的唯一成员。而在另一些情况下，零售商自己可能在确保产品安全方面发挥着非常重要的作用，或者可以在确保安全问题上对制造者施加压力，因此，零售商的严格责任成为促进安全的额外激励因素。制造者和零售商承担严格责任，可以对受伤的原告提供最大的保护，这对于被告来说不是不公平的，因为他们可以在持续的商业关系中调整彼此间保护的成本。因此，作为向公众销售商品的零售商，Maywood Bell 对所售缺陷汽车造成的人身伤害应当承担严格的侵权责任……

尽管原告希望依据《统一买卖法》保证理论要求 Maywood Bell 承担严格责任，但是他们经过辩护，同时提供了所有能够确立严格的侵权责任事实的实质性证据。因此，初审法院在所谓的保证诉因上指示陪审团作出对 Maywood Bell 有利的裁断是错误的……

撤销对福特汽车公司有利的驳回判决。维持在过失诉因上对 Maywood Bell Ford 有利的判决，撤销在所有其他方面对 Maywood Bell Ford 有利的判决。

Gibson 大法官和 Schauer 法官、Mccomb 法官、Peters 法官、Tobriner 法官以及 Peek 法官赞同。

66. Sheckells v. AGV Corp., 987 F.2d 1532 (11th Cir. 1993)

美国联邦上诉法院第十一巡回法庭

Birch 巡回法院法官主笔：

John Sheckells 是不具有行为能力的成年人，其生父和监护人 Charles Sheckells 作为原告，基于法院在一起产品责任诉讼中作出了有利于被告 AGV 的简易判决，而提起了上诉。有利于 AGV 的简易判决一部分得到支持，一部分被撤销。

I. 背景

John Sheckells 在路上骑摩托车时撞上了碎石，车辆因失去控制而造成 John 受伤。事故发生时，他佩戴了一顶由 AGV 生产的头盔。Sheckells 代表他的儿子，起诉 AGV，指控头盔的设计和制造存在缺陷，而对于头盔在受到合理的可预见性碰撞时不会提供有效的保护，被告没有作出警示。在上诉时，Sheckells 放弃了头盔缺陷设计理由，而只依据未尽警示义务的诉由要求上诉。

头盔在购买时，内部贴有一个警示标签，指出实际上"一些合理的可预

to protect against severe injury or death." In addition, the helmet was packaged with a consumer notice that informs the purchaser that "your helmet is the single most important piece of safety equipment you own and should be treated as such." The notice further states that "NO HELMET, including your AGV helmet, can protect the wearer against all foreseeable impacts" and that "NO WARRANTY OR REPRESENTATION IS MADE AS TO THIS PRODUCT'S ABILITY TO PROTECT THE USER FROM ANY INJURY OR DEATH. THE USER ASSUMES ALL RISKS."

In opposition to summary judgment, Sheckells offered the deposition testimony of Dr. Joseph L. Burton, the Chief Medical Examiner for the City of Atlanta. With regard to the failure to warn claim, Dr. Burton testified that Department of Transportation and Snell Memorial Foundation impact tests are conducted at speeds of only 15 to 20 miles an hour and that no motorcycle helmet marketed today provides any assurance of protecting the wearer from facial or brain injury at speeds of 30 or 45 miles an hour. Further, he opined that the average purchaser of a helmet would not know these facts.

The district court entered summary judgment in favor of AGV on the failure to warn theory on the ground that it was open and obvious that the AGV helmet would not protect an operator traveling at 30 to 45 miles an hour. Sheckells appeals the grant of summary judgment.

II. Discussion...

In this diversity action, AGV's duty to warn of hazards posed by the use of its products is determined by Georgia law....Under Georgia law, a manufacturer is subject to liability for failure to warn if it "(a) knows or has reason to know that the chattel is or is likely to be dangerous for the use for which it is supplied, and (b) has no reason to believe that those for whose use the chattel is supplied will realize its dangerous condition and (c) fails to exercise reasonable care to inform them of its dangerous condition or of the facts which make it likely to be dangerous." Greenway v. Peabody Intl. Corp., 163 Ga. App. 698, 703, 294 S.E.2d 541, 545-546 (1982) (quoting Restatement (Second) of Torts §388). Georgia law imposes no duty on a manufacturer to warn of a danger associated with the use of its product if that danger is open or obvious.

> There is no duty resting upon the manufacturer or seller to warn of a product-connected danger which is obvious, or of which the person who claims to be entitled to warning knows, should know, or should, in using the product, discover.

294 S.E.2d at 546 (quoting Annotation, Products Liability—Duty to Warn, 76 A.L.R.2d 9, 28-29 (1961)).

At his deposition, Dr. Burton testified that, although no motorcycle helmet on the market today would provide any assurance of protecting an operator from facial or brain injury at a speed of 30 to 45 miles an hour, "the average buyer of a helmet would not know that." Dr. Burton also

见性碰撞可能超出了该头盔防止严重受伤或死亡的能力"。此外，头盔的包装上也有一个消费者提示，告知购买者"你的头盔是保护你安全最重要的单个装备，应该照此对待"。该提示还进一步指出，"所有头盔，包括你的 AGV 头盔都不能保护你免受所有的可预见性碰撞的伤害"，"无任何的保证或表述说明该产品可以保护使用者免于遭受任何伤害或死亡。使用者自担所有风险"。

Sheckells 对简易判决结果提出了反对意见，并出示了亚特兰大市首席体检师 Joseph L. Burton 的宣誓书面证词。关于未尽警示义务的主张，Burton 医生作证说，交通部和 Snell Memorial 基金的碰撞实验是在 15 到 20 英里的时速下进行的，今天市场上销售的所有摩托车头盔，在 30 或 45 英里的时速下都无法保证为佩戴者提供面部或脑部的保护。而且，他认为头盔的普通购买者不知道这些事实。

联邦地区法院依据未尽警示义务理论作出了有利于 AGV 的简易判决，其理由是，AGV 头盔在 30 至 45 英里时速下无法保护佩戴者的安全，这是公开且明显的事实。Sheckells 对简易判决提起了上诉。

II. 讨论……

在这一跨州诉讼中，AGV 对使用其产品可能存在的危险进行警示的义务由佐治亚州法律确定……佐治亚州法律规定，制造者应该为未尽警示义务承担责任的条件是："（a）制造者知道或有理由知道使用其产品存在或可能存在危险；（b）没有理由相信产品的使用者会认识到产品的危险性；（c）在告知使用者产品具有的危险性，或者可能造成产品产生危险性的事实方面，没有尽到合理的注意义务。" Greenway v. Peabody Intl. Corp., 163 Ga. App. 698, 703, 294 S.E.2d 541, 545–546（1982）案（引用了《美国侵权法·第二次重述》第 388 条）。佐治亚州法律规定，如果危险是公开或明显的，制造者没有义务对使用产品而产生的危险进行警示。

> 制造者或出售者没有义务对与产品有关的显著危险进行警告，或者对主张有权要求作出警告的人知道、应该知道或在使用产品时应该发现的危险进行警告。

294 S.E.2d at 546 [引用了 Annotation, Products Liability—Duty to Warn, 76 A.L.R.2d 9, 28–29（1961）]。

Burton 医生在他的书面证词中作证说，尽管市面上销售的所有摩托车头盔都不能保证佩戴者在 30 至 45 英里时速的情况下不会受到面部或头部伤害，

testified that representations made by vendors of motorcycles and helmets may lull a purchaser into a false sense of security regarding the amount of protection provided by a helmet. Dr. Burton concluded that, in order to dispel this impression, some warning should accompany the helmet to educate the user that the helmet provides no significant protection at speeds exceeding 30 to 45 miles an hour. Thus, Dr. Burton's deposition, viewed in the light most favorable to the plaintiff, suggests that the failure of a motorcycle helmet to protect the wearer at speeds over 30 to 45 miles an hour is not an open or obvious danger.

AGV presented no evidence tending to show that it is open or obvious that its helmet would not protect the wearer at speeds of 30 to 45 miles an hour. That the parties' experts agree that no helmet currently marketed could protect a wearer traveling at speeds of 45 miles an hour does not mean that this fact is patent to a purchaser. Presumably, these experts are "expert" for the reason that they possess knowledge not generally shared with the public. As noted by the Greenway court, the focus of the open or obvious danger rule is upon "those for whose use the chattel is supplied." 294 S.E.2d at 545-546.

The district court relied on several Georgia cases for the proposition that "it is a matter of common knowledge that operating a motorcycle carries with it certain inherent dangers." While recognizing the inherent hazard of operating a motorcycle, these cases do not establish as a matter of Georgia law that safety precautions, such as a helmet, openly and obviously provide insignificant protection at speeds of 30 to 45 miles an hour. Further, those cases where the Georgia courts have concluded that a peril associated with a product is open or obvious suggest that summary judgment was inappropriate based on the factual record before the district court. The Georgia courts have determined that, under certain circumstances, operating a product without the safety features included by the manufacturer is an open or obvious hazard. See, e.g., Weatherby v. Honda Motor Co., 195 Ga. App. 169, 393 S.E.2d 64, 67 (1990) (danger in operating motorcycle with uncapped fuel tank is open and obvious). Additionally, the Georgia cases reveal that the observable absence of a safety feature is likely to be considered an open and obvious danger. In each of these cases, however, the absence of the safety feature in question was apparent to the purchaser by a simple visual inspection. By contrast, it is not obvious from an observation of the AGV helmet that this product provides only minimal protection against collision when the motorcycle is operated at speeds of 30 to 45 miles an hour. Conceivably, a purchaser might expect more from "the single most important piece of safety equipment" that he or she owns. Further, Dr. Burton's testimony suggests that the limited degree of protection afforded by wearing a helmet is not common knowledge. The evidence presented by the plaintiff was sufficient to raise an issue of fact regarding the open or obvious nature of this hazard. Thus, in granting summary judgment for AGV with respect to the failure to warn claim, the district court erred by resolving a material and genuinely disputed issue of fact against the plaintiff.

"但是普通的头盔购买者并不知道这一点"。Burton 医生还作证说,摩托车和头盔的卖家可能会诱导购买者产生错误的感觉,认为头盔可以为他们提供不切实际的保护。Burton 医生总结认为,为了打消消费者的这种印象,应该在头盔上附带一些警示信息,以告知消费者在时速达到 30 至 45 英里时头盔无法为他们提供实质性的保护。因此,从最有利于原告的角度来看,Burton 医生的书面证词显示,摩托车头盔无法在时速达到 30 至 45 英里时保护佩戴者的安全,并非一个公开或显著的危险。

AGV 没有出示任何证据证明头盔在 30 至 45 英里时速的情况下无法保护佩戴者的安全的事实,具有公开性和显著性。尽管当事各方的专家证人都认为,当下市场上销售的头盔无法在 45 英里的时速下保护佩戴者的安全,但是这并不意味着这样一个事实对于购买者来说具有显著性。可以说,这些专家之所以是"专家",主要因为他们通常具有公众所不具有的知识。正如 Greenway 案的审理法院提到的,公开或显著危险的规则关注的焦点在于"提供产品用以满足其使用人"。(294 S.E.2d at 545–546.)

联邦地区法院依据佐治亚州的一些案例,提出"骑摩托车本身就具有一定的危险性,这是常识性问题"。虽然这些案例认定骑摩托车具有一定的危险性,但是却没有以佐治亚州法律的形式确定一条规则,即采取安全防护措施,如佩戴头盔,公开且显著地无法为时速在 30 至 45 英里的佩带者提供实质性的保护。此外,佐治亚州法院在一些案件中判定与产品有关的危险具有公开性和显著性,这表明以联邦地区法院已有的以事实记录为基础的简易判决不具有适当性。佐治亚州法院已经确定,在某些情况下,如果产品不具有制造者所考量的安全特征,操作这种产品便具有公开或显著的危险性。例如,参见 Weatherby v. Honda Motor Co., 195 Ga. App. 169, 393 S.E.2d 64, 67(1990)案(摩托车的油箱没有盖子,驾驶这样的摩托车具有公开且显著的危险性)。此外,佐治亚州的案件还传达出一个信息——明显缺少一些安全特征也可以被认作具有公开且显著的危险性。然而,在这些案件中,购买者只需要简单用肉眼检查一下便可以发现这些安全项目的缺失。相反,观察 AGV 头盔却并不容易发现摩托车在 30 至 45 英里的时速下发生碰撞,头盔提供的保护十分有限。可以想象,购买者可能会从"保护安全最重要的单个装备"那里产生更多的预期。而且,Burton 医生的证词还表明,佩戴头盔所提供的保护有限,这并非一个常识。原告提供的证据十分充分,引发了一个有关该头盔的公开或显著特性的事实问题。因此,就被告没有尽到警示义务的诉讼主张,联邦地区法院作出了有利于 AGV 的简易判决,联邦地区法院以对原告不利的方式

AGV further contends that summary judgment was appropriate based on either of two issues not reached by the district court. First, AGV argues that John Sheckells did not read the allegedly inadequate warnings, and, thus, the failure to warn was not a proximate cause of his injuries. AGV relies on John Sheckells's deposition testimony that he did not remember reading the warning label affixed to the helmet or the literature that was packaged with the helmet. John Sheckells did not testify that he did not read the warnings, only that he did not remember doing so. Based on the factual record before the district court, it is possible that this failure to remember was due to his memory loss, suffered as a result of the accident. Additionally, Charles Sheckells testified at his deposition that he discussed the consumer warnings with his son at the time the helmet was purchased. Therefore, there is a genuine dispute of material fact as to proximate cause, and summary judgment is inappropriate.

AGV also maintains that summary judgment was proper since the warnings included with the helmet were adequate as a matter of law. The district court did not reach this issue. The consumer information packaged with the helmet explains that no helmet "can protect the wearer against all foreseeable impacts." While this warning informs the purchaser that certain foreseeable impacts exceed the helmet's capacity to protect the wearer, it falls short of informing the purchaser that the helmet will not provide any significant degree of protection at speeds of 30 to 45 miles an hour. Dr. Burton's testimony, viewed in the light most favorable to Sheckells, establishes a lack of consumer awareness of the degree of protection provided by a helmet at median and high speeds. AGV has not, at this stage of the litigation, proffered sufficient facts to show that this warning was sufficient as a matter of law.

The consumer information sheet also informs the purchaser that no warranty or representation is made as to the helmet's ability to protect the user from any injury or death and that the user assumes all risks. AGV contends that this statement, couched in language typically used in disclaimers of legal responsibility, also serves as a warning to purchasers. Whether this language was sufficient to warn the user that the helmet, which was described in the consumer information as "the single most important piece of safety equipment you own," would provide no significant protection at speeds of over 30 to 45 miles an hour is, at this stage of the proceeding, a disputed issue of fact.

III. Conclusion

The grant of summary judgment in favor of AGV is affirmed with regard to the claim of defective design or manufacture. In granting summary judgment on the failure to warn theory, however, the district court erred by resolving a disputed and material issue of fact regarding the open or obvious nature of the limited protection provided by AGV's helmet. Summary judgment on the failure to warn claim is therefore reversed.

解决了一个重要的和真正的有关事实的争议点，这样的做法存在错误。

AGV 还提出，根据联邦地区法院没有研究的两个问题，简易判决具有合理性。首先，AGV 指出，虽然原告指控警示说明不充分，但是 John Sheckells 并没有阅读警示说明，因此，没有尽到警示义务并不是其受伤的近因。AGV 的依据是 John Sheckells 的书面证词，在书面证词中 John Sheckells 说他不记得阅读过附在头盔上的警示标签，或者头盔包装里的说明文字。John Sheckells 并没有作证说自己没有阅读过警示信息，只是说自己不记得是否读过。根据提交给联邦地区法院的事实记录，John Sheckells 不记得的原因有可能是失忆造成的，而造成失忆的原因则是这起事故。此外，Charles Sheckells 在书面证词中作证说，在购买头盔时，他与儿子讨论过消费者警示信息。因此，关于近因问题，确实存在重要事实的真正争议，简易判决是不恰当的。

AGV 还主张，由于头盔包含的警示信息作为一个法律问题是充分的，因此简易判决是恰当的。联邦地区法院并没有研究这个问题。头盔包装里的消费者信息解释道，任何头盔"都无法保护佩带者免受所有可预见性的碰撞的伤害"。尽管这条警示告诉购买者，某些可预见性的碰撞超出了头盔保护佩戴者的能力，但是却没有告知消费者在 30 至 45 英里的时速下头盔无法提供实质性的保护。从最有利于 Sheckells 的角度来审视 Burton 医生的证词，可以看出，在中等速度或高速下，消费者并没有意识到头盔可以提供多大的保护。诉讼到了这一步，AGV 并没有提供足够的事实来说明在法律问题上警示信息具有充分性。

消费者信息文书还告知购买者，并不保证或宣称头盔有能力保护使用者免受任何伤害或死亡，使用者自己承担所有风险。AGV 指出这条规定是法律免责条款中经常使用的语言，对于购买者来说也是一种警示。在消费者信息文书中，头盔被形容为"保护你安全最重要的单一装备"，在时速达到 30 至 45 英里时无法提供实质性的保护，这种措辞对于使用者来说是否起到了充分的警示作用，在诉讼的这一个阶段，这也是一个有关事实的争议点。

III. 结论

有关设计缺陷或制造缺陷的主张，维持有利于 AGV 的简易判决。不过，由于 AGV 头盔提供保护有限是否属于一个公开或显著的特征，是具有争议的和重要的事实问题，联邦地区法院对于没有尽到警示义务的主张也作出了简易判决而存在错误。因此，撤销有关未尽到警示义务的简易判决。

Section 2. English Law: From Negligence to Strict Liability

67. A v National Blood Authority [2001] 3 All ER 289

Queen's Bench Division, High Court, United Kingdom

The claimants had been infected with Hepatitis C (the virus) through blood transfusions which had used blood or blood products obtained from infected donors. They brought actions for damages against the defendants, the authorities responsible for the production of blood and blood products. During the period when most of the claimants were infected, the risk of such infection through blood transfusions, though known to the medical profession, was impossible to avoid, either because the virus itself had not yet been discovered or because there was no way of testing for its presence in blood. Accordingly, the claims were brought not in negligence, but under the Consumer Protection Act 1987 which implemented Council Directive (EEC) 85/374 (on the approximation of the laws, regulations and administrative provisions of the member states concerning liability for defective products). Under that directive, a producer was liable for damage caused by a defect in his product. By virtue of art 6(1), a product was defective when it did not provide the safety which a person was entitled to expect, taking all circumstances into account, including the presentation of the product, the use to which it could reasonably be expected that the product would be put and the time when the product was put into circulation. Article 7(e) provided the producer with a defence if he could establish that the state of scientific and technical knowledge at the time when he put the product into circulation was not such as to enable 'the existence of the defect' to be discovered. On the trial of the six lead cases, the defendants accepted that a producer's liability under art 6 was irrespective of fault. They nevertheless contended that, in assessing whether the infected blood was defective, the unavoidability of the risk was a circumstance to be taken into account, and that the most that the public was entitled to expect was that all reasonably available precautions had been carried out, not that the blood would be 100% clean. In so contending, the defendants submitted that the infected blood was to be regarded as an inherently risky standard product (ie one which performed as the producer intended) rather than a non-standard product (ie a product which was deficient or inferior in terms of safety from the standard product, and whose harmful characteristic, not present in the standard product, had caused the material injury or damage). They also relied on the fact that they were obliged to produce blood and had no alternative but to supply it to hospitals and patients, as a service to society. Alternatively, the defendants sought to rely on the art 7(e) defence, contending that an unavoidable risk qualified for protection under it if the producer was unable to discover, by means of accessible information, the defect in a particular product.

BURTON J

第二节 英国法：从过失责任到严格责任

67. A v National Blood Authority [2001] 3 All ER 289

联合王国高等法院王座分庭

各原告因为在输血的时候被输入了丙肝病毒感染者的血液，或者使用了这样的血液制品，因而也都感染了丙肝病毒。他们因此起诉了几个负责采集血液和制造血液制品的机构，请求损害赔偿。在大多数的原告感染丙肝病毒期间，丙肝病毒能够通过输血传播的风险，虽然已经为医疗界所知，但是却是不可避免的。这或许是因为当时尚未发现丙肝病毒的存在，又或许是因为当时缺乏检测血液中存在丙肝病毒的技术手段。正因如此，各原告并未提起过失之诉，而是将其诉讼请求建立在 1987 年《消费者保护法》之上。该法是为了贯彻《欧共体理事会第 85/374 号指令》而颁布的（该指令是为了统一各成员国关于缺陷产品的法律、规章和管理规定）。根据该指令，生产者应该为其产品缺陷造成的损害承担责任。根据该法第 6 条第 1 款的规定，产品的缺陷是指，在考量了所有的情节后作出的判断下，产品不具有人们有权预期的安全性。这些考量的情节包括：产品的使用说明、可以合理预见的产品的使用情况、产品投入流通的时间。第 7 条第 e 项则为生产者提供了一种抗辩事由：生产者可以通过证明，当产品投入流通之时，利用当时的科学技术知识尚不足以发现缺陷的存在。在审理本判决涉及的这六起案件时，各被告都承认第 6 条所调整的生产者责任并不以过错为要件。然而，他们也主张，要判断被感染的血液是否属于缺陷产品，应该考虑到血液被感染的风险是不可避免的；公众有权预期的，最多是被告已经进行了所有的可以进行的合理的预防措施，而不是血液是百分之百干净的。为了配合这种主张，被告宣称，被感染的这批血液应该被看作"固有危险产品"（即符合生产者预期的产品），而不是"不达标产品"（即产品有缺陷，或者相比于达标产品在安全性上更低劣，这些不存在于达标产品中的有害特征，造成了严重的伤害或者损失）。他们同时还主张他们有义务生产血液制品，也必须向医院和病人提供这些血液制品，这是他们为社会提供的服务。除了援引第 6 条第 1 款，被告还援引第 7 条第 e 项以作为抗辩事由。被告主张如果生产者无法通过已知的信息来发现特定产品中的缺陷，那么无法避免的风险则属于该条规定的被告可以援引的事由。

Burton 法官主笔：

Cause of action

The claims the subject matter of this trial are not in negligence, but are put against the defendants by way of 'strict' or 'objective' liability by virtue of the CPA, which implemented in the United Kingdom the European Union (then the EEC) Product Liability Directive of 1985:Council Directive (EEC) 85/374 (on the approximation of the laws, regulations and administrative provisions of the member states concerning liability for defective products). The directive is not, in any event in this action, said to be directly enforceable against the defendants by the claimants, who rely for their cause of action on the CPA. However, as below appears, the European Commission complained, by application lodged at the Court of Justice of the European Communities on 20 September 1995, that the United Kingdom Government had not fulfilled its obligations under the directive and under the EC Treaty by implementing the CPA in the terms it had. Although the Court of Justice dismissed that application, it is apparent from the judgment of the Court of Justice, reported as *European Commission v UK*Case C–300/95 [1997] All ER (EC) 481, that, there not at that stage having been any decisions of the English courts, nor indeed any facts before the Court of Justice, the Court of Justice was concluding that, whatever be the precise terms of the CPA, the United Kingdom *would* so implement and construe the CPA as to be consistent with the directive—not least by virtue of s 1(1) of the CPA, which reads as follows: 'Part I shall have effect for the purpose of making such provision as is necessary in order to comply with the Product Liability Directive and shall be construed accordingly.' Consequently both parties have during this trial almost exclusively concentrated on the terms of the directive, on the basis that, in so far as the wording of the CPA, in relation to matters which have been the subject matter of particular issue in this case, differs from the equivalent articles in the directive, it should not be construed differently from the directive; and consequently the practical course was to go straight to the fount, the directive itself. As will be seen, the arguments were directed mainly to the true and properconstruction of art 6 of the directive (the equivalent being s 3 of the CPA) and art 7(e) (the equivalent being s 4(1)(e)), and consequently it is with those articles, and not the relevant sections, with which this judgment will be primarily, if not exclusively, concerned. It is conceded for the purpose of these proceedings that the blood or blood products by which the claimants were infected are products within the meaning of the CPA and the directive, and that the defendants' production of blood was, for the purpose of the directive, an industrial process.

...

The relevant articles are as follows:

Article 1

The producer shall be liable for damage caused by a defect in his product.

Article 4

The injured person shall be required to prove the damage, the defect and the causal

诉由

本案并非过失之诉；原告起诉被告的依据是"严格"或者"客观"责任。这种责任是由消费者保护法所确立的，同时也是为了在英国贯彻欧盟（当时的欧共体）1985年的关于产品责任的指令：《欧共体理事会第85/374号指令》（该指令的目的是为了统一各成员国关于缺陷产品的法律、规章和管理规定）。在本案中，无论如何都不能认为原告可以直接依据该指令来起诉被告；该指令是必须要通过消费者保护法才能起作用的。然而如下所示，欧盟委员会在其1995年9月20日向欧洲共同体法院提出的申请中，声称英国现在施行的《消费者保护法》并未履行其在上述指令下和欧盟条约下的义务。虽然欧洲法院驳回了欧盟委员会的申请，但是根据欧洲法院的判决［欧盟委员会诉英国，案号：C-300/95（1997）All ER（EC）481］，英国法院现阶段并未判决任何相关的案件，因此欧洲法院并没有任何事实可以审理。欧洲法院的结论则是：无论《消费者保护法》的措辞是什么，英国一定会在执行该法和解释该法时，使其与欧共体的指令一致；特别是考虑到《消费者保护法》的第1条第1款，该款规定："实施第一部分是为了贯彻执行《产品责任指令》，因此对其的解释应该按照相应的方法进行。"因此，在本次庭审中，双方的关注点都主要集中于欧共体的指令，因为就本案争议焦点的有关问题而言，就算《消费者保护法》的措辞和欧共体指令的措辞有什么不一致的地方，对《消费者保护法》的解释也不能和对共同体指令中相应的条文的解释不一致。这样，务实的做法是回溯到本源，也就是欧共体指令本身。如下所述，双方的争议主要是围绕如何正确地解释指令第6条（相当于《消费者保护法》的第3条）和指令第7条第e款（对应《消费者保护法》的第4条第1款第e项）。因此，本判决书将涉及的主要是（如果不说是只是）指令的条文，而非《消费者保护法》的条文。双方都同意为了本案审理的目的，原告所感染的血液和血液制品属于《消费者保护法》和欧共体指令所指的"产品"；被告制作血液制品的过程，则属于欧共体指令所称的工业过程。

……

相关法条如下：

第1条

生产者应为其产品的缺陷所造成的损害，承担责任。

第4条

受害人应当证明其损害，产品的缺陷，以及产品的缺陷和其损害之间的

relationship between defect and damage.

Article 6

1. A product is defective when it does not provide the safety which a person is entitled to expect, taking all circumstances into account, including: (a) the presentation of the product; (b) the use to which it could reasonably be expected that the product would be put; (c) the time when the product was put into circulation.

2. A product shall not be considered defective for the sole reason that a better product is subsequently put into circulation.

Article 7

The producer shall not be liable as a result of this Directive if he proves: (a) that he did not put the product into circulation; or (b) that, having regard to the circumstances, it is probable that the defect which caused the damage did not exist at the time when the product was put into circulation by him or that this defect came into being afterwards; or (d) that the defect is due to compliance of the product with mandatory regulations issued by the public authorities; or (e) that the state of scientific and technical knowledge at the time when he put the product into circulation was not such as to enable the existence of the defect to be discovered.

...

(i) As to art 6, the claimants assert that, with the need for proof of negligence eliminated, consideration of the conduct of the producer, or of a reasonable or legitimately expectable producer, is inadmissible or irrelevant. Therefore questions of avoidability cannot and do not arise: what the defendants could or should have done differently; whether there were any steps or precautions reasonably available; and whether it was impossible to take any steps by way of prevention or avoidance, or impracticable or economically unreasonable. Such are not 'circumstances' falling to be considered within art 6. In so far as the risk was known to blood producers and the medical profession, it was not known to the public at large (save for those few patients who might ask their doctor, or read the occasional article about blood in a newspaper) and no risk that any percentage of transfused blood would be infected was accepted by them.

(ii) The defendants assert that the risk was known to those who mattered, namely the medical profession, through whom blood was supplied. Avoiding the risk was impossible and unattainable, and it is not and cannot be legitimate to expect the unattainable. Avoidability or unavoidability is a circumstance to be taken into account within art 6. The public did not and/or was not entitled to expect 100% clean blood. The most they could legitimately expect was that all legitimately expectable (reasonably available) precautions—or in this case tests—had been taken or carried out. The claimants must therefore prove that they were legitimately entitled to expect more, and/ or must disprove the unavoidability of the harmful characteristic. There would need to be an investigation as to whether it was impossible to avoid the risk and/or whether the producers had

因果关系。

第6条

1. 产品的缺陷是指，在考量了所有的情节后作出的判断下，产品不具有人们有权预期的安全性；这些情节包括：（a）产品的使用说明；（b）可以合理预见的产品的使用情况；（c）产品投入流通的时间。

2. 仅仅因为之后有更好的产品投入流通，并不能认为某产品有缺陷。

第7条

生产者并不承担本指令所要求的责任，如果其证明：（a）其并未将产品投入流通；（b）相关的情况很可能说明造成损害的缺陷在产品投入流通时尚不存在，或者说明缺陷是投入流通之后产生的；（d）产品的缺陷是因为要使产品符合强制性规定的要求而产生的；（e）当产品投入流通之时，利用当时的科学技术知识尚不足以发现缺陷的存在。

……

（i）对于第6条，原告主张，因为不用证明被告的过失，所以生产者或者合理而可以预期的生产者，应当如何行事便是无关的情节了。因此，被告是否有避免感染的可能性这一问题，便没有必要讨论了：被告可以且应当有不同的作为；是否存在对风险的合理预防措施；防止或者避免感染的措施是否不可能，是否难以实行，是否经济上不合理这些都不属于第6条所考虑的"情节"。血液生产者和医疗界知晓感染的风险，然而公众却并不知情（除了个别的会询问医生的病人，或者会偶尔在报纸上读到有关血液的文章的病人），因此用来输血的血液有一定比例可能已经被感染的风险，无论比例是多少，这个风险都并不被公众所接受。

（ii）被告则主张，对感染的风险，关键人群（也就是从事输血活动的医疗界）是知晓的。避免这种风险是不可能的，也是客观上达不到的，而我们没有办法合情合理地去指望客观上达不到的要求。因此，风险是否可以避免，便完全属于第6条规定的应当纳入考量的情节。公众并未预期，也无权指望血液百分之百是干净的。他们最多能合情合理地指望的，不过是生产者已经做了所有可以合情合理可预期的（适度可行的）预防措施，在本案中则是各种测试。原告因此必须证明，他们有权合情合理地指望更多的东西，或者推翻被告对感染不可避免这一点的证明。对于风险是否不可能避免，或者对于生产者是否已经采取了所有可以合情合理地可预期的预防措施，是应该进行调查的。现在已经进行了的这个调查和对被告过失的调查很像，它调查的也

taken all legitimately expectable steps. In so far as there was thus an investigation analogous to, or involving similar facts to, an investigation into negligence, it was not an investigation of negligence by the individual producer and was necessary and, because it was not an investigation of fault, permissible. ...

...

The dispute therefore is as to what further, if anything, falls to be considered within 'all circumstances'. There is no dispute between the parties, as set out in para 31(i) and (ii) above, that consideration of the fault of the producer is excluded; but does consideration of 'all circumstances' include consideration of the conduct to be expected from the producer, the level of safety to be expected from a producer of that product? The parties agree that the starting point is theparticular product with the harmful characteristic, and if its inherent nature and intended use (eg poison) are dangerous, then there may not need to be any further consideration, provided that the injury resulted from that known danger. However, if the product was not intended to be dangerous, that is the harmful characteristic was not intended, by virtue of the intended use of the product, then there must be consideration of whether it was safe and the level of safety to be legitimately expected. At this stage, the defendants assert that part of the investigation consists of what steps could have been taken by a producer to avoid that harmful characteristic. The defendants assert that conduct is to be considered not by reference to identifying the individual producer's negligence, but by identifying and specifying the safety precautions that the public would or could reasonably expect from a producer of the product. The exercise is referred to as a balancing act; the more difficult it is to make safe, and the more beneficial the product, the less is expected and vice versa, an issue being whether a producer has complied with the safety precautions reasonably to be expected. ... The claimants, however, assert that, given that it is common ground that the article imposes liability irrespective of fault, the exercise of considering what could or should have been done by the producer is an impermissible and irrelevant exercise, which lets questions of fault back in by the back door.

Non-standard products

In any event, however, the claimants make a separate case in relation to the blood products here in issue: namely that they are what is called in the United States 'rogue products' or 'lemons', and in Germany 'Ausreisser'—escapees or'off the road' products. These are products which are isolated or rare specimens which are different from the other products of a similar series, different from the products as intended or desired by the producer. ... Thus a *standard* product is one which is and performs as the producer intends. A *non-standard* product is one which is different, obviously because it is deficient or inferior in terms of safety, from the standard product: and where it is the harmful characteristic or characteristics present in the non-standard product, but not in the standard product, which has or have caused the material injury or damage. Some Community

是跟构成过失类似的事实。但是这个调查并不是对单个生产者的过失调查，因此是必要的。由于这个调查并不是对过错的调查，因此属于可采纳的证据。

……

因此，本案的争议即为，除了列举的那些事项，是否还有其他的事项属于"所有的情节"，如果有，是哪些？双方在上文第 31 段（i）和（ii）两个小段里，已经明确了被告的过错不属于这里的可以考虑的情节，然而，生产者的行为、某个产品的生产者所能带来的安全性，这些情节是否属于可以考虑的情节呢？双方同意问题讨论的基点是产品具有某种有害的特征，而如果这种特征是固有的，且生产者所打算的用途就是危险的（比如毒药），那就不需要再有什么别的考虑了（肯定不成立产品责任），只要损害来源于前述已知的危险。然而，如果根据生产者所打算的产品的用途，并不能将其看作危险品，即产品的有害的特征并非生产者所打算的，那么我们就需要考虑产品是不是安全，以及产品的安全性是否符合可以合情合理的可预期程度。在目前的阶段，被告主张调查的部分内容是围绕生产者所能采取的避免这些有害特征的措施。被告主张，考量生产者的行为，并不是为了确定某个生产者的过失，而是为了确定公众可能会对产品的生产者所采取的安全措施有何种合理的预期。对公众预期的考量被视为一种平衡，产品的安全越难以保证，产品的益处越多，公众的预期就应该越少；反之亦然。这样，争议的焦点就应该是，生产者是否采取了公众所合理期望的安全措施……原告则主张，鉴于双方都同意第 6 条所设立的责任是不问过错的，考量生产者能够做什么或者应该做什么属于无关的事项，否则其实是把过错要件偷偷摸摸地给加回来了，因此其不能被采纳为证据。

不达标产品

对于本案中的血液产品，原告还有另一个主张：即它们属于美国所说的"流氓产品"或者"柠檬产品"，或者德国所说的"Ausreisser"——偏离正轨的产品。这种产品是指那些和类似系列的产品不同、和生产者所打算的样子不同的、孤立的或者个别的产品……标准产品的性质和性能符合生产者的预期。而不达标产品则是和标准产品不同的产品，很显然是因为其有缺陷，或者安全性更低才不同的。而造成了严重的人身损害或者财产损失的有害特征，则只在不达标产品中存在，而不在达标产品中存在。欧盟的某些成员国在贯彻指令时，特别规定了生产不达标产品的责任：对不达标产品，自动视为存在第 6 条所说的缺陷，意大利和西班牙就通过明文立法的方式这

jurisdictions in implementing the directive have specifically provided that there will be liability for 'non-standard' products, ie that such will automatically be defective within art 6: Italy and Spain have done so by express legislation…

…

Conclusions on Article 6

I do not consider it to be arguable that the consumer had an actual expectation that blood being supplied to him was not 100% clean, nor do I conclude that he had knowledge that it was, or was likely to be, infected with Hepatitis C. It is not seriously argued by the defendants, notwithstanding some few newspaper cuttings which were referred to, that there was any public understanding or acceptance of the infection of transfused blood by Hepatitis C. Doctors and surgeons knew, but did not tell their patients unless asked, and were very rarely asked. It was certainly, in my judgment, not known and accepted by society that there was such a risk…

I do not consider that the legitimate expectation of the public at large is that legitimately expectable tests will have been carried out or precautions adopted. Their legitimate expectation is as to the safeness of the product (or not). The court will act as what Dr Bartl called the appointed representative of the public at large, but in my judgment it is impossible to inject into the consumer's legitimate expectation matters which would not by any stretch of the imagination be in his actual expectation. He will assume perhaps that there are tests, but his expectations will be as to the safeness of the blood. In my judgment it is as inappropriate to propose that the public should not 'expect the unattainable'—in the sense of tests or precautions which are impossible—at least unless it is informed as to what is unattainable or impossible, as it is to reformulate the expectation as one that the producer will not have been negligent or will have taken all reasonable steps.

In this context I turn to consider what is intended to be included within 'all circumstances' in art 6. I am satisfied that this means all *relevant* circumstances. It is quite plain to me that (albeit that Professor Stapleton has been pessimistic about its success) the directive was intended to eliminate proof of fault or negligence. I am satisfied that this was not simply a legal consequence, but that it was also intended to make it easier for claimants to prove their case, such that not only would a consumer not have to prove that the producer did not take reasonable steps, or all reasonable steps, to comply with his duty of care, but also that the producer did not take all legitimately expectable steps either.

…

I conclude therefore that *avoidability* is not one of the *circumstances* to be taken into account within art 6.

…

Further, in my judgment, the infected bags of blood were non-standard products. I have already recorded that it does not seem to me to matter whether they would be categorised in US

规定……

……

对第 6 条的结论

我不认为消费者预料到了提供给他们的血液并不是百分之百干净的观点是合理的,我也不认为他们知道或者可能知道他们会感染丙肝。被告除了提供了几页报纸,并没有很认真地论证公众知道或者接受他们可能感染丙肝的风险。医生们倒是知道,但是他们只有在病人询问时才会告知这个事实,而病人却很少去问。在我看来,社会公众并不知道,也不接受感染这种疾病的风险。

我不认为公众可以合情合理地预期的仅仅是生产者对产品做的合理可预期的测试,或者采取的预防措施。公众合情合理的预期,应该是直接关于产品的安全性的(或者是产品的不安全性的)。法院确实需要扮演 Bartl 博士所说的"公众的代表"的角色,然而在我看来,公众所合理预期的内容,是不可能包括那些匪夷所思的东西的。公众确实有可能假设生产者会对产品做测试,但是他的预期只会是血液是安全的。在我看来,说公众"不能指望不可能达到的事"(即公众应该预见到某些测试或者预防措施是不可能的),这种说法是不恰当的,除非公众被告知了完全避免产品缺陷是无法做到的或是不可能的。如果公众确实被告知了,那么这会将公众的预期变更为:生产者并无过失且已经采取所有合理的措施来避免产品的缺陷。

由此而论,我将讨论一下第 6 条所说的"所有情节"到底包含什么内容。我认为这里的"所有情节"的意思是所有有关的情节。对我而言,指令的目的在于取消原告对过错或者过失的举证责任,这一点是再明显不过的了。指令的目的并不仅仅是发生法律效果,它的目的是为了让原告胜诉变得更容易,因此消费者不但不需要证明生产者没有采取其注意义务下的某些合理的措施或者全部的合理措施,而且消费者同样不需要证明的,还有生产者没有采取所有的可以合情合理地期望的措施。

……

因此,我的结论是,"缺陷的不可避免性"并非第 6 条所说的是可以被考虑的情节。

……

另外,在我看来,这些被污染了的血包是未达标产品。我已经表示我并不在意这些产品在美国侵权法上会被看作存在制造或者设计缺陷。总之,这

tort law as manufacturing or design defects. They were in any event different from the norm which the producer intended for use by the public.(i) I do not accept that all the blood products were equally defective because all of them carried the risk. That is a very philosophical approach. It is one which would, as Mr Forrester pointed out, be equally apt to a situation in which one tyre in one million was defective because of an inherent occasional blip in the strength of the rubber's raw material. The answer is that the test relates to the *use* of the blood bag. For, and as a result of, the intended use, 99 out of 100 bags would cause no injury and would not be infected, unlike the 100th. (ii) Even in the case of standard products such as drugs, side-effects are to my mind only capable of being 'socially acceptable' if they are made known. ... But I am satisfied, as I have stated above, that the problem was not *known* to the consumer. However, in any event, I do not accept that the consumer expected,or was entitled to expect, that *his* bag of blood was defective even if (which I have concluded was not the case) he had any knowledge of any problem. I do not consider, ... that he was expecting or entitled to expect a form of Russian roulette. That would only arise if, contrary to my conclusion, the public took that as socially acceptable ... For such knowledge and acceptance there would need to be at the very least publicity and probably express warnings, and even that might not ... be sufficient.

Accordingly I am quite clear that the infected blood products in this case were non-standard products (whether on the basis of being manufacturing or design defects does not appear to me to matter). Where, as here, there is a harmful characteristic in a *non-standard* product, a decision that it is defective is likely to be straightforward, and I can make my decision accordingly. However, the consequence of my conclusion is that 'avoidability' is also not in the basket of *circumstances*, even in respect of a harmful characteristic in a *standard* product. So I shall set out what I consider to be the structure for consideration under art 6. It must be emphasised that safety and intended, or foreseeable, use are the lynchpins: and, leading on from these, what legitimate expectations there are of safety in relation to foreseeable use. ...

The first step must be to identify the harmful characteristic which caused the injury (art 4). In order to establish that there is a defect in art 6, the next step will be to conclude whether the product is standard or non-standard. This will be done (in the absence of admission by the producer) most easily by comparing the offending product with other products of the same type or series produced by that producer. If the respect in which it differs from the series includes the harmful characteristic, then it is, for the purpose of art 6, non-standard. If it does not differ, or if the respect in which it differs does not include the harmful characteristic, but all the other products, albeit different, share the harmful characteristic, then it is to be treated as a standard product.

Non-standard products

The *circumstances* specified in art 6 may obviously be relevant—the product may be a second—as well as the circumstances of the supply. But it seems to me that the primary issue in

些血包和生产者打算给公众使用的标准是不一致的。（ⅰ）我并不认同这样的说法：因为所有的血液产品都有风险，所以，所有的血液产品都是一样有缺陷的。这是非常哲学家的说法。正如 Forrester 先生指出的那样，这种说法也同样适用于轮胎的场合：轮胎可能有百万分之一的概率有缺陷，因为橡胶原料存在偶尔发生但是属于固有性质的小问题。问题的关键还是要看血包的使用情况。按照生产者的预期，百分之九十九的血包并不会被感染，因此不会造成损害；只有剩下的百分之一会这样。（ⅱ）就算是对达标产品，比如药品，在我看来副作用也只有在为公众所知的情况下，才属于"社会能接受的"……如前所述，公众并不知道感染风险这一事实，已经足够了。然而，就算消费者是知晓这种风险的存在的（我已经说过这不是事实），我也不认为消费者会对他的血包的缺陷有预期。我并不认为……消费者会对类似俄罗斯轮盘赌的事情有预期。只有在公众都认为这种风险是社会可以接受时，这种和我的结论不同的预期才会存在……要让公众知晓并接受这种风险，那至少是需要一定的宣传的，还需要有明文的警告，而且就算有这些也不一定足够证明公众知晓并接受这种风险。

所以，我非常清楚本案中受感染的血液制品是不达标产品（是因为制造缺陷还不达标，还是因为设计缺陷不达标，在我看来并不重要）。如同本案这样，如果不达标产品具有某种有害特征，那么显而易见法官就很有可能去判决产品是有缺陷的；而我也会这样判决。然而我的结论还要更进一层，那就是就算是在达标产品中，致害特征也并不属于受害人应该预期的情节。现在我要陈述我所认为的考量第6条的方法。第6条中强调的关键词是"安全性"和"生产者所意图的（或可预见的）使用情况"。从这里出发，我们就可以知道，用户可以合情合理地期望的是与可预期的用途相关的安全性。

第一步要做的是确定导致了损害的致害特征（第4条）。为了证明产品存在第6条所说的缺陷，下一步要做的是确定产品是达标的还是非达标的。这主要是靠比较致害产品和该生产商生产的其他同类型的或者同系列的产品。若二者并没有什么不同，或者不同点并不包含那些有害特征，而是所有的产品都具有这种有害特征，那么就应当将致害产品视作达标产品。

非达标产品

显然，第6条所列举的那些情节肯定是相关的——产品本身的性质是另一个相关的情节——产品的供应情况也是相关的情节。然而对我来说，在涉及非达标产品时最重要的问题是公众是否接受了产品可能是不达标的这一特

relation to a non-standard product may be whether the public at large accepted the non-standard nature of the product—ie they accept that a proportion of the products is defective (as I have concluded they do not in this case). That, as discussed, is not of course the end of it, because the question is of *legitimate* expectation, and the court may conclude that the expectation of the public is too high or too low. But manifestly questions such as warnings and presentations will be in the forefront. However, I conclude that the following are not relevant: (i) avoidability of the harmful characteristic—ie impossibility or unavoidability in relation to precautionary measures; (ii) the impracticality, cost or difficulty of taking such measures; and (iii) the benefit to society or utility of the product (except in the context of whether—with *full information* and *proper knowledge*—the public does and ought to accept the risk). ...

...

Standard products

If a standard product is unsafe, it is likely to be so as a result of alleged error in design, or at any rate as a result of an allegedly flawed system. The harmful characteristic must be identified, if necessary with the assistance of experts. The question of presentation/time/circumstances of supply/social acceptability etc will arise as above. The sole question will be safety for the foreseeable use. If there are any comparable products on the market, then it will obviously be relevant to compare the offending product with those other products, so as to identify, compare and contrast the relevant features. There will obviously need to be a full understanding of how the product works—particularly if it is a new product, such as a scrid, so as to assess its safety for such use. Price is obviously a significant factor in legitimate expectation, and may well be material in the comparative process. But again it seems to me there is no room in the basket for: (i) what the producer could have done differently; and (ii) whether the producer could or could not have done the same as the others did.

...

JUDGMENT

For the reasons set out at length during its course, I give judgment for the claimants on the issues before me. ...

征，即他们是否接受一定比例的产品其实是有缺陷的（我已经表示在本案中公众对此并不接受）。讨论了这些当然并不是结束，因为这里实际是"合情合理的预期"，因此法院可以认为公众的预期太高了或者太低了。当然，生产者的警告和对产品的描述都是很重要的情节。然而，我认为下列的情节是无关的：（i）致害特征的不可避免性——即预防措施是不可能的，或无法避免损害；（ii）采取措施的不可行性，如采取措施的费用不可能，或者采取措施的困难度；（iii）产品对社会的好处或者产品的作用（除非是为了证明公众在掌握全部的信息和正确的知识的前提下，是接受或者应该接受这种风险）……

……

达标产品

如果达标产品是不安全的，这很可能是因为某种所谓的设计错误，或者有可能是因为某种系统瑕疵。我们必须要找到致害特征，在必要的情况下由专家协助寻找。有关使用说明、投入流通的时间、供应状况、社会的接受度等问题，和不达标产品一样都需要讨论。这些问题其实都是为了解决一个问题：产品为了可预见的用途的安全性。若市场上存在同类的产品，那么很显然需要比较致害产品和其他同类产品，以确定并比较相关的特征。很显然我们需要了解产品的工作原理（特别是当涉及新品的时候，比如代币券）以便评估其在这种用途上的安全性。然而我需要再次指出，需要考量的情节并不包括（i）生产者是否本可以不这样做；（ii）生产者是否本可以做到或不做别的生产者所做的。

……

判决

依据我在这个过程中作出的长篇论证，针对摆在我面前的这些争议焦点，我判决支持原告的主张……

Chapter 8. Damages

Section 1. Medical Expenses

68. Williams v. Bright, 230 A.D.2d 548, 658 N.Y.S.2d 910, appeal dismissed, 90 N.Y.2d 935, 686 N.E.2d 1368 (1997)

Appellate Division, Supreme Court of New York, United States

Wallach, Justice.

Plaintiff Robbins was a passenger in an automobile driven by her 70-year-old father on an upstate highway. An eyewitness saw the car veer off the road at about 65 MPH and turn over in a culvert on adjoining farmland. There was circumstantial evidence that the driver, who had driven with this plaintiff and other family members early that morning from New York City to Plattsburgh and was returning the same day, had fallen asleep at the wheel. This was conduct that the jury found to be both negligent and a proximate cause of the accident. On this appeal, defendants, who include the lessors of the vehicle, do not seriously contest liability; the main issue is the trial court's treatment of plaintiff Robbins' alleged failure to mitigate damages due to her religious beliefs as a Jehovah's Witness.

The central question for us, on appellate review, is not merely the admeasurement of plaintiff's damages under the application of traditional tort law standards, but the broader controversy involving plaintiff's beliefs and their proper effect upon her monetary award. That, in turn, obliges us to grapple with grave constitutional issues ordinarily not involved in a motor vehicle accident—even one as tragic and catastrophic as this one.

I.

For a hundred years it has been settled law in this state that a party who claims to have suffered damage by the tort of another is bound "to use reasonable and proper efforts to make the damage as small as practicable"..., and if an injured party allows the damages to be unnecessarily enhanced, the incurred loss justly falls upon him.

Plaintiff Robbins suffered a severely damaged left hip, as well as a painful injury to her right knee. Her own expert testified that if these injuries were not alleviated by well recognized and universally accepted surgical procedures, her prognosis was for a wheelchair-bound life because

第八章　损害赔偿金

第一节　医疗费用

68. Williams v. Bright, 230 A.D.2d 548, 658 N.Y.S.2d 910, appeal dismissed, 90 N.Y.2d 935, 686 N.E.2d 1368 (1997)

美国纽约州最高法院上诉庭

Wallach 法官主笔：

原告 Robbins 是一辆机动车上的乘客，该车由她 70 岁的父亲在该州北部的一条公路上驾驶。一名目击者看到汽车以大约 65 英里/小时的速度偏离道路，翻进了附近农田的涵洞里。间接证据表明，司机驾驶汽车，与原告和其他家庭成员在早晨离开纽约市，开往匹兹堡市，当天返回，后来司机趴在方向盘上睡着了。陪审团判定这种行为既有过失又是事故的近因。在本上诉中，包括汽车出租人在内的被告未努力进行争辩；主要问题是初审法院对由于原告 Robbins 作为耶和华见证会（Jehovah's Witness）成员的宗教信仰，而被指控未能进行减轻伤害的处理。

在受理上诉审议时，对我们来说，核心的问题不仅仅包括根据传统的侵权法标准的适用来分配原告的损害赔偿金，还包括更广泛的争议，这涉及原告的信仰及其对于赔偿金额的适当影响。这就迫使我们在机动车事故中——即使是像该事故那样的灾难性悲剧——解决通常并不涉及的重大宪法问题。

I.

一百多年以来，本州的法律确定，声称由于另一方的侵权行为，受到伤害的一方有义务"实施合理和适当的行为尽量减少伤害"……并且如果受害人使伤害不必要地加重，则产生的损失应由其承担。

原告 Robbins 左髋严重受伤，并且右膝受到疼痛性损害。她本人的专家证实，如果这些伤害不通过外科手术缓解，她的预后将是轮椅上的生活，

of the inevitability of necrotic development in the bone structure of these limbs. Moreover, all the experts agreed that the surgical intervention available to this plaintiff (52 years of age at the time of the accident) offered her the prospect of a good recovery and a near normal life. However, Robbins, a devout Jehovah's Witness, presented proof (chiefly from her own hospital records) that she was obliged to refuse these recommended surgeries because her church prohibits the blood transfusions they would necessarily entail.

In accordance with settled law, the New York pattern jury instruction on the subject of damage mitigation refers to the actions of "a reasonably prudent person" and measures the duty to mitigate in accordance with that standard. Although the trial court acquainted the jury with the existence of that standard, it charged that in this case the standard to be applied was something very different:

> You have to accept as a given that the dictates of her religion forbid blood transfusions.
>
> And so you have to determine ... whether she ... acted reasonably as a Jehovah's Witness in refusing surgery which would involve blood transfusions.
>
> Was it reasonable for her, not what you would do or your friends or family, was it reasonable for her given her beliefs, without questioning the validity or the propriety of her beliefs?

In abandoning the "reasonably prudent person" test in favor of a "reasonable Jehovah's Witness" standard, over defendants' objection, the trial court perceived the issue as involving this plaintiff's fundamental right to the free exercise of her religion, protected by the First Amendment to the United States Constitution . . . prohibits any law "respecting an establishment of religion, or prohibiting the free exercise thereof." Essentially, the court held that if the jury were permitted to assess this plaintiff's refusal to accept additional surgery without total deference to her religious beliefs, it would unlawfully restrain "the free exercise" of her Jehovah's Witness faith and would thus be constitutionally prohibited. In effect, this plaintiff's religious beliefs were held, as a matter of law, to relieve her of any legal obligation to mitigate damages under the same standard required of all other persons similarly situated who do not share similar religious convictions. . . .

In our view, the analysis of the trial court contained many flaws. The first error was in defining the fundamental issue as whether any jury verdict could be permitted to conflict with this plaintiff's "religious belief that it may be better to suffer present pain than to be barred from entering the Kingdom of Heaven" (167 Misc. 2d, at 318, 632 N.Y.S.2d 760). With all due deference, this is not the question that should have been presented; to put it in this manner inevitably skews the result.

No one suggests that the State, or, for that matter, anyone else, has the right to interfere with that religious belief. But the real issue here is whether the consequences of that belief must be

因为这些部位的骨骼将会不可避免地坏死。而且，所有专家都同意，对原告（事故发生时52岁）的手术介入将使其有希望康复，过上基本正常的生活。然而，Robbins是虔诚的耶和华见证会成员，她证明（主要来自本人的病历）自己必须拒绝这些外科建议，因为她的教派禁止这些外科手术必须进行的输血。

根据确定的法律，关于伤害减轻的纽约州示范性陪审团指示涉及"合理谨慎人"的行为，并且根据该标准衡量减轻义务。虽然初审法院告知了陪审团该标准的存在，但是在本案件中初审法院指示该标准的适用非常不同：

你们必须接受该前提：她的宗教信条禁止输血。

因此你们必须确定……在拒绝涉及输血的外科手术时，她是否……作为耶和华见证会成员合理地行事。

她的行为不是你们或你们的朋友或家人愿意实施的行为，但对她来说是否合理？根据她的信仰，对她来说是否合理？不要质疑她的信仰的合理性或适当性。

在放弃"合理谨慎人"检验标准而适用"合理的耶和华见证会成员"标准时，否定了被告的反对，初审法院将该问题视为涉及原告宗教信教自由的基本权利，该权利受到《美国宪法第一修正案》的保护……禁止任何法律"确立国教或禁止信教自由"。实质上，法院判定，如果允许陪审团评估原告拒绝接受额外的外科手术的事实而不完全尊重其宗教信仰，则会非法限制她对耶和华见证会教义的"自由信仰"，这是宪法所禁止的。实际上，作为法律问题，原告的宗教信仰使其免于根据要求发生类似情况，但不具有类似宗教信仰的所有其他人的标准，来履行减轻伤害的法律义务……

我们认为，初审法院的分析存在许多缺陷。第一项错误存在于将基本问题确定为是否允许任何陪审团的裁断与原告的以下宗教信仰相冲突："遭受目前的疼痛好过不被准许进入天国。"（167 Misc. 2d, at 318, 632 N.Y.S.2d 760）恕我直言，这不是应当提出的问题；以这种方式处理会不可避免地扭曲结果。

没有人认为州政府或任何其他人有权干涉宗教信仰。但在这里，真正的问题是该信仰的后果导致的损害赔偿金是否必须由非受伤信徒的其他人支付。

fully paid for here on earth by someone other than the injured believer. According to the trial court, the State has little interest in enforcing its general rule of damage mitigation simply to rescue a wrongdoer from the full consequences of his tortious conduct. . . .

Of course, the State does not have any interest in the question of who wins this lawsuit, or the extent to which one party prevails over the other. But the State does have a compelling interest in assuring that the proceedings before its civil tribunals are fair, and that any litigant is not improperly advantaged or disadvantaged by adherence to a particular set of religious principles....

An order emanating from a State court constitutes "state action" which, under the Fourteenth Amendment, would trigger First Amendment protections. The trial court's instruction to the jurors on mitigation directed them to pass upon the reasonableness of plaintiff Robbins' objection, on religious grounds, to a blood transfusion. The fallacy in this instruction was that the jury never received any evidence pertaining to the rationale of her religious convictions, nor how universally accepted they may have been by members of her faith. True, there were entries in her medical records that she refused blood transfusions because she was a Jehovah's Witness, and there was brief testimony (in the context of presenting her diminished physical capabilities) that she attended Jehovah's Witness prayer services. But there was no evidence of the basis for the religious prohibition of blood transfusions. The charge thus created a sham inquiry; instead of framing an issue on how plaintiff Robbins' religious beliefs impacted on mitigation, the court foreclosed the issue in her favor without any supporting evidence. Let us recall, the jurors were told that they must ask themselves whether this plaintiff's refusal to accept a blood transfusion was reasonable, "given her beliefs, without questioning the validity" of those beliefs. Having thus removed from the jury's consideration any question as to the validity (that is to say, the reasonableness) of plaintiff Robbins' religious convictions, the court effectively directed a verdict on the issue.

Of course, the alternative—the receipt of "expert" testimony on this subject—presents an even worse prospect. Such evidence, if any conflict developed, would present a triable issue as to whether the conviction against transfusions was heretical—or orthodox—within the Jehovah's Witness faith.

The State may not endorse religion or any particular religious practice. The trial court, in accepting the sincerity of plaintiff Robbins' beliefs as a given and asking the jury to consider the reasonableness of her actions only in the context of her own religion, effectively provided government endorsement to those beliefs. American courts have no business endorsing or condemning the truth or falsity of anyone's religious beliefs. ...

An extraordinary example of the perils of such an excursion is the recent Minnesota case of Lundman v. McKown, 530 N.W.2d 807, 828, *cert. denied,* 516 U.S. 1099, 116 S. Ct. 828, 133 L. Ed. 2d 770, where damages were awarded against a Christian Scientist stepfather who blocked conventional treatment that, to a medical certainty, would have saved a young child's life. Here

初审法院认为，州政府几乎不关注仅仅为了使不法行为人免于承担侵权行为的全部后果，而执行减轻伤害的一般规则……

当然，州政府不关注谁胜诉的问题，也不关注一方胜过另一方的程度。但是，本州必须注意确保其民事法庭的程序公正合理，并且任何诉讼当事人不会由于遵守特定的宗教原则，而不合适地处于有利地位或不利地位……

来自一家州法院的命令构成"州行为"，根据《美国宪法第十四修正案》，该行为将启动《美国宪法第一修正案》的保护。初审法院对于陪审员关于减轻伤害的指令，要求他们判断原告 Robbins 依据宗教反对输血的合理性。该指令中的谬误是陪审团从未获得有关她的宗教信念的基本原理的证据，也未获得这些信念在该宗教信徒中的接受程度。她的病历表明，因为她是耶和华见证会成员，所以拒绝输血，并且有简要的证词（在表示她丧失生理机能的背景下）表明她参加过耶和华见证会的祈祷仪式。然而，没有证据表明该宗教禁止输血。因此，该指令构成了虚假询问；法院没有质疑原告 Robbins 的宗教信仰如何影响减轻伤害，而是在没有任何支持性证据的情况下排除了该问题，从而对她有利。我们知道陪审员曾经被告知必须确定原告拒绝接受输血是否合理，"根据她的信仰，不要质疑她的信仰的有效性"。法院要求陪审团不考虑原告 Robbins 的宗教信念的有效性（即合理性），从而有效地主导了对于该争议的裁断。

当然，替代方案——接受"专家"的证词——导致了更糟糕的前景。如果争议继续发展，则该证据会产生可裁判性的问题：在耶和华见证会的信仰中——反对输血的信念是异端信念——还是正统信念。

州政府不能认可宗教或任何特别的宗教习惯。初审法院接受原告 Robbins 信仰的真实性，要求陪审团仅在她自己的宗教的背景下考虑她的行为的合理性，从而有效地表明政府对于这些信仰的认可。美国法院无权认可或谴责任何人的宗教信仰的真实性或虚假性……

这种离题危险性的特例是最近明尼苏达州的案件，参见 Lundman v. McKown, 530 N.W.2d 807, 828, cert. denied, 516 U.S. 1099, 116 S. Ct. 828, 133 L. Ed. 2d 770 案。在该案件中，作为基督教科学派（Christian Scientist）教徒的继父阻止常规治疗，而在医学上这种治疗一定会挽救儿童的生命。本案中的儿

was a healthy 11-year-old boy who succumbed to a sudden onset of juvenile diabetes, a disease that is easily diagnosable and treatable by conventional medical practice. Instead, his mother and stepfather enlisted the services of Christian Science practitioners who provided only "spiritual treatment." The child's condition deteriorated rapidly, and he died three days later. There was evidence that a shot of insulin administered as late as two hours before death could have saved him. A wrongful death action was commenced by the child's natural father and older sister against the mother and stepfather, the various spiritual practitioners and the Christian Science Church itself. A jury awarded compensatory damages against all defendants in the amount of $5.2 million (reduced on post-trial motion to $1.5 million), and $9 million in punitive damages against the church.

The Minnesota Court of Appeals overturned the verdict against the church and its officials, but upheld the portion of the award against the mother, stepfather and local practitioners. In reaching that conclusion, the appellate court allowed itself to become deeply entangled in ecclesiastical matters regarding the tenets of the Christian Science faith. The trial court, in awarding damages against the mother and stepfather, had applied the reasonable person standard of care. The Court of Appeals ruled, to the contrary, that the proper standard was that of the "reasonable Christian scientist," but then went on to hold, as a matter of law, that a new trial was not warranted because the reasonable Christian Scientist would necessarily have concluded (as did the jury under the reasonable person standard) that the life-or-death interest of the child should have prevailed and dictated conventional medical treatment .... In other words, the appellate court undertook to evaluate the reasonableness of various practices and tenets of the Christian Science faith....We should firmly decline to follow that rarely trodden and perilous path.

II.

In espousing the objective standard and remanding this matter for a new trial, we take note of an obvious problem with strict adherence to the pattern jury instruction that is provided as a general guide. We conclude that the unmodified application of that formulation would work an injustice in this case, as well as in others of a similar nature. It seems apparent to us that a person in plaintiff Robbins' position must be permitted to present to the jury the basis for her refusal of medical treatment; otherwise, the jury would simply be left with the fact of her refusal, without any explanation at all. Once such evidence is (as it should be) received, the court is called upon to instruct the jurors as to how such evidence should affect their deliberations. Addressing this issue, we hold that the pattern jury instruction must be supplemented here with the following direction:

> In considering whether the plaintiff acted as a reasonably prudent person, you may consider the plaintiff's testimony that she is a believer in the Jehovah's Witness faith, and that as an adherent of that faith, she cannot accept any medical treatment

童是一名 11 岁的男孩，突发儿童糖尿病，该病通过常规疗法很容易诊断和治疗。然而，他的母亲和继父却请来基督教科学派术士，仅提供"信仰治疗"。男孩的病情迅速恶化，3 天后死亡。有证据表明，最迟在死亡前两小时进行一次胰岛素注射就能挽救男孩的生命。男孩的生父和姐姐提起不法致死诉讼，控告生母和继父、各种信仰疗法术士和基督教科学派教会本身。陪审团裁断所有被告承担 520 万美元（根据审后申请减少至 150 万美元）的补偿性损害赔偿金，教会承担 900 万美元的惩罚性损害赔偿金。

明尼苏达州上诉法院推翻了对于教会及其成员的判决，但维持了对于生母、继父和当地术士的判决。在作出判决时，上诉法院被深深卷入有关基督教科学派教义的教会事宜中。在判定生母和继父缴纳损害赔偿金时，初审法院适用了合理人注意标准。相反，上诉法院判定适当的标准是"合理的基督教科学派教徒"标准，但是作为法律问题，认定没有必要重审，因为合理的基督教科学派教徒必然会决定（如陪审团根据合理人标准所作的）儿童的生死利益优先，需要进行常规治疗……换言之，上诉法院着手评估基督教科学派的各种惯例和教义的合理性……我们应当坚定地拒绝这种罕见又危险的途径。

Ⅱ.

在支持客观标准并将该案件发回重审时，我们注意到严格遵守作为一般指导的示范性陪审团指示存在着明显问题。我们认为，在本案中以及性质类似的其他案件中适用未修正的表述会产生不公正。对我们而言，很明显，必须允许处于原告 Robbins 位置的人向陪审团展示拒绝治疗的证据；否则，陪审团只会获得拒绝的事实，而不能得到任何解释。如果获得了该证据（也应当获得），则要求法院指示陪审员该证据应该如何影响其审议。提出该问题后，我们认为示范性陪审团指示必须补充以下指示：

  在考虑原告是否作为合理谨慎的人行事时，你们可以考虑原告的以下证词：她是耶和华见证会的信徒，为了遵守信仰，她不能接受需要输血的治疗。我指示你们，在确定原告是否尽到对所受伤害的合理注意义务，该信仰以及你们听到的所有其他证据是需要考虑的因素，然而，请记住，

which requires a blood transfusion. I charge you that such belief is a factor for you to consider, together with all the other evidence you have heard, in determining whether the plaintiff acted reasonably in caring for her injuries, keeping in mind, however, that the overriding test is whether the plaintiff acted as a reasonably prudent person, under all the circumstances confronting her.

...Our modification of the PJI charge is intended to strike a fair balance between the competing interests of these parties. And in pursuit of that goal, we reiterate that the court is not to permit the introduction of any "theological" proof, by way of either expert or lay testimony, as to the validity of religious doctrine, nor should the court issue any instructions whatsoever on that score....

Accordingly, the judgment ... should be reversed, on the law and the facts, without costs, and the matter remanded for new trial on damages alone.

Nardelli and Tom, JJ., concur with Wallach, J.

69. Coyne v. Campbell, 11 N.Y.2d 372, 183 N.E.2d 891 (1962)

Court of Appeals of New York, United States

Froessel, J.

On July 5, 1957, plaintiff sustained a whiplash injury when his automobile was struck in the rear by a motor vehicle driven by defendant. Inasmuch as plaintiff is a practicing physician and surgeon, he received medical treatment, physiotherapy and care from his professional colleagues and his nurse, and incurred no out-of-pocket expenses therefor. Nevertheless, in his bill of particulars, he stated that his special damages for medical and nursing care and treatment amounted to $2,235. The trial court ruled that the value of these services was not a proper item of special damages, and that no recovery could be had therefor since they had been rendered gratuitously. He thus excluded evidence as to their value. The sole question here presented is the correctness of this ruling.

In the leading case of Drinkwater v. Dinsmore (80 N.Y. 390) we unanimously reversed a plaintiff's judgment entered upon a jury verdict, because defendant was precluded from showing that plaintiff had been paid his wages by his employer during the period of his incapacitation. We held such evidence admissible on the theory that plaintiff was entitled to recover only his pecuniary losses, of which wages gratuitously paid were not an item. With respect to medical expenses, we stated (p. 393) that "the plaintiff must show what he paid the doctor, and can recover only so much as he paid or was bound to pay." Although decided more than 80 years ago, the *Drinkwater* case has continuously been and still is recognized as the prevailing law of this State.

As recently as 1957, the Legislature declined to enact a proposed amendment to the Civil

高于一切的检验标准是，原告在她所面临的所有情况下，是否如合理谨慎的人一样行事。

……我们对于示范性陪审团指示的修改旨在公平地实现各方利益的平衡。为了达到这一目标，我们重申法院不应允许通过专家或普通人的证言引入有关宗教教义的任何"神学"证据，也不应就此发出任何指令……

因此，根据法律和事实，该判决……应当被撤销，不包括诉讼费用，本案就损害赔偿金发回重审。

Nardelli 和 Tom 法官赞同 Wallach 法官的意见。

69. Coyne v. Campbell, 11 N.Y.2d 372, 183 N.E.2d 891 (1962)

美国纽约州上诉法院

Froessel 法官主笔：

1957 年 7 月 5 日，原告因为他的汽车被被告驾驶的机动车追尾而过度扭伤颈椎。由于原告是一名执业的内外科医师，因此得到了同事及其护士所实施的医疗、理疗和护理，没有产生需实际支付的费用。然而，在他的详情起诉状中，他主张医疗护理费用的特殊损害赔偿金为 2,235 美元。初审法院裁定，这些服务的价值不构成特殊损害赔偿金的适当项目，因为它们是无偿提供的，所以不能获得赔偿。因此，裁定排除了有关其价值的证据。这里提出的唯一问题是该裁定的正确性。

在指导性案例 Drinkwater v. Dinsmore（80 N.Y. 390）案中，我们一致撤销了根据陪审团裁断作出的对原告有利的判决，因为排除了被告证明雇主在原告无能力期间已经向其支付工资的情况。我们认为，基于以下理论该证据是可以被采纳的：原告有权仅获得金钱损失补偿，其中无偿获得的工资不是一个项目。关于医疗费用，我们认为（案卷第 393 页）："原告必须证明他向医生支付的金额，并且仅能获得他已经支付或必须支付的金额。"虽然 Drinkwater 案的判决是在八十多年前作出的，但是直到现在仍被视为本州的主流法律。

1957 年，立法机构拒绝颁布一项《民事执业法》（Civil Practice Act）的

Practice Act, the avowed purpose of which (1957 Report of N.Y. Law Rev. Comm., p. 223) was "to abrogate the rule of Drinkwater v. Dinsmore, 80 N.Y. 390 (1880) and to conform New York law to the rule followed in most states that payments from collateral sources do not reduce the amount recoverable in a personal injury action."... The Legislature and not the judiciary is the proper body to decide such a policy question involving the accommodation of various interests. We should not now seek to assume their powers and overrule their decision not to change the well-settled law of this State. No matter what may be the rule in other jurisdictions, *Drinkwater* is still the law in this State.

We find no merit in plaintiff's contention that the medical and nursing services for which damages are sought were supported by consideration. Plaintiff testified that he did not have to pay for the physiotherapy, and his counsel confirmed the fact that "these various items were not payable by the doctor nor were they actual obligations of his, and that he will not have to pay them."

Plaintiff's colleagues rendered the necessary medical services gratuitously as a professional courtesy. It may well be that as a result of having accepted their generosity plaintiff is under a moral obligation to act for them in a similar manner, should his services ever be required; such need may never arise, however, and in any event such a moral obligation is not an injury for which tort damages, which "must be compensatory only" may be awarded. A moral obligation, without more, will not support a claim for legal damages. ...

We are also told that the physiotherapy treatments which plaintiff received from his nurse consumed approximately two hours per week, and that they were given during the usual office hours for which she received her regular salary. Plaintiff does not claim that he was required to or in fact did pay any additional compensation to his nurse for her performance of these duties, and, therefore, this has not resulted in compensable damage to plaintiff.

Finally, we reject as unwarranted plaintiff's suggestion that our decision in Healy v. Rennert (9 N.Y.2d 202, 206) casts doubt on the continued validity of the *Drinkwater* rule in a case such as the instant one. In *Healy,* we held that it was error to permit defendants to establish on cross-examination that plaintiff was a member of a health insurance plan and that he was receiving increased disability pension benefits. In that case, however, the plaintiff had given value for the benefits he received; he paid a premium for the health insurance, and had worked for 18 years, in order to be eligible for the disability retirement benefits. We were not confronted with—and did not attempt to pass upon—a situation where the injured plaintiff received wholly gratuitous services for which he had given no consideration in return and which he was under no legal obligation to repay. In short, insurance, pension, vacation and other benefits which were contracted and paid for are not relevant here. Gratuitous services rendered by relatives, neighbors and friends are not compensable.

修正案草案（1957 Report of N.Y. Law Rev. Comm., p.223），其公开声明的目的是，"废除 Drinkwater v. Dinsmore, 80 N.Y. 390（1880）案的规则，使纽约州法符合大多数州遵循的规则，即在人身伤害诉讼中，平行来源的支付不会使赔偿金额减少"……决定各种利益调节政策问题的适当机构是立法机构而非司法部门。目前我们不应寻求夺取他们的权力，并推翻他们不改变本州稳定法律的判决。无论在其他法域是何种规则，Drinkwater 案仍然是本州的法律。

原告辩称，产生损害赔偿金的医疗和护理服务存在对价，我们认为没有依据。原告作证说，他不必为理疗付款，并且他的律师确认"这些项目不是该医生应支付的，也不是他的实际的债务，他不必支付"的事实。

作为职业礼节，原告的同事免费提供了必要的医疗服务。因为接受了他们的慷慨行为，所以如果他们需要原告的服务，则原告很有可能出于道德义务以类似的方式为他们提供服务，然而，该需求可能永远也不会产生，并且无论如何该道德义务不是一项可以请求侵权损害赔偿的伤害，而且损害赔偿金"必须仅为补偿性的"。仅有道德义务而没有其他，不会支持合法损害赔偿金要求……

我们还获悉，护士对原告实施的理疗每周大约需要两个小时，并且在她获得正常薪金的工作时间进行。原告未声称他必须或实际上向护士支付了多余的报酬，因此，这不会导致原告遭受可补偿的损失。

最后，我们拒绝了原告没有根据的提议，即认为我们在 Healy v. Rennert（9 N.Y.2d 202,206）案中的判决，使人对 Drinkwater 案的规则在本案中的持续有效性产生了怀疑。在 Healy 案中，我们认为，在交叉询问中允许被告证明以下事实是错误的：原告是健康保险计划成员，并且正在接受已经增加的残疾抚恤金收益。然而，在该案中，原告已经为其获得的收益提供了价值：他为健康保险支付保险费，并且已经工作了 18 年，旨在有资格获得残疾退休福利。我们未面对并且未试图判断以下情况：受伤的原告不用为完全的无偿服务提供对价，也没有报答的法律义务。简言之，签有合同并且进行支付的保险、抚恤金、休假和其他福利与本案都没有关系。亲属、邻居和朋友提供的无偿服务不具有可赔偿性。

... It would hardly be fair in a negligence action, where damages are compensatory and not punitive, to change the *Drinkwater* rule of long standing in the face of the Legislature's refusal to do so, and to punish a defendant by requiring him to pay plaintiff for a friend's generosity. If we were to allow a plaintiff the reasonable value of the services of the physician who treated him gratuitously, logic would dictate that the plaintiff would then be entitled to the reasonable value of such services, despite the fact that the physician charged him but a fraction of such value. Such a rule would involve odd consequences, and in the end simply require a defendant to pay a plaintiff the value of a gift.

The judgment appealed from should be affirmed.

Chief Judge Desmond (concurring). The reason why this plaintiff cannot include in his damages anything for physicians' bills or nursing expense is that he had paid nothing for those services. …

Settled and consistent precedents provide the answer to the question posed by this appeal. Neither justice nor morality require a different answer. Diminution of damages because medical services were furnished gratuitously results in a windfall of sorts to a defendant but allowance of such items although not paid for would unjustly enrich a plaintiff.

I vote to affirm.

Fuld, J. (dissenting). It is elementary that damages in personal injury actions are awarded in order to compensate the plaintiff, but, under an established exception, the collateral source doctrine—which we recognized in Healy v. Rennert (9 N.Y.2d 202)—a wrongdoer will not be allowed to deduct benefits which the plaintiff may have received from another source. To put the matter broadly, the defendant should not be given credit for an amount of money, or its equivalent in services, received by the plaintiff from other sources. "The rationale of the collateral source doctrine in tort actions," it has been said, "is that a tort-feasor should not be allowed to escape the pecuniary consequences of his wrongful act merely because his victim has received benefit from a third party" (Note, 26 Fordham L. Rev. 372, 381).

In the *Healy* case, this court held that, if one is negligently injured by another, the damages recoverable from the latter are diminished neither (1) by the fact that the injured party has been indemnified for his loss by insurance effected by him nor (2) by the fact that his medical expenses were paid by HIP or some other health insurance plan (p. 206). In the case before us, the plaintiff suffered injuries and required medical and nursing care. He had no health insurance, but he received the necessary medical care and services from fellow doctors without being required to pay them in cash. In addition, he received physiotherapy treatments from the nurse employed by him in his office and to whom he, of course, paid a salary.

I fail to see any real difference between the situation in Healy v. Rennert and the case now before us. In neither case was the injured person burdened with any charges for the medical

……在过失责任诉讼中，损害赔偿金具有补偿性，而非惩罚性，如果面对立法机构的拒绝而改变多年的 Drinkwater 案规则，并且要求被告因原告朋友的慷慨而向原告付款，从而惩罚被告，则难谓公平。如果我们允许原告获得对其进行无偿治疗的医生服务的合理价值，则逻辑性在于原告有权获得该服务的合理价值，尽管医生仅向其收取了该价值的一小部分。该规则会产生古怪的结果，到最后只不过是要求被告向原告支付赠品的价值。

被上诉的判决应当予以维持。

Desmond 大法官（协同）。原告不能将医生账单或护理费用纳入损害赔偿金的原因是他未为这些服务付款……

稳定且一致的先例，为本上诉提出的问题提供了答案。公正和道德都不需要不同的答案。无偿提供的医疗服务导致的损害赔偿金减少造成被告获得意外收入，但许可未付款的该类项目将会使原告的行为构成不当得利。

我投票维持原判。

Fuld 法官（反对）。在人身损害诉讼中给予损害赔偿金从而对原告进行赔偿是基本考虑，但根据既定的例外，即我们在 Healy v. Rennert（9 N.Y.2d 202）案中采纳的平行来源学说，不能允许不法行为人扣除原告可能已从另一来源获得的收益。推而广之，被告不应将原告从其他来源获得的资金或等值服务记在自己账上。"侵权诉讼中的平行来源学说的基本原理在于，侵权行为人不应仅仅因为受害人从第三方获得收益就获准逃避其不法行为带来的金钱赔偿义务"（Note, 26 Fordham L. Rev. 372, 381）。

在 Healy 案中，本法院认为，如果某人因另一人的过失而被伤害，则从后者获得的损害赔偿金不能因以下事实而减少：（1）受害人生效的保险已经对其损失进行了赔偿；（2）HIP（健康保险计划）或其他健康保险计划已经支付其医疗费用（案卷第 206 页）。在我们面临的案件中，原告受伤，需要医治和护理。他没有医疗保险，但却获得了来自同事的必要医治，并且无需以现金付款。另外，他在自己的办公室获得了所雇用的护士提供的理疗，当然，他向其支付薪金。

我没有看到 Healy v. Rennert 案和我们面前的案例之间的真正差别。在两个案件中，受害人都未支付医疗费用，因此当要求被告为这些服务或相

services rendered and, accordingly, when the defendant is required to pay as "damages" for those services or their value, such damages are no less "compensatory" in the one case than in the other. Nor do I understand why a distinction should be made depending upon whether the medical services were rendered gratuitously or for a consideration. What difference should it make, either to the plaintiff or to the defendant, whether an injured plaintiff has his medical bills taken care of by an insurer or by a wealthy uncle or by a fellow doctor? Certainly, neither the uncle, who acted out of affection, nor the doctor, impelled by so-called professional courtesy, intended to benefit the tort-feasor.

The crucial question in cases such as this is whether the tort-feasor would, in fairness and justice, be given credit for the amounts, or their equivalent in services, which the plaintiff has received from some collateral source. The collateral source doctrine is not, and should not be, limited to cases where the plaintiff had previously paid consideration (in the form of insurance premiums, for instance) for the benefit of services which he receives or where there has been a payment of cash or out-of-pocket expenses. The rationale underlying the rule is that a wrongdoer, responsible for injuring the plaintiff, should not receive a windfall. Were it not for the fortuitous circumstance that the plaintiff was a doctor, he would have been billed for the medical services and the defendant would have had to pay for them. The medical services were supplied to help the plaintiff, not to relieve the defendant from any part of his liability or to benefit him. It should not matter, in reason, logic or justice, whether the benefit received was in return for a consideration or given gratuitously, or whether it represented money paid out or its equivalent in services.

The rule reflected by the decision in Drinkwater v. Dinsmore (80 N.Y. 390) is court made and, accordingly, since I believe … that it is not only "completely opposite to the majority rule," but also "unfair, illogical and unduly complex," I cannot vote for its perpetuation. Indeed, as I have already indicated, an even stronger case for its repudiation is made out by our recent decision in Healy v. Rennert (9 N.Y.2d 202, supra).

I would reverse the judgment appealed from and direct a new trial.

Judges Dye, Van Voorhis, Burke and Foster concur with Judge Froessel; Chief Judge Desmond concurs in a separate opinion; Judge Fuld dissents in an opinion.

Judgment affirmed.

70. Hunt v Severs [1994] 2 AC 350

House of Lords, United Kingdom

LORD BRIDGE

My Lords, a plaintiff who establishes a claim for damages for personal injury is entitled in English law to recover as part of those damages the reasonable value of services rendered to him

应价值支付"损害赔偿金"时,两件案例中的损害赔偿金具有同样的"补偿性"。我不理解为什么应当根据无偿还是有偿提供医疗服务进行区分。对于原告或被告来说,受伤原告的医疗费用由保险公司、有钱的叔父或同事承担有何区别?当然,慈爱的叔父或受职业礼节推动的同事,都无意使侵权行为人受益。

这个案例中的关键问题是,侵权行为人将原告从其他来源获得的资金或等值服务记在他账上是否公平和公正。平行来源学说不限于,也不应该限于以下情况:原告以前已经为所获得的服务支付报酬(例如以保险费的形式),或已经支付现金。该规则内在的基本原理是伤害原告的不法行为人不应获得意外之财。如果原告不是医生,就会为医疗服务付款,而被告也必须支付。医疗服务的提供是为了帮助原告,而不是为了使被告免除责任部分或使其受益。从道理、逻辑或公正的角度而言,所获得的收益是对价的报答还是无偿提供,抑或是代表金钱的支出还是等值服务,都无关紧要。

Drinkwater v. Dinsmore(80 N.Y. 390)案判决所反映的规则由法院制定,因此,由于我认为……它不但"与多数规则完全对立",而且"还不公平、不符合逻辑且过度复杂",所以,我不能投票赞成其继续有效。实际上,我已经指出,否定该规则更有说服力的案件是我们在 Healy v. Rennert(9 N.Y.2d 202, supra)案中作出的判决。

我宁可撤销上诉判决,并指示重审。

Dye 法官、Van Voorhis 法官、Burke 法官和 Foster 法官赞同法官 Froessel 的意见;Desmond 大法官在单独的意见中表示赞同;Fuld 法官反对。

维持原判。

70. Hunt v Severs [1994] 2 AC 350

联合王国上议院

Bridge 大法官主笔:

诸位大法官,原告主张在英格兰法上,提出人身损害赔偿的原告若能胜诉,是有权就亲友为其提供的必要的且无偿的照看服务请求被告作出合理的赔偿的。而本案中的关键争议点则是,若上述的自愿照看人是侵权者本人时,

gratuitously by a relative or friend in the provision of nursing care or domestic assistance of the kind rendered necessary by the injuries the plaintiff has suffered. The major issue which arises for determination in this appeal is whether the law will sustain such a claim in respect of gratuitous services in the case where the voluntary carer is the tortfeasor himself.

...

The law with respect to the services of a third party who provides voluntary care for a tortiously injured plaintiff has developed somewhat erratically in England. The voluntary carer has no cause of action of his own against the tortfeasor. The justice of allowing the injured plaintiff to recover the value of the services so that he may recompense the voluntary carer has been generally recognised, but there has been difficulty in articulating a consistent juridical principle to justify this result.

...

In *Cunningham v. Harrison* [1973] Q.B. 942 and *Donnelly v. Joyce* [1974] Q.B. 454 judgments were delivered by different divisions of the Court of Appeal on successive days. In *Cunningham* the wife of a severely disabled plaintiff, who had initially looked after him, had died before the trial. Lord Denning M.R. said, at pp. 951-952:

"Before dealing with I would like to consider what the position would have been if the wife had not died and had continued to look after her husband, as she had been doing. The plaintiff's advisers seem to have thought that a husband could not claim for the nursing services rendered by a wife unless the husband was legally bound to pay her for them. So, on their advice on 11 July 1972, an agreement was signed whereby the husband agreed to pay his wife £2,000 per annum in respect of her nursing services. We were told that such advice is often given by counsel in such cases as these when advising on evidence. I know the reason why such advice is given. It is because it has been said in some cases that a plaintiff can only recover for services rendered to him when he was legally liable to pay for them: see for instance *Kirkham v. Boughey* [1958] 2 Q.B. 338, 342 and *Janney v. Gentry (1966) 110 S.J. 408*. But, I think that view is much too narrow. It seems to me that when a husband is grievously injured - and is entitled to damages - then it is only right and just that, if his wife renders services to him, instead of a nurse, he should recover compensation for the value of the services that his wife has rendered. It should not be necessary to draw up a legal agreement for them. On recovering such an amount, the husband should hold it on trust for her and pay it over to her. She cannot herself sue the wrongdoer . . . but she has rendered services necessitated by the wrongdoing, and should be compensated for it. If she had given up paid work to look after him, he would clearly have been entitled to recover on her behalf; because the family income would have dropped by so much: see *Wattson v. Port of London Authority* [1969] 1 Lloyd's Rep. 95, 102, *per* Megaw J. Even though she had not been doing paid work but only domestic duties in the house, nevertheless all extra attendance on him certainly calls for

原告还有没有这样的权利?

……

在英国,关于允许就第三人为侵权案的受害者所提供的服务请求赔偿的法律的发展过程是曲折的。自愿为原告提供服务的照看者自己对于侵权人是没有诉权的。之所以要允许受害人就这种服务向被告请求赔偿,是因为这样他就能够给予自愿的照看人一定的补偿了,这就是这条规则背后的正义所在。这条规则逐渐获得了法律的认可,然而支撑其正当性的法律原则到底是什么,法院却一直很难一以贯之地阐释。

……

Cunningham v Harrison [1973] Q.B. 942 和 *Donnelly v Joyce* [1974] Q.B. 454 案的判决书是上诉法院的不同的分院做出的,且做出判决的日期前后相继。在 *Cunningham* 案中,原告严重残疾,其妻子一直在照顾他。但是在庭审前,妻子却去世了。丹宁勋爵表示(第 951-952 页):

"在我们讨论之前,我想先来谈一谈一种假设的情况:如果原告的妻子没有去世并一直照顾着她的丈夫,就如同她之前一直做的那样。原告的律师似乎认为丈夫是不能就妻子为其提供的护理服务请求损害赔偿的,除非丈夫对妻子有法定的支付义务。夫妻双方听从了律师的建议,并于 1972 年 7 月 11 日签订了一份协议,约定丈夫每年要为妻子提供的护理服务支付两千英镑。我们听说在这类案件中,律师经常会如此建议。我知道为什么律师要这么建议。那是因为在有些判例中,原告确实只能就付费服务请求损害赔偿:比如 *Kirkham v Boughey* [1958] 2 Q.B. 338, 342 and *Janney v Gentry*(1966)110 S.J. 408。然而,我认为这种看法太狭隘了。在我看来如果丈夫严重地受伤了,且也确实有权获得赔偿,那么就算是他的妻子而非专业的护士在照顾他,他妻子为其提供的服务也应该属于损害赔偿的范围。为了请求这种赔偿,夫妻双方没有任何必要先去起草一份合同。收到赔偿金后,丈夫应当作为妻子的信托受托人保管这笔金钱,然后之后再支付给妻子。妻子本身并不能起诉侵权人……然而她确实为侵权行为造成的损害提供了必要的服务,因此她是应当获得补偿的。若她因此放弃了带薪的工作来照顾丈夫,那么丈夫毋庸置疑是有权为妻子代为请求赔偿的;因此此时家庭的总收入是下降了很多的:参见 *Wattson v. Port of London Authority* [1969] 1 Lloyd's Rep. 95, compensation."

In *Donnelly v. Joyce* [1974] Q.B. 454, the injured plaintiff was a boy of six. His mother gave up her work for a period to provide necessary care for him and the disputed item in his claim related to the mother's loss of wages. The judgment of the court delivered by Megaw L.J. contains a lengthy review of the authorities, but the key passage relied on by the trial judge and the Court of Appeal in the instant case is at pp. 461-462, and reads:

"We do not agree with the proposition, inherent in Mr. Hamilton's submission, that the plaintiff's claim, in circumstances such as the present, is properly to be regarded as being, to use his phrase, 'in relation to someone else's loss,' merely because someone else has provided to, or for the benefit of, the plaintiff - the injured person - the money, or the services to be valued as money, to provide for needs of the plaintiff directly caused by the defendant's wrongdoing. The loss *is* the plaintiff's loss. The question from what source the plaintiff's needs have been met, the question who has paid the money or given the services, the question whether or not the plaintiff is or is not under a legal or moral liability to repay, are, so far as the defendant and his liability are concerned, all irrelevant. The plaintiff's loss, to take this present case, is not the expenditure of money to buy the special boots or to pay for the nursing attention. His loss is the existence of the need for those special boots or for those nursing services, the value of which for purposes of damages - for the purpose of the ascertainment of the amount of his loss - is the proper and reasonable cost of supplying those needs. That, in our judgment, is the key to the problem. So far as the defendant is concerned, the loss is not someone else's loss. It is the plaintiff's loss.

"Hence it does not matter, so far as the defendant's liability to the plaintiff is concerned, whether the needs have been supplied by the plaintiff out of his own pocket or by a charitable contribution to him from some other person whom we shall call the 'provider;' it does not matter, for that purpose, whether the plaintiff has a legal liability, absolute or conditional, to repay to the provider what he has received, because of the general law or because of some private agreement between himself and the provider; it does not matter whether he has a moral obligation, however ascertained or defined, so to do. The question of legal liability to reimburse the provider may be very relevant to the question of the legal right of the provider to recover from the plaintiff. That may depend on the nature of the liability imposed by the general law or the particular agreement. But it is not a matter which affects the right of the plaintiff against the wrongdoer."

102 一案中 Megaw 法官的意见。而就算妻子并无带薪的工作而是一直在家中进行家务劳动，她照顾丈夫也属于额外的劳动，而这种额外的劳动当然应当获得补偿。"

在 *Donnelly v Joyce* [1974] Q.B. 454 案中，6 岁的原告受伤了。其母放弃了工作来照顾他，于是他的请求赔偿的项目中包括了母亲丧失的工资。Megaw 上诉法院法官为法庭撰写的判决书用了很长的篇幅，引用了各种判例，但是一审法官和上诉法院就本案而言所依赖的最关键是在第 461 到 462 页的内容：

> 我们并不同意 Hamilton 先生在其陈述中所宣称的，原告在本案中所请求赔偿的是"他人的损失"（被告的话）：被告的侵权行为给原告造成了一些特别的需求，而别人为满足这种需求向原告提供了金钱，或者可以用金钱计算的服务。这里的损失就是原告的损失。至于原告的需求是通过什么渠道满足的、至于是谁来支付金钱或提供服务、至于原告是否负有补偿他们的道德或者法律的义务，就被告的责任而言，通通都是毫不相关的。原告的损失，以本案为例，并不是购买特殊靴子的钱或者支付特殊护理的费用。对特殊靴子的需要和特别护理的需要，这些需要存在本身就是他的损失。在确定赔偿损失金额的意义上，这些损失的数额就是满足这些需求所需要的正当且合理的费用。这在我们看来是问题关键之所在。就被告责任的角度看来，这种损失并不是他人的损失，而就是原告自己的损失。
>
> 因此，就被告对原告所负责任而言，原告是用其自己口袋里的钱来满足自己的需求，还是用别人（我们将其称为付出者）仁爱的付出来满足自己的需求，并不重要。就确定被告的责任而言，原告是否有义务要去补偿付出者，也并不重要，无论这种义务是绝对的还是有条件的，是法定的还是约定的；同样不重要的，还有他是否负有道德义务为此作出补偿，无论这种义务是多么有据可循。就付出者能否向原告请求补偿而言，原告是否具有对付出者的法律义务可能是很关键的问题。这可能取决于这个法定或约定的义务的性质。然而，就原告是否可以请求被告赔偿而言，这个问题一点也不重要。

With respect, I do not find this reasoning convincing. I accept that the basis of a plaintiff's claim for damages may consist in his need for services but I cannot accept that the question from what source that need has been met is irrelevant. If an injured plaintiff is treated in hospital as a private patient he is entitled to recover the cost of that treatment. But if he receives free treatment under the National Health Service, his need has been met without cost to him and he cannot claim the cost of the treatment from the tortfeasor. So it cannot, I think, be right to say that in all cases the plaintiff's loss is "for the purpose of damages . . . the proper and reasonable cost of supplying his needs."

...

It is nevertheless important to recognise that the underlying rationale of the English law, as all the cases before *Donnelly v. Joyce* [1974] Q.B. 454 demonstrate, is to enable the voluntary carer to receive proper recompense for his or her services and I would think it appropriate for the House to take the opportunity so far as possible to bring the law of the two countries into accord by adopting the view of Lord Denning M.R. in *Cunningham v. Harrison* [1973] Q.B. 942 that in England the injured plaintiff who recovers damages under this head should hold them on trust for the voluntary carer.

By concentrating on the plaintiff's need and the plaintiff's loss as the basis of an award in respect of voluntary care received by the plaintiff, the reasoning in *Donnelly v. Joyce* diverts attention from the award's central objective of compensating the voluntary carer. Once this is recognised it becomes evident that there can be no ground in public policy or otherwise for requiring the tortfeasor to pay to the plaintiff, in respect of the services which he himself has rendered, a sum of money which the plaintiff must then repay to him. If the present case had been brought in Scotland and the claim in respect of the tortfeasor's services made in reliance on section 8 of the Administration of Justice Act 1982, it would have been immediately obvious that such a claim was not sustainable.

The case for the plaintiff was argued in the Court of Appeal without reference to the circumstance that the defendant's liability was covered by insurance. But before your Lordships Mr. McGregor, recognising the difficulty of formulating any principle of public policy which could justify recovery against the tortfeasor who has to pay out of his own pocket, advanced the bold proposition that such a policy could be founded on the liability of insurers to meet the claim. Exploration of the implications of this proposition in argument revealed the many difficulties which it encounters. But I do not think it necessary to examine these in detail. The short answer, in my judgment, to Mr. McGregor's contention is that its acceptance would represent a novel and radical departure in the law of a kind which only the legislature may properly effect. At common law the circumstance that a defendant is contractually indemnified by a third party against a particular legal liability can have no relevance whatever to the measure of that liability.

恕我直言，我认为这种论证不能令人信服。我同意，原告请求损害赔偿的基础是其对照顾服务的需求，然而我并不同意"从什么样的来源来满足这个需求"，这是一个毫无关系的问题。如果受害人自费到医院治疗，那他可以请求赔偿医疗费。然而如果受害人是享受国家医保而获得治疗的，他的需求在他自己没有花钱的情况下就已经得到满足了，因此他并不能因为治疗的费用向侵权人请求赔偿。因此我们不能说以下这句话在任何情况下都有道理："在确定赔偿损失金额的意义上，这些损失的数额就是满足这些需求所需要的正当且合理的费用。"

……

我们有必要了解一下英格兰法律这么规定的理由是什么。在 *Donnelly v Joyce* [1974] Q.B. 454 案之前的所有判例都证明，这么规定是为了让自愿照顾者能就其提供的服务获得合理的补偿。而在我看来，上议院应该抓住机会调和这两地的法律。上议院应该采纳丹宁勋爵在 *Cunningham v Harrison* [1973] Q.B. 一案中的观点：收到赔偿金的受害人原告应当作为自愿照顾者的信托受托人来保管这笔金钱。

Donnelly v Joyce 案的核心在于明确原告的需求和原告的损失，是别人为原告提供自愿无偿的服务后要求被告向原告承担赔偿责任的原因。这样的论证由于强调了原告，使得我们的注意力没有放在补偿自愿照顾者，其实才是这种赔偿的中心意义之所在。在明确这一点之后，我们可以很清楚地看到，让侵权人就其自己为原告所提供的服务，向原告作出赔偿，是没有任何的公共政策或其他方面的正当性的。因为就算赔偿了这笔钱，最后还是会回到被告自己手中。若本案是在苏格兰提起的，且就被告付出的劳务而提起的损害赔偿的依据是1982年《司法运行法》第8条，那么我们立刻就可以看出这种诉讼理由是站不住脚的。

在上诉法院审理的阶段中，原告并没有提到被告是有保险的这一事实。然而，在诸位大法官面前，McGregor 先生虽然意识到很难找到一种公共政策原则去支持让侵权人从自己口袋里掏钱出来赔偿原告，但是却大胆地提出，让保险人来满足这样的请求，以作为这种政策的基础。如果我们想一想这种主张的后果，就会发现它会面临许多的困境。这里我就不一一讨论这些困境了。我只想简短地回答 McGregor 先生的主张：如果我们接受了他的意见，那么我们会严重偏离实在法，而这是只有立法机关才能做的事。在普通法上，被告能否通过合同让第三方代为履行某种法律责任与该种责任的衡量本身，是毫无关系的。

Section 2. Loss of Earnings

71. Ruzzi v. Butler Petroleum Company, 527 Pa. 1, 588 A.2d 1 (1991)

Supreme Court of Pennsylvania, United States

Papadakos, Justice.

...

Shockey also claims that Jarrell's testimony was contrary to the evidence. The basis of this claim is that at the time of trial Ruzzi was employed by AMG Sign Company at a less physically demanding job, but at the same salary he made before the injury. The error in this claim is that it ignores the difference between actual loss of earnings and loss of earning capacity. This court discussed the difference between these concepts as follows:

> The defendants contend that there was no evidence of impairment of earning power and that the fact that Bochar's wages were higher after the accident than before proves no deterioration of earning ability. A tortfeasor is not entitled to a reduction in his financial responsibility because, through fortuitous circumstances or unusual application on the part of the injured person, the wages of the injured person following the accident are as high or even higher than they were prior to the accident. Parity of wages may show lack of impairment of earning power if it confirms other physical data that the injured person has completely recovered from his injuries. Standing alone, however, parity of wages is inconclusive. The office worker, who loses a leg has obviously had his earning ability impaired even though he can still sit at a desk and punch a comptometer as vigorously as before. It is not the status of the immediate present which determines capacity for remunerative employment. Where permanent injury is involved, the whole span of life must be considered. Has the economic horizon of the disabled person been shortened because of the injuries sustained as the result of the tortfeasor's negligence? That is the test.

Bochar v. J.B. Martin Motors, Inc., 374 Pa. 240, 244, 97 A.2d 813, 815 (1953).... Shockey's claim is without merit, for the fact of Ruzzi's current employment at the same salary as before the injury does not, as this court explained in *Bochar,* negate his claim for a diminished earning capacity. Earning capacity has to do with the injured person's economic horizons, not his actual earnings, and the fact that Ruzzi was fortunate enough to earn as much as he had formerly earned, but at a new and less physically demanding job, does not establish that a loss of earning capacity, on these facts, is contrary to the evidence.

第二节 收入损失

71. Ruzzi v. Butler Petroleum Company, 527 Pa. 1, 588 A.2d 1 (1991)

美国宾夕法尼亚州最高法院

Papadakos 法官主笔：

……

Shockey 还声称，Jarrell 的证词与证据相反。该主张的依据是在初审期间，Ruzzi 受 AMG Sign 公司雇用，从事对身体情况要求较低的工作，但薪金与受伤前相同。该主张的错误在于忽视了实际的收入损失和收入能力损失之间的差异。本院讨论这两个概念之间的差异如下：

> 被告辩称，没有证据表明 Bochar 收入能力受损，并且 Bochar 的工资在事故后高于事故前，证明收入能力并未降低。凭借受害人的幸运或异常勤奋，事故后受害人的工资等于或高于事故前，侵权行为人无权因此减少金钱责任。工资的相等可以表明收入能力未受损，但前提是确认受害人完全恢复了其他身体指标。然而，仅仅工资相等不具决定性。失去一条腿的办公室工作人员的收入能力明显受损，即使他仍然坐在桌旁，像以前一样精力充沛地在敲击电脑键盘。当前状态不能决定有偿受雇的能力。如果涉及永久伤害，则必须考虑整个人生跨度。由于侵权行为人的过失而导致的伤害，是否缩小了伤残人士的经济视野，这才是检验标准。

Bochar v. J.B. Martin Motors, Inc., 374 Pa. 240, 244, 97 A.2d 813, 815（1953）……Shockey 的主张没有依据，因为正如本院在 Bochar 案中所解释的，Ruzzi 目前的薪金与受伤前相同并不能否定收入能力受损的主张。收入能力与受害人的经济视野有关，与实际收入无关，并且 Ruzzi 十分幸运，获得了与以前相同的收入，但这是新工作，对身体情况要求不高，上述事实不能证明收入能力受损与证据相反。

最终，Shockey 辩称，专家证词不可被采纳，因为其超出了 Jarrell 审前

Finally, Shockey contends that the expert testimony was inadmissible because it went beyond the scope of Jarrell's pretrial report. In particular, Shockey claims that although the pretrial report addresses future wage loss, it does not address diminished earning capacity, and thus, does not place Shockey on notice that the expert would testify as to diminished earning capacity. We disagree with Shockey's characterization of Jarrell's pre-trial report furnished to Shockey pursuant to pertinent discovery rules.

As stated earlier in *Bochar v. J.B. Martin Motors, Inc.*, lost earning capacity involves the question, "Has the economic horizon of the disabled person been shortened because of the injuries sustained as a result of the tortfeasor's negligence?"

Jarrell's report states that, based on his understanding of Dr. Flit's testimony, Ruzzi was permanently injured and would never again be able to perform work of the type he had performed before the accident. Instead, he would be limited to light duty work where he could frequently change positions and not lift over twenty pounds. Jarrell also stated, in the last paragraph of his report:

> It is based on AMG Sign Company's continuing willingness to provide Mr. Ruzzi with employment on an "as able to work, as light duty work is available" basis. Should that willingness cease or should AMG Sign Company go out of business, Mr. Ruzzi would have to re-enter the open labor market where he would face the well known difficulties of the unemployed handicapped. Their unemployment rate is typically twice that of the non-handicapped, and their average earnings are 54%-82% of those of the non-handicapped (Employer Attitudes Towards Hiring Persons With Disabilities, Human Resources Center publication, 1978).

At trial, Jarrell testified that "countless studies done on the earnings of an impaired handicap versus the earnings of a nonimpaired, nonhandicapped" person indicate that the handicapped person suffers a loss of 17% earning capacity.

Since lost earning capacity is the limitation of economic horizons, and since Jarrell's report describes not only the nature of Ruzzi's injuries, but also, in Jarrell's opinion, what would happen to Ruzzi were he forced to compete on an open job market, including a prediction that he would be able to earn no more than 82% of his former salary (an 18% loss of earning capacity), the testimony was within the scope of the report and it was not error to admit Jarrell's expert testimony.

The order of Superior Court is affirmed.

报告的范围。Shockey 特别表示，虽然审前报告提出了未来工资损失，但是未提出收入能力减少，因此未使 Shockey 注意到专家会证实收入能力减少。我们不同意 Shockey 对于依照相关披露规则向 Shockey 提供的 Jarrell 审前报告的描述。

如早在 Bochar v. J.B. Martin Motors, Inc. 案中就论述到的，收入能力丧失涉及以下问题："由于侵权行为人的过失而导致的伤害是否缩小了伤残人士的经济视野？"

Jarrell 的报告陈述到，根据他对 Flit 医生证词的理解，Ruzzi 永久受伤，不能再从事事故前的那种工作。他只能从事轻负荷的工作，需要经常改变姿势，不能升举超过 20 磅的物体。Jarrell 在报告的最后一段还表示：

> 这是基于 AMG Sign 公司根据"能够工作，从事轻负荷工作"的原则向 Ruzzi 先生提供工作的持续意愿。如果该意愿终止，或 AMG Sign 公司停业，Ruzzi 先生必须重新进入开放的劳务市场，面对众所周知的失业残疾人的困难。他们的失业率一般是非残疾人的两倍，平均收入是非残疾人的 54%～82%〔《雇主对于雇用残疾人的态度》（Employer Attitudes Towards Hiring Persons With Disabilities, Human Resources Center publication, 1978）〕。

在初审中，Jarrell 作证说，"有关受伤残疾人收入与未受伤非残疾人收入的无数研究"表明，残疾人遭受了收入能力 17% 的损失。

由于收入能力的丧失来自经济视野的限制，并且由于 Jarrell 的报告不但描述了 Ruzzi 受到的伤害，而且还描述了如果 Ruzzi 被迫在开放的劳务市场上竞争，Ruzzi 会遇到哪些困难，包括预测他能够获得不超过以前薪金的 82%（收入能力损失 18%），所以该证词属于报告范围，采纳 Jarrell 的专家证词并无错误。

维持高等法院的法庭命令。

72. Grayson v. Irvmar Realty Corp., 7 A.D.2d 436, 184 N.Y.S.2d 33 (1959)

Appellate Division, Supreme Court of New York, United States

Breitel, J.

The principal issue raised in this personal injury negligence case is whether the court, in permitting the jury to award substantial damages to plaintiff for impairment or frustration of her inchoate operatic career, committed error. In addition, defendant contends that the damages awarded are, in any event, excessive. Some question is also raised as to liability, but it does not merit discussion.

Plaintiff, a young woman who is engaged seriously in the study of music looking to the development of an operatic career, sustained a fractured leg and an alleged impairment of her hearing as a result of a fall on the sidewalk in front of defendant's premises. The act of negligence charged was the failure to light properly a construction sidewalk bridge. ... The jury awarded damages in the amount of $50,000.

There is no dispute that one tortiously injured may recover damages based upon the impairment of future earning capacity. There is also no dispute that the assessment of damages may be based upon future probabilities and is not confined to actual earnings prior to the accident. The unusual issue tendered in this case is whether there may be a similar assessment where the probability of future earnings is not based upon any prior actual engagement in the vocational earning of income. In that respect it is not unlike the situation in death actions where the pecuniary benefit to survivors must be determined with respect to children or very young people whose income potentiality has not yet been developed. The situation, on the other hand, is a little different, again, from that of young persons training for occupations, especially professions, where the probability of completion of training is high, and the resultant earning of at least a modal income is equally highly probable. The reason for this last difference is that in the case of persons of rare and special talents many are called but few are chosen. For those who are not chosen, the probabilities of exploiting their talents financially are minimal or totally negative. In this class would fall the musical artist, the professional athlete, and the actor.

It should be clear that one possessed of rare and special talents is entitled to recover damages for tortious injury to the development of those talents. This, too, may have a pecuniary value which is assessable, albeit without the degree of precision one would require in a commercial case. On this view, the court properly submitted to the jury the question of assessing the damages to plaintiff's operatic career, inchoate though it may have been. But, in the light of the proper distinctions, the jury's award of $50,000 was grossly excessive.

At the time of the accident plaintiff was twenty-one and had been graduated from high school. Since some undisclosed age as a child, she had studied music and singing. This included

72. Grayson v. Irvmar Realty Corp., 7 A.D.2d 436, 184 N.Y.S.2d 33 (1959)

美国纽约最高法院上诉庭

Breitel 法官主笔：

在该人身伤害过失案件中提出的主要问题是，法院允许陪审团因原告在歌剧事业上的初步发展受损或受挫而给予损害赔偿金是否存在错误。另外，被告辩称损害赔偿金超额。有关责任的一些问题也被提出，但不值得讨论。

原告是一名年轻女性，全身心投入音乐学习，希望在歌剧事业上有所发展。她在被告建筑物前的人行道上摔倒，造成腿部骨折，听力受损。受到指控的过失行为是未对人行便桥提供适当的照明……陪审团裁定损害赔偿金为5万美元。

受到侵权行为伤害的人由于未来收入能力受损，可以获得损害赔偿金，这是没有争议的；可以根据未来概率评估损害赔偿金并且不限于事故前的实际收入，这也是没有争议的。本案中提出的异常问题是，是否存在以下的类似评估：未来收入概率不是基于以前实际的职业收入。一方面，并非不同于以下死亡诉讼：幸存者获得的损害赔偿金必须基于收入潜力尚未开发的儿童或非常年轻的人；另一方面，本案又有点儿不同于以下的年轻人职业培训：完成培训的概率很高，至少获得一般收入的可能性同样很高。最后一点差异的理由在于，要求特殊天赋的情况下，许多人参与其中，但被选中的却很少。如果未选中，则在经济上开发其天赋的概率最低，或者是负数。这一类人包括音乐家、职业运动员和演员。

很明显，具有特殊才能的人有权因才能的开发受到侵权伤害而获得损害赔偿金。这也会产生可评估的金钱价值，虽然其精确程度不如商业案件所要求的那样。为此，法院适当地向陪审团提交以下问题：评估对于原告歌剧事业受损的损害赔偿金，虽然该事业尚处初期，但是根据适当的差异，陪审团裁断的5万美元过于超额。

在事故发生时，原告21岁，已经高中毕业。从证据未披露的某一童龄起，她就开始学习音乐和歌唱，包括接受5年的乐器教育。后来，一名专业声乐

five years of instrumental instruction. In the later years she had a professional teacher of voice and studied under an opera coach. When she left school she participated successively in operatic workshops. As part of her operatic studies it was necessary to learn the various foreign languages closely associated with classic opera. While engaged in her studies she made a large number of appearances, all without income, on the radio, in benefit performances, and in workshop-productions of opera. Her voice teacher and opera coach testified that she had a superior voice and, as a consequence, had a bright future, in their opinion, in the opera. There was testimony that plaintiff was preparing for a European debut.

Plaintiff sustained her injuries when she fell, catching her foot in a hole. Her leg was then fractured. At the same time her head struck the surface, as a result of which she claims she sustained an impairment of hearing. The alleged hearing impairment has largely cleared up, leaving, however, a sequela of an impairment of pitch. Although she has continued to study singing and made a number of appearances of the same character as she had made before the accident, it is claimed that the impairment of pitch has limited her performance and that this is likely to be permanent. This claim was supported by her voice teacher and by medical testimony. However, there was highly credible proof from an eminent physician selected from the court-designated medical panel, offered by defendant, to the effect that any impairment of hearing she had was due to a diseased condition which existed before the accident. The jury might well have, but did not, accept this testimony, despite still other proof that plaintiff had had ear trouble prior to the accident.

As already noted, it is undisputed that a person tortiously injured is entitled to recover for impairment of future earning capacity, without limitation to the actual earnings which preceded the accident. In death actions, and in the cases of injuries, involving very young people whose vocational potentialities have not yet been developed, the courts have allowed assessment of damages based on future, and not presently realized, earning capacity. ...

In the case of young people engaged in the study for occupations or professions requiring a great deal of preliminary or formal training the courts have also permitted the assessment of damages based on future earning potential after the training period would have been completed. And even in the case of singers, and presumably, therefore, in the case of other musical artists, some courts in other jurisdictions have had occasion to permit juries to assess damages based on future earning potential although at the time of the accident the would-be artist's career is inchoate.

On this analysis the jury in this case was very properly permitted to assess the damages with respect to plaintiff's inchoate operatic career. But the award it made was highly excessive.

It is at this point that the distinction must be made between persons who largely exploit native talents and those who exploit intensive training. It is notable that those who exploit rare and special talents may achieve exceedingly high financial rewards, but that the probability of selection for the great rewards is relatively low. On the other hand, those who, provided they have the intelligence

教师和歌剧教师对她进行指导。她离开学校后，进入了一家歌剧工作室。作为歌剧学习的一部分，有必要学习与经典歌剧密切相关的各种外语。在学习期间，她无偿参加了大量演出，包括在电台演出、慈善义演和工作室歌剧作品。她的声乐教师和歌剧教师作证说，她的嗓音非常棒，因此在歌剧事业上前途光明。有证词表明她正在准备欧洲首演。

原告摔倒后受伤，脚部陷入洞中，然后腿部骨折，同时头部撞击地面，因此原告声称听力受损。听力受损已经基本恢复，但却留下了音调受损的后遗症。虽然她继续学习歌唱，进行大量演出，角色与事故前相同，但是她声称音调受损已经限制了她的表演，并且可能会永久受损。她的声乐教师和医学证词对此予以支持。然而，法院指定的医学小组选择的卓越医生，通过被告提供的高度可信的证据表明，她的听力受损是事故前存在的疾病所致。陪审团有充分的理由接受该证词，但却并未接受，尽管还有其他证据表明原告在事故前患有耳疾。

如上所述，以下观点没有争议：遭受侵权行为伤害的人有权因未来收入能力受损而获得赔偿，不限于事故前的实际收入。在死亡诉讼和伤害案例中，非常年轻的人的职业潜能尚未开发，法院允许根据目前未实现的未来收入能力评估损害赔偿金……

在需要大量初步或正式培训进行职业学习的年轻人案件中，法院也允许根据培训期完成后的未来谋生潜力来评估损害赔偿金。即使对于歌手以及其他音乐家，其他法域的一些法院有时也允许陪审团根据未来谋生潜力评估损害赔偿金，虽然在事故发生时，未来艺术家的事业尚处于初期。

根据此分析，允许该案中的陪审团按照原告的初期歌剧事业评估损害赔偿金是非常正确的，但是裁定的金额严重超额。

正是在这一点上，必须区分依靠天赋的人和依靠强化培训的人。一方面，很明显，利用特殊天赋的人可能会获得很高的经济回报，但概率较低；另一方面，不十分依赖天赋的人，如果具有一定的智力，获得了机会，接受职业培训，则更有可能实现目标。

and opportunities, train for the more skilled occupations and professions, not so heavily dependent upon unusual native gifts, will more likely achieve their objectives.

The would-be operatic singer, or the would-be violin virtuoso, or the would-be actor, are not assured of achieving their objectives merely because they have some gifts and complete the customary periods of training. Their future is a highly speculative one, namely, whether they will ever receive recognition or the financial perquisites that result from such recognition. Nevertheless, the opportunities exist and those opportunities have an economic value which can be assessed, although, obviously, without any precision. But a jury may not assume that a young student of the opera who has certain gifts will earn the income of an operatic singer, even in the median group.

In determining, therefore, the amount to be recovered, the jury may consider the gifts attributed to plaintiff; the training she has received; the training she is likely to receive; the opportunities and the recognition she already has had; the opportunities she is likely to have in the future; the fact that even though the opportunities may be many, that the full realization of those opportunities is limited to the very few; the fact that there are many other risks and contingencies, other than accidents, which may divert a would-be vocal artist from her career; and, finally, that it is assessing directly not so much future earning capacity as the opportunities for a practical chance at such future earning capacity.

The foregoing factors to be considered must reflect substantial development in the would-be artist's career. Every gleam in a doting parent's eye and every self-delusion as to one's potentialities must be skeptically eradicated. The jury is not to assess within the limits of wishful thinking but is to assess the genuine potentialities, although not yet realized, as evidenced by objective circumstances. Thus viewed, plaintiff here was undoubtedly serious about her operatic career; but, except from her teachers, she had not achieved any spectacular or extraordinary recognition for her talents. It is not the dilettante interest that has a pecuniary value, but the genuine opportunity to engage in a serious artistic career. In this context no effort has been made to consider the possible issues, sometimes tendered, as to the compensability for artistic pursuits indulged in solely for self-enjoyment, but impaired as a result of tortious injury.

Based on the preceding discussion and the proof in this case, and allowing for the injury sustained by plaintiff to her leg, any verdict in excess of $20,000 is excessive. ...

Judgment reversed, on the law and on the facts, and a new trial granted, unless plaintiff stipulates to accept a judgment in the reduced amount of $20,000, in which event the judgment is modified in that respect and, as so modified, affirmed, with costs to defendant-appellant. Settle order on notice.

All concur except Valente and Mcnally, J.J., who concur in part and dissent in part. ...

未来的歌剧演唱家、小提琴演奏家或演员仅通过一些天赋和完整的常规培训并不能保证实现目标。他们的未来具有高度不确定性，即不能保证获得认可或由此认可而产生的经济收入。然而，机会是存在的，并且这些机会具有能够评估的经济价值，虽然并不精确。但陪审团不能认为具有某些天赋的年轻歌剧学生将获得歌剧演唱家的收入，即使是在中间水平。

因此，在确定赔偿金额时，陪审团可以考虑原告的天赋、已经接受的培训、可能将要接受的培训、已经获得的机会和认可、在未来可能获得的机会，即使机会很多，但是充分实现这些机会的情况很少。存在许多其他风险和意外（除事故外）可能会使未来的歌唱家离开她的事业。最后，未直接将这些未来收入的能力评估成使用这些能力的实际机会。

以上考虑因素必须反映未来艺术家职业的实际发展。溺爱子女的父母尚未实施的想法以及个人潜能的每种自欺都必须排除。陪审团不评估主观愿望，而是评估客观情况证明的真实潜力，虽然尚未实现。这样看来，原告无疑十分认真地对待自己的歌剧前途，但除了她的教师外，她尚未获得对其才能的特殊称赞。具有经济价值的并非是业余爱好，而是从事专业艺术工作的真正机会。在该背景下，有时会提出以下尚未考虑的问题：完全出于自我享受却由于侵权行为而受损的艺术追求的可补偿性。

根据上述讨论和本案证据以及原告的腿伤，任何超过2万美元的裁断都是超额的……

依据法律和事实，撤销原判，发回重审，除非原告保证接受减少到2万美元的判决。在此情况下判决作相应修改，修改后判决被维持，并承担被告（上诉人）的费用。待原告通知后确定法庭命令。

全部同意，除Valente法官和Mcnally法官外，他们部分同意，部分反对……

73. Pickett v British Rail Engineering Ltd [1980] AC 136

House of Lords, United Kingdom

LORD WILBERFORCE

My Lords, this appeal raises three questions as to the amount of damages which ought to have been awarded to Mr. Ralph Henry Pickett ("the deceased") against his employer, the respondent, for negligence and/or breach of statutory duty. From 1949 to 1974 Mr. Pickett was working for the respondent in the construction of the bodies of railway coaches, which work involved contact with asbestos dust. In 1974 he developed symptoms which proved to be of mesothelioma of the lung, of which he later died. On July 14, 1975, he issued a writ against the respondent claiming damages for personal injuries or physical harm. The respondent admitted liability but contested the issue of quantum of damages. The case came for trial before Stephen Brown J. who on October 12, 1976, awarded damages under various heads. Those in issue in this appeal were three: (1) £7,000 by way of general damages in respect of pain, suffering and loss of amenities; (2) £787.50 as interest on the £7,000 at 9 per cent. from the service of the writ; (3) £1,508.88 as a net sum in respect of loss of earnings. This sum was based on a finding that the deceased's expectation of life had been reduced to one year from the date of trial, and the loss of earnings related to that period, i.e. the period of likely survival. The judge also awarded £500 for loss of expectation of life, and the total for which he gave judgment was £14,947.64. Mr. Pickett appealed to the Court of Appeal against this judgment, but before the appeal was heard he died. An order to carry on the proceedings was made in favour of his widow as administratrix of his estate. The appeal was heard in November 1977. The Court of Appeal did not award any sum for loss of earnings beyond the survival period but increased the general damages award to £10,000, without interest. The administratrix now appeals to this House contending that a much larger amount ought to have been awarded in respect of loss of future earnings. She also claims that interest should be awarded on the general damages. The respondent appeals against the award of £10,000 general damages.

In 1974, when his symptoms became acute, the deceased was a man of 51 with an excellent physical record. He was a champion cyclist of Olympic standard, he kept himself very fit and was a non-smoker. He was leading an active life and cycled to work every day. He had a wife and two children. There was medical evidence at the trial as to his condition and prospects, which put his then expectation of life at one year: this the judge accepted. There can be no doubt that but for his exposure to asbestos dust in his employment he could have looked forward to a normal period of continued employment up to retiring age. That exposure, for which the respondent accepts liability, has resulted in this period being shortened to one year. It seems, therefore, strange and unjust that his claim for loss of earnings should be limited to that one year (the survival period) and that he should recover nothing in respect of the years of which he has been deprived (the lost years). But

73. Pickett v British Rail Engineering Ltd [1980] AC 136

联合王国上议院

Wilberforce 大法官主笔：

诸位大法官，本案涉及三个问题，这些问题关系到 Ralph Henry Pickett（死者）先生可以向他的雇主（即被上诉人。因为被上诉人的过失，或者因为被上诉人违反法定义务而导致对死者的侵权行为的发生）请求多少钱的损害赔偿金。自 1949 年起到 1974 年为止，Pickett 先生的工作是为被上诉人制造火车车厢，这个工作会接触到石棉尘埃。在 1974 年，死者身上开始出现一些症状，这些症状证明他罹患了肺部间质瘤，他最后也死于该疾病。在 1975 年 7 月 14 日，他起诉被上诉人，请求人身损害赔偿。被上诉人承认其负有责任，但是却不同意损害赔偿金的数额。该案一审由 Stephen Brown 法官审理，其于 1976 年 10 月 12 日判决被告须根据各种事项对原告作出损害赔偿。这些事项中，在本次上诉中有争议的有以下三点：（1）由原告遭受的痛苦和失去的生活中的美好事物产生的一般赔偿金 7 000 英镑；（2）从被告接到传票之日起按照年息 9% 计算前述 7 000 英镑支付的利息 787.5 英镑；（3）原告丧失的净收入 1 508.88 英镑。这个丧失的净收入的数额，来源于法院认定死者的预期寿命已经被缩短到庭审之日起的一年内，而这个丧失的净收入就是指他在可能的生存期内的收入。法官还判决支付给原告 500 英镑，以赔偿其失去的预期寿命；而法官支持的总赔偿额则是 14 947.65 英镑。Pickett 先生不满该判决，上诉到上诉法院，然而在上诉法院开始审理前，他就去世了。上诉法院决定由他的遗孀（也就是他的遗产管理人）替代他的位置，并继续诉讼程序。上诉法院在 1977 年 11 月审理了该案的上诉。上诉法院没有判决被告支付原告预计在其生存期之外丧失的收入，但是却将一般赔偿金提升到 1 万英镑，也没有判决被告支付利息。死者的遗产管理人现在向上议院上诉，请求就原告未来丧失的收入，给予更多的赔偿。她还请求被告应该支付一般赔偿金的利息。被上诉人也因不满 1 万英镑的一般赔偿金而上诉。

1974 年，死者的症状开始加剧前，他是个 51 岁的身体非常健康的人。那时他是奥运标准水平的冠军自行车运动员，健身，而且从不吸烟。他生活积极，每日骑行上班。他有一个妻子两个孩子。医疗证据在一审庭审中证明根据他的现状和对未来的预测，他的预期寿命只有一年了，一审法官采信了这一点。如果不是因为在工作中暴露在石棉尘埃下，他完全有希望继续工作到退休为止，这一点也是没有争议的。被告对他只能活 1 年一事，应该承担责任，因为这完全是因为他被暴露在石棉尘埃中。他对收入丧失的损害赔偿请求，被限制在了 1 年内（他的生存期）；对于他失去的日子，他不能就丧失的收入获得任何赔偿，这看起来奇怪而又不公。然而这就是一审法官和上诉法院的

this is the result of authority binding on the judge and the Court of Appeal: *Oliver v. Ashman* [1962] 2 Q.B. 210. The present is, in effect, an appeal against that decision.

Oliver v. Ashman is part of a complex of law which has developed piecemeal and which is neither logical nor consistent. Judges do their best to make do with it but from time to time cases appear, like the present, which do not appeal to a sense of justice. I shall not review in any detail the state of the authorities for this was admirably done by Holroyd Pearce L.J. in *Oliver v. Ashman*. The main strands in the law as it then stood were (1) the Law Reform (Miscellaneous Provisions) Act 1934 which abolished the old rule actio personalis moritur cum persona and provided for the survival of causes of action in tort for the benefit of the victim's estate. (2) The decision of this House in *Rose v. Ford* [1937] A.C. 826 that a claim for loss of expectation of life survived under the Act of 1934, and was not a claim for damages based on the death of a person and so barred at common law: see *Admiralty Commissioners v. S.S. Amerika (Owners)* [1917] A.C. 38. (3) The decision of this House in *Benham v. Gambling* [1941] A.C. 157 that damages for loss of expectation of life could only be given up to a conventional figure, then fixed at £200. (4) The Fatal Accidents Acts under which proceedings may be brought for the benefit of dependants to recover the loss caused to those dependants by the death of the breadwinner. The amount of this loss is related to the probable future earnings which would have been made by the deceased during "lost years." This creates a difficulty. It is assumed in the present case, and the assumption is supported by authority, that if an action for damages is brought by the victim during his lifetime, and either proceeds to judgment or is settled, further proceedings cannot be brought after his death under the Fatal Accidents Acts. If this assumption is correct, it provides a basis, in logic and justice, for allowing the victim to recover for earnings lost during his lost years. This assumption is based upon the wording of section 1 of the Act of 1846 (now section 1 of the Act of 1976) and is not supported by any decision of this House. It cannot however be challenged in this appeal, since there is before us no claim under the Fatal Accidents Acts. I think, therefore, that we must for present purposes act upon the basis that it is well founded, and that if the present claim, in respect of earnings during the lost years, fails, it will not be possible for a fresh action to be brought by the deceased's dependants in relation to them.

With this background, *Oliver v. Ashman* [1962] 2 Q.B. 210 may now be considered. I shall deal with it on authority and on principle. …

…

As to principle, the passage which best summarises the underlying reasons for the decision in *Oliver v. Ashman* [1962] 2 Q.B. 210 is the following *per* Willmer L.J. at p. 240:

> "… what has been lost by the person assumed to be dead is the opportunity to enjoy what he would have earned, whether by spending it or saving it. Earnings

判决结果，他们这么判决是因为受到一个判例的约束：*Oliver v Ashman* [1962] 2 Q.B. 210。这么看来，本次上诉针对的，其实是这个判例。

　　Oliver v Ashman 是一系列慢慢发展起来的实在法体系中的一个判例，这些体系并无逻辑，而且内部也缺乏融惯性。法官们只能竭尽所能地凑合着使用这个体系。然而时不时地还是会有类似本案这样的案件发生，这些案件如果用这个体系来判决会不符合人们的正义感。在这里我就不一一回顾这个问题的法律渊源了。Holroyd Pearce 上诉法院法官在 *Oliver v Ashman* 案的判决中已经很出色地完成了这个工作。当时，调整这个问题的主要的法律有：第一，1934 年《法律改革法（杂项法）》。该法废除了"人死则诉权消灭"的旧规则，允许为了死者遗产的利益，上诉的诉权继续存在。第二，上议院在 *Rose v Ford* [1937] A.C. 826 案中的判决。该判决确定因为前述 1934 年《法律改革法（杂项法）》的存在，为"预期寿命的丧失"而提起诉讼，不因死者的死亡而消灭，且该诉讼并非是为了死亡赔偿金，因此该诉讼并不会在普通法上被禁止：参见 *Admiralty Commissioners v S.S. Amerika (Owners)* [1917] A.C. 38。第三，上议院在 *Benham v Gambling* [1941] A.C. 157 案中的判决。该判决确定对预期寿命损失的赔偿数额，应该被限制在一个公认的数额内，当时确定这个数额为 200 英镑。第四，《死亡事故法》。该法规定死者的被供养人有权请求因为抚养者的死亡而丧失的收入。这个丧失的收入的数额是指死者在"失去的岁月"中可能获得的未来收入。这里有个困境：因为在这种情况下，有人认为（这种观点其实有实在法支持）若侵权行为的受害人在其生存期已经提起了损害赔偿请求的诉讼，无论该诉讼的结果最后是判决还是调解，根据《死亡事故法》，在他死后别人都不能就其死亡再提起诉讼。如果这种看法是正确的，那么允许受害人就其在"失去的岁月"中丧失的收入请求赔偿，就是有依据的，是有逻辑而正义的。这种想法是基于对 1846 年的《死亡事故法》的第 1 条（对应现行的 1976 年《死亡事故法》第 1 条）的解读，然而这种解读并没有上议院作出的判例来支持。然而在现在的上诉案件中，这种看法不应该被否定，因为我们审理的并不是依据《死亡事故法》而提起的诉讼。因此，我认为就本案而言我们应该认同这种看法是正确的；而且如果在本案中，对在丧失的日子中丧失的收入的赔偿请求没有得到支持，那么死者的被扶养人是不能再提出新的诉讼来请求对这部分损失进行赔偿的。

　　在这种背景下，我们可以来讨论 *Oliver v Ashman* [1962] 2 Q.B. 210 这个判例了。我会依据实在法和原则来讨论它……

　　　　……

　　就原则来说，最好的解释 *Oliver v Ashman* [1962] 2 Q.B. 210 一案背后的法理的文字，是 Willmer 上诉法院法官在 240 页撰写的：

　　　　……我们假定已经死亡的这个人所失去的其实是他享受自己挣来的

themselves strike me as being of no significance without reference to the way in which they are used. To inquire what would have been the value to a person in the position of this plaintiff of any earnings which he might have made after the date when ex hypothesi he will be dead strikes me as a hopeless task."

Or as Holroyd Pearce L.J. put it, at p. 230: "... what is lost is an expectation, not the thing itself."

My Lords, I think that these are instinctual sentences, not logical propositions or syllogisms - none the worse for that because we are not in the field of pure logic. It may not be unfair to paraphrase them as saying: "Nothing is of value except to a man who is there to spend or save it. The plaintiff will not be there when these earnings hypothetically accrue: so they have no value to him." Perhaps there are additional strands, one which indeed Willmer L.J. had earlier made explicit, that the whole process of assessment is too speculative for the courts to undertake; another that the only loss is a subjective one - an emotion of distress. but if so I would disagree with them. Assumptions, chances, hypotheses enter into most assessments, and juries had, we must suppose, no difficulties with them: the judicial approach, however less robust, can manage too. And to say that what calls for compensation is injured feelings does not provide an answer to the vital question which is whether, in addition to this subjective element, there is something objective which has been lost.

But is the main line of reasoning acceptable? Does it not ignore the fact that a particular man, in good health, and sound earning, has in these two things an asset of present value quite separate and distinct from the expectation of life which every man possesses? Compare him with a man in poor health and out of a job, is he not, and not only in the immediate present, a richer man? Is he not entitled to say, at one moment I am a man with existing capability to earn well for 14 years; the next moment I can only earn less well for one year? and why should he be compensated only for the immediate reduction in his earnings and not for the loss of the whole period for which he has been deprived of his ability to earn them? To the argument that "they are of no value because you will not be there to enjoy them" can he not reply, "yes they are: what is of value to me is not only my opportunity to spend them enjoyably, but to use such part of them as I do not need for my dependants, or for other persons or causes which I wish to support. If I cannot do this, I have been deprived of something on which a value - a present value - can be placed"?

I do not think that the problem can be solved by describing what has been lost as an "opportunity" or a "prospect" or an "expectation." Indeed these words are invoked both ways - by the Lords Justices as denying a right to recover (on grounds of remoteness, intangibility or speculation), by those supporting the appellant's argument as demonstrating the loss of some real asset of true value. The fact is that the law sometimes allows damages to be given for the loss of

钱的机会，他享受的方式可能是花掉它们，也可能是把它们存起来。然而这些他所挣得的钱如果不是拿来用，则在我看来就并不是什么重要的东西了。像原告这样的人很可能在未来的某个日期死去，然而他如果不死本来是可以挣到一些钱的。但是我却实在是看不出来这些钱对死后的他有什么价值。

或者就像 Holroyd Pearce 上诉法院法官在 230 页所说的："失去的是对事物的期望，而不是该事物本身。"

诸位大法官，我认为以上的说法其实是出于本能的，而非逻辑命题或者推理。当然，不是逻辑命题或者推理也无伤大雅，因为我们本就不是在一个纯粹逻辑的领域。我想我可以这么翻译一下他们的话："只有能花或者能存的东西，对一个人才是有价值的。原告对他这些理论上能挣得的收入并不能做这些事情，这样这些收入对他就没有价值。"当然也许还有额外的理由来支持这个说法，比如 Willmer 上诉法院法官之前明确提到的，评估这种损失的程序对法院来说太不确定了，法院没法完成这种工作；另一个理由则是这种损失是一种主观的损失，是一种精神损害。对于这种额外的理由我是无法赞同的。假设、机会、猜测在大部分的评估中都会存在，而且我们必须承认这些东西并没有对陪审团带来什么困难。法官来做这件事，就算有些不如人意，也并不是不可以。另外，要求赔偿的其实是受伤的情感，这并没有回答一个关键的问题：除主观的成分外，是不是有什么客观的东西其实也损失了？

（我们刚驳斥了那些额外的理由）那么主要的理由是否站得住脚呢？一个有可靠收入的健康人，就其未来的健康和未来收入其实有一种可以折现的价值；而这种人人都有的现值和预期寿命，难道是一回事吗？将这么一个人和一个失业而虚弱的人相比，难道不能说前者更富有，而且不仅仅是当下更富有吗？难道他不能说："之前我是一个有能力好好挣 14 年钱的人；之后我就只能挣得很少了，还只能挣 1 年了？"凭什么他只能就他即刻减少的收入获得赔偿，而不能就其被剥夺挣钱能力的整个期间的收入获得赔偿？对于那种"这些东西对你没有价值，因为你没法享用他们"的说法，难道他不能这么回应吗？"这些东西对我当然有价值：对我有价值的并不是我开开心心地花掉他们的机会，而是将那些我自己不用的部分用到我所抚养的人身上，或者用到其他人身上，或者用到我所支持的事业上。如果我不能做这些事了，我当然被剥夺了某些对我很有价值的东西，有现值的东西"。

有人觉得把原告的损失描述成"机会""前景"或者"预期"一类的词汇就能解决这里的问题，我认为并不能。其实正反两方都在用这些词汇实现自己的目的：上议院的大法官们用这些词汇来拒绝原告的这种赔偿请求（基于这些词

things so described (e.g., *Chaplin v. Hicks* [1911] 2 K.B. 786), sometimes it does not. It always has to answer a question which in the end can hardly be more accurately framed than as asking, "Is the loss of this something for which the claimant should and reasonably can be compensated?"

The respondent, in an impressive argument, urged upon us that the real loss in such cases as the present was to the victim's dependants and that the right way in which to compensate them was to change the law (by statute, judicially it would be impossible) so as to enable the dependants to recover their loss independently of any action by the victim. There is much force in this, and no doubt the law could be changed in this way. But I think that the argument fails because it does not take account, as in an action for damages account must be taken, of the interest of the victim. Future earnings are of value to him in order that he may satisfy legitimate desires, but these may not correspond with the allocation which the law makes of money recovered by dependants on account of his loss. He may wish to benefit some dependants more than, or to the exclusion of, others - this (subject to family inheritance legislation) he is entitled to do. He may not have dependants, but he may have others, or causes, whom he would wish to benefit, for whom he might even regard himself as working. One cannot make a distinction, for the purposes of assessing damages, between men in different family situations.

There is another argument, in the opposite sense - that which appealed to Streatfeild J. in *Pope v. D. Murphy & Son Ltd.* [1961] 1 Q.B. 222. Why, he asked, should the tortfeasor benefit from the fact that as well as reducing his victim's earnings capacity he has shortened his victim's life? Good advocacy but unsound principle, for damages are to compensate the victim not to reflect what the wrongdoer ought to pay.

My Lords, in the case of the adult wage earner with or without dependants who sues for damages during his lifetime, I am convinced that a rule which enables the "lost years" to be taken account of comes closer to the ordinary man's expectations than one which limits his interest to his shortened span of life. The interest which such a man has in the earnings he might hope to make over a normal life, if not saleable in a market, has a value which can be assessed. A man who receives that assessed value would surely consider himself and be considered compensated - a man denied it would not. and I do not think that to act in this way creates insoluble problems of assessment in other cases. In that of a young child (cf. *Benham v. Gambling* [1941] A.C. 157, neither present nor future earnings could enter into the matter: in the more difficult case of adolescents just embarking upon the process of earning (cf. *Skelton v. Collins* (1966) 115 C.L.R. 94) the value of "lost" earnings might be real but would probably be assessable as small.

There will remain some difficulties. In cases, probably the normal, where a man's actual dependants coincide with those for whom he provides out of the damages he receives, whatever they obtain by inheritance will simply be set off against their own claim. If on the other hand this coincidence is lacking, there might be duplication of recovery. To that extent injustice may be

汇反应出的"遥远性""无形性"和"猜测性"）；而支持上诉人的一方则因此认为其失去了某种确实有价值的真正的财产。而事实上法律有时候允许就这些不确定的损失请求损害赔偿［比如 *Chaplin v Hicks*（1911）2 K.B. 786］，而有时候又不允许。这样，我们就必须要回答一个问题，这个问题最准确的问法是："原告失去的这个东西，是不是应该获得补偿而且能够合理地得到补偿？"

被上诉人提出了一种令人印象深刻的观点。他向我们指出在这种情况下真正遭受损失的其实是受害人所抚养之人，因此正确的做法应该是修改成文法而不是通过判例改变规则，以使这些被抚养人能独立于受害人去请求损害赔偿。这种说法很有道理，而且毫无疑问法律就是可以这么改。然而这种说法是站不住脚的，因为它没能考虑到受害人的利益，而这在损害赔偿案件中是当然应该考虑的。未来收入对于受害人是有价值的，因为他可以用其满足自己的合法的愿望，但是他分配的方式可能并不同于法律分配"其被抚养人因为他丧失了未来收入，而获得的赔偿金"的方式。他可能希望给某个被抚养人多一些，不给某个被抚养人任何东西，这些都是法律所许可他做的（当然要受到继承法的限制）。他可能没有被抚养人，但是可能想帮助其他人或促进某些事业，甚至其工作的目标就是这些。在计算赔偿金时，我们不应该区分不同的家庭情况。

有另外一种反驳，Streatfeild 法官在 *Pope v D. Murphy & Son Ltd.* [1961] 1 Q.B. 222 案中非常喜欢这种反驳。他问到，凭什么我们要允许侵权人在受害人的赚钱能力已经减少的情况下，还要因为其寿命的缩短而得利？这是个很好的反驳，但是却并不成立。因为损害赔偿金是用来填补受害人的损害的，而不是用来反映侵权人应该赔多少的。

诸位大法官，当一个成年的工薪族在他生存期间提起损害赔偿请求时，无论他有没有被抚养人，我都认为那种将他"失去的岁月"列入考量因素的规则，比只允许他就被缩短了的余生请求赔偿的制度，要更接近常人的预期。一个人在能过正常生活时的收入对他是有利益的。这种利益可能不能拿到市场上去交易，但是一定是具有可以被评估的价值的。一个人若能获得这种价值，则他自己和旁人都会认为他获得了补偿。如果拒绝认定他这种价值，则他就没有获得补偿。我同样不认为这么做会产生别的案件中的那种不能解决的无法评估的问题。当受害人是个孩子时［参见 *Benham v Gambling*（1941）A.C. 157］，受害人现在的收入或者未来的收入都不能作为损害赔偿的考量因素；对于更加复杂的涉及刚开始挣钱的青少年的案件［参考 *Skelton v Collins*（1966）115 C.L.R. 94］，受害人所丧失的收入，可能是有价值的，但是数额却是微小的。

我们的做法还是会留下一些问题。很可能是多数的情况：一个人所抚养的人正好就是他希望用赔偿金来帮助的人，那么这些被抚养人通过继承得到的金钱就会和他们以自己的名义提起的损害赔偿请求相抵销。然而如果是相反的情况，就是说以上两种人并不重合时，就可能出现双重赔偿的问题。双

caused to the wrongdoer. But if there is a choice between taking a view of the law which mitigates a clear and recognised injustice in cases of normal occurrence, at the cost of the possibility in fewer cases of excess payments being made, or leaving the law as it is, I think that our duty is clear. We should carry the judicial process of seeking a just principle as far as we can, confident that a wise legislator will correct resultant anomalies.

Section 3. Non-Pecuniary Losses

74. Walters v. Hitchcock, 237 Kan. 31, 697 P.2d 847 (1985)

Supreme Court of Kansas, United States

McFarland, J. This is a medical malpractice action wherein plaintiff Lillian K. Walters received a $2,000,000 damage award against defendant C. Thomas Hitchcock, M.D. The defendant physician appeals from the jury's verdict and certain pretrial and posttrial rulings of the district court.

The facts may be summarized as follows. In December, 1979, a lump on the neck of Lillian Walters was discovered by her family physician. Mrs. Walters was, at the time, approximately 32 years of age, married, with four minor children. She was not employed outside the home. The family physician conducted a number of tests and advised her to consult with a surgeon. Mrs. Walters was seen by defendant Hitchcock, a surgeon, on January 7, 1980. As a result of the prior testing and his physical examination of her, Dr. Hitchcock recommended surgical removal of diseased areas of the thyroid gland. There were indications of a possibly malignant condition. Surgery was scheduled for January 22, 1980. Mrs. Walters was advised the operation was a relatively low risk procedure with an anticipated three-day hospital stay and a small residual scar.

The operation proceeded in what appeared at the time to be a routine manner. Specimens were sent to the pathology laboratory and no malignancy was detected. The patient was sutured and sent to the recovery room. One day later. Mrs. Walters' condition rapidly deteriorated. Her head ballooned in size, she became blind and suffered extreme respiratory distress. She was taken to the intensive care unit where a breathing tube was inserted. Shortly thereafter, Dr. Hitchcock was advised by the hospital pathology department that a one inch by one and one-half inch piece of esophagus tissue was connected to the thyroid specimen sent to the laboratory during surgery. Mrs. Walter's wound was now badly infected. She was taken to surgery. Dr. Hitchcock reopened the wound and observed a significant hole in the left front portion of her esophagus. He concluded that repair was not possible and sewed the esophagus shut—thereby closing it permanently.

At this point feeding was possible only through a tube inserted directly into Mrs. Walters' stomach. She regained her vision. Numerous hospitalizations and surgical procedures followed.

重赔偿确实可能对侵权人不公。然而我们面临这两种选择时，要么我们采取这种法律的观点，这种观点在一般情况下能减少显而易见的不公正，但是在少数的情况下可能会造成过度的赔偿；要么我们不让实在法维持原状。在这两种选择面前，我们该选哪一种，那是显而易见的。我们需要用私法程序来竭尽所能地寻找一种正义的原则；对在特别反常的情况下适用该原则造成的问题，我们应该相信立法者会改正它们。

第三节 非金钱损失

74. Walters v. Hitchcock, 237 Kan. 31, 697 P.2d 847 (1985)

美国堪萨斯州最高法院

McFarland 法官主笔：

这是一起医疗事故诉讼。原告 Lillian K. Walters 获得法院判决被告 C. Thomas Hitchcock 医学博士赔偿 200 万美元的损害赔偿金。作为医生的被告，不服陪审团的裁断以及联邦地区法院的某些审前和审后裁定，提出上诉。

本案的事实概述如下。1979 年 12 月，Lillian Walters 的家庭医生发现她的颈部出现一个肿块。Walters 夫人当时大约 32 岁，已婚，育有 4 个未成年孩子。她从未在外工作。家庭医生进行了大量检查，建议她咨询外科医生。Walters 夫人在 1980 年 1 月 7 日由被告外科医生 Hitchcock 进行诊断。根据之前的检查和对她进行的身体检查，Hitchcock 医生建议进行外科手术去除甲状腺上的病区，因为有迹象表明可能是恶性肿瘤。手术定于 1980 年 1 月 22 日进行。他告诉 Walters 夫人手术风险很低，预计住院 3 天，术后仅会留下很小的疤痕。

手术过程似乎十分正常。样本送至病理实验室，未发现恶性肿瘤。伤口缝合后，患者被送至加护病房。一天后，Walters 夫人的病情急剧恶化。她的头部开始膨胀，眼睛失明，呼吸极其困难。她被送至重症监护室，插入呼吸管。此后不久，医院病理室告知 Hitchcock 医生，尺寸为 1 英寸 ×1.5 英寸的食管组织与手术期间送至实验室的甲状腺样本连在一起。Walters 夫人的伤口严重感染。她进行了外科手术。Hitchcock 医生再次打开了伤口，看到食管左前部有一个大洞。他断定不可能修复，因此将食管缝合，从而使其永久闭锁。

Ultimately, colon interposition surgery was performed which involved making a sort of bypass esophagus from a portion of Mrs. Walters' colon. Additional facts relative to Mrs. Walters' condition and the quality of her life will be set forth in the discussion of the issue relative to the amount of damages awarded herein.

Mrs. Walters brought this action against Dr. Hitchcock based upon negligence in cutting into the esophagus and in failing to make prompt repair thereof. She sought $4,000,000 in damages. Dr. Hitchcock denied negligence and blamed the injury to the esophagus on the abnormal physiology of Mrs. Walters. The jury awarded Mrs. Walters $2,000,000 in damages and Dr. Hitchcock appeals therefrom.

The first issue on appeal concerns alleged misconduct of plaintiff's counsel during closing argument. In his closing argument plaintiff's counsel stated: "Who would sell their esophagus for $4 million? I would not sell mine."

Defendant contends this constitutes a prohibited "golden rule" argument. This term relates to arguments of counsel that jurors should place themselves in the position of the plaintiff. Such arguments are usually improper and may constitute reversible error. See 75 Am. Jur. 2d., Trial §282, pp. 357-358.

Plaintiff argues the remarks were not asking the jurors to place themselves in plaintiff's shoes, and were merely hypothetical in nature.

The remarks actually span two categories. The comment commencing "Who would sell. ..." is, we believe, a fair argument relative to claimed damages and is not a "golden rule" argument. The comment that counsel would not sell his esophagus for that sum is testimonial in nature as it is a statement of counsel's personal opinion. This is an improper argument. Does this improper comment constitute reversible error? We believe not. To constitute reversible error there must be a likelihood that the improper remarks changed the result of the trial. We have examined the record and conclude that, in the totality of the circumstances, the improper comment constituted only harmless error. ...

For his final issue, defendant challenges the size of the verdict. In his brief defendant states:

In advancing this argument, the defendant is definitely aware of the long line of Kansas cases on the subject and the guidelines that have evolved in those cases. The defendant realizes that the trial court will not be reversed in an order denying new trial *unless* the amount of the verdict, in light of the evidence, shocks the conscience of the appellate court.

Defendant, in support of his argument that the verdict was excessive, directs our attention to the following:

Plaintiff's medical bills by the time of trial were approximately $59,000.

2. There was no claim nor was the jury instructed with regard to lost wages or diminished future earning capacity as Mrs. Walters was not employed during the course of her 19-year

此时 Walters 夫人只能通过直接插入胃部的导管进食。她的视力恢复了。随后是长时间的住院治疗和大量外科手术。最后实施的是结肠间置术，也就是使用 Walters 夫人部分结肠构造一个迂回食管。有关 Walters 夫人的病情和生命质量的其他事实将在讨论损害赔偿金金额时陈述。

Walters 夫人起诉 Hitchcock 医生，基于因过失切开食管，并且未能及时修复。她索赔 400 万美元。Hitchcock 否认过失，将食管伤害归咎于 Walters 夫人的异常生理。陪审团裁定 Walters 夫人获得 200 万美元损害赔偿金，Hitchcock 医生提出上诉。

上诉的第一个争议点是所谓的原告律师在终结辩论时的不当行为。在终结辩论时，原告律师说道："谁愿意为 400 万美元卖掉食管？我不愿意卖我的。"

被告辩称，这构成了被禁止的"金箴"型辩论（Golden Rule Argument）。该术语涉及律师的以下观点：陪审员应该将其自身置于原告的位置上。这种观点通常是不适当的，可能会构成可撤销判决错误。（参见 75 Am. Jur. 2d., Trial §282, pp.357–358.）

原告辩称，以上表述并非请求陪审员将其自身置于原告的位置上，在本质上仅仅是假设。

这些表述实际上涉及两个方面。我们认为，开始的"谁愿意……"涉及所请求损害赔偿金的公平争辩，不是"金科玉律"型争辩。律师不愿为 400 万美元卖掉他的食管在性质上属于证明书，因为它表明律师的个人意见。这是不当辩论。该不当辩论是否会构成可撤销判决错误？我们认为不会。构成可撤销判决错误的条件是必须存在不当言论改变审判结果的可能性。我们检查了案卷，认为总体说来，该不当评论仅构成无害错误……

关于最后的争议，被告质疑裁断的金额。在其摘要中，被告表示：

在提出本论点时，被告明确知悉有关该主题的堪萨斯州的大量案例以及这些案例中的指导方针。被告意识到，初审法院不会撤销拒绝重审的命令，除非根据证据，裁定的金额震惊了上诉法院的良心。

被告为了支撑其裁断过当的观点，请我们注意以下因素：

1. 截至初审时，原告的医疗账单金额约为 59 000 美元。

2. 在工资损失或未来收入能力受损方面，未提出索赔，陪审团也未得到指示，因为 Walters 夫人在 19 年的婚姻期间未曾外出工作。

marriage.

3. The repair surgery and reconstruction by colon interposition were working properly at the time of trial, and no further surgery, with respect to the surgical complication that occurred during the thyroidectomy, was contemplated. . . . No further evidence was presented regarding future medical expenses.

The evidence herein bears out that medical science has done all that it can do to alleviate plaintiff's condition and no further surgery is contemplated, although the same is not ruled out. This does not mean the damage done to Mrs. Walters has been undone and that she has been restored to her previous condition. It simply means her condition cannot be helped by further surgery or treatment. The substitute esophagus fashioned from a part of Mrs. Walters' colon is, apparently, functioning as well as can be expected but that level of function is a source of permanent problems for Mrs. Walters. When she swallows, food does not automatically go to her stomach. It piles up in grotesque bulges in her throat and upper chest. It is necessary for her to manually massage the bulges downward to force the food to her stomach. The process is physically painful. As there is no valve to keep the contents of her stomach from traveling back up the makeshift esophagus, she cannot lie flat and must remain in a position where gravity will keep the contents of her stomach in place. Her condition is embarrassing, distasteful to persons around her, and a major obstacle to leading a normal life. She has serious ongoing digestive problems. At the time of trial her life expectancy was 41.9 years. The years between Mrs. Walters' injury and attainment of her present level of functioning were a nightmare of pain, disability, hospitalizations and surgical procedures. She has severe disfiguring scars on her neck and torso. Many activities, such as eating and sitting, continue to be painful.

After having reviewed the record, we conclude our collective conscience are not shocked by the size of the verdict herein.

The judgment is affirmed.

Schroeder, C.J., dissenting:

The magnitude of the verdict in this case is the result of trial error and what purports to be misconduct of the jurors. ...

By reason of the ... trial court errors and speculation on the part of the jurors, the magnitude of the verdict in this case demonstrates *prejudice on its face.* In light of the evidence it shocks my conscience.

The plaintiff, Lillian K. Walters, at the time of trial had a life expectancy of 41.9 years. Her medical bills at the time of trial were approximately $59,000. She made no claim for lost-earning capacity, or diminished earning capacity; no evidence of future surgery or medical expenses was presented. The $2 million verdict included $1,940,000 in the general damage categories.

On an annual basis this gives the plaintiff the principal sum of $47,733 per year for the rest

3. 修复手术和通过结肠间置进行的重建在初审时正常进行，并且在甲状腺切除术期间发生并发症是在预期之内的，因此无须进一步的手术……未提出有关未来医疗费用的进一步证据。

这里的证据证实，根据目前的医学水平，被告已经竭尽全力减轻原告的病情，并且没有进一步手术的计划，虽然并未排除这种考虑。这并非表示未对 Walters 夫人造成伤害以及她已经恢复到以前的状态，只是表明更多的手术或治疗已经于事无补。替代食管的那部分结肠很明显在发挥作用，但这种作用也给 Walters 夫人带来永久的麻烦。她吞咽食物时，食物不能直接进入胃部，而是怪异地堆积在喉咙的凸出部分和胸部上方。她必须用手向下按摩突出部分，使食物进入胃中。该过程令人十分痛苦。因为没有瓣膜阻止胃中食物返回替代食管，所以她不能平躺，必须保持固定姿势，通过重力使胃中食物处于原来的位置。她的状况令人困窘，使周围的人产生反感，正常生活被严重损害。消化方面也出现了严重问题。在初审时她的预期寿命是 41.9 岁。从受伤到目前的状态，Walters 夫人感觉像是一场噩梦，充斥着痛苦、残疾、住院治疗和外科手术。她的颈部和躯干上留下了损伤外貌的疤痕。吃饭和就坐等许多活动仍然会导致疼痛。

审核案卷后，我们认为我们的集体良心未因裁断金额大小而震惊。

维持原判。

Schroeder 大法官反对：

本案的裁断金额是初审错误和所称的陪审员不当行为的结果……

由于……初审法院和陪审员的猜测，本案的裁断金额显然存在偏见。根据证据，它震惊了我的良心。

在初审时，原告 Lillian K. Walters 的预期寿命为 41.9 岁。在初审时，她的医疗账单金额约为 59 000 美元。她未就收入能力丧失或降低提出索赔；无证据表明需要未来手术或医疗费用。200 万美元的裁断金额，包括一般损害赔偿金类别中的 194 万美元。

因此，原告在余生中将会获得每年 47 733 美元的本金。假设一半损害赔偿金用于支付费用和律师费，则将剩余的 100 万美元以 10% 的单利进行投资

of her life. Assuming one-half of the damage award is paid on expenses and attorney fees, the remaining $1 million invested at 10 percent simple interest (present interest rates compounded quarterly on money invested in C.D.'s will exceed 10 percent), payable annually, will provide an annual income of $100,000 without invading the principal sum invested.

The law in Kansas regarding an excessive verdict has been well defined. One of our leading cases is Kirk v. Beachner Construction Co., Inc., 214 Kan. 733, 522 P.2d 176 (1974). The rules there stated are confined to a situation which is based solely on the amount of the verdict. The case stands for the proposition that no verdict is right which more than compensates—and none is right which fails to compensate. The legal test is one of reasonable compensation.

In my opinion, courts of last resort must exercise a degree of economic judgment to provide stability in our free enterprise system if justice is to be administered fairly and within reason. Courts should not declare serious errors made by the trial court to be harmless, or permit a verdict permeated with speculation and conjecture to go unchallenged, particularly where the amount of the verdict is clearly excessive on its face and indicates prejudice.

Many articles appearing in journals and periodicals address the crisis in the medical profession. The tremendous growth in malpractice liability has resulted in higher insurance premiums which insured physicians pass along in higher prices to health care consumers. In DeVito, Abuse of Litigation: Plague of the Medical Profession, 56 N.Y. St. B.J. 23, 25 (1984), the author says:

The jury system is a free society's precious gift to its citizens. The adversary system within which it functions is an effective guardian of our rights, but, as obtains in any free society, these rights carry with them commensurate obligations and responsibilities. This is especially true of lawyers who, in their capacity as officers of the court, have a unique duty to preserve, protect and perpetuate the founding spirit of our judicial process. Abuse of that process, whether in civil or criminal law, whether by the courts or by lawyers, is to guarantee its ultimate demise. ...

Where state courts of last resort fail to respond with reasonable action to fairly administer justice, public opinion shifts the control to legislative bodies. In the 1985 session of the Kansas Legislature, Senate Bill No. 110 has been introduced by the Judiciary Committee. The Bill is designed to limit liability in malpractice actions of this nature. In the Journal of the Kansas Trial Lawyers Association, Vol. VIII, No. 4, p. 25, this legislation is described as "extremely regressive." Similar instances where state courts of last resort have failed to act with reason have resulted in legislation introduced in the Congress of the United States. Carryover bills in the 99th Congress from the 98th Congress are bills concerning Federal Trade Commission regulation of the Bar, and federal preemption of product liability law of the states.

It is respectfully submitted this court should reverse the trial court and grant a new trial on the ground of misconduct of counsel for the plaintiff in closing argument and, failing this, that the (simple interest)（以现行利率将钱投资到活期存款按季度进行复利计算将超过10%），每年分红，将获得除本金以外的10万美元的年收入。

堪萨斯州法律对于超额裁断有明确规定。我们的指导性案例之一是Kirk v. Beachner Construction Co., Inc., 214 Kan. 733, 522 P.2d 176（1974）案。其表明的规则限于完全基于裁断金额的情况。该案例代表以下观点：过度赔偿不适当，不赔偿也不适当。法定检验标准是合理赔偿检验标准。

我认为，为了公平合理地维护正义，终审法院必须实施一定程度的经济判断，从而为我们的自由企业制度提供稳定性。法院不应宣称初审法院犯下的严重错误是无害的，或允许弥漫着猜测和推测的裁断不受质疑，特别是裁断金额明显超额、存在偏见时。

杂志和期刊上的许多文章都提出了医疗职业的这种危机。医疗事故责任的急剧增加，导致保险费提高，以更高的价格保证医生能够承担对于患者的责任。参见DeVito的《滥用诉讼：医疗职业的苦恼》[Abuse of Litigation:Plague of the Medical Profession, 56 N.Y. St. B.J. 23, 25（1984）]。作者写道：

陪审团制度是自由社会赠与其公民的珍贵礼物。它所依托的对抗制诉讼制度，具有有效保护我们的权利的功能，但在任何自由社会，人们公认这些权利会带来同等的义务和责任。对于法律人来说尤其如此，他们具有作为法院工作人员的能力，承担独特义务来维护司法程序的基本精神。该程序的滥用，无论是民事法还是刑事法，无论是法院还是律师，都会导致它的终结……

如果州终审法院未能合理回应，从而维护公正，则公众意见将改变立法机构控制权。在堪萨斯州立法机构1985年会期上，司法委员会提出参议院议案第110号。该议案旨在限制此类医疗事故责任。在《堪萨斯州出庭律师协会期刊》（Journal of the Kansas Trial Lawyers Association, Vol. VIII, No.4, p.25）中，该立法被称为"十足的倒退"。各州终审法院未能合理行动的类似情况，已经导致美国国会提出立法。涵盖第98届国会遗留给第99届国会的议案涉及联邦贸易委员会对法律界的规范，以及美国联邦法优先于州产品责任法。

我恭敬地向本院提交建议，应当撤销初审法院的判决，基于原告律师在终结辩论中的不当行为批准重审，否则，法院应当基于对陪审团确定损害赔

court should remand the case for a hearing on the motion for new trial concerning the charge of misconduct on the part of the jury in fixing the damage award.

75. McDougald v. Garber, 73 N.Y.2d 246, 536 N.E.2d 372 (1989)

Court of Appeals of New York, United States

Wachtler, Chief Judge. This appeal raises fundamental questions about the nature and role of nonpecuniary damages in personal injury litigation. By nonpecuniary damages, we mean those damages awarded to compensate an injured person for the physical and emotional consequences of the injury, such as pain and suffering and the loss of the ability to engage in certain activities. Pecuniary damages, on the other hand, compensate the victim for the economic consequences of the injury, such as medical expenses, lost earnings and the cost of custodial care.

The specific questions raised here deal with assessment of nonpecuniary damages and are (1) whether some degree of cognitive awareness is a prerequisite to recovery for loss of enjoyment of life and (2) whether a jury should be instructed to consider and award damages for loss of enjoyment of life separately from damages for pain and suffering. We answer the first question in the affirmative and the second question in the negative.

I

On September 7, 1978, plaintiff Emma McDougald, then 31 years old, underwent a Caesarean section and tubal ligation at New York Infirmary. Defendant Garber performed the surgery; defendants Armengol and Kulkarni provided anesthesia. During the surgery, Mrs. McDougald suffered oxygen deprivation which resulted in severe brain damage and left her in a permanent comatose condition. This action was brought by Mrs. McDougald and her husband, suing derivatively, alleging that the injuries were caused by the defendants' acts of malpractice.

A jury found all defendants liable and awarded Emma McDougald a total of $9,650,102 in damages, including $1,000,000 for conscious pain and suffering and a separate award of $3,500,000 for loss of the pleasures and pursuits of life. The balance of the damages awarded to her were for pecuniary damages—lost earnings and the cost of custodial and nursing care. Her husband was awarded $1,500,000 on his derivative claim for the loss of his wife's services. On defendants' posttrial motions, the Trial Judge reduced the total award to Emma McDougald to $4,796,728 by striking the entire award for future nursing care ($2,353,374) and by reducing the separate awards for conscious pain and suffering and loss of the pleasures and pursuits of life to a single award of $2,000,000 (McDougald v. Garber, 132 Misc. 2d 457, 504 N.Y.S.2d 383). Her husband's award was left intact. On cross appeals, the Appellate Division affirmed (135 A.D.2d 80, 524 N.Y.S.2d 192) and later granted defendants leave to appeal to this court.

偿金额不当行为指示的重审,申请将案件发回听证。

75. McDougald v. Garber, 73 N.Y.2d 246, 536 N.E.2d 372 (1989)

美国纽约州上诉法院

Wachtler 大法官主笔:

该上诉提出了人身伤害诉讼中有关非金钱损害赔偿金的性质和角色的基本问题。非金钱损害赔偿金是受害人所受伤害造成的物质和精神后果的损害赔偿金,例如疼痛、痛苦和丧失从事某些活动的能力。金钱损害赔偿金是受害人所受伤害造成的经济后果的损害赔偿金,例如医疗费用、收入损失和照顾费用。

这里提出的具体问题涉及非金钱损害赔偿金的评估,包括:(1)某种程度的认知是否为获得丧失生活乐趣损害赔偿金的先决条件;(2)是否应当指示陪审团在考虑和裁定损害赔偿金时,将生活乐趣丧失损害赔偿金与疼痛和痛苦损害赔偿金分开。我们对第一个问题予以肯定,对第二个问题予以否定。

I.

1978年9月7日,31岁的原告 Emma McDougald 在 New York 医院接受剖腹产手术和输卵管结扎手术。被告 Garber 实施手术、被告 Armengol 和 Kulkarni 进行麻醉。在手术期间,McDougald 夫人发生缺氧,导致大脑严重受损,使其处于持续昏迷状态。McDougald 夫人提起诉讼,其丈夫提起派生诉讼,声称被告的医疗事故导致了伤害。

陪审团裁定所有被告对此负责,共计赔偿 Emma McDougald 9 650 102 美元,包括 100 万美元的疼痛和痛苦损害赔偿金以及 350 万美元的生活乐趣丧失损害赔偿金。其他部分是金钱损害赔偿金,用于赔偿收入损失以及照顾和护理费用。对于妻子的家务丧失,丈夫基于派生索赔获得 150 万美元的损害赔偿金。根据被告的审后申请,初审法官将 Emma McDougald 的损害赔偿金减至 4 796 728 美元,即取消全部未来护理费用(2 353 374 美元),并将独立的疼痛和痛苦损害赔偿金以及生活乐趣丧失损害赔偿金合并成一项,减至 200 万美元(McDougald v. Garber, 132 Misc. 2d 457, 504 N.Y.S.2d 383)。其丈夫的损害赔偿金不变。在交叉上诉后,上诉法院维持原判(135 A.D.2d 80, 524 N.Y.S.2d 192),后来准许被告向本院上诉。

II

...At trial, defendants sought to show that Mrs. McDougald's injuries were so severe that she was incapable of either experiencing pain or appreciating her condition. Plaintiffs, on the other hand, introduced proof that Mrs. McDougald responded to certain stimuli to a sufficient extent to indicate that she was aware of her circumstances. Thus, the extent of Mrs. McDougald's cognitive abilities, if any, was sharply disputed.

The parties and the trial court agreed that Mrs. McDougald could not recover for pain and suffering unless she were conscious of the pain. Defendants maintained that such consciousness was also required to support an award for loss of enjoyment of life. The court, however, accepted plaintiffs' view that loss of enjoyment of life was compensable without regard to whether the plaintiff was aware of the loss. Accordingly, because the level of Mrs. McDougald's cognitive abilities was in dispute, the court instructed the jury to consider loss of enjoyment of life as an element of nonpecuniary damages separate from pain and suffering. ...

We conclude that the court erred, both in instructing the jury that Mrs. McDougald's awareness was irrelevant to their consideration of damages for loss of enjoyment of life and in directing the jury to consider that aspect of damages separately from pain and suffering.

III

We begin with the familiar proposition that an award of damages to a person injured by the negligence of another is to compensate the victim, not to punish the wrongdoer. The goal is to restore the injured party, to the extent possible, to the position that would have been occupied had the wrong not occurred. To be sure, placing the burden of compensation on the negligent party also serves as a deterrent, but purely punitive damages—that is, those which have no compensatory purpose—are prohibited unless the harmful conduct is intentional, malicious, outrageous, or otherwise aggravated beyond mere negligence.

Damages for nonpecuniary losses are, of course, among those that can be awarded as compensation to the victim. This aspect of damages, however, stands on less certain ground than does an award for pecuniary damages. An economic loss can be compensated in kind by an economic gain; but recovery for noneconomic losses such as pain and suffering and loss of enjoyment of life rests on "the legal fiction that money damages can compensate for a victim's injury" (Howard v. Lecher, 42 N.Y.2d 109, 111, 397 N.Y.S.2d 363, 366 N.E.2d 64). We accept this fiction, knowing that although money will neither ease the pain nor restore the victim's abilities, this device is as close as the law can come in its effort to right the wrong. We have no hope of evaluating what has been lost, but a monetary award may provide a measure of solace for the condition created.

Our willingness to indulge this fiction comes to an end, however, when it ceases to serve the compensatory goals of tort recovery. When that limit is met, further indulgence can only result in

Ⅱ.

……在初审时，被告力图表明，McDougald 夫人受到严重伤害，从而不能感知疼痛或自身情况。而原告提交证据，证明 McDougald 夫人对于某些刺激作出的反应，足以表示她能够感知自己的情况。因此，双方对 McDougald 夫人的认知能力进行了激辩。

双方和初审法院同意，除非 McDougald 夫人能够感知疼痛，否则不能获得疼痛和痛苦损害赔偿金。被告主张，生活乐趣丧失损害赔偿金也需要得到神志清醒的支持。然而，法院接受了原告的观点，即无论原告是否能够感知生活乐趣的丧失，都需要对生活乐趣丧失进行赔偿。故此，因为对于 McDougald 夫人的认知能力存在争议，所以法院指示陪审团将生活乐趣丧失作为独立于疼痛和痛苦的非金钱损害赔偿金因素……

我们认为，该法院在以下两方面都犯下了错误：指示陪审团 McDougald 夫人的意识与生活乐趣丧失损害赔偿金无关；指示陪审团将该类损害赔偿金与疼痛和痛苦损害赔偿金分开。

Ⅲ.

我们从熟悉的主张开始：受到他人过失行为伤害的人获得损害赔偿金，是对受害人进行赔偿，而非惩罚不法行为人。目标是尽量使受害人恢复到伤害前的状态。诚然，使过失方承担赔偿责任也是一种威吓，但纯粹的惩罚性损害赔偿金——即非补偿性的是被禁止的，除非该有害行为是故意的、恶意的、恶劣的，或者其他加重到超过过失边界的情形。

非金钱损失损害赔偿金当然属于对于受害人的补偿。然而，这种损害赔偿金的依据与金钱损害赔偿金相比缺乏确定的依据。经济损失能够由同类的经济收入进行补偿，但疼痛和痛苦以及生活乐趣丧失等非经济损失的赔偿，是基于"金钱可以对受害人受到的伤害进行补偿的法律拟制"（Howard v. Lecher, 42 N.Y.2d 109, 111, 397 N.Y.S.2d 363, 366 N.E.2d 64）。我们接受这种拟制，承认虽然金钱既不能缓解疼痛又不能恢复受害人的能力，但是该方式是法律所能实施的纠正不法的最好方法。虽然我们无法评估已经损失了什么，但是金钱赔偿却可能为已经发生的情况提供慰藉。

然而，当这种拟制不再服务于侵权救济的补偿性目标时，我们对它的迁就就会达到尽头。当达到该限度后，进一步的放任只会导致对惩罚性损害赔

assessing damages that are punitive. The question posed by this case, then, is whether an award of damages for loss of enjoyment of life to a person whose injuries preclude any awareness of the loss serves a compensatory purpose. We conclude that it does not.

Simply put, an award of money damages in such circumstances has no meaning or utility to the injured person. An award for the loss of enjoyment of life "cannot provide with any consolation or ease any burden resting on him. …He cannot spend it upon necessities or pleasures. He cannot experience the pleasure of giving it away" (Flannery v. United States, 4th Cir., 718 F.2d 108, 111, *cert. denied,* 467 U.S. 1226, 104 S. Ct. 2679, 81 L. Ed. 2d 874).

We recognize that, as the trial court noted, requiring some cognitive awareness as a prerequisite to recovery for loss of enjoyment of life will result in some cases "in the paradoxical situation that the greater the degree of brain injury inflicted by a negligent defendant, the smaller the award the plaintiff can recover in general damages" (McDougald v. Garber, 132 Misc. 2d 457, 460, 504 N.Y.S.2d 383, supra). The force of this argument, however—the temptation to achieve a balance between injury and damages—has nothing to do with meaningful compensation for the victim. Instead, the temptation is rooted in a desire to punish the defendant in proportion to the harm inflicted. However relevant such retributive symmetry may be in the criminal law, it has no place in the law of civil damages, at least in the absence of culpability beyond mere negligence.

Accordingly, we conclude that cognitive awareness is a prerequisite to recovery for loss of enjoyment of life. We do not go so far, however, as to require the fact finder to sort out varying degrees of cognition and determine at what level a particular deprivation can be fully appreciated. With respect to pain and suffering, the trial court charged simply that there must be "some level of awareness" in order for plaintiff to recover. We think that this is an appropriate standard for all aspects of nonpecuniary loss. No doubt the standard ignores analytically relevant levels of cognition, but we resist the desire for analytical purity in favor of simplicity. A more complex instruction might give the appearance of greater precision but, given the limits of our understanding of the human mind, it would in reality lead only to greater speculation. We turn next to the question whether loss of enjoyment of life should be considered a category of damages separate from pain and suffering.

IV

There is no dispute here that the fact finder may, in assessing nonpecuniary damages, consider the effect of the injuries on the plaintiff's capacity to lead a normal life. Traditionally, in this State and elsewhere, this aspect of suffering has not been treated as a separate category of damages; instead, the plaintiff's inability to enjoy life to its fullest has been considered one type of suffering to be factored into a general award for nonpecuniary damages, commonly known as pain and suffering.

Recently, however, there has been an attempt to segregate the suffering associated with

偿金进行评估。本案提出的问题是：所受伤害使其不能感知损失的人的生活乐趣丧失损害赔偿金是否服务于补偿目标。我们认为不能。

简言之，在这种情况下，金钱赔偿对于受害人没有意义或效用。生活乐趣丧失损害赔偿金"不能提供安慰或缓解其负担……他不能用它满足需要或获得快乐。他不能体验支出带来的愉悦"。（参见 Flannery v. United States, 4th Cir., 718 F.2d 108, 111, cert. denied, 467 U.S. 1226, 104 S. Ct. 2679, 81 L. Ed. 2d 874）案。

我们认为，如初审法院所述，要求将某种认知意识作为生活乐趣丧失损害赔偿金的前提条件，将在一些案件中产生以下"自相矛盾的情况：被告因过失造成原告的大脑伤害越严重，原告获得的一般损害赔偿金越少"（McDougald v. Garber, 132 Misc. 2d 457, 460, 504 N.Y.S.2d 383, supra）。然而，这种观点的力量——实现伤害和损害赔偿金之间的平衡的诱惑，与对受害人进行有意义的赔偿无关。这种诱惑植根于根据伤害成比例地惩罚被告的愿望。无论这种报应性对称在刑法中有多么重要，在民事赔偿法中都没有适用余地，至少是在缺乏超过过失的可责难性时。

因此，我们认为，认知意识是生活乐趣丧失赔偿的前提条件。然而，我们并未要求事实认定者挑选各种认知，然后确定在何种水平上能够充分意识到特定的丧失。关于疼痛和痛苦，初审法院仅指示必须存在"某种程度的意识"才能对原告进行赔偿。我们认为，该标准适用于非金钱损失的所有方面。毫无疑问，该标准忽略了在分析上十分重要的认知水平，但我们抑制对于分析纯度的渴望而选择了简单化。更加复杂的指示可能会提供更高的精确度，但鉴于我们对人类头脑了解的有限性，这实际上只会导致更多猜测。接下来我们考察下一个问题，即生活乐趣丧失是否应当被视为独立于疼痛和痛苦的损害赔偿金类别。

Ⅳ.

在评估非金钱损害赔偿金时，事实认定者可能会考虑伤害对于原告正常生活能力的影响，这一点是没有争议的。在本州和其他法域，这种痛苦的损害赔偿金一直未被视为独立的损害赔偿金；原告不能充分享受生活的损害赔偿金，一直属于一般被称为疼痛和痛苦损害赔偿金的非金钱损害赔偿金的考量要素。

然而，最近出现一种尝试，旨在将身体疼痛与不能从事某种活动导致的

physical pain from the mental anguish that stems from the inability to engage in certain activities, and to have juries provide a separate award for each.

Some courts have resisted the effort, primarily on the ground that duplicative and therefore excessive awards would result. Other courts have allowed separate awards, noting that the types of suffering involved are analytically distinguishable. Still other courts have questioned the propriety of the practice but held that, in the particular case, separate awards did not constitute reversible error. ...

We do not dispute that distinctions can be found or created between the concepts of pain and suffering and loss of enjoyment of life. If the term "suffering" is limited to the emotional response to the sensation of pain, then the emotional response caused by the limitation of life's activities may be considered qualitatively different. But suffering need not be so limited—it can easily encompass the frustration and anguish caused by the inability to participate in activities that once brought pleasure. Traditionally, by treating loss of enjoyment of life as a permissible factor in assessing pain and suffering, courts have given the term this broad meaning.

If we are to depart from this traditional approach and approve a separate award for loss of enjoyment of life, it must be on the basis that such an approach will yield a more accurate evaluation of the compensation due to the plaintiff. We have no doubt that, in general, the total award for nonpecuniary damages would increase if we adopted the rule. That separate awards are advocated by plaintiffs and resisted by defendants is sufficient evidence that larger awards are at stake here. But a larger award does not by itself indicate that the goal of compensation has been better served.

The advocates of separate awards contend that because pain and suffering and loss of enjoyment of life can be distinguished, they must be treated separately if the plaintiff is to be compensated fully for each distinct injury suffered. We disagree. Such an analytical approach may have its place when the subject is pecuniary damages, which can be calculated with some precision. But the estimation of nonpecuniary damages is not amenable to such analytical precision and may, in fact, suffer from its application. Translating human suffering into dollars and cents involves no mathematical formula; it rests, as we have said, on a legal fiction. The figure that emerges is unavoidably distorted by the translation. Application of this murky process to the component parts of nonpecuniary injuries (however analytically distinguishable they may be) cannot make it more accurate. If anything, the distortion will be amplified by repetition.

Thus, we are not persuaded that any salutary purpose would be served by having the jury make separate awards for pain and suffering and loss of enjoyment of life. We are confident, furthermore, that the trial advocate's art is a sufficient guarantee that none of the plaintiff's losses will be ignored by the jury.

The errors in the instructions given to the jury require a new trial on the issue of nonpecuniary

精神痛苦分开，并且由陪审团为各自提供分别损害赔偿裁定额。

有些法院已经抵制该尝试，主要是因为这将会产生双重损害赔偿金，从而导致损害赔偿超额裁定。有些法院批准分别赔偿，指出痛苦类型在分析时可以区分。其他法院则质疑该做法的适当性，但认为在特定的案件中，分别的损害赔偿裁定额不构成可撤销判决错误……

我们无须争论疼痛和痛苦与丧失生活乐趣之间是否存在差别。如果术语"痛苦"限于对痛觉的情绪反应，则限制人的生活活动导致的情绪反应，可以视为具有不同性质。但无须这样来限制痛苦，因为它能够包含不能参加曾经带来快乐的活动导致的挫折和苦恼。一直以来，法院在评估疼痛和痛苦时，都将丧失生活乐趣视为许可的因素，从而使该术语具有广泛的含义。

如果我们放弃这种传统方法，准许将生活乐趣丧失损害赔偿金作为单独的类别，则必须基于以下依据，即该方法将会更精确地评估对原告的补偿。总之，如果我们采用该规则，非金钱损害赔偿金总额无疑会增加。原告支持而被告抵制损害赔偿金分类充分证明更多的损害赔偿金在此是存在争议的。但更多的损害赔偿金本身不能说明赔偿目标已经更好地实现了。

区分损害赔偿裁定额的支持者辩称，因为疼痛和痛苦与丧失生活乐趣能够区分，所以如果对于原告遭受的每种伤害进行充分补偿，就必须分别处理。我们并不同意。当对象是金钱损害赔偿金时，因为可以相对精确地进行计算，所以这种分析方法可能会发挥作用。但非金钱损害赔偿金的估计却不适用这种分析的精确，并且可能会出现问题。将人类痛苦转换成美元和美分没有数学公式，如我们所述，这是基于法律拟制。出现的数字不可避免地会被这种转换所扭曲。将该模糊程序适用于非金钱伤害的组成部分（无论它们如何能够通过分析进行区分）不能使其更加精确，甚至扭曲将会被重复放大。

因此，我们不认为要求陪审团区分疼痛和痛苦与生活乐趣丧失损害赔偿金能够用于有益的目的。而且，我们认为律师的技能足以保证陪审团不会忽视原告的损失。

向陪审团发出的指示中的错误，是要求重新审理给予原告 Emma

damages to be awarded to plaintiff Emma McDougald. Defendants' remaining contentions are either without merit, beyond the scope of our review or are rendered academic by our disposition of the case.

Accordingly, the order of the Appellate Division, insofar as appealed from, should be modified, with costs to defendants, by granting a new trial on the issue of nonpecuniary damages of plaintiff Emma McDougald, and as so modified, affirmed.

Titone, Judge (dissenting).

The majority's holding represents a compromise position that neither comports with the fundamental principles of tort compensation nor furnishes a satisfactory, logically consistent framework for compensating nonpecuniary loss. Because I conclude that loss of enjoyment of life is an objective damage item, conceptually distinct from conscious pain and suffering, I can find no fault with the trial court's instruction authorizing separate awards and permitting an award for "loss of enjoyment of life" even in the absence of any awareness of that loss on the part of the injured plaintiff. Accordingly, I dissent. …

The capacity to enjoy life—by watching one's children grow, participating in recreational activities, and drinking in the many other pleasures that life has to offer—is unquestionably an attribute of an ordinary healthy individual. The loss of that capacity as a result of another's negligent act is at least as serious an impairment as the permanent destruction of a physical function, which has always been treated as a compensable item under traditional tort principles. Indeed, I can imagine no physical loss that is more central to the quality of a tort victim's continuing life than the destruction of the capacity to enjoy that life to the fullest.

Unquestionably, recovery of a damage item such as "pain and suffering" requires a showing of some degree of cognitive capacity. Such a requirement exists for the simple reason that pain and suffering are wholly subjective concepts and cannot exist separate and apart from the human consciousness that experiences them. In contrast, the destruction of an individual's capacity to enjoy life as a result of a crippling injury is an objective fact that does not differ in principle from the permanent loss of an eye or limb. As in the case of a lost limb, an essential characteristic of a healthy human life has been wrongfully taken, and, consequently, the injured party is entitled to a monetary award as a substitute. …

Moreover, there is no need to establish the injured's awareness of the loss. The victim's ability to comprehend the degree to which his or her life has been impaired is irrelevant, since, unlike "conscious pain and suffering," the impairment exists independent of the victim's ability to apprehend it. Indeed, the majority reaches the conclusion that a degree of awareness must be shown only after injecting a new element into the equation. …

Ironically, the majority's expressed goal of limiting recovery for non-pecuniary loss to compensation that the injured plaintiff has the capacity to appreciate is directly undercut by

McDougald 的非金钱损害赔偿金。被告的其余争辩或者是没有依据的,或者超出了我们的复核范围,或者根据我们对于本案的处理被视为是纯理论的。

因此,在上诉范围内应当修改上诉分庭的命令,包含被告的费用,即允许重新审理原告 Emma McDougald 的非金钱损害赔偿金争议,并在修改后予以维持。

Titone 法官(反对意见)。

多数意见代表了一种妥协立场,这既不符合侵权损害赔偿的基本原则,又未提供赔偿非金钱损失的令人满意的一致逻辑框架。因为我认为,生活乐趣丧失是客观的损害项目,在概念上不同于有意识的疼痛和痛苦。所以我认为,即使是受伤的被告未感知丧失,初审法院批准分别损害赔偿裁定额和许可"生活乐趣丧失"损害赔偿金的指令,也没有错误。因此,我反对……

享受生活的能力——注视子女的成长、参加娱乐活动、沉醉于生活提供的其他欢乐——无疑是健康正常人的属性。由于他人的过失行为而丧失这种能力,至少与身体机能的永久破坏同样严重,根据传统的侵权法原则,这一直被视为可补偿的项目。我确实想象不出,有什么身体损害比破坏充分享受生活的能力更能影响侵权受害人的生活质量。

毫无疑问,获得"疼痛和痛苦"损害赔偿金需要表明存在某种程度的认知能力。该要求存在的简单原因是疼痛和痛苦是完全主观的概念,不能脱离人的意识。相比之下,致残伤害导致的享受生活能力的破坏是客观事实,在原则上,与眼睛或四肢的永久丧失没有区别。如果失去一个肢体,则健康人生的一项重要特征就会丧失,因此,受害人有权获得金钱赔偿……

而且,无须证实受害人对于丧失的感知。受害人理解生活受损程度的能力无关紧要,因为,与"有意识的疼痛和痛苦"不同,该损害独立于受害人理解它的能力。多数意见认为,只有向等式注入新的要素之后,才必须表明某种程度的意识……

具有讽刺意味的是,多数意见表明的将非金钱损失赔偿限于受伤原告能够感知的赔偿的目标,被多数意见为了"简单化"而采用的以下最终裁定所直接削弱:只要受伤原告"具有某种程度的意识"(无论多么微弱),

the majority's ultimate holding, adopted in the interest of "simplicity," that recovery for loss of enjoyment of life may be had as long as the injured plaintiff has " 'some level of awareness,' " however slight (majority opn., at 255, at 940 of 538 N.Y.S.2d, at 375 of 536 N.E.2d). Manifestly, there are many different forms and levels of awareness, particularly in cases involving brain injury. Further, the type and degree of cognitive functioning necessary to experience "pain and suffering" is certainly of a lower order than that needed to apprehend the loss of the ability to enjoy life in all of its subtleties. Accordingly, the existence of "some level of awareness" on the part of the injured plaintiff says nothing about that plaintiff's ability to derive some comfort from the award or even to appreciate its significance. Hence, that standard does not assure that loss of enjoyment of life damages will be awarded only when they serve "a compensatory purpose," as that term is defined by the majority.

In the final analysis, the rule that the majority has chosen is an arbitrary one, in that it denies or allows recovery on the basis of a criterion that is not truly related to its stated goal. In my view, it is fundamentally unsound, as well as grossly unfair, to deny recovery to those who are completely without cognitive capacity while permitting it for those with a mere spark of awareness, regardless of the latter's ability to appreciate either the loss sustained or the benefits of the monetary award offered in compensation. In both instances, the injured plaintiff is in essentially the same position, and an award that is punitive as to one is equally punitive as to the other. Of course, since I do not subscribe to the majority's conclusion that an award to an unaware plaintiff is punitive, I would have no difficulty permitting recovery to both classes of plaintiffs.

Having concluded that the injured plaintiff's awareness should not be a necessary precondition to recovery for loss of enjoyment of life, I also have no difficulty going on to conclude that loss of enjoyment of life is a distinct damage item which is recoverable separate and apart from the award for conscious pain and suffering. The majority has rejected separate recovery, in part because it apparently perceives some overlap between the two damage categories and in part because it believes that the goal of enhancing the precision of jury awards for nonpecuniary loss would not be advanced. However, the overlap the majority perceives exists only if one assumes, as the majority evidently has (see, majority opn., at 256-257, at 940-942 of 538 N.Y.S.2d, at 375-377 of 536 N.E.2d), that the "loss of enjoyment" category of damages is designed to compensate only for "the emotional response caused by the limitation of life's activities" and "the frustration and anguish caused by the inability to participate in activities that once brought pleasure", both of which are highly *subjective* concepts.

In fact, while "pain and suffering compensates the victim for the physical and mental discomfort caused by the injury; ... loss of enjoyment of life compensates the victim for the limitations on the person's life created by the injury," a distinctly objective loss (Thompson v. National R.R. Passenger Corp., [6th Cir., 621 F.2d 814, 824, *cert. denied,* 449 U.S. 1035, 101 S.

就能获得生活乐趣的丧失赔偿（参见 majority opn., at 255, at 940 of 538 N.Y.S.2d, at 375 of 536 N.E.2d）。很明显，有许多不同形式和水平的意识，特别是在涉及大脑伤害的案件中。而且，感知"疼痛和痛苦"所必需的认知功能的类型和程度，当然低于理解充分享受微妙生活的能力丧失所需的认知功能的类型和程度。因此，受伤原告具有"某种程度的意识"，不能证明原告有能力从损害赔偿金中获得一些安慰或感知其意义。所以，该标准不能保证只有在服务于"赔偿性目的"时，才能给予生活乐趣丧失损害赔偿金。

在最终的分析中，多数意见选择的规则是武断的，因为它们根据与所表明的目标实际无关的标准拒绝或允许赔偿。我认为以下观点是完全错误、明显不公平的：拒绝向完全失去认知能力的受害人赔偿，却允许向仅有一点儿意识的受害人赔偿，无论其感知伤害或损害赔偿金利益的能力如何。在这两种情况中，受伤的原告实质上处于同等状态，两种损害赔偿金具有同样的惩罚性。当然，因为我并不同意无意识的原告获得的赔偿具有惩罚性的多数意见结论，所以我在允许向两类原告进行赔偿时，不会存在困难。

认定受伤原告的意识不应成为获得生活乐趣丧失赔偿的必要前提后，进一步认定生活乐趣丧失是不同的伤害项目就没有困难，其损害赔偿金应当与有意识的疼痛和痛苦损害赔偿金区分开。多数意见拒绝区别赔偿，部分原因是明显感觉两种伤害存在重叠；部分原因是认为无助于实现提高非金钱损失赔偿陪审团裁定精确性的目标。然而，多数意见感觉到的重叠仅在以下情况下才出现：人们认为，如多数意见明显认为的（参见 majority opn., at 256-257, at 940-942 of 538 N.Y.S.2d, at 375-377 of 536 N.E.2d），"丧失乐趣"损害赔偿金旨在仅对"生命活动受限导致的情绪反应"和"不能参与曾经带来快乐的活动导致的挫折和苦恼"进行赔偿，这两者都是具有高度主观性的概念。

实际上，尽管"疼痛和痛苦损害赔偿金对伤害引起的受害人身体和精神不适进行赔偿；……生活乐趣丧失损害赔偿金对伤害引起的受害人生活受限（明显的客观损失）进行赔偿"（参见 Thompson v. National R.R. Passenger Corp., 6th Cir., 621 F.2d 814, 824, cert. denied, 449 U.S. 1035, 101 S. Ct. 611, 66 L.Ed.2d 497 案）。换言之，尽管受害人的"情绪反应"与"挫折和苦恼"是疼痛和痛苦赔偿的要素，但在"生活乐趣丧失"的标题下，多数意见确认

Ct. 611, 66 L.Ed.2d 497]). In other words, while the victim's "emotional response" and "frustration and anguish" are elements of the award for pain and suffering, the "limitation of life's activities" and the "inability to participate in activities" that the majority identifies are recoverable under the "loss of enjoyment of life" rubric. Thus, there is no real overlap, and no real basis for concern about potentially duplicative awards where, as here, there is a properly instructed jury.

Finally, given the clear distinction between the two categories of nonpecuniary damages, I cannot help but assume that permitting separate awards for conscious pain and suffering and loss of enjoyment of life would contribute to accuracy and precision in thought in the jury's deliberations on the issue of damages. …In light of the concrete benefit to be gained by compelling the jury to differentiate between the specific objective and subjective elements of the plaintiff's nonpecuniary loss, I find unpersuasive the majority's reliance on vague concerns about potential distortion owing to the inherently difficult task of computing the value of intangible loss. My belief in the jury system, and in the collective wisdom of the deliberating jury, leads me to conclude that we may safely leave that task in the jurors' hands.

For all of these reasons, I approve of the approach that the trial court adopted in its charge to the jury. Accordingly, I would affirm the order below affirming the judgment.

76. H West & Son Ltd v Shephard [1964] AC 326

House of Lords, United Kingdom

LORD MORRIS

(read by Lord Tucker). My Lords, the grievous injuries in respect of which, as has been held, liability rests upon the appellants, were sustained by the respondent on November 28, 1959. She was then 41 years of age, the wife of a devoted husband and the mother of three children. On that date she was removed to hospital in an unconscious condition. Her clinical state suggested that there was intracranial bleeding and an operation was performed on the same day in order to evacuate haemorrhages. There was also bruising of the underlying brain. Following the operation her level of consciousness lightened somewhat but she did not regain full consciousness. Later investigations suggested a marked degree of cerebral atrophy on the right side of the brain: there was asymmetry between the two hemispheres and a diffuse abnormality such as is often seen after head injuries with extensive cerebral contusion.

On March 1, 1961, she was transferred to another hospital. In reference to that date it was said that she was conscious and responded in a negative manner to examination but that she lay quite detached from her environment: there was no response to external painful stimuli except slight withdrawal by the right arm and she did not respond to any requests. A hospital report stated that "all four limbs were spastic, the arms more so than the legs and there was no voluntary movement

的"生命活动限制"和"不能参与活动"是可以赔偿的。因此，没有真正的重叠，并且在陪审团受到正确指示的情况下，担心出现双重赔偿也没有真正的依据。

最后，由于两类非金钱损害赔偿金存在明显区别，我不禁认为，允许将有意识的疼痛和痛苦损害赔偿金与生活乐趣丧失损害赔偿金分开会提高陪审团考虑损害赔偿金问题的精确度……根据要求陪审团对原告非金钱损失的主观与客观要素进行区分所获得的具体收益，我发现，由于计算无形损失价值的任务的固有困难，使得建立于对潜在扭曲的模糊忧虑之上的大多数意见并不具有说服力。我对于陪审团制度以及深思熟虑的陪审团的集体智慧的信任，使我认为可以放心地将该任务交给陪审员。

基于全部这些理由，我同意初审法院在向陪审团发出指令中采用的方法。因此，我宁可维持下级法院维持原判的命令。

76. H West & Son Ltd v Shephard [1964] AC 326

联合王国上议院

Morris 大法官主笔：

（由 Tucker 大法官所代为宣读。）各位大法官，被上诉人在 1959 年 11 月 28 日遭到了严重的伤害；上诉人已经被确认应该为此承担责任。被上诉人当时 41 岁，有一个爱她的丈夫和三个孩子。发生事故的当天，她被送到医院时已经失去了意识。经过检查，发现她颅内出血，于是在当日她就接受了手术，以排出淤血。她的大脑也有淤伤。手术之后，她恢复了一点意识，但是没有恢复到之前的程度。之后的检查发现她的右侧大脑严重萎缩；她的左右侧大脑不对称；在脑部撞伤中高发的扩散性异常也出现了。

1961 年 3 月 1 日，她被转到另一家医院。谈到当天的情况，据说她当时是有意识的，但是对检查却抱以消极的态度，且她对周围的环境完全不敏感：当受到外界的疼痛刺激时，她除了稍微缩回左臂之外，完全没有其他的反应；对于问她的任何问题她都没有回答。医院报告描述当时的情况："患者四肢都在抽搐；上肢比下肢抽搐得厉害；除了眼球能跟着移动物体移动之外，没有其他的自主活动。"

present beyond eye movements to follow a moving object."

By November 22, 1961, there had been a gradual increase in her awareness of and response to her surroundings and a little voluntary movement was returning to the head and right arm. She could see and hear and she appeared to understand simple requests, though very slowly. In medical language her state was said to be that of "post-traumatic spastic quadriplegia and intellectual deficit."

A report dated February 16, 1962, recorded that there has been a slight improvement in her mental condition in that she showed some signs of recognition of relatives and members of the nursing staff and had responded to commands by moving her right hand. She could appreciate the difference between articles of food that she liked or disliked, her means of indication being by means of facial expressions.

Her husband, a witness at the trial, noticed that in November, 1961, there was some improvement in her condition. Though she remains unable to speak she has been able to indicate colour in that when her husband mentioned a colour she touched a coloured card which was held up in front of her: she could just lift her hand from the bed cover and extend a finger so as to touch the card. When her husband mentioned a number up to but not beyond the number nine she could touch a card with the mentioned number on it. Accepting the husband's evidence the learned judge at the trial held that though she cannot speak at all she must be able, to a certain extent, to understand what is said to her.

She needs continuous nursing care in hospital with hourly or two-hourly feeding by tube. Although her general condition (apart from her neurological condition) is good, she is at great risk from the development of chest and other infections. She will require full-time hospital nursing for the period that her life continues and there is no prospect of any further improvement in her condition.

On a consideration of the evidence, and balancing the possibilities, the learned judge held that she had an expectation of life "somewhere in the neighbourhood of five years." On that basis her life from the date of the accident for a period of over seven years will have been lived in the condition and subject to the deprivations which I have summarised.

The award of damages made by the learned judge at the trial on May 3, 1962, included (a) a sum of £500, the agreed special damages which covered the respondent's loss of earnings down to the date of trial; (b) £600 for future loss of earnings; (c) £500 for loss of expectation of life; and (d) £17,500 general damages. In the Court of Appeal no challenge was made of the sums awarded under (a), (b) and (c) above. The challenge which was made of the amount of the general damages failed.

My Lords, the damages which are to be awarded for a tort are those which, "so far as money can compensate will give the injured party reparation for the wrongful act and for all the natural

到 1961 年 11 月 22 日，她的知觉开始恢复，她开始逐渐对外界环境做出回应，头部和右臂也能稍微活动了。她能看能听，而且她似乎能理解简单的问题，虽然理解得很慢。用一个概念医学术语来说，她的状态属于"创伤后痉挛性四肢麻痹，伴随着智力减损"。

1962 年 2 月 16 日的一份报告记录了她的大脑功能有一定的提升。有迹象表明她能认识亲人和护理人员，并且能根据指令移动其右手。她能用面部表情表达自己辨别喜欢的食物和不喜欢的食物。

其丈夫作为庭审时的证人，证明在 1961 年 11 月，她的状况有所好转。虽然依然不能说话，但是丈夫说一个颜色词汇时，她能用手触碰放在她面前的相应的颜色卡：她能将手从床垫上抬起，并伸出手指去触碰颜色卡。当丈夫说出一个不超过 9 的数字时，她可以触碰写有相应数字的卡片。博学的一审法官在庭审时接受了丈夫的证词，并判定虽然她并不能说话，但是在某种程度上她能理解别人跟她说的话。

她需要持续的住院护理，需要每隔一小时或两小时用导管来喂食物。虽然她的整体情况很好（除了神经系统），但其胸部或者其他地方的感染很可能加剧。她的余生都需要全日制的住院护理，也没有进一步好转的希望。

基于这些证据并运用概率平衡法，博学的一审法官认定她的预期寿命"大概是五年"。这样看来，从车祸发生时算起，她能活七年；这七年间，她都将活在我刚才描述的被剥夺了很多正常人拥有的东西的状况下。

1962 年 5 月 3 日，博学的一审法官判决被上诉人可以获得以下损害赔偿：首先是一笔 500 英镑的双方达成共识的特别赔偿金（用来赔偿经济损失的叫作特别赔偿金），旨在赔偿被上诉人从车祸发生到庭审时的收入损失；其次是一笔 600 英镑的赔偿金，旨在赔偿未来的收入损失；再次是一笔 500 英镑的赔偿金，旨在赔偿被上诉人丧失的预期寿命；最后是一笔 17 500 英镑的一般赔偿金（用来赔偿非金钱损失的叫作一般赔偿金）。上诉到上诉法院时，前三项赔偿金双方没有争议。对于一般赔偿金的数额则有争议。

诸位大法官，我们要允许侵权行为的受害人获得损害赔偿金的情形，应当是那些"只要金钱能够赔偿，就能弥补受害人因为侵权行为及其自然

and direct consequences of the wrongful act."(*Admiralty Commissioners v. S.S. Susquehanna*.) The words "so far as money can compensate" point to the impossibility of equating money with human suffering or personal deprivations. A money award can be calculated so as to make good a financial loss. Money may be awarded so that something tangible may be procured to replace something else of like nature which has been destroyed or lost. But money cannot renew a physical frame that has been battered and shattered. All that judges and courts can do is to award sums which must be regarded as giving reasonable compensation. In the process there must be the endeavour to secure some uniformity in the general method of approach. By common assent awards must be reasonable and must be assessed with moderation. Furthermore, it is eminently desirable that so far as possible comparable injuries should be compensated by comparable awards. When all this is said it still must be that amounts which are awarded are to a considerable extent conventional.

In the process of assessing damages judges endeavour to take into account all the relevant changes in a claimant's circumstances which have been caused by the tortfeasor. These are often conveniently described as "heads of damage." …

If there has been some serious physical injury which as the result of skilled medical attention has happily not necessitated the enduring of pain then it will follow that there will be no question of including in an award any sum as compensation for the enduring of pain. If someone has been made unconscious so that pain is not felt the like result will follow. Damages are awarded as a fair compensation for that which has in fact happened and will not arise in respect of anything that has not happened.

…

Certain particular questions have been raised. How are general damages affected if at all by the fact that the sufferer is unconscious? How are they affected, if at all, if it be the fact that the sufferer will not be able to make use of any money which is awarded?

The first of these questions may be largely answered if it is remembered that damages are designed to compensate for such results as have actually been caused. If someone has been caused pain then damages to compensate for the enduring of it may be awarded. If, however, by reason of an injury someone is made unconscious either for a short or for a prolonged period with the result that he does not feel pain then he needs no monetary compensation in respect of pain because he will not have suffered it. Apart from actual physical pain it may often be that some physical injury causes distress or fear or anxiety. If, for example, injuries include the loss of a leg there may be much physical suffering, there will be the actual loss of the leg (a loss the gravity of which will depend upon the particular circumstances of the particular case) and there may be (depending upon particular circumstances) elements of consequential worry and anxiety. One part of the affliction (again depending upon particular circumstances) may be an inevitable and constant awareness of the deprivations which the loss of the leg entails. These are all matters which judges take into

而直接的后果的情形"（*Admiralty Commissioners v S.S. Susquehanna.*）"只要金钱能够赔偿"这句话，表明金钱（的损失）和人受到的痛苦以及被剥夺的身体机能不能被同等看待。我们可以计算出能够赔偿经济损失的赔偿金的数额。金钱能让受害人获得某些有形的东西，以替代他被毁坏或灭失的类似的东西。然而金钱并不能重塑破损的身体。法官和法院能做的，是判决给予受害人一个合理的赔偿数额。在这个过程中，他们所用的一般的计算方法在不同的案件中必须尽量做到一致。按照公意，赔偿金的数额应该是合理的、适度的。另外，类似的损害应当由类似的赔偿填补，这是我们都非常希望实现的价值。除此之外，赔偿金的数额还需要在很大程度上符合大众的预期。

在计算赔偿金时，法官尽力考虑所有的由侵权人造成的原告生活状况的变化。这些变化一般被称为"损失项目"……

如果人身损害虽然严重，但是高明的医术让患者并未感到疼痛，那么就没有必要在赔偿金中包含任何的数额来补偿疼痛。一个没有知觉的人感受不到疼痛，因此也就不需要因为疼痛补偿他。损害赔偿金是为了弥补确实发生了的损害的，对于没有发生的事情当然不能要求赔偿。

……

另外，还是有些具体问题要回答。受害人没有知觉了，是否影响一般赔偿金的数额，如果是，怎么影响？在受害人没有能力使用获得的赔偿金时，一般赔偿金的数额是否受到影响，如果是，怎么影响？

如果我们能记得损害赔偿金是为了弥补确实产生了的后果，第一个问题基本上就可以回答了。如果一个人感受到了痛苦，那么因为这种痛苦就可能获得赔偿。然而，如果一个人因为受伤而失去了知觉因而感觉不到痛苦（无论是短时间的还是长时间的），那么就没有必要给他金钱赔偿，因为它没有承受这种疼痛。除了身体的疼痛，很可能某些人身损害可能会导致忧伤、恐惧或者焦虑。比如若人身损害导致受害人失去了一条腿，受害人会承受极大的身体上的痛苦，他会确确实实失去一条腿（严重程度取决于具体案件的具体情况），他也可能附带地感到担心和焦虑（这也取决于具体情况）。这种担心和焦虑的一个原因可能是受害人无法避免常常想到自己失去了一条腿（是不是确实担心和焦虑也取决于具体的情况）。以上这些事实都是法官要考虑的。还需要考虑的是受害人生存期间的长短，因为在整个生存期间内他都将被剥

account. In this connection also the length of the period of life during which the deprivations will continue will be a relevant factor (see *Rose v. Ford*).

To the extent to which any of these last-mentioned matters depend for their existence upon an awareness in the victim it must follow that they will not exist and will not call for compensation if the victim is unconscious. An unconscious person will be spared pain and suffering and will not experience the mental anguish which may result from knowledge of what has in life been lost or from knowledge that life has been shortened. The fact of unconsciousness is therefore relevant in respect of and will eliminate those heads or elements of damage which can only exist by being felt or thought or experienced. The fact of unconsciousness does not, however, eliminate the actuality of the deprivations of the ordinary experiences and amenities of life which may be the inevitable result of some physical injury.

If damages are awarded to a plaintiff on a correct basis it seems to me that it can be of no concern to the court to consider any question as to the use that will thereafter be made of the money awarded. It follows that if damages are assessed on a correct basis there should not then be a paring down of the award because of some thought that a particular plaintiff will not be able to use the money. In assessing damages there may be items which will only be awarded if certain needs of a plaintiff are established. A particular plaintiff may have to have provision made for some future form of transport: a particular plaintiff may have to have provision made for some special future attention or some special treatment or medication. If, however, some reasonable sum is awarded to a plaintiff as compensation for pain endured or for the loss of past or future earnings or for ruined years of life or lost years of life the use to which a plaintiff puts such sum is a matter for the plaintiff alone. A rich man, merely because he is rich and is not in need, is not to be denied proper compensation; nor is a thrifty man merely because he may keep and not spend.

…

LORD PEARCE

The loss of happiness of the individual plaintiffs is not, in my opinion, a practicable or correct guide to reasonable compensation in cases of personal injury to a living plaintiff. A man of fortitude is not made less happy because he loses a limb. It may alter the scope of his activities and force him to seek his happiness in other directions. The cripple by the fireside reading or talking with friends may achieve happiness as great as that which, but for the accident, he would have achieved playing golf in the fresh air of the links. To some ancient philosophers the former kind of happiness might even have seemed of a higher nature than the latter, provided that the book or the talk were such as they would approve. Some less robust persons, on the other hand, are prepared to attribute a great loss of happiness to a quite trivial event. It would be lamentable if the trial of a personal injury claim put a premium on protestations of misery and if a long face was the only safe passport to a large award. Under the present practice there is no call for a parade of personal

夺以上说到的这些东西。（参考 Rose v. Ford）.

以上说到的这些受害人的损失是否存在，取决于受害人是否有意识，如果受害人没有意识，那这些损失就不存在了，因此受害人就不能获得相应的损害赔偿。失去知觉的人不会感到疼痛，不会因为知晓生命中失去了什么或者知晓生命被缩短了而感到精神痛苦。因此受害人失去知觉这一事实，与那些只有在受害人能感受到、想到或者经历到的赔偿事项是有相关性的；这一事实将阻却受害人主张这些赔偿事项。然而，受害人失去知觉这一事实并不能否认受害人因为人身损害而不可避免地被剥夺了日常生活的经历，被剥夺了生命的美好。

如果已经根据正确的原因，确定应该判决给予原告损害赔偿金，那么在我看来这笔损害赔偿金之后怎么用，对法庭来说是不需要考虑的问题。某个原告可能需要储备一些钱来应付未来的交通问题；某个原告可能需要储备一些钱来应付未来的看护问题、治疗问题或者药品问题。然而，如果原告获得了一笔合理数额的赔偿金，以补偿他感受到的疼痛、他丧失的过去或者未来的收入，或者他被毁掉的和失去的人生，那么原告怎么用这笔钱只是他自己的事。富人并不仅仅因为他富有，他不需要钱，而就要被剥夺正当的赔偿请求权；节俭的人也并不仅仅因为他会把钱存起来而不花掉，就要被剥夺这样的权利。

......

Pearce 大法官主笔：

人身侵害案件中，我不认为去赔偿原告失去的快乐是可行的、正确的、合理的。坚毅的人并不会因为失去了一条腿而有多悲伤。因为失去了腿，他可选择的行为的类型可能发生变化，他可能被迫去别的地方寻找快乐。一个残疾人，在火堆旁读书、与朋友闲聊获得的快乐，可能并不亚于如果他没有遇到事故时在林克斯球场（一种高尔夫球场 golf course 的类型）的新鲜空气中打高尔夫球的快乐。对某些先哲来说，前者的快乐甚至比后者更高级，如果他们对书或者闲聊满意的话。而没有那么坚强的人，则可能因为一点点琐事而不开心好久。如果人身侵害案件的审理关键居然是卖惨，如果拉长脸就能获得巨额赔偿，那该是多么可悲啊。在现行法的做法下，原告没有任何必要去大倒苦水。原告开开心心地承认他和以前一样高兴，依然可能获得对其受

unhappiness. A plaintiff who cheerfully admits that he is happy as ever he was, may yet receive a large award as reasonable compensation for the grave injury and loss of amenity over which he has managed to triumph. ...

Section 4. Punitive or Exemplary Damages

77. State Farm Mutual Automobile Insurance Company v. Campbell, 123 S. Ct. 1513 (2003)

District Court of Appeal of Florida, United States

Justice Kennedy delivered the opinion of the Court.

We address once again the measure of punishment, by means of punitive damages, a State may impose upon a defendant in a civil case. The question is whether, in the circumstances we shall recount, an award of $145 million in punitive damages, where full compensatory damages are $1 million, is excessive and in violation of the Due Process Clause of the Fourteenth Amendment to the Constitution of the United States.

I

In 1981, Curtis Campbell (Campbell) was driving with his wife, Inez Preece Campbell, in Cache County, Utah. He decided to pass six vans traveling ahead of them on a two-lane highway. Todd Ospital was driving a small car approaching from the opposite direction. To avoid a head-on collision with Campbell, who by then was driving on the wrong side of the highway and toward oncoming traffic, Ospital swerved onto the shoulder, lost control of his automobile, and collided with a vehicle driven by Robert G. Slusher. Ospital was killed, and Slusher was rendered permanently disabled. The Campbells escaped unscathed....

In the ensuing wrongful death and tort action, Campbell insisted he was not at fault. Early investigations did support differing conclusions as to who caused the accident, but "consensus was reached early on by the investigators and witnesses that Mr. Campbell's unsafe pass had indeed caused the crash."...Campbell's insurance company, petitioner State Farm Mutual Automobile Insurance Company (State Farm), nonetheless decided to contest liability and declined offers by Slusher and Ospital's estate (Ospital) to settle the claims for the policy limit of $50,000 ($25,000 per claimant). State Farm also ignored the advice of one of its own investigators and took the case to trial, assuring the Campbells that "their assets were safe, that they had no liability for the accident, that State Farm would represent their interests, and that they did not need to procure separate counsel."... To the contrary, a jury determined that Campbell was 100 percent at fault, and a judgment was returned for $185,849, far more than the amount offered in settlement.

At first State Farm refused to cover the $135,849 in excess liability. Its counsel made this clear to the Campbells: " 'You may want to put for sale signs on your property to get things

到的严重伤害和对其失去的生活中的美好事物的合理赔偿，而且他可能完全能够克服这些痛苦……

第四节 惩罚性或惩戒性损害赔偿金

77. State Farm Mutual Automobile Insurance Company v. Campbell, 123 S. Ct. 1513 (2003)

美国佛罗里达州联邦地方上诉法院

由 Kennedy 法官发表法院的意见。

通过一个州在民事案件中可能对被告施加的惩罚性损害赔偿金的方式，我们再次提出处罚尺度问题。问题是，在我们叙述的情形下，1.45 亿美元惩罚性损害赔偿金（全部补偿性损害赔偿金为 100 万美元）是否超额，以及是否违反《美国宪法第十四修正案》的正当程序条款。

I.

1981 年，Curtis Campbell（Campbell）与妻子 Inez Preece Campbell 在犹他州 Cache 县驾车行驶。在双车道公路上，他决定超越前面的 6 辆货车。这时，Todd Ospital 驾驶一辆小轿车从对面驶来。Campbell 这时已经处于对向车道，为了避免迎头相撞，Ospital 将车转向路肩，但车失去了控制，与 Robert G. Slusher 驾驶的机动车相撞。Ospital 当场死亡，Slusher 永久残疾。Campbell 夫妇幸免于难……

在随后的不法致死和侵权诉讼中，Campbell 坚称自己没有过错。对于谁造成事故的早期调查显示了不同结论，但"调查人员和目击者在早期一致认为 Campbell 先生的危险超车造成了碰撞"。……Campbell 的保险公司，原告 State Farm Mutual 机动车保险公司（以下简称"State Farm"）却决定对责任提出异议，拒绝 Slusher 和 Ospital 的遗产继承人（以下简称"Ospital"）提出的保单限额 5 万美元的和解要求（每位索赔者 2.5 万美元）。State Farm 还无视本公司一位调查人员的建议，将案件提交法院审理，并向 Campbell 夫妇保证"他们的资产十分安全，对事故没有责任，State Farm 将会代表他们的权益，他们无须聘请单独的辩护律师"。……结果陪审团裁定 Campbell 承担 100% 责任，宣布损害赔偿金为 185 849 美元，远高于和解提出的金额。

State Farm 起初拒绝支付额外的 135 849 美元。其律师向 Campbell 夫妇明确表示："你们可能需要在房产上贴上待售标签来解决问题。"……State Farm

moving.' " …Nor was State Farm willing to post a supersedeas bond to allow Campbell to appeal the judgment against him. Campbell obtained his own counsel to appeal the verdict. During the pendency of the appeal, in late 1984, Slusher, Ospital, and the Campbells reached an agreement whereby Slusher and Ospital agreed not to seek satisfaction of their claims against the Campbells. In exchange the Campbells agreed to pursue a bad faith action against State Farm and to be represented by Slusher's and Ospital's attorneys. The Campbells also agreed that Slusher and Ospital would have a right to play a part in all major decisions concerning the bad faith action. No settlement could be concluded without Slusher's and Ospital's approval, and Slusher and Ospital would receive 90 percent of any verdict against State Farm.

In 1989, the Utah Supreme Court denied Campbell's appeal in the wrongful death and tort actions. …State Farm then paid the entire judgment, including the amounts in excess of the policy limits. The Campbells nonetheless filed a complaint against State Farm alleging bad faith, fraud, and intentional infliction of emotional distress. The trial court initially granted State Farm's motion for summary judgment because State Farm had paid the excess verdict, but that ruling was reversed on appeal. …On remand State Farm moved *in limine* to exclude evidence of alleged conduct that occurred in unrelated cases outside of Utah, but the trial court denied the motion. At State Farm's request the trial court bifurcated the trial into two phases conducted before different juries. In the first phase the jury determined that State Farm's decision not to settle was unreasonable because there was a substantial likelihood of an excess verdict.

Before the second phase of the action against State Farm we decided *BMW of North America, Inc. v. Gore*, 517 U.S. 559, L.Ed.2d 809 (1996), and refused to sustain a $2 million punitive damages award which accompanied a verdict of only $4,000 in compensatory damages. Based on that decision, State Farm again moved for the exclusion of evidence of dissimilar out-of-state conduct. …The trial court denied State Farm's motion. …

The second phase addressed State Farm's liability for fraud and intentional infliction of emotional distress, as well as compensatory and punitive damages. The Utah Supreme Court aptly characterized this phase of the trial:

State Farm argued during phase II that its decision to take the case to trial was an 'honest mistake' that did not warrant punitive damages. In contrast, the Campbells introduced evidence that State Farm's decision to take the case to trial was a result of a national scheme to meet corporate fiscal goals by capping payouts on claims company wide. This scheme was referred to as State Farm's 'Performance, Planning and Review,' or PP&R, policy. To prove the existence of this scheme, the trial court allowed the Campbells to introduce extensive expert testimony regarding fraudulent practices by State Farm in its nation-wide operations. Although State Farm moved prior to phase II of the trial for the exclusion of such evidence and continued to object to it at trial, the trial court ruled that such evidence was admissible to determine whether State Farm's conduct in

也不愿提供中止执行保证书，以使 Campbell 能够上诉。Campbell 聘请了律师提出上诉。1984 年年末，在上诉期间，Slusher、Ospital 和 Campbell 夫妇达成协议，Slusher 和 Ospital 同意不向 Campbell 夫妇索赔。作为交换条件，Campbell 夫妇同意针对 State Farm 基于恶意诉因起诉，由 Slusher 和 Ospital 的律师代理。Campbell 夫妇还同意 Slusher 和 Ospital 有权参与有关恶意诉讼的所有重要决定。未经 Slusher 和 Ospital 批准，不得进行和解，并且 Slusher 和 Ospital 将获得 State Farm 支付的损害赔偿金的 90%。

1989 年，犹他州最高法院驳回了 Campbell 在不法致死和侵权诉讼中的上诉……State Farm 支付了全部损害赔偿金，包括超出保单限额的部分。随后，Campbell 夫妇控告 State Farm 恶意、欺诈以及故意施加精神伤害。初审法院最初批准 State Farm 的即席判决申请，因为 State Farm 已经支付了额外损害赔偿金，但该判决在上诉后被撤销……案件发回重审后，State Farm 提出了防止偏见申请以排除在犹他州外的无关案件中发生的行为的证据，但初审法院驳回了该申请。根据 State Farm 的请求，初审法院将审理分成两个阶段，由不同的陪审团审理。在第一阶段，陪审团裁定 State Farm 的不和解决策是不合理的，因为超额裁断具有实质可能性。

在第二阶段开始之前，我们对 BMW of North America, Inc. v. Gore, 517 U.S. 559, L.Ed.2d 809（1996）案进行了判决，拒绝支持 200 万美元的惩罚性损害赔偿金裁定（补偿性损害赔偿金仅 4 000 美元）。根据该判决，State Farm 再次请求排除无关的州外行为证据……初审法院驳回了 State Farm 的请求……

第二阶段处理 State Farm 的欺诈和故意施加精神伤害责任以及补偿性和惩罚性损害赔偿金事宜。犹他州最高法院对该阶段进行了适当的描述：

State Farm 在第二阶段辩称，它作出的将案件提交法院审理的决定是"诚实的错误"，不能证明惩罚性损害赔偿金的正当性。Campbell 夫妇提交证据，表明 State Farm 作出的将案件提交法院审理的决定是一项全国计划的结果，旨在通过设定公司范围的索赔要求支出的上限实现公司财务目标。该计划被称为 State Farm 的"绩效、规划和审核"或 PP&R 计划。为了证明该计划的存在，初审法院允许 Campbell 夫妇提交广泛的专家证词，证明 State Farm 在全国业务中实施欺诈行为。虽然 State Farm 在初审第二阶段开始前请求排除该证据，并且在初审时继续表示反对，但是初审法院裁定该证据可接受，能够确定 State Farm 在 Campbell 案件中的行为是否确实有恶意并且极端恶劣，从而

the Campbell case was indeed intentional and sufficiently egregious to warrant punitive damages. …

Evidence pertaining to the PP&R policy concerned State Farm's business practices for over 20 years in numerous States. Most of these practices bore no relation to third-party automobile insurance claims, the type of claim underlying the Campbells' complaint against the company. The jury awarded the Campbells $2.6 million in compensatory damages and $145 million in punitive damages, which the trial court reduced to $1 million and $25 million respectively. Both parties appealed.

The Utah Supreme Court sought to apply the three guideposts we identified in *Gore, supra*, … and it reinstated the $145 million punitive damages award. Relying in large part on the extensive evidence concerning the PP&R policy, the court concluded State Farm's conduct was reprehensible. The court also relied upon State Farm's "massive wealth" and on testimony indicating that "State Farm's actions, because of their clandestine nature, will be punished at most in one out of every 50,000 cases as a matter of statistical probability," …and concluded that the ratio between punitive and compensatory damages was not unwarranted. Finally, the court noted that the punitive damages award was not excessive when compared to various civil and criminal penalties State Farm could have faced, including $10,000 for each act of fraud, the suspension of its license to conduct business in Utah, the disgorgement of profits, and imprisonment. …We granted certiorari. …

II

We recognized in *Cooper Industries, Inc. v. Leatherman Tool Group, Inc.*, 532 U.S. 424, … that in our judicial system compensatory and punitive damages, although usually awarded at the same time by the same decisionmaker, serve different purposes. …Compensatory damages "are intended to redress the concrete loss that the plaintiff has suffered by reason of the defendant's wrongful conduct."… (citing Restatement (Second) of Torts §903, pp. 453-454 (1979)). By contrast, punitive damages serve a broader function; they are aimed at deterrence and retribution. *Cooper Industries, supra*….

While States possess discretion over the imposition of punitive damages, it is well established that there are procedural and substantive constitutional limitations on these awards. …The reason is that "elementary notions of fairness enshrined in our constitutional jurisprudence dictate that a person receive fair notice not only of the conduct that will subject him to punishment, but also of the severity of the penalty that a State may impose."…To the extent an award is grossly excessive, it furthers no legitimate purpose and constitutes an arbitrary deprivation of property.…

Although these awards serve the same purposes as criminal penalties, defendants subjected to punitive damages in civil cases have not been accorded the protections applicable in a criminal proceeding. This increases our concerns over the imprecise manner in which punitive damages

证明惩罚性损害赔偿金裁定是正当的……

有关 PP&R 政策的证据涉及 State Farm 在很多州超过 20 年的经营行为。大多数行为与第三方机动车保险索赔无关，该类索赔是 Campbell 夫妇控告该公司的基础。陪审团裁断 Campbell 夫妇获得 260 万美元的补偿性损害赔偿金和 1.45 亿美元的惩罚性损害赔偿金。初审法院将其分别减至 100 万美元和 2500 万美元。双方均提出上诉。

犹他州最高法院寻求适用上述 Gore 案中确认的三项准则，恢复了 1.45 亿美元的惩罚性损害赔偿金。法院主要依据有关 PP&R 政策的广泛证据，认为 State Farm 的行为应受谴责。法院还采用了以下证据：State Farm 的"大量财富"；证词："State Farm 的行为具有隐秘性，根据统计学概率，每 5 万起案件中至多有 1 起会受到惩罚……"因此，法院认为惩罚性损害赔偿金和补偿性损害赔偿金之间的比率并非不正当。最后，法院表示，与 State Farm 可能面临的以下各种民事和刑事处罚，包括每次欺诈行为 1 万美元、吊销在犹他州的营业执照、退还非法所得利润、与监禁等相比，该惩罚性损害赔偿金并非超额……我们批准了调卷令……

Ⅱ.

在 Cooper Industries, Inc. v. Leatherman Tool Group, Inc., 532 U.S. 424 案中，我们认为，在我们的司法体系中，补偿性损害赔偿金和惩罚性损害赔偿金虽然通常由同一决策者在同一时间裁定，但是出于不同目的……补偿性损害赔偿金"旨在补偿被告的不当行为使原告遭受的具体损失"……[引用《侵权法重述·第二次》第 903 条，pp. 453-454（1979）]。相比之下，惩罚性损害赔偿金服务于更广泛的功能，旨在阻吓和惩罚。Cooper Industries, supra……

尽管各州具有施加惩罚性损害赔偿金的裁量权，但是已经确立对于这些裁定的大量程序性和宪法性限制……原因在于"我们的宪法学理所昭示的基本公平概念要求一个人收到的公平提示不仅包含使其遭到惩罚的行为，还包含一个州施加的惩罚程度"……如果裁断金额明显超额，则无助于合法目的，并且构成对财产的任意剥夺……

虽然这些损害赔偿裁定服务于与刑事处罚相同的目的，但是在民事案件中支付惩罚性损害赔偿金的被告，并未获得刑事程序中适用的保护。这就增加了我们对于以不准确的方式管理惩罚性损害赔偿金制度的担忧。我们已经

systems are administered. We have admonished that "punitive damages pose an acute danger of arbitrary deprivation of property. Jury instructions typically leave the jury with wide discretion in choosing amounts, and the presentation of evidence of a defendant's net worth creates the potential that juries will use their verdicts to express biases against big businesses, particularly those without strong local presences."...

In light of these concerns, in *Gore supra*, ... we instructed courts reviewing punitive damages to consider three guideposts: (1) the degree of reprehensibility of the defendant's misconduct; (2) the disparity between the actual or potential harm suffered by the plaintiff and the punitive damages award; and (3) the difference between the punitive damages awarded by the jury and the civil penalties authorized or imposed in comparable cases. ... We reiterated the importance of these three guideposts in *Cooper Industries* and mandated appellate courts to conduct *de novo* review of a trial court's application of them to the jury's award. ... Exacting appellate review ensures that an award of punitive damages is based upon an 'application of law, rather than a decisionmaker's caprice.' ...

III

Under the principles outlined in *BMW of North America, Inc. v. Gore*, this case is neither close nor difficult. It was error to reinstate the jury's $145 million punitive damages award. We address each guidepost of *Gore* in some detail.

A

"The most important indicium of the reasonableness of a punitive damages award is the degree of reprehensibility of the defendant's conduct." ... We have instructed courts to determine the reprehensibility of a defendant by considering whether: the harm caused was physical as opposed to economic; the tortious conduct evinced an indifference to or a reckless disregard of the health or safety of others; the target of the conduct had financial vulnerability; the conduct involved repeated actions or was an isolated incident; and the harm was the result of intentional malice, trickery, or deceit, or mere accident. ... The existence of any one of these factors weighing in favor of a plaintiff may not be sufficient to sustain a punitive damages award; and the absence of all of them renders any award suspect. It should be presumed a plaintiff has been made whole for his injuries by compensatory damages, so punitive damages should only be awarded if the defendant's culpability, after having paid compensatory damages, is so reprehensible as to warrant the imposition of further sanctions to achieve punishment or deterrence. ...

Applying these factors in the instant case, we must acknowledge that State Farm's handling of the claims against the Campbells merits no praise. The trial court found that State Farm's employees altered the company's records to make Campbell appear less culpable. State Farm disregarded the overwhelming likelihood of liability and the near-certain probability that, by taking the case to trial, a judgment in excess of the policy limits would be awarded. State Farm amplified

告诫,"惩罚性损害赔偿金造成随意剥夺财产的危险。对陪审团的指令,一般使陪审团在选择金额时拥有很大的裁量权,并且被告资产净值的证据出示,使陪审团有可能在裁断时产生对大企业的偏见,特别是在当地没有较强影响力的企业"……

根据这些担心,在前引 Gore 案中……我们指示审核惩罚性损害赔偿金的法院考虑以下三项准则:(1)被告的不当行为应受谴责的程度;(2)原告受到的实际伤害或潜在伤害与其获得的惩罚性损害赔偿金之间的差异;(3)陪审团裁定的惩罚性损害赔偿金与可比案例中批准或施加的民事惩罚之间的差异……我们在 Cooper Industries 案中重申了这三项准则,命令上诉法院再次审核初审法院将这些准则适用于陪审团裁定的情况……严格的上诉审核确保惩罚性损害赔偿金裁定是基于"法律的适用,而不是决策者的任性"……

Ⅲ.

根据 BMW of North America, Inc. v. Gore 案中概述的原则,本案既不和 Gore 案相似也不困难。恢复陪审团的 1.45 亿美元惩罚性损害赔偿金是错误的。我们将一定程度地细察 Gore 案中的每项准则。

A

"惩罚性损害赔偿金裁定合理性的最重要标志是被告行为应受谴责的程度"……我们已经指示法院通过考虑以下因素确定被告应受谴责的程度:造成的损害是身体伤害还是经济损失;侵权行为表明不关心还是肆意漠视他人的健康或安全;行为的目标是否具有经济脆弱性;该行为涉及重复的行动,还是仅为孤立的事故;伤害是有意的恶意、欺骗或者谎言的结果,还是仅仅是事故……有利于原告的任何一种因素的存在,可能不足以支持惩罚性损害赔偿金裁定;如果所有因素都不存在,则使得任何裁定都可疑。应当假设,通过补偿性损害赔偿金已经对原告进行了伤害补偿,因此只有在支付补偿性损害赔偿金后,被告的行为应受谴责足以证明进一步制裁的正当性,在实现惩罚或阻吓的情况下,才应裁定惩罚性损害赔偿金……

通过在本案中适用这些因素,我们必须承认,State Farm 对于 Campbell 夫妇遭受的索赔处理失当。初审法院发现 State Farm 的员工修改了公司记录,使 Campbell 的可责难性降低。State Farm 无视承担责任的巨大可能性,以及将案件提交法院审理后出现超过保单限额裁定的几乎肯定的可能性。State

the harm by at first assuring the Campbells their assets would be safe from any verdict and by later telling them, postjudgment, to put a for-sale sign on their house. While we do not suggest there was error in awarding punitive damages based upon State Farm's conduct toward the Campbells, a more modest punishment for this reprehensible conduct could have satisfied the State's legitimate objectives, and the Utah courts should have gone no further.

This case, instead, was used as a platform to expose, and punish, the perceived deficiencies of State Farm's operations throughout the country. The Utah Supreme Court's opinion makes explicit that State Farm was being condemned for its nationwide policies rather than for the conduct directed toward the Campbells. 65 P.3d at 1143 ("The Campbells introduced evidence that State Farm's decision to take the case to trial was a result of a national scheme to meet corporate fiscal goals by capping payouts on claims company wide"). This was, as well, an explicit rationale of the trial court's decision in approving the award, though reduced from $145 million to $25 million. … ("The Campbells demonstrated, through the testimony of State Farm employees who had worked outside of Utah, and through expert testimony, that this pattern of claims adjustment under the PP&R program was not a local anomaly, but was a consistent, nationwide feature of State Farm's business operations, orchestrated from the highest levels of corporate management").

The Campbells contend that State Farm has only itself to blame for the reliance upon dissimilar and out-of-state conduct evidence. The record does not support this contention. From their opening statements onward the Campbells framed this case as a chance to rebuke State Farm for its nationwide activities. …("You're going to hear evidence that even the insurance commission in Utah and around the country are unwilling or inept at protecting people against abuses"); …("This is a very important case. …It transcends the Campbell file. It involves a nationwide practice. And you, here, are going to be evaluating and assessing, and hopefully requiring State Farm to stand accountable for what it's doing across the country, which is the purpose of punitive damages"). This was a position maintained throughout the litigation. In opposing State Farm's motion to exclude such evidence under *Gore*, the Campbells' counsel convinced the trial court that there was no limitation on the scope of evidence that could be considered under our precedents. …

A State cannot punish a defendant for conduct that may have been lawful where it occurred. …Nor, as a general rule, does a State have a legitimate concern in imposing punitive damages to punish a defendant for unlawful acts committed outside of the State's jurisdiction. Any proper adjudication of conduct that occurred outside Utah to other persons would require their inclusion, and, to those parties, the Utah courts, in the usual case, would need to apply the laws of their relevant jurisdiction. *Phillips Petroleum Co. v. Shutts,* 472 U.S. 797. …

Here, the Campbells do not dispute that much of the out-of-state conduct was lawful where it occurred. They argue, however, that such evidence was not the primary basis for the punitive damages award and was relevant to the extent it demonstrated, in a general sense, State Farm's

Farm 放大了伤害，即首先向 Campbell 夫妇保证他们的资产不会失去，然后在判决后告诉他们在房产上贴上待售标志。虽然我们并未表示根据 State Farm 对于 Campbell 夫妇的做法裁定惩罚性损害赔偿金有错误，但是对这种应受谴责的行为实施适度的惩罚就能实现该州的合法目标，犹他州法院不应走得更远。

本案实际上是一个平台，来揭露惩罚发现的 State Farm 全国业务的缺陷。犹他州最高法院的意见表明，State Farm 受到谴责的原因是其全国性政策，而非针对 Campbell 夫妇的行为。65 P.3d at 1143（"Campbell 夫妇提交证据，表明 State Farm 作出的将案件提交法院审理的决定是一项全国计划的结果，旨在通过设定公司范围的索赔要求支出的上限实现公司财务目标"）。这也是初审法院批准裁定的明确理由，虽然从 1.45 亿美元减至 2500 万美元……（"Campbell 夫妇通过在犹他州外工作的 State Farm 员工的证词以及专家证词证明，根据 PP&R 计划调整索赔的模式不是局部异常，而是 State Farm 业务在全国的一致性特征，由公司最高管理层制定"）。

Campbell 夫妇声称，由于对不同的州外行为证据的依赖，仅 State Farm 自身应受责备。案卷记载法院不支持这种观点。从开庭陈述起，Campbell 夫妇一直将本案作为指责 State Farm 的全国活动的机会……（"你们将会听到以下证据：即使是犹他州和全国的保险委员会也不愿或不能保障人们免受伤害"）……（"这是非常重要的案件……它超越了 Campbell 案。它涉及全国行为。你们在这里准备评估，并且有希望要求 State Farm 对其在全国的做法承担责任，这是惩罚性损害赔偿金的目的"）。这是整个诉讼中保持的立场。在反对 State Farm 根据 Gore 案排除该证据的请求时，Campbell 夫妇的辩护律师使初审法院相信，根据判例，对于所考虑的证据的范围没有限制……

一个州不能就在发生地合法的行为惩罚被告……作为一般规则，一个州也不应担心因在州外实施的非法行为向被告施加惩罚性损害赔偿金不合法。对于在犹他州外对其他人实施的行为的正确判决需要考虑这些人，并且在一般情况下，犹他州法院需要对此适用其相关法域的法律。例如，参见 Phillips Petroleum Co. v. Shutts, 472 U.S. 797 案……

在这里，Campbell 夫妇并未怀疑大多数州外行为在发生地是合法的。然而，他们认为，该证据不是惩罚性损害赔偿金的主要依据，而是在一般的意

motive against its insured. Brief for Respondents 46-47 ("Even if the practices described by State Farm were not malum in se or malum prohibitum, they became relevant to punitive damages to the extent they were used as tools to implement State Farm's wrongful PP&R policy"). This argument misses the mark. Lawful out-of-state conduct may be probative when it demonstrates the deliberateness and culpability of the defendant's action in the State where it is tortious, but that conduct must have a nexus to the specific harm suffered by the plaintiff. A jury must be instructed, furthermore, that it may not use evidence of out-of-state conduct to punish a defendant for action that was lawful in the jurisdiction where it occurred. …

For a more fundamental reason, however, the Utah courts erred in relying upon this and other evidence: The courts awarded punitive damages to punish and deter conduct that bore no relation to the Campbells' harm. A defendant's dissimilar acts, independent from the acts upon which liability was premised, may not serve as the basis for punitive damages. A defendant should be punished for the conduct that harmed the plaintiff, not for being an unsavory individual or business. Due process does not permit courts, in the calculation of punitive damages, to adjudicate the merits of other parties' hypothetical claims against a defendant under the guise of the reprehensibility analysis, but we have no doubt the Utah Supreme Court did that here. …Punishment on these bases creates the possibility of multiple punitive damages awards for the same conduct; for in the usual case nonparties are not bound by the judgment some other plaintiff obtains. …

The Campbells have identified scant evidence of repeated misconduct of the sort that injured them. Nor does our review of the Utah courts' decisions convince us that State Farm was only punished for its actions toward the Campbells. Although evidence of other acts need not be identical to have relevance in the calculation of punitive damages, the Utah court erred here because evidence pertaining to claims that had nothing to do with a third-party lawsuit was introduced at length. Other evidence concerning reprehensibility was even more tangential. For example, the Utah Supreme Court criticized State Farm's investigation into the personal life of one of its employees and, in a broader approach, the manner in which State Farm's policies corrupted its employees. …The Campbells attempt to justify the courts' reliance upon this unrelated testimony on the theory that each dollar of profit made by underpaying a third-party claimant is the same as a dollar made by underpaying a first-party one. …For the reasons already stated, this argument is unconvincing. The reprehensibility guidepost does not permit courts to expand the scope of the case so that a defendant may be punished for any malfeasance, which in this case extended for a 20-year period. In this case, because the Campbells have shown no conduct by State Farm similar to that which harmed them, the conduct that harmed them is the only conduct relevant to the reprehensibility analysis.

B

Turning to the second *Gore* guidepost, we have been reluctant to identify concrete

义上证明了 State Farm 对于被保险人的动机。被告答辩摘要 46-47（"即使 State Farm 描述的行为并非本质上违法或者法律禁止的违法，只要是用作实施 State Farm 不法的 PP&R 计划的工具，则也与惩罚性损害赔偿金有关"）。该论证并不正确。被告合法的州外行为在构成侵权行为的州证明其蓄意性和可责难性时，可以作为证据，但行为必须与原告遭受的具体伤害有关。而且，必须指示陪审团不能就发生地法域合法的行为使用州外行为证据惩罚被告……

然而，由于更根本的理由，犹他州法院错误地依赖了该证据和其他证据：法院裁定惩罚性损害赔偿金惩罚和阻止与 Campbell 夫妇受到的伤害无关的行为。被告的不同行为，独立于受责行为，不能作为惩罚性损害赔偿金的依据。被告受到处罚的原因应当是伤害原告的行为，而不是作为令人憎恶的个人或企业。正当程序不允许法院在计算惩罚性损害赔偿金时，假借可谴责性分析裁定其他方对于被告的假设索赔的是非。但在这里，犹他州最高法院无疑采取了这种做法……在此基础上的惩罚创建了对同一行为裁定多重惩罚性损害赔偿金的可能性；因为在一般情况下，非当事人不受其他原告获得的裁决的约束……

Campbell 夫妇已经确认了伤害他们的重复不当行为的证据不足。我们对于犹他州法院裁决的审核也未使我们相信，State Farm 仅因对 Campbell 夫妇的行为而受罚。虽然在计算惩罚性损害赔偿金时其他行为的证据无需同样相关，但是犹他州法院在这里犯了错误，因为最终提交的有关索赔的证据与第三方诉讼无关，与涉及可谴责性的其他证据更是无关。例如，犹他州最高法院批评 State Farm 调查一名员工的个人生活，以及 State Farm 的计划使员工堕落的方式……Campbell 夫妇试图根据以下理论证明法院依赖该无关证词是正当的：向第三方索赔者少付损害赔偿金获得的 1 美元利润，与向第一方索赔者少付损害赔偿金获得的 1 美元是相同的……由于已经陈述的理由，该论证没有说服力。可谴责性准则不允许法院扩展案件范围，使被告可因任何不当行为受罚，而在本案中扩大到 20 年的范围。在本案中，因为 Campbell 夫妇未表明与伤害他们的行为类似的 State Farm 的行为，所以伤害他们的行为是涉及可谴责性分析的唯一行为。

B

关于第二项 Gore 准则，我们不愿意确立对于原告受到的伤害或潜在伤害

constitutional limits on the ratio between harm, or potential harm, to the plaintiff and the punitive damages award. *Gore, supra*, at 582, 116 S. Ct. 1589 ("We have consistently rejected the notion that the constitutional line is marked by a simple mathematical formula, even one that compares actual *and potential* damages to the punitive award"); …We decline again to impose a bright-line ratio which a punitive damages award cannot exceed. Our jurisprudence and the principles it has now established demonstrate, however, that, in practice, few awards exceeding a single-digit ratio between punitive and compensatory damages, to a significant degree, will satisfy due process. In *Haslip*, in upholding a punitive damages award, we concluded that an award of more than four times the amount of compensatory damages might be close to the line of constitutional impropriety. 499 U.S., at 23-24. …We cited that 4-to-1 ratio again in *Gore*. 517 U.S., at 581. … The Court further referenced a long legislative history, dating back over 700 years and going forward to today, providing for sanctions of double, treble, or quadruple damages to deter and punish. … While these ratios are not binding, they are instructive. They demonstrate what should be obvious: Single-digit multipliers are more likely to comport with due process, while still achieving the State's goals of deterrence and retribution, than awards with ratios in range of 500 to 1, … or, in this case, of 145 to 1.

Nonetheless, because there are no rigid benchmarks that a punitive damages award may not surpass, ratios greater than those we have previously upheld may comport with due process where "a particularly egregious act has resulted in only a small amount of economic damages." …The converse is also true, however. When compensatory damages are substantial, then a lesser ratio, perhaps only equal to compensatory damages, can reach the outermost limit of the due process guarantee. The precise award in any case, of course, must be based upon the facts and circumstances of the defendant's conduct and the harm to the plaintiff.

In sum, courts must ensure that the measure of punishment is both reasonable and proportionate to the amount of harm to the plaintiff and to the general damages recovered. In the context of this case, we have no doubt that there is a presumption against an award that has a 145-to-1 ratio. The compensatory award in this case was substantial; the Campbells were awarded $1 million for a year and a half of emotional distress. This was complete compensation. The harm arose from a transaction in the economic realm, not from some physical assault or trauma; there were no physical injuries; and State Farm paid the excess verdict before the complaint was filed, so the Campbells suffered only minor economic injuries for the 18-month period in which State Farm refused to resolve the claim against them. The compensatory damages for the injury suffered here, moreover, likely were based on a component which was duplicated in the punitive award. Much of the distress was caused by the outrage and humiliation the Campbells suffered at the actions of their insurer; and it is a major role of punitive damages to condemn such conduct. Compensatory damages, however, already contain this punitive element. …

The Utah Supreme Court sought to justify the massive award by pointing to State Farm's

与惩罚性损害赔偿金之间的比率的具体宪法限制。Gore, supra, at 582,116 S. Ct. 1589 案（"我们一直否定以下观念：宪法界限由简单的数学公式标记，即使是实际和潜在的损害赔偿金与惩罚性损害赔偿金进行对比"）；……我们也拒绝强行设定惩罚性损害赔偿金不能超越的明确界限比率。然而，我们的法理学及其目前所确立的原则表明，很显著地在实际中的超过惩罚性损害赔偿金和补偿性损害赔偿金之间的一位数比率的裁决几乎是不能符合正当程序的。在 Haslip 案中，在支持惩罚性损害赔偿金裁定时，我们认为超过补偿性损害赔偿金四倍的裁定可能接近于违宪界限。499 U.S., at 23-24……我们再次引用 Gore. 517 U.S., at 581 中的 4:1 比率……法院进一步提及漫长的立法历史，追溯到 700 年前，又回到今天，规定双倍、三倍或四倍损害赔偿金的制裁，旨在阻吓和惩罚……虽然这些比率不具有约束力，但是却具有指导性。它们证明什么应当是明显的：尽管仍然要实现该州的阻吓和惩罚目标，但是对具有 500:1……或本案中的 145:1 范围内的比率的裁定来说，一位数比率更有可能符合正当程序。

然而，因为没有惩罚性损害赔偿金裁定不能超越的严格基准，所以在以下情形中，高于我们以前支持的比率的情况可能符合正当程序："极端恶劣的行为仅导致少量经济损失。"……但是反之亦然。如果补偿性损害赔偿金很高，则较小的比率（可能只有等于补偿性损害赔偿金）能够达到正当程序准许的最远界限。当然，在任何案件中，精确的裁定必须基于被告行为和原告所受伤害的事实和环境。

总之，法院必须确保惩罚尺度十分合理，并且与原告受到的伤害和获得的一般损害赔偿金成比例。在本案中，我们不怀疑存在反对具有 145:1 比率的裁决的假定。在本案中，补偿性损害赔偿金很高；Campbell 夫妇因一年半的精神损害获得了 100 万美元的损害赔偿金。这是完全的补偿。伤害来源于经济领域的交易，而非来自身体受袭或外伤；没有身体伤害；State Farm 在控告前支付了额外的损害赔偿金，因此 Campbell 夫妇在 18 个月中仅遭受了轻微的经济损失，在此期间，State Farm 拒绝解决针对他们的索赔。而且，在这里遭受的伤害的补偿性损害赔偿金可能是基于在惩罚性损害赔偿金中加倍的组成部分。大部分精神损害来自保险公司的行为导致的侮辱和羞辱；谴责该类行为是惩罚性损害赔偿金的主要作用。然而，补偿性损害赔偿金已经包含这种惩罚因素……

犹他州最高法院寻求通过指出以下情况证明高额损害赔偿金裁定的正当

purported failure to report a prior $100 million punitive damages award in Texas to its corporate headquarters; the fact that State Farm's policies have affected numerous Utah consumers; the fact that State Farm will only be punished in one out of every 50,000 cases as a matter of statistical probability; and State Farm's enormous wealth. ...Since the Supreme Court of Utah discussed the Texas award when applying the ratio guidepost, we discuss it here. The Texas award, however, should have been analyzed in the context of the reprehensibility guidepost only. The failure of the company to report the Texas award is out-of-state conduct that, if the conduct were similar, might have had some bearing on the degree of reprehensibility, subject to the limitations we have described. Here, it was dissimilar, and of such marginal relevance that it should have been accorded little or no weight. The award was rendered in a first-party lawsuit; no judgment was entered in the case; and it was later settled for a fraction of the verdict. With respect to the Utah Supreme Court's second justification, the Campbells' inability to direct us to testimony demonstrating harm to the people of Utah (other than those directly involved in this case) indicates that the adverse effect on the State's general population was in fact minor.

The remaining premises for the Utah Supreme Court's decision bear no relation to the award's reasonableness or proportionality to the harm. They are, rather, arguments that seek to defend a departure from well-established constraints on punitive damages. While States enjoy considerable discretion in deducing when punitive damages are warranted, each award must comport with the principles set forth in *Gore*. Here the argument that State Farm will be punished in only the rare case, coupled with reference to its assets (which, of course, are what other insured parties in Utah and other States must rely upon for payment of claims) had little to do with the actual harm sustained by the Campbells. The wealth of a defendant cannot justify an otherwise unconstitutional punitive damages award. ... ("Wealth provides an open-ended basis for inflating awards when the defendant is wealthy. ...That does not make its use unlawful or inappropriate; it simply means that this factor cannot make up for the failure of other factors, such as 'reprehensibility,' to constrain significantly an award that purports to punish a defendant's conduct"). The principles set forth in *Gore* must be implemented with care, to ensure both reasonableness and proportionality.

C

The third guidepost in *Gore* is the disparity between the punitive damages award and the "civil penalties authorized or imposed in comparable cases."...We note that, in the past, we have also looked to criminal penalties that could be imposed. ...The existence of a criminal penalty does have bearing on the seriousness with which a State views the wrongful action. When used to determine the dollar amount of the award, however, the criminal penalty has less utility. Great care must be taken to avoid use of the civil process to assess criminal penalties that can be imposed only after the heightened protections of a criminal trial have been observed, including, of course, its higher standards of proof. Punitive damages are not a substitute for the criminal process, and the

性；指出 State Farm 未能向公司总部报告以前在德克萨斯州受到的 1 亿美元惩罚性损害赔偿金的处罚；State Farm 的计划影响众多犹他州消费者的事实；根据统计学概率，每 5 万起案件中至多有 1 起会使 State Farm 受到惩罚的事实；State Farm 的巨大财富……因为犹他州最高法院在适用比率准则时讨论了得克萨斯州的裁定，所以我们在这里讨论一下该裁定。然而，对得克萨斯州裁定应当仅在可谴责性准则的背景下分析。公司未能报告得克萨斯州裁定是州外行为，根据我们陈述的限制，如果行为类似，则可能会涉及可谴责性程度。在这里，该行为是不同的行为，具有很小的重要性或根本不重要。该裁定在第一方诉讼中作出；在该案中未判决；后来以裁断金额的一部分进行了和解。关于犹他州最高法院的第二项理由，Campbell 夫妇不能向我们提交证明犹他州居民（不包括本案直接涉及的人）受害的证词，表明对于该州居民的不利影响实际很小。

犹他州最高法院裁决的剩余部分与损害赔偿金的合理性以及与伤害的成比例性无关。这些观点是在寻求对违反的辩护。尽管各州在推断何时准许惩罚性损害赔偿金时享有很大的裁量权，但每项裁定必须符合 Gore 案中陈述的原则。State Farm 几乎不会受到惩罚并且提及其资产（犹他州和其他州的其他被保险人当然必须依赖这一点，从而获得损害赔偿金）与 Campbell 夫妇遭受的实际伤害几乎没有关系。被告的财富不能证明在其他方面违宪的惩罚性损害赔偿金裁定是正当的……["在被告很富有时，财富提供了提高损害赔偿金的无限制依据……这不会使它的使用非法或不适当；这仅意味着该因素不能补偿其他因素的缺乏（例如可谴责性），从而大量限制主张惩罚被告行为的裁定"]。Gore 案中陈述的原则必须谨慎实施，以确保其合理性和成比例性。

C

Gore 案中的第三项准则是惩罚性损害赔偿金裁定与"可比案例中批准或施加的民事惩罚"之间的差异……我们注意到，过去我们也期望能够施加刑事处罚……刑事处罚的存在确实与一个州看待不当行为的严肃性有关。然而，在用于确定损害赔偿金金额时，刑事处罚的作用不大。必须十分谨慎，以避免使用民事程序评估刑事处罚，因为只有在实施刑事审判的增强保护（当然包括更高的证据标准）后才能施加刑事处罚。惩罚性损害赔偿金不是刑事程序的替代，刑事制裁的微弱可能性不会自动支持惩罚性损害赔偿金裁定。

remote possibility of a criminal sanction does not automatically sustain a punitive damages award.

Here, we need not dwell long on this guidepost. The most relevant civil sanction under Utah state law for the wrong done to the Campbells appears to be a $10,000 fine for an act of fraud ... an amount dwarfed by the $145 million punitive damages award. The Supreme Court of Utah speculated about the loss of State Farm's business license, the disgorgement of profits, and possible imprisonment, but here again its references were to the broad fraudulent scheme drawn from evidence of out-of-state and dissimilar conduct. This analysis was insufficient to justify the award.

IV

An application of the *Gore* guideposts to the facts of this case, especially in light of the substantial compensatory damages awarded (a portion of which contained a punitive element), likely would justify a punitive damages award at or near the amount of compensatory damages. The punitive award of $145 million, therefore, was neither reasonable nor proportionate to the wrong committed, and it was an irrational and arbitrary deprivation of the property of the defendant. The proper calculation of punitive damages under the principles we have discussed should be resolved, in the first instance, by the Utah courts.

The judgment of the Utah Supreme Court is reversed, and the case is remanded for proceedings not inconsistent with this opinion.

It is so ordered.

...

The Court dismisses the evidence describing and documenting State Farm's PP&R policy and practices as essentially irrelevant, bearing "no relation to the Campbells' harm."... It is hardly apparent why that should be so. What is infirm about the Campbells' theory that their experience with State Farm exemplifies and reflects an overarching underpayment scheme, one that caused "repeated misconduct of the sort that injured them," ...? The Court's silence on that score is revealing: Once one recognizes that the Campbells did show "conduct by State Farm similar to that which harmed them," ...it becomes impossible to shrink the reprehensibility analysis to this sole case, or to maintain, at odds with the determination of the trial court ... that "the adverse effect on the State's general population was in fact minor," *ante*, at 1525.

Evidence of out-of-state conduct, the Court acknowledges, may be "probative when it demonstrates the deliberateness and culpability of the defendant's action in the State where it is tortious. ..." "Other acts" evidence concerning practices both in and out of State was introduced in this case to show just such "deliberateness" and "culpability." The evidence was admissible, the trial court ruled: (1) to document State Farm's "reprehensible" PP&R program; and (2) to "rebut State Farm's assertion that its actions toward the Campbells were inadvertent errors or mistakes in judgment."...Viewed in this light, there surely was "a nexus"...between much of the "other acts" evidence and "the specific harm suffered by the Campbells."...

在这里，我们无须详述该准则。根据犹他州法律，对于伤害 Campbell 夫妇的不当行为的最适当民事制裁，似乎是对于欺诈行为的 1 万美元罚款……与 1.45 亿美元惩罚性损害赔偿金相比简直微不足道。犹他州最高法院推测 State Farm 营业执照的吊销、退还非法所得利润，以及可能的监禁，但在这里它再次提及来自州外不同行为证据的广泛的欺诈计划。该分析不足以证明裁定的正当性。

Ⅳ.

将 Gore 准则适用于本案的事实，特别是基于已经裁定的高额补偿性损害赔偿金（其中的一部分包含惩罚因素），可能会证明等于或接近补偿性损害赔偿金的惩罚性损害赔偿金裁定是正当的。因此，1.45 亿美元的惩罚性损害赔偿金既非合理，亦非与从事的不法行为相称，这是无理和武断地剥夺被告财产。犹他州法院首先应当解决的是根据我们讨论的原则正确计算惩罚性损害赔偿金。

撤销犹他州最高法院的判决，案件发回重审，其诉讼程序不能不符合本意见。

特此发出法庭命令。

……

法院不考虑被认为在本质上与 State Farm 的 PP&R 计划和行为无关的描述和记录的证据，认为"与 Campbell 夫妇受到的伤害无关"……为什么应当这样并不明确。Campbell 夫妇的以下理论为什么缺乏效力：他们与 State Farm 接触的经验证明和反映了导致"伤害他们的该类不当行为不断重复"的整个少付计划。法院在这一点上的沉默表明：一旦确认 Campbell 夫妇指出"State Farm 的行为与伤害他们的行为类似"，就不可能将可谴责性分析缩小至本案，或主张（与初审法院的判决不同）……"对于该州居民的不利影响实际上很小"。

法院承认，州外行为的证据"在被告行为具有侵权性的州证明被告行为的蓄意性和可责难性时，可能能够提供证明"……在本案中引入有关州内和州外行为的"其他行为"证据仅旨在表明"蓄意性"和"可责难性"。可接受该证据，并且初审法院裁定：（1）记录 State Farm 的"可责"PP&R 计划；（2）"驳回 State Farm 的以下主张：其对于 Campbell 夫妇的行为是无意中的错误或判断错误。"……由此看来，大部分"其他行为"证据和"Campbell 夫妇受到的具体伤害"之间确实存在"关联"……

When the Court first ventured to override state-court punitive damages awards, it did so moderately. The Court recalled that "in our federal system, States necessarily have considerable flexibility in determining the level of punitive damages that they will allow in different classes of cases and in any particular case." *Gore*, 517 U.S., at 568…Today's decision exhibits no such respect and restraint. No longer content to accord state-court judgments "a strong presumption of validity."…the Court announces that "few awards exceeding a single-digit ratio between punitive and compensatory damages, to a significant degree, will satisfy due process."…Moreover, the Court adds, when compensatory damages are substantial, doubling those damages "can reach the outermost limit of the due process guarantee."…In a legislative scheme or a state high court's design to cap punitive damages, the handiwork in setting single-digit and 1-to-1 benchmarks could hardly be questioned; in a judicial decree imposed on the States by this Court under the banner of substantive due process, the numerical controls today's decision installs seem to me boldly out of order.

…

I remain of the view that this Court has no warrant to reform state law governing awards of punitive damages. …Even if I were prepared to accept the flexible guides prescribed in *Gore*, I would not join the Court's swift conversion of those guides into instructions that begin to resemble marching orders. For the reasons stated, I would leave the judgment of the Utah Supreme Court undisturbed. …

78. Rookes v Barnard [1964] AC 1129

House of Lords, United Kingdom

LORD DEVLIN

There are certain categories of cases in which an award of exemplary damages can serve a useful purpose in vindicating the strength of the law and thus affording a practical justification for admitting into the civil law a principle which ought logically to belong to the criminal. I propose to state what these two categories are; and I propose also to state three general considerations which, in my opinion, should always be borne in mind when awards of exemplary damages are being made. I am well aware that what I am about to say will, if accepted, impose limits not hitherto expressed on such awards and that there is powerful, though not compelling, authority for allowing them a wider range. …

The first category is oppressive, arbitrary or unconstitutional action by the servants of the government. I should not extend this category—I say this with particular reference to the facts of this case—to oppressive action by private corporations or individuals. Where one man is more powerful than another, it is inevitable that he will try to use his power to gain his ends; and if his

法院最初大胆推翻州法院的惩罚性损害赔偿金裁定时，是适度进行的。法院回述道："在我们的联邦制度中，各州必然十分灵活地确定不同类别的案件和具体案件的惩罚性损害赔偿金水平。"Gore, 517 U.S., at 568……今天的裁决未显示这种尊重和克制。不再满足于赋予州法院的判决"有力的有效性假设"……法院表示"在超过惩罚性损害赔偿金和补偿性损害赔偿金之间的一位数比率的裁决中，在显著程度上，几乎没有能够符合正当程序的"……而且，法院补充说，在补偿性损害赔偿金很高时，损害赔偿金加倍"能够达到正当程序准许的最远界限"……在立法方案或州高等法院确定惩罚性损害赔偿金上限的设计中，建立一位数和1:1基准的工作几乎不会受到质疑。我认为，在本法院以实质性正当程序的名义向各州发布的司法命令中，今天的判决建立的数字控制显然存在问题。

……

我仍然认为，本法院没有改革有关惩罚性损害赔偿金裁定的州法律的正当理由……我即使准备接受 Gore 案中规定的灵活指导，也不会参与本法院迅速将这些引导转化为开始类似于出发令的指示。基于上述理由，我宁可不干涉犹他州最高法院的判决……

78. Rookes v Barnard [1964] AC 1129

联合王国上议院

Devlin 大法官

在某些情况下，惩罚性赔偿可以很好地维护法律权威，因此可以有效地论证为什么我们要将一个逻辑上属于刑法的原则纳入民法中。下面我将说明以上两种情况是什么；此外，我还将提出三点在判决给予惩罚性赔偿时需要考量的因素。我很清楚我要说的一旦被接受，会对惩罚性赔偿施加一些目前还没有的限制，而且目前有很多有力的判例（虽然我认为它们欠缺说服力）允许在更大的范围给予惩罚性赔偿。

第一种类型的情况是政府公务员做出的压迫、武断或者违宪的行为。我不能把这种类型扩展到私人公司或者自然人所做出的压迫行为上，我刚提到的这个问题恰恰就是本案的情况。一个人比另一个人强的时候，前者不可避免地会用他的强大来实现其目的；如果他的力量比对方强大得多，我们也许

power is much greater than the other's, he might, perhaps, be said to be using it oppressively. If he uses his power illegally, he must of course pay for his illegality in the ordinary way; but he is not to be punished simply because he is the more powerful. In the case of the government it is different, for the servants of the government are also the servants of the people and the use of their power must always be subordinate to their duty of service. It is true that there is something repugnant about a big man bullying a small man and, very likely, the bullying will be a source of humiliation that makes the case one for aggravated damages, but it is not, in my opinion, punishable by damages.

Cases in the second category are those in which the defendant's conduct has been calculated by him to make a profit for himself which may well exceed the compensation payable to the plaintiff. I have quoted the dictum of Erle C.J. in *Bell v. Midland Railway Co.* Maule J. in *Williams v. Currie* suggests the same thing; and so does Martin B. in an obiter dictum in *Crouch v. Great Northern Railway Co.* It is a factor also that is taken into account in damages for libel; one man should not be allowed to sell another man's reputation for profit. Where a defendant with a cynical disregard for a plaintiff's rights has calculated that the money to be made out of his wrongdoing will probably exceed the damages at risk, it is necessary for the law to show that it cannot be broken with impunity. This category is not confined to moneymaking in the strict sense. It extends to cases in which the defendant is seeking to gain at the expense of the plaintiff some object—perhaps some property which he covets—which either he could not obtain at all or not obtain except at a price greater than he wants to put down. Exemplary damages can properly be awarded whenever it is necessary to teach a wrongdoer that tort does not pay.

To these two categories which are established as part of the common law there must of course be added any category in which exemplary damages are expressly authorised by statute.

I wish now to express three considerations which I think should always be borne in mind when awards of exemplary damages are being considered. First, the plaintiff cannot recover exemplary damages unless he is the victim of the punishable behaviour. The anomaly inherent in exemplary damages would become an absurdity if a plaintiff totally unaffected by some oppressive conduct which the jury wished to punish obtained a windfall in consequence.

Secondly, the power to award exemplary damages constitutes a weapon that, while it can be used in defence of liberty, as in the *Wilkes case*, can also be used against liberty. Some of the awards that juries have made in the past seem to me to amount to a greater punishment than would be likely to be incurred if the conduct were criminal; and, moreover, a punishment imposed without the safeguard which the criminal law gives to an offender. I should not allow the respect which is traditionally paid to an assessment of damages by a jury to prevent me from seeing that the weapon is used with restraint. It may even be that the House may find it necessary to follow the precedent it set for itself in *Benham v. Gambling*, and place some arbitrary limit on awards of

可以说他"压迫地"使用了它的力量。如果他使用力量的方式是非法的，按照一般情况他毋庸置疑地要为这种违法付出代价，然而他并不会仅仅因为他更强大就要被惩罚。在涉及政府的时候，情况又不一样了。因为公务员是为政府服务的，也是为人民服务的；而公务员使用他们的权力时，必须受到他们为人民服务的义务的限制。强者欺凌弱者，确实令人厌恶。欺凌也常常确实会让受害人蒙羞，因此会增加损害赔偿金。然而，在我看来这并不是说我们在用损害赔偿金惩罚欺凌。

第二种类型的情况则是被告经过计算，发觉其行为可以获利，且所获之利远远超过对原告的损害赔偿数额。我引用了 Erle 首席法官在 *Bell v Midland Railway Co.* 案中的附带意见。Maule 法官在 *Williams v Currie* 案中也是同样的意见。同样的还有财税法院 Martin 法官在 *Crouch v Great Northern Railway Co.* 案中的附带意见。在诽谤案中，这也是一个需要考量的因素：一个人不能靠出卖另外一个人的声誉赚钱。玩世不恭、目无原告之权利的被告可能发现他从他做的坏事中能得到的钱，比他可能要给出的赔偿金要多，这时法律就要告诉他，他不可能违法了还什么事都没有。这种类型并不局限于那种被告可以在严格意义上挣到钱的情形。它同样包括被告在损害原告利益的前提下，获得了某些东西，这可能是某处他觊觎的地产：他如果不是靠损害原告的利益，则要么完全不可能获得这个地产，要么就要付出比他实际支付的多得多的价金。只要有必要教训侵权人通过侵权行为不可能获利，我们就有必要让他支付惩罚性赔偿金。

除了上述两类普通法发展起来的类型外，成文法所明确规定的惩罚性赔偿当然也属于授权的类型。

我现在要来说一说我认为在给出惩罚性赔偿时需要考量的三项因素。首先，要获得惩罚性赔偿的原告必须是应该惩罚的行为的受害人。惩罚性赔偿天然是反常的，而如果陪审团仅仅因为要惩罚一个压迫行为，就允许一个完全没有受到该行为侵害的原告获得一笔天降横财，这种反常将变成荒谬。

其次，给予惩罚性赔偿的权力是一件武器，它既可以用来捍卫自由，就像 *Wilkes* 案那样，也可以损害自由。在我看来，之前的有些案件中陪审团所判决的惩罚性赔偿，是比刑罚还重的惩罚。这种惩罚在被做出时，侵权人还没有刑法给犯罪嫌疑人提供的保护。传统上，我们都尊重陪审团对损害赔偿金的计算。然而不能因为这种尊重就否认这种武器应该有节制地适用。上议院可能会遵循自己在 *Benham v Gambling* 案中作出的先例，在给予惩罚性赔偿的时候加上某些任意而武断的限制。然而，只是劝陪审团下手温和一点

damages that are made by way of punishment. Exhortations to be moderate may not be enough.

Thirdly, the means of the parties, irrelevant in the assessment of compensation, are material in the assessment of exemplary damages. Everything which aggravates or mitigates the defendant's conduct is relevant.

Thus a case for exemplary damages must be presented quite differently from one for compensatory damages; and the judge should not allow it to be left to the jury unless he is satisfied that it can be brought within the categories I have specified. But the fact that the two sorts of damage differ essentially does not necessarily mean that there should be two awards. In a case in which exemplary damages are appropriate, a jury should be directed that if, but only if, the sum which they have in mind to award as compensation (which may, of course, be a sum aggravated by the way in which the defendant has behaved to the plaintiff) is inadequate to punish him for his outrageous conduct, to mark their disapproval of such conduct and to deter him from repeating it, then it can award some larger sum. If a verdict given on such direction has to be reviewed upon appeal, the appellate court will first consider whether the award can be justified as compensation and if it can, there is nothing further to be said. If it cannot, the court must consider whether or not the punishment is, in all the circumstances, excessive. There may be cases in which it is difficult for a judge to say whether or not he ought to leave to the jury a claim for exemplary damages. In such circumstances, and in order to save the possible expense of a new trial, I see no objection to his inviting the jury to say what sum they would fix as compensation and what additional sum, if any, they would award if they were entitled to give exemplary damages.

79. Cassell v Broome [1972] AC 1027

House of Lords, United Kingdom

LORD REID

The award of exemplary damages meant that the plaintiff, by being given more than on any view could be justified as compensation, was being given a pure and undeserved windfall at the expense of the defendant, and that in so far as the defendant was being required to pay more than could possibly be regarded as compensation he was being subjected to pure punishment.

I thought and still think that that is highly anomalous. It is confusing the function of the civil law which is to compensate with the function of the criminal law which is to inflict deterrent and punitive penalties. Some objection has been taken to the use of the word "fine" to denote the amount by which punitive or exemplary damages exceed anything justly due to the plaintiff. In my view the word "fine" is an entirely accurate description of that part of any award which goes beyond anything justly due to the plaintiff and is purely punitive.

…

是不够的。

最后，双方当事人的行为在计算填补性的赔偿金时是无关紧要的，但是在计算惩罚性赔偿金时则非常关键。任何可能加重或减轻被告行为的性质的因素，都是相关的。

综上，惩罚性赔偿的案件和填补性赔偿的案件大有不同。除非法官确信案件属于我刚才所说的类型，法官不应该让陪审团来决定赔偿金的数额。虽然这两种赔偿金本质上不同，但是这并不是说我们要判定两种赔偿金。如果一个案件中，给予惩罚性赔偿金是正确的，法官应该这么引导陪审团：当且仅当陪审员们认为自己脑中确定的填补性赔偿金的数额（填补性的赔偿金的数额当然也是可能因为被告对原告的行为而加大的）不足以惩罚被告那骇人听闻的行为时、不足以表达自己对这种行为的反对时、不足以防止他再犯时，陪审员们才应该在填补性的赔偿金以上增加一些数额。如果在上诉案中需要重审陪审员的决定，上诉法院应当先考察陪审员所决定的赔偿金是否属于填补性的，如果是，那就没什么好说的了；如果不是，法院则应当根据所有的情况，考量对被告的惩罚是否过重。某些情况下法官无法判定到底应不应该让陪审团来决定惩罚性赔偿金。这时，为了避免发回重审的麻烦，法官完全可以让陪审团决定两次：第一次决定他们认为合理的填补性赔偿金的数额；第二次则决定如果他们有权作出惩罚性赔偿的决定，这个额外的赔偿金数额应当是多少。

79. Cassell v Broome [1972] AC 1027

联合王国上议院

Reid 大法官

对惩罚性赔偿的裁决，意味着原告获得了用任何观点都无法证明有理的巨额赔偿，这纯粹就是一笔不恰当的横财，而这笔横财是以被告的利益为代价的，因为被告支付了远远大于应该支付的赔偿金数额，可以说被告其实得到了纯粹的惩罚。

我曾经认为，现在也认为惩罚性赔偿是不正常的。它混淆了民法的填补损失功能和刑法的威慑和惩罚的功能。有人反对用"罚款"这个词来描述惩罚性赔偿金高出原告所应得的那部分份额。而我却觉得"罚款"这个词用来描述任何高出原告应得的、作为纯粹对被告惩罚的那部分赔偿金，都是非常准确的。

……

I think that the objections to allowing juries to go beyond compensatory damages are overwhelming. To allow pure punishment in this way contravenes almost every principle which has been evolved for the protection of offenders. There is no definition of the offence except that the conduct punished must be oppressive, high-handed, malicious, wanton or its like - terms far too vague to be admitted to any criminal code worthy of the name. There is no limit to the punishment except that it must not be unreasonable. The punishment is not inflicted by a judge who has experience and at least tries not to be influenced by emotion: it is inflicted by a jury without experience of law or punishment and often swayed by considerations which every judge would put out of his mind. and there is no effective appeal against sentence. All that a reviewing court can do is to quash the jury's decision if it thinks the punishment awarded is more than any twelve reasonable men could award. The court cannot substitute its own award. The punishment must then be decided by another jury and if they too award heavy punishment the court is virtually powerless. It is no excuse to say that we need not waste sympathy on people who behave outrageously. Are we wasting sympathy on vicious criminals when we insist on proper legal safeguards for them? The right to give punitive damages in certain cases is so firmly embedded in our law that only Parliament can remove it. But I must say that I am surprised by the enthusiasm of Lord Devlin's critics in supporting this form of palm tree justice.

...

LORD WILBERFORCE

It cannot lightly be taken for granted, even as a matter of theory, that the purpose of the law of tort is compensation, still less that it ought to be, an issue of large social import, or that there is something inappropriate or illogical or anomalous (a question-begging word) in including a punitive element in civil damages, or, conversely, that the criminal law, rather than the civil law, is in these cases the better instrument for conveying social disapproval, or for redressing a wrong to the social fabric, or that damages in any case can be broken down into the two separate elements. As a matter of practice English law has not committed itself to any of these theories: it may have been wiser than it knew.

80. Kuddus v Chief Constable of Leicestershire Constabulary [2001] UKHL 29, [2002] 2 AC 122

House of Lords, United Kingdom

LORD NICHOLLS

The arguments for and against exemplary damages need no rehearsing. They are familiar enough, and they are set out clearly in the Law Commission's report. In the end, and in respectful agreement with the views expressed by Lord Wilberforce in *Broome v Cassell & Co Ltd* [1972] AC 1027, 1114, the feature I find most striking is the extent to which the principle of exemplary

我认为不允许陪审团给出超过填补性赔偿的数额是很有道理的。允许像这样的纯粹惩罚性的措施，基本上与历年发展而来的所有旨在保护侵权人的原则相冲突。对于可以要求惩罚性赔偿的侵权行为我们并没有定义，除了说受到惩罚的行为必须是残酷的、横暴的、恶毒的和肆虐的或者这一类的形容词。然而这样的词汇实在是太模糊了，是无法被任何值得提到的刑法典所接受的，而且对惩罚也没有限制，除了说这种惩罚必须适当。再者这种惩罚也不是由有经验的，至少是试着不被情绪影响的法官做出的，而是由没有法律经验的陪审团做出的，这样的惩罚决定经常被任何法官都认为不应当考虑的因素所左右。对于这样的惩罚，也没有有效的上诉机制。如果法院认为这种惩罚是十二个理性人所不可能做出的，其能做的也只是推翻陪审团的决定，法院并不能自己去给出一个赔偿金的数额。在法院推翻这个数额之后，另一个陪审团又可以再决定惩罚，如果这次数额又太高了，法院能做的其实就很少了。我们没有理由说，我们不必对凶暴之人浪费我们的同情心。我们对于凶狠的罪犯都提供正当程序保护，难道我们是在对他们浪费同情心？允许惩罚性赔偿，这在某些情况下是我们的法律里根深蒂固的观念，这只有议会能去除。然而我必须说，对Devlin大法官的批评者们支持这种"棕榈树司法"①的狂热，我真的很惊讶。

......

Wilberforce大法官

即便是作为一种理论这么认为，我们也不能理所应当地认为侵权法的目的就是补偿，更不能认为侵权法的目的就应该是补偿，因为这毕竟是一个对社会很重要的问题，或者认为在民事赔偿金中加入一点惩罚性的成分有什么不恰当的，有什么不合逻辑的或者有什么不正常的（这个词经常会引发问题）；或者认为刑法比民法更适合在这类案件中表达社会的不满，救济对社会结构的破坏；或者在所有的情况下，赔偿金都能被分解为泾渭分明的两部分。事实上英格兰法并没有把自己限制在以上任何一种理论中：它可能没有意识到自己这样做是多么明智。

80. Kuddus v Chief Constable of Leicestershire Constabulary [2001] UKHL 29, [2002] 2 AC 122

联合王国上议院

Nicholls大法官

我们没有必要再赘述支持和反对惩罚性赔偿的意见了。我们对此已经非

---

① 穆斯林国家的民事法官坐在棕榈树下，不以先例与典籍为依据的司法，指不考虑法律原则和法律规定而作出裁判.这种做法对具体案件可能达到公正的结果，但如果对每一案件都单独决定，则类似的案件将难以保持统一。

damages continues to have vitality. The availability of exemplary damages has played a significant role in buttressing civil liberties, in claims for false imprisonment and wrongful arrest. From time to time cases do arise where awards of compensatory damages are perceived as inadequate to achieve a just result between the parties. The nature of the defendant's conduct calls for a further response from the courts. On occasion conscious wrongdoing by a defendant is so outrageous, his disregard of the plaintiff's rights so contumelious, that something more is needed to show that the law will not tolerate such behaviour. Without an award of exemplary damages, justice will not have been done. Exemplary damages, as a remedy of last resort, fill what otherwise would be a regrettable lacuna.

This experience has not been confined to this country. Exemplary damages continue to discharge a role, perceived to be useful and valuable, in other common law jurisdictions. Indeed, the restrictions on exemplary damages imposed by *Rookes v Barnard* and *Broome v Cassell & Co Ltd* did not strike a receptive chord, for instance, in Canada, Australia or New Zealand. Outside the United Kingdom *Rookes v Barnard* received a generally negative reception.

If exemplary damages are to continue as a remedial tool, as recommended by the Law Commission after extensive consultation, the difficult question which arises concerns the circumstances in which this tool should be available for use. Stated in its broadest form, the relevant principle is tolerably clear: the availability of exemplary damages should be coextensive with its rationale. As already indicated, the underlying rationale lies in the sense of outrage which a defendant's conduct sometimes evokes, a sense not always assuaged fully by a compensatory award of damages, even when the damages are increased to reflect emotional distress.

In *Rookes v Barnard* [1964] AC 1129, 1226, Lord Devlin drew a distinction between oppressive acts by government officials and similar acts by companies or individuals. He considered that exemplary damages should not be available in the case of non-governmental oppression or bullying. Whatever may have been the position 40 years ago, I am respectfully inclined to doubt the soundness of this distinction today. National and international companies can exercise enormous power. So do some individuals. I am not sure it would be right to draw a hard-and-fast line which would always exclude such companies and persons from the reach of exemplary damages. Indeed, the validity of the dividing line drawn by Lord Devlin when formulating his first category is somewhat undermined by his second category, where the defendants are not confined to, and normally would not be, government officials or the like.

...

LORD SCOTT

I agree with Lord Nicholls that the question whether exemplary damages are available in misfeasance in public office cases cannot be answered without first asking whether exemplary damages *should* be available in misfeasance cases. And that question cannot be answered without

常熟悉，而且在法律委员会的报告里也写得很清楚。对 Wilberforce 大法官在 *Broome v Cassell & Co Ltd* [1972] AC 1027 案中的表述，我敬重地同意。这其中最让我惊讶的，是惩罚性赔偿原则居然依然如此有生命力。惩罚性赔偿的存在，对保护非法拘禁和非法逮捕案件中的公民自由，起着极大的作用。时常会有这类案件产生，其中填补性的赔偿金并不足以在双方当事人之间实现正义的结果，被告行为的性质可能需要法庭进一步回应。在被告的行为实在是太骇人听闻、他对原告权利的无视实在是太无礼的场合，我们需要一点别的东西来告诉他"你的行为法律不会容忍"。没有惩罚性赔偿，正义是无法实现的。惩罚性赔偿作为一种最后的救济措施，如果不存在，将构成一个遗憾的漏洞，而它的存在则填补了这个漏洞。

我们的这种经验并非仅仅适用于我国。在其他的英美法系法域，惩罚性赔偿都起到了很宝贵的作用。说真的，*Rookes v Barnard* 和 *Broome v Cassell & Co Ltd* 案中应用的对惩罚性赔偿的限制在其他国家比如加拿大、澳大利亚和新西兰都没有产生共鸣。在英国以外，*Rookes v Barnard* 案受到的一般都是负面评价。

如果我们要继续适用惩罚性赔偿作为救济措施，正如法律委员会在广泛听取意见之后建议的那样，我们将面临一个困难的问题：这种工具在什么样的场合下才该使用？以其最广泛的形式陈述，相关的原则其实还是比较清楚的：什么时候可以用惩罚性赔偿，要看惩罚性赔偿背后的原理。如前所述，这个背后的原理是被告的行为引起了公愤，这种公愤并不能完全由填补性的赔偿金所平息，即使我们已经提高了赔偿金的数额，以反映受害人所遭受的精神损害。

在 *Rookes v Barnard* [1964] AC 1129, 1226 一案中，Devlin 法官认为应当区别对待政府官员的压迫行为和私人公司、个人的压迫行为。他认为对非政府的主体实施的压迫或者欺凌行为不应该适用惩罚性赔偿。四十年前的情况暂且不论，但是我恭敬地怀疑今天仍存在这种区分的合理性。全国性的公司或者跨国公司有能力行使巨大的权力。某些个人也能行使巨大的权力。我不认为我们划分一条泾渭分明的线将所有的公司和个人都排除出惩罚性赔偿的适用范围是一件正确的事。其实 Devlin 法官画的这条线已经在一定程度上被他的第二种类型所侵蚀了。第二种类型并不局限于政府官员一类的主体，而且一般情况下也并不涉及政府官员之类的人。

……

Scott 大法官

我赞同 Nicholls 大法官的意见：要回答是不是应该在公职人员行为失当案件中适用惩罚性赔偿，关键是先要回答在这种情况下适用这种赔偿应不应该。而要回答这个问题，又必须先考量民法中惩罚性赔偿的作用和性质。涉

considering the role and propriety of exemplary damages in the civil law. The law regarding exemplary damages did not become fossilised and set in stone when Lord Devlin pronounced in 1964 (*Rookes v Barnard* [1964] AC 1129) or when the seven members of the House pronounced in 1972 (*Broome v Cassell & Co Ltd* [1972] AC 1027). Since then the common law has flowed on. One of the great developments of the common law since the time of *Rookes v Barnard* has been in the area of public law and judicial review to which Lord Diplock referred. Oppressive, arbitrary and unconstitutional acts by members of the executive can be remedied through civil proceedings brought in the High Court. The remedies the court can provide include awards of damages, declarations of right and, in most cases, injunctions. The developments since Lord Diplock's remarks in *Broome v Cassell & Co Ltd* have transformed the ability of the ordinary citizen to obtain redress. The continuing need in the year 2001 for exemplary damages as a civil remedy in order to control, deter and punish acts falling within Lord Devlin's first category is not in the least obvious.

My noble and learned friend, Lord Hutton, has referred, as examples, to two cases in Northern Ireland where in his view the award of exemplary damages served a valuable purpose in restraining the arbitrary and outrageous use of executive power and in vindicating the strength of the law. In one case (*Lavery v Ministry of Defence* [1984] NI 99) a soldier was the wrongdoer. The Ministry of Defence was the defendant. In the other case (*Pettigrew v Northern Ireland Office* [1990] NI 179), prison officers were the wrongdoers. The Northern Ireland Office was the defendant. In each case the conduct of the wrongdoer, or wrongdoers, was outrageous and fell squarely within Lord Devlin's first category. But I do not follow why an appropriate award of aggravated damages would not have served to vindicate the law just as effectively as the fairly moderate awards of exemplary damages that were made. The condemnation by the trial judge of the conduct in question would have been expressed no differently. As to deterrence, in a case where the defendant is not the wrongdoer, and the damages are in any event going to be met out of public funds, how can it be supposed that the award of exemplary damages adds anything at all to the deterrent effect of the trial judge's findings of fact in favour of the injured person and his condemnation of the conduct in question? The proposition that exemplary damage awards against such defendants as the Ministry of Defence or the Northern Ireland Office, or, for that matter, the Chief Constable of Leicestershire Constabulary, can have a deterrent effect is, in my respectful opinion, fanciful.

…

My Lords, I view the prospect of any increase in the cases in which exemplary damages can be claimed with regret. I have explained already why I regard the remedy as no longer serving any useful function in our jurisprudence. Victims of tortious conduct should receive due compensation for their injuries, not windfalls at public expense.

及惩罚性赔偿的法律并没有固化在 1964 年 Devlin 大法官发表的意见[*Rookes v Barnard*（1964）AC 1129]，也没有固化在 1972 年上议院的七名大法官发的表意见[*Broome v Cassell & Co Ltd*（1972）AC 1027]。在这之后，普通法一直在发展。在 *Rookes v Barnard* 案后普通法最重要的发展是在公法领域和司法审查领域，这点 Diplock 大法官已经提到。行政人员做出的压迫、武断和违宪行为可以通过民事程序在高等法院得到救济。高等法院可以提供损害赔偿金、确认权利和禁止令等救济措施。这项发生在 Diplock 大法官在 *Broome v Cassell & Co Ltd* 案的判决书中表达的意见之后的改革，已经改善了普通公民获得救济的能力。2001 年我们是否还需要继续用惩罚性赔偿作为民事救济措施，以控制、阻却和惩罚 Devlin 大法官所列举的第一类情况，便不是那么显而易见了。

我高贵而博学的朋友 Hutton 大法官举例提到了两个北爱尔兰的案件。这两个案件在他看来，惩罚性赔偿在制止任意、粗暴地使用行政权力和维护法律的权威方面发挥了宝贵的作用。在其中的一个案子中[*Lavery v Ministry of Defence*（1984）NI 99]侵权人是移民士兵，国防部则是被告。在另一起案件中[*Pettigrew v Northern Ireland Office*（1990）NI 179]，侵权人是狱警，北爱尔兰事务办公室则是被告。在两起案件中，侵权人的行为都是骇人听闻的，因而都属于 Devlin 大法官所说的第一种类型。然而，我不太能理解为什么合理地提高填补性的赔偿金不能实现维护法律权威的目的，而非要用惩罚性赔偿（虽然这里的惩罚性赔偿也并不太极端）。判决填补性的损害赔偿也同样能表达一审法官对违法行为的谴责。至于威慑功能，对于一个被告人并不是行为人本人，而赔偿金肯定是由公款提供的案件，我们如何能认为判决被告支付惩罚性赔偿金能产生更大的威慑作用？一审法官认定事实支持受害人并谴责相关恶行已经在威慑违法行为了。认为像国防部、北爱尔兰办公室或者在本案中的莱切斯特警察局长这样的被告承担了惩罚性赔偿，其违法行为就会受到威慑，恕我直言，这不过是幻想罢了。

……

诸位大法官，未来在很多案件中都将判决惩罚性赔偿，我对此感到非常遗憾。我已经解释过了为什么在我们的法理上，惩罚性赔偿这种救济措施已经没有任何有用的功能了。侵权行为的受害人应该获得的是对其损害的应有赔偿，而不是由公众买单的横财。

Chapter 9. Dignitary Wrongs and Intentional Infliction

Section 1. Assault

81. Read v Coker [1853] 13 C.B. 850, 138 ER 1437

Court of Common Pleas, United Kingdom

The cause was tried before Talfourd, J., at the first sitting in London in Easter Term last. The facts which appeared in evidence were as follows:—The plaintiff was a paper-stainer, carrying on business in the City Road, upon premises which he rented of one Molineux, at a rent of 8s. per week. In January 1852, the rent being sixteen weeks in arrear, the landlord employed one Holliwell to distrain for it. Holliwell accordingly seized certain presses, lathes, and other trade fixtures, and, at the plaintiff's request, advanced him 16£ upon the security of the goods, for the purpose of paying off the rent. The plaintiff, being unable to redeem his goods, on the 23rd of February applied to the defendant for assistance. The goods were thereupon sold to the defendant by Holliwell, on the part of Read, for 25£. 11s.6d.; and it was agreed between the plaintiff and the defendant, that the business should be carried on for their mutual benefit, the defendant paying the rent of the premises and other outgoings, and allowing the plaintiff a certain sum weekly.

The defendant becoming dissatisfied with the speculation, dismissed the plaintiff on the 22nd of March. On the 24th, the plaintiff came to the premises, and refusing to leave when ordered by the defendant, the latter collected together some of his workmen, who mustered round the plaintiff, tucking up their sleeves and aprons, and threatened to break his neck if he did not go out; and, fearing that the men would strike him if he did not do so, the plaintiff went out. This was the assault complained of in the first count. Upon this evidence, the learned judge left it to the jury to say, whether there was an intention on the part of the defendant to assault the plaintiff, and whether the plaintiff was apprehensive of personal violence if he did not retire. The jury found for the plaintiff on this count, damages one farthing....

Byles, Serjt., on a former day in this term, in pursuance of leave reserved to him at the trial, moved for a rule nisi to enter the verdict for the defendant...or for a new trial on the ground of misdirection, and that the verdict was not warranted by the evidence. That which was proved... clearly did not amount to an assault....To constitute an assault, there must be something more than

第九章　不法侵害尊严与故意致人精神损害

第一节　威吓

81. Read v Coker [1853] 13 C.B. 850, 138 ER 1437

联合王国民事诉讼法院

本案曾经在伦敦上一个复活节开庭期（Easter Term[①]）进行第一次开庭，由 Talfourd 法官进行审理。经由证据证实的案件事实如下：原告是一位壁纸匠，在 City 路上营业，其营业场所是从一位名叫 Molineux 的人手中以每星期 8 先令承租的。1852 年 1 月份，因拖欠 16 个星期的租金，房主雇佣一位叫做 Holliwell 的人来为房租而扣押财物。于是，Holliwell 扣押了一定数量的模具、木板条以及其他的营业装潢材料。此外，应原告的要求，Holliwell 基于那些货物的担保预付他 16 英镑以付清租金。原告因不能赎回他的货物，于 2 月 23 日请求被告的帮助。于是，那些货物被 Holliwell 卖给被告，就 Read 而言，价格是 25 英镑 11 先令 6 便士。[②] 原告与被告商定应当基于双方共同利益而营业。被告支付场所租金和其他开支，并每周给予原告一些钱。

被告因对原告的投机行为不满意，让原告在 3 月 22 日离开。3 月 24 日，原告来到营业场所，不顾被告的命令而拒绝离开。被告召集他的一些工人将原告围在当中，卷起袖子和围裙，并威胁如果他不离开，就将他的脖子扭断。原告因害怕如果他不照做的话，将被那些人殴打，于是离开了。这是第一次开庭被提起的威吓。基于这个证据，博学的法官留给陪审团去判断的问题是，如果原告不离开，其是否害怕受到人身伤害。陪审团在就此问题作出了有利于原告的事实认定。裁决了一法新[③]赔偿金……

Byles 高级律师，在该开庭期的前一天，依照初审预留给他的许可，为该

[①] "Easter Term" 一词，是指英国法律曾经规定的复活节开庭期，从 4 月 15 日一直延续到 5 月 8 日。复活节开庭期于 1875 年被废止。——译者注
[②] 英镑（Pound）为英国的本位货币单位，由英格兰银行发行。辅币单位原为先令（Shilling）和便士（Penny），1 英镑等于 20 先令，1 先令等于 12 便士。1971 年 2 月 15 日，英格兰银行实行新的货币进位制，辅币单位改为新便士（New Penny），1 英镑等于 100 新便士。原文为"25 £.11s. 6d."，这三个符号是拉丁文（单数/复数）"libra/librae""solidus/solidi"和"denarius/denarii"的缩写。——译者注
[③] 1956 年前，英国还流通一种名为"法新"（Farthing）的铜币，面值是便士的 1/4。——译者注

a threat of violence. An assault is thus defined in Buller's Nisi Prius, p. 15,—"An assault is an attempt or offer, by force or violence, to do a corporal hurt to another, as, by pointing a pitchfork at him, when standing within reach; presenting a gun at him; drawing a sword, and waving it in a menacing manner, &c. But no words can amount to an assault, though perhaps they may in some cases serve to explain a doubtful action, as, if a man were to lay his hand upon his sword, and say, 'If it were not assize time, he would not take such language'; the words would prevent the action from being construed to be an assault, because they shew he had no intent to do him any corporal hurt at that time: Tuberville v. Savage, 1 Mod. 3."…[Jervis, C.J. If a man comes into a room, and lays his cane on the table, and says to another, "If you don't go out, I will knock you on the head," would not that be an assault?] Clearly not: it is a mere threat, unaccompanied by any gesture or action towards carrying it into effect. The direction of the learned judge as to this point was erroneous. He should have told the jury, that, to constitute an assault, there must be an attempt, coupled with a present ability to do personal violence to the party; instead of leaving it to them, as he did, to say what the plaintiff thought, and not what they (the jury) thought was the defendant's intention. There must be some act done denoting a present ability and an intention to assault.

…

Jervis, C.J. I am of opinion that this rule…must be discharged. If anything short of actual striking will in law constitute an assault, the facts here clearly shewed that the defendant was guilty of an assault. There was a threat of violence exhibiting an intention to assault, and a present ability to carry the threat into execution.…

Maule, Cresswell, and Talfourd, JJ., concurring. Rule discharged.…

82. Beach v. Hancock, 27 N.H. 223 (1853)

Superior Court of Judicature of New Hampshire, United States

Trespass, for an assault.

Upon the general issue it appeared that the plaintiff and defendant, being engaged in an angry altercation, the defendant stepped into his office, which was at hand, and brought out a gun, which he aimed at the plaintiff in an excited and threatening manner, the plaintiff being three or four rods distant. The evidence tended to show that the defendant snapped the gun twice at the plaintiff, and that the plaintiff did not know whether the gun was loaded or not, and that, in fact, the gun was not loaded.

The court ruled that the pointing of a gun, in an angry and threatening manner, at a person three or four rods distant, who was ignorant whether the gun was loaded or not, was an assault, though it should appear that the gun was not loaded, and that it made no difference whether the gun was snapped or not.

被告作出的裁定申请一个可撤销的裁决……或者以错误指示为由申请一次新的审判，此项裁断没有得到此项证据证实。那就证明……显然不是威吓……要构成一项威吓，必须至少需要一项对暴力的恐惧。因此，在 Buller 所著《初审》（Nisi Prius）一书的第 15 页，威吓被界定为"威吓是一种企图或意图，通过武力或者暴力，去对另一个人实施有形的伤害。例如，将干草叉指着站在触手可及地方的人；把手枪指着射程内的人；抽出宝剑，并以有威胁性的方式挥舞着，等等。但是，没有话语能够构成一项威吓，尽管或许他们可能通过一些例子来解释一项值得怀疑的行为，譬如，如果一个人将手放在他的宝剑上，同时说，'如果没有裁判时间，他不会说这样的话'。这些话可能避免这样的行为被理解为一项威吓，因为它们表明他没有在那时实施有形伤害的企图：Tuberville v. Savage, 1 Mod. 3"……[Jervis 首席法官：假如一个人进入一个房间，并将他的手杖放到桌子上，对其他人说，"如果你们不出去的话，我将敲击你们的脑袋"。这难道不是一种威吓吗？] 显然不是：如果未伴随着任何实施效果的手势或者行为的话，它仅仅是一种威胁。渊博的法官就此所作出的指示是错误的。他本应当告知陪审团的是，构成一种威吓，必须具备一项企图，同时伴随一种向对方实施人身伤害的现实能力；而不是将问题留给他们，如其所言，认定原告想到的是什么，而不是陪审团想到的是什么，这是被告的意图。必须存在一些已做出的行为来表明一种现实的能力和实施威吓的企图。

……

Jervis 首席法官：我的意见是这项裁决……必须被撤销。假如任何缺乏实际存在的、显著的意图的事项在法律上构成威吓，这些事实清晰地表明被告构成威吓。一种暴力的威胁表明威吓的企图，而一种现实的能力则将这种威胁付诸实施……

Maule 法官、Cresswell 法官和 Talfourd 法官赞同。此项裁决被撤销……

82. Beach v. Hancock, 27 N.H. 223 (1853)

美国新罕布什尔州高等法院

威吓的侵害诉讼。

就一般性问题，看起来原告与被告之间曾经发生过一场激烈的口角。被告走进他的办公室，迅速地取出一把手枪，并以一种兴奋而令人恐惧的方式将枪口指向 15—20 米之外的原告。证据趋于表明被告对准原告两次扣动扳机，而原告不知道其手枪中是否装有子弹。证据还证实，实际上该手枪中并未装有子弹。

法院裁定，以一种兴奋、令人警觉的方式将手枪指向距离 15—20 米之外的一个不知枪中是否装有子弹的人。尽管该枪中没有子弹，但该行为已构成

The court, among other things, instructed the jury that, in assessing the damages, it was their right and duty to consider the effect which the finding of light or trivial damages in actions for breaches of the peace, would have to encourage a disregard of the laws and disturbances of the public peace.

The defendant excepted to these rulings and instructions.

The jury, having found a verdict for the plaintiff, the defendant moved for a new trial by reason of said exceptions.

Gilcrest, C.J....One of the most important objects to be attained by the enactment of laws and the institutions of civilized society is, each of us shall feel secure against unlawful assaults. Without such security society loses most of its value. Peace and order and domestic happiness, inexpressively more precious than mere forms of government, cannot be enjoyed without the sense of perfect security. We have a right to live in society without being put in fear of personal harm. But it must be a reasonable fear of which we complain. And it surely is not unreasonable for a person to entertain a fear of personal injury, when a pistol is pointed at him in a threatening manner, when, for aught he knows, it may be loaded, and may occasion his immediate death. The business of the world could not be carried on with comfort, if such things could be done with impunity.

We think the defendant guilty of an assault, and we perceive no reason for taking any exception to the remarks of the court. Finding trivial damages for breaches of the peace, damages incommensurate with the injury sustained, would certainly lead the ill-disposed to consider an assault as a thing that might be committed with impunity. But, at all events, it was proper for the jury to consider whether such a result would or would not be produced.

Judgment on the verdict.

83. Stephens v Myers (1830) 4 C & P 349, 172 ER 735

Nisi Prius, United Kingdom

It appeared, that the plaintiff was acting as chairman, at a parish meeting, and sat at the head of a table, at which table the defendant also sat, there being about six or seven persons between him and the plaintiff. The defendant having, in the course of some angry discussion, which took place, been very vociferous, and interrupted the proceedings of the meeting, a motion was made, that he should be turned out, which was carried by a very large majority. Upon this, the defendant said, he would rather pull the chairman out of the chair, than be turned out of the room ; and immediately advanced with his fist clenched toward the chairman, but was stopt by the churchwarden, who sat next but one to the chairman, at a time when he was not near enough for any blow he might have meditated to have reached the chairman; but the witnesses said, that it seemed to them that he was

殴击侵权，至于是否扣动手枪扳机亦在所不论。

除其他外，法官在指示陪审团确定赔偿金数额时说，这是基于他们的权利和义务来考虑裁决的结果，如果对侵害安宁之诉讼作出数额上微不足道的损害赔偿裁决，则无异于鼓励无视法律和破坏治安之行为的再发生。

被告对裁决及指示提出异议。

陪审团作出了支持原告的裁决，而被告则基于上述异议的理由申请重新审理。

Gilcrest大法官……制定法律和构建文明社会的最为重要的目标之一是，我们每一个人应当在面临不法殴击时感受到安全。欠缺此种安全的社会丢掉了它最为重要的价值。除非拥有最佳的安全感，否则，比单纯的治理形式更为珍贵的和平、秩序以及家庭幸福将无法享有。我们有权利生活在一个不会为人身伤害而恐慌的社会。但是，必须对我们所抱怨的保持合理恐慌。当一把手枪被以令人惊悚的方式指向某一个人，而他无从知晓枪中是否装有子弹，并可能导致他立即死亡时，背负这种人身伤害的恐惧对于他来说确实是不合理的。如果可以不受惩罚地从事此类事情，社会将不会以令人舒适的方式运转。

我们认为被告构成殴击侵权，并且我们想象不出任何可用于反对法院判决的理由。如果对侵害安宁的行为判处微不足道的损害赔偿金，与受害人所承受伤害不相称的损害赔偿金，将确定地诱使不怀好意的想法，即殴击行为是一件可以实施而不受惩罚的行为。但是，无论如何，陪审团对这种结果能否发生的考虑是恰当的。

基于裁断作出判决。

83. Stephens v Myers (1830) 4 C & P 349, 172 ER 735

联合王国民事初审法院

审理查明：原告作为教区会议的主席，坐在桌子的首位；被告也坐在这张桌子旁，他和原告之间隔了六七个人。被告在争执中大吵大闹，因此打乱了会议的进程。会议作出决议要求他离开，大多数会议成员都同意这个决议。被告对此说到，他宁愿把主席从椅子上扔出去，也不会离开会议室，同时他立即紧握拳头走向主席。教堂的保安阻止了被告，且此时他离主席尚有一段距离，因此他就算想打也无法殴打到主席。然而证人表示，他们认为被告走向主席时确实具有殴打他的意图。

advancing with an intention to strike the chairman.

Spankie, Serjt., for the defendant, upon this evidence, contended, that no assault had been committed, as there was no power in the defendant, from the situation of the parties, to execute his threat—there was not a present ability—he had not the means of executing his intention at the time he was stopt.

Tindal, C. J., in his summing up to the jury, said—It is not every threat, when there is no actual personal violence, that constitutes an assault, there must, in all cases, be the means of carrying the threat into effect. The question I shall leave to you will be, whether the defendant was advancing at the time, in a threatening attitude, to strike the chairman, so that his blow would almost immediately have reached the chairman, if he had not been stopt; then, though he was not near enough at the time to have struck him, yet if he was advancing with that intent, I think it amounts to an assault in law. If he was so advancing, that, within a second or two of time, he would have reached the plaintiff, it seems to me it is an assault in law. If you think he was not advancing to strike the plaintiff, then only can you find your verdict for the defendant; otherwise you must find it for the plaintiff, and give him such damages as you think the nature of the case requires.

Verdict for the plaintiff—Damages 1 shilling

Section 2. False Imprisonment

84. Whittaker v. Sanford, 110 Me. 77, 85 A. 399 (1912)

Supreme Judicial Court of Maine, United States

Savage, J. Action for false imprisonment. The plaintiff recovered a verdict for $1100. The case comes up on defendant's exceptions and motion for a new trial.

…

…The court instructed the jury that the plaintiff to recover must show that the restraint was physical, and not merely a moral influence, that it must have been actual physical restraint, in the sense that one intentionally locked into a room would be physically restrained, but not necessarily involving physical force upon the person; that it was not necessary that the defendant, or any person by his direction, should lay his hand upon the plaintiff, that if the plaintiff was restrained so that she could not leave the yacht Kingdom by the intentional refusal to furnish transportation as agreed, she not having it in her power to escape otherwise, it would be a physical restraint and unlawful imprisonment. We think the instructions were apt and sufficient. If one should, without right, turn the key in a door, and thereby prevent a person in the room from leaving, it would be the simplest form of unlawful imprisonment. The restraint is physical. The four walls and the locked door are physical impediments to escape. How is it different when one who is in control of a vessel

Spankie 律师代表原告，依据上述事实，主张被告并未实施威吓的行为，因为按照当时双方的情况，他是没有能力去实现他的威胁的。他在被保安阻止的时候并没有能力去实现他的意图。

Tindal 首席法官如此指导陪审团：在没有现实的人身暴力时，并非所有的威胁都构成威吓。要构成威吓，被告无论如何都必须拥有将其威胁付诸实施的手段。陪审团要回答的问题是，被告走向主席的时候，是否具有威胁要殴打他的意图，如果他当时没有被制止便几乎能接触到主席。虽然当时他离原告还不够近，因此并不能实际殴打他，但是如果他走向原告时确实有这样的意图，那么在我看来这就构成了法律上的威吓行为。如果他走得足够靠近，一两秒内他就将接触到原告，那么在我看来这就构成了法律上的威吓行为。如果你们认为被告走向原告并不是为了殴打他，那么你们只能裁断支持被告；否则你们必须裁断支持原告获得你们认为合适数额的赔偿金。

陪审团裁断支持原告获得一先令的损害赔偿。

第二节　非法拘禁

84. Whittaker v. Sanford, 110 Me. 77, 85 A. 399 (1912)

美国缅因州最高法院

Savage 法官主笔：这是一起以非法拘禁为由提起的诉讼。原告获得了一项金额为 1 100 美元的裁断。本案源于被告的异议以及对重新审理的申请。

……

……法院指示陪审团：想获得赔偿的原告必须证明所受人身自由的限制是有形的，而不仅仅是道德上的压力，它必须是对人身自由实际的、有形的限制，在这个意义上，一个人被故意锁到房间里大概属于对人身自由的有形限制，但并不必然要求对这个人实施了有形的暴力。被告或者受其指使的其他人没有必要必须用手摁住原告。假设原告被以拒绝使用先前约定的交通工具的方式限制了人身自由，导致她不能离开"王国号"游艇。除此以外，她没有其他办法逃离。这就是有形的身体自由限制和非法拘禁。我们认为这个指示是适当的、充分的。如果一个没有法定权利的人拧锁上的钥匙，并因此阻止了屋里的一个人离开，这可能是最简单的非法拘禁。人身自由的限制是有形的。四面墙和锁着的门是逃跑的有形障碍物。当一位掌管着一艘停泊在

at anchor, within practical rowing distance from the shore, who has agreed that a guest on board shall be free to leave, there being no means to leave except by rowboats, wrongfully refuses the guest the use of a boat? The boat is the key. By refusing the boat he turns the key. The guest is as effectually locked up as if there were walls along the sides of the vessel. The restraint is physical. The impassable sea is the physical barrier....

But the damages awarded seem to us manifestly excessive. The plaintiff, if imprisoned, was by no means in close confinement. She was afforded all the liberties of the yacht. She was taken on shore by her husband to do shopping and transact business at a bank. She visited neighboring islands with her husband and children, on one of which they enjoyed a family picnic. The case lacks the elements of humiliation and disgrace that frequently attend false imprisonment. She was respectfully treated as a guest in every way, except that she was restrained from quitting the yacht for good and all.

The certificate will be,

Exceptions overruled. If the plaintiff remits all of the verdict in excess of $500, within 30 days after the certificate is received by the clerk, motion overruled; otherwise, motion sustained.

85. Sindle v. New York City Transit Authority, 33 N.Y.2d 293, 307 N.E.2d 245 (1973)

Court of Appeals of New York, United States

Jasen, J. At about noon on June 20, 1967, the plaintiff, then 14 years of age, boarded a school bus owned by the defendant, New York City Transit Authority, and driven by its employee, the defendant Mooney. It was the last day of the term...and the 65 to 70 students on board the bus were in a boisterous and exuberant mood. Some of this spirit expressed itself in vandalism, a number of students breaking dome lights, windows, ceiling panels and advertising poster frames. There is no evidence that the plaintiff partook in this destruction.

The bus made several stops at appointed stations. On at least one occasion, the driver admonished the students about excessive noise and damage to the bus. When he reached the Annadale station, the driver discharged several more passengers, went to the rear of the bus, inspected the damage and advised the students that he was taking them to the St. George police station.

The driver closed the doors of the bus and proceeded, bypassing several normal stops. As the bus slowed to turn onto Woodrow Road, several students jumped without apparent injury from a side window at the rear of the bus. Several more followed, again without apparent harm, when the bus turned onto Arden Avenue.

At the corner of Arden Avenue and Arthur Kill Road, departing from its normal route, the bus turned right in the general direction of the St. George police station. The plaintiff, intending to

距岸边有可行的划船距离的船舶之人,曾同意一位在船上的客人可以自由离开,但除了乘划艇外没有其他方式可以离开,其无正当理由地拒绝该客人使用划艇。这种情况有怎样的不同呢?这艘划艇就是"钥匙"。他通过拒绝使用划艇的方式转动了"门上的钥匙"。这名客人就像船舶的四周有墙一样,被有效地关押。这种人身自由的限制就是有形的。那片无法穿越的海就是有形的屏障……

然而,被判处的赔偿金,在我们看来,显然是过重的。这名原告假如被拘禁的话,绝不是密闭的拘禁。她在游艇上被给予全部的行动自由。她曾被丈夫带上岸购物并在一家银行从事交易活动。她和丈夫、孩子们一道游览临近的岛屿,并在其中一个岛上享用了家庭野餐。该案欠缺非法拘禁中经常具备的蒙羞和耻辱等要素。除了被阻止永久地离开游艇外,她每天像客人一样被恭敬地款待。

法院通知会载明,

异议被推翻。如果原告在收到法官助理所送达的法院文件 30 日内放弃全部超过 500 美元的裁断,则撤销申请;否则,维持申请。

85. Sindle v. New York City Transit Authority, 33 N.Y.2d 293, 307 N.E.2d 245 (1973)

美国纽约州上诉法院

Jasen 法官主笔:大约在 1967 年 6 月 20 日的中午,当时年仅 14 岁的原告乘坐被告纽约市政运输管理局的一辆校车,而该车由其雇员、另一名被告 Mooney 驾驶。这是那学期的最后一天……车上的 65—70 名学生正处于喧闹而兴奋的情绪中。这种情绪自身表现为故意的破坏行为,许多学生砸坏了车厢的顶灯、窗户、车厢顶板以及广告牌。没有证据表明原告参加了这项破坏活动。

汽车在一些预设的站点停车。这名司机不止一次地告诫学生不要喧闹,以及损坏车辆。当他到达 Annadale 站点时,司机卸下一些乘客,走到车辆的尾部,检查了损害并告诉剩下的学生们他将把他们送到 St. George 警察局。

司机关闭车门继续前进,避开了许多正常的停靠点。当汽车缓慢地驶上 Woodrow 路,许多学生从车辆尾部的一个窗户中跳下,没有明显受伤。当车辆行至 Arden 大街时,更多的学生仿效,同样没有明显的伤害。

在 Arden 大街与 Arthur Kill 路拐角处,该车驶离正常的线路,右转驶向 St. George 警察局。原告试图从汽车上跳下,已将他自己置于右后侧的窗户上。

jump from the bus, had positioned himself in a window on the right-rear side. Grasping the bottom of the window sill with his hands, the plaintiff extended his legs (to mid-thigh), head and shoulders out of the window. As the bus turned right, the right rear wheels hit the curb and the plaintiff either jumped or fell to the street. The right rear wheels then rolled over the midsection of his body, causing serious personal injuries.

The plaintiff, joined with his father, then commenced an action to recover damages for negligence and false imprisonment. At the outset of the trial, the negligence cause was waived and plaintiffs proceeded on the theory of false imprisonment. At the close of the plaintiffs' case, the court denied defendants' motion to amend their answers to plead the defense of justification. The court also excluded all evidence bearing on the justification issue.

We believe that it was an abuse of discretion for the trial court to deny the motion to amend and to exclude the evidence of justification. It was the defendants' burden to prove justification—a defense that a plaintiff in an action for false imprisonment should be prepared to meet—and the plaintiffs could not have been prejudiced by the granting of the motion to amend. The trial court's rulings precluded the defendants from introducing any evidence in this regard and were manifestly unfair. Accordingly, the order of the Appellate Division must be reversed and a new trial granted.

In view of our determination, it would be well to outline some of the considerations relevant to the issue of justification. In this regard, we note that, generally, restraint or detention, reasonable under the circumstances and in time and manner, imposed for the purpose of preventing another from inflicting personal injuries or interfering with or damaging real or personal property in one's lawful possession or custody is not unlawful....Also, a parent, guardian or teacher entrusted with the care or supervision of a child may use physical force reasonably necessary to maintain discipline or promote the welfare of the child.

Similarly, a school bus driver, entrusted with the care of his student-passengers and the custody of public property, has the duty to take reasonable measures for the safety and protection of both—the passengers and the property. In this regard, the reasonableness of his actions—as bearing on the defense of justification—is to be determined from a consideration of all the circumstances. At a minimum, this would seem to import a consideration of the need to protect the persons and property in his charge, the duty to aid the investigation and apprehension of those inflicting damage, the manner and place of the occurrence, and the feasibility and practicality of other alternative courses of action.

With regard to the proper measure of damages, an ancillary but nevertheless important question of law is presented—namely, whether a plaintiff's negligence in attempting to extricate himself from an unlawful confinement should diminish his damages for bodily injuries sustained as a result of the false imprisonment. In this regard, plaintiff has been awarded damages of $500 for mental anguish and $75,000 for bodily injuries. The plaintiff father has been awarded damages

原告用手抓住窗户的下边，将腿（至大腿的中部）、头以及肩膀伸出窗外。在车辆右转时，车辆的右后部碰到路缘，原告不是跳到就是跌到了街上。右后车轮从他上腹部碾过，造成严重的身体伤害。

原告以及原告的父亲，以过失侵权和非法拘禁为由提起了损害赔偿诉讼。在初审开始时，原告放弃过失侵权的诉因而以非法拘禁为由继续诉讼。在原告的诉讼结束时，法院拒绝了被告将其答辩状修改为以正当理由为基础的申请。法院也排除了与正当理由相关的全部证据。

我们认为，初审法院拒绝修改申请以及排除正当性证据是滥用自由裁量权的行为。被告负有正当理由的举证责任——对非法拘禁之诉中的原告应当准备去满足之事项的抗辩——并且原告们会因为准许修改判决书的申请而遭受侵害。初审法院在这点上拒绝被告提交相关证据的决定显然是不公平的。因此，应当撤销分庭命令并准许重审本案。

在我们看来，最好概括与正当理由相关的一些原则。在这一点上，我们注意到，一般来讲，为了阻止某人伤害他人或毁坏他人合法占有的动产及不动产的行为，如果是在适当的情况下以适当的方式及时做出的，对人身自由的合理限制或扣押不是违法的……同样，对儿童负有照顾和管理义务的父母、监护人或者老师可以采用合理的适当体罚方式以维持纪律或提升儿童的福祉。

校车司机通常都被看作学生乘客的照顾者和公共财物的看管者，他有义务承担起采取合适措施保护学生和公共财产的双重职责。在这种情况下，校车司机当时行为的合理性——也就是他为自己辩护时所称的正当理由——必须同时从这些方面来考量。至少，有几个因素需要考量：保护学生安全和财产完好的责任、协助警方调查公共财产被破坏的义务、被告采取行动的方式和场合以及当时是否存在有更加合理可行的替代方法。

在损害赔偿的合理确定方面，一个辅助性但很重要的法律问题是，原告因试图从不法拘禁中脱身的过失，是否应当减少非法拘禁所导致之人身伤害的赔偿金数额。对此，原告已经获得500美元的精神损害赔偿金以及75 000美元的人身伤害赔偿金。原告的父亲已经获得750美元的服务丧失赔偿金以及5 797美元的医疗费用赔偿金。

of $750 for loss of services and $5,797 for medical expenses.

Where the damages follow as a consequence of the plaintiff's detention without justification an award may include those for bodily injuries. And although confinement reasonably perceived to be unlawful may invite escape, the person falsely imprisoned is not relieved of the duty of reasonable care for his own safety in extricating himself from the unlawful detention. In this regard, it has been held that alighting from a moving vehicle, absent some compelling reason, is negligence per se. Therefore, upon retrial, if the trier of fact finds that plaintiff was falsely imprisoned but that he acted unreasonably for his own safety by placing himself in a perilous position in the window of the bus preparatory to an attempt to alight, recovery for the bodily injuries subsequently sustained would be barred.

For the reasons stated, the order of the Appellate Division should be reversed and the case remitted for a new trial.

Fuld, C.J., and Burke, Breitel, Gabrielli, Jones and Wachtler, JJ., concur.

Order reversed, without costs, and a new trial granted.

86. Bird v Jones (1845) 7 QB 742, 115 ER 668

Court of Queen's Bench, United Kingdom

Coleridge J.

These facts, stated shortly, and, as I understand them, are in effect as follows. A part of a public highway was inclosed, and appropriated for spectators of a boat race, paying a price for their seats. The plaintiff was desirous of entering this part, and was opposed by the defendant: but, after a struggle, during which no momentary detention of his person took place, he succeeded in climbing over the inclosure. Two policemen were then stationed by the defendant to prevent, and they did prevent, him from passing onwards in the direction in which he declared his wish to go: but he was allowed to remain unmolested where he was, and was at liberty to go, and was told that he was so, in the only other direction by which he could pass. This he refused for some time, and, during that time, remained where he had thus placed himself.

These are the facts ... And I am of opinion that there was no imprisonment. To call it so appears to me to confound partial obstruction and disturbance with total obstruction and detention. A prison may have its boundary large or narrow, visible and tangible, or, though real, still in the conception only; it may itself be moveable or fixed : but a boundary it must have ; and that boundary the party imprisoned must be prevented from passing; he must be prevented from leaving that place, within the ambit of which the party imprisoning would confine him, except by prison-breach. Some confusion seems to me to arise from confounding imprisonment of the body with mere loss of freedom: it is one part of the definition of freedom to be able to go whithersoever

作为没有正当理由的拘禁原告的后果，损害赔偿金可能包括对身体伤害的一些赔偿事项。尽管被合理地理解为非法拘禁可能诱使逃脱，但被非法拘禁的人并没有免除其从非法拘禁逃脱过程中对自身安全所负有的合理注意义务。对此，曾有判决认为，从一辆行驶中的车上跳下，而缺少有说服力的理由，构成法律上的当然过失。因此，在重新审理的时候，如果陪审团认定原告受到非法拘禁，但他从汽车窗户试图跳下的行为将其自身安全置于不合理的危险境地，随后被确认的人身伤害损害赔偿将被阻却。

基于上述理由，应当撤销上诉分庭的命令，本案发回重审。

Fuld 大法官和 Burke 法官、Breitel 法官、Gabrielli 法官、Jones 法官以及 Wachtler 法官赞同。

撤销命令，包括诉讼费用，准许重审。

86. Bird v Jones (1845) 7 QB 742, 115 ER 668

联合王国高等法院王座分庭

Coleridge 法官

据我所知，本案的事实可以概述如下：一段公路被封闭起来作为赛艇比赛观众的观赛区，其中的座位则是收费的。原告希望进入这段公路，但是却被被告阻止了。双方发生了一些争执，但被告并未拘束原告的人身。原告则在争执之后成功地爬上了围栏。两名警察被派过来阻止原告朝着他所希望的方向前进，他们也确实做到了。然而，原告被允许不受影响地待在原地，或者从另外一边离开。他持续拒绝了这些选项一段时间，在那期间他待在原地。

以上就是本案的事实……我对此的意见是本案被告不构成非法拘禁。认为这构成非法拘禁的观点其实是混淆了"阻碍一个人的部分前进方向"和"完全阻碍一个人的移动"或者说"将他监禁"。一所监狱的边界可能大或小，实在或者虚拟；边界可能能移动或者是固定的，然而一所监狱它必须是有边界的，而且被监禁的人是没有办法越过边界的，他除了越狱是无法离开监禁者希望监禁他的范围的。在我看来，这是混淆了拘禁一个人的身体和仅仅剥夺他的部分自由。自由的定义中的一点就是一个人可以去任何他想去的地方，

one pleases; but imprisonment is something more than the mere loss of this, power; it includes the notion of restraint within some limits defined by a will or power exterior to our own.

...

Patteson J.

This was an action of trespass for an assault and false imprisonment. The pleas were: as to the assault, son assault demesne; as to the imprisonment, that the plaintiff, before the imprisonment, assaulted the defendant, wherefore the defendant gave him into custody. ... I have no doubt that, in general, if one man compels another to stay in any given place against his will, he imprisons that other just as much as if he locked him up in a room: and I agree that it is not necessary, in order to constitute an imprisonment, that a man's person should be touched. I agree, also, that the compelling a man to go in a given direction against his will may amount to imprisonment. But I cannot bring my mind to the conclusion that, if one man merely obstructs the passage of another in a particular direction, whether by threat of personal violence or otherwise, leaving him at liberty to stay where he is or to go in any other direction if he pleases, he can be said thereby to imprison him. He does him wrong, undoubtedly, if there was a right to pass in that direction, and would be liable to an action on the case for obstructing the passage, or of assault, if, on the party persisting in going in that direction, he touched his person, or so threatened him as to amount to an assault. But imprisonment is, as I apprehend, a total restraint of the liberty of the person, for however short a time, and not a partial obstruction of his will, whatever inconvenience it may bring on him.

...

Lord Denman C.J.

I have not drawn up a formal judgment in this case, because I hoped to the last that the arguments which my learned brothers would produce in support of their opinion might alter mine.

...

I had no idea that any person in these times supposed any particular boundary to be necessary to constitute imprisonment, or that the restraint of a man's person from doing what he desires ceases to be an imprisonment because he may find some means of escape. It is said that the party here was at liberty to go in another direction. I am not sure that in fact he was, because the same unlawful power which prevented him from taking one course might, in case of acquiescence, have refused him any other. But this liberty to do something else does not appear to me to affect the question of imprisonment. As long as I am prevented from doing what I have a right to do, of what importance is it that I am permitted to do something else? How does the imposition of an unlawful condition shew that I am not restrained? If I am locked in a room, am I not imprisoned because I might effect my escape through a window, or because I might find an exit dangerous or inconvenient to myself, as by wading through water or by taking a route so circuitous that my necessary affairs would suffer by delay. It appears to me that this is a total deprivation of liberty

然而拘禁不止失去这种自由。拘禁的定义是要把一个人困在一个外在于他自己的意志或权利所确定的范围内。

……

Patteson 法官

本案的诉由是威吓和非法拘禁。被告的抗辩如下：对于威吓的指控，被告指出是原告先威吓他的。对于非法拘禁的指控，原告在被拘禁之前威吓了被告，被告因此才限制了他的自由……在一般意义上，我认为如果一个人强迫另一个人待在特定的地方，和这个人把另一个人锁在房间里一样，都是拘禁。我也承认，要构成拘禁并不需要触碰到被拘禁者的身体。我同样认同，强迫一个人一定要按照某个方向移动，可能属于拘禁。然而，如果仅仅是阻碍一个人朝着某个方向移动，就算是通过人身暴力威胁的方式，但是却给了他待在原地的自由和从其他方向离开的自由，我就很难赞同在这种情况下说前者拘禁了后者。如果后者有权利朝这被阻碍的方向前进，那么前者毫无疑问侵害了后者的权利，可能要承担阻碍后者前进的责任；如果前者因为后者非要走这个方向而对他动了手，或者对他做出了相当于威吓的威胁，也可能要承担威吓之诉的责任。然而在我看来，拘禁要求的是对一个人的人身的全面的限制，时间可以很短，但是一定不能只是部分地阻碍了他的意志，无论这给他带来了多大的不便。

……

首席大法官 Denman

对本案我还没有最后的结论，因为我希望我那博学的同僚们能在最后关头，用支撑他们观点的论证改变我的观点。

……

我不知道今天居然还有人认为要构成拘禁必须要有特定的边界，或者认为只要一个人有逃出去的方法，那么妨害他做他想做的事情就不是拘禁。据说本案当事人可以自由地从另外的方向离开。我不清楚这是不是事实，因为不让他朝一个方向移动的非法力量，也完全可以在他默许的情况下不允许他朝任何其他方向移动。然而（就算这是事实），一个人有权做某件别的事，并不能改变他是不是被拘禁了的事实。如果我不能做某件我有权做的事，我有权做其他事到底有什么意义？有人对我的自由施加了一个非法的要求，难道我没有被限制？如果我被锁在房间里，仅仅因为我可以跳窗逃走，或者因为我能发现其他的危险又不方便的出口，比如说从水中趟过去或者绕远路从而耽误了我的正事，难道就可以说我没有被拘禁？在我看来，这些都属于对一个人的自由的完全剥夺，因为行使自由是为了一定目的的，这些是对这种

with reference to the purpose for which he lawfully wished to employ his liberty: and, being effected by force, it is not the mere obstruction of a way, but a restraint of the person.

...

87. Davidson v Chief Constable of North Wales and another [1994] 2 All ER 597

Court of Appeal, United Kingdom

H, a friend of the plaintiff, purchased a cassette at a store and, having made the purchase, returned to the cassette counter where the plaintiff was waiting. They stood there talking before leaving the store. A store detective who had observed them standing at the cassette counter gained the impression that they had left without paying for the cassette and telephoned the police. When two police officers arrived the store detective told them that the plaintiff had taken the cassette without paying and pointed them out. The officers arrested the plaintiff and H on suspicion of shoplifting. H denied that he had taken anything dishonestly and produced the cassette but was unable to produce the receipt as he had thrown it away. The plaintiff remained silent. The plaintiff and H were taken to the police station but were released after two hours when the police received a message from the shop assistant who had served H confirming that he had paid for the cassette. The plaintiff brought an action against, inter alia, the store detective's employers for false imprisonment. At the trial of the action the police officers gave evidence that they had exercised their own judgment in arresting the plaintiff and H acting on the information received from the store detective. The judge withdrew the case from the jury on the grounds that the police officers were protected by s 24(6) of the Police and Criminal Evidence Act 1984 because they had had reasonable grounds to make the arrest and since they had acted independently of the store detective there was no case to answer. The plaintiff appealed.

SIR THOMAS BINGHAM

This is an appeal against a decision of Judge Roberts given in the Llangefni County Court on 12 December 1991. The decision appealed against was made in the course of the hearing of a civil claim for false imprisonment which was proceeding before the learned judge and a jury and was to the effect that the case should be withdrawn from the jury.

It is pertinent to observe that the evidence of the two police officers was adduced by the plaintiff at the hearing before the learned judge and was accordingly not the subject of cross-examination. It is plain on the facts that Mrs Yates herself did not arrest, imprison, detain or restrain the plaintiff's liberty directly in any way herself. She gave information to the police constables and according to their evidence they acted on it. If she is liable, therefore, it can only be through the police constables either as her agents or, as Mr Clover who appears for the appellants would prefer to put it, as persons whom she procured to act as they did. It is however plain, as I

目的的剥夺。如果这种剥夺是通过暴力完成的，这就不仅仅是阻碍了一个人朝着一个方向前进，也是对人身自由的限制。

……

87. Davidson v Chief Constable of North Wales and another [1994] 2 All ER 597

联合王国上诉法院

H 是原告的朋友。他在商店买了一盘磁带，付完钱后又回到了磁带柜台去找原告。他们在磁带柜台附近聊了一会儿，然后就离开了。商店的保安看到他们站在磁带柜台旁边，以为他们没有付钱就走了，因此就报了警。警察到了之后，商店保安告诉警官原告拿了磁带没给钱，并指认了他们。警官以涉嫌盗窃为由逮捕了原告和 H。H 否认他们拿了任何不该拿的东西，并拿出磁带给警官看，但是他却拿不出收据了，因为收据被他扔了。原告则一直保持着沉默。原告和 H 被带到了派出所。两个小时后，警察收到服务 H 的店员的信息，证明了 H 确实给了钱的，因此警察便把两人放了。原告起诉了包括商店保安的雇主在内的一系列的人，理由是非法拘禁。一审庭审时，警官作证说他们是按照自己的判断来逮捕原告和 H 的，但是信息是商店保安提供的。法官没有让陪审团来裁断，其理由是由于警官们作出的逮捕决定有正当的依据，因此他们受到 1984 年《警察和刑事证据法》第 24 条第 6 款的保护。由于警官们并不是按照商店保安的指示在行事，从而无需让陪审团来回答任何问题，原告因此上诉。

Thomas Bingham 爵士

本次上诉的案件是 Roberts 法官 1991 年 12 月 12 日在 Llangefni 郡法院所作出的判决。被上诉的判决是在一起针对非法拘禁的民事诉讼中作出的，由博学的法官和一个陪审团审理。判决的结果是该案件应从陪审团处撤回。

需要注意的是，两位警官的证词是原告提供的，而不是交叉询问的结果。显而易见的是，Yates 女士并未亲自直接地逮捕、拘禁原告或者限制原告的自由。她仅仅只是把信息告诉了警官，而警官依据她给的信息行事。如果她要承担责任，那只能是在为警官承担替代责任。而警官则是她的代理人，或者按照上诉人的律师 Clover 先生的说法，她促成了警官的行为。然而同样显而

have indicated, that the police constables acted under s 24(6) of the Police and Criminal Evidence Act 1984. It was accepted that they had reasonable suspicion and acted in pursuance of that section and it is accepted that their action was proper. It, therefore, is correct, as the learned judge observed, that a somewhat anomalous situation arises if the appellant's case is correct, since the defendant would be liable for an act of persons who were not themselves liable in respect of what they had done.

The high watermark of the appellant's case derives from answers which Mrs Yates gave when she was cross-examined by counsel for the plaintiff. In the course of a series of answers she said that she expected information given by a store detective such as herself to carry weight with police officers. She intended and expected the police officers to act upon it. They had always done so in the past. She had never known of any occasion when they had failed to do so and accordingly she regarded the arrest as made on her behalf or for her.

…

Accordingly, as it would seem to me, the question which arose for the decision of the learned judge in this case was whether there was information properly to be considered by the jury as to whether what Mrs Yates did went beyond laying information before police officers for them to take such action as they thought fit and amounted to some direction, or procuring, or direct request, or direct encouragement that they should act by way of arresting these defendants. He decided that there was no evidence which went beyond the giving of information. Certainly there was no express request. Certainly there was no encouragement. Certainly there was no discussion of any kind as to what action the police officers should take.

The crux of Mr Clover's submission is that this case is different from the case in which an ordinary member of the public gives information to a police officer because this is a store detective, somebody better informed than an ordinary member of the public as to what was likely to happen upon making a complaint, and somebody with a very clear intention and expectation as to what would happen. No doubt the store detective did have an intention and expectation as to what would happen. The fact remains that the learned judge to my mind quite correctly held that what Mrs Yates did and said in no way went beyond the mere giving of information, leaving it to the officers to exercise a discretion which on their unchallenged evidence they did as to whether they should take any action or not.

In those circumstances the learned judge was, as I think, entirely correct to withdraw the matter from the jury since it seems to me inevitable that had he left it to the jury, and had the jury found for the plaintiff, that verdict would have been open to challenge in this court which would have led to its being overruled. I, therefore, dismiss this appeal.

Staughton LJ.

Whether a request by itself is sufficient to make a person liable does not arise in this case.

易见的是，如前所述，警官是在按照 1984 年《警察和刑事证据法》第 24 条第 6 款行事。双方都承认警官采取的措施是基于合理的怀疑，是在按照 24 条第 6 款行事，因此其行为是正当的。正如博学的一审法官所讲的，支持上诉人的话会导致很奇怪的结果，因为被告要为他人的行为承担责任，而并非他人自己为自己的行为承担责任。

上诉人最占上风的时候是在交叉询问的时候，当时原告律师让 Yates 女士说出了很多东西。她回答了一系列的问题。她说她预料到了她作为商店保安所提供的信息在警方那里分量是很重的。她料想到警官会依她所提供的信息来行事。他们之前都是这么做的。她不知道有哪次警察没有这么做。因此她认为警官对原告的逮捕其实是代表她而做出的，或者是为她做出的。

......

由此而言，在我看来，本案博学的一审法官要判决的问题，其实是根据现有的信息，判决是否要由陪审团来判断 Yates 女士的行为仅仅是为警方提供信息供他们参考，还是在指导、促成或者直接请求、直接鼓励警方去逮捕这些人。一审法官最后认定，并没有证据证明 Yates 女士做了比提供信息更多的事。她显然并没有明示请求警官去逮捕原告和 H。她并没有鼓励警官去这么做。她显然并没有讨论警官应该采取何种行动。

Clover 先生的关键主张是本案和一般的公众向警方提供信息的情形是不同的，这种不同是因为本案涉及的是商店保安，而商店保安是比一般公众更知晓他报警的后果的，商店保安显然也很希望发生这种后果。毫无疑问，商店保安确实是希望发生这种后果。然而这并不能改变博学的一审法官的观点是对的。Yates 女士的所作所为，没有在任何一种意义上超过了提供信息，且她提供的信息是为警官的自由裁量作参考的，这已经由警方自己的无可辩驳的证词所证明。

综上所述，在我看来，博学的一审法官不让陪审团来裁断这个问题是完全正确的。因为如果他这么做了而陪审团又裁断支持了原告，那么这个裁断在本庭也会被推翻的。因此，我驳回上诉。

Staughton 上诉法院法官

一个请求本身是否足以让一个人承担责任，这个问题其实并不是本案的争

What is clear in the passage I have read is that merely giving information is not enough. That does not give rise to false imprisonment. Mrs Yates did no more than that. However much one may look at evidence and analyse what possible consequences might or would arise from the information which she gave, the fact is that all she did was give the information.

I too would dismiss this appeal.

WAITE LJ.

I agree the appeal should be dismissed for the reasons given by the Sir Thomas Bingham MR and Staughton LJ.

Section 3. Intentional Infliction of Mental Upset

88. State Rubbish Collectors Association v. Siliznoff, 38 Cal. 2d 330, 240 P.2d 282 (1952)

Supreme Court of California, United States

Traynor, J. On February 1, 1948, Peter Kobzeff signed a contract with the Acme Brewing Company to collect rubbish from the latter's brewery. Kobzeff had been in the rubbish business for several years and was able to secure the contract because Acme was dissatisfied with the service then being provided by another collector, one Abramoff. Although Kobzeff signed the contract, it was understood that the work should be done by John Siliznoff, Kobzeff's son-in-law, whom Kobzeff wished to assist in establishing a rubbish collection business.

Both Kobzeff and Abramoff were members of the plaintiff State Rubbish Collectors Association, but Siliznoff was not. The by-laws of the Association provided that one member should not take an account from another member without paying for it. Usual prices ranged from five to ten times the monthly rate paid by the customer, and disputes were referred to the board of directors for settlement. After Abramoff lost the Acme account he complained to the association, and Kobzeff was called upon to settle the matter. Kobzeff and Siliznoff took the position that the Acme account belonged to Siliznoff, and that he was under no obligation to pay for it. After attending several meetings of plaintiff's board of directors Siliznoff finally agreed, however, to pay Abramoff $1,850 for the Acme account and join the association. The agreement provided that he should pay $500 in 30 days and $75 per month thereafter until the whole sum agreed upon was paid. Payments were to be made through the association, and Siliznoff executed a series of promissory notes totaling $1,850. None of these notes was paid, and in 1949 plaintiff association brought this action to collect the notes then payable. Defendant cross-complained and asked that the notes be cancelled because of duress and want of consideration. In addition he sought general and exemplary damages because of assaults made by plaintiff and its agents to compel him to join the association and pay Abramoff for the Acme account. The jury returned a verdict against

议问题。就我所读的本案的案情来说，很明显的是仅仅提供信息是不足以让一个人承担责任的。这种行为本身并不构成非法拘禁。Yates 女士所做的，也仅仅是提供信息而已。不论我们再努力地从证据中寻找蛛丝马迹，去看她提供的信息到底产生了什么后果，也不能改变她所做的仅仅是提供信息而已这样一个事实。

我同样驳回上诉。

Waite 上诉法院法官

我同意应该驳回上诉，掌卷法官 Thomas Bingham 爵士和 Staughton 上诉法院法官已经给出了理由。

第三节 故意致人精神损害

88. State Rubbish Collectors Association v. Siliznoff, 38 Cal. 2d 330, 240 P.2d 282 (1952)

美国加利福尼亚州最高法院

Traynor 法官主笔：1948 年 2 月 1 日，Peter Kobzeff 与 Acme 酿造公司订立了一份从后者的酿酒厂收集垃圾的合同。Kobzeff 曾经从事多年垃圾收集业务并且有能力保证合同的履行，因为 Acme 公司对曾承担该业务的另一个叫做 Abramoff 的垃圾收集人的服务不甚满意。尽管 Kobzeff 签订了合同，但是据了解该工作应当由 Kobzeff 的女婿 John Siliznoff 完成，Kobzeff 希望他协助从事垃圾收集业务。

Kobzeff 与 Abramoff 都是原告州垃圾收集人协会的成员，但 Siliznoff 不是。协会章程规定成员除了购买之外，不应当从其他成员那里取得业务。由购买者支付的通常价格是每月费用的 5—10 倍，并且争议被提交董事会进行和解。在 Abramoff 丢掉 Acme 公司的业务之后，他向协会投诉，然后 Kobzeff 被叫来解决问题。Kobzeff 和 Siliznoff 所秉持的立场是，Acme 公司的业务是 Siliznoff 的，并且他没有义务购买它。在参加原告董事会的多轮会议之后，Siliznoff 最终同意，为 Acme 公司的业务向 Abramoff 支付 1 850 美元并加入协会。该协议规定他应当在 30 日内支付 500 美元，此后每月支付 75 美元直至其同意的全部数额支付完毕。付款将通过协会履行，并且 Siliznoff 签发了总金额为 1 850 美元的几张本票。那几张本票中没有一张被付款，原告协会遂于 1949 年提起本诉讼，请求接受票据并付款。被告提起反诉并主张票据的签发系出于强制胁迫，且没有对价，故所签票据应被撤销。此外，他请求一般性及惩罚性赔偿，理由是原告实施威吓行为以及其代理人强迫被告加入协会并向 Abramoff 购买 Acme 公司的业务。陪审团在本诉部分作出不利于原告而有利于被告的裁决，在反

plaintiff and for defendant on the complaint and for defendant on his cross-complaint. It awarded him $1,250 general and special damages and $7,500 exemplary damages. The trial court denied a motion for a new trial on the condition that defendant consent to a reduction of the exemplary damages to $4,000. Defendant filed the required consent, and plaintiff has appealed from the judgment.

Plaintiff's primary contention is that the evidence is insufficient to support the judgment. Defendant testified that shortly after he secured the Acme account, the president of the association and its inspector, John Andikian, called on him and Kobzeff. They suggested that either a settlement be made with Abramoff or that the job be dropped, and requested Kobzeff and defendant to attend a meeting of the association. At this meeting defendant was told that the association "ran all the rubbish from that office, all the rubbish hauling," and that if he did not pay for the job they would take it away from him. "'We would take it away, even if we had to haul for nothing'... One of them mentioned that I had better pay up, or else." Thereafter, on the day when defendant finally agreed to pay for the account, Andikian visited defendant at the Rainier Brewing Company, where he was collecting rubbish. Andikian told defendant that "'We will give you up till tonight to get down to the board meeting and make some kind of arrangements or agreements about the Acme Brewery, or otherwise we are going to beat you up.'...He says he either would hire somebody or do it himself. And I says, 'Well, what would they do to me?' He says, well, they would physically beat me up first, cut up the truck tires or burn the truck, or otherwise put me out of business completely. He said if I didn't appear at that meeting and make some kind of an agreement that they would do that, but he says up to then they would let me alone, but if I walked out of that meeting that night they would beat me up for sure." Defendant attended the meeting and protested that he owed nothing for the Acme account and in any event could not pay the amount demanded. He was again told by the president of the association that "that table right there the board of directors ran all the rubbish collecting in Los Angeles and if there was any routes to be gotten that they would get them and distribute them among their members...." After two hours of further discussion defendant agreed to join the association and pay for the Acme account. He promised to return the next day and sign the necessary papers. He testified that the only reason "they let me go home, is that I promised that I would sign the notes the very next morning." The president "made me promise on my honor and everything else, and I was scared, and I knew I had to come back, so I believe he knew I was scared and that I would come back. That's the only reason they let me go home." Defendant also testified that because of the fright he suffered during his dispute with the association he became ill and vomited several times and had to remain away from work for a period of several days.

Plaintiff contends that the evidence does not establish an assault against defendant because the threats made all related to action that might take place in the future; that neither Andikian nor members of the board of directors threatened immediate physical harm to defendant. We have concluded, however, that a cause of action is established when it is shown that one, in the absence

诉部分则裁决被告胜诉。它判决给被告 1 250 美元的一般及特别赔偿，以及 7 500 美元的惩罚性赔偿。在被告同意将惩罚性赔偿降至 4 000 美元的前提下，一审法院驳回了重新审理之申请。被告提交符合要求的同意书，而原告已就判决提起上诉。

原告的首要主张是支持判决的证据不足。被告作证说，在其得到 Acme 公司的业务后不久，协会主席及其监察员 John Andikian 拜访了他和 Kobzeff。他们建议要么与 Abramoff 达成和解，要么放弃该工作，并要求 Kobzeff 和被告参加协会的一个会议。在该会议上，被告被告知协会"从该处掌管所有的垃圾业务和垃圾运送"，以及如果他不购买此业务他们将从他那里拿走它。"'我们将取走它，即使我们运送而得不到任何报酬'……他们中的一个人说我最好全部付清，要不然就……"此后，在被告最终同意购买该业务的那一天，Andikian 会见了正在 Rainier 酿造公司收集垃圾的被告。Andikian 告诉被告，"'直到今晚我们将对于你认真考虑董事会议以及达成有关 Acme 酿造公司的某种安排或协议不再抱有希望，或者不然我们将要毒打你'……他说他要么雇佣他人或者亲自动手做这件事。而我说，'好的，他们将如何对付我呢？'他说，他们可能对我进行身体上的殴打，切碎卡车的轮胎或烧毁卡车，或者让我完全失业。他说如果我不出席那次会议并达成他们想要的某种协议，到那时他将令我孤立无援，要是我走出那晚的会场，他们肯定会打我"。被告参加了会议并主张他在 Acme 业务上并无任何亏欠，而且不管在什么情况下都不能支付被要求数额的金钱。他再次被协会主席告知："就在这张桌子上的董事会掌管洛杉矶的全部垃圾收集业务，如果有任何可以取得的垃圾收集途径，他们都会取得并在其成员之间分配……"经过两个多小时的进一步磋商，被告同意加入协会并购买收集 Acme 公司的垃圾业务。他承诺于次日偿还并签署必要的文件。他作证说，唯一的理由使"他们让我回家，就是我承诺我将于次日上午签发票据"。主席"让我以我的荣誉以及其他所有的东西来确保承诺，我感到惊恐，我知道我不得不回来，当然我也相信他知道我害怕了，并且我会回来。这是他们让我回家的唯一的理由"。被告还举证说明，因为其与州垃圾协会的交涉，其精神上很害怕，并且因此生病，多次呕吐，多日无法工作。

原告认为证据不能证实其对被告实施了威吓行为，因为恐惧所造成的任何相关反应，可能在将来发生。Andikian 与董事会成员之威胁都不会造成被

of any privilege, intentionally subjects another to the mental suffering incident to serious threats to his physical well-being, whether or not the threats are made under such circumstances as to constitute a technical assault.

In the past it has frequently been stated that the interest in emotional and mental tranquillity is not one that the law will protect from invasion in its own right. As late as 1934 the Restatement of Torts took the position that "The interest in mental and emotional tranquillity and, therefore, in freedom from mental and emotional disturbance is not, as a thing in itself, regarded as of sufficient importance to require others to refrain from conduct intended or recognizably likely to cause such a disturbance." (Restatement, Torts, §46, Comment *c*.) The Restatement explained the rule allowing recovery for the mere apprehension of bodily harm in traditional assault cases as an historical anomaly (§24, Comment *c*), and the rule allowing recovery for insulting conduct by an employee of a common carrier as justified by the necessity of securing for the public comfortable as well as safe service. (§48, Comment *c*.)

The Restatement recognized, however, that in many cases mental distress could be so intense that it could reasonably be foreseen that illness or other bodily harm might result. If the defendant intentionally subjected the plaintiff to such distress and bodily harm resulted, the defendant would be liable for negligently causing the plaintiff bodily harm. (Restatement, Torts, §§306, 312.) Under this theory the cause of action was not founded on a right to be free from intentional interference with mental tranquillity, but on the right to be free from negligent interference with physical well-being. A defendant who intentionally subjected another to mental distress without intending to cause bodily harm would nevertheless be liable for resulting bodily harm if he should have foreseen that the mental distress might cause such harm.

The California cases have been in accord with the Restatement in allowing recovery where physical injury resulted from intentionally subjecting the plaintiff to serious mental distress.

The view has been forcefully advocated that the law should protect emotional and mental tranquillity as such against serious and intentional invasions and there is a growing body of case law supporting this position. In recognition of this development the American Law Institute amended section 46 of the Restatement of Torts in 1947 to provide…

There are persuasive arguments and analogies that support the recognition of a right to be free from serious, intentional, and unprivileged invasions of mental and emotional tranquillity. If a cause of action is otherwise established, it is settled that damages may be given for mental suffering naturally ensuing from the acts complained of, and in the case of many torts, such as assault, battery, false imprisonment, and defamation, mental suffering will frequently constitute the principal element of damages. In cases where mental suffering constitutes a major element of damages it is anomalous to deny recovery because the defendant's intentional misconduct fell short of producing some physical injury.

告遭受即刻的、实质的伤害。然而，我们认为在证实不存在任何特免的情况下，故意致他人精神损害，并对该他人的有形健康造成严重威胁，无论此情形所产生的威胁是否构成法律上的威吓，一个诉因得以成立。

在过去曾被反复表明的是，精神安宁并不是一种以法律权利的名义予以保护的利益。直到1934年的《侵权法重述》所采取的见解是，"精神安宁利益，即免受精神损害的自由，其自身并不是禁止他人以故意或放任的方式实施产生此类损害行为的足够重要的理由"。（《侵权法重述》第46条评论c。）此重述表明过去准许对传统的威吓侵权案件中身体上之伤害的单纯警觉进行赔偿的规则（第24条评论c），从历史上看是罕见而不寻常的，而有的规则基于保障公众享受舒适、安全服务的必要性，准许就公共运输业的员工对乘客的冒犯行为，请求损害赔偿（第48条评论c）。

然而，该重述承认在许多案件中精神痛苦是如此得强烈，以至于可以合理地预见疾病或者其他身体上的伤害可能发生。如果被告故意致使原告遭受此类痛苦和由此而产生的身体伤害，被告将对其过失地引发原告之人身伤害承担赔偿责任（《侵权法重述》第302条和第312条）。基于此理论，诉因不是建立在免受故意侵害心灵安宁的权利之上，而是建立在一种免受过失侵害身体健康的权利之上。一个故意致他人遭受精神痛苦而无意产生身体伤害的被告，假如他本应预见此精神痛苦可能导致此种伤害，他仍将对所产生的身体伤害承担赔偿责任。

已经与重述保持一致的加利福尼亚州判例，允许对故意致原告严重精神痛苦所产生的人身损害进行赔偿。

有观点已经强有力地主张，法律应当保护精神安宁以反对严重的且故意的侵害行为，而正在增长中的判例法支持了此立场。认识到该发展的美国法律协会在1947年修改了《侵权法重述》第46条，并规定……

有说服力的论据和类推支持确立一种使精神安宁免受严重的、故意的且无特免之侵害的权利。假如该诉因得以确立，将对被诉行为所直接产生的精神损害给予赔偿，而在许多诸如威吓、殴击、非法拘禁以及诽谤案件中，精神损害将经常成为损害赔偿的重要条件。在精神损害成为损害赔偿的主要条件的案件中，因为被告的故意侵权行为未能造成人身损害，而拒绝赔偿是反常的。

It may be contended that to allow recovery in the absence of physical injury will open the door to unfounded claims and a flood of litigation, and that the requirement that there be physical injury is necessary to insure that serious mental suffering actually occurred. The jury is ordinarily in a better position, however, to determine whether outrageous conduct results in mental distress than whether that distress in turn results in physical injury. From their own experience jurors are aware of the extent and character of the disagreeable emotions that may result from the defendant's conduct, but a difficult medical question is presented when it must be determined if emotional distress resulted in physical injury. Greater proof that mental suffering occurred is found in the defendant's conduct designed to bring it about than in physical injury that may or may not have resulted therefrom.

That administrative difficulties do not justify the denial of relief for serious invasions of mental and emotional tranquillity is demonstrated by the cases recognizing the right of privacy. Recognition of that right protects mental tranquillity from invasion by unwarranted and undesired publicity. As in the case of the protection of mental tranquillity from other forms of invasion, difficult problems in determining the kind and extent of invasions that are sufficiently serious to be actionable are presented. Also the public interest in the free dissemination of news must be considered. Nevertheless courts have concluded that the problems presented are not so insuperable that they warrant the denial of relief altogether.

In the present case plaintiff caused defendant to suffer extreme fright. By intentionally producing such fright it endeavored to compel him either to give up the Acme account or pay for it, and it had no right or privilege to adopt such coercive methods in competing for business. In these circumstances liability is clear....

Plaintiff contends finally that the damages were excessive. The question of excessiveness is addressed primarily to the discretion of the trial court, and an award that stands approved by that court will not be disturbed on appeal unless it appears that the jury was influenced by passion or prejudice. With respect to the general damages the trial court concluded that the jury was not so influenced, and on the record before us we cannot say that it was. The excessiveness, if any, of the award of exemplary damages was cured by the trial court's reduction of those damages to $4,000.

The judgment is affirmed. Gibson, C.J., Shenk, Edmonds, Carter, Schauer, and Spence, JJ., concurred.

89. Ford v. Revlon, Inc., 153 Ariz. 38, 734 P.2d 580 (1987)

Supreme Court of Arizona, United States

Facts

Leta Fay Ford worked for the purchasing department of Revlon, Inc. (Revlon) in Phoenix,

有人可能认为，允许缺乏人身损害的损害赔偿将为没有事实依据的诉讼以及洪水般的诉讼打开阀门；还认为，人身损害要件对于确保严重精神损害的实际出现是必要的。然而，陪审团通常站在一个更为有利的位置，去判断令人难以忍受的行为是否导致精神损害，而不是接着判断此精神损害是否导致人身损害。基于他们自身的经验，陪审员们知道被告行为所导致的原告不良情绪的程度与性质，但是在必须判断精神损害是否引发人身损害的时候，就提出了一个难懂的医学问题。精神损害发生的更重要的证明是查明引起其发生的被告之行为，而不是人身损害可能或不可能由其导致。

那些确认了隐私权的判例表明，即便存在管理上的困难，我们依然应该给严重的被侵害了精神安宁的受害者提供救济。对该权利的承认保护精神安宁不受非法的和不被欢迎的公开行为侵害。在保护精神安宁免受其他形式之侵害的情况下，所提出的难题是确定侵害行为的种类和程度是否具有可诉讼的足够严重性。在新闻的自由传播中公共利益同样必须予以考量。不过，法院已经判定所提交的问题并没有达到无法克服的程度以至于彻底地拒绝给予司法救济。

在本案中原告导致被告陷入极端的恐惧。通过故意制造此种恐惧，它试图迫使被告要么放弃 Acme 公司的业务，要么花钱购买，而在商业竞争中它没有权利或特免采取这样的强制方法。在这些情形中责任是显然的……

最后，原告主张损害赔偿超额。超额问题的提出主要针对的是初审法院的自由裁量，并且除非证明陪审团受到激情或偏见的影响，否则该法院所核准的赔偿金将不受上诉行为的影响。对于一般赔偿，初审法院判定陪审团没有受到此等影响，而基于我们面前的案卷，我们无法说它是。如果真有的话，惩罚性赔偿的超额已经通过初审法院将其降至 4 000 美元的行为得以弥补。

维持原判。Gibson 大法官和 Shenk 法官、Edmonds 法官、Carter 法官以及 Schauer 法官赞同。

89. Ford v. Revlon, Inc., 153 Ariz. 38, 734 P.2d 580 (1987)

美国亚利桑那州最高法院

事实

Leta Fay Ford 受雇于亚利桑那州 Phoenix 市的 Revlon 公司的销售部门（以

Arizona. She began her employment in 1973 as a secretary. She worked her way up to junior buyer and buyer positions over the ten years of her employment at Revlon. In October 1979, Revlon hired Karl Braun as the new manager for the purchasing department, which made him Ford's supervisor.

On 3 April 1980, Braun invited Ford to a dinner ostensibly to discuss business away from the office. Ford agreed and met Braun at a Phoenix restaurant. The business discussion, however, turned to more personal topics. At the end of the dinner, Ford started to leave. Braun told her that she was not going anywhere and to sit down because he planned to spend the night with her. When Ford rejected his advances, Braun told her, "you will regret this." Ford testified at trial that after this incident her working relationship with Braun was strained and uncomfortable. Ford did not report the dinner incident nor the adverse working atmosphere to Revlon management.

On 3 May 1980, Revlon held its annual service awards picnic. Braun followed Ford for most of the day....

Later in May of 1980, Ford began a series of meetings with various members of Revlon management to report her complaints. Ford first spoke with the Phoenix Revlon comptroller, Robert Lettieri, who had authority to recommend hiring, firing, discipline, and promotions. Ford told him about the incidents with Braun and that she was afraid of Braun and wanted help. Lettieri said that he would speak to someone in personnel about her complaint and that she also should talk to personnel.

In early June of 1980, Ford spoke to Cecelia Domin, the personnel manager for the clerical and technical group in the Phoenix plant. In the Revlon management hierarchy, Domin reported directly to the director of personnel and worked with the plant manager of executives. When meeting with Domin, Ford was very emotional, her hands were shaking, and she was crying. Ford told Domin about the incidents and said that she was afraid of Braun. On 23 June 1980, Ford spoke to Robert Kosciusko, the personnel manager for executives. Ford also told him about the incidents, that she was afraid of Braun, and that the strain was making her sick.

In August of 1980, Ford met again with Domin and additionally with Martin Burstein, the director of personnel at the Phoenix plant. Again Ford complained about the incidents and told them that she was afraid of Braun. Burstein told Ford that he would talk to a Revlon vice president and that he would get back to her. Also in August, Ford spoke to John Maloney, a manager in receiving and stores. Maloney suggested that Ford contact Marie Kane at Revlon headquarters in New Jersey. Kane, a manager of human resources, was a "trouble shooter" and a veteran of the Phoenix personnel department.

In November of 1980, Ford telephoned Kane in New Jersey to report her concerns about Braun and her frustrations about the work situation. At this time, it had been six months since Ford first complained of Braun's conduct and no action had been taken. Kane then reported the details

下简称"Revlon")。她在 1973 年以一名秘书的身份开始了她的雇佣生涯。她受雇于 Revlon 从事了长达 10 年的客户分布管理工作。在 1979 年 10 月，Revlon 雇用 Karl Braun 作为销售部门的新经理，这使得他成为 Ford 的上司。

在 1980 年 4 月 3 日，Braun 以讨论工作为名邀请 Ford 离开办公室去吃饭。Ford 同意并在 Phoenix 的一家餐馆见到 Braun。但是，这场工作讨论转向更多的私人话题。在就餐结束时，Ford 准备离开。Braun 告诉她不要去其他地方并要求其坐下，因为他准备与她过夜。当 Ford 拒绝他的勾引后，Braun 对她说："你将为此而后悔。" Ford 在初审中作证说，在此事之后她与 Braun 的工作关系变得紧张和不愉快。Ford 没有将就餐事件以及不利的工作环境向 Revlon 的管理层汇报。

在 1980 年 5 月 3 日，Revlon 举行年度工作奖励野餐会。Braun 用这天的多数时间跟踪 Ford……

在 1980 年 5 月的稍后时间里，Ford 开始与 Revlon 管理层的各位成员展开一系列的会面来诉说她的不满。Ford 首先和 Phoenix 市的 Revlon 公司有权建议雇用、解聘、处罚以及晋升的审计官员 Robert Lettieri 会谈。Ford 告诉他有关与 Braun 发生的事以及她对 Braun 感到害怕并寻求帮助。Lettieri 说他会把她的抗议告诉人事部门的人，并且她也应当告知人事部门。

在 1980 年 6 月初，Ford 告诉了在 Phoenix 工厂负责文书和技术类工作的人事经理 Cecelia Domin。在 Revlon 公司的管理层中，Domin 直接告诉了人事主管还要求与公司的执行经理一道处理此事。在见到 Domin 的时候，Ford 的情绪非常激动，她的双手颤抖，并且一直在哭泣。Ford 向 Domin 诉说那件事并且说她对 Braun 感到害怕。在 1980 年 6 月 23 日，Ford 与负责行政的人事经理 Robert Kosciusko 交谈。Ford 同样告诉他那件事，她对 Braun 感到害怕，并且极度的紧张让她变得心烦意乱。

在 1980 年 8 月，Ford 再次会见 Domin 以及 Phoenix 工厂的人事主管 Martin Burstein。Ford 再次投诉了那件事并且告诉他们她害怕 Braun。Burstein 对 Ford 说他将与 Revlon 的一位副总裁谈话并回复她。同样在 8 月，Ford 告诉了 John Maloney，这是一位负责收购和仓储的经理。Maloney 建议 Ford 去联系在新泽西州 Revlon 公司总部的一位名叫 Marie Kane 的人力资源经理，她是一位"解决麻烦的能手"，并且是 Phoenix 公司人事部门的一位"老兵"。

在 1980 年 11 月，Ford 给在新泽西州的 Kane 打电话诉说她对 Braun 的焦虑以及她对工作处境的沮丧。此时，自从 Ford 首次对 Braun 抱怨以来，已经过去 6 个月，而公司未采取任何行动。Kane 随后将与 Ford 的谈话细节汇报

of her conversation with Ford to her boss, David Coe, the vice president of industrial relations and operations. Kane also informed Coe that Ford was becoming ill because of the problem. Coe's response was that the matter was not their concern at the corporate level and that the matter should be sent back to the local level and handled in Phoenix. Coe instructed Kane to telephone Burstein so that he could solve the problem. Kane did speak to Burstein, who promised to take care of the problem immediately.

When, as of December 1980, no action had been taken on Ford's complaint, Ford telephoned Kane again and informed her that Braun was continuing his harassment by calling her into his office and telling her that he wanted to destroy her, that she made him nervous, and that so long as she worked for him she was never going to go anywhere. He also called her into his office and did not allow her to sit down and would stare at her and not speak to her. According to Ford, Kane responded that it was a lot to absorb and that she would have to talk to someone else about it and that she would get back to Ford. After a few days had elapsed and Kane had not telephoned Ford, Ford again called Kane, who was out, and left a message. It was January 1981 before Kane returned Ford's call. Kane told Ford that the situation was too hot for her to handle and that she did not want to be involved. Kane suggested that Ford put the matter in the back of her mind and try to forget the situation. Around this time, Ford also contacted Gene Tucker, a corporate Equal Employment Opportunity (EEO) specialist, and asked him for help. Tucker said that he would have to talk to Harry Petrie, the vice president of industrial relations and personnel in New York. Tucker did not get back to Ford.

During the time of the harassment, Ford developed high blood pressure, a nervous tic in her left eye, chest pains, rapid breathing, and other symptoms of emotional stress. Ford felt weak, dizzy, and generally fatigued. Ford consulted a physician about her condition.

On 23 February 1981, Ford submitted a written request for a transfer out of the purchasing department. On 24 February 1981, Braun placed Ford on a 60-day probation because of her allegedly poor work performance. On 25 February 1981, a meeting finally was held in personnel at Ford's demand so she could have something done about her situation with Braun. Ford was able to have Tucker arrange a meeting with them and with Domin and Burstein. Ford again gave the details of her complaint against Braun and her fear of him. Ford also submitted a handwritten complaint which read in part:

> I want to officially register a charge of sexual harassment and discrimination against K. Braun.
> I am asking for protection from Karl Braun. I have a right to be protected.
> I am collapsing emotionally and physically and I can't go on.

给她的老板，负责产业关系与运行的副总裁 David Coe。Kane 同时向 Coe 告知 Ford 因该问题而陷入病态。Coe 的回应是该问题并不是公司层面所关切的，并且该问题应当反馈给基层并由 Phoenix 公司处理。Coe 指示 Kane 给 Burstein 打电话以便他能够解决该问题。Kane 确实告诉了 Burstein，他承诺立即处理此事。

到 1980 年 12 月为止，公司对 Ford 的控诉没有采取任何行动。Ford 再次给 Kane 打电话说 Braun 仍然在骚扰她，还叫她去办公室说想毁灭她，是她使得他紧张，并且她为他工作以来她从来没有打算去其他地方。他也叫她去他的办公室而不允许她坐下并默不作声地盯着她。根据 Ford 的报告，Kane 回应说她需要一些时间去告诉其他人这件事并给她回音。几天过后，Kane 未给 Ford 打电话。Ford 再次给 Kane 打电话但她出差了，于是留下一条信息。直到 1981 年 1 月 Kane 才给 Ford 回了电话。Kane 对 Ford 说这种局面对她而言太棘手而不能处理，并且她不想被牵扯进来。Kane 建议 Ford 将这件事埋在心底并忘了此事。在此前后，Ford 还联系了一位公司平等就业机会（EEO）专家 Gene Tucker 并向他寻求帮助。Tucker 说他一定会将此事告诉在纽约市负责工业关系和人事的副总裁 Harry Petrie。Tucker 没有回复 Ford。

在被骚扰期间，Ford 患上了高血压、左眼神经性痉挛、胸痛、气短以及精神紧张等症状。Ford 感到虚弱、眩晕并且全身乏力。Ford 向一位医生咨询了她的健康状况。

在 1981 年的 2 月 23 日，Ford 递交了一份调离销售部的书面请求。1981 年 2 月 24 日，Braun 给了 Ford 一个 60 日的察看期，理由是她工作表现糟糕。在 1981 年 2 月 25 日，应 Ford 的要求人事部召开了一个会议来解决她与 Braun 之间的事。Ford 要求 Tucker 安排一场由他们和 Domin、Burstein 参加的会议。Ford 再次陈述了她对 Braun 控诉的细节以及她对他的恐惧。Ford 也递交了一份手写的控告，其中一部分写着：

> 我想正式对 K. Braun 提起有关性骚扰和歧视的控告。
> 我正在请求免受 Karl Braun 侵扰的保护。我有得到保护的权利。
> 我正从精神上和肉体上崩溃，并且我不能再坚持了。

At this meeting on 25 February 1981, Braun was called in and confronted. After the meeting, Burstein and Domin told Ford that Braun would be closely monitored. Burstein also testified that he investigated Ford's allegation, which he said took him about three weeks.

Not until three months later, on 8 May 1981, however, did Burstein submit a report on Ford's complaint to vice president Coe; the report confirmed Ford's charge of sexual assault and recommended that Braun be censured. On 28 May 1981, a full year and one month after Braun's initial act of harassment, Braun was issued a letter of censure from Revlon.

In October of 1981, Ford attempted suicide.

On 5 October 1981, Revlon terminated Braun. Braun testified at trial that the reason given him for his termination was that he did not fit into the Revlon organization, partially because of the way he handled the "Ford situation."

In April of 1982, Ford sued both Braun and Revlon for assault and battery, and for intentional infliction of emotional distress.

The jury found Braun liable for assault and battery but not liable for intentional infliction of emotional distress. The jury found Revlon liable for intentional infliction of emotional distress but not liable for assault and battery. Damages awarded to Ford by the jury were assessed against Braun in the amount of $100 compensatory damages and $1,000 punitive damages, and assessed against Revlon in the amount of $10,000 compensatory damages and $100,000 punitive damages. Only Revlon appealed. Therefore, the only issue on appeal was whether Revlon was liable for intentional infliction of emotional distress. The court of appeals in a memorandum decision reversed the judgment of the trial court, holding that since Braun (as agent) was found not guilty of intentional infliction of emotional distress, then Revlon (as principal) could not be found guilty. We granted review because we disagreed with this limitation on the liability of Revlon.

Independent Tort Liability of the Employer

The court of appeals held that Revlon could not be liable for intentional infliction of emotional distress if Braun was not liable. The court of appeals stated:

> Even though the jury found Braun did assault Ford on May 3, 1980, it found that the assault and his subsequent acts, whatever they were found to be, were insufficient to hold him liable for intentional or reckless infliction of emotional distress. Revlon's liability is inextricably tied to the acts of Braun. Since Braun's acts did not constitute intentional or reckless infliction of emotional distress, then the inaction of Revlon on Ford's complaint certainly could not reach that level.

We disagree. Admittedly, when the master's liability is based solely on the negligence of his servant, a judgment in favor of the servant is a judgment in favor of the master. DeGraff v.

在 1981 年 2 月 25 日的会议上，Braun 被叫来并当面对证。在会后，Burstein 和 Domin 对 Ford 说 Braun 已经被严密监视了。Burstein 同时表示他将调查 Ford 的指控，他说他需要 3 周的时间。

但是，直到 3 个月后，即 1981 年 5 月 8 日，Burstein 才向公司副总裁 Coe 递交了一份有关 Ford 抗议的报告；该报告认可了 Ford 的性骚扰指控并认为 Braun 应该受到谴责。在 1981 年 5 月 28 日，即在 Braun 首次骚扰行为之后的一整年零一个月，Braun 签收了一份来自 Revlon 公司的谴责信。

在 1981 年 10 月，Ford 试图自杀。

在 1981 年 10 月 5 日，Revlon 解雇了 Braun。Braun 在初审中作证说他被解雇的理由是他不适合 Revlon 公司的工作，也部分因为他对"Ford 问题"的处理方法。

在 1982 年 4 月，Ford 以威吓、殴击以及故意致人精神损害为由起诉 Braun 和 Revlon 公司。

陪审团裁决 Braun 承担威吓和殴击的侵权责任，但不承担故意致人精神损害的责任。陪审团裁决 Revlon 公司承担故意致人精神损害的责任，但不承担威吓和殴击的侵权责任。陪审团裁决 Braun 向 Ford 支付 100 美元的补偿性赔偿金以及 1 000 美元的惩罚性损害赔偿金，并裁决 Revlon 公司支付 1 万美元的补偿性赔偿金以及 10 万美元的惩罚性损害赔偿金。只有 Revlon 公司提起上诉。于是，上诉的唯一争议问题是 Revlon 公司是否承担故意致人精神损害的赔偿责任。上诉法院在一份简式判决书中撤销了初审法院的判决。判决既然 Braun（作为代理人）被认定不为故意致人精神损害承担责任，而 Revlon 公司（作为被代理人）不能被认定为有责任。我们决定重审，因为我们不同意对 Revlon 公司责任的限制。

独立的雇主侵权责任

上诉法院认为如果 Braun 不承担故意致人精神损害的责任，Revlon 公司则不能承担责任。上述法院说：

> 尽管陪审团认定 Braun 在 1980 年 5 月 3 日构成威吓侵权，威吓及他的后续行为，不论它们如何被认定，是不足以判决他承担故意或放任地致人精神损害的责任的。Revlon 公司的责任不可避免地与 Braun 的行为绑在一起。既然 Braun 的行为不构成故意或放任地致人精神损害，则 Revlon 公司在 Ford 控诉上的不作为肯定不能达到那个程度。

我们不同意。诚然，雇主责任仅基于其雇员的过失行为，一份有利于雇员的判决就是一份有利于雇主的判决。参见 DeGraff v. Smith, 62 Ariz. 261, 157

Smith, 62 Ariz. 261, 157 P.2d 342 (1945). When the negligence of the master is independent of the negligence of the servant, the result may be different. As noted by the court of appeals:

We recognize that where there is independent negligence on the part of the master, the master may be liable, apart from his derivative liability for his servant's wrongful acts. In such a case, a judgment in favor of the servant will not ordinarily bar a recovery against the master. However, the master must have "'been guilty of acts on which independently of the acts of the servant, liability may be predicated.'"

We believe that the analysis should be the same in intentional tort cases. In a case factually similar to this one, the U.S. Court of Appeals for the Fourth Circuit recognized that a corporation could be liable for intentional infliction of emotional distress because its supervisor was aware of the sexual harassment of an employee by a manager and failed to stop it even though the *underlying* harassment might not rise to the level of either assault and battery or intentional infliction of emotional distress. Davis v. United States Steel Corp., 779 F.2d 209, 211 (4th Cir. 1985). The Fourth Circuit held that although the acts and behavior of the manager were despicable, they did not rise to the level of providing a basis for recovery by the complainant against the corporation for assault and battery or intentional infliction of emotional distress. The court went on to say, however, that "the situation is otherwise with respect to failure to take any action." Id. at 212. We believe that Revlon's failure to investigate Ford's complaint was independent of Braun's abusive treatment of Ford.

Is Revlon Liable for Intentional Infliction of Emotional Distress?

Elements of the tort of intentional infliction of emotional distress have been set out by this court, relying upon the language of the Restatement of Torts.

The three required elements are: *first*, the conduct by the defendant must be "extreme" and "outrageous"; *second*, the defendant must either intend to cause emotional distress or recklessly disregard the near certainty that such distress will result from his conduct; and *third*, severe emotional distress must indeed occur as a result of defendant's conduct.

We believe that the conduct of Revlon met these requirements. First, Revlon's conduct can be classified as extreme or outrageous. Ford made numerous Revlon managers aware of Braun's activities at company functions. Ford did everything that could be done, both within the announced policies of Revlon and without, to bring this matter to Revlon's attention. Revlon ignored her and the situation she faced, dragging the matter out for months and leaving Ford without redress. Here is sufficient evidence that Revlon acted outrageously.

Second, even if Revlon did not intend to cause emotional distress, Revlon's reckless disregard of Braun's conduct made it nearly certain that such emotional distress would in fact occur. Revlon knew that Braun had subjected Ford to physical assaults, vulgar remarks, that Ford continued to feel threatened by Braun, and that Ford was emotionally distraught, all of which led to a

P.2d 342（1945）案。当雇主的过失行为独立于雇员的过失行为时，结果可能不同。正如上诉法院所言：

我们认为，除了对其雇员的侵权行为所负的派生责任，雇主存在独立的过失行为，要对此承担责任。在这样的案件中，一份有利于雇员的判决通常不会阻却从雇主处获得救济。但是，雇主必须"已经对独立于雇员行为的行为负有责任，责任可能被预见"。

我们相信此分析同样适用于故意侵权案件。在一个事实与本案类似的案件中，美国第四巡回上诉法院认定一家公司可能承担故意致人精神损害的责任，因为其管理人知道一个经理对其雇员实施性骚扰但未能阻止它，即使潜在的骚扰行为尚未达到威吓、殴击或者故意致人精神损害的程度。参见 Davis v. United States Steel Corp., 779 F.2d 209, 211（4th Cir. 1985）案。第四巡回法院判决尽管这名经理的行为和举止应当受到谴责，但是它们未达到为以威吓、殴击或者故意致人精神损害为由的诉讼提供赔偿依据的程度。但是，法院继续说："这种情况与未能采取任何行动有关。"（Id. at 212.）我们认为，Revlon 公司未能调查 Ford 的控诉，是独立于 Braun 对 Ford 的污秽行为。

Revlon 是否承担故意致人精神损害责任？

故意致人精神损害的侵权构成要件，本法院根据侵权法重述的语句而确定。

这三个构成要件是：第一，Revlon 的行为必须是"极端"且"令人难以忍受"的；第二，被告必须故意导致精神损害或者近乎鲁莽地忽视此损害将由他的行为造成的几近确定性；第三，严重精神损害必须确实作为被告行为的结果发生。

我们相信 Revlon 的行为满足这些要件。第一，Revlon 的行为能被归入极端且令人难以忍受的行为。Ford 让 Revlon 的许多经理知道 Braun 在公司业务上的行为。Ford 做了能够做的每一件事，在 Revlon 公司已公布的政策之内或之外，以引起 Revlon 公司的注意。Revlon 公司漠视她以及她所面对的情况，将此事拖延数个月并置 Ford 于无救济的境地。这里有足够的证据证明 Revlon 公司的行为令人难以忍受。

第二，虽然 Revlon 公司没有造成精神损害的意图，但是 Revlon 公司几近鲁莽地漠视 Braun 之行为造成此类精神损害实际发生的几近确定性。Revlon 公司知道 Braun 已经使 Ford 遭受人身威胁及粗鲁的言辞。Ford 继续受到 Braun 的威胁，并且 Ford 变得精神错乱，身体健康出现问题。尽管 Ford 提出

manifestation of physical problems. Despite Ford's complaints, Braun was not confronted for nine months, and then only upon *Ford's* demand for a group meeting. Another three months elapsed before Braun was censured. Revlon not only had actual knowledge of the situation but it also failed to conduct promptly any investigation of Ford's complaint.

Third, it is obvious that emotional distress did occur. Ample evidence, both medical and otherwise, was presented describing Ford's emotional distress. Ford testified about her emotional distress and her development of physical complications caused by her stressful work environment. The evidence convinced the jury, which found that emotional distress had occurred.

We also note that Revlon had set forth a specific policy and several guidelines for the handling of sexual harassment claims and other employee complaints, yet Revlon recklessly disregarded these policies and guidelines. Ford was entitled to rely on the policy statements made by Revlon.

Once an employer proclaims a policy, the employer may not treat the policy as illusory. We hold that Revlon's failure to take appropriate action in response to Ford's complaint of sexual harassment by Braun constituted the tort of intentional infliction of emotional distress.

Arizona Workers' Compensation Law

Revlon contends that this matter is controlled by Arizona Workers' Compensation laws and not by tort law. We disagree. Ford's severe emotional distress injury was found by the jury to be not unexpected and was essentially nonphysical in nature. As the trial court stated:

> Evidence established that this tort was committed through defendant's action and inaction to plaintiff's complaints made over a period in excess of eight months. Such action and inaction and the resulting emotional injury to the plaintiff were therefore not "unexpected," accidental, or physical in nature so as to limit plaintiff's recovery to the workmen's compensation claim under A.R.S. §§23-1021(B) and 1043.01(B).

Ford v. Revlon, Inc., No. C-457854, slip op. at 15 (Super. Ct. Maricopa County, June 15, 1984). A.R.S. §23-1021(B) provides, in relevant part, that

> Every employee covered by insurance in the state compensation fund who is injured by accident arising out of and in the course of employment...shall be paid such compensation....

A.R.S. §23-1043.01(B) sets forth the limiting standard for compensation under the statute for physiological injury. This section states: "A mental injury...shall not be considered a personal injury by accident...and is not compensable...unless...unexpected, unusual or extraordinary stress...or some physical injury...was a substantial contributing cause."

控诉,但是 Braun 长达 9 个月未受到调查,并仅应 Ford 的要求开了一次集体会议。在 Braun 被申斥之前又过了 3 个月。Revlon 公司不但已经实际知晓相关情况,而且未能对 Ford 的控告及时进行任何调查活动。

第三,显然精神损害确已发生。在医疗和其他方面已递交了足够的证据,用以证明 Ford 的精神损害。Ford 证实了由于她紧张的工作环境造成的精神损害以及并发症。证据说服了陪审团,从而认定精神损害已经发生。

我们也注意到,Revlon 公司已经针对性骚扰及其他雇员控诉的问题制定了一项特殊政策和几项指导方针,但是 Revlon 公司极其漠视这些政策和指导方针。Ford 有权依赖 Revlon 公司作出的这些政策主张权利。

一旦雇主宣布了一项政策,雇主就不能将这政策不当回事。我们认为,Revlon 公司未能采取适当的措施来回应 Ford 对 Braun 性骚扰的控告。这就构成故意致人精神损害的侵权行为。

亚利桑那州的劳工赔偿法

Revlon 公司主张本案由亚利桑那州劳工赔偿法而不是侵权法调整。我们不予认可。陪审团所认定的 Ford 的严重精神损害不是出乎意料的并且是非人身性的。正如初审法院所言:

> 证据确认该侵权是通过原告控告被告长达 8 个月的作为和不作为而实施的。因此,这样的作为和不作为,以及对原告所造成的精神损害,并非"出乎意料的"、意外的或者人身性的,限制了原告依据 A.R.S.§§23-1021 (B) 以及 1043.01(B) 的规定以劳工赔偿为由行使损害赔偿权。

Ford v. Revlon, Inc., No.C-457854, slip op. at 15(Super. Ct. Maricopa County, June 15, 1984)。A.R.S. § 23-1021(B)相关部分的规定是:

> 每一名由州赔偿基金的保险承保的雇员被产生于雇佣期间的事故所伤害……应当被支付此类赔偿金……

A.R.S. § 23-1021(B)对该法中的生理学上的损害赔偿设置了限制性标准。该条规定:"精神损害……不应被认定为事故导致的人身伤害……并且不具可赔偿性……除非……不可预料的、异乎寻常的或者异常严重的……或者其他的有形损害……构成一项实质性要件。"

The acts by Braun and Revlon were not "accidents." Indeed, the jury found both parties liable for the intentional offenses in which they engaged: Braun for assault and battery and Revlon for emotional distress. An injured employee may enforce common-law liability against his or her employer if not encompassed by statute.

The decision of the court of appeals is vacated. The judgment of the trial court is reinstated.

Gordon, C.J., and Jack D. H. Hays, Retired J., concur.

…

90. Wainwright v Home Office [2003] UKHL 53, [2004] 2 AC 406

House of Lords, United Kingdom

LORD BINGHAM

[1] My Lords, I have had the advantage of reading in draft the opinion of my noble and learned friend, Lord Hoffmann. I agree with it, and for the reasons which he gives I would dismiss this appeal.

LORD HOFFMANN

[2] My Lords, on 15 August 1996 Patrick O'Neill was taken into custody on a charge of murder and held at Armley Prison, Leeds. The prison authorities suspected that while awaiting trial he was dealing in drugs. They did not know how he obtained his supplies but people who visit prisoners are a common source of drugs and other contraband. So the governor gave instructions that anyone who wanted an open visit with Patrick O'Neill had first to allow himself (or herself) to be strip searched. Rule 86(1) of the Prison Rules 1964 (SI 1964/388) (consolidated 1998) confers a power in general terms to search any person entering a prison.

[3] Strip searching is controversial because having to take off your clothes in front of a couple of prison officers is not to everyone's taste. Leeds Prison has internal rules designed to reduce the embarrassment as far as possible. They are modelled on the code of practice issued to the police. The search must take place in a completely private room in the presence of two officers of the same sex as the visitor. The visitor is required to expose first the upper half of his body and then the lower but not to stand completely naked. His body (apart from hair, ears and mouth) is not to be touched. Before the search begins, the visitor is asked to sign a consent form which outlines the procedure to be followed.

[4] On 2 January 1997 Patrick O'Neill's mother Mrs Wainwright, together with her son Alan (Patrick's half-brother) went to visit him. A prison officer told them that they would have to be strip-searched. They reluctantly agreed and prison officers took them to separate rooms where they were asked to undress. They did as they were asked but both found the experience upsetting. Some time afterwards (it is unclear when) they went to a solicitor who had them examined by

Braun 和 Revlon 公司的行为不是"事故"。的确，陪审团认定双方负有故意冒犯的责任。Braun 负有威吓和殴击的责任而 Revlon 公司负有精神损害的责任。如果法律未规定，则一名受到伤害的雇员可以迫使他的雇主承担普通法上的赔偿责任。

上诉法院的判决被撤销。初审法院的判决被恢复。

Gordon 大法官和退休法官 Jack D.H. Hays 赞同。

……

90. Wainwright v Home Office [2003] UKHL 53, [2004] 2 AC 406

联合王国上议院

Bingham 大法官

[1][①] 诸位大法官，我有幸提前读到了我那高贵而博学的朋友，Hoffmann 大法官的意见草稿。我认同他的意见，根据他给出的意见，我驳回上诉。

Hoffmann 大法官

[2] 诸位大法官，1996 年 8 月 15 日，Patrick O'Neill 因被指控谋杀而被收监于丽兹的 Armley 监狱。监狱当局怀疑在等候审判的期间，他吸食了毒品。他们并不知道他是如何获得毒品的，但是毒品或者其他违禁品流入监狱的一个通常的渠道是通过探监的人带进来。监狱长因此命令任何要探视 Patrick O'Neill 的人都需要先同意被裸体搜查。1964 年《监狱规则》（SI1964/388）的第 86 号规则第 1 款概括地授予狱方权力以搜查任何进入监狱的人。

[3] 裸体搜查是有争议的，因为并不是每个人都喜欢在狱警面前脱衣服的。丽兹监狱规定了内部规则来尽量减少裸体搜查给人造成的难堪。他们的内部规定是仿照警方的操作规程来制定的。裸体搜查必须在完全私密的房间中进行，而且必须有两名和探视者性别相同的警官在场。探视者须要先裸露上半身，再裸露下半身，但是不会全裸。狱警也不能触碰他的身体（除了头发，耳朵和嘴）。在搜查开始之前，狱方会要求探视者先签署一份同意书，同意书上会载明搜查的程序。

[4] 1997 年 1 月 2 日，Patrick O'Neill 的母亲 Wainwright 夫人和她的孩子 Alan（Patrick 的同母异父兄弟）一起去探视他。一位狱警告诉他们需要裸体搜查。他们不太情愿地答应了，狱警也将他们带到了不同的房间脱光检查。

---

① 英国上议院、上诉法院自 2001 年起，高等法院自 2002 年起，分别推行了 neutral citation 案例汇编体系。与之前相比，其重要的特点之一就是，案例每段都有了段号，起到方便定位和引用的效果。——编者注

a psychiatrist. He concluded that Alan (who had physical and learning difficulties) had been so severely affected by his experience as to suffer post-traumatic stress disorder. Mrs Wainwright had suffered emotional distress but no recognised psychiatric illness.

[5] Mrs Wainwright and Alan commenced an action against the Home Office on 23 December 1999, just before the expiry of the limitation period.

[6] Judge McGonigal, who heard the action in the Leeds County Court, said that the searches could not be justified as a proper use of the statutory power conferred by rule 86(1). He gave two reasons. The first was that the strip searching of the Wainwrights was an invasion of their privacy which exceeded what was necessary and proportionate to deal with the drug smuggling problem. Although the prison officers honestly believed that they had a right under the rules to search the Wainwrights, they should not have done so because it would have been sufficient to search Patrick O'Neill after they left. The second reason was that the prison authorities had not adhered to their own rules. The Court of Appeal agreed with the second reason but not the first. Lord Woolf CJ, who has considerable experience of the administration of prisons, said that a search of Patrick O'Neill would have been inadequate. It followed that "on the findings of the judge, searching, if it had been properly conducted, was perfectly appropriate": [2002] QB 1334 , 1351, para 54. On the other hand, Lord Woolf CJ agreed that if there were clearly laid down restrictions on how the search was to be conducted, conduct which did not observe those restrictions could not (if otherwise actionable) be justified.

[7] The conclusion of both the judge and the Court of Appeal was therefore that the searches were not protected by statutory authority. But that is not enough to give the Wainwrights a claim to compensation. The acts of the prison officers needed statutory authority only if they would otherwise have been wrongful, that is to say, tortious or in breach of a statutory duty. People do all kinds of things without statutory authority. So the question is whether the searches themselves or the manner in which they were conducted gave the Wainwrights a cause of action.

[13] The Court of Appeal did not agree with the judge's extensions of the notion of trespass to the person and did not consider that (apart from the battery, which was unchallenged) the prison officers had committed any other wrongful act.

[14] The Wainwrights appeal to your Lordships' House. Their … counsel proposed that if a general tort of invasion of privacy seemed too bold an undertaking, the House could comply with the Convention in respect of this particular invasion by an extension of the principle in *Wilkinson v Downton* [1897] 2 QB 57.

…

[36] I turn next to the … argument based upon *Wilkinson v Downton* [1897] 2 QB 57. This is a case which has been far more often discussed than applied. Thomas Wilkinson, landlord of the Albion public house in Limehouse, went by train to the races at Harlow, leaving his wife

他们都按照狱警所说的做了，但是都觉得这段经历不太舒服。一段时间之后（到底是多久不太清楚）他们去咨询了律师，律师则让他们做了个心理检查。心理医生的结论是这段经历对 Alan（他有身体残疾和学习障碍）造成了严重的伤害，他患上了创后应激障碍。Wainwright 夫人虽然也遭受了精神痛苦，但是并没有发现她患上了精神疾病。

[5] Wainwright 夫人和 Alan 于是在 1999 年 12 月 23 日起诉了内政部。他们起诉的日期刚好在诉讼时效届满之前。

[6] McGonigal 法官在丽兹郡法院审理了此案。他认为监狱不能用第 86 号规则第 1 款授予的权力来为其裸体搜查的做法辩护。他给出了两个理由来支持他的结论。第一个理由是对 Wainwright 一家的搜查侵犯了他们的隐私，而且这种侵犯的程度是远远超过为了解决偷运毒品这一问题所必须采取的措施的限度的，也是与这种需求不成比例的。虽然狱警们诚实地以为他们是根据监狱规定是有权搜查 Wainwright 一家的，但是他们却不该这么做，因为他们完全可以通过其家人走后搜查 Patrick O'Neill 来实现他们的目的。第二个理由则是监狱当局并未遵守他们自己制定的规定。上诉法院同意了第二个理由，反对第一个理由。Woolf 首席大法官是有很丰富的管理监狱的经验的。他说只搜查 Patrick O'Neill 是不够的。因此"根据一审法官对事实的认定，这种搜查如果是按照正确的方式进行的，就是完全合适的"。[（2002）QB 1334, 1351, 第 54 段]。然而另一方面，Woolf 首席大法官也同意如果存在清晰的关于应该如何进行搜查的规定，那么不遵守这些规定也是不正当的，是可诉的。

[7] 这样看来，一审法官和上诉法院的结论都是裸体检查并不能以制定法授权作为正当化的理由。然而仅仅这一点并不足以支持 Wainwright 一家的损害赔偿请求。狱警的行为只有在如果不授权就是违法时（或者说如果不授权就构成侵权或者说违反了法定的义务时），才需要制定法授权作为正当化事由。人们做大多数的事情都不需要制定法授权。所以，本案的争议焦点其实是，裸体搜查本身，或者进行裸体搜查的方式，是不是足以支持 Wainwright 一家的诉求。

[13] 上诉法院并不认同一审法官对人身侵害一词的概念做的扩张解释，除了没有争议的殴击，他们同时不认为狱警实施了任何其他的侵权行为。

[14] Wainwright 一家上诉到本院。他们的律师主张，如果对隐私的侵犯实在太过分，那么上议院可以通过扩张解释 *Wilkinson v Downton* [1897] 2 QB 57 案确立的原则来实现在侵犯隐私方面对《欧洲人权公约》的遵守。

……

[36] 我现在就来讨论一下基于 *Wilkinson v Downton* [1897] 2 QB 57 案的这种主张。这个判例争议很大，因而很少适用。Thomas Wilkinson 是位于

Lavinia behind the bar. Downton was a customer who decided to play what he would no doubt have described as a practical joke on Mrs Wilkinson. He went into the Albion and told her that her husband had decided to return in a horse-drawn vehicle which had been involved in an accident in which he had been seriously injured. The story was completely false and Mr Wilkinson returned safely by train later that evening. But the effect on Mrs Wilkinson was dramatic. Her hair turned white and she became so ill that for some time her life was thought in danger. The jury awarded her £100 for nervous shock and the question for the judge on further consideration was whether she had a cause of action.

[37] The difficulty in the judge's way was the decision of the Privy Council in *Victorian Railway Comrs v Coultas* (1888) 13 App Cas 222, in which it had been said that nervous shock was too remote a consequence of a negligent act (in that case, putting the plaintiff in imminent fear of being run down by a train) to be a recoverable head of damages. Wright J distinguished the case on the ground that Downton was not merely negligent but had intended to cause injury. Quite what the judge meant by this is not altogether clear; Downton obviously did not intend to cause any kind of injury but merely to give Mrs Wilkinson a fright. The judge said, however, at p 59, that as what he said could not fail to produce grave effects "upon any but an exceptionally indifferent person", an intention to cause such effects should be "imputed" to him.

[38] The outcome of the case was approved and the reasoning commented upon by the Court of Appeal in *Janvier v Sweeney* [1919] 2 KB 316. During the First World War Mlle Janvier lived as a paid companion in a house in Mayfair and corresponded with her German lover who was interned as an enemy alien on the Isle of Man. Sweeney was a private detective who wanted secretly to obtain some of her employer's documents and sent his assistant to induce her to co-operate by pretending to be from Scotland Yard and saying that the authorities wanted her because she was corresponding with a German spy. Mlle Janvier suffered severe nervous shock from which she took a long time to recover. The jury awarded her £250.

[39] By this time, no one was troubled by Victorian *Railway Comrs v Coultas* 13 App Cas 222. In *Dulieu v White & Sons* [1901] 2 KB 669 the Divisional Court had declined to follow it; Phillimore J said, at p 683, that in principle "terror wrongfully induced and inducing physical mischief gives a cause of action". So on that basis Mlle Janvier was entitled to succeed whether the detectives intended to cause her injury or were merely negligent as to the consequences of their threats. Duke LJ observed, at p 326, that the case was stronger than *Wilkinson v Downton* [1897] 2 QB 57 because Downton had intended merely to play a practical joke and not to commit a wrongful act. The detectives, on the other hand, intended to blackmail the plaintiff to attain an unlawful object.

[40] By the time of *Janvier v Sweeney* [1919] 2 KB 316, therefore, the law was able comfortably to accommodate the facts of *Wilkinson v Downton* [1897] 2 QB 57 in the law of

Limehouse 的 Albion 酒馆的老板。他坐火车去 Harlow 参加比赛，因此把他的妻子 Lavinia 留在了酒吧里。顾客 Downton 想对 Wilkinson 太太恶作剧。他来到 Albion 酒馆，然后告诉她，她丈夫坐的马车出事了，她丈夫受伤很严重。这完全是个瞎编的故事，Wilkinson 先生平安地回来了，坐的是火车。但是这个瞎编的故事给 Wilkinson 造成了很大的伤害。她急白了头，也一病不起，很长时间人们都以为她快死了。陪审团以精神损害为由，判决被告支付 100 英镑的赔偿金；而法官要考虑的，则是原告是否真的有合理的诉由。

[37] 审理 Wilkinson 案的 Wright 法官面临一个难题，这个难题就是枢密院的判例 Victorian Railway Comrs v Coultas（1888）13 App Cas 222。这个判例确立的规则是，对于过失行为（被告在 Victorian 案中的过失行为是让原告害怕会被火车撞），精神损害属于在因果链条上太过遥远的结果，因此不能作为可赔偿的损害项目。Wright 法官则指出这两个案件并不一样，因为 Downton 并不仅仅是过失，他其实是故意想造成损害的。Wright 法官此话的意思并不是太清楚。Downton 显然并不希望造成任何损害，他仅仅是想吓一吓 Wilkinson 太太。然而在 59 页，Wright 法官说道，由于被告所说的话是一定会给人造成巨大的影响的，"除非听话的人是特别无情的人"，因此应当"推定"被告具有造成这种影响的故意。

[38] Wilkinson 案的结论被上诉法院所赞同，同时在 Janvier v Sweeney [1919] 2 KB 316 案中，上诉法院还评论了前者的推理。在第一次世界大战期间，Janvier 小姐是一名付费伴侣，居住在 Mayfair 的一所房子中。她的德国情人被关押在马恩岛。她和他通着信。Sweeney 是个私家侦探，他想秘密地弄到一些 Janvier 小姐的雇主的文件，于是派他的助手去让她合作。他的助手伪装成苏格兰场的警官，然后告诉她有关部门要抓她，因为她在和德国间谍通信。Janvier 小姐遭受了巨大的精神损害，她花了很长时间才康复。陪审团裁断她应该获得 250 英镑的赔偿。

[39] 在 Janvier 案之前，没有人把 Victorian Railway Comrs v Coultas 13 App Cas 222 案当一回事。在 Dulieu v White & Sons [1901] 2 KB 669 案中，Divisional 法院就拒绝遵循 Victorian Railway Comrs 案的先例。在 Janvier 案中，Phillimore 法官在第 683 页说，原则上"给人造成的不正当的恐怖，给人造成了身体上的伤害的恐怖，均可构成诉由"。由此，Janvier 小姐是能够胜诉的，无论这里的侦探是意图对她造成伤害，还是仅仅是过失地忽略了他的威胁的后果。在第 326 页，Duke 上诉法院法官指出，Janvier 案比 Wilkinson v Downton [1897] 2 QB 57 案更该支持原告，因为 Downton 只是想搞个恶作剧，并不想实施侵权行为。而侦探是意图通过敲诈原告来实现非法的目的。

[40] 这样，在 Janvier v Sweeney [1919] 2 KB 316 案的时代，在法律上，

nervous shock caused by negligence. It was unnecessary to fashion a tort of intention or to discuss what the requisite intention, actual or imputed, should be. Indeed, the remark of Duke LJ to which I have referred suggests that he did not take seriously the idea that Downton had in any sense intended to cause injury.

[41] Commentators and counsel have nevertheless been unwilling to allow *Wilkinson v Downton* [1897] 2 QB 57 to disappear beneath the surface of the law of negligence. Although, in cases of actual psychiatric injury, there is no point in arguing about whether the injury was in some sense intentional if negligence will do just as well, it has been suggested (as the claimants submit in this case) that damages for distress falling short of psychiatric injury can be recovered if there was an intention to cause it. This submission was squarely put to the Court of Appeal in *Wong v Parkside Health NHS Trust* [2003] 3 All ER 932 and rejected. Hale LJ said that before the passing of the Protection from Harassment Act 1997 there was no tort of intentional harassment which gave a remedy for anything less than physical or psychiatric injury. That leaves *Wilkinson v Downton* with no leading role in the modern law.

[42] In *Khorasandjian v Bush* [1993] QB 727, the Court of Appeal, faced with the absence of a tort of causing distress by harassment, tried to press into service the action for private nuisance. In *Hunter v Canary Wharf Ltd* [1997] AC 655, as I have already mentioned, the House of Lords regarded this as illegitimate and, in view of the passing of the 1997 Act, unnecessary. I did however observe, at p 707:

> "The law of harassment has now been put on a statutory basis ... and it is unnecessary to consider how the common law might have developed. But as at present advised, I see no reason why a tort of intention should be subject to the rule which excludes compensation for mere distress, inconvenience or discomfort in actions based on negligence ... The policy considerations are quite different."

[43] Mr Wilby said that the Court of Appeal in Wong's case should have adopted this remark and awarded Ms Wong damages for distress caused by intentional harassment before the 1997 Act came into force. Likewise, the prison officers in this case did acts calculated to cause distress to the Wainwrights and therefore should be liable on the basis of imputed intention as in *Wilkinson v Downton* [1897] 2 QB 57.

[44] I do not resile from the proposition that the policy considerations which limit the heads of recoverable damage in negligence do not apply equally to torts of intention. If someone actually intends to cause harm by a wrongful act and does so, there is ordinarily no reason why he should not have to pay compensation. But I think that if you adopt such a principle, you have to be very careful about what you mean by intend. In *Wilkinson v Downton* Wright J wanted to water down

Wilkinson v Downton [1897] 2 QB 57 案的事实是可以适用过失造成的精神损害的规则的。这时并不一定要以过失侵权来起诉，也不需要去讨论被告是何种过失，是真正的过失还是推定的过失。事实上，Duke 上诉法院法官的话表明他对于 Downton 是故意造成的损害这种看法，并没有认真对待。

[41] 然而，评论者和律师们不愿意 Wilkinson v Downton [1897] 2 QB 57 案淹没在过失之诉的汪洋之中。虽然在涉及确实存在精神损害的场合，的确没有必要去讨论损害是不是被告故意造成的，因为证明过失就够了。然而有人却认为（就像本案的原告这样）就算不存在确实存在的精神损害，只要有精神痛苦，如果被告是故意造成原告精神痛苦的，那么原告就可以请求损害赔偿。在 Wong v Parkside Health NHS Trust [2003] 3 All ER 932 案中，上诉法院否认了这种观点。Hale 上诉法院法官认为在 1997 年《防止性骚扰法》之前，并不存在会为不足以达到身体或者精神损害程度的痛苦提供救济的，针对故意骚扰的侵权之诉。这样，在现代法上，Wilkinson v Downton 案就没有引领性的作用了。

[42] 在 Khorasandjian v Bush [1993] QB 727 案中，上诉法院因为当时并不存在针对造成了精神痛苦的骚扰的侵权之诉，因此想利用私有妨害之诉来为原告提供救济。如前所述，在 Hunter v Canary Wharf Ltd [1997] AC 655 案中，上议院认为这不是合情合理的；又由于 1997 年《防止性骚扰法》的颁布，这种做法不再必要。然而，我在第 707 页评论道：

> 有关骚扰的规则现在有了成文法的基础……因而我们没有必要去考虑在普通法上它会如何发展。然而就目前的情况来看，我想不明白为什么故意侵权要受到过失侵权规则的限制：这种限制是只排除了精神痛苦、不便和不适的诉讼获得损害赔偿……这两种侵权的政策考量是完全不同的。

[43] Wilby 先生认为当时上诉法院应该在 Wong 案中采纳这种意见，判决 Wong 女士可以因为故意骚扰造成的精神痛苦而获得损害赔偿，即便是在 1997 年《防止性骚扰法》生效之前。同样，本案中的狱警也对 Wainwright 一家造成了同样的痛苦，因此应当根据 Wilkinson v Downton [1897] 2 QB 57 案的原理被推定为存在过失，应对此承担责任。

[44] 我并不收回我的意见，我依然认为限制过失侵权中的可赔偿损害的范围的政策考量因素，并不适用于故意侵权。若某人意图对他人造成伤害，并且也实际这么做了，那么通常来说没有什么理由支持他不支付赔偿。然而如果我们要采纳这么一个原则，那么对于"意图（故意）"一词的含义，我

the concept of intention as much as possible. He clearly thought, as the Court of Appeal did afterwards in *Janvier v Sweeney* [1919] 2 KB 316, that the plaintiff should succeed whether the conduct of the defendant was intentional or negligent. But the Victorian Railway Comrs case 13 App Cas 222 prevented him from saying so. So he devised a concept of imputed intention which sailed as close to negligence as he felt he could go.

[45] If, on the other hand, one is going to draw a principled distinction which justifies abandoning the rule that damages for mere distress are not recoverable, imputed intention will not do. The defendant must actually have acted in a way which he knew to be unjustifiable and either intended to cause harm or at least acted without caring whether he caused harm or not. Lord Woolf CJ, as I read his judgment [2002] QB 1334, 1350, paras 50-51, might have been inclined to accept such a principle. But the facts did not support a claim on this basis. The judge made no finding that the prison officers intended to cause distress or realised that they were acting without justification in asking the Wainwrights to strip. He said, at paragraph 83, that they had acted in good faith and, at paragraph 121, that: "The deviations from the procedure laid down for strip-searches were, in my judgment, not intended to increase the humiliation necessarily involved but merely sloppiness."

[46] Even on the basis of a genuine intention to cause distress, I would wish, as in *Hunter's case* [1997] AC 655, to reserve my opinion on whether compensation should be recoverable. In institutions and workplaces all over the country, people constantly do and say things with the intention of causing distress and humiliation to others. This shows lack of consideration and appalling manners but I am not sure that the right way to deal with it is always by litigation. The Protection from Harassment Act 1997 defines harassment in section 1(1) as a "course of conduct" amounting to harassment and provides by section 7(3) that a course of conduct must involve conduct on at least two occasions. If these requirements are satisfied, the claimant may pursue a civil remedy for damages for anxiety: section 3(2) . The requirement of a course of conduct shows that Parliament was conscious that it might not be in the public interest to allow the law to be set in motion for one boorish incident. It may be that any development of the common law should show similar caution.

[47] In my opinion, therefore, the claimants can build nothing on *c*. It does not provide a remedy for distress which does not amount to recognised psychiatric injury and so far as there may be a tort of intention under which such damage is recoverable, the necessary intention was not established. I am also in complete agreement with Buxton LJ [2002] QB 1334, 1355-1356, paras 67-72, that *Wilkinson v Downton* has nothing to do with trespass to the person.

们就必须格外小心。Wilkinson v Downton 案中 Wright 法官希望尽可能地解构故意一词的内涵。就如上诉法院之后在 Janvier v Sweeney [1919] 2 KB 316 案中的判决那样，他肯定地认为无论被告的行为是故意还是过失，原告都应该胜诉。然而 Victorian Railway Comrs case 13 App Cas 222 案不允许他这么说。他因此创造了"推定故意"这么一个概念，然后让这个概念无限逼近"过失"。

[45] 若从另一方面讲，我们通过区分故意或者过失来支持抛弃掉"仅仅是精神痛苦无法获得损害赔偿"的规则，那么仅仅引入"推定故意"的概念是不够的。被告必须确实地以他明知是不正当的方式行事，且他需要是意图造成损害，或者至少是不关心会不会造成损害。Woolf 首席大法官［我宣读了他的判决书（2002）QB 1334, 1350, 第 50 至 51 段］可能是支持做这种区分的。然而本案的事实并不支持以此作为起诉的依据。一审法官并未查明狱警是意图造成原告的精神痛苦的，也未查明狱警意识到他们要求 Wainwright 一家脱衣服是不正当的。一审法官在第 83 段表示，警官们的行为是善意的。而在 121 段他则表示："警官们对裸体搜查程序的偏离，在我看来并非是意图增加对原告的羞辱，而仅仅是做事草率的结果。"

[46] 即使是真的故意造成精神痛苦的情形，我依然希望如同 Hunter's case [1997] AC 655 案一样，对该不该支持赔偿一事保留一点意见。在全国的各种机构、各种工作场所，人们都在做着说着各种事，目的都是想给别人造成精神痛苦或者羞辱。这种行为确实显示出他们缺乏对他人的关心，行为的方式也是骇人听闻的，然而我不确定对付这样的行为一定要用到诉讼。1997 年《防止骚扰法》在第 1 条第 1 款将骚扰定义为"一系列的"构成骚扰的行为；在第 7 条第 3 款则规定这"一系列的行为"至少要发生两次。如果上述的要件都满足，那么原告可以提起民事诉讼对造成的焦虑请求损害赔偿：第 3 条第 2 款。"一系列行为"这个要件，显示议会意识到了，仅仅因为一次粗野的行为就动用法律来解决，可能并不符合公共利益。而普通法的发展也应该对此采取类似的警惕态度。

[47] 综上，在我看来 Wilkinson v Downton [1897] 2 QB 57 案并不能对原告有多大的用处。这个判例并没有确立不构成精神损害的精神痛苦可以获得救济的规则。而如果要说故意侵权下这种精神痛苦也是可以赔偿的，那么本案中原告并没有证明被告具有那种必要的"故意"。同样，我完全赞同 Buxton 上诉法院法官的意见［（2002）QB 1334, 1355-1356, paras 67-72］，Wilkinson v Downton 案和人身侵害之诉没有任何关系。

Chapter 10. Defamation

Section 1. US Law: Constitutional Issues

91. Gertz v. Robert Welch, Inc., 418 U.S. 323, 94 S. Ct. 2997, 41 L. Ed. 2d 789 (1974)

Supreme Court, United States

Mr. Justice Powell delivered the opinion of the Court.

This Court has struggled for nearly a decade to define the proper accommodation between the law of defamation and the freedoms of speech and press protected by the First Amendment. With this decision we return to that effort. We granted certiorari to reconsider the extent of a publisher's constitutional privilege against liability for defamation of a private citizen.

I

In 1968 a Chicago policeman named Nuccio shot and killed a youth named Nelson. The state authorities prosecuted Nuccio for the homicide and ultimately obtained a conviction for murder in the second degree. The Nelson family retained petitioner Elmer Gertz, a reputable attorney, to represent them in civil litigation against Nuccio.

...

III

We begin with the common ground. Under the First Amendment there is no such thing as a false idea. However pernicious an opinion may seem, we depend for its correction not on the conscience of judges and juries but on the competition of other ideas. But there is no constitutional value in false statements of fact. Neither the intentional lie nor the careless error materially advances society's interest in "uninhibited, robust, and wide-open" debate on public issues. New York Times Co. v. Sullivan, 376 U.S., at 270. They belong to that category of utterances which "are no essential part of any exposition of ideas, and are of such slight social value as a step to truth that any benefit that may be derived from them is clearly outweighed by the social interest in order and morality." Chaplinsky v. New Hampshire, 315 U.S. 568, 572 (1942).

Although the erroneous statement of fact is not worthy of constitutional protection, it is nevertheless inevitable in free debate....Our decisions recognize that a rule of strict liability that compels a publisher or broadcaster to guarantee the accuracy of his factual assertions may lead to

第十章 诽 谤

第一节 美国法：宪法性问题

91. Gertz v. Robert Welch, Inc., 418 U.S. 323, 94 S. Ct. 2997, 41 L. Ed. 2d 789 (1974)

美国联邦最高法院

Powell 法官表达了法院的意见。

本法院已经花费了近十年的时间确定诽谤法与《宪法第一修正案》保护的言论及出版自由之间的适宜关系。通过本判决我们回到这一主题。我们发出调卷令，重新考虑针对发布者的宪法性特免的范围。

Ⅰ.

1968 年，芝加哥警察 Nuccio 开枪杀死青年 Nelson。州检察机关指控 Nuccio 杀人，最后法院判为二级谋杀罪。Nelson 的家人聘请著名律师 Elmer Gertz，代表他们向 Nuccio 提起民事诉讼。

……

Ⅲ.

我们从共同基础开始。根据第一修正案，不存在虚假思想。无论一项意见看起来是多么有害，对于它的纠正也不能依赖于法官和陪审团的良心，而是要取决于其他观点的论争。但是对于事实的虚假陈述没有宪法性价值。故意说谎和疏忽造成的错误都不会大力推动社会去关注"不受抑制、热烈和完全开放的"公共问题辩论。New York Times Co. v. Sullivan, 376 U.S., at 270. 它们属于以下言论类型："不属于任何意见阐述的重要部分，只具有微小的社会价值，它们所产生的效益显然不及秩序和道德的社会效益。"Chaplinsky v. New Hampshire, 315 U.S. 568, 572（1942）。

虽然对于事实的错误陈述不值得宪法性保护，但是在自由辩论中是不可避免的……我们认为，强迫发布者或广播者保证其事实陈述的准确性的严格责任规则可能会导致无法忍受的自我审查。要求媒体仅通过证明所有有害陈

intolerable self-censorship. Allowing the media to avoid liability only by proving the truth of all injurious statements does not accord adequate protection to First Amendment liberties....The First Amendment requires that we protect some falsehood in order to protect speech that matters.

The need to avoid self-censorship by the news media is, however, not the only societal value at issue. If it were, this Court would have embraced long ago the view that publishers and broadcasters enjoy an unconditional and indefeasible immunity from liability for defamation. Such a rule would indeed obviate the fear that the prospect of civil liability for injurious falsehood might dissuade a timorous press from the effective exercise of First Amendment freedoms. Yet absolute protection for the communications media requires a total sacrifice of the competing value served by the law of defamation.

The legitimate state interest underlying the law of libel is the compensation of individuals for the harm inflicted on them by defamatory falsehoods. We would not lightly require the State to abandon this purpose, for, as Mr. Justice Stewart has reminded us, the individual's right to the protection of his own good name "reflects no more than our basic concept of the essential dignity and worth of every human being—a concept at the root of any decent system of ordered liberty. The protection of private personality, like the protection of life itself, is left primarily to the individual states under the Ninth and Tenth Amendments. But this does not mean that the right is entitled to any less recognition by this Court as a basic of our constitutional system." Rosenblatt v. Baer, 383 U.S. 75, 92-93 (1963) (opinion of Stewart, J.)....

We have no difficulty in distinguishing among defamation plaintiffs. The first remedy of any victim of defamation is self-help—using available opportunities to contradict the lie or correct the error and thereby to minimize its adverse impact on reputation. Public officials and public figures usually enjoy significantly greater access to the channels of effective communication and hence have a more realistic opportunity to counteract false statements than private individuals normally enjoy. Private individuals are therefore more vulnerable to injury, and the state interest in protecting them is correspondingly greater.

More important than the likelihood that private individuals will lack effective opportunities for rebuttal, there is a compelling normative consideration underlying the distinction between public and private defamation plaintiffs. An individual who decides to seek governmental office must accept certain necessary consequences of that involvement in public affairs. He runs the risk of closer public scrutiny than might otherwise be the case. And society's interest in the officers of government is not strictly limited to the formal discharge of official duties. As the Court pointed out in Garrison v. Louisiana, 379 U.S. 64, 77 (1964), the public's interest extends to "anything that might touch on an official's fitness for office....Few personal attributes are more germane to fitness for office than dishonesty, malfeasance, or improper motivation, even though these characteristics may also affect the official's private character."

述的真实性而避免承担责任,并不能充分保护第一修正案赋予的自由权利……第一修正案要求我们保护某种谬误,从而保护重要的言论。

然而,新闻媒体避免自我审查并非问题的唯一一社会价值。如果真是问题的唯一社会价值,则本法院很久以前就会采纳以下观点:发布者和广播者享受无限制的和不能撤销的诽谤责任豁免权。这样的规则确实会消除以下恐惧:对于有害谎言民事责任的预期可能会阻止胆小的媒体有效实施第一修正案赋予的自由。然而,对于媒体的绝对保护,需要完全牺牲诽谤法保护的竞争性价值。

对于诽谤法,政府所关注的是被虚假消息损害的个人能够得到赔偿。我们不会轻易要求该州放弃这一目的,因为,正如 Stewart 法官所提醒的,私人保护自己的名誉的权利"反映的不过是每个人的尊严和价值的基本概念,这一概念是任何有序自由的优良系统的基础。对于私人人格的保护,正如保护生命本身一样,主要由各州根据第九和第十修正案实施。但这并非表示本法院未充分将该权利视为我们的宪法体系的基础"。Rosenblatt v. Baer, 383 U.S. 75, 92-93(1963)(Stewart 法官的意见)……

区分诽谤不同的原告并不困难。诽谤受害人首先要进行的补救是自助——利用各种机会驳斥谎言或纠正错误,从而将对名誉的不利影响最小化。公职官员和公众人物通常更容易接触有效沟通渠道,因此更加现实地能够获得多于普通人的机会反击虚假陈述。普通人更容易受到伤害,所以保护他们的州利益更大。

比普通人缺乏有效反驳机会的可能性更重要的是,存在强制性的标准化考虑,成为区分公共和私人诽谤原告的基础。决定寻求政府部门的个人必须接受参与公共事务的某些必然结果。他面临更深入的公众审查的风险。社会对于政府官员的关注,并非严格局限于官员职责的正式履行。正如本法院在 Garrison v. Louisiana, 379 U.S. 64, 77(1964)案中所指出的,公众的关注扩展至"可能涉及官员是否尽职的任何事情……与是否尽职关系最密切的私人品质莫过于不诚实、渎职或不正当的动机,即使这些特征可能也会影响官员的性格"。

Those classed as public figures stand in a similar position. Hypothetically, it may be possible for someone to become a public figure through no purposeful action of his own, but the instances of truly involuntary public figures must be exceedingly rare. For the most part those who attain this status have assumed roles of especial prominence in the affairs of society. Some occupy positions of such persuasive power and influence that they are deemed public figures for all purposes. More commonly, those classed as public figures have thrust themselves to the forefront of particular public controversies in order to influence the resolution of the issues involved. In either event, they invite attention and comment.

Even if the foregoing generalities do not obtain in every instance, the communications media are entitled to act on the assumption that public officials and public figures have voluntarily exposed themselves to increased risk of injury from defamatory falsehoods concerning them. No such assumption is justified with respect to a private individual. He has not accepted public office nor assumed an "influential role in ordering society." Curtis Publishing Co. v. Butts,...388 U.S., at 164 (opinion of Warren, C.J.). He has relinquished no part of his interest in the protection of his own good name, and consequently he has a more compelling call on the courts for redress of injury inflicted by defamatory falsehood. Thus, private individuals are not only more vulnerable to injury than public officials and public figures; they are also more deserving of recovery.

For these reasons we conclude that the States should retain substantial latitude in their efforts to enforce a legal remedy for defamatory falsehood injurious to the reputation of a private individual....

We hold that, so long as they do not impose liability without fault, the States may define for themselves the appropriate standard of liability for a publisher or broadcaster of defamatory falsehood injurious to a private individual. This approach provides a more equitable boundary between the competing concerns involved here. It recognizes the strength of the legitimate state interest in compensating private individuals for wrongful injury to reputation, yet shields the press and broadcast media from the rigors of strict liability for defamation. At least this conclusion obtains where, as here, the substance of the defamatory statement "makes substantial danger to reputation apparent." This phrase places in perspective the conclusion we announce today. Our inquiry would involve considerations somewhat different from those discussed above if a State purported to condition civil liability on a factual misstatement whose content did not warn a reasonably prudent editor or broadcaster of its defamatory potential. Such a case is not now before us, and we intimate no view as to its proper resolution.

IV

Our accommodation of the competing values at stake in defamation suits by private individuals allows the States to impose liability on the publisher or broadcaster of defamatory falsehoods on a less demanding showing than that required by *The New York Times*. This

公众人物的情况与此类似。假设某人有可能并非有目的地成为公众人物，但这种情况极其罕见。大多数公众人物在社会事务中都发挥着特别突出的作用。一些人的说服力和影响力十分强大。更常见的是，公众人物冲向特殊公共争议的前沿，旨在影响相关问题的解决。无论如何，他们都引发了关注和评论。

即使以上普遍性并非适用于每种情况，媒体也有权根据以下假设行事：公职官员和公众人物自愿面临不断增加的诽谤性谬误伤害的风险。对于普通人来说，这种假设没有理由。普通人没有接受公职，"在维护社会秩序方面也没有影响力"。Curtis Publishing Co. v. Butts, ... 388 U.S., at 164（Warren 大法官的意见）。他未放弃保护自身名誉的权利，因此更强烈地要求法院救济诽谤性谬误造成的伤害。所以，与公职官员和公众人物相比，普通人不但更容易受到伤害，而且更应得到救济。

根据以上理由，我们认为，各州应当大幅度地保留对于私人名誉受到诽谤性谬误损害的法律救济……

我们认为，只要各州正当地施加责任，就可以针对发布伤害普通人的诽谤性谬误的发布者或广播者确定适宜的责任标准。这种方法提供了这里涉及的竞争性利害关系之间更衡平的界限。它认可了普通人在名誉受到不正当损害而应当得到补偿时州的合法利益，同时也使新闻和广播媒体免于严苛的诽谤责任。至少该结论适用于类似本案的以下情况：诽谤陈述的实质"显然严重损害名誉"。该表述准确地阐明了我们今天宣布的结论。如果一个州打算对事实性错误陈述的民事责任进行限制，并且错误陈述的内容并未警告合理审慎的编辑或广播员诽谤的可能性，则我们的质询涉及的因素将会略微不同于以上讨论。我们目前没有这样的案例，我们对如何正确处理不发表意见。

Ⅳ.

在私人提起的诽谤诉讼中，考量其所涉及的各种互相冲突的价值，各州可以规定，出版者和广播者承担责任的条件低于纽约时报一案的要求。根据某些考量因素，纽约时报案确立了对诽谤官员的豁免，这种豁免还延伸到了其他公众人物的场合。要得到前述的结论，我们并不需要认为这些考量因素

conclusion is not based on a belief that the considerations which prompted the adoption of the *The New York Times* privilege for defamation of public officials and its extension to public figures are wholly inapplicable to the context of private individuals. Rather, we endorse this approach in recognition of the strong and legitimate state interest in compensating private individuals for injury to reputation. But this countervailing state interest extends no further than compensation for actual injury. For the reasons stated below, we hold that the States may not permit recovery of presumed or punitive damages, at least when liability is not based on a showing of knowledge of falsity or reckless disregard for the truth.

The common law of defamation is an oddity of tort law, for it allows recovery of purportedly compensatory damages without evidence of actual loss. Under the traditional rules pertaining to actions for libel, the existence of injury is presumed from the fact of publication. Juries may award substantial sums as compensation for supposed damage to reputation without any proof that such harm actually occurred. The largely uncontrolled discretion of juries to award damages where there is no loss unnecessarily compounds the potential of any system of liability for defamatory falsehood to inhibit the vigorous exercise of First Amendment freedoms. Additionally, the doctrine of presumed damages invites juries to punish unpopular opinion rather than to compensate individuals for injury sustained by the publication of a false fact. More to the point, the States have no substantial interest in securing for plaintiffs such as this petitioner gratuitous awards of money damages far in excess of any actual injury.

We would not, of course, invalidate state law simply because we doubt its wisdom, but here we are attempting to reconcile state law with a competing interest grounded in the constitutional command of the First Amendment. It is therefore appropriate to require that state remedies for defamatory falsehood reach no farther than is necessary to protect the legitimate interest involved. It is necessary to restrict defamation plaintiffs who do not prove knowledge of falsity or reckless disregard for the truth to compensation for actual injury. We need not define "actual injury," as trial courts have wide experience in framing appropriate jury instructions in tort action. Suffice it to say that actual injury is not limited to out-of-pocket loss. Indeed, the more customary types of actual harm inflicted by defamatory falsehood include impairment of reputation and standing in the community, personal humiliation, and mental anguish and suffering. Of course, juries must be limited by appropriate instructions, and all awards must be supported by competent evidence concerning the injury, although there need be no evidence which assigns an actual dollar value to the injury.

We also find no justification for allowing awards of punitive damages against publishers and broadcasters held liable under state-defined standards of liability for defamation. In most jurisdictions jury discretion over the amounts awarded is limited only by the gentle rule that they not be excessive. Consequently, juries assess punitive damages in wholly unpredictable amounts

完全不适用于普通人的场合。我们同意这种方法是因为认可在私人名誉受损赔偿方面强大而合法的州利益。但是这种补偿性的州利益的扩展不会超过实际伤害的赔偿。根据以下理由，我们认为，至少在责任并至少在判定责任并非基于熟知何为谎言或对于真实性的极其漠视时，各州不能批准推定性的或惩罚性损害赔偿金。

诽谤普通法是侵权法上的怪事，因为它批准据称是补偿性的损害赔偿金，而无须证明实际损失。根据有关书面诽谤诉讼的传统规则，发生伤害的推定基于发布的事实。陪审团可以根据假设的名誉侵害裁决实质性的损害赔偿金，而无须证明该侵害确实存在。在没有损失的情况下陪审团基本不受控制地自由裁量损害赔偿金增加了以下可能性：任何诽谤性谬误责任体系禁止充分行使第一修正案赋予的自由。另外，推定损害赔偿金原则导致陪审团惩罚不受欢迎的意见，而不是根据虚假事实的发布造成的伤害向普通人予以赔偿。更加重要的是，各州尚未重视类似于本案原告获得远超实际伤害的没有必要的损害赔偿金的案件。

我们当然不会仅仅因为怀疑智慧就废除其他州法，但在这里我们试图使州法律符合以第一修正案宪法性命令为基础的竞争性利益。因此，应当要求诽谤性谬误的州救济不超过保护相关合法利益的必要救济。有必要将不能证明知悉虚假性或极其漠视真实性的诽谤原告获得的赔偿限制在实际伤害赔偿范围内。我们无须定义"实际伤害"，因为初审法院在制定侵权诉讼中适宜的陪审团指示方面拥有丰富经验。只要说实际伤害不限于现金损失就足够了。实际上，诽谤性谬误造成的实际伤害，更常见的类型包括社会声望和地位受损、个人受辱、精神痛苦等。当然，陪审团必须受适宜指示的限制，并且所有判决必须由有关伤害的有力证据支持，虽然并不需要对伤害赋予实际金钱价值的证据。

我们还发现，根据州确定的诽谤责任标准，允许对负有责任的发布者和广播者处以惩罚性损害赔偿金没有正当性。在大多数法域中，陪审团对于损害赔偿金额的自由裁量权仅由宽松的不得超额的规则限制。因此，陪审团裁定的惩罚性损害赔偿金金额完全不可预测，与实际伤害没有必然联系。而且，他们仍然有选择性地自由裁量惩罚不受欢迎的观点表达。与推定损害赔偿金法律学说类似，判定惩罚性损害赔偿金的陪审团的自由裁量权，不必要地加

bearing no necessary relation to the actual harm caused. And they remain free to use their discretion selectively to punish expressions of unpopular views. Like the doctrine of presumed damages, jury discretion to award punitive damages unnecessarily exacerbates the danger of media self-censorship, but, unlike the former rule, punitive damages are wholly irrelevant to the state interest that justifies a negligence standard for private defamation actions. They are not compensation for injury. Instead, they are private fines levied by civil juries to punish reprehensible conduct and to deter its future occurrence. In short, the private defamation plaintiff who establishes liability under a less demanding standard than that stated by *New York Times* may recover only such damages as are sufficient to compensate him for actual injury.

V

Notwithstanding our refusal to extend the *New York Times* privilege to defamation of private individuals, respondent contends that we should affirm the judgment below on the ground that petitioner is either a public official or a public figure. There is little basis for the former assertion....

Respondent's characterization of petitioner as a public figure raises a different question. That designation may rest on either of two alternative bases. In some instances an individual may achieve such pervasive fame or notoriety that he becomes a public figure for all purposes and in all contexts. More commonly, an individual voluntarily injects himself or is drawn into a particular public controversy and thereby becomes a public figure for a limited range of issues. In either case such persons assume special prominence in the resolution of public questions.

Petitioner has long been active in community and professional affairs. He has served as an officer of local civil groups and of various professional organizations, and he has published several books and articles on legal subjects. Although petitioner was consequently well-known in some circles, he had achieved no general fame or notoriety in the community. None of the prospective jurors called at the trial had ever heard of petitioner prior to this litigation, and respondent offered no proof that this response was atypical of the local population. We would not lightly assume that a citizen's participation in community and professional affairs rendered him a public figure for all purposes. Absent clear evidence of general fame or notoriety in the community, and pervasive involvement in the affairs of society, an individual should not be deemed a public personality for all aspects of his life. It is preferable to reduce the public figure question to a more meaningful context by looking to the nature and extent of an individual's participation in the particular controversy giving rise to the defamation.

In this context it is plain that petitioner was not a public figure. He played a minimal role at the coroner's inquest, and his participation related solely to his representation of a private client. He took no part in the criminal prosecution of officer Nuccio. Moreover, he never discussed either the criminal or civil litigation with the press and was never quoted as having done so. He plainly did not thrust himself into the vortex of this public issue, nor did he engage the public's attention

剧了媒体自我审查的危险，但与前一规则不同的是，惩罚性损害赔偿金与州利益完全无关，而州利益证明私人诽谤诉讼的过失标准是正确的。惩罚性损害赔偿金不是对于伤害的赔偿，而是民事陪审团为了惩罚应受指责的行业并且预防再次发生而征收的私人罚款。简而言之，根据低于 *New York Times* 案陈述的要求的标准确定责任的私人诽谤原告仅可获得足以赔偿实际伤害的损害赔偿金。

V.

尽管我们拒绝将 *New York Times* 案特免扩展至对于普通人的诽谤，但是被告辩称，我们应当维持原判，理由是原告不是公职官员就是公众人物。上述主张几乎没有依据……

被告将原告描述为公众人物，提出了一个不同的问题。这种指定可能基于两项可选依据之一。在一些情况下，某人可能会获得名声或者恶名，成为公众人物。更常见的情况是，某人有意投身于或无意陷入特殊的公共争议中，因此成为有限领域内的公众人物。在任何一种情况下，在解决公共问题中该类人员特别突出。

原告长期积极从事社会和专业活动。他在当地民间团体和各种专业组织任职，出版和发表了若干法律著作和文章。因此，虽然原告在某些领域十分有名，但是在社会上还没有一般性的名声或者恶名。在审理时召集的将任陪审员在诉讼前都未听说过原告，并且被告不能证明这种反应不是当地人的典型反应。我们不会轻易假定公民参与社会活动和专业活动就会使其成为公众人物。如果缺乏已成为公众人物以及全面参与社会事务的清晰证据，则不能将某人视为其生活全部内容的公众人物。更可取的是将公众人物问题缩减为更有意义的背景，即考察该人员参与导致诽谤的特定争议的性质和程度。

在这种背景下，很明显原告不是公众人物。在验尸官做死因调查时他发挥的作用最小，他的参与仅涉及代表私人客户。他未参与针对警官 Nuccio 的刑事起诉。而且，他从未与媒体讨论过刑事或民事诉讼，并且也无人提起他曾经从事该类事务。很明显，他没有涉足这一公共争议的漩涡，也没有吸引公众的注意力从而试图影响事件的结果。我们认为，初审法院为了本诉讼的

in an attempt to influence its outcome. We are persuaded that the trial court did not err in refusing to characterize petitioner as a public figure for the purpose of this litigation.

We therefore conclude that the *New York Times* standard is inapplicable to this case and that the trial court erred in entering judgment for respondent. Because the jury was allowed to impose liability without fault and was permitted to presume damages without proof of injury, a new trial is necessary. We reverse and remand for further proceedings in accord with this opinion.

It is so ordered.

92. Milkovich v. Lorain Journal Co., 497 U.S. 1, 110 S. Ct. 2695, 111 L. Ed. 2d 1 (1990)

Supreme Court, United States

Chief Justice Rehnquist delivered the opinion of the Court. Respondent J. Theodore Diadiun authored an article in an Ohio newspaper implying that petitioner Michael Milkovich, a local high school wrestling coach, lied under oath in a judicial proceeding about an incident involving petitioner and his team which occurred at a wrestling match. Petitioner sued Diadiun and the newspaper for libel, and the Ohio Court of Appeals affirmed a lower court entry of summary judgment against petitioner. This judgment was based in part on the grounds that the article constituted an "opinion" protected from the reach of state defamation law by the First Amendment to the United States Constitution. We hold that the First Amendment does not prohibit the application of Ohio's libel laws to the alleged defamations contained in the article.

…bore the heading "Maple beat the law with the 'big lie,' " beneath which appeared Diadiun's photograph and the words "TD Says." The carryover page headline announced " … Diadiun says Maple told a lie." The column contained the following passages:

…A lesson was learned (or relearned) yesterday by the student body of Maple Heights High School, and by anyone who attended the Maple-Mentor wrestling meet of last Feb. 8.

A lesson which, sadly, in view of the events of the past year, is well they learned early.

It is simply this: If you get in a jam, lie your way out.

If you're successful enough, and powerful enough, and can sound sincere enough, you stand an excellent chance of making the lie stand up, regardless of what really happened.

The teachers responsible were mainly Maple wrestling coach, Mike Milkovich, and former superintendent of schools, H. Donald Scott.

Anyone who attended the meet, whether he be from Maple Heights, Mentor, or impartial observer, knows in his heart that Milkovich and Scott lied at the hearing after each having given his solemn oath to tell the truth.

But they got away with it.

Is that the kind of lesson we want our young people learning from their high school

目的拒绝将原告描述为公众人物是正确的。

因此,我们认定,New York Times 案的标准不适用于本案,并且初审法院错误地作出有利于被告的判决。因为允许陪审团在没有过错的情形下施加责任,并且允许推定损害赔偿金而无须证明伤害,所以有必要进行重审。我们撤销原判,发回根据本意见重审。

特此发出法庭命令。

92. Milkovich v. Lorain Journal Co., 497 U.S. 1, 110 S. Ct. 2695, 111 L. Ed. 2d 1 (1990)

美国联邦最高法院

Rehnquist 大法官表达了法院的意见。Respondent 法官主笔:Theodore Diadiun 在俄亥俄州的一家报纸上发表了一篇文章,指出当地的中学摔跤教练 Michael Milkovich 在司法程序中宣誓后说谎。该程序涉及摔跤比赛中发生的一起事故,与原告及其团队有关。原告提起诉讼,指控 Diadiun 和报纸书面诽谤。下级法院作出不利于原告的简易判决,俄亥俄州上诉法院维持原判。该判决部分地基于以下理由:该文章构成的"意见"受到《美国宪法第一修正案》的保护,不适用州诽谤法。我们认为,第一修正案未禁止将俄亥俄州的诽谤法用于文章中包含的所谓书面诽谤。

……标题为"Maple 以'弥天大谎'战胜了法律",下面是 Diadiun 的照片和短语"TD 说"。翻到次页的标题是"……Diadiun 说 Maple 撒了谎"。该栏包含以下段落:

……昨天,Maple Heights 中学的学生以及去年 2 月 8 日参与了 Maple-Mentor 摔跤比赛的任何人都上了(或再上了)一课。

鉴于去年的活动,这是可悲的一课,好在能够提前上了。

很简单:如果陷入困境,就通过说谎摆脱。

如果你足够成功,足够强大,似乎足够真诚,你就有绝佳的机会使谎言成立,无论是否真正发生。

需要负责的教师主要包括 Maple 的摔跤教练 Mike Milkovich 和前学校督导 H. Donald Scott。

参与了比赛的任何人,无论是来自 Maple Heights 或 Mentor,还是作为公正的观众,都深知 Milkovich 和 Scott 在听证会上说谎,而此前他们都庄严宣誓说出真相。

但他们逃脱了惩罚。

我们是否希望孩子们从中学管理者和教练那里受到这种教育?

administrators and coaches?

I think not.

Petitioner commenced a defamation action against respondents…alleging that the headline of Diadiun's article and the 9 passages quoted above "accused plaintiff of committing the crime of perjury, an indictable offense in the State of Ohio, and damaged plaintiff directly in his lifetime occupation of coach and teacher, and constituted libel per se."

…We now reverse.

Since the latter half of the 16th century, the common law has afforded a cause of action for damage to a person's reputation by the publication of false and defamatory statements.

In Shakespeare's Othello, Iago says to Othello:

Good name in man and woman, dear my lord,

Is the immediate jewel of their souls.

Who steals my purse steals trash;

'Tis something, nothing;

'Twas mine, 'tis his, and has been slave to thousands;

But he that filches from me my good name

Robs me of that which not enriches him,

And makes me poor indeed.

Act III, scene 3.

Defamation law developed not only as a means of allowing an individual to vindicate his good name, but also for the purpose of obtaining redress for harm caused by such statements. As the common law developed in this country, apart from the issue of damages, one usually needed only allege an unprivileged publication of false and defamatory matter to state a cause of action for defamation. The common law generally did not place any additional restrictions on the type of statement that could be actionable. Indeed, defamatory communications were deemed actionable regardless of whether they were deemed to be statements of fact or opinion. See, e.g., Restatement of Torts, §§565-567. As noted in the 1977 Restatement (Second) of Torts §566, Comment *a*:

Under the law of defamation, an expression of opinion could be defamatory if the expression was sufficiently derogatory of another as to cause harm to his reputation, so as to lower him in the estimation of the community or to deter third persons from associating or dealing with him.…The expression of opinion was also actionable in a suit for defamation, despite the normal requirement that the communication be false as well as defamatory.…This position was maintained even though the truth or falsity of an opinion—as distinguished from a statement of fact—is not a matter that can be objectively determined and truth is a complete defense to a suit for defamation.

However, due to concerns that unduly burdensome defamation laws could stifle valuable public debate, the privilege of "fair comment" was incorporated into the common law as an

我想不是。

原告向被告提起诽谤诉讼……声称 Diadiun 文章的标题和以上引用的 9 段话"指控原告犯有在俄亥俄州可招致起诉的伪证罪,直接损害原告作为教练和教师的终身职业,构成当然书面诽谤"。

……现在我们予以撤销。

自从 16 世纪下半叶以来,普通法已经提供通过发布虚假和诽谤陈述损害私人名誉的诉因。

在莎士比亚的《奥赛罗》(Othello)中,埃古(Iago)对奥赛罗说[①]:

无论男和女,尊敬的阁下,
名誉是灵魂中无上之宝,
偷我的钱袋的人不过是偷走一把铜臭钱;
固然有点价值,实在算不得什么;
钱原是我的,如今变成他的,从前更曾为千万人做过奴隶;
但是他若夺去我的名誉,
于他不见得有利,
对我却是一件损失哩。
(第三幕,第三场。)

诽谤法不仅是普通人维护名誉的方式,还是对诽谤陈述导致的伤害的救济。随着普通法在美国的发展,除损害赔偿金问题外,人们通常仅需要声称无特免地发布虚假和诽谤事宜表明诽谤诉讼的理由。普通法一般不对可起诉的陈述施加额外限制。事实上,诽谤陈述被视为可起诉,无论被视为事实陈述还是意见。参见《侵权法重述·第二次》第 565-567 条。在 1977 年出版的《侵权法重述·第二次》第 566 条,评论 a 指出:

根据诽谤法,如果意见的表达对于另一人的贬抑,足以造成其名誉受损,从而降低其社会评价,或阻吓第三人与其交往或接洽,则该表达具有诽谤性……在诽谤诉讼中也可起诉意见表达,尽管通常要求该表达具有虚假性和诽谤性……该立场始终保持,即使意见的真实性或虚假性区别于事实的陈述,不能客观确定,而意见的真实性对于诽谤诉讼却是完全的抗辩。

然而,由于担心过度繁重的诽谤法会抑制有益的公共辩论,"公正评论"将特免纳入了普通法,作为对于诽谤诉讼的正面抗辩。"'公正评论'原则在

[①] 此处采纳了梁实秋先生的译文。因原译文缺少"dear my lord"部分,译者予以了增补。参见梁实秋译:《奥赛罗》,中国广播电视出版社 2001 年版,第 125—127 页。——译者注

affirmative defense to an action for defamation. "The principle of 'fair comment' afforded legal immunity for the honest expression of opinion on matters of legitimate public interest when based upon a true or privileged statement of fact." 1 F. Harper & F. James, Law of Torts §5.28, p. 456 (1956) .... As this statement implies, comment was generally privileged when it concerned a matter of public concern, was upon true or privileged facts, represented the actual opinion of the speaker, and was not made solely for the purpose of causing harm. See Restatement of Torts, supra, §606. "According to the majority rule, the privilege of fair comment applied only to an expression of opinion and not to a false statement of fact, whether it was expressly stated or implied from an expression of opinion." Restatement (Second) of Torts, supra, §566, Comment *a*. Thus under the common law, the privilege of "fair comment" was the device employed to strike the appropriate balance between the need for vigorous public discourse and the need to redress injury to citizens wrought by invidious or irresponsible speech.

...

Respondents would have us recognize, in addition to the established safeguards discussed above, still another First Amendment-based protection for defamatory statements which are categorized as "opinion" as opposed to "fact." For this proposition they rely principally on the following dictum from our opinion in *Gertz* v. Robert Welch, Inc., 418 U.S. 323, 94 S. Ct. 2997, 41 L. Ed. 2d 789 (1974)]:

Under the First Amendment there is no such thing as a false idea. However pernicious an opinion may seem, we depend for its correction not on the conscience of judges and juries but on the competition of other ideas. But there is no constitutional value in false statements of fact.

418 U.S., at 339-340, 94 S. Ct., at 3007.

Read in context,...the fair meaning of the passage is to equate the word "opinion" in the second sentence with the word "idea" in the first sentence. Under this view, the language was merely a reiteration of Justice Holmes' classic "marketplace of ideas" concept. See Abrams v. United States, 250 U.S. 616, 630, 40 S. Ct. 17, 22, 63 L. Ed. 1173 (1919) (Holmes, J., dissenting) ("The ultimate good desired is better reached by free trade in ideas...the best test of truth is the power of the thought to get itself accepted in the competition of the market").

Thus we do not think this passage from *Gertz* was intended to create a wholesale defamation exemption for anything that might be labeled "opinion."...Not only would such an interpretation be contrary to the tenor and context of the passage, but it would also ignore the fact that expressions of "opinion" may often imply an assertion of objective fact.

If a speaker says, "In my opinion John Jones is a liar," he implies a knowledge of facts which lead to the conclusion that Jones told an untruth. Even if the speaker states the facts upon which he bases his opinion, if those facts are either incorrect or incomplete, or if his assessment of them is erroneous, the statement may still imply a false assertion of fact. Simply couching such statements

对真实或特许的事实陈述的基础上,为对合法公共利益事宜意见的诚实表达提供了法律豁免"。1 F. Harper & F. James 的《侵权法》[Law of Torts, § 5.28, p. 456(1956)]……。该陈述表示,在以下情况中评论通常获得特免:该评论涉及公共利益,基于真实或特免的事实,代表发言者的真实意见,不仅是为了造成伤害。参见前引《侵权法重述》第606条。"根据多数规则,公正评论特免仅适用于意见的表达,不适用于事实的虚假陈述,无论在意见表达中是明确的还是隐含的陈述"。参见前引《侵权法重述·第二次》第566条评论 a。因此,根据普通法,"公正评论"特免作为工具用于寻求以下两者之间的平衡:热烈的公共讨论的需求,与救济诽谤或不负责任的言论造成公民的伤害。

……

除了以上讨论的既定保护外,被告还让我们认可另一项基于第一修正案的对于属于"意见"而非"事实"的诽谤陈述的保护。该主张主要基于我们在 Gertz v. Robert Welch, Inc., 418 U.S. 323, 94 S. Ct. 2997, 41 L. Ed. 2d 789(1974)案中的法官附带意见:

根据第一修正案,不存在虚假思想。无论一项意见看起来是多么有害,对于它的纠正也不能依赖于法官和陪审团的良心,而是要取决于其他观点的论争。但是对于事实的虚假陈述没有宪法性价值。

418 U.S., at 339-340. 94 S. Ct., at 3007。

根据上下文阅读……该段的正确含义是第二句中的词语"意见"(opinion)等同于第一句中的词语"思想"(idea)。根据这一观点,语言仅仅是 Holmes 法官经典的"思想市场"理念的重审。[参见 Abrams v. United States, 250 U.S. 616,630,40 S. Ct. 17, 22, 63 L. Ed. 1173(1919)案(Holmes 法官反对)("最终的良好期望通过思想的自由贸易更好地实现……真相的最佳检验是思想的力量使其在市场竞争中被接受")]。

因此我们不认为来自 Gertz 案的该段旨在创建对于可能标记为"意见"的事物的整批诽谤豁免……这种解释不仅违反该段的要旨和背景,还无视以下事实:"意见"的表达可能通常会隐含对于客观事实的断言。

如果发言者说"在我看来,John Jones 是说谎者",则表示他知道事实,从而得出 Jones 说谎的结论。即使发言者陈述他的意见依据的是事实,如果这些事实不正确或不完整,或他对事实的评估出现错误,则发言者的陈述仍会包含对于事实的虚假表达。仅根据意见表达陈述不能消除这些含义,并且"在

in terms of opinion does not dispel these implications; and the statement, "In my opinion Jones is a liar," can cause as much damage to reputation as the statement, "Jones is a liar."...

Apart from their reliance on the *Gertz* dictum, respondents do not really contend that a statement such as, "In my opinion John Jones is a liar," should be protected by a separate privilege for "opinion" under the First Amendment. But they do contend that in every defamation case the First Amendment mandates an inquiry into whether a statement is "opinion" or "fact," and that only the latter statements may be actionable. They propose that a number of factors developed by the lower courts (in what we hold was a mistaken reliance on the *Gertz* dictum) be considered in deciding which is which. But we think the "breathing space" which "freedoms of expression require in order to survive," is adequately secured by existing constitutional doctrine without the creation of an artificial dichotomy between "opinion" and fact.

Foremost...a statement on matters of public concern must be provable as false before there can be liability under state defamation law, at least in situations, like the present, where a media defendant is involved. Thus, unlike the statement, "In my opinion Mayor Jones is a liar," the statement, "In my opinion Mayor Jones shows his abysmal ignorance by accepting the teachings of Marx and Lenin," would not be actionable....A statement of opinion relating to matters of public concern which does not contain a provably false factual connotation will receive full constitutional protection.

Next, ...for statements that cannot "reasonably be interpreted as stating actual facts" about an individual....This provides assurance that public debate will not suffer for lack of "imaginative expression" or the "rhetorical hyperbole" which has traditionally added much to the discourse of our Nation.

The *New York Times-Butts* and *Gertz* culpability requirements further ensure that debate on public issues remains "uninhibited, robust, and wide-open," New York Times [Co. v. Sullivan], 376 U.S., at 270, 84 S. Ct., at 720 [(1964)]. Thus, where a statement of "opinion" on a matter of public concern reasonably implies false and defamatory facts regarding public figures or officials, those individuals must show that such statements were made with knowledge of their false implications or with reckless disregard of their truth. Similarly, where such a statement involves a private figure on a matter of public concern, a plaintiff must show that the false connotations were made with some level of fault as required by *Gertz*.

We are not persuaded that, in addition to these protections, an additional separate constitutional privilege for "opinion" is required to ensure the freedom of expression guaranteed by the First Amendment. The dispositive question in the present case then becomes whether or not a reasonable factfinder could conclude that the statements in the Diadiun column imply an assertion that petitioner Milkovich perjured himself in a judicial proceeding. We think this question must be answered in the affirmative....This is not the sort of loose, figurative or hyperbolic language which

我看来，John Jones 是说谎者"的陈述造成的名誉损害，可以等同于"Jones 是说谎者"的陈述……

除了依赖 Gertz 案中的法官附带意见之外，被告并未真正主张根据第一修正案，"在我看来，John Jones 是说谎者"这样的陈述应当由另外的"意见"特免保护。但是，他们确实声称在每一件诽谤案件中，第一修正案要求质询一项陈述是"意见"还是"事实"，并且只有后者才可起诉。他们提出，下级法院在确定是"意见"还是"事实"时，应当考虑许多因素（我们认为是对于 Gertz 案法官附带意见的错误依赖）。但是，我们认为，"表达自由所需的""呼吸空间"由现有的宪法性法律学说充分保护，无须创建"意见"和"事实"的人为对立。

最重要的是……根据州诽谤法确定责任之前必须能够证明对于公共利益事宜的陈述为谎言，至少是在本案这样的情况下，即涉及作为媒体的被告。因此，与"在我看来，Jones 市长是说谎者"的陈述不同，"在我看来，Jones 市长通过接受马克思和列宁的学说显示了他的极端无知"的陈述，不可起诉……不包含可证明虚假的事实含义的有关公共利益事宜的一项意见陈述将获得全面的宪法性保护。

接下来，对于不能"被合理地解释为陈述有关私人的真正事实"的陈述……这就确保了公共辩论不会因为缺少以下因素而受损：一直为我们国家的讨论添彩的"富于想象的表达"或"辞藻华丽的夸张"。

New York Times-Butts 案和 Gertz 案的可责难性要求进一步确保有关公共问题的辩论保持"不受抑制、热烈和完全开放"。New York Times[Co. v. Sullivan], 376 U.S., at 270, 84 S. Ct., at 720 [（1964）] 因此，如果有关公共利益事宜的"意见"陈述合理地表明有关公众人物或公职人员的虚假和诽谤事实，则这些个人必须证实作出这些陈述具有以下前提：知悉其虚假含义，或极其漠视真实性。类似的，如果该类陈述涉及有关公共利益事宜的普通人，则原告必须证明虚假含义的表达具有 Gertz 案要求的某种错误。

我们不认为除了这些保护外，还需要对"意见"赋予额外的独立宪法性特免，以确保第一修正案保证的表达自由。在本案中，决定性的问题是理性的事实认定者是否能够认定 Diadiun 专栏中的陈述表示原告 Milkovich 在司法程序中作伪证。我们认为对该问题必须给予肯定的回答……这不是否定以下印象的散漫、比喻或夸张语言：作者严肃地表示原告犯有伪证罪。文章的主

would negate the impression that the writer was seriously maintaining petitioner committed the crime of perjury. Nor does the general tenor of the article negate this impression.

We also think the connotation that petitioner committed perjury is sufficiently factual to be susceptible of being proved true or false. A determination of whether petitioner lied in this instance can be made on a core of objective evidence by comparing, *inter alia,* petitioner's testimony.

The numerous decisions discussed above establishing First Amendment protection for defendants in defamation actions surely demonstrate the Court's recognition of the Amendment's vital guarantee of free and uninhibited discussion of public issues. But there is also another side to the equation; we have regularly acknowledged the "important social values which underlie the law of defamation," and recognize that "society has a pervasive and strong interest in preventing and redressing attacks upon reputation." Rosenblatt v. Baer, 383 U.S. 75, 86, 86 S. Ct. 669, 676, 15 L. Ed. 2d 597 (1966). Justice Stewart in that case put it with his customary clarity:

The right of a man to the protection of his own reputation from unjustified invasion and wrongful hurt reflects no more than our basic concept of the essential dignity and worth of every human being—a concept at the root of any decent system of ordered liberty.

The destruction that defamatory falsehood can bring is, to be sure, often beyond the capacity of the law to redeem. Yet, imperfect though it is, an action for damages is the only hope for vindication or redress the law gives to a man whose reputation has been falsely dishonored.

Id., at 92-93, 86 S. Ct., at 679-680 (Stewart, J., concurring).

We believe our decision in the present case holds the balance true. The judgment is reversed and the case remanded for further proceedings not inconsistent with this opinion.

Reversed.

...

Section 2. English Law: Definition, Remedies, and Free Speech

93. Cassidy v Daily Mirror [1929] 2 KB 331

Court of Appeal, United Kingdom

SCRUTTON L.J.

The facts in this case are simple. A man named Cassidy, who for some reason also called himself Corrigan and described himself as a General in the Mexican Army, was married to a lady who also called herself Mrs. Cassidy or Mrs. Corrigan. Her husband occasionally came and stayed with her at her flat, and her acquaintances met him. Cassidy achieved some notoriety in racing circles and in indiscriminate relations with women, and at a race meeting he posed, in company with a lady, to a racing photographer, to whom he said he was engaged to marry the

旨也不否定这种印象。

我们还认为原告犯有伪证罪的含义充分依据事实，易于证实或证伪。确定原告是否说谎可以依据客观证据进行，尤其是对比原告的证词等。

以上讨论展示了第一修正案保护诽谤诉讼被告的大量案例，确实证实了法院认可第一修正案对于自由和不被抑制地讨论公共问题的重要保证作用。但是，平衡还有另一边；我们通常了解"作为诽谤法基础的重要社会价值"，并且认可"社会普遍重视预防和救济名誉侵害"。在 Rosenblatt v. Baer, 383 U.S. 75, 86, 86 S. Ct. 669, 676, 15 L. Ed. 2d 597（1966）案中，Stewart 法官以其惯有的清晰度指出：

一个人保护自己的名誉免遭不当侵犯和非法伤害的权利，仅仅反映了我们对人类基本尊严和价值的根本观念——这一概念植根于任何一个有序自由的得体的制度之中。

诚然，诽谤性谬误导致的破坏通常超出法律的救济能力，然而，虽然损害赔偿金诉讼并不完美，但是却是法律给予蒙羞者的唯一的辩护或救济希望。

Id., at 92–93, 86 S. Ct., at 679–680（Stewart 法官，赞同）。

我们认为我们在本案中的裁决真正做到了此种平衡。撤销判决，本案发回重审，未来审理不能不符合本意见。

撤销原判。

……

第二节 英国法：定义、救济与言论自由

93. Cassidy v Daily Mirror [1929] 2 KB 331

联合王国上诉法院

Scrutton 上诉法院法官

本案案情很简单。一个叫 Cassidy 的男人，因为某些原因又自称 Corrigan，并称自己是墨西哥军队的将军。他娶了一名女士，这名女士自称 Cassidy 夫人或者 Corrigan 夫人。她的丈夫偶尔会来到她的公寓和她一起生活一段时间，她的熟人们也都见过他。Cassidy 先生在赛马圈有些名声，但同时也因为和女人的风流关系而声名狼藉。在一次赛马会上，他和另一名女士在一起，并让赛马摄影师给他俩拍照。他对赛马摄影师说他将娶这位女士，摄影师可以公

lady and the photographer might announce it. The photographer, without any further inquiry, sent the photograph to the Daily Mirror with an inscription: "Mr. M. Corrigan, the race horse owner, and Miss X" - I omit the name - "whose engagement has been announced," and the Daily Mirror published the photograph and inscription. This paper was read by the female acquaintances of Mrs. Cassidy or Mrs. Corrigan, who gave evidence that they understood from it that that lady was not married to Mr. M. Corrigan and had no legal right to take his name, and that they formed a bad opinion of her in consequence. Mrs. Cassidy accordingly brought an action for libel against the newspaper setting out these words with an innuendo, meaning thereby that the plaintiff was an immoral woman who had cohabited with Corrigan without being married to him.

At the trial counsel for the defendants objected that the words were not capable of a defamatory meaning. McCardie J. held that they were; the jury found that they did reasonably bear a defamatory meaning and awarded the plaintiff 500 pounds. damages. The damages were high, but the plaintiff called considerable evidence of damage to social reputation, and the defendants' solicitors suggested, when the plaintiff alleged she was married to Mr. Corrigan, that there must be some mistake; and even after she had produced her marriage certificate, did not admit the marriage. It is not possible to interfere with the damages, and some allegations of misdirection and wrongful admission of evidence came to nothing.

The real questions involved were: (1.) Was the alleged libel capable of a defamatory meaning? (2.) As the defendants did not know the facts which caused the friends of Mrs. Cassidy to whom they published the words to draw defamatory inferences from them about the plaintiff, were they liable for those inferences?

Now the alleged libel does not mention the plaintiff, but I think it is clear that words published about A may indirectly be defamatory of B. For instance, "A is illegitimate." To persons who know the parents those words may be defamatory of the parents. Or again, "A has given way to drink; it is unfortunately hereditary"; to persons who know A's parents these words may be defamatory. Or "A holds a D. Litt. degree of the University at X, the only one awarded." To persons who know B, who habitually describes himself (and rightly so) as "D. Litt. of X," these words may be capable of a defamatory meaning. Similarly, to say that A is a single man or a bachelor may be capable of a defamatory meaning if published to persons who know a lady who passes as Mrs. A and whom A visits. ... I do not agree with some dicta to the effect that if words are capable of several meanings, some defamatory and some innocent, they should not be left to the jury. I agree with the view expressed arguendo by Sir Montague Smith in the case of *Simmons v. Mitchell*: "The judge must decide if the words are reasonably capable of two meanings; if he so decide, the jury must determine which of the two meanings was intended;" and by "intended" I understand that a man is liable for the reasonable inferences to be drawn from the words he used, whether he foresaw them or not, and that if he scatters two-edged and ambiguous statements broadcast, without knowing

布这件事。这位摄影师没有做任何查证，就把合影照片发送给了《每日镜报》，并附上这段话："M. Corrigan 先生，赛马的主人，已经宣布和 X 小姐（我省去她的姓名）订婚。"《每日镜报》则刊登了这张照片和这段话。Cassidy 夫人或者叫 Corrigan 夫人的女性熟人读到了这张报纸，根据这张报纸给出的证据，她们认为 Corrigan 夫人并没有和 M. Corrigan 先生结婚，也无权使用他的姓氏。她们因此对她产生了很坏的印象。Cassidy 夫人因此对报社提起了诽谤之诉。她宣称报社刊登的这些话是在含沙射影地表示她是个和 Corrigan 姘居但却没有嫁给他的不正经的女人。

在庭审过程中，被告的律师反对原告的意见，声称被告发表的文字并没有任何诽谤的意思。McCardie 法官却认为有这个意思；陪审团也认为这些文字确实有诽谤的意思，因此裁断原告可以获得 500 英镑的赔偿。这个赔偿金的数额确实很高，但是原告出示了大量证据证明她的社会评价的损失。被告律师则辩称，原告声称自己嫁给 Corrigan 先生的言论一定有错误之处，甚至在原告出示了结婚证之后，被告律师也并不相信他们结婚了。干涉赔偿金数额是不可能的，而被告律师声称一审法官对陪审团的指导错误以及庭审时采纳了很多不该采纳的证据的说法都是站不住脚的。

本案真正的问题其实是：第一，原告所宣称的具有诽谤意味的文字是不是真的能解读出诽谤的意思？第二，被告其实并不知道他们的读者，Cassidy 夫人的朋友们会从他们的文章中推断出诽谤性的结论，那么这时被告要为这种推断承担责任吗？

诚然，原告所宣称诽谤的文字其实并没有提到原告，然而媒体发表的关于 A 的文字是可能间接地对 B 产生诽谤作用的，这一点我认为是显而易见的。比如，"A 是个私生子"这句话。对于认识 A 的父母的人来说，这句话其实是在诽谤他的父母。还有，"A 是个烂酒鬼，这是随根儿的"。这句话对认识 A 的父母的人来说，也是在诽谤他的父母。还有，"A 获得了 X 大学的文学博士学位，这是历史上头一份儿"。若有个 B 经常宣称自己是 X 大学的文学博士，而且他又确实是，那么对认识 B 的人来说，这些话就是对 B 的诽谤。同样，报道说 A 是单身也完全可能有诽谤的意思，如果某个女士宣称自己是 A 夫人并且经常被 A 拜访，且如果知晓这些事的人读到了这个报道……我不同意某些判决的附带意见的说法，说如果一段文字可能有多种理解方式，有的理解方式是在诽谤他人，有的则不是，那么这时候法官是不能把判断是否诽谤的任务交给陪审团的。我赞同 Mongtague Smith 爵士在 *Simmons v Mitchell* 案中，对一种假定情况所表达的意见："法官应当判断一段话是否可能有两种不同的解读；如果他认为是，那么就需要陪审团来判断到底是哪一种解读的意思是说话者所意图的。"这里，"意图"一词的意思按照我的理解，是要求一个

or making inquiry about facts material to the statements he makes and the inferences which may be drawn from them, he must be liable to persons who, knowing those facts, draw reasonable inferences from the words he publishes. ...

In my view the words published were capable of the meaning "Corrigan is a single man," and were published to people who knew the plaintiff professed to be married to Corrigan; it was for the jury to say whether those people could reasonably draw the inference that the so-called Mrs. Corrigan was in fact living in immoral cohabitation with Corrigan, and I do not think their finding should be interfered with.

But the second point taken was that the defendants could not be liable for the inference drawn, because they did not know the facts which enabled some persons to whom the libel was published, to draw an inference defamatory of the plaintiff. ... In my view ... it is impossible for the person publishing a statement which, to those who know certain facts, is capable of a defamatory meaning in regard to A, to defend himself by saying: "I never heard of A and did not mean to injure him." If he publishes words reasonably capable of being read as relating directly or indirectly to A and, to those who know the facts about A, capable of a defamatory meaning, he must take the consequences of the defamatory inferences reasonably drawn from his words.

It is said that this decision would seriously interfere with the reasonable conduct of newspapers. I do not agree. If publishers of newspapers, who have no more rights than private persons, publish statements which may be defamatory of other people, without inquiry as to their truth, in order to make their paper attractive, they must take the consequences, if on subsequent inquiry, their statements are found to be untrue or capable of defamatory and unjustifiable inferences. No one could contend that "M. Corrigan, General in the Mexican Army," was "a source in whom we have full confidence." To publish statements first and inquire into their truth afterwards, may seem attractive and up to date. Only to publish after inquiry may be slow, but at any rate it would lead to accuracy and reliability.

In my opinion the appeal should be dismissed with costs.

...

RUSSELL L.J.

Liability for libel does not depend on the intention of the defamer; but on the fact of defamation. If you once reach the conclusion that the published matter in the present case amounts to or involves a statement that Mr. Corrigan is an unmarried man, then in my opinion those persons who knew the circumstances might reasonably consider the statement defamatory of the plaintiff. The statement being capable of a meaning defamatory to the plaintiff, it was for the jury upon the evidence adduced to decide whether the plaintiff had been libelled or not.

It was said that it would be a great hardship on the defendants if they were made liable in consequence of a statement innocent on its face and published by them in good faith. The answer

人为他的话中可以合理地推断出来的意思承担责任，无论他是否预见到了这种推断出来的意思。如果他把一段模棱两可的话广而告之，而不管他的话涉及的重要方面是不是事实，也不管别人能从他的话中推断出什么，他当然应该对那些既知道事实，又从他的话中推断出了一些合理的意思的人负责……

在我看来，本案中的报道完全可以解读出"Corrigan 是个单身汉"这样的意思，而且这个报道也被认识以 Corrigan 夫人自居的原告的一些人读到了，这时，需要陪审团来判断这些人是否可能从报道中推断出所谓的 Corrigan 夫人其实不过是和 Corrigan 姘居而已，而陪审团的裁断，我认为我们不能干涉。

另一个问题是，（有人可能会说）被告并不应当为别人对他的报道的推断承担责任，因为他并不知道有些人会从他的报道中推断出某种诽谤性的信息……在我看来……一个人发表了一段话，这段话对知道某些事实的人可能意味着对 A 产生诽谤的效果，这时这个人是不可能如此抗辩的："我从没听说过 A 这号人，因此我不可能有侵害他的意思。"如果他说的话可以被合理地理解为直接或者间接涉及 A，且对于那些知道和 A 有关的事实的人可能被理解为诽谤的意思，那么这个人就必须承担这种合理推断出来的诽谤意思的后果。

有人说我们的决定会严重干扰报社的运营。我认为这是胡说八道。报社相比个人并没有更多的权利，因此如果报社为了吸引读者发表了对他人的诽谤性文字而不去查证事实到底是什么，那么当后来查证发现他们的文字并不真实，还可能被诽谤性地或者不正当地解读，他们当然要为此承担责任。没人敢说"Corrigan 先生，墨西哥军队的将军"是个"我们都全心全意信任的信息来源"。先发表文章再查证事实，对报社可能是更有吸引力的做法，也能保证新闻的及时性。先查证了再发表，虽然慢，但是无论如何都会呈现更准确且更值得信赖的内容。

我认为应驳回上诉，上诉人应承担诉讼费。

……

Russell 上诉法院法官

对诽谤是否承担责任并不取决于诽谤者的主观心态是什么，而是取决于诽谤的事实。如果你读了本案中的报道得出的结论是 Corrigan 先生是个单身汉，那么在我看来对那些知道情况的人来说，他们可以合理地认为这个报道是对原告的诽谤。既然报道是可能被解读为对原告的诽谤的，那么就需要由陪审团根据出示的证据来判断原告到底有没有真的被诽谤。

有人说，如果要被告因为他们善意地发表的，表面看起来是无害的文字而承担责任，这会对他们造成极大的困难。对这种装可怜的做法，可能应该

to this appeal for sympathy seems to be to point out that, in stating to the world that Mr. Corrigan was an unmarried man (for that construction is the foundation of their liability), they in fact stated that which was false. From a business point of view no doubt it may pay them not to spend time or money in making inquiries, or verifying statements before publication; but if they had not made a false statement they would not now be suffering in damages. They are paying a price for their methods of business.

...

For these reasons I agree with Scrutton L.J. that the appeal fails.

94. John v MGN Ltd [1997] QB 586 p 752

Court of Appeal, United Kingdom

SIR THOMAS BINGHAM MR

Part 2: The principles of law relating to damages in defamation

Introduction

It is standard practice for plaintiffs in defamation actions to claim damages and also an injunction against repetition of the publication complained of. If the action is compromised, the defendant ordinarily undertakes not to repeat the publication. If the action goes to trial and the plaintiff wins and recovers damages, the defendant ordinarily undertakes not to repeat the publication and if he is unwilling to give that undertaking an injunction restraining him from further publication will usually be granted. But it is the award of damages, not the grant of an injunction (in lieu of an undertaking), which is the primary remedy which the law provides on proof of this tort, both because, save in exceptional cases, the grant of an injunction in practice follows and is dependent on success in recovering damages, and also because an injunction, while giving the plaintiff protection against repetition in future, gives him no redress for what has happened in the past. It is to an award of damages that a plaintiff must look for redress, and the principles governing awards of damages are accordingly of fundamental importance in ensuring that justice is done to plaintiffs and defendants and that account is taken of such public interests as may be involved.

Compensatory damages

The successful plaintiff in a defamation action is entitled to recover, as general compensatory damages, such sum as will compensate him for the wrong he has suffered. That sum must compensate him for the damage to his reputation; vindicate his good name; and take account of the distress, hurt and humiliation which the defamatory publication has caused. In assessing the appropriate damages for injury to reputation the most important factor is the gravity of the libel; the more closely it touches the plaintiff's personal integrity, professional reputation, honour,

这样回应,即指出当报社向全世界宣布 Corrigan 先生是个单身汉时(这种解读是他们责任的基础),他们其实是在宣传虚假的东西。从商业策略的角度看,在发表之前不花时间或金钱去询问、核实内容无疑是划算的,但是如果他们没有发表虚假内容,他们也就不会承担责任。他们是在为他们的商业模式付费。

……

基于以上原因,我赞同 Scrutton 上诉法院法官的意见,应驳回上诉。

94. John v MGN Ltd [1997] QB 586 p 752

联合王国上诉法院

掌卷法官 Thomas Bingham 爵士

第二部分:关于诽谤赔偿金的法律原则

介绍

在诽谤案中,原告通行的做法是既请求损害赔偿,又请求禁止令以禁止诽谤内容的再次传播。若双方和解,被告一般会承诺不再传播相关内容。如果案件进入到庭审阶段,且原告胜诉并获得了赔偿金,那么被告一般会承诺不再传播相关的内容;若被告不愿意做出这样的承诺,那么一般法院会判决禁止令以禁止被告再次传播相关内容。然而在证明了侵权存在的前提下,原告获得的最主要的救济措施,还是损害赔偿金而不是禁止令(禁止令是为了替代被告不再传播相关内容的承诺)。这是因为两方面的原因。一方面,除了极端的案件外,法院判决禁止令的前提是原告成功地获得了损害赔偿金;另一方面,禁止令只能在未来保护原告,但是却不能救济已经发生的损失。原告必须寻求对于损害赔偿金的裁决而获得救济,因此,关于损害赔偿金裁决的原则,在保证原被告间的公正和考虑可能涉及的公共利益方面,具有基础性的重要作用。

填补性赔偿金

胜诉的原告有权获得一般性的填补性赔偿金,其金额由他因侵权行为而遭受的损失来确定。赔偿金的金额应当足够补偿其名声的损失;足够恢复他的良好名誉;还应当考虑到他因被诽谤所遭受的痛苦、伤害和羞辱。在评估对名誉损害的补偿金的数额时,最重要的因素是诽谤的严重程度,诽谤的言论越涉及原告的人格尊严、职业名声、荣誉、勇气、忠诚和其他的重要的人

courage, loyalty and the core attributes of his personality, the more serious it is likely to be. The extent of publication is also very relevant: a libel published to millions has a greater potential to cause damage than a libel published to a handful of people. A successful plaintiff may properly look to an award of damages to vindicate his reputation: but the significance of this is much greater in a case where the defendant asserts the truth of the libel and refuses any retraction or apology than in a case where the defendant acknowledges the falsity of what was published and publicly expresses regret that the libellous publication took place. It is well established that compensatory damages may and should compensate for additional injury caused to the plaintiff's feelings by the defendant's conduct of the action, as when he persists in an unfounded assertion that the publication was true, or refuses to apologise, or cross-examines the plaintiff in a wounding or insulting way. Although the plaintiff has been referred to as "he" all this of course applies to women just as much as men.

There could never be any precise, arithmetical formula to govern the assessment of general damages in defamation, but if such cases were routinely tried by judges sitting alone there would no doubt emerge a more or less coherent framework of awards which would, while recognising the particular features of particular cases, ensure that broadly comparable cases led to broadly comparable awards. This is what has happened in the field of personal injuries since these ceased to be the subject of trial by jury and became in practice the exclusive preserve of judges. There may be even greater factual diversity in defamation than in personal injury cases, but this is something of which the framework would take account.

The survival of jury trial in defamation actions has inhibited a similar development in this field. Respect for the constitutional role of the jury in such actions, and judicial reluctance to intrude into the area of decision-making reserved to the jury, have traditionally led judges presiding over defamation trials with juries to confine their jury directions to a statement of general principles, eschewing any specific guidance on the appropriate level of general damages in the particular case. While some distinguished judges (for example, Diplock L.J. in *McCarey v. Associated Newspapers Ltd. (No. 2)* [1965] 2 Q.B. 86, 109) have considered that juries should be informed in broad terms of the conventional level of awards for personal injuries, not by way of analogy but as a check on the reasonableness of an award which the jury are considering, this has not been an authoritative view: see *Broome v. Cassell & Co. Ltd.* [1972] A.C. 1027, 1071. Even in the rare case when a personal injury claim was to be tried by a jury it was thought inappropriate that a jury should be informed of the conventional level of awards (*Ward v. James* [1966] 1 Q.B. 273, 302), a striking departure from the modern practice when judges are sitting alone.

Whatever the theoretical attractions of this approach, its practical disadvantages have become ever more manifest. A series of jury awards in sums wildly disproportionate to any damage conceivably suffered by the plaintiff has given rise to serious and justified criticism of the

格要素，诽谤就越严重。诽谤言论的传播程度也是非常关键的：向一百万人传播的诽谤言论就比向少数人传播的诽谤言论更可能造成损害。胜诉的原告可以正当地获得损害赔偿金来恢复他的名誉，然而这事在被告坚持声称其言论是正确的且拒绝撤回或道歉的场合，比在被告承认其言辞的错误且公开表示对于诽谤言论的歉意的场合，要重要得多。毋庸置疑的还有：填补性的赔偿金应当能够填补原告因为被告在诉讼之中的行为而遭受的额外的伤害，比如被告毫无依据地坚持他的言论是正确的；拒绝道歉；或在交叉询问原告的时候伤害他或者侮辱他。这里我用了"他"来支撑原告，我所说的其实既适用于女性又适用于男性。

如何计算诽谤案中名誉损失的赔偿金，是没有精确的公式的，但是如果这类案件是由法官自己来审判的话，毫无疑问会产生比较确定的架构。这种架构在考虑到特殊案件的特殊特征的前提下，能够保证类似案件的原告获得数额大致相同的赔偿金。在人身损害领域中，由于案件不再由陪审团来审理而在实践中成为了法官的禁脔，因此这种架构就确实产生了。诽谤案件相比于人身损害案件，其不同案件间的事实的不同点可能更多，但是这种框架是会考虑到这一点的。

诽谤案件还是可能由陪审团来审理，因此阻碍了这种框架在这个领域的发展。因为要尊重陪审团在这类案件中的宪法性角色，也因为法官不愿意干涉陪审团的决定权，在有陪审团参与的诽谤案件中，传统上法官只会向陪审团作出很原则性的指导，从而避免就"某个具体案件中何种程度的一般赔偿金合适"这一问题作出指导。虽然某些著名的法官［比如 *McCarey v Associated Newspapers Ltd.*（*No. 2*）（1965）2 Q.B. 86, 109 案中的 Diplock 上诉法院法官］认为应该更进一步告知陪审团人身损害赔偿金的惯常数额，其方法也不是告诉他们类似的案件是怎么做的，而是让他们给出一个数额后由法官来判断这个数额是否合理。但是这样的观点并非权威观点：参见 *Broome v Cassell & Co. Ltd.* [1972] A.C. 1027, 1071。在很少见的由陪审团来审判的人身损害案件中，法官们也认为告知陪审团惯常的赔偿金数额是不恰当的［*Ward v James*（1966）1 Q.B. 273, 302］。这和由法官自己来审理这类案件的现代做法非常不同。

这种不干涉陪审团的做法有很多理论上的好处，但是它在实践中的坏处已经清楚显示。一系列的陪审团给出的损害赔偿金的数额，都和可以想象的原告遭受的损害，完全不成比例。导致给出这种虚高的赔偿金的程序，因此也受到

procedures leading to such awards. This has not been the fault of the juries. Judges, as they were bound to do, confined themselves to broad directions of general principle, coupled with injunctions to the jury to be reasonable. But they gave no guidance on what might be thought reasonable or unreasonable, and it is not altogether surprising that juries lacked an instinctive sense of where to pitch their awards. They were in the position of sheep loosed on an unfenced common, with no shepherd.

While the Court of Appeal reaffirmed the fundamental soundness of the traditional approach in *Sutcliffe v. Pressdram Ltd.* [1991] 1 Q.B. 153, the court did in that case recommend trial judges to draw the attention of juries to the purchasing power of the award they were minded to make, and of the income it would produce... This was thereafter done, and juries were reminded of the cost of buying a motor car, or a holiday, or a house. But judges were still constrained by authority from steering the jury towards any particular level of award.

Following enactment of section 8(2) of the Courts and Legal Services Act 1990 and the introduction of R.S.C., Ord. 59, r. 11(4) in its present form the Court of Appeal was for the first time empowered, on allowing an appeal against a jury's award of damages, to substitute for the sum awarded by the jury such sum as might appear to the court to be proper.

...

Any legal process should yield a successful plaintiff appropriate compensation, that is, compensation which is neither too much nor too little. That is so whether the award is made by judge or jury. No other result can be accepted as just. But there is continuing evidence of libel awards in sums which appear so large as to bear no relation to the ordinary values of life. This is most obviously unjust to defendants. But it serves no public purpose to encourage plaintiffs to regard a successful libel action, risky though the process undoubtedly is, as a road to untaxed riches. Nor is it healthy if any legal process fails to command the respect of lawyer and layman alike, as is regrettably true of the assessment of damages by libel juries. We are persuaded by the arguments we have heard that the subject should be reconsidered. This is not a field in which we are bound by previous authority (*Sutcliffe v. Pressdram Ltd.* [1991] 1 Q.B. 153, 178) but it is necessary for us to review the arguments which have found favour in the past.

In considering the criticisms of the present lack of guidance which is given to juries on the issue of compensatory damages we have examined four possible changes in the present practice: (a) Reference to awards by other juries in comparable actions for defamation. (b) Reference to awards approved by the Court of Appeal or substituted by the Court of Appeal in accordance with R.S.C., Ord. 59, r. 11(4) . (c) Reference to the scale of damages awarded in actions for personal injuries. (d) Submissions by counsel as to the appropriate award coupled with some guidance by the judge as to the appropriate bracket.

了严厉的批评，这种批评也是完全恰当的。这其实并非陪审员的错。法官不得不将对陪审团的指导局限于大的原则上，最多要求陪审团作出的禁止令要合理。但是法官并没有指导陪审团什么是合理的，什么是不合理的。对赔偿金多少才合理这个问题，陪审员是缺乏判断直觉的，这一点也并不奇怪。陪审员们就像是在没有围栏的草地上散放，却没有牧羊人来管理的羊群一样。

虽然在 *Sutcliffe v Pressdram Ltd.* [1991] 1 Q.B. 153 案中，上诉法院还是再次确认了传统的不介入陪审团的决定的做法是完全正确的。但是上诉法院在该案中还是建议一审法官要让陪审员注意一下他们想要决定的损害赔偿金数额的购买力，还有这个数额的金钱可以产生的被动收益……一审法官之后确实这么做了。他让陪审员想想买辆车要多少钱，度一次假要多少钱，买栋房子要多少钱。然而判例依然不允许一审法官去引导陪审员决定赔偿金的具体数额。

1990年《法院和法律服务法》第 8 条第 2 款和现在形式的《最高法院规则》第 59 号命令第 11 号规则第 4 款颁布之后，上诉法院第一次有权在同意对陪审团作出的损害赔偿金的裁断上诉时，用自己认为合理的赔偿金数额替代陪审团作出的数额。

……

法律程序应该能够让原告获得合理数额的赔偿金。所谓合理，就是说金额不能过高也不能过低。不管是法官还是陪审团来做这个决定，都应该是这样。除此之外的数额，都不能被认为是公正的。然而不断有证据表明，诽谤案的赔偿金数额太高了，高到脱离了一般人在生活中所遇到的东西的价值。这样做最明显的效果是对被告太不公正。但是鼓励原告把成功的诽谤诉讼（虽然其程序毫无疑问是有风险的）当作不交税的暴富之路，也是不符合公共利益的。而如果法律程序不能要求法律人和外行对法律给予同样的尊重，这种程序也是不健康的，很遗憾，诽谤案的陪审团决定损害赔偿金的程序就是这样得不健康。有很多人提议对这个问题应该重新考虑，我们认为这些提议说得对。对于这个问题，我们并不受到先例的约束（*Sutcliffe v Pressdram Ltd.* [1991] 1 Q.B. 153, 178），但是我们有必要重新审视之前那些支持这种做法的理由。

现在的做法是不给陪审团就填补性赔偿金的数额做具体指导。很多人都批评这种做法。我们考察了四种实践中发生的变化：第一是参考其他类似的诽谤案件中陪审团给出的赔偿金数额；第二是参考上诉法院所同意的数额，或者上诉法院自己根据《最高法院规则》第 59 号命令第 11 号规则第 4 款所作出的替代数额；第三是参考人身损害案件中给出的赔偿金的大小；第四是参考律师关于合理赔偿金数额的意见和法官提出的合适的赔偿金的范围。

Other awards in actions for defamation

We wholly agree with the ruling in the *Rantzen* case that juries should not at present be reminded of previous libel awards by juries. Those awards will have been made in the absence of specific guidance by the judge and may themselves be very unreliable markers.

The position may change in the future if the additional guidance which we propose later in this judgment is given and proves to be successful. As was pointed out in the course of argument, however, comparison with other awards is very difficult because the circumstances of each libel are almost bound to be unique. Furthermore, the corpus of such awards will be likely to become unwieldy and time would be expended on the respective parties pointing to features which were either similar or dissimilar in the other cases.

Awards approved or substituted by the Court of Appeal

We agree with the ruling in the *Rantzen* case that reference may be made to awards approved or made by the Court of Appeal. As and when a framework of awards is established this will provide a valuable pointer to the appropriate level of award in the particular case. But it is plain that such a framework will not be established quickly: it is now five years since section 8(2) of the Act of 1990 and Ord. 59, r. 11(4) came into force, and there is no case other than Gorman, *Rantzen* and Smith in which the court has itself fixed the appropriate level of award.

It is true that awards in this category are subject to the same objection that time can be spent by the parties on pointing to similarities and differences. But, if used with discretion, awards which have been subjected to scrutiny in the Court of Appeal should be able to provide *some* guidance to a jury called upon to fix an award in a later case.

Reference to damages in actions for personal injuries

In *Broome v. Cassell & Co. Ltd.* [1972] A.C. 1027, 1071-1072, Lord Hailsham of St. Marylebone L.C. gave his reason for rejecting comparison with awards of damages for personal injuries. He said:

> In actions of defamation and in any other actions where damages for loss of reputation are involved, the principle of restitutio in integrum has necessarily an even more highly subjective element. Such actions involve a money award which may put the plaintiff in a purely financial sense in a much stronger position than he was before the wrong. Not merely can he recover the estimated sum of his past and future losses, but, in case the libel, driven underground, emerges from its lurking place at some future date, he must be able to point to a sum awarded by a jury sufficient to convince a by-stander of the baselessness of the charge. As Windeyer J. well said in *Uren v. John Fairfax & Sons Pty. Ltd.*, 117 C.L.R. 115 , 150: 'It seems to me that, properly speaking, a man defamed does not get compensation *for* his damaged reputation.

其他诽谤案中陪审团裁断的赔偿金

我们完全赞同 Rantzen 案的判决：现阶段并不需要告知陪审团之前的案件中陪审团都裁断给出了多少赔偿金。那时陪审团所作出的有关赔偿金的裁断都没有法官的具体指导，因此可能并不能作为可靠的借鉴标准。

如果像我们的判决书中建议的那样，陪审团能获得法官更多的指导，且这种指导被证明是成功的，那么未来情况是可能改变的。然而，正如我们之前所指出的，与其他案件的赔偿金数额做比较是非常困难的，因为每起诽谤案件都注定是独一无二的。另外，以前的陪审团作出的赔偿金裁断所依赖的各种因素可能非常复杂，这样大量的时间会被消耗在比较本案和他案的相同点和不同点上。

其他案件中被上诉法院所同意或者为上诉法院所改判的赔偿金

我们同意 Rantzen 案的意见，可以参考上诉法院同意或者改判的赔偿金。当判断赔偿金数额的框架建立起来后，具体案件便有了判断依据。然而很明显，这样的框架不可能很快搭起来：1990 年《法院和法律服务法》第 8 条第 2 款和 59 号命令第 11 号规则第 4 款已经生效 5 年了，然而上诉法院只在 Gorman、Rantzen 和 Smith 这几个案件中自己确定了赔偿金的数额。

诚然，要参考这种类型的判例来确定赔偿金，还是会遇到之前同样的问题：双方当事人会花时间去指出本案和他案的相同点和不同点。然而，如果运用得当，上诉法院所审查过的赔偿金数额是可以为之后案件的陪审团提供一些指导价值的。

参考人身伤害案件中的赔偿金

在 *Broome v Cassell & Co. Ltd.* [1972] A.C. 1027, 1071-1072 案中，Hailsham 大法官拒绝比较诽谤案和人身伤害案的赔偿金。他的理由是：

> 在诽谤案或者其他有关名声损失的案件中，完全赔偿原则的构成要件必然有更多的主观判断。这类案件的赔偿金很可能在金钱意义上让原告处于比侵权行为发生前更好的状态。他不但可以获得对他过去或者未来损失的赔偿，而且为了避免案中流传的诽谤言论在未来某天又突然冒出来，陪审团必须要同意他提出的赔偿金额，以让局外人知道这种诽谤是多么无中生有。正如 Windeyer 法官在 *Uren v John Fairfax & Sons Pty. Ltd.*, 117 C.L.R. 115, 150 案中说的那样："我认为严格来说诽谤案的受害人并不是为了弥补他受损的名声所以要获得赔偿金。他获得赔偿金是因为他的名

He gets damages *because* he was injured in his reputation, that is simply because he was publicly defamed. For this reason, compensation by damages operates in two ways—as a vindication of the plaintiff to the public and as consolation to him for a wrong done. Compensation is here a solatium rather than a momentary recompense for harm measurable in money.' This is why it is not necessarily fair to compare awards of damages in this field with damages for personal injuries. Quite obviously, the award must include factors for injury to the feelings, the anxiety and uncertainty undergone in the litigation, the absence of apology, or the reaffirmation of the truth of the matters complained of, or the malice of the defendant. The bad conduct of the plaintiff himself may also enter into the matter …

This reasoning would weigh strongly against any attempt to equiparate damages for personal injuries and damages for defamation. It would not weigh so heavily, if at all, against reference to conventional levels of award for personal injuries as a check on the reasonableness of a proposed award of damages for defamation.

…

It has often and rightly been said that there can be no precise correlation between a personal injury and a sum of money. The same is true, perhaps even more true, of injury to reputation. There is force in the argument that to permit reference in libel cases to conventional levels of award in personal injury cases is simply to admit yet another incommensurable into the field of consideration. There is also weight in the argument, often heard, that conventional levels of award in personal injury cases are too low, and therefore provide an uncertain guide. But these awards would not be relied on as any exact guide, and of course there can be no precise correlation between loss of a limb, or of sight, or quadriplegia, and damage to reputation. But if these personal injuries respectively command conventional awards of, at most, about £52,000, £90,000 and £125,000 for pain and suffering and loss of amenity (of course excluding claims based on loss of earnings, the cost of care and other specific financial claims), juries may properly be asked to consider whether the injury to his reputation of which the plaintiff complains should fairly justify any greater compensation. The conventional compensatory scales in personal injury cases must be taken to represent fair compensation in such cases unless and until those scales are amended by the courts or by Parliament. It is in our view offensive to public opinion, and rightly so, that a defamation plaintiff should recover damages for injury to reputation greater, perhaps by a significant factor, than if that same plaintiff had been rendered a helpless cripple or an insensate vegetable. The time has in our view come when judges, and counsel, should be free to draw the attention of juries to these comparisons.

…

声受损了，换言之，仅仅是因为他被诽谤了他就能获得赔偿。这样，赔偿金其实起到了两个作用：为原告向公众澄清事实；为原告提供对侵权行为的抚慰。此处的赔偿与其说是对他所受损害的金钱填补，不如说是一种抚慰金。"这就是为什么把这个领域的赔偿金和人身损害案的赔偿金比较可能并不公平的原因。显然，赔偿金应当考虑到对情感的伤害、受害人在诉讼中所感受到的焦虑和不安、被告有没有道歉、被告是不是在坚持诽谤言论是真的、被告的主观恶性等。原告的恶行也应当作为考量的因素……

以上的说理坚决反对将人身损害案和诽谤案的赔偿金画等号。然而它对"通过参考人身损害案的赔偿金标准来判断诽谤案的赔偿金是否合理"这种做法，反对的程度没有那么大（如果非要说它反对的话）。
……

常有人说，人身损害是不能用精确的金钱标准来衡量的。在名声损害的问题上，这句话可能更对。这种说法是很有道理的：将人身损害赔偿的常规标准引入诽谤案件，只不过是把另一种无法衡量的因素引入了诽谤案赔偿金的判断问题中。同样有道理的还有这种常听到的说法：常规的人身损害案的赔偿金数额实在是太低了，因此作为指导标准只会产生不确定的结果。但是，我们在判断诽谤案的赔偿金的时候，当然不会将人身损害案的标准当作严格的指导标准。诚然，断肢、失明或者瘫痪和名声损失之间没有精确的联系。然而，假设以上的这些人身损害类型中，对身体的痛苦和生命中失去的美好事物（当然要排除失去的收入、护理费用和其他经济损失）的赔偿金的数额一般最多是 52 000 英镑、90 000 英镑和 125 000 英镑，那么要求陪审团考虑一下对名声损害的补偿是不是有理由比以上这些损失的补偿还大，便是恰当的了。我们应当把人身损害案件中的通常的赔偿金额的范围看作是公平的，除非法院和议会后来作出了修改。如果诽谤案的原告因为他名声受损就可以获得比残疾的原告或者成为植物人的原告更多的赔偿，这在我看来简直就是对公共意志的侮辱。我认为现在已经是时候允许法官和律师去提请陪审团注意下人身损害的赔偿金是多少，然后跟诽谤案作比较了。
……

Reference to an appropriate award and an appropriate bracket

It has been the invariable practice in the past that neither counsel nor the judge may make any suggestion to the jury as what would be an appropriate award. ...

...

We have come to the conclusion, however, that the reasons which have been given for prohibiting any reference to figures are unconvincing. Indeed, far from developing into an auction (and we do not see how it could), the process of mentioning figures would in our view induce a mood of realism on both sides.

...

In personal injury actions it is now commonplace for the advocates on both sides to address the judge in some detail on the quantum of the appropriate award. Any apprehension that the judge might receive a coded message as to the amount of any payment into court has not to our knowledge been realised. The judge is not in any way bound by the bracket suggested, but he finds it helpful as a check on his own provisional assessment. We can for our part see no reason why the parties' respective counsel in a libel action should not indicate to the jury the level of award which they respectively contend to be appropriate, nor why the judge in directing the jury should not give a similar indication. The plaintiff will not wish the jury to think that his main object is to make money rather than clear his name. The defendant will not wish to add insult to injury by underrating the seriousness of the libel. So we think the figures suggested by responsible counsel are likely to reflect the upper and lower bounds of a realistic bracket. The jury must of course make up their own mind and must be directed to do so. They will not be bound by the submission of counsel or the indication of the judge. If the jury make an award outside the upper or lower bounds of any bracket indicated and such award is the subject of appeal, real weight must be given to the possibility that their judgment is to be preferred to that of the judge.

The modest but important changes of practice described above would not in our view undermine the enduring constitutional position of the libel jury. Historically, the significance of the libel jury has lain not in their role of assessing damages but in their role of deciding whether the publication complained of is a libel or no. The changes which we favour will, in our opinion, buttress the constitutional role of the libel jury by rendering their proceedings more rational and so more acceptable to public opinion.

95. Derbyshire County Council v Times Newspapers [1993] AC 534

House of Lords, United Kingdom

LORD KEITH.

My Lords, this appeal raises, as a preliminary issue in an action of damages for libel,

参考律师和法官所主张的金额范围

律师和法官都不能对陪审员提出合理的赔偿金数额是多少的建议,这在过去是不可变更的通例……

……

然而我们现在的结论却是禁止律师和法官提到具体的赔偿金数字的理由是没有说服力的。提到数字其实并不会发展成拍卖会(我们不知道怎么可能变成拍卖会),在我们看来这样做只会让双方都感到没有那么虚幻。

……

在人身损害案中,现在的通行做法是双方律师都可以向法官陈述决定赔偿金数额的细节和向其建议合适的数额。有人可能会担心法官会因为这种诱导性的建议而在判断赔偿金数额时产生定式思维,然而据我们所知这种事并没有发生。法官并没有在任何意义上被律师建议的范围所束缚,相反,法官们会觉得这些建议很有用,可以用来检查并修正自己暂时作出的判断。我们找不到理由来反对在诽谤案中让双方的律师去告知陪审团他们认为合适的赔偿金数额,也找不到理由去反对法官对陪审团做类似的指导。原告并不想让陪审团认为他是想发一笔横财而不是想找回清白的名声。被告并不想在原告已经遭受损害的基础上再冒犯他,因此并不会对诽谤的程度轻描淡写。因此我们认为负责任的律师所提出的数额应该能反映合理的赔偿金的上下限范围。陪审团的裁断当然应该由他们自己来作出,法官也应该指导他们自己作出裁断。陪审团并不会被律师的建议和法官的指导所束缚。若陪审团给出的赔偿金的数额高于或者低于法官给出的范围,且赔偿金的数额是上诉的标的,则必须真正重视他们的裁断优先于法官的可能性。

我们这里提议的改变是很微小的,但也是很重要的。这种改变在我们看来并不会减损在诽谤案中陪审团那历史悠久的宪法地位。历史上诽谤案中的陪审团的角色之所以很重要,并不是因为他们要决定赔偿金的数额,而是因为他们要判断涉案言论是不是诽谤。我们提议的这种改变只会巩固诽谤案陪审团的宪法角色,只会让他们的判断过程更理性,更能被公众所接受。

95. Derbyshire County Council v Times Newspapers [1993] AC 534

联合王国上议院

Keith 大法官

诸位大法官,本次上诉的一个先决问题是地方政府机关是否有权对评价

the question whether a local authority is entitled to maintain an action in libel for words which reflect on it in its governmental and administrative functions. ...

...

There are ... features of a local authority which may be regarded as distinguishing it from other types of corporation, whether trading or non-trading. The most important of these features is that it is a governmental body. Further, it is a democratically elected body, the electoral process nowadays being conducted almost exclusively on party political lines. It is of the highest public importance that a democratically elected governmental body, or indeed any governmental body, should be open to uninhibited public criticism. The threat of a civil action for defamation must inevitably have an inhibiting effect on freedom of speech. In City of Chicago v. Tribune Co. (1923) 139 N.E. 86 the Supreme Court of Illinois held that the city could not maintain an action of damages for libel. Thompson C.J. said, at p. 90:

> 'The fundamental right of freedom of speech is involved in this litigation, and not merely the right of liberty of the press. If this action can be maintained against a newspaper it can be maintained against every private citizen who ventures to criticise the ministers who are temporarily conducting the affairs of his government. Where any person by speech or writing seeks to persuade others to violate existing law or to overthrow by force or other unlawful means the existing government, he may be punished . . . but all other utterances or publications against the government must be considered absolutely privileged. While in the early history of the struggle for freedom of speech the restrictions were enforced by criminal prosecutions, it is clear that a civil action is as great, if not a greater, restriction than a criminal prosecution. If the right to criticise the government is a privilege which, with the exceptions above enumerated, cannot be restricted, then all civil as well as criminal actions are forbidden. A despotic or corrupt government can more easily stifle opposition by a series of civil actions than by criminal prosecutions ...'

After giving a number of reasons for this, he said, at p. 90:

> 'It follows, therefore, that every citizen has a right to criticise an inefficient or corrupt government without fear of civil as well as criminal prosecution. This absolute privilege is founded on the principle that it is advantageous for the public interest that the citizen should not be in any way fettered in his statements, and where the public service or due administration of justice is involved he shall have the right to speak his mind freely.'

其统治和管理职能的言论提起诽谤之诉……

……

地方政府机关具有某些特征，使其与营利和非营利的其他类型的组织相区别。其最重要的特征便是它是政府机关。另外，它是民主选举的政府机关，而民主选举的程序在今天基本上是由政党政治主宰的。公众对民选的政府机关或者任何类型的政府机关的批评，都不应该受到限制，这对公众来说是最重要的事之一。如果政府机关能以诽谤为依据提起民事诉讼，那么言论自由是一定会受到限制的。在 *City of Chicago v Tribune Co.*（1923）139 N.E. 86 案中，伊利诺伊州最高法院认为芝加哥市并不具有提起诽谤之诉的资格。Thompson 首席大法官在第 90 页说道：

> 本案涉及的不仅仅是新闻自由，还涉及作为基本人权的言论自由。如果可以对报社提起诽谤之诉，那么这种诉讼也是可以由任何敢对暂时从事政府工作的部长提出批评意见的公民提起的。一个人如果用口头或者书面的言词煽动他人违反现行法或者用暴力或其他手段推翻现政府，那么这个人是应该受到惩罚的……然而除此以外的言论是完全不应该受到起诉的威胁的。虽然在言论斗争史的早期，政府限制言论自由一般都适用刑事诉讼的方式，但是很显然，民事诉讼对言论自由的限制如果不是比刑事诉讼更大，也是会达到差不多的效果的。如果批评政府的权利在除了上列例外的情况之外应该得到保护，那么政府无论是提起民事诉讼还是刑事诉讼都应该是被禁止的。专横的或者腐败的政府通过一系列的民事诉讼来扼杀对其的反对，甚至比用刑事诉讼还简单……

在为他的结论寻找了多个理由之后，在第 90 页，他说：

> 因此每个公民都有权批评低效而腐败的政府，且有权不因此而受到刑事指控。这种绝对的权利是建筑在这样一项原则之上的：为了公共利益，公民的言论不应该受到任何的限制；当涉及公共服务或者司法公正的时候，他有权把他所想的自由地说出来。

These propositions were endorsed by the Supreme Court of the United States in New York Times Co. v. Sullivan (1964) 376 U.S. 254 , 277. While these decisions were related most directly to the provisions of the American Constitution concerned with securing freedom of speech, the public interest considerations which underlaid them are no less valid in this country. What has been described as 'the chilling effect' induced by the threat of civil actions for libel is very important. Quite often the facts which would justify a defamatory publication are known to be true, but admissible evidence capable of proving those facts is not available. This may prevent the publication of matters which it is very desirable to make public...

...

I regard it as right for this House to lay down that not only is there no public interest favouring the right of organs of government, whether central or local, to sue for libel, but that it is contrary to the public interest that they should have it. It is contrary to the public interest because to admit such actions would place an undesirable fetter on freedom of speech. ...

...

In the case of a local authority temporarily under the control of one political party or another it is difficult to say that the local authority as such has any reputation of its own. Reputation in the eyes of the public is more likely to attach itself to the controlling political party, and with a change in that party the reputation itself will change. A publication attacking the activities of the authority will necessarily be an attack on the body of councillors which represents the controlling party, or on the executives who carry on the day to day management of its affairs. If the individual reputation of any of these is wrongly impaired by the publication any of these can himself bring proceedings for defamation. Further, it is open to the controlling body to defend itself by public utterances and in debate in the council chamber.

The conclusion must be, in my opinion, that under the common law of England a local authority does not have the right to maintain an action of damages for defamation. That was the conclusion reached by the Court of Appeal, which did so principally by reference to article 10 of the European Convention for the Protection of Human Rights and Fundamental Freedoms (1953) (Cmd. 8969) , to which the United Kingdom has adhered but which has not been enacted into domestic law. Article 10 is in these terms:

> '1. Everyone has the right to freedom of expression. This right shall include freedom to hold opinions and to receive and impart information and ideas without interference by public authority and regardless of frontiers. ... 2. The exercise of these freedoms, since it carries with it duties and responsibilities, may be subject to such formalities, conditions, restrictions or penalties as are prescribed by law and are necessary in a democratic society, in the interests of national security, territorial

美国最高法院在 New York Times Co. v. Sullivan（1964）376 U.S. 254, 277 案中支持了这种观点。虽然与美国法院的判决直接相关的大多都是美国宪法中的言论自由条款，但是这背后对公共利益的考量在我们国家也是适用的。诽谤之诉的威胁造成的寒蝉效应是非常严重的。所谓的诽谤言论其实经常是真话，只是没有证据证明其所说的事实是真的。这种情况常常会阻碍公众希望知道的事实被公之于众……

……

我认为本院的以下观点是正确的：允许无论是中央还是地方政府有权以诽谤为由起诉，不但没有公共利益来支持这么做，而且如果让他们这么做还会违反公共利益。之所以这是违反公共利益的，是因为如果允许这样的诉讼，那么言论自由必将受到我们所不希望的限制……

……

地方政府都是在这个或者那个政党的控制之下的，因此很难说这样的地方政府有自己独立的名声。地方政府的名声在公众看来和执政的党派联系更紧密，且随着执政党的更迭，地方政府的名声也会改变。批评政府的报道是肯定也会批评它的执委会的，而执委会是代表执政党的；也可能会批评执行日常事务的执行官员。如果上述个人的名誉因为报道而被不法地侵犯了，那么他们都可以自己提起诽谤之诉。另外，控制政府的团体完全可以通过发表公开声明的方式或者在会议厅里辩论的方式来为自己辩护。

我的结论就是，在英格兰的普通法下，地方的政府机关是没有权利提起诽谤之诉的。上诉法院也得出了这个结论。上诉法院得出这个结论主要是依据《欧洲保护人权和基本自由公约》（1953）（以下简称《公约》）（Cmd. 8969）第 10 条的规定。该规定英国也是遵守的，但是还没有被转换为国内法。第 10 条规定：

　　1. 人人享有言论自由的权利。此项权利应当包括持有主张的自由，以及在不受公共机构干预和不分国界的情况下，接受和传播信息和思想的自由…… 2. 行使上述各项自由，因为同时负有义务和责任，所以必须接受法律所规定的和民主社会所必需的程式、条件、限制或者是惩罚的约束。这些约束是基于对国家安全、领土完整或者公共安全的利益，为

integrity or public safety, for the prevention of disorder or crime, for the protection of health or morals, for the protection of the reputation or rights of others, for preventing the disclosure of information received in confidence, or for maintaining the authority and impartiality of the judiciary.'

My Lords, I have reached my conclusion upon the common law of England without finding any need to rely upon the European Convention. My noble and learned friend, Lord Goff of Chieveley, in *Attorney-General v. Guardian Newspapers Ltd. (No. 2)* [1990] 1 A.C. 109, 283-284, expressed the opinion that in the field of freedom of speech there was no difference in principle between English law on the subject and article 10 of the Convention. I agree, and can only add that I find it satisfactory to be able to conclude that the common law of England is consistent with the obligations assumed by the Crown under the Treaty in this particular field.

For these reasons I would dismiss the appeal. It follows that *Bognor Regis Urban District Council v. Campion* [1972] 2 Q.B. 169 was wrongly decided and should be overruled.

了防止混乱或者犯罪,保护健康或者道德,为了保护他人的名誉或者权利,为了防止秘密收到的情报泄露,或者为了维护司法官员的权威与公正的因素的考虑。

诸位大法官,我得出的有关英格兰普通法上的结论并没有依赖《公约》。我那高贵而博学的朋友,Goff 大法官,在 *Attorney-General v Guardian Newspapers Ltd.* (*No. 2*) [1990] 1 A.C. 109, 283-284 案中,认为在言论自由的领域中,英格兰法和《公约》第 10 条并没有什么区别。我同意这种意见;英格兰普通法和女王陛下根据《公约》必须履行的义务是相符合的,对于这个结论我感到很欣慰。

综上所述,我要驳回上诉。因此 *Bognor Regis Urban District Council v Campion* [1972] 2 Q.B. 169 案的判决是错误的,应该被推翻。

Chapter 11. Invasion of Privacy

Section 1. Invasion of Privacy in US Law

96. Hamberger v. Eastman, 106 N.H. 107, 206 A.2d 239 (1964)

Supreme Court of New Hampshire, United States

The plaintiffs, husband and wife, brought companion suits for invasion of their privacy against the defendant who owned and rented a dwelling house to the plaintiffs....

The declaration in the suit by the husband reads as follows:

"In a plea of the case, for that the defendant is the owner of a certain dwelling house...which was, and still is, occupied by the plaintiff and his family as a dwelling house on a weekly rental basis; that said dwelling house is located adjacent to and abutting other land of the defendant whereon the defendant maintains his place of residence, together with his place of business.

"That, sometime during the period from October, 1961, to October 15, 1962, the defendant, wholly without the knowledge and consent of the plaintiff, did willfully and maliciously invade the privacy and sanctity of the plaintiff's bedroom, which he shared with his wife in their dwelling house, by installing and concealing a listening and recording device in said bedroom; that this listening and recording device, which was concealed in an area adjacent to the bed occupied by the plaintiff and his wife was attached and connected to the defendant's place of residence by means of wires capable of transmitting and recording any sounds and voices originating in said bedroom.

"That, on or about October 15, 1962, plaintiff discovered the listening and recording device which defendant had willfully and maliciously concealed in his bedroom, and the plaintiff, ever since that time and as a direct result of the actions of the defendant, has been greatly distressed, humiliated, and embarrassed and has sustained and is now sustaining, intense and severe mental suffering and distress, and has been rendered extremely nervous and upset, seriously impairing both his mental and physical condition, and that the plaintiff has sought, and still is under, the care of a physician; that large sums have been, and will be in the future, expended for medical care and attention; that because of his impaired mental and physical condition, the plaintiff has been and still is unable to properly perform his normal and ordinary duties as a father and as a husband, and has been unable to properly perform his duties at his place of employment, and has been otherwise

第十一章 侵犯隐私

第一节 美国法上的侵犯隐私之诉

96. Hamberger v. Eastman, 106 N.H. 107, 206 A.2d 239 (1964)

美国新罕布什尔州最高法院

原告是一对夫妇，被告将自己的住宅出租给原告，原告以侵犯隐私提起同类诉讼……

丈夫诉称：

"在本案的一项事实主张中，被告是该特定住宅的所有者，……原告和他的家人过去、现在仍然以周租的形式占有住宅。这个住宅紧挨并毗邻被告的其他土地，被告居住在那，也是他做生意的地方。

1961年10月至1962年10月15日这段时间，被告在完全没有告知原告也未经原告同意的情况下，通过在起居室安装并隐藏听录装置，蓄意和恶意地侵犯他和妻子共同享有神圣不可侵犯的起居室隐私。听录装置紧挨原告和他妻子所有的床，且与被告的住处相连，通过无线装置传送和记录起居室的所有声音。

大约在1962年10月15日，原告发现了被告在他房间蓄意和恶意地隐藏的听录装置，被告这一行为的直接后果是，原告从那一刻起觉得受到严重伤害、屈辱和尴尬，巨大的、严重的精神痛苦一直持续到现在，也感到极度紧张和烦恼，严重破坏了他的精神和身体健康，原告从那时起一直都在接受一位医生的照顾。医疗保健和照顾费用会相当庞大。由于原告的精神和身体健康遭到破坏，他已经不能承担作为父亲和丈夫应尽的基本义务，也不能适当履行他所受雇职位的义务。他在其他方面也严重受损"。

greatly injured."

The declaration in the suit by the wife is identical, with appropriate substitutes of the personal pronoun, and omission of the allegation of inability to perform duties at her place of employment.

In both actions the defendant moved to dismiss on the ground that on the facts alleged, no cause of action is stated. The Court...reserved and transferred the cases to the Supreme Court without ruling.

Kenison, C.J. The question presented is whether the right of privacy is recognized in this state. There is no controlling statute and no previous decision in this jurisdiction which decides the question. Inasmuch as invasion of the right of privacy is not a single tort but consists of four distinct torts, it is probably more concrete and accurate to state the issue in the present case to be whether this state recognizes that intrusion upon one's physical and mental solitude or seclusion is a tort....

We have not searched for cases where the bedroom of husband and wife has been "bugged" but it should not be necessary—by way of understatement—to observe that this is the type of intrusion that would be offensive to any person of ordinary sensibilities. What married "people do in the privacy of their bedrooms is their own business so long as they are not hurting anyone else." Ernst and Loth, For Better or Worse 79 (1952). The Restatement, Torts, §867 provides that "a person who unreasonably and seriously interferes with another's interest in not having his affairs known to others...is liable to the other." As is pointed out in Comment d "liability exists only if the defendant's conduct was such that he should have realized that it would be offensive to persons of ordinary sensibilities. It is only where the intrusion has gone beyond the limits of decency that liability accrues. These limits are exceeded where intimate details of the life of one who has never manifested a desire to have publicity are exposed to the public...."

The defendant contends that the right of privacy should not be recognized on the facts of the present case as they appear in the pleadings because there are no allegations that anyone listened or overheard any sounds or voices originating from the plaintiffs' bedroom. The tort of intrusion on the plaintiffs' solitude or seclusion does not require publicity and communication to third persons although this would affect the amount of damages....The defendant also contends that the right of privacy is not violated unless something has been published, written or printed and that oral publicity is not sufficient. Recent cases make it clear that this is not a requirement.

If the peeping Tom, the big ear and electronic eavesdropper (whether ingenious or ingenuous) have a place in the hierarchy of social values, it ought not to be at the expense of a married couple minding their own business in the seclusion of their bedroom who have never asked for or by their conduct deserved a potential projection of their private conversations and actions to their landlord or to others. Whether actual or potential such "publicity with respect to private matters of purely personal concern is an injury to personality. It impairs the mental peace and comfort of

妻子在起诉状中的陈述是相同的,只是将代词作了合理替换,并省略掉其不能履行受雇职位义务的主张。

在这一诉讼中,被告以鉴于指控的事实、原告起诉理由不足为由,申请驳回。法院……推迟该案,并未判决就将案件移送至最高法院。

Kenison 大法官主笔:隐私权在该州是否被认可是有待解决的问题。在本法域,还没有主导性的立法,也没有先例决定这一问题。鉴于侵犯隐私权不是一种侵权行为而是包含四种不同的侵权行为,可能在本案中确定的是,本州是否认可对一个人身心独处或者隐秘的侵扰构成一种侵权,这可能是更清楚和正确的……

我们并未对夫妻卧室被"窃听"的案例进行检索。我们也没有必要以轻描淡写的方式认为这是对具有一般感知能力的任何人都具有冒犯性的一种侵扰。"只要不伤害任何其他人,已婚的人在私人房间的所为是他们自己的事情"。(参见 Ernst & Loth 的《不论好坏》[For Better or Worse 79(1952)])《侵权法重述》第 867 条规定,"一个人不合理且严重地干涉他人利益,且未将自己事务告知他人,……应该对该他人承担责任"。像在评论 d 中所指出的:"只有被告的行为使他认识到这对人的一般感知具有冒犯性,他才会承担责任。即只有侵扰超出正当行为的限制才会产生责任。人们从未表示有公开意愿的私密生活细节被公开披露时,就超出了该限制……"

被告争辩道,隐私权在本案起诉状所述事实中不应得到认可,因为起诉状中没有主张其他人听到或偶尔听到从原告卧室传出的声音。虽然会影响赔偿的数额,但是对原告独处或者隐秘的侵扰的侵权行为,并不要求公开性或者传播给第三人……被告还认为,除非有相关事宜被公开、撰写或者出版,否则隐私权没有被侵害,只有口头公开是不充分的。近期的案例显示这并非要件。

如果偷窥癖、大耳朵和电子窃听者(不管是巧妙的还是坦率的)在社会价值等级中有一席之地,也不应以牺牲已婚夫妇卧室的隐秘为代价,他们从未以语言要求或行为显示,要将他们的私人谈话和行为暴露给房东和其他人。不管是实际的还是潜在的,"对纯粹私人相关事务的公开,对个人都是一种伤害。它破坏了精神的宁静和个人生活的舒适,它导致的伤害甚至比单纯肉体

the individual and may produce suffering more acute than that produced by a mere bodily injury." III Pound, Jurisprudence 58 (1959). The use of parabolic microphones and sonic wave devices designed to pick up conversations in a room without entering it and at a considerable distance away makes the problem far from fanciful.

It is unnecessary to determine the extent to which the right of privacy is protected as a constitutional matter without the benefit of statute. For the purposes of the present case it is sufficient to hold that the invasion of the plaintiffs' solitude or seclusion, as alleged in the pleadings, was a violation of their right of privacy and constituted a tort for which the plaintiffs may recover damages to the extent that they can prove them. "Certainly, no right deserves greater protection, for, as Emerson has well said, 'solitude, the safeguard of mediocrity, is to genius the stern friend.'" Ezer, Intrusion on Solitude: Herein of Civil Rights and Civil Wrongs, 21 Law in Transition 63, 75 (1961).

The motion to dismiss should be denied.

Remanded.

All concurred.

97. Shulman v. Group W Productions, Inc., 18 Cal. 4th 200, 955 P.2d 469, 74 Cal. Rptr. 2d 843 (1998)

Supreme Court of California, United States

Werdegar, Justice....

In the present case, we address the balance between privacy and press freedom in the commonplace context of an automobile accident. Plaintiffs, two members of a family whose activities and position did not otherwise make them public figures, were injured when their car went off the highway, overturning and trapping them inside. A medical transport and rescue helicopter crew came to plaintiffs' assistance, accompanied on this occasion by a video camera operator employed by a television producer. The cameraman filmed plaintiffs' extrication from the car, the flight nurse and medic's efforts to give them medical care during the extrication, and their transport to the hospital in the helicopter. The flight nurse wore a small microphone that picked up her conversations with other rescue workers and with one of the plaintiffs. This videotape and sound track were edited into a segment that was broadcast, months later, on a documentary television show, *On Scene: Emergency Response*. Plaintiffs, who consented neither to the filming and recording nor to the broadcasting, allege the television producers thereby intruded into a realm of personal privacy and gave unwanted publicity to private events of their lives.

The trial court granted summary judgment for the producers on the ground that the events depicted in the broadcast were newsworthy and the producers' activities were therefore protected under the First Amendment to the United States Constitution. The Court of Appeal reversed,

伤害还要严重"。这句话出自 III Pound 的《法理学》[Jurisprudence 58（1959）]。使用抛物面反射镜式传声器和声波装置，在不进入房间并隔有相当距离的情况下，接收房间内谈话信息，这使得该问题远非稀奇。

在没有立法利益的情况下，讨论隐私权在何种程度上作为宪法问题被保护是没有必要的。依本案目的，侵犯原告声称的独处或者隐秘，即侵犯了他们的隐私权，构成侵权，原告据此只要能够证明受到多大程度的伤害，就能够获得多少赔偿，这就够了。"当然，没有权利值得更多保护，正如 Emerson 所讲，独处，平凡人物的守护者，对天才人物来说是位严厉的朋友"。这句话出自 Ezer 的《侵扰独处：在民事权利与民事不法之中》[Intrusion on Solitude: Herein of Civil Rights and Civil Wrongs, 21 Law in Transition 63, 75（1961）]。

驳回起诉的申请应当被拒绝。

发回重审。

全体法官赞同。

97. Shulman v. Group W Productions, Inc., 18 Cal. 4th 200, 955 P.2d 469, 74 Cal. Rptr. 2d 843 (1998)

美国加利福尼亚州最高法院

Werdegar 法官主笔：……

本案中，我们讨论汽车事故在一般情境之下的隐私和出版自由的平衡。原告是一个家庭的两个成员，根据他们的活动和身份，不能认为他们是公众人物，他们因为汽车驶出高速公路翻倒困在车里而受伤。一个医疗运输和营救直升机小组对原告实施了救助，同时，由一个受雇于电视节目制片人的摄影师陪同。摄影师拍摄了原告从车里被救出，机上护士和医生在实施医疗救助中做出的努力，以及通过直升机将原告运往医院的过程。机上护士戴了耳麦以便于她与其他救助者和原告之一交流。这个视频和音带经过编辑，几个月之后在一个电视纪录节目中播放，题为"现场：紧急反应"。原告既未同意录像、录音，更未同意播放，原告主张电视节目制片人因此侵扰了个人隐私领域，把他们生活中的私人事件进行了不必要的公开。

初审法院作出了有利于制片人的简易判决，理由是节目中描述的事件是有新闻价值的，制片人的活动受到《美国联邦宪法第一修正案》的保护。上诉法院撤销判决，认为……初审法院在原告的两项侵扰诉讼中都存在法律错

finding...legal error on the trial court's part as to both plaintiffs' intrusion claims. Agreeing with some, but not all, of the Court of Appeal's analysis, we conclude summary judgment was improper]as to their cause of action for intrusion....

Discussion

Influenced by Dean Prosser's analysis of the tort actions for invasion of privacy (Prosser, Privacy (1960), 48 Cal. L. Rev. 381) and the exposition of a similar analysis in the Restatement Second of Torts sections 652A-652E. California courts have recognized...the privacy cause of action pleaded by plaintiffs here:...intrusion into private places, conversations or other matters....

II. Intrusion

Of the four privacy torts identified by Prosser, the tort of intrusion into private places, conversations or matter is perhaps the one that best captures the common understanding of an "invasion of privacy."...

As stated in Miller v. National Broadcasting Co., 232 Cal. Rptr. 668 (1986) and the Restatement,...the action for intrusion has two elements: (1) intrusion into a private place, conversation or matter, (2) in a manner highly offensive to a reasonable person. We consider the elements in that order.

We ask first whether defendants "intentionally intruded, physically or otherwise, upon the solitude or seclusion of another," that is, into a place or conversation private to....To prove actionable intrusion, the plaintiff must show the defendant penetrated some zone of physical or sensory privacy surrounding, or obtained unwanted access to data about, the plaintiff. The tort is proven only if the plaintiff had an objectively reasonable expectation of seclusion or solitude in the place, conversation or data source.

Cameraman Cooke's mere presence at the accident scene and filming of the events occurring there cannot be deemed either a physical or sensory intrusion on plaintiffs' seclusion. Plaintiffs had no right of ownership or possession of the property where the rescue took place, nor any actual control of the premises. Nor could they have had a reasonable expectation that members of the media would be excluded or prevented from photographing the scene; for journalists to attend and record the scenes of accidents and rescues is in no way unusual or unexpected.

Two aspects of defendants' conduct, however, raise triable issues of intrusion on seclusion. First, a triable issue exists as to whether both plaintiffs had an objectively reasonable expectation of privacy in the interior of the rescue helicopter, which served as an ambulance. Although the attendance of reporters and photographers at the scene of an accident is to be expected, we are aware of no law or custom permitting the press to ride in ambulances or enter hospital rooms during treatment without the patient's consent. Other than the two patients and Cooke, only three people were present in the helicopter, all Mercy Air staff. As the Court of Appeal observed, "it is neither the custom nor the habit of our society that any member of the public at large or its

误。我们部分同意上诉法院的分析,我们认为就他们的侵扰诉因作出简易判决并不合适……

讨论

受 Prosser 院长对侵犯隐私侵权诉讼的分析(Prosser 的《隐私》[1960],48 Cal.L.Rev.381)和《侵权法重述·第二次》第 652A 至 652E 条相似分析阐述的影响,加州法院已经认可……原告提起的隐私诉因:……侵扰私人空间、谈话或者其他事项……

Ⅱ. 侵扰

在 Prosser 所认可的四种隐私侵权行为中,侵扰他人私人空间、谈话或者事项可能最能把握"侵犯隐私"的一般理解。

像在 Miller v. National Broadcasting Co., 232 Cal. Rptr. 668(1986)案和《侵权法重述》中所述的……侵扰诉讼有两个要件:(1)侵扰私人空间、谈话或者事项;(2)以一种对理性人来讲高度冒犯性的方式。我们按这个顺序讨论一下这两个要件。

我们首先询问被告是否"物质性地或者以其他方式,故意侵扰他人的独处或者隐秘",即侵入的私人空间和私人谈话……要证明可诉的侵扰,原告必须展示,被告进入原告隐私环境的物质性的和可感知到的区域,或者以不必要的途径获得关于原告的数据。只有原告对该空间、谈话或者数据来源存在对隐秘或者独处的客观的合理期待,才能构成侵权。

摄影师 Cooke 仅仅出现在事故现场,并对发生的事件录像,既不能认为是物质性的,又不能认为是可感知地侵扰了原告的隐秘。原告对于营救发生地的财产既没有占有又不享有所有权,也不对不动产实际控制。他们也没有合理地期待媒体工作人员应该被排除或避免现场拍照,因为记者参与并记录事故和营救现场绝非不正常和不可期待的。

然而,被告行为的两个方面存在侵扰隐秘的可裁判性争点:第一,二原告是否对提供救护车的营救直升机内部的隐私有客观上的合理期待,这是一个可裁判性争点。虽然事故现场可以预期记者和摄影者的参与,但是我们没发现任何法律或习俗在未经病人同意的情况下,允许媒体工作人员乘坐救护车或者在治疗期间进入医院。除了两个病人和 Cooke,直升机内只有三个人,都是 Mercy Air 公司的工作人员。就像上诉法院所评论的,"一般大众的任何成

media representatives may hitch a ride in an ambulance and ogle as paramedics care for an injured stranger."

Second, Ruth was entitled to a degree of privacy in her conversations with Carnahan and other medical rescuers at the accident scene, and in Carnahan's conversations conveying medical information regarding Ruth to the hospital base. Cooke, perhaps, did not intrude into that zone of privacy merely by being present at a place where he could hear such conversations with unaided ears. But by placing a microphone on Carnahan's person, amplifying and recording what she said and heard, defendants may have listened in on conversations the parties could reasonably have expected to be private....

Whether Ruth expected her conversations with Nurse Carnahan or the other rescuers to remain private and whether any such expectation was reasonable are, on the state of the record before us, questions for the jury. We note, however, that several existing legal protections for communications could support the conclusion that Ruth possessed a reasonable expectation of privacy in her conversations with Nurse Carnahan and the other rescuers. A patient's conversation with a provider of medical care in the course of treatment including emergency treatment, carries a traditional and legally well-established expectation of privacy....

Ruth's claim requires her...only to prove that she had an objectively reasonable expectation of privacy in her conversations. Whether the circumstances of Ruth's extrication and helicopter rescue would reasonably have indicated to defendants, or to their agent, Cooke, that Ruth would desire and expect her communications to Carnahan and the other rescuers to be confined to them alone, and therefore not to be electronically transmitted and recorded, is a triable issue of fact in this case....

We turn to the second element of the intrusion tort, offensiveness of the intrusion.... The *Miller* court explained that determining offensiveness requires consideration of all the circumstances of the intrusion, including its degree and setting and the intruder's "motives and objectives." The *Miller* court concluded that reasonable people could regard the camera crew's conduct in filming a man's emergency medical treatment in his home, without seeking or obtaining his or his wife's consent, as showing "a cavalier disregard for ordinary citizens' rights of privacy" and, hence, as highly offensive.

We agree with the *Miller* court that all the circumstances of an intrusion, including the motives or justification of the intruder, are pertinent to the offensiveness element. Motivation or justification becomes particularly important when the intrusion is by a member of the print or broadcast press in the pursuit of news material. Although, as will be discussed more fully later, the First Amendment does not immunize the press from liability for torts or crimes committed in an effort to gather news, the constitutional protection of the press does reflect the strong societal interest in effective and complete reporting of events, an interest that may—as a matter of tort

员或者它的媒体代表搭乘救护车，在一个受伤的陌生人接受医疗人员护理的同时盯着看，这既不是我们社会的习俗也不是习惯"。

第二，在事故现场，Ruth 确实对其和 Carnahan 与其他的救援人员的谈话，以及 Carnahan 和医院之间的关于 Ruth 的情况的谈话，享有一定的隐私权。也许仅仅因为 Cooke 在现场，能不带辅助设备就听到这些谈话，我们不能说他就侵犯了 Ruth 的隐私权。但是，Cooke 在 Carnahan 身上装了一个能放大并记录她的话的麦克风，这样被告就能听到那些本来应该是私下进行的谈话。

不管 Ruth 是否期待她与 Carnahan 护士和其他营救者的谈话属于隐私，不管这个期待是否合理，根据我们面前案卷的情况，这属于陪审团的问题。然而，我们注意到，几个已经存在的对谈话的法律保护可支持这样的结论，Ruth 在她与 Carnahan 和其他营救者的谈话中对隐私拥有合理期待。病人在治疗，包括紧急诊治过程中与医疗提供者的对话，是传统的和法律上广泛认可的可期待的隐私……

根据 Ruth 获救时的情况，被告或者其代理人 Cooke，是否应该知道 Ruth 期待 Carnahan 以及其他的救援人员之间与她的谈话要保密，也就是说不能被传播或录音，这应该是一个需要审理的争议焦点。

我们转到侵扰侵权行为的第二个要件，侵扰的冒犯性。……Miller 案中，法院解释道，要确定冒犯性，需要考虑侵扰所有的情节，包括它的程度、背景和侵扰者的"动机和目标"。Miller 案中，法院认为，未寻求或获得他或他妻子的同意下，摄影组在接受紧急医疗的人家里拍摄救助过程的行为，表现出"傲慢地漠视普通民众的隐私权"，因此，理性人可能会认为这具有高度冒犯性。

我们赞同 Miller 案中法院的意见，包括侵扰隐私的动机和正当性在内的所有构成侵扰的情节对冒犯性要件来讲是恰当的。出版和广播机构成员在新闻采集时进行侵扰的，其动机或者正当性就显得格外重要。虽然《美国联邦宪法第一修正案》并未豁免媒体机构努力采集新闻导致的侵权或者犯罪导致的责任，但是对媒体机构的宪法保护确实反映了有效并全面报导事件带来的强大的社会利益，这种利益——作为一个侵权法的法律问题，使本来被认为具有冒犯性的侵扰具有正当性。

因此，在确定记者侵扰私人事项（即物理空间、谈话或者数据）是否具

law—justify an intrusion that would otherwise be considered offensive.

In deciding, therefore, whether a reporter's alleged intrusion into private matters (i.e., physical space, conversation or data) is "offensive" and hence actionable as an invasion of privacy, courts must consider the extent to which the intrusion was, under the circumstances, justified by the legitimate motive of gathering the news. Information collecting techniques that may be highly offensive when done for socially unprotected reasons—for purposes of harassment, blackmail or prurient curiosity, for example—may not be offensive to a reasonable person when employed by journalists in pursuit of a socially or politically important story....

The mere fact the intruder was in pursuit of a "story" does not, however, generally justify an otherwise offensive intrusion; offensiveness depends as well on the particular method of investigation used. At one extreme, " 'routine...reporting techniques,' " such as asking questions of people with information...could rarely, if ever, be deemed an actionable intrusion. At the other extreme, violation of well-established legal areas of physical or sensory privacy—trespass into a home or tapping a personal telephone line, for example—could rarely, if ever, be justified by a reporter's need to get the story. Such acts would be deemed highly offensive even if the information sought was of weighty public concern; they would also be outside any protection the Constitution provides to newsgathering.

Between these extremes lie difficult cases, many involving the use of photographic and electronic recording equipment. Equipment such as hidden cameras and miniature cordless and directional microphones are powerful investigative tools for newsgathering, but may also be used in ways that severely threaten personal privacy. California tort law provides no bright line on this question; each case must be taken on its facts.

On this summary judgment record, we believe a jury could find defendants' recording of Ruth's communications to Carnahan and other rescuers, and filming in the air ambulance, to be " 'highly offensive to a reasonable person.' " With regard to the depth of the intrusion, a reasonable jury could find highly offensive the placement of a microphone on a medical rescuer in order to intercept what would otherwise be private conversations with an injured patient. In that setting, as defendants could and should have foreseen, the patient would not know her words were being recorded and would not have occasion to ask about, and object or consent to, recording. Defendants, it could reasonably be said, took calculated advantage of the patient's "vulnerability and confusion." Arguably, the last thing an injured accident victim should have to worry about while being pried from her wrecked car is that a television producer may be recording everything she says to medical personnel for the possible edification and entertainment of casual television viewers.

For much the same reason, a jury could reasonably regard entering and riding in an ambulance—whether on the ground or in the air—with two seriously injured patients to be an

有"冒犯性",并因此作为侵犯隐私具有可诉性时,法院必须考虑新闻采集的合法性动机在何种程度上使侵扰具有正当性。因为社会所不保护的原因——如以骚扰、敲诈或者淫秽的好奇为目的而进行的信息收集技术可能具有很大的冒犯性,当记者用来调查社会或政治上重要新闻题材时,对理性人来说并不具有冒犯性……

仅仅是侵扰者在追寻"题材"这一事实本身并不一般性地使本来具有冒犯性的侵扰合理化,冒犯也取决于调查所使用的特殊方式。在一个极端,一般性的报道技术,比如询问知情人,很少被认为属于可诉的对隐私的侵犯。在另一个极端,侵犯明确的属于隐私权的领域(可能是物理上的,也可能是感官意义上的)时,比如非法侵入住宅或者窃听他人的电话,仅仅因为记者需要获取题材就被正当化了,这样的情形也是很少的。这些行为被认为具有高度冒犯性,即使获得的信息具有重大公共价值,它们也超出了宪法对新闻采集提供的任何保护。

疑难案件处于这两个极端之间,大多涉及摄像和电子录音设备的使用。隐藏的摄像头和微型无绳定向麦克风在新闻采集中是强有力的工具,但也可以以严重威胁个人隐私的方式使用。加利福尼亚州侵权法对此问题没有明确规定,每个案件都取决于具体事实。

在简易判决案卷中,我们相信陪审团可以认定被告录制 Ruth 与 Carnahan 以及其他救助者谈话,并在空中救护车中录像,"对理性人来讲具有高度冒犯性"。至于侵扰的深度,一个理性的陪审团可以认为,截听救助者配戴麦克风与受伤病人的私人谈话具有高度冒犯性。在那一情境下,被告应该能够预见,病人并不知晓她的谈话被录音,也没有机会询问、反对或者同意是否录音。可以说,被告是有计划地利用了病人的"脆弱与混淆"。存在争议的是,当事故中受伤的受害者在车中被窥探时,她最后一项担心的事情是电视节目制片人录制她对医疗人员说的每句话,目的是让不熟悉的电视观众获得可能的启发和娱乐。

基于同样原因,陪审团可以合理地认为进入并乘坐载着两个严重受伤病人的救护车——不管是在陆地还是在空中——是极其过分的对被期待为隐秘空间的侵扰。再者,至少在本案中,原告很难注意到谁跟随他们,并询问每个人的情况,最后决定同意或反对他们在场。陪审团可以合理地相信,对人

egregious intrusion on a place of expected seclusion. Again, the patients, at least in this case, were hardly in a position to keep careful watch on who was riding with them, or to inquire as to everyone's business and consent or object to their presence. A jury could reasonably believe that fundamental respect for human dignity requires the patients' anxious journey be taken only with those whose care is solely for them and out of sight of the prying eyes (or cameras) of others.

Nor can we say as a matter of law that defendants' motive—to gather usable material for a potentially newsworthy story—necessarily privileged their intrusive conduct as a matter of common law tort liability. A reasonable jury could conclude the producers' desire to get footage that would convey the "feel" of the event—the real sights and sounds of a difficult rescue—did not justify either placing a microphone on Nurse Carnahan or filming inside the rescue helicopter. Although defendants' purposes could scarcely be regarded as evil or malicious (in the colloquial sense), their behavior could, even in light of their motives, be thought to show a highly offensive lack of sensitivity and respect for plaintiffs' privacy. A reasonable jury could find that defendants, in placing a microphone on an emergency treatment nurse and recording her conversation with a distressed, disoriented and severely injured patient, without the patient's knowledge or consent, acted with highly offensive disrespect for the patient's personal privacy comparable to, if not quite as extreme as, the disrespect and insensitivity demonstrated in *Miller*.

Turning to the question of constitutional protection for newsgathering, one finds the decisional law reflects a general rule of *nonprotection:* the press in its newsgathering activities enjoys no immunity or exemption from generally applicable laws. "It is clear that the First Amendment does not invalidate every incidental burdening of the press that may result from the enforcement of civil and criminal laws of general applicability. Under prior cases, otherwise valid laws serving substantial public interests may be enforced against the press as against others, despite the possible burden that may be imposed."…

Defendants enjoyed no constitutional privilege, merely by virtue of their status as members of the news media, to eavesdrop…or otherwise to intrude tortiously on private places, conversations or information.…

As should be apparent from the above discussion, the constitutional protection accorded newsgathering, if any, is far narrower than the protection surrounding the publication of truthful material; consequently, the fact that a reporter may be seeking "newsworthy" material does not in itself privilege the investigatory activity. The reason for the difference is simple: the intrusion tort, unlike that for publication of private facts, does not subject the press to liability for the contents of its publications. Newsworthiness, as we stated earlier, is a complete bar to liability for publication of private facts and is evaluated with a high degree of deference to editorial judgment. The same deference is not due, however, when the issue is not the media's right to publish or broadcast what they choose, but their right to intrude into secluded areas or conversations in pursuit of publishable

的尊严的基本尊重要求在病人忧虑的旅程中只需要必须照顾他们的人陪伴，绝不要被其他眼睛（或者照相机）所窥探。

我们不能说，作为法律问题，被告的为有潜在新闻价值的题材收集有用资料的动机是一个普通法侵权责任问题，有必要使他们的侵扰性行为拥有特免。一个理性的陪审团可以认为，制片人渴望传达事件"感觉"的镜头——一次艰难营救的真实见闻——既不能使Carnahan护士戴耳麦，又不能使在直升机内摄影的行为具有正当性。虽然被告的目的难以被认为是邪恶或者恶毒的（通俗意义上），但是依据他们的动机，他们的行为由于缺乏对原告隐私的感知和尊重显现出高度冒犯性。一个理性的陪审团可以发现，被告让急救护士戴耳麦并录制她与痛苦的、不能辨别方向的、严重受伤的原告之间的谈话，且原告并不知晓或同意的这一不尊重原告个人隐私的行为具有高度冒犯性，即使没有那么极端，与Miller案所展示的无礼和麻木相比也是差不多的。

现在转向新闻采集的宪法保护问题，判例法形成了不予保护的一般性规则：在新闻采集活动中，媒体机构在一般适用的法律上没有豁免或者免除。"清楚的是，宪法第一修正案并未使在执行民事和刑事法律的一般适用中所产生的媒体机构的每一项伴随性负担无效。根据先前判例，保护实质公共利益本应有效的法律可能会同样适用于媒体机构，而不考虑可能会施加的负担"……

仅仅因为他们作为新闻媒体成员的地位，被告不享有任何宪法性特免来窃听……或者侵权性地侵扰私人空间、私人谈话或者信息……

经过上面讨论就应该看出，对新闻采集的宪法保护比对发布真实性材料的法律保护要狭窄得多。结果是，记者寻求有"新闻价值"材料的事实本身并不能使调查活动拥有特免。存在这个区别的原因很简单：不像公开个人隐私，侵扰侵权行为并非因为新闻机构公布的内容而追究其责任。像我们先前所说的，新闻价值性对公开个人隐私的责任是完全阻却的，以对编辑判断的高度尊重来评估。然而，当该争点并非新闻媒体有权发布或者播放，而他们仅有权在追寻可发布的材料时进入隐秘范围或谈话，同样的尊重是不正当的。宪法最多可能会排除"给新闻采集者不能允许的负担"的侵权责任。

material. At most, the Constitution may preclude tort liability that would "place an impermissible burden on newsgatherers."

Defendants urge a rule more protective of press investigative activity. Specifically, they seek a holding that "when intrusion claims are brought in the context of newsgathering conduct, that conduct be deemed protected so long as (1) the information being gathered is about a matter of legitimate concern to the public and (2) the underlying conduct is lawful (i.e., was undertaken without fraud, trespass, etc.)." Neither tort law nor constitutional precedent and policy supports such a broad privilege.

As to constitutional policy, we repeat that the threat of infringement on the liberties of the press from intrusion liability is minor compared with the threat from liability for publication of private facts....But no constitutional precedent or principle of which we are aware gives a reporter general license to intrude in an objectively offensive manner into private places, conversations or matters merely because the reporter thinks he or she may thereby find something that will warrant publication or broadcast.

Conclusion...

The state may not intrude into the proper sphere of the news media to dictate what they should publish and broadcast, but neither may the media play tyrant to the people by unlawfully spying on them in the name of newsgathering. Summary judgment for the defense was...improper as to the cause of action for invasion of privacy by intrusion....

Chin, Justice,...dissenting....

I dissent...from the plurality's holding that plaintiffs' "intrusion" cause of action should be remanded for trial....

Ruth's expectations notwithstanding, I do not believe that a reasonable trier of fact could find that defendants' conduct in this case was "highly offensive to a reasonable person," the test adopted by the plurality. Plaintiffs do not allege that defendants, though present at the accident rescue scene and in the helicopter, interfered with either the rescue or medical efforts, elicited embarrassing or offensive information from plaintiffs, or even tried to interrogate or interview them. Defendants' news team evidently merely recorded newsworthy events "of legitimate public concern" as they transpired. Defendants' apparent motive in undertaking the supposed privacy invasion was a reasonable and nonmalicious one: to obtain an accurate depiction of the rescue efforts from start to finish. The event was newsworthy, and the ultimate broadcast was both dramatic and educational, rather than tawdry or embarrassing.

No illegal trespass on private property occurred, and any technical illegality arising from defendants' recording Ruth's conversations with medical personnel was not so "highly offensive" as to justify liability. Recording the innocuous, inoffensive conversations that occurred between Ruth and the nurse assisting her and filming the seemingly routine, though certainly newsworthy,

被告寻求对媒体机构调查性活动保护性更强的规则。特别是，他们寻求认定"当在新闻采集背景下提起侵扰诉讼时，行为只要满足如下要求即被认为应该得到保护：（1）采集的信息是关于公众合法关注的事项；（2）基本行为是合法的（即没有以欺骗、侵入等方式从事）"。不管是侵权法还是宪法先例以及法律目的都不支持这种宽泛的特免。

至于宪法性法律目的，我们重申，因侵扰责任带来的侵犯媒体自由的威胁，比公开私人事务责任的威胁要小……但我们并未找到我们知晓的任何宪法判例或者其原则，仅仅因为记者认为他或她的一些发现有必要出版或播放，就给他或她以客观上冒犯性的方式侵扰私人空间、谈话或事项以概括许可。

结论……

州不应侵扰新闻媒体的合适领域去指示应该发布和播放的内容，新闻媒体也不能专断地以新闻采集的名义非法窥探人们的生活。对以侵扰方式侵犯隐私的诉因作出利于被告方的简易判决……并不合适……

Chin 法官……撰写反对意见……：

我反对……原告"侵扰"诉因被发回重审的相对多数意见……

虽然 Ruth 存有期待，但是我不相信一个理性的事实认定者会认为本案中被告的行为对理性人"具有高度冒犯性"，这是相对多数意见所适用的标准。原告并未主张被告在事故营救现场和直升机内，干扰了营救或者医疗上的努力，从原告那里得到了令人尴尬或冒犯性的信息，甚至试图询问或采访他们。被告的新闻小组很明显仅仅在录制发生的有新闻价值的正如被人们所知的"公众合法关注"的事件。在从事这一被认为是侵犯隐私的行为中，被告明显的动机是合理且非恶意的：期望准确描述从头到尾的营救努力。该事件具有新闻价值，最终的播放既引人注目又很有教育意义，而非拖沓或者令人尴尬。

没有发生任何对私有财产的侵入，被告录制 Ruth 与医疗人员谈话导致的任何技术上的非法性并未具有如此"高度冒犯性"而足以导致责任。录制 Ruth 和陪同护士之间无伤大雅的、非冒犯性的谈话，看似常规却当然具有新闻价值，搭乘直升机可能从技术上侵犯了原告的私人"空间"，但我认为并未"高度冒犯性地"侵犯他们的隐私。

helicopter ride may have technically invaded plaintiffs' private "space," but in my view no "highly offensive" invasion of their privacy occurred.

We should bear in mind we are not dealing here with a true "interception"—e.g., a surreptitious wiretap by a third party—of words spoken in a truly private place—e.g., in a psychiatrist's examining room, an attorney's office, or a priest's confessional. Rather, here the broadcast showed Ruth speaking in settings where others could hear her, and the fact that she did not realize she was being recorded does not ipso facto transform defendants' newsgathering procedures into *highly* offensive conduct within the meaning of the law of intrusion.

In short, to turn a jury loose on the defendants in this case is itself "highly offensive" to me. I would reverse the judgment of the Court of Appeal with directions to affirm the summary judgment for defendants on all causes of action.

98. Godbehere v. Phoenix Newspapers, Inc., 162 Ariz. 335, 783 P.2d 781 (1989)

Supreme Court of Arizona, United States

Feldman, Vice Chief Justice.

Richard G. Godbehere, a former Maricopa County Sheriff, and several deputies and civilian employees of the sheriff's office (plaintiffs) brought this action against Phoenix Newspapers, Inc., the publisher of The Arizona Republic and Phoenix Gazette, and fourteen editors and reporters of the two newspapers (publishers), for libel and false light invasion of privacy. The trial court granted publishers' motion to dismiss for failure to state a claim as to the invasion of privacy claims, but refused to dismiss the other counts of the complaint. Plaintiffs appealed and the court of appeals affirmed. We granted review to determine whether Arizona should recognize a cause of action for false light invasion of privacy, and if so, what the proper standard should be....

Facts

In the spring and summer of 1985, publishers printed over fifty articles, editorials, and columns (the publications) about plaintiffs' various law enforcement activities. The publications stated that the plaintiffs engaged in illegal activities, staged narcotics arrests to generate publicity, illegally arrested citizens, misused public funds and resources, committed police brutality, and generally were incompetent at law enforcement. Plaintiffs alleged in their eighteen-count complaint that the publications were false, damaged their reputations, harmed them in their profession, and caused them emotional distress. Publishers moved to dismiss all eighteen counts of the complaint for failure to state a claim, and the court dismissed the false light invasion of privacy claims....

On appeal, plaintiffs argued that Arizona should follow the Restatement (Second) of Torts §652E (1977) (hereafter Restatement), which provides in part:

我们应该记住，我们并非在处理真正的"拦截信号"问题。例如，第三方偷偷窃听真正私人空间的谈话，比如精神病医生的检查室、律师办公室或者牧师的忏悔室。这里，广播播放了 Ruth 在能被他人听到的情境中的谈话，她未意识到她在被录音，根据事实本身并不会使被告的新闻采集程序变成侵扰法律意义上的高度冒犯性的行为。

总之，放任陪审团对本案被告判决本身，对我就是"高度冒犯性的"。我宁可撤销上诉法院的判决，并给出对所有诉因维持有利于被告的简易判决的指示。

98. Godbehere v. Phoenix Newspapers, Inc., 162 Ariz. 335, 783 P.2d 781 (1989)

美国亚利桑那州最高法院

Feldman 副大法官主笔：

前 Maricopa 县行政司法官 Richard G. Godbehere、司法官办公室的几位副手和文职雇员（以下简称"原告"），对 Phoenix Newspapers, Inc. 和 The Arizona Republic and Phoenix Gazette 的出版商以及两家报社的 14 名编辑和记者（以下简称"出版商"）基于书面诽谤和歪曲暴露侵犯隐私提起诉讼。初审法院以起诉理由不足为由准许出版商的驳回侵犯个人隐私诉讼的申请，但拒绝驳回起诉状的其他诉因。原告提起上诉，上诉法院维持原判。我们同意司法审查以确定亚利桑那州是否应该认可歪曲暴露侵犯隐私的诉因，以及如果认可，那么合适的标准是什么……

事实

1985 年春夏，出版商刊登了关于原告各种执法活动的超过 50 篇的文章、社论和专栏文章（以下简称"出版物"）。这些出版物表明，原告从事非法活动、使用麻醉逮捕引起公众注意、非法逮捕公民、滥用公共基金和资源、犯有警察暴行，总体来说无能力胜任执法工作。原告在他们 18 项诉因的起诉状中称，这些出版物是虚假的，损害了他们的名誉，给他们的职业带来伤害，并且导致精神损害。出版商以起诉理由不足为由申请驳回起诉状的全部 18 项诉因。法院驳回了歪曲暴露侵犯隐私的诉因……

上诉中，原告主张，亚利桑那州应该遵循 1977 年《侵权法重述·第二次》第 652E 条，该条部分地作出了规定：

One who gives publicity to a matter concerning another that places the other before the public in a false light is subject to liability to the other for invasion of his privacy, if

(a) the false light in which the other was placed would be highly offensive to a reasonable person, and

(b) the actor had knowledge of or acted in reckless disregard as to the falsity of the publicized matter and the false light in which the other would be placed.

Discussion...

B. Privacy in Arizona

Arizona first recognized an action for invasion of privacy in Reed v. Real Detective Publishing Co., 63 Ariz. 294, 162 P.2d 133 (1945). Reed involved the unauthorized publication of the plaintiff's photograph. Subsequently, our court of appeals recognized the Restatement's four-part classification of the tort.

Although most jurisdictions that recognize a cause of action for invasion of privacy have adopted the Restatement standard of "highly offensive to a reasonable person" or a similar standard, Arizona courts of appeals' decisions have imposed a stricter standard. Rather than following the Restatement, these decisions have held that where the damage alleged is emotional, the plaintiff must prove the elements of the tort of intentional infliction of emotional distress in addition to proving invasion of privacy. To recover for invasion of privacy, a plaintiff must show that the defendant's conduct was "extreme and outrageous." No other state requires a plaintiff to prove that the defendant committed "outrage" in a false light action.

Publishers urge this court to adopt the court of appeals' view. They argue that there is no need for an independent tort of false light invasion of privacy because the action overlaps two other recognized torts: defamation and intentional infliction of emotional distress. These, publishers contend, cover the field and permit recovery in meritorious cases, thus making the false light action an unnecessary burden on the media's first amendment rights. To consider this argument, we must examine the distinctions between the false light action and the torts of intentional infliction of emotional distress and defamation.

C. False Light Invasion of Privacy and Intentional Infliction of Emotional Distress

Arizona has turned to Restatement §46 to define intentional infliction of emotional distress, also known as the tort of outrage. This section provides:

(1) one who by extreme and outrageous conduct intentionally or recklessly causes severe emotional distress to another is subject to liability for such emotional distress, and if bodily harm to the other results from it, for such bodily harm.

如果一个人公开了一件事。这件事会歪曲他人的形象，则该人因侵犯他人的隐私而对其承担责任，如果：

（a）将该他人置于歪曲暴露对理性的人来说是高度冒犯的；且

（b）该行为人知道或者极其漠视该被公开事务的虚假性，以及该他人将被歪曲暴露。

讨论……

B. 亚利桑那州的隐私

亚利桑那州首次在 Reed v. Real Detective Publishing Co., 63 Ariz. 294, 162 P.2d 133（1945）案中确认了侵犯个人隐私的诉讼。Reed 未经原告授权刊登了原告的照片。结果，我们的上诉法院认可了《侵权法重述·第二次》对侵权行为的四分法分类。

虽然多数认可侵犯隐私诉因的法域，都已经采纳了《侵权法重述·第二次》的"理性人高度冒犯性"标准或类似标准，但是亚利桑那州上诉法院的判决采用了更严厉的标准。这些判决没有遵循《侵权法重述·第二次》，认为如果主张精神损害赔偿，原告不仅要证明侵犯了隐私，还必须证明故意导致精神损害的构成要件。原告因侵犯隐私而获得赔偿，就必须证明被告的行为是"极端且令人难以忍受的"。没有任何州要求原告在歪曲暴露诉讼中证明被告犯下"暴行"。

出版商敦促本法院采纳上诉法院的观点。他们主张，歪曲暴露侵犯隐私没有必要成为独立侵权行为，因为该诉因与已被认可的两类侵权行为相重叠：诽谤和故意导致精神损害。出版商主张，值得称赞的案例中已经涵盖了该领域并允许获得救济，因此，歪曲暴露是对媒体的《宪法第一修正案》所设立的权利的不必要负担。要考察这一主张，我们必须审查歪曲暴露侵犯隐私行为与故意导致精神损害侵权行为及诽谤侵权行为的区别。

C. 歪曲暴露侵犯隐私与故意导致精神损害

亚利桑那州通过《侵权法重述·第二次》第 46 条来定义故意导致精神损害，也被称为暴行侵权行为。该条规定：

（1）以极端且令人难以忍受的行为故意或鲁莽地使他人遭受严重的精神痛苦的人，应对该精神痛苦承担责任；如果因此导致身体上的伤害，也应就该身体上的伤害承担责任。

The element of "extreme and outrageous conduct" requires that plaintiff prove defendant's conduct exceeded "all bounds usually tolerated by decent society...and caused mental distress of a very serious kind."...

Publishers emphasize that actions for both intentional infliction of emotional distress and invasion of privacy provide compensation for emotional distress or damage to sensibility. Thus, the injury from both torts is similar. Although this may be true, the fact that two different actions address the same injury is no reason to refuse to recognize torts that protect against different wrongful conduct. For example, three victims may suffer broken legs in the following ways: (1) a defendant negligently drives a car into the first victim's car; (2) a defendant's defective product injures the second victim; and (3) a defendant, without justification, attacks the third. Each victim would have a different tort claim: negligence, strict liability, and battery. The fact that each victim suffers the same type of injury does not preclude recognizing separate tort actions. Each tort theory developed separately to deter and provide redress against a different type of wrongful conduct.

Thus, the fact that outrage and invasion of privacy both provide redress for emotional injury does not persuade us that the actions are "merged" or that plaintiffs should be required to prove the former in an action for the latter. The outrage tort protects against conduct so extreme that it would induce "an average member of the community...to exclaim, 'outrageous!'" Restatement §46 Comment *d*. False light invasion of privacy, however, protects against the conduct of knowingly or recklessly publishing false information or innuendo that a "reasonable person" would find "highly offensive." Although false publication may constitute outrageous conduct and vice versa, it is also true that the same wrongful conduct will not always satisfy the elements of both tort actions. Because each action protects against a different type of tortious conduct, each has its place, and the common injury should not abrogate the action.

Nor do we believe that recognizing the false light action without requiring plaintiffs to prove outrage will circumvent the "stringent standards" of the emotional distress tort. The standards for proving false light invasion of privacy are quite "stringent" by themselves. For example, the plaintiff in a false light case must prove that the defendant published with knowledge of the falsity or reckless disregard for the truth. This standard is as stringent as the intentional infliction of emotional distress requirement that the plaintiff prove the defendant "intentionally or recklessly caused" the emotional distress....

We conclude, therefore, that the two torts exist to redress different types of wrongful conduct. Situations exist where a jury could find the defendant's publication of false information or innuendo was not outrageous but did satisfy the false light elements. Thus, we believe the tort action for false light invasion of privacy provides protection against a narrow class of wrongful conduct that falls short of "outrage," but nevertheless should be deterred.

"极端且令人难以忍受的行为"的要件,要求原告证明,被告行为超过了"正当社会所通常能容忍的程度……以一种非常严重的方式导致精神痛苦"……

出版商强调,故意导致精神损害和侵犯隐私诉因都为精神痛苦和情感伤害提供赔偿。因此,两种侵权的伤害是相似的。虽然这可能是正确的,但是两个不同诉因救济同样的伤害这一事实,不能使拒绝认可针对不同不法行为的侵权行为具有任何理由。如三个受害人以以下方式遭受断腿:(1)被告过失地开车撞上了第一个受害人的车;(2)被告有缺陷的产品伤害了第二个受害人;(3)被告毫无正当理由地攻击了第三个受害人。每个受害人都将有不同的侵权诉讼:过失、严格责任和殴击。每个受害人遭受同等类型的伤害这一事实并不会妨碍认可单独的侵权行为类型。每一侵权理论都单独发展去阻吓不同的不法行为并提供救济。

因此,暴行和侵犯隐私诉因都为精神伤害提供救济,这一事实并不能说服我们,我们认为,诉讼应合并或者原告应该在前一诉讼中被要求证明后一诉讼中应证明的内容。暴行侵权保护受极端行为侵害的对象,它会导致"社区的一般成员……惊呼'令人难以忍受'!"参见《侵权法重述·第二次》第46条评论d。而歪曲暴露侵犯隐私,防范了被"理性人"认为是"高度冒犯的"有意识地或者鲁莽地发布虚假信息或隐射的行为。虽然虚假发布也可能是令人难以忍受的行为,但是反之亦然。同样正确的是,同一个不法行为不会总是满足两种侵权诉因的构成要件。因为每种诉因都针对不同的侵权行为,各自为政,共同的伤害不应废除诉因。

我们也不相信,不要求原告证明暴行而认可歪曲暴露诉因,会绕开精神损害侵权行为的"严格标准"。歪曲暴露侵犯隐私的证明标准本身就很"严格"。例如,原告在一起歪曲暴露的案件中,必须证明被告知晓虚假或者极其漠视真实性而发布。这一标准与故意导致精神损害中,要求原告能够证明被告"故意或鲁莽地"导致精神损害一样严格……

我们因此认为,这两种侵权行为独立存在以矫正不同的不法行为。陪审团可认定被告公开披露虚假信息或隐射并非令人难以忍受,但的确满足了歪曲暴露的构成要件。因此,我们相信侵犯隐私的歪曲暴露诉讼的侵权是针对一小类并非"暴行"、但仍应被阻吓的不法行为。

D. Invasion of Privacy and Defamation

A second argument advanced by publishers is that little distinction exists between a tort action for false light invasion of privacy and one for defamation. Thus, because defamation actions are available, they argue, Arizona need not recognize false light invasion of privacy. Again, we disagree

Although both defamation and false light invasion of privacy involve publication, the nature of the interests protected by each action differs substantially. A defamation action compensates damage to reputation or good name caused by the publication of false information. To be defamatory, a publication must be false and must bring the defamed person into disrepute, contempt, or ridicule, or must impeach plaintiff's honesty, integrity, virtue, or reputation.

Privacy, on the other hand, does not protect reputation but protects mental and emotional interests. Under this theory, a plaintiff may recover even in the absence of reputational damage, as long as the publicity is unreasonably offensive and attributes false characteristics. However, to qualify as a false light invasion of privacy, the publication must involve "a major misrepresentation of the plaintiff's character, history, activities or beliefs," not merely minor or unimportant inaccuracies. Restatement §652E Comment *c*.

Another distinction between defamation and false light invasion of privacy is the role played by truth. To be defamatory, a publication must be false, and truth is a defense. A false light cause of action may arise when something untrue has been published about an individual, or when the publication of true information creates a false implication about the individual. In the latter type of case, the false innuendo created by the highly offensive presentation of a true fact constitutes the injury.

Thus, although defamation and false light often overlap, they serve very different objectives. The two tort actions deter different conduct and redress different wrongs. A plaintiff may bring a false light invasion of privacy action even though the publication is not defamatory, and even though the actual facts stated are true....

F. Free Speech Considerations

As in defamation, a public official in a false light action must always show that the defendant published with knowledge of the false innuendo or with reckless disregard of the truth. Any doubt about the application of the actual malice element of the false light tort to public figures has been eliminated. In Hustler Magazine, Inc. v. Falwell, 485 U.S. 46, 108 S. Ct. 876, 99 L. Ed. 2d 41 (1988), the Supreme Court held that a public figure plaintiff must prove Times v. Sullivan actual malice in order to recover for intentional infliction of emotional distress. Although *Hustler* was an intentional infliction case, the language used by the Court is so broad that it applies to any tort action relating to free speech, particularly "in the area of public debate about public figures." See *Hustler,* 485 U.S. at 53, 108 S. Ct. at 881. Additional protection for free speech comes from the principle that

D. 侵犯隐私与诽谤

出版商提出的第二项主张是，歪曲暴露侵犯隐私的侵权行为与诽谤侵权行为区别很小。他们因此主张，由于诽谤诉因是可行的，亚利桑那州不需要确认歪曲暴露侵犯隐私诉因。我们仍不同意。

一方面，虽然诽谤和歪曲暴露侵犯隐私都涉及发布，但是每种诉因所保护的利益本质不同。诽谤诉因是对因发布虚假信息所造成的名誉或者好名声的损失而进行补偿。要构成诽谤，发布内容必须是虚假的，必须使被诽谤的人声名狼藉，被轻视或者被奚落，或者怀疑原告的诚实、正直、道德或名誉。

另一方面，隐私并不保护名誉而保护精神和情感利益。在这一理论之下，即使原告名誉没有遭受损失，只要发布是不合理冒犯且具有虚假的特征，原告就可获得赔偿。然而，作为歪曲暴露侵犯隐私的侵权行为，发布必须涉及"原告品质、历史、行为或信仰的重要虚假陈述"，而不仅仅是轻微的或者不重要的、不准确的。参见《侵权法重述·第二次》第652E条评论c。

诽谤和歪曲暴露侵犯隐私的另一区别是真实性所起到的作用。要构成诽谤，发布内容必须是虚假的，真实性构成抗辩。发布个人不真实信息可导致歪曲暴露侵犯隐私诉讼成立，或者发布个人真实信息产生虚假含义也可构成歪曲暴露。在后一种案件中，具有高度冒犯性的真实信息所产生的虚假隐射也构成损害。

因此，虽然诽谤和歪曲暴露侵犯隐私经常重叠，但是它们服务于不同的目标。两种不同的侵权诉因阻吓不同的行为，矫正不同的不法行为。即使发布内容并非诽谤性的，阐述的实际事实也是真实的，原告仍可以提起歪曲暴露侵犯隐私诉讼……

F. 言论自由的考虑

如同在诽谤诉讼中，歪曲暴露侵犯隐私诉讼中的公职官员，必须证明被告知晓虚假隐射或者极端漠视的真实性。任何对公众人物歪曲暴露侵犯隐私的侵权行为适用实质恶意要件的疑虑已经被消除。联邦最高法院在 Hustler Magazine, Inc. v. Falwell, 485 U. S. 46, 108 S. Ct. 876, 99 L. Ed. 2d 41（1988）案中，判决作为公众人物的原告必须证明 Times v. Sullivan 案中的实质恶意，才能基于故意导致精神损害而获得赔偿。虽然 Hustler 案是故意致害案件，但是法院使用的语言如此广泛以至于可适用于与言论自由相关的任何侵权诉因，特别是"对公众人物公开争论的一些领域"。参见 Hustler, 485 U. S. at 53, 108 S. Ct. at 881。对言论自

protection for privacy interests generally applies only to private matters....

G. Is False Light Available in This Case?

Finally, publishers contended that even if we recognize false light actions, the action does not lie in this case. They argue that not only do the publications discuss matters of public interest, but plaintiffs have no right of privacy with respect to the manner in which they perform their official duties. We agree....

A number of jurisdictions take the position that because false light is a form of invasion of privacy, it must relate only to the private affairs of the plaintiff and cannot involve matters of public interest. It is difficult to conceive of an area of greater public interest than law enforcement. Certainly the public has a legitimate interest in the manner in which law enforcement officers perform their duties. Therefore, we hold that there can be no false light invasion of privacy action for matters involving official acts or duties of public officers.

Consequently, we adopt the following legal standard: A plaintiff cannot sue for false light invasion of privacy if he or she is a public official and the publication relates to performance of his or her public life or duties. We do not go so far as to say, however, that a public official has no privacy rights at all and may never bring an action for invasion of privacy. Certainly, if the publication presents the public official's private life in a false light, he or she can sue under the false light tort, although actual malice must be shown.

The Supreme Court has held that "the public official designation applies at the very least to those among the hierarchy of government employees who have, or appear to the public to have, substantial responsibility for or control over the conduct of governmental affairs." Rosenblatt v. Baer, 383 U.S. 75, 85, 86 S. Ct. 669, 676, 15 L. Ed. 2d 597 (1966). Police and other law enforcement personnel are almost always classified as public officials. The publications at issue concern the discharge of their public duties and do not relate to private affairs. Therefore, plaintiffs have no claim for false light invasion of privacy.

We affirm the trial court's dismissal of the false light claim. Because we disagree with the court of appeals' reasoning, we vacate that opinion and remand to the trial court for further proceedings consistent with this opinion.

Section 2. Invasion of Privacy in English Law

99. Wainwright v Home Office [2003] UKHL 53, [2004] 2 AC 406

House of Lords, United Kingdom

LORD HOFFMANN

[15] My Lords, let us first consider the proposed tort of invasion of privacy. Since the famous

由的额外保护产生于对隐私利益的保护只限于私人事项的原则……

歪曲暴露适用于本案吗？

最后，出版商争辩道，即使我们认可歪曲暴露侵犯隐私诉因，它也不适用于本案。他们主张，不仅是出版物讨论的公共利益事项，还有原告履行公职的方式都使他们没有隐私权。我们同意……

一些法域持有如下立场，即因为歪曲暴露是侵犯隐私的形式之一，它必须只与原告的私人事项有关，不能涉及公共利益事项。很难想象还有比执法更重要的公共利益领域了。当然，公众在执法人员履行职责的方式中存在合法利益。因此，我们认定，涉及公职行为或者公务人员职责的事项不存在歪曲暴露侵犯隐私诉因。

结果，我们采纳以下法律标准：如果他或她是公职官员，出版物是关于他或她的公共生活或职责的履行，那么原告不能提起歪曲暴露侵犯隐私诉讼。然而，我们不能走得太远去说，公职官员根本没有隐私权，且可能永远不能提起侵犯隐私的诉讼。当然，如果出版物以他人歪曲暴露的方式展示了公职官员的私生活，他或她可以针对歪曲暴露侵犯隐私的侵权行为提起诉讼，但必须证明实质恶意。

联邦最高法院判决，"公职官员头衔适用于那些至少是属于对于实施政府事务行为负有重要责任或具有控制权，或对于公众来说看起来是如此的政府雇员层次的政府雇员"。Rosenblatt v. Baer, 383 U. S. 75, 85, 86 S. Ct. 669, 676, 15 L. Ed. 2d 597（1966）案。警署和其他执法部门一直被认定为公职官员系列。存在争议的出版物涉及披露他们的公共义务，与私人事务没有关系。因此，原告不能提起歪曲暴露侵犯隐私诉讼。

我们维持初审法院对歪曲暴露侵犯隐私诉讼的驳回。因为我们不同意上诉法院的分析，我们废止其意见书，发回初审法院依据本意见书进一步审理。

第二节 英国法上的侵犯隐私之诉

99. Wainwright v Home Office [2003] UKHL 53, [2004] 2 AC 406

联合王国上议院

Hoffmann 大法官主笔：

[15] 诸位大法官，我们先来考察一下所谓的"侵犯隐私之诉"。自从 Warren 和 Brandeis 那篇著名的论文《隐私权》[*"The Right to Privacy"*（1890）

article by Warren and Brandeis ("The Right to Privacy" (1890) 4 Harvard LR 193) the question of whether such a tort exists, or should exist, has been much debated in common law jurisdictions. Warren and Brandeis suggested that one could generalise certain cases on defamation, breach of copyright in unpublished letters, trade secrets and breach of confidence as all based upon the protection of a common value which they called privacy or, following Judge Cooley (Cooley on Torts, 2nd ed (1888), p 29) "the right to be let alone". They said that identifying this common element should enable the courts to declare the existence of a general principle which protected a person's appearance, sayings, acts and personal relations from being exposed in public.

[16] Courts in the United States were receptive to this proposal and a jurisprudence of privacy began to develop. It became apparent, however, that the developments could not be contained within a single principle; not, at any rate, one with greater explanatory power than the proposition that it was based upon the protection of a value which could be described as privacy. Dean Prosser, in his work on *The Law of Torts,* 4th ed (1971), p 804, said that:

> "What has emerged is no very simple matter ... it is not one tort, but a complex of four. To date the law of privacy comprises four distinct kinds of invasion of four different interests of the plaintiff, which are tied together by the common name, but otherwise have almost nothing in common except that each represents an interference with the right of the plaintiff 'to be let alone'."

[17] Dean Prosser's taxonomy divided the subject into (1) intrusion upon the plaintiff's physical solitude or seclusion (including unlawful searches, telephone tapping, long-distance photography and telephone harassment) (2) public disclosure of private facts and (3) publicity putting the plaintiff in a false light and (4) appropriation, for the defendant's advantage, of the plaintiff's name or likeness. These, he said, at p 814, had different elements and were subject to different defences.

[18] The need in the United States to break down the concept of "invasion of privacy" into a number of loosely-linked torts must cast doubt upon the value of any high-level generalisation which can perform a useful function in enabling one to deduce the rule to be applied in a concrete case. English law has so far been unwilling, perhaps unable, to formulate any such high-level principle. There are a number of common law and statutory remedies of which it may be said that one at least of the underlying values they protect is a right of privacy. Sir Brian Neill's well known article "Privacy: a challenge for the next century" in Protecting Privacy (ed B Markesinis, 1999) contains a survey. Common law torts include trespass, nuisance, defamation and malicious falsehood; there is the equitable action for breach of confidence and statutory remedies under the Protection from Harassment Act 1997 and the Data Protection Act 1998. There are also extra-legal

4 Harvard LR 193〕发表以来,这种诉由是否存在于实在法上,或者是否应该存在,在普通法国家一直以来都是个有争议的问题。Warren 和 Brandeis 认为,我们可以把一些诽谤案、未公开发表信件中的侵犯版权案、侵犯商业秘密案、侵犯保密协议案等概括为对某种共同价值的保护,这种共同价值被称为隐私,或者按照 Cooley 法官的说法,"不受干扰的权利"(《Cooley 说侵权法》,1888 年第二版,第 29 页)。他们认为确定了这种共同价值,就可以让法院确认一种一般原则的存在,这种原则能保护一个人的外表、言论、行为和人际关系不会被暴露在公众面前。

[16] 美国法院接受了这样的观点,并且发展出了有关隐私的一个判例法系统。然而,非常清楚的是,这套系统是不能被一个统一的原则所涵盖的;至少一个统一的原则的解释力并不大于那种认为这套系统是为了保护多个被称为隐私的价值的观点的。Prosser 院长在其著作《侵权法》第四版(1971)第 804 页中说:

> 这个领域的发展不是一件简单的事……并不是只有一种侵权之诉,而是有四种。今天,隐私领域的侵权规则其实调整的是对四种不同的原告权利的侵犯。这四种侵权行为共享一个名字,但是除此之外其实并没有什么共同点,除了一点,就是它们都是"不受干扰的权利"的推论。

[17] Prosser 院长将侵犯隐私分为以下几种情况:第一是侵入原告的私人空间(包括非法搜查、电话窃听、在较远距离拍摄或者电话骚扰);第二是向公众泄露私人事实;第三是错误报道他人隐私;第四是为了被告的利益盗用原告的姓名或类似之事务。他在《侵权法》第四版(1971)第 814 页认为这些不同的侵犯隐私的类型有不同构成要件和抗辩事由。

[18] 在美国,侵犯隐私权这个概念需要被分解成几个相关性很弱的侵权类型,这让人怀疑一个(称为"侵犯隐私"的)上位概念的价值:(这个概念本来的)作用是为了让人在遇到具体案件的时候能从(给定的上位规则中)抽象出适用的规则。英格兰法到目前为止并不愿意去构建这样的上位规则,当然也可能是由于没有能力这么做。普通法和成文法上有许多的救济措施,这些救济措施所保护的价值,至少可以说其中之一是跟隐私有关的权利。Brian Neill 爵士所著的著名论文《隐私:下个世纪的挑战》(载《保护隐私》,B Markesinis 编著,1999)一文列举了这些措施。普通法上的诉由有人身侵害、妨害、诽谤和恶意虚假陈述;衡

remedies under Codes of Practice applicable to broadcasters and newspapers. But there are gaps; cases in which the courts have considered that an invasion of privacy deserves a remedy which the existing law does not offer. Sometimes the perceived gap can be filled by judicious development of an existing principle. The law of breach of confidence has in recent years undergone such a process: see in particular the judgment of Lord Phillips of Worth Matravers MR in *Campbell v MGN Ltd* [2003] QB 633. On the other hand, an attempt to create a tort of telephone harassment by a radical change in the basis of the action for private nuisance in *Khorasandjian v Bush* [1993] QB 727 was held by the House of Lords in *Hunter v Canary Wharf Ltd* [1997] AC 655 to be a step too far. The gap was filled by the 1997 Act.

[19] What the courts have so far refused to do is to formulate a general principle of "invasion of privacy"? (I use the quotation marks to signify doubt about what in such a context the expression would mean) from which the conditions of liability in the particular case can be deduced.

...

[32] Nor is there anything in the jurisprudence of the European Court of Human Rights which suggests that the adoption of some high level principle of privacy is necessary to comply with article 8 of the Convention. The European Court is concerned only with whether English law provides an adequate remedy in a specific case in which it considers that there has been an invasion of privacy contrary to article 8(1) and not justifiable under article 8(2) . So in *Earl Spencer v United Kingdom* 25 EHRR CD 105 it was satisfied that the action for breach of confidence provided an adequate remedy for the Spencers' complaint and looked no further into the rest of the armoury of remedies available to the victims of other invasions of privacy. Likewise, in *Peck v United Kingdom* (2003) 36 EHRR 719 the court expressed some impatience, at paragraph 103, at being given a tour d'horizon of the remedies provided and to be provided by English law to deal with every imaginable kind of invasion of privacy. It was concerned with whether Mr Peck (who had been filmed in embarrassing circumstances by a CCTV camera) had an adequate remedy when the film was widely published by the media. It came to the conclusion that he did not.

[33] Counsel for the Wainwrights relied upon Peck's case as demonstrating the need for a general tort of invasion of privacy. But in my opinion it shows no more than the need, in English law, for a system of control of the use of film from CCTV cameras which shows greater sensitivity to the feelings of people who happen to have been caught by the lens. For the reasons so cogently explained by Sir Robert Megarry V-C in *Malone v Metropolitan Police Comr* [1979] Ch 344, this is an area which requires a detailed approach which can be achieved only by legislation rather than the broad brush of common law principle.

[34] Furthermore, the coming into force of the Human Rights Act 1998 weakens the argument for saying that a general tort of invasion of privacy is needed to fill gaps in the existing remedies. Sections 6 and 7 of the Act are in themselves substantial gap fillers; if it is indeed the

平法上的诉由则是违反保密义务；提供救济措施的成文法是《1997年防止骚扰法》和《1998年数据保护法》。适用于广播业和报社的《操作守则》也提供了一些法律以外的救济途径。然而法律漏洞依然存在；法庭认为，有些案件依然存在侵犯隐私的情况，也应该提供救济，但是现行法却没有提供救济。有时候法官在发现这种漏洞之后，可以通过发展现行法上已有的原则来填补漏洞。调整违反保密义务的规范中，法官就是这么做的：特别参见 Phillips 大法官在 *Campbell v MGN Ltd* [2003] QB 633 案中的意见。但是，当 *Khorasandjian v Bush* [1993] QB 727 尝试通过激进地改变私有妨害之诉的构成要件而创建一种新的电话骚扰之诉时，上诉法院在 *Hunter v Canary Wharf Ltd* [1997] AC 655 案中却判决这种尝试太过了。这个漏洞是在1997年《防止骚扰法》中才被填上的。

[19] 英格兰法院到目前为止拒绝建构一种通用的"侵犯隐私"的原则（我之所以打上引号，是因为这个词语在这种情况下到底是什么意思，我尚有疑问）并根据这个原则演绎得出某个具体案件中责任的要件。

……

[32] 欧洲人权法院的判例也并不认为其成员国的法律中必须存在某种高位阶的隐私权原则，才符合《公约》第8条的规定。欧洲法院所关心的，只是具体案件中英格兰法是否为违反《公约》第8条第1款且无法为第8条第2款所正当化的侵犯隐私的行为提供足够的救济。在 *Earl Spencer v United Kingdom* 25 EHRR CD 105 案中，欧洲法院满足于"违反保密义务之诉"已经足够为 Spencers 提供救济了，因此并没有更进一步去考察其他类型的侵犯隐私行为的受害者到底能获得什么样的救济措施。类似的，在 *Peck v United Kingdom*（2003）36 EHRR 719 案中，欧洲法院在判决书第103段表示了某种不满，因为当事人给他们列举了一长串英格兰法已经提供或者将要提供的，应对每一种能想到的隐私侵权类型的救济措施。该案的关键是，当拍到 Peck 先生的视频在媒体上广泛流传的时候，他是否有足够的救济措施（Peck 先生被闭路电视拍到了很尴尬的场面）。欧洲法院的结论是他没有足够的救济措施。

[33] Wainwright 一家的律师以 Peck 案为依据主张我们是多么需要一种一般性的侵权之诉。然而在我看来，这个案子所显示的不过是英格兰法多么需要建立一个系统来监控对某些闭路电视所拍片段的使用，这些片段中被镜头拍到的人可能比别的片段中的人更敏感。在 *Malone v Metropolitan Police Comr* [1979] Ch 344 案中，Robert Megarry V-C 爵士提出了很有说服力的理由，证明了这个领域需要成文法来制定很详细的规则而不是粗糙的普通法原则。

case that a person's rights under article 8 have been infringed by a public authority, he will have a statutory remedy. The creation of a general tort will, as Buxton LJ pointed out in the Court of Appeal [2002] QB 1334, 1360, para 92, pre-empt the controversial question of the extent, if any, to which the Convention requires the state to provide remedies for invasions of privacy by persons who are not public authorities.

...

[48] Counsel for the Wainwrights submit that unless the law is extended to create a tort which covers the facts of the present case, it is inevitable that the European Court of Human Rights will find that the United Kingdom was in breach of its Convention obligation to provide a remedy for infringements of Convention rights. In addition to a breach of article 8, they say that the prison officers infringed their Convention right under article 3 not to be subjected to degrading treatment.

[49] I have no doubt that there was no infringement of article 3. The conduct of the searches came nowhere near the degree of humiliation which has been held by the European Court of Human Rights to be degrading treatment ...

[50] In the present case, the judge found that the prison officers acted in good faith and that there had been no more than "sloppiness" in the failures to comply with the rules. The prison officers did not wish to humiliate the claimants ...

[51] Article 8 is more difficult. Buxton LJ thought [2002] QB 1334, 1352, para 62, that the Wainwrights would have had a strong case for relief under section 7 if the 1998 Act had been in force. Speaking for myself, I am not so sure. Although article 8 guarantees a right of privacy, I do not think that it treats that right as having been invaded and requiring a remedy in damages, irrespective of whether the defendant acted intentionally, negligently or accidentally. It is one thing to wander carelessly into the wrong hotel bedroom and another to hide in the wardrobe to take photographs. Article 8 may justify a monetary remedy for an intentional invasion of privacy by a public authority, even if no damage is suffered other than distress for which damages are not ordinarily recoverable. It does not follow that a merely negligent act should, contrary to general principle, give rise to a claim for damages for distress because it affects privacy rather than some other interest like bodily safety: compare *Hicks v Chief Constable of South Yorkshire Police* [1992] 2 All ER 65.

[52] Be that as it may, a finding that there was a breach of article 8 will only demonstrate that there was a gap in the English remedies for invasion of privacy which has since been filled by sections 6 and 7 of the 1998 Act. It does not require that the courts should provide an alternative remedy which distorts the principles of the common law.

[53] I would therefore dismiss the appeal.

[34] 另外，随着《1998年人权法》的出台，那种认为需要一般性的侵犯隐私之诉来填补现行救济措施的阙如的观点，也被削弱了。该法第6条和第7条能起到非常好的填补损害的作用：如果确实是公共机关侵害了个人的权利，根据《公约》第8条的规定，受害人能获得成文法上的救济。而若要创设一种一般性的侵犯隐私之诉，那么正如Buxton上诉法院法官在[2002] QB 1334, 1360, para 92中指出的那样，这样具有争议性的问题，"《公约》是否以及在何种程度上可以要求国家对非公共机关侵犯隐私提供救济"，将在没有得到回答的情况下就被直接绕过了。

......

[48] Wainwright一家的律师主张除非创设一种侵权之诉以涵盖本案的事实，否则欧洲人权法院不可避免地会认为英国违反了为侵犯公约权利提供救济的公约义务。原告认为狱方除了违反了《公约》第8条，同时也违反了《公约》第3条所规定的不得让人受到侮辱性的对待。

[49] 我认为狱方没有违反《公约》第3条，这是没有疑问的。进行搜查的程度远不及欧洲人权法院认为有辱人格的侮辱程度……

[50] 本案中，一审法官认定狱警的行为是善意的，他们之所以没有遵守相关的搜查规则，是因为"粗心大意"。狱警并不希望侮辱原告……

[51] 而狱警是否违反了《公约》第8条则是个更难回答的问题。Buxton上诉法院法官认为Wainwright一家根据1998年《人权法》第7条的规定很可能获得救济。我对这一点不是很肯定。虽然《公约》第8条确实保障隐私权，但是我并不认为《公约》适用到本案会得出任何权利受到侵犯都需要给予损害赔偿的结论，不管被告行为是故意的、过失的，还是意外事件。不小心走错了宾馆的房间是一回事，躲在人家的衣柜里偷拍照片是另一回事。《公约》第8条可能会为公共机关故意侵犯隐私提供救济，即便受害人所受损害不过是一般不可能获得赔偿的纯粹精神痛苦。但这并不是说，我们能不顾一般原则，允许受害人在加害人是纯粹的过失时，也能因为仅仅是影响了隐私权的痛苦（而不是影响其他的利益，比如身体的安全）就获得赔偿：试比较 *Hicks v Chief Constable of South Yorkshire Police* [1992] 2 All ER 65。

[52] 就算我们发现这是对《公约》第8条的违反，也只能证明英格兰法上曾经在救济问题上有漏洞，而现在这个漏洞已经被1998年《人权法》第6条和第7条所填补了。这并不能证明法院应当提供额外的扭曲普通法原则的救济措施。

[53] 因此我要驳回上诉。

100. Campbell v Mirror Group Newspapers Ltd [2004] UKHL 22, [2004] 2 AC 457

House of Lords, United Kingdom

LORD NICHOLLS

[1] My Lords, Naomi Campbell is a celebrated fashion model. Hers is a household name, nationally and internationally. Her face is instantly recognisable. Whatever she does and wherever she goes is news.

[2] On 1 February 2001 the "Mirror" newspaper carried as its first story on its front page a prominent article headed "Naomi: I am a drug addict". The article was supported on one side by a picture of Miss Campbell as a glamorous model, on the other side by a slightly indistinct picture of a smiling, relaxed Miss Campbell, dressed in baseball cap and jeans, over the caption "Therapy: Naomi outside meeting". The article read:

> "Supermodel Naomi Campbell is attending Narcotics Anonymous meetings in a courageous bid to beat her addiction to drink and drugs. The 30-year-old has been a regular at counselling sessions for three months, often attending twice a day. Dressed in jeans and baseball cap, she arrived at one of NA's lunchtime meetings this week. Hours later at a different venue she made a low-key entrance to a women-only gathering of recovered addicts. Despite her £14m fortune Naomi is treated as just another addict trying to put her life back together. A source close to her said last night: 'She wants to clean up her life for good. She went into modelling when she was very young and it is easy to be led astray. Drink and drugs are unfortunately widely available in the fashion world. But Naomi has realised she has a problem and has bravely vowed to do something about it. Everyone wishes her well.' Her spokeswoman at Elite Models declined to comment."

[3] The story continued inside, with a longer article spread across two pages. The inside article was headed "Naomi's finally trying to beat the demons that have been haunting her". The opening paragraphs read:

> "She's just another face in the crowd, but the gleaming smile is unmistakeably Naomi Campbell's. In our picture, the catwalk queen emerges from a gruelling two-hour session at Narcotics Anonymous and gives a friend a loving hug. This is one of the world's most beautiful women facing up to her drink and drugs addiction—and clearly winning. The London-born supermodel has been going to NA meetings for the past three months as she tries to change her wild lifestyle. Such is her commitment to

100. Campbell v Mirror Group Newspapers Ltd [2004] UKHL 22, [2004] 2 AC 457

联合王国上议院

Nicholls 大法官

[1] 诸位大法官，Naomi Campbell 是个著名的模特。她在国内和国外都家喻户晓。人人都能一下就认出她的脸。她做什么、去哪里都是新闻。

[2] 2001 年 2 月 1 日，《镜报》在其头版头条刊登了一篇著名的文章《娜奥米：我是个瘾君子》。这篇文章的一幅配图是 Campbell 小姐光鲜亮丽的模特照，另一幅配图则是一张模糊的照片，照片中的 Campbell 小姐微笑而放松，戴着棒球帽，穿着牛仔裤；第二幅照片的说明文字是"治疗：娜奥米在互助会外"。这篇文章说道：

> 超模 Naomi Campbell 勇敢地向她的酒瘾和毒瘾开战了。她参加了匿名戒毒互助会。三个月来，这位 30 岁的超模已经是戒毒会的常客了，她经常一天要参加两次戒毒会。这天，她穿着牛仔裤戴着棒球帽来参加戒毒会举办的每周午餐会。几个小时之后，在另一个地方她低调地参加了一个仅限女性的成功戒毒者的聚会。尽管她拥有 1 400 万英镑的财富，Naomi 此时不过是那些希望自己的生活回到正常的吸毒者中的一个。昨晚，她身边的一位知情人说："她想要彻底改变自己的生活。她很小的时候就进入了模特这行，因此很容易误入歧途。不幸的是，酒精和毒品在时尚界随处可见。但是 Naomi 意识到了她的问题，并且勇敢地发誓要解决它。所有人都祝她顺利。她在 Elite Models（精英模特公司）的发言人拒绝对此发表意见。"

[3] 这个故事在一篇更长的占了两个版面的内版文章中继续着。这个内版文章的标题是"Naomi 对纠缠她的魔鬼的最后一击"。该文章开头一段是这样的：

> 她看起来淹没在了人群里。然而那闪耀的笑容告诉我们，她就是 Naomi Campbell。我们这里拍到的是猫步女王在紧张的两小时的互助会后和朋友热烈拥抱的场景。这是世界上最美的女人之一在对抗她的毒瘾和酒瘾——显然她胜利了。在过去的三个月以来，这位伦敦出生的超模一直在参加戒毒会，她想改变她混乱的生活方式。她致力于解决

conquering her problem that she regularly goes twice a day to group counselling ... To the rest of the group she is simply Naomi, the addict. Not the supermodel. Not the style icon."

[4] The article made mention of Miss Campbell's efforts to rehabilitate herself, and that one of her friends said she was still fragile but "getting healthy". The article gave a general description of Narcotics Anonymous therapy, and referred to some of Miss Campbell's recent publicised activities. These included an occasion when Miss Campbell was rushed to hospital and had her stomach pumped. She claimed it was an allergic reaction to antibiotics and that she had never had a drug problem: but "those closest to her knew the truth".

[5] In the middle of the double page spread, between several innocuous pictures of Miss Campbell, was a dominating picture over the caption "Hugs: Naomi, dressed in jeans and baseball hat, arrives for a lunchtime group meeting this week". The picture showed her in the street on the doorstep of a building as the central figure in a small group. She was being embraced by two people whose faces had been pixelated. Standing on the pavement was a board advertising a named café. The article did not name the venue of the meeting, but anyone who knew the district well would be able to identify the place shown in the photograph.

[6] The general tone of the articles was sympathetic and supportive with, perhaps, the barest undertone of smugness that Miss Campbell had been caught out by the "Mirror". The source of the newspaper's information was either an associate of Miss Campbell or a fellow addict attending meetings of Narcotics Anonymous. The photographs of her attending a meeting were taken by a freelance photographer specifically employed by the newspaper to do the job. He took the photographs covertly, while concealed some distance away inside a parked car.

[7] In certain respects the articles were inaccurate. Miss Campbell had been attending Narcotics Anonymous meetings, in this country and abroad, for two years, not three months. The frequency of her attendance at meetings was greatly exaggerated. She did not regularly attend meetings twice a day. The street photographs showed her leaving a meeting, not arriving, contrary to the caption in the newspaper article.

The proceedings and the further articles

[8] On the same day as the articles were published Miss Campbell commenced proceedings against MGN Ltd, the publisher of the "Mirror". The newspaper's response was to publish further articles, this time highly critical of Miss Campbell. On 5 February 2001 the newspaper published an article headed, in large letters, "Pathetic". Below was a photograph of Miss Campbell over the caption "Help: Naomi leaves Narcotics Anonymous meeting last week after receiving therapy in her battle against illegal drugs". This photograph was similar to the street scene picture published on 1 February. The text of the article was headed "After years of self-publicity and illegal drug

自己的问题,因此常常一天要参加两次集体讨论会……对互助会的其他成员来说,她就是 Naomi,一名瘾君子,而不是什么超模,不是什么时尚偶像。

[4] 这篇文章提到了 Campbell 小姐改过自新的努力,也提到她的朋友说她虽然依旧脆弱,但是在慢慢康复。这篇文章大概地介绍了一下匿名戒毒互助疗法,也提到了最近 Campbell 的一些已经被报道过的事。比如那次 Campbell 冲进医院洗胃。她当时声称她是因为对抗生素过敏才去的,她没有吸毒的问题,但是"那些和她亲近的人知道事情的真相"。

[5] 这个占用了两个版面的文章中间,除了几张 Campbell 小姐无伤大雅的照片,还有一张很重要的照片,这张照片所配的说明文字是"拥抱:穿牛仔裤戴棒球帽的 Naomi 来参加这周的集体午餐会"。这张照片中,她站在一栋建筑门外的大街上,是一群人的中心人物。两个人拥抱着她,他们俩的脸都打了马赛克。人行道上则竖立着一块广告牌,宣传的是一家著名的咖啡馆。这篇文章没有提到聚会的地点,但是熟悉这块区域的人可以确定这张照片是在哪里拍的。

[6] 这篇文章总的基调还是对原告表示同情和支持的,也许作者对于《镜报》抓到了 Campbell 小姐的新闻这事有点洋洋得意。报社的信息来源或许是 Campbell 小姐的一位伙伴,或许就是和她一起参加戒毒互助会的其他瘾君子。她参加互助会的照片是一位报社特别雇佣的自由摄影师拍摄的。他藏在一段距离之外的一辆车上偷偷摸摸地拍了这张照片。

[7] 报道的某些方面并不准确。Campbell 小姐在国内外参加戒毒互助会已经两年了,而不是只有三个月。她参加的频率也被夸张了,她并不是经常一天参加两次。拍到她站在街上的那些照片,其实是在她离开互助会时拍的而不是如解释文字所说是刚到时拍的。

审判程序和之后的文章

[8] 这些文章登报的当天,Campbell 小姐就起诉了 MGN 集团,《镜报》的出版商。作为回应,报社又刊登了几篇文章,不过这次都是在批评 Campbell 小姐了。2001 年 2 月 5 日该报发表了一篇用大写字母书写标题,名为"可怜虫"的文章。文章的标题下方是一张照片,解释文字是"救救我:Naomi 上周在接受药物滥用治疗后离开了匿名互助会"。这张照片和 2001 年 2 月 1 日所刊登的那几张拍到她站在街上的照片很类似。这篇文章的开头是这样的:"虽然经年累月地自我宣传和滥用药物,Naomi Campbell 却抱怨被侵犯

abuse, Naomi Campbell whinges about privacy." The article mentioned that "the Mirror revealed last week how she is attending daily meetings of Narcotics Anonymous". Elsewhere in the same edition an editorial article, with the heading "No hiding Naomi", concluded with the words: "If Naomi Campbell wants to live like a nun, let her join a nunnery. If she wants the excitement of a show business life, she must accept what comes with it."

[9] Two days later, on 7 February, the "Mirror" returned to the attack with an offensive and disparaging article. Under the heading "Fame on you, Ms Campbell", an article referred to her plans "to launch a campaign for better rights for celebrities or 'artists' as she calls them". The article included the sentence: "As a campaigner, Naomi's about as effective as a chocolate soldier."

[10] In the proceedings Miss Campbell claimed damages for breach of confidence and compensation under the Data Protection Act 1998. The article of 7 February formed the main basis of a claim for aggravated damages. Morland J [2002] EWHC 499 (QB) upheld Miss Campbell's claim. He made her a modest award of £2,500 plus £1,000 aggravated damages in respect of both claims. The newspaper appealed. The Court of Appeal, comprising Lord Phillips of Worth Matravers MR, Chadwick and Keene LJJ, allowed the appeal and discharged the judge's order: [2003] QB 633. Miss Campbell has now appealed to your Lordships' House.

Breach of confidence: misuse of private information

[11] In this country, unlike the United States of America, there is no over-arching, all-embracing cause of action for "invasion of privacy": see *Wainwright v Home Office* [2004] AC 406 . But protection of various aspects of privacy is a fast developing area of the law, here and in some other common law jurisdictions. The recent decision of the Court of Appeal of New Zealand in *Hosking v Runting* [2004] NZCA 34 is an example of this. In this country development of the law has been spurred by enactment of the Human Rights Act 1998.

[12] The present case concerns one aspect of invasion of privacy: wrongful disclosure of private information. The case involves the familiar competition between freedom of expression and respect for an individual's privacy. Both are vitally important rights. Neither has precedence over the other. The importance of freedom of expression has been stressed often and eloquently, the importance of privacy less so. But it, too, lies at the heart of liberty in a modern state. A proper degree of privacy is essential for the well-being and development of an individual. And restraints imposed on government to pry into the lives of the citizen go to the essence of a democratic state: see La Forest J in *R v Dyment*[1988] 2 SCR 417, 426.

[13] The common law or, more precisely, courts of equity have long afforded protection to the wrongful use of private information by means of the cause of action which became known as breach of confidence. A breach of confidence was restrained as a form of unconscionable conduct, akin to a breach of trust. Today this nomenclature is misleading. The breach of confidence label harks back to the time when the cause of action was based on improper use of information

了隐私。"这篇文章提到了"《镜报》在上周揭露了她参加匿名戒毒互助会的每日会议"。报纸上另一处的社论文章则以"Naomi别藏了"为标题，以下面的文字结束："如果Naomi Campbell想当个尼姑，她应该去尼姑庵。如果她要的是娱乐圈的名利场，她就应当接受这里会有的一切。"

[9] 两天后的2月7日，《镜报》对于原告的起诉，以更具攻击性和轻蔑语调的文章回应。这文章的标题是"你真有名啊，Campbell小姐"，其中提到"她要发起一项让名人或者她所称的'艺术家'获得更多权利的运动"。这文章还包括这样的句子："作为运动发起者，Naomi就跟巧克力糖兵一样有本事。"

[10] 在庭审中，Campbell小姐以被告违反了保密义务以及《1998年数据保护法》的赔偿金规定为由，主张自己应当获得损害赔偿金。2月7日的文章则是请求加重赔偿的基本依据。Morland法官在[2002] EWHC 499（QB）中支持了Campbell小姐的请求。在这两项主张下，他判决她受到严重损害并获得巨额赔偿金：2500英镑的基本赔偿金和1000英镑的加重赔偿金。报社因此上诉。上诉法院（合议庭成员：Phillips大法官，Chadwick和Keene上诉法院法官）在[2003] QB 633中支持了上诉，驳回了原判。Campbell小姐因此向上议院上诉。

违反保密义务：对私有信息的滥用

[11] 和美国不同，我国并没有抽象的侵犯隐私之诉：参见 *Wainwright v Home Office* [2004] AC 406。但是对隐私的不同方面的保护，在我国和其他的普通法法域中都在快速地发展着。最近新西兰上诉法院判决的 *Hosking v Runting* [2004] NZCA 34案就是个例子。1998年《人权法》的颁布大大促进了这种发展。

[12] 本案涉及侵犯隐私之诉的一个方面：非法泄露他人的私有信息。本案涉及言论自由和对他人隐私的尊重这两个方面的冲突。这二者都是极其重要的权利。不能说一种优先于另一种。言论自由的重要性是经常被强调的问题，而且理论发展已经很完善了；而隐私权的重要性就没有那么受重视了。但是隐私权也是现代国家中自由的核心方面。适度的隐私对于个人的福祉和发展至关重要。对政府窥探公民生活的种种限制，则是民主国家的真髓：参见 *La Forest J in R v Dyment* [1988] 2 SCR 417, 426。

[13] 普通法或者更确切地说衡平法院很早就通过一种称为"违反保密义务"的诉由向被他人非法使用私有信息的受害人提供保护了。当时要提起违反保密义务之诉，需要侵权人的行为如同违反信托义务那样过分才行。如今，这种命名法具有误导性。"违反保密义务之诉"听起来就像是旧时代的诉由，当时要提起这个诉讼需要一个人不正当地使用了别人秘密告诉他的信息。要

disclosed by one person to another in confidence. To attract protection the information had to be of a confidential nature. But the gist of the cause of action was that information of this character had been disclosed by one person to another in circumstances "importing an obligation of confidence" even though no contract of non-disclosure existed: see the classic exposition by Megarry J in *Coco v A N Clark (Engineers) Ltd* [1969] RPC 41, 47-48. The confidence referred to in the phrase "breach of confidence" was the confidence arising out of a confidential relationship.

[14] This cause of action has now firmly shaken off the limiting constraint of the need for an initial confidential relationship. In doing so it has changed its nature. In this country this development was recognised clearly in the judgment of Lord Goff of Chieveley in *Attorney General v Guardian Newspapers Ltd (No 2)* [1990] 1 AC 109, 281. Now the law imposes a "duty of confidence" whenever a person receives information he knows or ought to know is fairly and reasonably to be regarded as confidential. Even this formulation is awkward. The continuing use of the phrase "duty of confidence" and the description of the information as "confidential" is not altogether comfortable. Information about an individual's private life would not, in ordinary usage, be called "confidential". The more natural description today is that such information is private. The essence of the tort is better encapsulated now as misuse of private information.

[15] In the case of individuals this tort, however labelled, affords respect for one aspect of an individual's privacy. That is the value underlying this cause of action. An individual's privacy can be invaded in ways not involving publication of information. Strip searches are an example. The extent to which the common law as developed thus far in this country protects other forms of invasion of privacy is not a matter arising in the present case. It does not arise because, although pleaded more widely, Miss Campbell's common law claim was throughout presented in court exclusively on the basis of breach of confidence, that is, the wrongful *publication* by the "Mirror" of private *information* .

[16] The European Convention on Human Rights, and the Strasbourg jurisprudence, have undoubtedly had a significant influence in this area of the common law for some years. The provisions of article 8 , concerning respect for private and family life, and article 10 , concerning freedom of expression, and the interaction of these two articles, have prompted the courts of this country to identify more clearly the different factors involved in cases where one or other of these two interests is present. Where both are present the courts are increasingly explicit in evaluating the competing considerations involved. When identifying and evaluating these factors the courts, including your Lordships' House, have tested the common law against the values encapsulated in these two articles. The development of the common law has been in harmony with these articles of the Convention: see, for instance, *Reynolds v Times Newspapers Ltd* [2001] 2 AC 127, 203-204.

[17] The time has come to recognise that the values enshrined in articles 8 and 10 are now part of the cause of action for breach of confidence. As Lord Woolf CJ has said, the courts have

法律来提供保护，这个信息就需要具有秘密的性质。但是这里的"秘密"是指信息是一个人在"会产生保密义务"的情况下告诉另一个人的，并不需要一定有保密协议的存在：参见 Megarry 法官在 *Coco v A N Clark（Engineers）Ltd* [1969] RPC 41, 47-48 案中所做的经典论述。"违反保密义务"这个表达中所说的保密，其意思产生于一个需要保密的关系。

[14] 现在这个诉由连"最初的保密关系"这个要件都不需要了，这样做其实改变了它的性质。在我国，这种变化在 Goff 大法官为 *Attorney General v Guardian Newspapers Ltd（No 2）*[1990] 1 AC 109, 281 案所撰写的判决中得到了明确的承认。现在法律要求一个人在收到一个他知道或者应该知道属于保密的信息时，都要承担"保密义务"。其实即便这样要求也还是有些不妥。现在我们还在使用"保密义务"这样的表达方式，还在将涉及的信息称为"秘密"，这样的做法是不太正确的。关于一个人私人生活的信息在一般语境下是不会被称为"秘密"的。在今天，更自然的称谓应该是"私有信息"。因此在今天，这个诉由的核心应该被表述为"对私有信息的滥用"。

[15] 这个诉由无论叫什么名字，都是为了保证对个人隐私的某个方面的尊重，这就是这个诉由背后的价值。除了发布私有信息，一个人的隐私还可能以其他方式被侵犯。裸体搜查就是个例子。但是普通法在保护其他类型的隐私侵犯这个问题上发展到什么程度了，不是本案中需要解决的问题。它之所以不是本案中的问题，是因为 Campbell 小姐的请求一直都是完全建立在"违反保密义务"这一点上的（虽然她所主张的东西可能看起来比这更多一点），换言之是建立在《镜报》对其私有信息的非法公布之上的。

[16] 这几年《公约》和欧洲人权法院的判例在这个问题上毫无疑问对普通法有很大的影响。涉及对私人生活和家庭生活的尊重的《公约》第 8 条和涉及言论自由的《公约》第 10 条以及这两条的互相配合，使得我国法院在遇到有关这两种利益之一或者两者都有的案件时能更清楚地确定相关的因素。当这两种利益都存在时，现在的法院越来越明确地表示要考虑这两种互相冲突的因素。在确定和考量这些因素时，包括本院在内的法院都要基于《公约》的这两个法条来考察普通法。普通法的发展是随着《公约》的这两个法条的发展而发展的：参考比如 *Reynolds v Times Newspapers Ltd* [2001] 2 AC 127, 203-204。

[17] 承认《公约》第 8 条和第 10 条所传递的价值也是"违反保密义务之诉"的价值，这个已经是大势所趋。首席大法官 Woolf 说，法院可以通过将《公约》

been able to achieve this result by absorbing the rights protected by articles 8 and 10 into this cause of action: *A v B plc* [2003] QB 195, 202, para 4. Further, it should now be recognised that for this purpose these values are of general application. The values embodied in articles 8 and 10 are as much applicable in disputes between individuals or between an individual and a non-governmental body such as a newspaper as they are in disputes between individuals and a public authority.

[18] In reaching this conclusion it is not necessary to pursue the controversial question whether the European Convention itself has this wider effect. Nor is it necessary to decide whether the duty imposed on courts by section 6 of the Human Rights Act 1998 extends to questions of substantive law as distinct from questions of practice and procedure. It is sufficient to recognise that the values underlying articles 8 and 10 are not confined to disputes between individuals and public authorities. This approach has been adopted by the courts in several recent decisions, reported and unreported, where individuals have complained of press intrusion. A convenient summary of these cases is to be found in Gavin Phillipson's valuable article "Transforming Breach of Confidence? Towards a Common Law Right of Privacy under the Human Rights Act" (2003) 66 MLR 726 , 726-728.

[19] In applying this approach, and giving effect to the values protected by article 8 , courts will often be aided by adopting the structure of article 8 in the same way as they now habitually apply the Strasbourg court's approach to article 10 when resolving questions concerning freedom of expression. Articles 8 and 10 call for a more explicit analysis of competing considerations than the three traditional requirements of the cause of action for breach of confidence identified in *Coco v A N Clark (Engineers) Ltd* [1969] RPC 41.

[20] I should take this a little further on one point. Article 8(1) recognises the need to respect private and family life. Article 8(2) recognises there are occasions when intrusion into private and family life may be justified. One of these is where the intrusion is necessary for the protection of the rights and freedoms of others. Article 10(1) recognises the importance of freedom of expression. But article 10(2), like article 8(2), recognises there are occasions when protection of the rights of others may make it necessary for freedom of expression to give way. When both these articles are engaged a difficult question of proportionality may arise. This question is distinct from the initial question of whether the published information engaged article 8 at all by being within the sphere of the complainant's private or family life.

[21] Accordingly, in deciding what was the ambit of an individual's "private life" in particular circumstances courts need to be on guard against using as a touchstone a test which brings into account considerations which should more properly be considered at the later stage of proportionality. Essentially the touchstone of private life is whether in respect of the disclosed facts the person in question had a reasonable expectation of privacy.

[22] Different forms of words, usually to much the same effect, have been suggested from

第 8 条和第 10 条所保护的权利吸收到这个诉由中, 以实现这个目的: *A v B plc* [2003] QB 195, 202, 第 4 段。另外, 为了这个目的,《公约》所保护的价值应该具有一般的适用性。第 8 条和第 10 条所保护的价值, 既在个人之间又在个人和非政府的组织之间适用, 同时也在个人和公共机关之间适用。

[18] 要得出我刚才说的这个结论, 其实没有必要去讨论《公约》本身的适用范围是不是这么大的争议问题, 也没有必要去讨论 1998 年《人权法》第 6 条所施加的义务是不是也包括和程序不一样的实体法问题。我们只需要承认《公约》第 8 条和第 10 条承载的价值并不局限于个人和公共机关之间。最近的一些有关个人起诉媒体侵权的案件的判决(有的公布了, 有的没有公布)显示这种观点已经被法院所接受。Gavin Phillipson 在其很有价值的论文《改造违反保密义务之诉? 在〈人权法〉下朝着普通法中的隐私权前进》[(2003) 66 MLR 726, 726-728] 中总结了这些案件。

[19] 为了贯彻这种观点, 也为了让《公约》第 8 条所保护的价值得到实现, 法院可以参考《公约》第 8 条的结构, 就跟他们在解决言论自由的问题时习惯于参考欧洲人权法院对第 10 条的观点一样。《公约》第 8 条和第 10 条相比 *Coco v A N Clark (Engineers) Ltd* [1969] RPC 41 案确定的"违反保密义务之诉"的三个传统要件, 要求更明确地分析相互冲突的这两个因素。

[20] 我要进一步讨论一下一个要点。《公约》第 8 条第 1 款规定了对私人生活和家庭生活的尊重; 第 2 款则规定了某些情况下对私人生活和家庭生活的侵入也是正当的。这样的情形之一是当有必要保护他人的权利和自由时。《公约》第 10 条第 1 款则规定了言论自由的重要性, 但是第 10 条第 2 款, 就像第 8 条第 2 款一样, 规定了有些情况下为了保护他人的权利, 言论自由也是需要让位的。当以上这些法条都要适用时, 就会产生一个很难解决的比例问题。这个比例问题和最初的被告刊登的信息是否因为属于原告的私人生活或者家庭生活而触发《公约》第 8 条这个问题, 是两个不同的问题。

[21] 因此, 如果要解决的问题是具体情况下一个人的"私人生活"的范围是什么, 那么法院需要警惕不要将"比例问题"阶段才需要考量的因素当作判断标准。判断"私人生活"的标准应该是被泄露的信息所指向的那个人(在信息被泄露前)是否可以合理地期望(这个信息属于)隐私。

[22] (界定"私人生活"), 人们有时会使用不同词句, 但其揆一也。美国法学会在《侵权法重述·第二次》(1977) 第 625D 条中, 使用的说法

time to time. The American Law Institute, *Restatement of the Law, Torts,* 2d (1977), section 652D, uses the formulation of disclosure of matter which "would be highly offensive to a reasonable person". In *Australian Broadcasting Corpn v Lenah Game Meats Pty Ltd* (2001) 208 CLR 199, 226, para 42, Gleeson CJ used words, widely quoted, having a similar meaning. This particular formulation should be used with care, for two reasons. First, the "highly offensive" phrase is suggestive of a stricter test of private information than a reasonable expectation of privacy. Second, the "highly offensive" formulation can all too easily bring into account, when deciding whether the disclosed information was private, considerations which go more properly to issues of proportionality; for instance, the degree of intrusion into private life, and the extent to which publication was a matter of proper public concern. This could be a recipe for confusion.

The present case

[23] I turn to the present case and consider first whether the information whose disclosure is in dispute was private. Mr Caldecott placed the information published by the newspaper into five categories: (1) the fact of Miss Campbell's drug addiction; (2) the fact that she was receiving treatment; (3) the fact that she was receiving treatment at Narcotics Anonymous; (4) the details of the treatment—how long she had been attending meetings, how often she went, how she was treated within the sessions themselves, the extent of her commitment, and the nature of her entrance on the specific occasion; and (5) the visual portrayal of her leaving a specific meeting with other addicts.

[24] It was common ground between the parties that in the ordinary course the information in all five categories would attract the protection of article 8. But Mr Caldecott recognised that, as he put it, Miss Campbell's "public lies" precluded her from claiming protection for categories (1) and (2). When talking to the media Miss Campbell went out of her way to say that, unlike many fashion models, she did not take drugs. By repeatedly making these assertions in public Miss Campbell could no longer have a reasonable expectation that this aspect of her life should be private. Public disclosure that, contrary to her assertions, she did in fact take drugs and had a serious drug problem for which she was being treated was not disclosure of private information. As the Court of Appeal noted, where a public figure chooses to present a false image and make untrue pronouncements about his or her life, the press will normally be entitled to put the record straight: [2003] QB 633, 658. Thus the area of dispute at the trial concerned the other three categories of information.

[25] Of these three categories I shall consider first the information in categories (3) and (4), concerning Miss Campbell's attendance at Narcotics Anonymous meetings. In this regard it is important to note this is a highly unusual case. On any view of the matter, this information related closely to the fact, which admittedly could be published, that Miss Campbell was receiving treatment for drug addiction. Thus when considering whether Miss Campbell had a reasonable expectation of privacy in respect of information relating to her attendance at Narcotics Anonymous meetings the relevant question can be framed along the following lines: Miss Campbell having

是披露"可能会对一个理性人非常冒犯"的信息。在 *Australian Broadcasting Corpn v Lenah Game Meats Pty Ltd*（2001）208 CLR 199, 226 para 42 中 Gleeson 首席大法官说了一段高引用率的话，这段话的意思和侵权法重述差不多。有两个原因让我们要谨慎使用这种说法。第一个原因是，"非常冒犯"这个表达给人一种感觉，就是对"私人信息"的判断标准要高于"合理地期望（这个信息属于）隐私"这个标准。第二个原因是，"非常冒犯"这个表达会让人在考虑被披露的信息是否属于私人信息这一步时，就去考虑应该之后再考虑的"比例问题"的相关因素，比如，对他人私人生活的侵入程度以及报道属于正当的公众事务的程度。这样做可能会造成混乱。

本案

[23] 我们回到本案，先考量一下被泄露的信息是否属于私人信息。Caldecott 先生将《镜报》所刊登的信息分为五类：（1）Campbell 小姐的毒瘾；（2）她在接受治疗；（3）她在匿名戒毒互助会接受治疗；（4）治疗的细节——她参加戒毒会多久了，她去那里的频率，她在戒毒会中是如何被治疗的，她投入的程度以及某次特定集会时她的情况；（5）在某次特定会议，她和其他瘾君子离开时的照片。

[24] 双方都认同，在一般情况下，五类信息的泄漏都可以用《公约》第8条来保护。但是 Caldecott 先生认为，由于 Campbell 小姐公开地撒了谎，因此她在第一类和第二类信息上就不能受到保护了。Campbell 小姐在媒体面前卖人设，说她跟那些时尚模特不一样，她就从来不吸毒。Campbell 小姐不断向公众这么说，因此她对于她这方面的生活依然属于私人生活，就没法抱有合理预期了。这样向公众披露和她的话相反的事实，即她确实吸毒且还有很严重的毒瘾并因此接受治疗，就不属于泄漏私人信息了。上诉法院的意见是，如果公众人物要给自己营造假人设或者发表不实之言，那么新闻媒体通常就有权把他戳穿：参见 [2003] QB 633, 658。这样在庭审中争论的，就只有后三种类型的信息。

[25] 在后面这三种类型的信息中，我将先考察第三类和第四类，这两种类型涉及 Campbell 小姐参加匿名戒毒会的事。在这方面，需要注意的是，这个案子很不寻常。这两类信息从任何角度看，都和 Campbell 小姐在接受戒毒治疗这事有关，而这已经确定是可以报道的了。因此要考量 Campbell 小姐是否有合理的期望将她参加匿名戒毒会这事当作隐私，我们需要考虑的是这个问题：Campbell 小姐在将她的毒瘾和对毒瘾的治疗放到公共领域之后，更进

put her addiction and treatment into the public domain, did the further information relating to her attendance at Narcotics Anonymous meetings retain its character of private information sufficiently to engage the protection afforded by article 8?

[26] I doubt whether it did. Treatment by attendance at Narcotics Anonymous meetings is a form of therapy for drug addiction which is well known, widely used and much respected. Disclosure that Miss Campbell had opted for this form of treatment was not a disclosure of any more significance than saying that a person who has fractured a limb has his limb in plaster or that a person suffering from cancer is undergoing a course of chemotherapy. Given the extent of the information, otherwise of a highly private character, which admittedly could properly be disclosed, the additional information was of such an unremarkable and consequential nature that to divide the one from the other would be to apply altogether too fine a toothcomb. Human rights are concerned with substance, not with such fine distinctions.

[27] For the same reason I doubt whether the brief details of how long Miss Campbell had been undergoing treatment, and how often she attended meetings, stand differently. The brief reference to the way she was treated at the meetings did no more than spell out and apply to Miss Campbell common knowledge of how Narcotics Anonymous meetings are conducted.

[28] But I would not wish to found my conclusion solely on this point. I prefer to proceed to the next stage and consider how the tension between privacy and freedom of expression should be resolved in this case, on the assumption that the information regarding Miss Campbell's attendance at Narcotics Anonymous meetings retained its private character. At this stage I consider Miss Campbell's claim must fail. I can state my reason very shortly. On the one hand, publication of this information in the unusual circumstances of this case represents, at most, an intrusion into Miss Campbell's private life to a comparatively minor degree. On the other hand, non-publication of this information would have robbed a legitimate and sympathetic newspaper story of attendant detail which added colour and conviction. This information was published in order to demonstrate Miss Campbell's commitment to tackling her drug problem. The balance ought not to be held at a point which would preclude, in this case, a degree of journalistic latitude in respect of information published for this purpose.

[29] It is at this point I respectfully consider Morland J fell into error. Having held that the details of Miss Campbell's attendance at Narcotics Anonymous had the necessary quality of confidentiality, the judge seems to have put nothing into the scales under article 10 when striking the balance between articles 8 and 10. This was a misdirection. The need to be free to disseminate information regarding Miss Campbell's drug addiction is of a lower order than the need for freedom to disseminate information on some other subjects such as political information. The degree of latitude reasonably to be accorded to journalists is correspondingly reduced, but it is not excluded altogether.

一步的关于她参加匿名戒毒互助会的信息是否依然具有足够隐私信息的性质，以致可以适用《公约》第 8 条？

[26] 我觉得不适用。参加戒毒互助会是治疗毒瘾的一种著名的、被广泛使用且为人所接受的手段。披露 Campbell 小姐选择这种手段来治疗，并不比披露一个手脚骨折的病人打了石膏或者披露一个癌症病人在接受化疗更为严重。（她在接受戒毒治疗）的信息虽然在一般情况下是非常隐私的信息，但是已经变得可以披露了，（她在参加戒毒会这样的）额外的信息是很平常的，也是前者的自然延伸，因此如果要区分后者和前者，那就是在把信息做太细微的区分了。人权关注的是重要的权利，而不是细微的区分。

[27] 基于同样的理由，Campbell 小姐在接受治疗、她多久参加一次聚会这样的信息，也并无不同（都是可以披露的）。对于 Campbell 小姐在戒毒互助会的情况的简要描述不过是在阐述一般情况下戒毒互助会是如何运作的，只是这里用到了 Campbell 小姐做例子。

[28] 但是我的结论并不是仅仅建立在这一点上的。我希望能进一步到下一个阶段，在假设关于 Campbell 小姐参加匿名戒毒会的信息确实具有私人信息的性质的前提下，考量隐私权和言论自由之间的冲突关系在本案中怎么解决。在这个阶段我也认为 Campbell 小姐的诉讼请求会失败。我可以很快地陈述我的理由。一方面，发布这方面的信息在本案这种不同寻常的情况下最多算作对 Campbell 小姐私人生活的轻微的侵入；另一方面，如果不发布这种信息则会使得合情合理又充满同情的新闻报道丧失相应的细节，而这些细节会给报道增添色彩和可信度。发布这些信息是为了展示 Campbell 小姐为解决毒瘾问题而下的决心。这时（隐私权和言论自由的）平衡就不能停在一个会让新闻记者在这个方面失去自由的点上。

[29] 在这一点上，我诚恳地认为 Morland 法官犯了错误。他认定 Campbell 小姐参加戒毒互助会的细节具有秘密的性质，但是他在对第 8 条和第 10 条作平衡时，好像没有重视第 10 条。这就错了。传播有关 Campbell 小姐毒瘾的信息没有传播其他类型的信息重要，比如政治信息。因此记者享有的自由就要相应地减少一些，但是不能完全排除这种自由。

[30] There remains category (5): the photographs taken covertly of Miss Campbell in the road outside the building she was attending for a meeting of Narcotics Anonymous. I say at once that I wholly understand why Miss Campbell felt she was being hounded by the "Mirror". I understand also that this could be deeply distressing, even damaging, to a person whose health was still fragile. But this is not the subject of complaint. Miss Campbell, expressly, makes no complaint about the taking of the photographs. She does not assert that the taking of the photographs was itself an invasion of privacy which attracts a legal remedy. The complaint regarding the photographs is of precisely the same character as the nature of the complaints regarding the text of the articles: the information conveyed by the photographs was private information. Thus the fact that the photographs were taken surreptitiously adds nothing to the only complaint being made.

[31] In general photographs of people contain more information than textual description. That is why they are more vivid. That is why they are worth a thousand words. But the pictorial information in the photographs illustrating the offending article of 1 February 2001 added nothing of an essentially private nature. They showed nothing untoward. They conveyed no private information beyond that discussed in the article. The group photograph showed Miss Campbell in the street exchanging warm greetings with others on the doorstep of a building. There was nothing undignified or distrait about her appearance. The same is true of the smaller picture on the front page. Until spotted by counsel in the course of preparing the case for oral argument in your Lordships' House no one seems to have noticed that a sharp eye could just about make out the name of the café on the advertising board on the pavement.

[32] For these reasons and those given by my noble and learned friend, Lord Hoffmann, I agree with the Court of Appeal that Miss Campbell's claim fails.

LORD HOFFMANN

[36] My Lords, the House is divided as to the outcome of this appeal, but the difference of opinion relates to a very narrow point which arises on the unusual facts of this case. The facts are unusual because the plaintiff is a public figure who had made very public false statements about a matter in respect of which even a public figure would ordinarily be entitled to privacy, namely her use of drugs. It was these falsehoods which, as was conceded, made it justifiable, for a newspaper to report the fact that she was addicted. The division of opinion is whether in doing so the newspaper went too far in publishing associated facts about her private life. But the importance of this case lies in the statements of general principle on the way in which the law should strike a balance between the right to privacy and the right to freedom of expression, on which the House is unanimous. The principles are expressed in varying language but speaking for myself I can see no significant differences.

...

[49] ... Until the Human Rights Act 1998 came into force, there was no equivalent in

[30] 还剩下第五种类型：拍到的 Campbell 小姐站在举办匿名戒毒会的大楼外面的大街上的照片。我完全理解为什么 Campbell 小姐感到她被《镜报》骚扰了。同样我理解这对她这样一个还没有康复的人来说是很痛苦的，甚至是破坏性的。但是这并不是她起诉的内容。Campbell 小姐的起诉并没有依据她被拍照一事。她并没有宣称她的隐私被侵犯是因为被拍照了，因此需要救济。她关于照片的起诉依据和关于文章的起诉依据是同样的性质：照片所表达的信息是私人信息。因此照片是偷偷摸摸地拍的这事并没有给她的起诉增加任何东西。

[31] 通常来说，人物照片比文字描述含有更多的信息。这就是为什么照片更生动，这也就是为什么一图胜千言。但是 2001 年 2 月 1 日的文章所配图片表达的信息并没有让这篇文章变得含有更多的私人信息。这些图片并没有什么不恰当的内容。它们所表达的私人信息并不比系争文章所表达得多。那张集体照显示的是 Campbell 小姐在街上在楼房门口和大家热情地打招呼。这对于她的形象并没有任何贬损。头版那张小一些的照片也是这样。在律师为本院的口头辩论做准备之前，都没有人发现人行道上的广告牌可以让眼尖的人发现咖啡馆的地址。

[32] 基于以上的原因，还基于我高贵而博学的朋友 Hoffmann 大法官所给出的原因，我同意上诉法院的意见，Campbell 小姐的诉讼请求应该被驳回。

Hoffmann 大法官

[36] 诸位大法官，本院就该如何对待上诉这事上有两种不同意见，但是这种意见的不同是因为本案不同寻常的事实而产生的。本案的事实之所以不同寻常是因为原告作为一名公众人物在公众面前做了虚假陈述，但是陈述的主体涉及的却是公众人物也享有隐私权的事项，即她吸毒这件事。正是因为她的虚假陈述（她也承认她说了假话），使得报社报道她实际上是瘾君子一事有了正当性。我们的争论在于报社在报道这事的过程中，有没有对她的私人生活报道得太过分。本案最重要的问题是如何平衡隐私权和言论自由的一般原则，这一点我们都一致同意。这种原则的具体说法有很多种，但是就我自己而言，我觉得它们之间没有根本的不同。

……

[49] ……在 1998 年《人权法》生效之前，英格兰国内法上并没有类似《公

English domestic law of article 8 of the European Convention or the equivalent articles in other international human rights instruments which guarantee rights of privacy. So the courts of the United Kingdom did not have to decide what such guarantees meant. Even now that the equivalent of article 8 has been enacted as part of English law, it is not directly concerned with the protection of privacy against private persons or corporations. It is, by virtue of section 6 of the 1998 Act, a guarantee of privacy only against public authorities. Although the Convention, as an international instrument, may impose upon the United Kingdom an obligation to take some steps (whether by statute or otherwise) to protect rights of privacy against invasion by private individuals, it does not follow that such an obligation would have any counterpart in domestic law.

[50] What human rights law has done is to identify private information as something worth protecting as an aspect of human autonomy and dignity. And this recognition has raised inescapably the question of why it should be worth protecting against the state but not against a private person. There may of course be justifications for the publication of private information by private persons which would not be available to the state—I have particularly in mind the position of the media, to which I shall return in a moment—but I can see no logical ground for saying that a person should have less protection against a private individual than he would have against the state for the publication of personal information for which there is no justification. Nor, it appears, have any of the other judges who have considered the matter.

[51] The result of these developments has been a shift in the centre of gravity of the action for breach of confidence when it is used as a remedy for the unjustified publication of personal information. It recognises that the incremental changes to which I have referred do not merely extend the duties arising traditionally from a relationship of trust and confidence to a wider range of people. As Sedley LJ observed in a perceptive passage in his judgment in *Douglas v Hello! Ltd* [2001] QB 967, 1001, the new approach takes a different view of the underlying value which the law protects. Instead of the cause of action being based upon the duty of good faith applicable to confidential personal information and trade secrets alike, it focuses upon the protection of human autonomy and dignity—the right to control the dissemination of information about one's private life and the right to the esteem and respect of other people.

...

[78] I would ...dismiss the appeal.

...

BARONESS HALE

[147] I start ... from the fact—indeed, it is common ground—that *all* of the information about Miss Campbell's addiction and attendance at NA which was revealed in the "Daily Mirror" article was both private and confidential, because it related to an important aspect of Miss Campbell's physical and mental health and the treatment she was receiving for it. It had also

约》第 8 条或类似的其他保障隐私权的国际人权法规范的规定。因此英国法院无须判断这些规定到底是什么意思。即使现在《公约》第 8 条已经被内化成了英格兰法的一部分，英格兰法上也并没有直接保护隐私免受私人或者公司侵犯的规定。1998 年《人权法》第 6 条是保护隐私免受公共机关的侵犯。虽然《公约》作为国际法规范可以给英国施加一定的义务让其采取措施（可能是制定成文法，可能是其他措施）以保护隐私权免受私人的侵犯，但是这并不是说在国内法上一定能找到这样的义务。

[50] 人权法所做的，是确认私人信息作为人的自主和尊严的一部分，是值得保护的。这种确认不可避免会提出一个问题：即为什么只保护隐私免受来自国家的侵害而不保护免受私人的侵害。当然，并不是说所有的私人能够援引的用来将发布别人私人信息正当化的事由，国家也都可以援引——我尤其能想到的是媒体的地位，这个问题我待会儿再说——但是说一个人的私人信息在毫无理由的情况下被他人发布时，如果该他人是私人而不是国家，那么信息被发布的人获得的保护应该更少，我认为这个说法就没有任何逻辑基础在里面。似乎也没有其他考虑过此事的法官。

[51] 以上这些变化发展的结果是，当"违反保密义务之诉"被用来救济不正当的发布私人信息时，我们考察的重点变了。我刚才所提到的这些逐渐的变化并不仅仅增加了保密义务的范围：从传统上的信托或者保密关系增加到拘束更广泛的人群。正如 Sedley 上诉法院法官在 *Douglas v Hello! Ltd* [2001] QB 967 案中极富洞察力的观点，新做法对于这个诉由所保护的价值采取了不同的看法。它不认为这个诉由是建立在适用于秘密私人信息或者商业秘密这类东西的善意义务之上的，它强调的是保护人的自主和尊严——控制有关自己私人生活信息传播的权利，受到他人尊重的权利。

……

[78] 我将……驳回上诉。

……

Hale 大法官

[147] 我从以下事实开始陈述，这些事实是双方所公认的：所有的为《每日镜报》所报道的有关 Campbell 小姐的毒瘾和她参加戒毒会的事实都是私人的信息，也是应该保密的信息，因为这些信息涉及 Campbell 小姐的身心健康和她接受的治疗。同样，这些信息来源于内部人员，他违反了保密义务。但

been received from an insider in breach of confidence. That simple fact has been obscured by the concession properly made on her behalf that the newspaper's countervailing freedom of expression did serve to justify the publication of some of this information. But the starting point must be that it was all private and its publication required specific justification.

[148] What was the nature of the freedom of expression which was being asserted on the other side? There are undoubtedly different types of speech, just as there are different types of private information, some of which are more deserving of protection in a democratic society than others. Top of the list is political speech. The free exchange of information and ideas on matters relevant to the organisation of the economic, social and political life of the country is crucial to any democracy. Without this, it can scarcely be called a democracy at all. This includes revealing information about public figures, especially those in elective office, which would otherwise be private but is relevant to their participation in public life. Intellectual and educational speech and expression are also important in a democracy, not least because they enable the development of individuals' potential to play a full part in society and in our democratic life. Artistic speech and expression is important for similar reasons, in fostering both individual originality and creativity and the free-thinking and dynamic society we so much value. No doubt there are other kinds of speech and expression for which similar claims can be made.

[149] But it is difficult to make such claims on behalf of the publication with which we are concerned here. The political and social life of the community, and the intellectual, artistic or personal development of individuals, are not obviously assisted by pouring over the intimate details of a fashion model's private life. However, there is one way in which the article could be said to be educational. The editor had considered running a highly critical piece, adding the new information to the not inconsiderable list of Miss Campbell's faults and follies detailed in the article, emphasising the lies and hypocrisy it revealed. Instead he chose to run a sympathetic piece, still listing her faults and follies, but setting them in the context of her now-revealed addiction and her even more important efforts to overcome it. Newspaper and magazines often carry such pieces and they may well have a beneficial educational effect.

[150] The crucial difference here is that such pieces are normally run with the co-operation of those involved. Private people are not identified without their consent. It is taken for granted that this is otherwise confidential information. The editor did offer Miss Campbell the opportunity of being involved with the story but this was refused. Her evidence suggests that she was concerned for the other people in the group. What entitled him to reveal this private information about her without her consent?

[151] The answer which she herself accepts is that she had presented herself to the public as someone who was not involved in drugs. It would have been a very good thing if she were not. If other young women do see her as someone to be admired and emulated, then it is all to the good if

是以上这些很清楚的事实变得有些复杂了,因为原告承认报社拥有(和她的隐私)相冲突的言论自由,而这一自由能够让发表某些关于她的私人信息合理化。但是我们的出发点一定是要发表这些属于私人的信息,需要特别的正当化事由。

[148] 那么被告所宣称言论自由的性质是什么呢?毫无疑问,言论的类型是多种多样的,就像隐私的类型是多种多样的一样,有的类型值得在民主社会中获得比另一些类型更多的保护。最值得保护的是政治言论,能自由地交换关于经济社会和政治生活的意见对民主来说至关重要。没有这种自由,一个社会是不能被称作民主的。这种自由包括揭露公众人物,特别是选任官的信息的自由,这些信息如果不是因为涉及这些公众人物对公共生活的参与,本来都是私人信息。智力性的和教育性的言论对民主社会也很重要,特别是因为这类信息能让个人增长能力,以参与社会和民主生活。艺术性的言论也因为类似原因很重要,这种言论能促进个人的创造力和我们所珍视的允许人自由思考的有活力的社会的形成。无疑还存在其他类型的我们可以说同样的话的言论。

[149] 但是本案中我们很难为了报社的利益说这样的话。社群的政治或社会生活,个人的智力、艺术能力和发展显然并不会因为我们知道了某个时尚模特私人生活的细节就得到促进。当然,在有一个意义上我们可以说这些报道是有教育意义的。编辑曾经考虑要写一篇批评文章,要在Campbell小姐那已经不少的错误和蠢事清单上再增加点信息,要强调她的谎言和伪善。但是最后他选择写一篇支持性的文章,虽然依然列举了她的错误和蠢事,但是背景是她的毒瘾(现在已经众所周知)和她戒毒的努力,后者更重要。报纸和杂志经常刊登这样的文章,这样的文章也很有教育意义。

[150] 然而本案的不同点在于,一般情况下这种文章都是需要涉事者同意的。在未经涉事者同意时,不会点明他们的身份。理所当然这些都是应该保密的信息。编辑曾经请求Campbell小姐参与到报道中来,但是她拒绝了。她的证词是她要考虑到互助会里的其他人。那么编辑凭什么能在未经她同意时,就披露这些私人信息呢?

[151] 对这个问题,她自己都能接受的答案是,她在公众面前把自己打扮成了一个从不沾毒品的人。如果她真的不沾毒品,那确实是好事。如果其他

she is not addicted to narcotic substances. It might be questioned why, if a role model has adopted a stance which all would agree is beneficial rather than detrimental to society, it is so important to reveal that she has feet of clay. But the possession and use of illegal drugs is a criminal offence and a matter of serious public concern. The press must be free to expose the truth and put the record straight.

[152] That consideration justified the publication of the fact that, contrary to her previous statements, Miss Campbell had been involved with illegal drugs. It also justified publication of the fact that she was trying to do something about it by seeking treatment. It was not necessary for those purposes to publish any further information, especially if this might jeopardise the continued success of that treatment.

[153] The further information includes the fact that she was attending Narcotics Anonymous meetings, the fact that she had been doing so for some time, and with some regularity, and the photographs of her either arriving at or leaving the premises where meetings took place. All of these things are inter-related with one another and with the effect which revealing them might have upon her. Revealing that she was attending Narcotics Anonymous enabled the paper to print the headline "Naomi: I am a drug addict", not because she had said so to the paper but because it could assume that she had said this or something like it in a meeting. It also enabled the paper to talk about the meetings and how she was treated there, in a way which made it look as if the information came from someone who had been there with her, even if it simply came from general knowledge of how these meetings work. This all contributed to the sense of betrayal by someone close to her of which she spoke and which destroyed the value of Narcotics Anonymous as a safe haven for her.

[154] Publishing the photographs contributed both to the revelation and to the harm that it might do. By themselves, they are not objectionable. Unlike France and Quebec, in this country we do not recognise a right to one's own image: cfAubry v Éditions Vice-Versa Inc [1998] 1 SCR 591 . We have not so far held that the mere fact of covert photography is sufficient to make the information contained in the photograph confidential. The activity photographed must be private. If this had been, and had been presented as, a picture of Naomi Campbell going about her business in a public street, there could have been no complaint. She makes a substantial part of her living out of being photographed looking stunning in designer clothing. Readers will obviously be interested to see how she looks if and when she pops out to the shops for a bottle of milk. There is nothing essentially private about that information nor can it be expected to damage her private life. It may not be a high order of freedom of speech but there is nothing to justify interfering with it.

[155] But here the accompanying text made it plain that these photographs were different. They showed her coming either to or from the NA meeting. They showed her in the company of others, some of whom were undoubtedly part of the group. They showed the place where the

的年轻女性崇拜她模仿她,那么她没有毒瘾这事是件大好事。我们可能会问,如果一个明星模特持有一种对社会有益无害的观点,那为什么要戳穿她在说谎呢?因为持有和使用毒品是刑事犯罪,也是公众所非常关心的事情。媒体当然要有权去自由地揭露真相,澄清是非。

[152] 以上的理由可以支持对 Campbell 小姐吸毒的报道(这事她之前说谎了)。它也可以支持对她正在接受治疗的报道。但是它并不能支持对更进一步的信息的报道,特别是如果这么做会阻碍后续的治疗。

[153] 这些更进一步的信息包括她在参加匿名戒毒会,包括她参加戒毒会已经一段时间且比较频繁,包括她到达或者离开聚会场所时的照片。这些事都是相互关联的,披露它们会对她有影响。披露她在参加戒毒互助会,报社就能用"Naomi:我是瘾君子"做标题,这不是因为她这么说,而是因为可以推断她会在戒毒会上说类似的话。这么做也让报社在谈到戒毒会和她的治疗时能给人一种信息来自她身边人的感觉,虽然这不过是戒毒会运作的常识。这些给人感觉她身边的人背叛了她,并且摧毁了作为避风港的匿名戒毒会对她的价值。

[154] 刊登照片会揭露一些事实,但是也可能会造成一些损害。刊登照片本身并不会让人反感。不像法国和魁北克,我国并不承认肖像权:参见 *Aubry v-ditionsVice-Versa Inc* [1998] 1 SCR 591。我们目前并没有承认,偷拍本身会让照片的内容变成秘密。被拍照的行为本身必须属于私人信息的(才能起诉)。如果照片是关于 Naomi Campbell 在路上开展她的工作且报社也是这么表示的,那么原告就不能起诉。她就是靠神采奕奕地穿着时尚服饰照相来工作的。她到商店买牛奶,读者们显然会对她看起来怎样感兴趣。这种信息没有什么私人信息的特征,也没有人认为公布这种信息会对她的私人生活有什么损害。拍这种照片的自由可能不算非常重要的言论自由的类型,但是也没有什么理由去妨害这种自由。

[155] 但是本案中照片所配的文字表明,这些照片不同于刚才举的例子。这些照片显示她到达戒毒会或者从戒毒会出来,也显示了她由其他人陪同,其中的一些人无疑是同她一起参加戒毒会的人。这些照片显示了拍摄地点,任何熟悉那里的人都能认出这些地点。"一图胜千言",因为图片让文字更有影响力;另外图片也增加了文字的信息。如果照片上没有广告牌,这些照片

meeting was taking place, which will have been entirely recognisable to anyone who knew the locality. A picture is "worth a thousand words" because it adds to the impact of what the words convey; but it also adds to the information given in those words. If nothing else, it tells the reader what everyone looked like; in this case it also told the reader what the place looked like. In context, it also added to the potential harm, by making her think that she was being followed or betrayed, and deterring her from going back to the same place again.

[156] There was no need to do this. The editor accepted that even without the photographs, it would have been a front page story. He had his basic information and he had his quotes. There is no shortage of photographs with which to illustrate and brighten up a story about Naomi Campbell. No doubt some of those available are less flattering than others, so that if he had wanted to run a hostile piece he could have done so. The fact that it was a sympathetic story is neither here nor there. The way in which he chose to present the information he was entitled to reveal was entirely a matter for him. The photographs would have been useful in proving the truth of the story had this been challenged, but there was no need to publish them for this purpose. The credibility of the story with the public would stand or fall with the credibility of "Mirror" stories generally.

[157] The weight to be attached to these various considerations is a matter of fact and degree. Not every statement about a person's health will carry the badge of confidentiality or risk doing harm to that person's physical or moral integrity. The privacy interest in the fact that a public figure has a cold or a broken leg is unlikely to be strong enough to justify restricting the press's freedom to report it. What harm could it possibly do? Sometimes there will be other justifications for publishing, especially where the information is relevant to the capacity of a public figure to do the job. But that is not this case and in this case there was, as the judge found, a risk that publication would do harm. The risk of harm is what matters at this stage, rather than the proof that actual harm has occurred. People trying to recover from drug addiction need considerable dedication and commitment, along with constant reinforcement from those around them. That is why organisations like Narcotics Anonymous were set up and why they can do so much good. Blundering in when matters are acknowledged to be at a "fragile" stage may do great harm.

[158] The trial judge was well placed to assess these matters. He could tell whether the impact of the story on her was serious or trivial. The fact that the story had been published at all was bound to cause distress and possibly interfere with her progress. But he was best placed to judge whether the additional information and the photographs had added significantly both to the distress and the potential harm. He accepted her evidence that it had done so. He could also tell how serious an interference with press freedom it would have been to publish the essential parts of the story without the additional material and how difficult a decision this would have been for an editor who had been told that it was a medical matter and that it would be morally wrong to publish it.

[159] The judge was also obliged by section 12(4)(b) of the 1998 Act, not only to have

不过是告诉读者上面的人的长相。但是在本案中,这些照片也告诉了读者拍摄的地点。在本案的情景下,这些照片让她觉得自己被跟踪或者被背叛了,因此不会再回到同样的地方,这增加了潜在的危害。

[156] 但是报社编辑并不需要这么做。编辑承认就算没有这些照片,依然可以完成这篇头版报道。他有基本信息也有原告说的话。他也不缺用来配 Naomi Campbell 的故事的图片。无疑这些照片中,有的照片对原告没有那么友好,因此如果他想撰写一篇批评原告的文章,他是完全可以这么做的。这篇报道是支持原告的这一点不重要。他选择什么形式来呈现他有权揭露的信息完全是他自己的事。这些照片在故事的真实性被质疑时,对于证明这一真实性是有用的,但是为了这个目的是没有必要发布它们的。这篇报道在公众中的可信度,跟《镜报》文章一般性的可信度是正相关的。

[157] 以上这些情节的权重是个度的问题。并不是所有的关于一个人身体情况的表达都是需要保密的,或者会对这个人的身体或者精神造成伤害。公众人物如果腿不能动了或者伤了腿这事,其中的隐私利益很可能是不足以支持限制媒体报道这事的自由的。这么做能有什么危害呢?有时候报道这种事有额外的理由,特别是如果相关信息关乎这个公众人物还能不能履职。但是这不是本案的情形。在本案的情形中,如同一审法官认定的那样,被告的报道可能是有风险的。在这个阶段证明存在风险的可能即可,不需要证明损害已经发生。试图戒毒的人需要恰当的指导和决心,还需要周围人的支持。这就是为什么匿名互助戒毒会这类组织建立的原因,也是它们的效果那么好的原因。在事情还在"脆弱"阶段就贸然进入,可能会造成严重的损害。

[158] 一审法官正确地考察了这些情节。他可以去判断这个报道对她的影响是大是小。她的故事被报道本身肯定会对她造成精神痛苦,也很可能会干扰她的治疗进程。但是一审法官最主要是去判断这些额外的信息和照片是否增加了她的精神痛苦和可能的损害。一审法官接受了她的证据,判断确实增加了。他也可以判断只报道重要部分而省去额外的材料会多大程度上妨碍新闻自由,以及对于一个被告知这是一个医疗事件且报道这些事是不道德的编辑,其决定不使用这些额外材料是多么困难。

[159] 一审法官根据 1998 年《人权法》第 12 条第 4 款第 b 项的规定,不

particular regard to the importance of the Convention right to freedom of expression, but also to any relevant privacy code. The Press Complaints Commission Code of Practice supports rather than undermines the conclusion he reached:

> 3. *Privacy*
>
> (i) Everyone is entitled to respect for his or her private and family life, home, health and correspondence. A publication will be expected to justify intrusions into any individual's private life without consent. (ii) The use of long lens photography to take pictures of people in private places without their consent is unacceptable. Note— Private places are public or private property where there is a reasonable expectation of privacy.
>
> *The public interest*
>
> There may be exceptions to the clauses marked where they can be demonstrated to be in the public interest.
>
> 1. The public interest includes: (i) Detecting or exposing crime or a serious misdemeanour. (ii) Protecting public health and safety. (iii) Preventing the pubic from being misled by some statement or action of an individual or organisation ...

This would appear to expect almost exactly the exercise conducted above and to lead to the same conclusion as the judge.

I would therefore allow this appeal and restore the order of the judge.

...

但应该理解公约中言论自由的重要性，而且应该理解任何相关的隐私权规范。传媒投诉委员会的操作守则支持而不是反对他作出的结论：

3. 隐私

（i）每个人都有权要求他的或者她的私人生活和家庭生活、住宅、健康和通信获得尊重。未经允许侵入他人的私人生活的报道是需要有理由的。（ii）未经他人同意用长焦镜头拍摄他人的私有地点或私人生活是不被允许的。注意——私有地点是指在公共或者私人的地产中，人们可以对隐私有合理的期望的地点。

公共利益

能够证明存在公共利益的，上款可以存在例外。

1. 公共利益包括（i）对犯罪或者严重的不法行为的侦查或者揭露。（ii）对公共健康和安全的保护。（iii）对公众被个人或组织的言论或行为误导的防止……

上面这段话所要求的行为几乎就是被告的行为。根据这段话也可以得出和一审法官一样的结论。

因此，我支持上诉，恢复一审判决的效力。

……

巨人已逝、巨著长存（代后记）

每年圣诞节前夕，我都会给在康奈尔大学访学时的联合导师 James A. Henderson Jr. 教授发邮件问好，并汇报一年来的工作情况，总能得到教授的回复，这也是十年来与 Henderson 教授保持联系的一种方式。去年年底，书稿初成，原计划出版的消息，第一个想告诉的海外教授就是 Henderson 教授。但我的 2019 年圣诞节问候邮件，却被退回了。上网一查才知道，教授已经于 2019 年 7 月 2 日仙逝，享年 81 岁。我看着康奈尔大学法学院网站上纪念教授的文章，久久不能平静。回想起教授的音容笑貌，既清晰又模糊。回国任教后，曾经邀请过教授到中国来讲学，但他年事已高，无法长途飞行，这也成为我终生的遗憾。

一、已逝的巨人

Henderson 教授是美国法律协会《侵权法重述·第三次·产品责任编》的联合报告人，在美国参议院和众议院多次就侵权法、产品责任法和保险法作证，还担任了美国历史上最复杂的大规模侵权诉讼——"9·11"世贸大厦责任人诉讼的特别主事（Special Master）。他作为侵权法和产品责任法领域"学术巨人"的影响力已经不需要我来作更多的介绍，但是有一件事情在 Henderson 教授的简历上是看不到的。那就是他曾经在飞机上与一位试图进入机舱干扰飞行的醉酒者英勇搏斗，为此还获得了美国联邦航空管理局（FAA）专门颁发的奖章。我听说此事后，好奇地问他："您是怎么鼓起勇气去和这个醉酒者搏斗的？"他说："我坐飞机回 Ithaca，如果飞机掉下去，我就没法见到我妻子和孩子了。所以，我很生气，就冲过去把他压到我的身下，一直到飞机安全降落。"关于这个"把他压到我的身下"的形象，按照名著 *Prosser, Wade and Schwartz's Torts* 唯一健在的作者 Victor Schwartz 先生和我开玩笑的说法，他绕着 Henderson 教授走一圈要很长时间。这是因为，Schwartz 先生体型精瘦，而 Henderson 教授则很魁梧。

在美国访学期间，受 Henderson 教授推荐，我有幸受邀参加了 2008 年 11 月 13 日在 Brooklyn Law School 召开的《侵权法重述·第三次·产品责任编》发布 10 周年纪念研讨会（The Products Liability Restatement: Was it a Success？）当

时我还在读博士，囊中羞涩，交不起 200 美元的注册费。Henderson 教授得知我的难处后，又专门给会议主办者，也是该重述的联合报告人 Aaron D. Twerski 打电话，免除了我的参会费用。

2009 年 4 月 2—3 日，也是在 Henderson 教授的推荐下，我受邀到 Wake Forest Law School 参加由 Michael D. Green 教授主办的《侵权法重述·第三次·物质和精神损害责任编》研讨会：A Symposium on the Third Restatement of Torts。那次会议可以说是巨星云集，我印象尤其深刻的是，包括 Dan Dobbs 教授在内的美国侵权法领域引用率排名前 10 的学者悉数到场。Henderson 教授不仅积极地把我推荐给各位大家，还特别叮嘱我不用坐在他身边陪他，要多和其他学者交流。正是在该次会议上，我与刚接任欧洲侵权法与保险法研究中心主任的 Ken Oliphant 教授相识，才有了后来促成 Helmut Koziol 教授和杨立新教授筹建世界侵权法学会的契机。

二、长存的巨著

第一次见到 The Torts Process 这本书，是我 2004 年在中国人民大学法学院刚开始读硕士的时候，中信出版社以《侵权程序法》为书名影印出版了该书第六版。[①] 当时的第一印象是，书很厚，英文书名特别；中文书名直译虽无可厚非，但所指并非一目了然。因为我当时已经确定了侵权法作为主要研究方向。"非典"过后正好有一位长辈资助了我 1 000 元用于购书，就买了这本当时看起来挺贵的英文原版，可惜当时也没细读全书。

2005 年年底，高等教育出版社出版了潘维大教授编著的《英美侵权行为法案例解析》，那时我已经开始准备考博，见到此书，如获至宝。尽管该书装帧精美，由于反复翻看、逐页批注，今天特意拿出来，竟然发现书有些脱页。2006 年夏季，潘维大教授来中国人民大学访问，杨立新教授把我介绍给他，并商定好我到东吴大学短期交换事宜。当时到我国台湾地区交流很是困难，2007 年 9 月，经过层层审批，通过香港转机，我终于来到宝岛，再次见到潘维大教授，并获赠该书对应的繁体版。尽管该书 1997 年初版的案例选择参考了 Prosser, Wade and Schwartz's Torts: Cases and Materials[②]，2002 年修订版又参考了 Marc A. Franklin 教授和 Robert L. Rabin 教授编写的 Tort Law and

---

[①] 参见〔美〕小詹姆斯·A. 亨德森、理查德·N. 皮尔逊、约翰·A. 西里西艾诺：《侵权程序法》（第六版），中信出版社 2003 年版。

[②] See Prosser, Wade and Schwartz's Torts: Cases and Materials (9th ed.), Foundation Press, 1994.

Alternatives: Cases and Materials[1]，但我在东吴大学学习期间，潘维大教授实际使用的教材却是 James A. Henderson Jr. 教授、Richard N. Pearson 教授和 John A. Siliciano 编写的 *The Torts Process*[2]。我认真地对比了三本英文原著的案例，发现所选案例重合度较高，甚至节选内容都较为一致，我当时想，大概这就是判例法的通说吧。

2008 年，我在康奈尔大学访学期间，在图书馆特别找到 *The Torts Process* 1975 年第一版[3]，可惜未能买到样书以作纪念。正好 2007 年该书出版了第七版[4]，很荣幸获赠该书第一作者 Henderson 教授的亲笔签名版。2009 年年初，我转到耶鲁大学法学院继续访学，该书第七版新增的第三作者 Douglas A. Kysar 教授担任我的导师，他当然也使用该书作为教材。

2012 年，*The Torts Process* 第八版[5]出版，但因为翻译版权的原因，2014 年 4 月我主持翻译的《美国侵权法：实体与程序（第七版）》[6]由北京大学出版社出版，只能在部分译者注中说明美国侵权法的最新进展。2017 年，该书更名为 *The Torts Process: Cases and Materials*[7]出版了第九版。考虑到大部头译作不大可能，也没有太大必要出版新版，我就考虑出版一本英美侵权法教材，来吸收该书最新的判例选择进展。以上就是本书的来历。希望本书能够与 *The Torts Process* 长期同步更新下去，让这本巨著以这种特别的方式，在中文世界产生持久的影响力。

巨人已逝、巨著长存！愿 Henderson 教授九泉有知。谨以本书，纪念 Henderson 教授！

学生：王竹

己亥年大寒于马六甲

---

[1] See Marc A. Franklin and Robert L. Rabin, *Tort Law and Alternatives: Cases and Materials (6th ed.)*, Foundation Press, 1996.

[2] See James A. Henderson Jr., Richard N. Pearson and John A. Siliciano, *The Torts Process (6th ed.)*, Aspen Law & Business, 2003.

[3] See James A. Henderson Jr. and Richard N. Pearson, *The Torts Process*, Little, Brown & Company (1975).

[4] See James A. Henderson Jr. and Richard N. Pearson, Douglas A. Kysar and John A. Siliciano, *The Torts Process (7th ed.)*, Aspen Publisher, 2007.

[5] See James A. Henderson Jr., Richard N. Pearson, Douglas A. Kysar, *The Torts Process (8th ed.)*, Wolters Kluwer, 2012.

[6] 参见〔美〕小詹姆斯·A. 亨德森、理查德·N. 皮尔森、道格拉斯·A. 凯萨、约翰·A. 西里西艾诺：《美国侵权法：实体与程序》（第七版），王竹、丁海俊、董春华、周玉辉译，王竹审校，北京大学出版社 2014 年版。

[7] See James A. Henderson Jr., Richard N. Pearson and Douglas A. Kysar, *The Torts Process: Cases and Materials (9th ed.)*, Wolters Kluwer, 2017.